THE UNIVER

Personality

Personality

Description,
Dynamics,
and Development

Susan C. Cloninger
Russell Sage College

W. H. Freeman and Company
New York

Part opening and chapter opening illustration by Theo Rudnak

Library of Congress Cataloging-in-Publication Data

Cloninger, Susan C., 1945-
    Personality: description, dynamics, and development/ Susan C. Cloninger
       p. cm.
    Includes bibliographical references and index.
    ISBN 0-7167-2825-7 (hardcover)
    1. Personality.   I. Title.
BF698.C54 1996
155—dc20   95-48100
                                                      CIP

Printed in the United States of America

Third Printing, 2000

To Shirley and Butch

CONTENTS IN BRIEF

CONTENTS

PREFACE

The field of personality is, for me, one of the most exciting yet frustrating areas of psychology. It aims to bring systematic theory and scientific rigor to the most fundamental questions of who we are and how we got that way. Answers show themselves in snatches and hints but refuse to be grasped, like a hologram that suggests forms but is not itself the firm and substantive stuff that we seek. Sometimes I think those of us who become addicted to this field are like young children who pester adults with their incessant "Why?" Without those questions, life would seem simpler, but we would miss so much understanding, awe, and the thrill of the quest.

How Should the Field Be Organized?
Reorienting from Theories toward Research

Our questions are tough. The answers are still under investigation and, as Chapter 1 considers further, experts disagree about how this investigation should be conducted. Researchers may be able to set such issues aside to focus on a smaller puzzle, but how can we teach such a field in the classroom? Should the first (and often only) personality course be organized around traditional theories, which provide familiar anchors but may seem old-fashioned? Or should we instead turn our attention to current research, risking a feeling of fragmentation and a fear that much of our course content will be obsolete in a few years? There are many fields where knowledge is mushrooming, but few where the foundations seem as uncertain as in personality. What is the role of broad theories, largely metaphorical, devised by therapists to guide their understanding and intervention? Are these broad theories suitable guides for research? How can we reconcile such theories with newer approaches, more self-consciously scientific in language, that are devised to guide researchers rather than to guide clinicians? Is it not foolish to expect the same theories to be optimal for both purposes? As the field of personality has become more self-consciously scientific in its methods, the legacy of clinical theory, written in bold form by Freud, Jung,

Adler, Horney, and others, has taken on a historic flavor.

What are we to make of this movement from traditional theories based in therapy to modern approaches designed primarily to guide research? In some ways, the move toward scientific rigor is a step forward, because such scientific methods do help sort truth from error. In some ways, it is a step back, because (as Abraham Maslow warned) we have lost sight of some of the larger issues and applications of our understanding while playing the game of research. I would like to have it both ways, as those familiar with my earlier text in personality theory must know. Forced to choose, though, I would have to admit that, because we are still asking fundamental questions about personality that may require drastic theoretical revisions, the largely fossilized traditional theories may not serve us in the future. Like old maps, they are picturesque and offer vital insights into our historical vision, but they may not be accurate enough for the tasks we face today. Worse than the erroneous details is the fact that these theories are too simple, like old maps that portrayed the world as flat. The world needs a three-dimensional representation. Personality, too, is three-dimensional (at least). Let's look at it with a "3-D" perspective. What might that be?

The 3 D's of Personality

By organizing this book as I have, I suggest that current personality research can find an organizing framework in three fundamental questions. How shall we *describe* personality? What are the *dynamics* that make us function? How do we *develop* the personalities that we do? Part One considers the first question, the description of personality, which is fundamental to any discussion of personality. Chapter 2 considers how everyday people describe personality and how researchers have built upon these lay descriptions, refining the concept of personlality traits. Chapter 3 discusses historic theoretical controversies over personality traits and presents several current models of personality traits that guide

researchers. Chapter 4 examines differences in personality between men and women and among racial and ethnic groups, discussing the precautions that must be taken in conducting and interpreting such comparative research. In contrast to this focus on comparisons across people, Chapter 5 examines historic and current approaches to studying unique individuals.

It is not enough to describe people; we must also understand why they behave as they do. Historic theories of personality, beginning with Freud's psychoanalytic theory, have addressed this question, but such historic approaches have been revised and reconceptualized by modern researchers. Part Two of this book considers this second question, the dynamics of personality. The psychoanalytic assertion that we are motivated by unconscious reasons has not only guided therapists; many of its assertions (for example, concerning dreams, hypnosis, and sexuality) have also been tested by researchers, as presented in Chapter 6. Researchers in the tradition of Henry Murray have considered other unconscious motives: achievement, affiliation, power, and fear of success, presented in Chapter 7 with related current theoretical approaches and research. Chapter 8 considers personality dynamics from the perspective of stress and coping, including alternative ways of coping and their effectiveness, and research relating personality to physical diseases. The self, presented in Chapter 9, is central to personality dynamics as people strive for self-esteem and self-knowledge and base their life choices on beliefs about themselves.

Personality develops over time, and we cannot understand adults without also considering the impact of their developmental history and current developmental tasks, presented in Part Three. Chapter 10 presents the results of longitudinal research examining personality continuity and change over time and discusses theories of development and major developmental tasks at various stages of life. Development is also influenced by biological variation considered in Chapter 11, including heredity and temperament. Emotions are considered here as a phenomenon that has physiological as well as experiential implications, and the evolutionary perspective toward personality is presented. Personality dynamics are considered in Chapter 12 from a social perspective, which discusses the relationship between personality and major social tasks (education, work, love and marriage, parenting, political life, and religion). As we see in Chapter 13, culture provides a context for personality, reflected in cross-cultural studies and in studies of the impact of race, ethnicity, and gender on personality. Chapter 14 concludes by integrating the discussion of the 3 D's: description, dynamics, and development, and by considering research strategies in perspective.

These three questions must be answered or we cannot understand personality. The answers, of course, are intertwined in a way that is not always apparent in a form, like a book, that must take a linear format. The interconnections do show when the same topic (such as culture, or emotion, or achievement) appears in more than one chapter. If you could see my writing area, with its multiple indexing system and ever changing piles of reading material, you would know that I do not think of these as three separate questions. Their answers must be coordinated. I take heart from now popular chaos theory, that describes emergent order from what seems to be huge numbers of small processes. But we may not see the patterns if we look only at the details. Our perspectives must be 3-D.

Among the challenges to understanding personality, one of the greatest is that personality is influenced by many levels of experience, from the biochemistry of our bodies to the cultural institutions that shape and sometimes thwart our human striving, from the fleeting intuitions and images of our unconscious to the conscious logic of reason, from the private and personal to the social and community experience. We must ponder all levels, and we must also strive to understand how these levels interrelate. Another challenge is the question of individual differences. Describing how personality varies from one person to another has traditionally been a major focus of

personality psychologists, and we consider descriptive models early in the text. Such understanding is limited, however, unless we also consider the personality processes that influence us all—the dynamic and developmental processes considered in Parts Two and Three.

Personality is an empirical field, claiming the status of science. Although we derive from our everyday life experience ideas that go beyond our science, we must resist the impulse to accept these ideas without testing them sufficiently.

The commitment to science demands an appreciation of sound methods for making observations. In this text, research methods are considered in boxed features. By examining research methods in close connection with specific substantive issues, students can better understand the methods and their importance. This understanding is essential to evaluate research findings and determine whether or not they apply to a given situation or person.

For the student, the text includes several pedagogical features:

• Research Strategies Boxes in each chapter explain specific methods for conducting research.

• Chapter Summaries list, in bulleted format, the major points of the chapter.

• Glossaries in each chapter define terms introduced in that chapter. These terms are printed in boldface in the text.

• Thought Questions challenge students to evaluate what they have learned critically.

For the Instructor

Instructors will find that the 3-D organization provides a logical framework for modifying the course according to their particular goals and interests. With my co-author, I present suggestions for lectures and class activities in the *Instructor's Manual*, which also includes test questions in multiple choice, true-false, and essay format. I welcome your comments and suggestions. My e-mail address is: clonis@sage.edu.

Acknowledgments

There are many people to thank for their support and guidance during the writing of this book. Susan Finnemore Brennan, my editor, first suggested this book. She has had a great deal to do with its final shape; she coaxed a better organization from me than the one I first proposed and is master of the art of making a small suggestion at just the moment when it will have a major impact. Like a gardener, she has pruned a little, imagined what could be, and known when to simply be patient and trust that there was something growing somewhere during apparently dormant periods. Susan has now edited me through two books and we are looking forward to our third. She has collaborated with a fantastic group of professionals at W. H. Freeman and Company: Travis Amos directed the photography program, finding photographs that provoke thought as well as providing a welcome break in the text. Diane Cimino Maass supervised the final editing and production, making the words and the art appear as you see and managing cheerfulness when this tardy author deserved far less. Blake Logan designed the interior, Paul Rohloff coordinated manufacturing, and Sheridan Sellers composed this book, making each part of the process go more smoothly than I could have imagined. I would also like to thank Amy Sheridan for her kind assistance. Several reviewers have made suggestions at various stages of the book. Their reactions have improved the text, although none of them would agree with everything in the final product; perhaps I ought to have taken more of their advice. Thanks to the reviewers: A. R. Allgeier, Bowling Green University; Marvin Brodsky, University of Manitoba; Bernardo J. Carducci, Indiana University Southeast; Russell Cropanzano, Colorado State University; Scott J. Dickman, University of Massachusetts at Dartmouth; Karen G. Duffy, SUNY Genesco; Barry Fritz, Quinnipiiac College; Sherryl Goodman, Emory University; Sharon D. Herzberger, Trinity College; James J. Johnson, Illinois State University; Laura King, Southern Methodist University; David C. Munz, St. Louis University; Robert Nadon, Brock University (St. Catharines, Ontario); Brian Stagner, Texas A & M University; J. Kevin Thompson, University of Southern Florida; and Jerry S. Wiggins, University of British Columbia.

I have been fortunate to find wise and supportive counsel among my colleagues and friends at Russell Sage College, especially my colleagues in the Psychology Department; many patient and helpful librarians; especially Jane Neale, who prepared the subject index; and accommodating college administrators, whose granting of a sabbatical leave has permitted me to finish this book and begin the next. My family, like good families everywhere, cheer what they don't always understand, and so I thank Dad, Mom, Shirley, Butch (whom all but his sisters call Clyde), and John. In the later stages of the book, my mother died unexpectedly, and I want particularly to thank my therapist, Pearl Mindell, for helping me to find a new balance between grieving, growing, and going on with life's commitments and opportunities.

Sue Cloninger

Personality

1

Introduction

THERE IS NO QUESTION that scientific research has transformed human life. Advances in energy, transportation, communication—the legacy of scientific knowledge about the physical world—have changed our lives in countless ways. Have we learned comparable lessons about human personality? No, but perhaps the comparison is unfair. Scientific researchers have explored personality only since the 1930s (Pervin, 1990). In many ways, we are still struggling to identify the questions and issues that need to be addressed. Even so, much has been discovered, and our research findings are already being applied to practical problems. Personality tests are used to advise people about career choices, for example, and research on the debatable accuracy of memories is considered by the judicial system when accusations of sexual abuse are brought to court.

The Field of Personality

The field of personality psychology draws from the rest of psychology and from the natural and social sciences broadly. One definition of personality focuses on the functioning of the individual person; it defines **personality** as *the psychological functioning of the individual person.* It encompasses the diverse qualities of individuals and the influences on their psychological functioning. Biological variations, social influences, cognitive factors, childhood experiences, individual goals and choices, and other

Most people would agree that children who have loving parents are likely to develop better personalities, but how would we go about testing this idea scientifically?

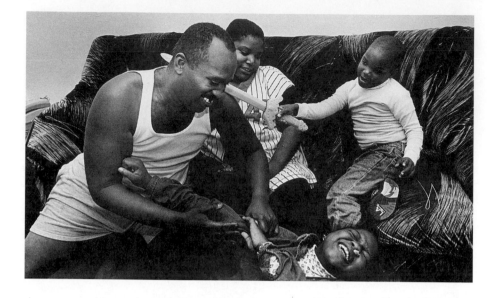

aspects of personality have been described by various theorists and researchers as components of personality.

The range of topics that personality researchers study is limited only by commitment to the **scientific method.** Science judges the truth of statements based on the *empirical method.* That is, statements are accepted or rejected after systematic investigation and verification of observations by independent observers. For example, many people believe that loving parents produce well-adjusted children, but a scientist would not accept such a statement without evidence based on the observation of facts. What facts would be relevant? Do we mean "parents who spend a lot of time with their children will have children who get good evaluations on behavior from their teachers"? Or "parents who do not hit their children will have children who win popularity contests"? Each of these specific predictions about what will be observed in a scientific study is called a **hypothesis.** The scientific method requires that we accept statements as true only if the hypotheses that correspond to them are confirmed by observation.

It is no easy matter to apply scientific methods to the study of personality. It is not easy to state the beliefs that we wish to test in the precise terms required by scientific hypotheses. In addition, we bring to this field preconceptions that may bias our observations and limit the questions we ask. For example, past generations of researchers asked about the influence of mothers on their children's development, ignoring the impact of fathers because of their assumptions about women's role in the family and men's role at work. (When I was analyzing data in a national sample, I stumbled across the finding in a small portion of the sample that parental unemployment seemed to be associated with a reduction in crime and violence in schools. I was told to drop the idea rather than to examine the association systematically. The belief that unemployment could have any beneficial effects was so contrary to the preconceived idea that work is good that empirical data were deemed irrelevant.) Beliefs about "human nature" are ingrained in our consciousness and are held far more tenaciously than the tentative hypotheses that science requires. Science demands that hypotheses be discarded if they are not confirmed by observation; our beliefs are often harder to shake. Our closeness to the subject of personality poses difficulties different from those of the scientists who probed the structure of the atom or the functioning of the cell.

Despite its limitations, the scientific approach is appealing because it offers a method for distinguishing beliefs that are true from those that are false. Rather than giving up science in areas close to our individual experiences, we should recognize that the discipline of science is particularly important in this field. Nonetheless, the methods of science were developed for studying the natural world, not human experience. As we shall see in this chapter, questions have been raised about applying scientific methods to personality; some adaptation of these methods may be necessary.

Can the scientific approach be reconciled with our preconceived understandings of personality? Insights about personality are found in literature, religion, and human tradition. Yet a systematic comparison of these insights with scientific studies of personality would be an ambitious undertaking. Science aspires to be value-free, but the field of personality is not a purely academic undertaking. Throughout its history, the study of personality has been influenced by the concerns of clinicians, who try to help people to live better lives. Is it now possible to create a value-free environment for such research, or at least an environment in which our values do not distort our observations?

The State of the Field

What is the current state of the field of personality? Methodologically, important developments have occurred in the procedures that scientists use in their research. We have developed increasingly sophisticated measurements, and our techniques for analyzing data have also evolved to exploit the capacities of modern computers. Conceptually, however, the overriding impression is that the field is in turmoil. Decisions about what to study seem driven by available measures and statistical methods, personal interests, funding realities, and current fads, rather than by a broadly shared vision of research priorities.

Where might such a shared vision of priorities come from? According to Thomas Kuhn (1970), *normal science* occurs when scientists share a common **paradigm.** They agree on the fundamental assumptions and methodology of their discipline. This makes it possible for each scientist to work on some manageable piece of the endeavor, secure in the knowledge that the work will advance the discipline. Physics, a more mature science than psychology, has shared assumptions about matter and energy that are fundamental to all physicists' work. The study of personality, in contrast, does not have a common paradigm that is the basis for everyone's work. When a person feels anxious, for example, is this a sign that unconscious conflicts have become activated? Is the anxiety caused by aspects of the environment that are reminiscent of unpleasant times in the past? Is it a sign that the person is thinking maladaptive thoughts? Does it stem from a lack of courage to be true to one's inner nature? Is anxiety a reflection of a biological activation that is more typical of some people than of others? Each of these characterizations would be accepted by some psychologists and rejected by others. More troubling, because personality psychologists start with different assumptions, they do not agree about how research should be done, and they routinely find research to be irrelevant to their own understandings of personality when it is conducted by those whose guiding assumptions are different from their own.

Some of the competing viewpoints are described briefly in Table 1.1. These various perspectives are usually called *theories*, although occasionally this usage is criticized because the term *theory* implies a highly systematic formal statement that is consistently presented. As suggested in the table, those who try to advance the understanding of anxiety or other phenomena don't agree about whether we should study the anxious person's dreams, environment, thoughts, potential, or responses on questionnaires. Such disagreement limits the extent to which researchers can build on the work of others. It is as though there are dozens of construction workers building a house, but each has a different plan. Hans Eysenck compares the situation to the building of the Tower of Babel (Eysenck, 1986a). Perhaps the modules will fit together, but it seems unlikely.

Why are there so many competing perspectives in personality? Perhaps the field is too broad ever to be unified by one paradigm. Perhaps scientists have brought their diverse common sense explanations of personality to the laboratory. Perhaps personality psychologists do not know how to do scientific research. Eysenck (1986a) blames psychologists for being too undisciplined, ignorant, and lazy to conduct good systematic scientific work. It may be more accurate, however (and certainly more compassionate), to note that the discipline is still quite young in the family of sciences. Shared paradigms emerge over time. Personality is still developing.

The Two Traditions Influencing Personality Researchers

Two different traditions, **clinical psychology** and academic psychology, have influenced the field of personality. Many of the best known personality theorists were clinicians: Freud, Jung, Adler, Horney, Rogers, Kelly, and others. Clinical psychologists focus on how people adapt to everyday life, and they often intervene to improve the lives of individuals (particularly those suffering emotional disturbances) through therapy. Clinicians study

TABLE **1.1** **Major Theoretical Perspectives in Personality**

Major perspectives	Typical approach to personality
Trait approach	Assumes that each individual has stable personality characteristics (traits)
	Seeks to develop questionnaires to measure traits
Psychoanalytic approach	Assumes that people are motivated by unconscious emotional conflicts originating in childhood
	Seeks to understand the unconscious through dreams, free association, and creative products
Cognitive approach	Assumes that people's thoughts and beliefs are central to personality
	Seeks to measure people's thoughts and beliefs and to understand how they lead to behavior in specific situations
Humanistic approach	Assumes that people have an innate tendency to develop their full human potential; that is, to become self-actualized
	Seeks to describe fully developed people and the social conditions that foster personal growth

each person in depth. They generally describe their observations in words, rather than in quantitative scores, and they more often report individual case studies than statistical analyses of groups. (There are exceptions, of course. A tradition of *clinical research* has developed, in which the diagnostic and treatment concerns of practitioners are addressed through research, and many clinicians also hold academic positions.)

A second tradition shaping the field of personality is **academic psychology,** which emphasizes research and theory-building. Cattell, Allport, Murray, Bandura, and Mischel, among others, are well-known researchers and personality theorists. In addition, many researchers are known for their work on specialized topics, rather than for proposing broad theories of personality. Typically, researchers study groups of people, rather than individuals. They examine selected aspects of personality, rather than attempting to grasp the whole person (Carlson, 1971). They almost always express their observations as numbers and report statistical analyses.

The Clinical Tradition Therapists use theories of personality that have evolved in clinical practice. In many cases, these theories have been extended to the "normal," nonclinical population as well. Sigmund Freud, for example, boasted that his theory was not merely a clinical theory; he claimed that it was a general psychological theory. Carl Rogers's client-centered theory has suggested applications beyond the consulting room to the work environment and to schools.

Clinically derived approaches generally stress the adaptive behavior of the whole person; that is, how the person copes with the stresses and challenges of life. They do not limit their focus to one or two aspects of personality, such as a limited set of personality traits. Consider how one renowned clinician, Erik Erikson, describes the process of dream interpretation. A male patient dreamt the following:

> *There was a big face sitting in a buggy of the horse-and-buggy days. The face was completely empty, and there was horrible, slimy, snaky hair all around it. I am not sure it wasn't my mother. (Erikson, 1958, p. 71)*

Erikson's interpretation of this dream cites causes from diverse sources: the patient's anxiety; his childhood experiences with his mother, his uncertainty about the therapist's approval, the therapist's physical appearance, Biblical imagery, and more. In psychoanalytic terms, the dream was "overdetermined." That is, it had many causes that combined in condensed form in the dream.

Clearly, clinicians use intuition to decipher such dreams. In one sense, this openness to many causes is a virtue, because it reflects the complexity of human personality. The method considers the whole person, rather than one isolated aspect, such as the person's level of anxiety. (In contrast, an empirical researcher in academic psychology would be more likely to consider a limited number of traits.) Clinical observation permits the discovery of phenomena that surprise the observer, such as the effects of some childhood experiences. In contrast, the academic researcher's controlled experiment generally constrains subjects' behavior considerably, thus eliminating the possibility of most observations that were not planned in advance.

The openness of the clinical method poses serious methodological problems. It relies extensively on the particular clinician's observational abilities. Would another clinician make the same report of a particular clinical session? Often not. If the interpretations of the clinical method are so equivocal, how can they be the basis of scientific progress? Many have voiced doubts. Predictions are difficult to specify in advance. Observations are not generally open to confirmation by an independent observer. These factors prevent the clinical setting from being an appropriate place for the scientific verification of theories. One critic (Eysenck, 1986a) dismisses a major clinical theory, Freud's psychoanalysis, as "pseudoscience," along with parapsychology (which includes the study of extrasensory perception, astrology, and other alleged phenomena that are not taken seriously by most scientists). His criticism extends to other well-known theories, including those of Jung and Maslow.

If science seeks to identify the causes of observed phenomena through testing in controlled situations, clinical psychology is not that sort of science. It is committed to the understanding of individual lives, which are full of complexities that cannot be controlled. It seeks to understand the meanings of an individual life and so has been called a "hermeneutic" (interpretative) science (Edelson, 1985; Manicas & Secord, 1983; Ricoeur, 1977). Like the study of history, psychoanalysis applies general principles to the understanding of individual events, with all their complexities and uncontrolled influences (Manicas & Secord, 1983).

Not everyone dismisses psychoanalysis as unscientific (Bromley, 1990; Wallace, 1989). Many who are sympathetic to psychoanalysis, however, recognize that science requires data collection and analysis beyond what is needed to conduct therapy (Grünbaum, 1984; Holzman, 1985; Jones & Windholz, 1990; Kline, 1987a; Rubinstein, 1980; Shulman, 1990; Wallerstein, 1986; Weiss, 1988). Many other clinical approaches have been devised to guide therapy, and some of these are easier (compared to psychoanalysis) to reconcile with the demands of science.

The Academic Tradition

In its early years as an academic discipline, psychology was closely allied with philosophy. Psychologists took pride, however, in becoming independent from philosophy. They sought to replace logical analysis with experimental research. Psychology has advanced as an experimental science more easily in some fields than in others. Sensation, perception, and learning lend themselves to experimental investigation more readily than does personality, because their variables can be isolated and controlled more easily. Before considering these difficulties, however, what are the distinguishing characteristics of the research tradition? What does "science" demand?

The Method of Science

Science is distinguished by its method. According to the method of science, *independent observers must verify data*. If only one person makes an observation, how can we know whether it corresponds to reality or was an aberration or an error? If several people independently make the same observation, we are more confident of their reports. According to this criterion, the study of private experience is problematic. If I have a headache, can anyone else observe it? Perhaps my report that I have a headache is accompanied by measures that other people *can* observe, such as an abnormal EEG recording. In such a case, they will probably accept my report as accurate, even though no one else can observe the headache directly. If no such corroborative evidence is available, however, others may dismiss my report of a headache as untrustworthy, perhaps a neurotic ploy to achieve attention. When the data of interest are inherently private, this criterion of science poses a dilemma. Shall we refuse to study private phenomena, as B. F. Skinner advocates? Shall we trust reports of private experience, as Carl Rogers proposes? A cynic might suggest giving up the scientific study of personality entirely. Or we might question the wisdom of accepting this requirement and a philosophy of science that is so inhospitable to the subject matter of this particular field, as Carl Rogers did (Hutterer, 1990).

A second requirement of the scientific method is that hypotheses be stated in a form that can be tested by empirical observation. A hypothesis is a prediction about what will be observed. The prediction is made before the observation. In this way, it is different from an after-the-fact understanding. For example, after a person has committed suicide, friends, family, and therapists may see evidence that clearly pointed to the tragedy. Such "*post*diction," however, is not an adequate substitute, practically or theoretically, for the *pre*diction required by the scientific method. Hindsight, common wisdom tells us, is always 20–20.

The hypothesis must specify, clearly and unambiguously, what observations will confirm it and what will disconfirm it. It cannot be vague. Consider the prediction, "Student behavior at midterm will be influenced by stress." What would confirm this hypothesis? Studying hard? Overeating? Sleeping excessively? Getting drunk? Arguing? Being unusually quiet? A person who believes the statement is likely to be able to find supporting evidence. The hypothesis is stated too imprecisely, however, to indicate what evidence would *refute* it, so it is not acceptable as a scientific hypothesis. Quite possibly, all those behaviors could be influenced by stress, and in some individuals each could be more frequent at midterm. Until we can predict with more precision, though, we are simply explaining, not predicting. Science demands more.

Third, the scientific method demands that *hypotheses be derived from theory.* Friends may predict accurately that "Leslie will be late for work on Monday," but this prediction has nothing to do with science. It is particularistic, contributing nothing to the task of science, which is to build a general conceptual understanding of the phenomena of interest: a **theory.** Theories consist of a network of propositions that describe, in abstract terms, the connections among concepts. These abstract statements (such as the example presented earlier in the chapter, "loving parents produce well-adjusted children") are translated into concrete, observable form; that is, hypotheses. Science is particularly impressive when, based on theory, a prediction is made that otherwise would not be expected, and when that hypothesis is confirmed by observation.

Does science demand mathematics? Many people would say yes, thinking of the sophisticated measures and mathematical analyses of physics and other hard sciences. Statistical procedures have become a ritual in the scientific process of theory-testing, but a ritual often done inadequately (Rosnow & Rosenthal, 1989). Paul Meehl (1990) advocates increased mathematical training for psychological researchers. In principle, though, "the essence of the scientific method is not mathematics, but logic" (Corsini, 1986, p. 483), and so the use of mathematics is not a necessary criterion for scientific adequacy. The field of personality should not be judged by apparent mathematical sophistication. Rather, we should focus critical attention on the logic,

RESEARCH STRATEGIES ●-----------------------------

Alternative Interpretations of the Same Observation

A child is watching television and sees the television character strangle a doll with a jump rope. Afterwards, the child does the same thing with a toy doll and a jump rope of his own.

This seems like a simple phenomenon. Certainly, events like this happen often in life and are among the phenomena that a personality psychologist strives to understand. Yet this simple event can be interpreted in many different ways. Competing assumptions, based on alternative theoretical assumptions, call attention to different aspects of the observation. They give different explanations and suggest different lines of research to elaborate understanding of this simple phenomenon.

Consider the possibilities:

• The child is motivated by a desire to be like powerful models. (Research suggestion: The more powerful the model, the more frequent the imitation. Social learning theorists have explored this issue.)

• The child has been influenced by strong situational forces. (Research implication: Pay attention to aspects of the situation, but ignore characteristics of the child. Behaviorists adopt this perspective.)

• The child is exhibiting behavior characteristic of a violent culture. (Research suggestion: Explore whether children in less violent cultures behave differently. Awareness of culture has been uncommon in personality research but is of increasing interest to researchers.)

• The child is expressing an innate aggressive tendency. (Research implication: Expect to find similar or alternative expressions of aggression universally. Psychoanalytic approaches discuss such innate tendencies.)

• The child is expressing his own personal aggressive tendencies, which were released by the television program. (Research implication: Expect to find that television elicits such behavior in children who show other evidence of aggression, but not in less aggressive children. Cognitive social learning theorists explore such issues.)

• The child is doing what he likes best, selecting from among many behaviors seen on television the one that he prefers most. (Research implication: See whether children who don't like strangling and jump ropes so much exhibit less of this behavior.) (Slife & Rychlak, 1982, found this, from a teleological "logical learning theory" perspective.)

Researchers in personality have been guided by their theoretical assumptions to explore various aspects of this simple behavior. Some describe the behavior; others the situation; others his inner motivations; others the child's choices. Research can enlighten, but theories, formal or informal, paradigmatic or simply offered tentatively, tell us where to point the light. The guiding assumptions of research are crucially important. Of course, as we shall consider later in this text, the methodological know-how is also important.

the theoretical reasoning, behind the numbers. See the Research Strategies box for a discussion of how alternative interpretations can be made of the same observations.

The Research Tradition within Personality

Personality has been an academic (as opposed to a clinical) discipline for more than half a century. One marker of its birth as an academic discipline is Gordon Allport's offering of the first personality course in the United States in the 1930s. Although Allport was more interested in theory than in research methods, his course and accompanying textbook brought the study of personality to psychology, releasing it from the nonempirical traditions of philosophy and psychotherapy.

Not everyone is convinced that personality is really a scientific field. Hans Eysenck, for one, doubts that personality is a scientific discipline, citing its lack of a shared paradigm as a major failure; he suggests that his own theory offers a viable paradigm, but one that has limited adherents (Eysenck, 1986a). He is particularly harsh toward psychoanalysis: "Psychoanalysis is a religious, not a scientific movement, hence its success and its continuation in spite of failure by all scientific criteria" (Eysenck, 1986a, p. 6). Academic researchers, such as Eysenck, often express criticism of the scientific failures of clinically based approaches to personality. These theories simply may not be amenable to scientific test at present, whatever other merits they may have (Meehl, 1990). Yet even within the academic world, the field of personality is deeply divided.

Cronbach's "Two Disciplines" of Scientific Psychology

Differences among strategies of academic research are so great that one often-cited observer, Lee Cronbach (1957), dubbed them the "two disciplines" of scientific psychology. Although these two disciplines exist throughout psychology, they are particularly debated in the field of personality.

The *two disciplines of scientific psychology* are set apart by their methods of research. **Experimental psychology** manipulates variables in controlled situations to examine cause-effect relationships. Have you ever suspected that you did badly on a test because the room was noisy, making you feel stressed? To test this hypothesis, an experimental psychologist would divide subjects randomly into two groups. An experimental group would be exposed to a loud noise, intended to make them feel stressed. A second group, called the "control group," would be kept in a quiet room. The

Researchers sometimes observe personality in unusual and unnatural laboratory situations in order to understand personality. While these "twists and bends" do not occur in everyday life, they do help to isolate causes and understand how personality functions.

researcher would have both groups take the same performance test. If the experimental group did less well, it could be concluded that the noisy environment caused their lower performance.

In contrast, **correlational psychology** does not manipulate variables. Instead, it examines the theorized causes of behavior as they naturally occur. Such causes are measured, rather than manipulated. Measurement can take many forms, including questionnaires, observer ratings, and physiological measurements. A researcher in this tradition might give subjects a questionnaire to determine how much stress they report in their lives. The subjects would also take a performance test. If those who reported more life stress did worse on the performance test than those who reported less life stress, then the researcher could conclude that high stress *predicts* a performance deficit. It may be tempting to conclude that stress "causes" the performance deficit, but this conclusion is not warranted in a correlational study. It could also be that the causes are reversed (poor performance may cause stress) or that some third variable, such as physical illness, causes both high stress and poor performance.

The "two disciplines" examine different aspects of psychology. One studies individual differences among people; the other studies the impact of situations. Correlational psychology analyzes existing aspects of the person that influence behavior. Experimental psychology investigates situations, manipulated by the experiment, for their effects. Of course, both person and situation have an impact, and in a broader sense, they combine to influence the outcome. They often *interact*, meaning that the impact of situations varies from person to person or, stated differently, that people respond differently to the same situation (Cronbach, 1957, 1975; Endler & Edwards, 1986). Research strategies that investigate both kinds of effects simultaneously, the effects of situations and of individual differences among people, have become increasingly common in personality research (Cervone, 1991).

Experimental and correlational approaches are not equal contenders for respect in the scientific community. The accepted scientific method is better matched to experimental than to correlational research (Mishler, 1990). Experimental research offers unambiguous interpretations, whereas correlational research can often be explained in more than one way, as we saw in the example just discussed. Correlations, even when predicted in advance and replicated across studies, do not constitute clear tests of theoretical predictions. For one thing, many variables are correlated for complex, probably unknowable, reasons (Meehl, 1990). Nature does not guarantee that everything else, except the researcher's variable of interest, is equal.

Correlational research justifies prediction, but not causal interpretation. That, at any rate, is the traditional view. More recently, it has been argued that causal interpretations sometimes *can* be made from correlational studies (for example, Rorer, 1990, p. 705). Sophisticated correlational designs, such as structural equation modeling, are used to test causal models; though the method does not allow a positive proof of causality, it permits causal models to be falsified (West, 1986). At this point, a simple general rule is sufficient: experimental research tests cause-effect relationships; correlational research does not.

Personality Measurement

Correlational researchers in personality have developed highly refined ways of measuring personality. This effort is called **psychometrics,** the measurement of personality. Psychometricians develop instruments to assess the personality differences among individuals. Psychometricians have developed many personality tests, and some of these are used in clinical and counseling psychology, as well as in research (Bubenzer, Zimpfer & Mahrle, 1990; Costa, 1991; Lubin et al., 1985). Some popular instruments are the Minnesota Multiphasic Personality Inventory (MMPI), the Myers-Briggs Type Indicator (MBTI), and the Rorschach inkblot test.

Measurement takes many forms. People may be presented with true-false or multiple-choice questions to answer in written form. They may write their answers as sentences or describe their thoughts orally to the researcher. They may make up imaginative stories or tell what they see in blots of ink. They may be filmed so that their facial expressions or body language can be analyzed. They may not even know that they are being measured, if a researcher surreptitiously watches them through a one-way mirror or in a public place. Whatever the source of the data, measurement involves taking these observations and translating them into codes or numbers so that the data can be systematically analyzed.

These measurements are sometimes categorical, as when we categorize facial expressions as "smiles" or "frowns." This level of measurement is called *qualitative measurement*. People can be classified into various groups, much as we might sort silverware into bins for knives, forks, and spoons. Clinicians think of patients as members of groups based on their diagnosis (schizophrenics, depressed individuals, and so forth). A diagnosis, because it is a statement about group membership, illustrates a qualitative measure. More often, individual differences are expressed as *quantitative measurement*. That is, a dimension of personality is proposed, and people possess varying amounts of that characteristic. To describe people's intelligence, for example, we need a whole range of numbers: 100, 110, 150, 90, and so on. Most personality traits, such as conscientiousness, openness, and extraversion, are quantitative. People are given a score on a measure of extraversion, rather than simply being categorized as extraverts or introverts, for example. Each level of measurement has its usefulness. Qualitative measures answer questions of "What kind?": "What kind of facial expression?" "What kind of illness?" Quantitative measures answer questions of "How much?": "How happy?" "How depressed?"

Whether qualitative or quantitative, measurements must fulfill two criteria of testing: good tests are *reliable*, and they are *valid*. By **reliability,** we mean that the measurement is dependable. It is not influenced very much by random fluctuations that would make it inconsistent. An unreliable personality test might tell you one day that you are introverted and the next day that you are extraverted. Such a test would have little value. Given a choice, would you prefer to have a speedometer in your car that reliably gave you the same reading when you were going the same speed, or one that was erratic, sometimes registering higher and sometimes lower? If you care to know how fast you are going, obviously you need a reliable speedometer. Without reliability, no measure can be trusted.

A reliable measuring instrument, though, is not necessarily accurate. For example, a speedometer may consistently register 10 miles per hour lower than the car is actually moving: it is reliable, but not accurate. Still, it could be useful, if we remember to make an appropriate adjustment for the biased reading. Certainly it is better than looking at the radio dial and interpreting it as a measure of speed!

By **validity,** we mean that the test measures what the test-giver is trying to measure, rather than something else. If a person scores high on a test of psychotic thinking but is not psychotic, the test is not valid. Such a result could occur if the test is not understood by the test-taker; for example, if the test-taker does not understand English well enough to give reasonable answers. The test would not be valid for this person, but it still could be valid for people who *do* speak English well. The reliability and validity of tests can never be assumed, but must be demonstrated through research and may vary from one group of people to another, and one setting to another.

Measuring and Improving Reliability   The most straightforward way to measure reliability is simply to give the test twice to the same group of subjects and compare their scores. This procedure is called **test-retest reliability.** If the same people tend to score high the second time as scored high the first time, while those who scored low the first time score low the second, the test is reliable. The statistic most often used to measure such reliability is the **correlation coefficient (r).** The maximum possible correlation coefficient is 1. A test with a reliability of .85 is more dependable than one with a reliability of only .60.

There is, however, a difficulty with the test-retest reliability method. It is intended to determine how much random error is present in the measuring instrument, and it does that well in some cases; for example, if we are measuring the weight of rocks or watching people through a one-way mirror and rating their behavior. In these cases, the first and second tests are independent assessments of what we are trying to measure; the first measurement cannot influence the second. Often, though, tests use a self-report format, requiring subjects to respond to questionnaires. People are likely to remember what they have answered before; most people try to be consistent. Even if they were guessing at questions the first time (so that there was a lot of random error; that is, unreliability), they try to repeat their answers the second time. This inflates the correlation, leading us to believe erroneously that the measure is more reliable than it really is and to underestimate the effect of chance on people's scores.

How can we avoid this problem and get a more meaningful estimate of the reliability of the test? Several strategies are possible. One technique is to assess the **alternate forms reliability** of the test. Two entirely different tests, intended to measure the same characteristic, are written. The same group of subjects takes both tests, and the correlation between the two scores is computed. If there is only one form of the test, reliability can be estimated by the **split half reliability** method. One score is computed using only half of the items (the odd-numbered items, for example) and another score from the other half (the even-numbered items). The correlation between these two measures gives a reliability estimate. However it is calculated, the higher the reliability, the better. Measures that are not sufficiently reliable are not dependable for measuring traits in individuals, and they will not show dependable associations with other variables in research.

If reliability is so important, how can it be improved? Researchers often use the following strategies:

1. Delete from the test any items that do not correlate with the other items, because they reduce the reliability of the whole measure. (Test constructors begin with a very large pool of potential items and pick actual items by looking for those that correlate highly with one another.)

2. Standardize the circumstances under which the test is administered, to avoid inconsistencies due to situational influences. Read standard instructions to all subjects.

3. Make the test longer. It is the total score that matters. The longer the test, the more consistent the total score, since variation from item to item tends to cancel out.

4. If scoring the measure is not a simple mechanical process, improve scoring methods to be sure that various coders agree. For example, if researchers are evaluating subjects' responses to inkblots or ambiguous pictures, describe scoring procedures in a coding manual and train coders to use it in a standard way.

Evaluating Validity How do we know that a measurement is accurate? A measurement is *valid* if it measures what it sets out to measure. People often agree with the results of personality tests that they have taken, even when these results are simply vague and general statements that could be applied to nearly anyone (like horoscopes). This phenomenon is called the **Barnum effect** (Dickson & Kelly, 1985; Furnham & Schofield, 1987). People are readily convinced that personality tests are accurate; they do not differentiate meaningful tests from those that don't say anything particular about them. Therefore, people's judgments are not a good basis for evaluating the validity of personality tests.

Instead, the validity of psychological tests must be established by research. One strategy is to demonstrate that the test accurately predicts what one would expect. This technique is called **predictive validity.** For example, a measure of suicide risk would have high predictive validity if people who got high scores more often committed suicide in the future than did those who got low scores. The test predicts a *criterion;* in this case, suicide. With other types of validity, the criterion does not have to occur in the future. It can be measured at the same time as the test, in which case the term **concurrent validity** is used. For example, a test of "social interest" is significantly correlated with the number of close friends that people report they have (Watkins & Hector, 1990).

Sometimes tests predict a criterion, but one that doesn't seem to be convincing evidence for the validity of the test. For example, a measure of general intelligence, the Australian Army General Classification test, predicts midlife mortality (O'Toole & Stankov, 1992). Yet this prediction adds nothing to our confidence in the test as a measure of intelligence. Neither does it make it a measure of health. What, besides prediction, is needed to establish validity?

Construct validity is established by an accumulation of research from several studies, showing that the pattern of results is what would be expected from the theoretical conceptualization (Cronbach & Meehl, 1955). The Australian intelligence test described above would be more convincing if it predicted what we expect from an intelligence test: grades, occupational status, and so on. Why mortality? There is no theoretical reason to expect more intelligent people to live longer. We might imagine a reason: that intelligence is an overall rating of one's ability to adapt and therefore to survive. Perhaps our theory of intelligence should be expanded to include this idea. Does that mean, though, that any measurement that predicts longevity is a measure of intelligence? Theory would also need to explain how to distinguish intelligence from other characteristics, such as health consciousness, that also predict longevity. Such theoretical developments occur often in scientific fields, with each step tested by research. In essence, construct validation requires that a *theory* be shown to be valid because it generates many predictions that are confirmed by research; it is not simply a matter of accepting a particular test (Landy, 1986). Such validation is "problematic in a deep theoretical sense, rather than . . . a technical problem to be solved by more rigorous rules and procedures" (Mishler, 1990, p. 417). In fact, validation of theories is the central task of science.

Personality, Social Values, and Scientific Objectivity

Conceptions about personality are entrenched in law and tradition. For example, legal decisions rest on the assumption that people generally have "free will," thus making them responsible for their actions, but it is also assumed that such free will can be lost under certain other circumstances (including insanity and extreme emotional distress). Tradition tells us that women are more nurturant and less mathematically gifted than men. Given such strong traditional conceptions, can personality really be studied objectively?

There is the danger that we will simply look for evidence to support what we already believe. Social psychologists have found that people often show such a **confirmation bias,** looking for evidence of shyness in people they believe to be shy or of immorality in those they consider to be immoral. It's harder to prove someone is wrong about you than to confirm what they already believe. In the same way, the ultimate truths about personality will be more difficult to discover if we seek them hampered by erroneous beliefs.

Worse, these beliefs are not simply wrong but are tenaciously embedded in our whole system of values. Thomas Kuhn, discussing the history of the discovery that the Earth is not the center of the universe, pointed out that heliocentrism (the fact that the sun is the center of our solar system) is "more than a strictly astronomical issue" (Kuhn, 1970, p. 150). It challenged the fervent belief that humans were in a unique, privileged status in God's creation. Similarly, many ideas about personality, including free will, genetic determination, and the qualities that are considered mentally healthy, are not simply scientific issues. Increasingly, psychologists have recognized that values influence their theories and research (Lyddon, 1991). Of course, we may find that science confirms our beliefs, but we cannot be scientists unless we are open to the possibility of disconfirmation.

Impetus for theoretical change has come from some directions based on social values and political convictions. Feminists have challenged assumptions about personality that they claim reflect the biases of a culture's commitment to traditional sex roles (Crawford & Marecek, 1989; Torrey, 1987). The feminist argument is "that scientific knowledge cannot be neutral or objective because it is structured by power relations which are not only unequal across the boundaries of gender but also across the dimensions of class and race" (Lyddon, 1991, p. 269). Some feminists claim that the research methods used by mainstream personality researchers, which manipulate variables and ignore social context, are biased and do not meet feminist concerns (Ballou, 1990; Lykes & Stewart, 1986; Marecek, 1989). Others, however, have challenged this viewpoint (Peplau & Conrad, 1989).

Members of racial minorities contend that theories ignore various influences on personality experienced by individuals who are not white. Social change (and how quickly the world changes!) is even said to influence conceptions of personality. For instance, the individual (rather than the group) has been particularly important in our modern era; our ancestors stressed community more than individuality. This heightened awareness of individuality may be fading, however, as our society becomes sensitive to the interrelationship among various cultures, within North America and around the world (Sampson, 1989).

Underlying such challenges to traditional perspectives is the understanding that psychology does not simply discover objective reality. The *social constructionist* position recognizes that the discipline helps to create (not simply discover) its "truths" (Gergen, 1985; Hampson, 1988). Studying the achievements of males and the nurturance of females solidifies these characteristics. Investigating men's nurturant potential and women's ability to lead helps to bring about these potentialities. Such science is not entirely "objective," of course, though we must guard against distortion. Perhaps a science of psychology cannot be objective, in the sense of the traditional view that scientists study but do not influence the objects of their study. So concluded Roger Sperry, a Nobel Prize winner well known for his research in neuropsychology (Sperry, 1986). This field is shaped, consciously or unconsciously, by the values of researchers, and its findings have implications for those values, as well as the potential to help steer the course of cultural change. What kind of science is this? What is science? We need to reconsider the fundamentals.

Philosophy of Science

Whether prompted by a concern with values or by a recognition that the theories that direct personality research are in need of clearer conceptualization, scholars in the field of personality are increasingly rethinking the philosophical assumptions of the field. According to Sigmund Koch,

> *Psychology is necessarily the most philosophy-sensitive discipline in the entire gamut of disciplines that claim empirical status. We cannot discriminate a so-called variable, pose a research question, choose or invent a method, project a theory, stipulate a psychotechnology, without making strong presumptions of philosophical cast about the nature of our human subject matter—presumptions that can be ordered to age-old contexts of philosophical discussion. Even our nomenclature for the basic fields of specialized research within psychology (e.g., sensation, perception, cognition, memory, motivation, emotion, etc.) has its origin in philosophy."* (Koch, 1981, p. 267.)

A clearer understanding of the philosophical assumptions of science can help researchers to investigate personality more effectively. Many who work in the field have questioned the philosophical assumptions, often unstated, upon which theory and research are based. They argue that the older assumptions, rooted in the physical sciences of the last century, are no longer adequate. What are these traditional assumptions of the philosophy of science? Why are they being challenged? What has been offered to replace them?

Scientific theory and research are based upon the philosophy of *logical positivism* and the *hypothetico-deductive method.*

Logical Positivism

The philosophy of **logical positivism** has shaped the scientific methods acceptable in much of the study of personality and in psychology generally. What is this philosophical position? First, logical positivism asserts that knowledge is obtained from data provided by the senses. Observation provides knowledge. Intuition, enlightenment, and divine inspiration are outside the realm of science. Subjective experience has no place in this philosophy. Strictly logical statements are accepted, but only those based on logical *deduction*, not *induction.*

Second, logical positivism avoids explanations of phenomena in terms of abstract concepts that cannot be observed. This approach has "a thorough-going hostility to unobservable or theoretical entities" (O'Hear, 1989, p. 109). Instead of "deeper" causes, logical positivism describes

How shall we try to understand these people? Should we describe their passion? Their need for love? Or should we leave such language to less scientific disciplines and describe their behavior more objectively? Personality has been studied in a variety of ways, reflecting different answers to fundamental philosophical questions about science.

causes in terms of associations among events that are directly observable (O'Hear, 1989, p. 108).

Some psychologists have adopted the philosophy of logical positivism more strongly than have others. In particular, logical positivism has been closely associated with behaviorism (Turner, 1967). B. F. Skinner's radical behaviorism fits this philosophy well. He argued that theoretical terms are unnecessary (Skinner, 1950), and he observed behavior in great detail. Skinner attributed the causes of behavior to environmental variables that could be directly observed, such as a pellet of food given to a hungry rat. Others have deviated from the tenets of logical positivism but have been criticized as being less scientific because of these deviations. Sigmund Freud explained psychological phenomena in terms of such abstract "metapsychological" concepts as "libido," which could not be directly observed, and he has been the target of frequent criticism for this. Humanists, too, often discuss dimensions of personality (such as "self-actualization") that are relatively difficult to describe in terms of observable phenomena.

Are the assumptions of logical positivism necessary for science? Although they are accepted by radical behaviorists, most observers question the notion that logical positivism defines good science. It is often rejected as an outdated philosophy of science. Psychologists have often modeled their understandings of science after physics. Yet physicists have not adopted logical positivism. "Physicists have never had any reluctance to talk about things that are in principle unobservable (e.g., atoms, quarks, black holes), but psychologists, thinking that they were being scientific, competed with one another to see who could be the most rigorous—that is, the most objective" (Rorer, 1990, p. 705). Perhaps psychology's greater distrust of unobservable explanations is that so many of these (moral character, demonic possession, and so forth) are the basis of views of human nature that psychology seeks to replace.

The Hypothetico-Deductive Method

Unlike logical positivism, the **hypothetico-deductive method** remains central to the scientific method as it is practiced in psychology today, when formal theoretical statements are put to the test. How does this method work? First, there is a formal *theory*, consisting of statements at an abstract level. Erik Erikson, for example, proposed a theory stating that each person develops throughout life in eight stages. These statements are amplified into a whole network of related assertions. Erikson's theory identified a central conflict for each of the eight stages, described a healthy and an unhealthy outcome of the conflict, predicted that people who have early unhealthy outcomes will be handicapped in resolving later conflicts in a healthy manner, and so on (Erikson, 1959).

Then, by a process of logical deduction, predictions (hypotheses) are made about observations that could be made in the real world if the abstract theory were true. The researcher then looks for these real-world observations. If they are *not* observed, the theory can be rejected. If they *are* observed, the theory is still tenable. In the case of Erikson's theory, researchers have developed measures of his developmental stages and have shown that these measures are related as hypothesized to one another and to other variables, such as patterns of friendships, fear of death, and satisfaction with college (Cloninger, 1993). A theory is never unambiguously proved, because there may be other abstract theories that would make the same predictions, but at least it has withstood an empirical test. That is, the theory has been stated in such a way that it could be proved wrong, and it has withstood this test of **falsifiability** (Popper, 1959).

The more predictions are tested and confirmed, the more the theory is likely to be accepted. If a theory, first proposed tentatively, has been broadly successful in making predictions and explaining observations, it may become the prevailing model or paradigm for the area of study (Kuhn, 1970). A few unconfirmed predictions, on the other hand, do not necessarily lead to rejection of the theory. Perhaps the process of deducing predicted observations from the theory is flawed, rather than the theory itself. There may be inadequate observations that do not correspond well to the theory; alternative measures might find what was predicted, after all.

Kuhn's View of Scientific Progress

Thomas Kuhn has described the progress of science as a series of revolutions. When a prevailing paradigm (generally accepted theory) can no longer explain observations, it gives way to a competing paradigm. Although Kuhn's model is not universally accepted (see, for example, Leahey, 1992), he is the most widely cited philosopher of science. His work is often cited in personality journals, despite the fact that it was based on the natural sciences, and despite Kuhn's warning that the social and behavioral sciences might not follow the model of the natural sciences (Coleman & Salamon, 1988).

When Kuhn observed social scientists and saw something different from what he had observed in natural scientists,

> *I was struck by the number and extent of the overt disagreements between social scientists about the nature of legitimate scientific problems and methods. [This is not the case in astronomy, physics, chemistry, biology.] Attempting to discover the source of that difference [from the other sciences] led me to recognize the role in scientific research of what I have since called "paradigms." These I take to be universally recognized scientific achievements that for a time provide model problems and solutions to a community of practitioners. (Kuhn, 1970, p. viii)*

A perusal of many texts in personality theory will attest to the large number of theories: psychoanalytic theory (in many variations), behaviorism, cognitive behaviorism, humanistic theory, and so on. To some observers, this means that the field has competing paradigms (Leahey, 1992). A theory is not necessarily a paradigm, however, and other observers maintain that psychology is in a preparadigm phase (Kornfeld, 1990). This conclusion is supported by the similarity of personality psychology today with Kuhn's description of the field of physical optics before Newton, in its preparadigm phase:

> *Though the field's practitioners were scientists, the net result of their activity was something less than science. Being able to take no common body of belief for*

granted, each writer on physical optics felt forced to build his field anew from its foundations. In doing so, his choice of supporting observation and experiment was relatively free, for there was no standard set of methods or of phenomena that every optical writer felt forced to employ and explain. Under these circumstances, the dialogue of the resulting books was often directed as much to the members of other schools as it was to nature. That pattern is not unfamiliar in a number of creative fields today, nor is it incompatible with significant discovery and invention. It is not, however, the pattern of development that physical optics acquired after Newton and that other natural sciences make familiar today. (Kuhn, 1970, p. 13)

Personality theory is still waiting for its Newton. No one paradigm has been adopted (Sarason, 1989). If the natural sciences are an appropriate model (and we have no guarantee that they are), a common paradigm seems desirable. It would provide researchers with clearer direction for their efforts. Presumably, they could accomplish more by building on one another's research. On the other had, such unification may be unwise at present. Perhaps more progress could be achieved by increased attention to theoretical developments (Meehl, 1990; Serlin, 1987). Premature synthesis is likely to bring more confusion than integration (Walsh & Peterson, 1985), and it would end debate over philosophical and theoretical issues that may need further consideration.

Philosophical Issues in Personality Theory

It is clear that there is no consensus in the field about which model should guide personality research. Competing models, from various sources, each have adherents. Major issues divide these theories. Let us consider the most important of them. Then we will examine a way to organize our thinking about scientific research in personality in the absence of a unifying paradigm.

Reductionism

At one level, people can be thought of as biological organisms made up of active cells. Thought itself involves the firing of neurons in the brain and the transmission of information across synapses. To what extent can psychological processes be explained entirely in neurological terms? That is the question of **reductionism.** Can all of personality be reduced to such a description? Perhaps it can, in principle. (Not everyone would agree with this, however.) Certainly, though, something is lost in a solely neurological description.

Personality psychology is part of a broad spectrum of interrelated sciences, each borrowing from the next and each obligated not to contradict the clearly replicated observations of the other disciplines. Neuroscience, in particular, has made discoveries about the biological bases of experience that personality psychology should not contradict. One of the most well known of these findings is the difference in function between the left and right cerebral hemispheres of the brain, although there are others (Derryberry & Tucker, 1991). Cerebral hemisphere specialization seems to provide a neurological basis for the different functions of creativity and language, of art and logic. The more abstract descriptions of these psychological functions seem to be confirmed when they can be related to distinct neurological bases.

Merle Turner asserts that "there are no logical barriers, and perhaps no technological ones, to reductionism in psychology and . . . all explanations of behavior can in principle be reduced to the language of neurophysiology" (Turner, 1967, p. 335). Even if this is so, neurology will not make psychology obsolete. Why not? In part, the answer is practical. Neuroscience has much to learn. Observations of the functioning of human personality can be made globally, but the task of tracing these observations to specific neural mechanisms lags far behind. Consider this analogy. In principle, medicine may be reduced to cell physiology, but in practice, medicine remains a necessary field for describing (and treating) disease. Similarly, in practical terms, neurology cannot replace psychology.

Beyond this practical issue, the phenomena studied by personality psychology can never be wholly understood from a neurological perspective. The reductionistic model asserts that higher order phenomena are determined by lower order phenomena (for example, psychological experience is determined by neural events). Yet in human personality, the whole is more than the sum of the parts. Roger Sperry (1987, 1990) argues for an alternative model, in which higher order developments in the nervous system take on causal functions. Sperry calls this position "emergent determinism." Therefore, reduction to biological processes cannot fully explain psychological phenomena (Bunge, 1990), any more than a musical concert can be reduced to the physics of sound.

No science exists in isolation. Each is related to other sciences (as biology is related to chemistry) and to the nonscientific realm. The relationship of personality to these other areas can help us to understand some of its dilemmas. Personality borrows from many areas of psychology and from other sciences. Yet it is distinctive in its emphasis on the functioning of the whole person. From the physiological sciences, especially neurology, personality psychologists learn to consider the abilities and limitations of the body that influence the functioning of the individual. From disciplines that describe the social world, including sociology and history, personality psychologists consider the life tasks and pressures that confront individuals: socioeconomic stressors, war, and so on. Within psychology, developmental psychologists provide descriptions of the capacities and developmental tasks of a person that vary with age, helping personality psychologists to better understand the processes by which personality is shaped. Experimental psychologists have provided methodologies for assessing the impact of specific situations on behavior. Clinical psychologists and other therapists have a particularly close relationship with personality theory, since they observe personality functioning and change at close range.

Determinism

Traditionally, science presumes that the phenomena being studied have causes and that these causes can be discovered through scientific methods; this is the assumption of **determinism.** This assumption conflicts with the concept of **free will,** which has played a prominent role in culture for centuries.

Personality theories have varying perspectives on determinism. Some, like behaviorism and psychoanalysis, assume determinism. Others, like humanism, emphasize free will and choice. The term *telic* is often used to describe these nondeterministic approaches that emphasize choice and goals. The telic (also called "teleological") view asserts "that the person behaves for the sake of a freely formulated plan, design, or predication" (Slife, 1981a, p. 221).

Are such free choices outside the realm of scientific study? Are they inconsistent with physical reality? Some thinkers have argued that the uncertainty principle of subatomic particles that is recognized by modern physics provides a scientific basis for accepting free will and other nondeterministic assumptions at the level of human personality (for example, Keutzer, 1984). This leap may be unwarranted (McLarty, 1990; Wallace, 1986), but it does provide a powerful metaphor.

Research on telic approaches is exceedingly difficult, because psychological research methods have been adapted from sciences in which free will is not an issue. In the physical sciences, forces outside the objects studied are sufficient to describe the phenomena. No physicist would agree that a rock falls to Earth because it *wants* to unite with Earth. How could such a theory be falsified?

We can ask people about their desires and goals. Yet if their responses predict their behavior, that still is not convincing evidence that the desires *cause* the behavior, because the method is correlational, not experimental. Psychologists must decide whether collecting data about people's choices and plans is central to their task or a diversion from more important questions. Some theorists have been working on this methodological dilemma, trying to develop research strategies that support a telic theory of human personality (Howard, Youngs & Siatczynski, 1989; Rychlak, 1981a, 1981b, 1984a, 1988). Success has been limited, however. Observations that sup-

Our private thoughts and feelings are of interest to personality psychologists, though it is challenging to know how to study them scientifically.

port a teleological theory also can be interpreted from a deterministic perspective.

The concept of free will, even if not itself verifiable through research, serves as a meta-assumption, influencing researchers to collect data on people's choices and intentions (Sappington, 1990). Increasingly, psychologists are using "concepts such as *conscious choice* and *purpose* to predict and account for data" (Sappington, 1990, p. 26). Even if people's choices are, in principle, determined rather than free, they cannot, in practical terms, be predicted from lower order explanations. What seems to be "free will" in ordinary language is not inherently irreconcilable with scientific determinism (Kimble, 1989).

Subjective Experience

A person's thoughts, feelings, fears, and other aspects of subjective experience are privately known but publicly unobservable. How can science, which demands the validation of observations by independent observers, deal with such phenomena? Radical behaviorists, led by B. F. Skinner, excluded private subjective experience from their scientific research (Moore, 1985, 1990). For Skinner, private experience exists, but it is incidental, not a cause of behavior (Creel, 1980; Natsoulas, 1983; Skinner, 1987). In contrast, humanists claim that subjective experience is central to the experience of being human. It provides a key to the higher order determinants of personality, will and striving (Maslow, 1966; Rogers, 1973). Even

TABLE 1.2 Personality Description, Dynamics, and Development

Personality description	Describes the major dimensions of personality (traits); develops tests to measure these traits in individuals; describes differences among groups in their typical traits
Personality dynamics	Considers the factors that influence the day-to-day functioning of a person, including unconscious and conscious motivations, self-concept, and coping mechanisms
Personality development	Considers how personality is formed, including influences from biological factors such as genetics and experiential factors such as childhood experiences in the family and adult experiences in work, marriage, and other social roles

the subjective experience of the researcher may play a legitimate part in the research enterprise, although that researcher must also maintain a degree of objectivity (Hutterer, 1990).

Psychologists do not agree, then, about how to include subjective experience in personality theories. Some say that subjective experience can be explained in terms of simple learning mechanisms. Others say that it can be explained within a deterministic model but requires higher order cognitive concepts (Miller, 1988; Staats, 1987, 1993). Still others maintain that no deterministic model can account for phenomenal experience. This is a central issue that must be resolved if personality theory is ever to agree on a shared paradigm.

Three Questions to Direct Research in Personality

Given the lack of a consensus paradigm to guide research in the field of personality, how shall research be directed? One approach is to continue as a pluralistic discipline, with several schools of thought, each continuing more or less in isolation from the others. Unfortunately, this approach leaves the observations of each school of thought relatively unavailable to the other schools. For the most part, observations from other schools are seen as irrelevant, because they depend upon the conceptualizations and measurements of alien approaches. As the metaphor at the beginning of this chapter suggested, the field is like builders without a common plan. Obviously, this is inefficient. Yet the conceptual disagreements that divide the field are too great to expect a common paradigm to emerge soon. Is there any way that the findings derived from personality research can be conceptualized so that they will be more accessible across theoretical divisions?

One approach to devising a common plan is to describe the observations in terms of issues that transcend theoretical boundaries. Broad questions guide research. Three such concerns constitute the organizing framework for this book. First, how shall personality be described? Can the same descriptions of personality traits that describe one person be used for another? What is the most meaningful way to describe individual differences? How different are people, anyway? Second, how shall we understand personality dynamics? What motivates people? What needs, unconscious pressures, or concepts of self, influence people's behavior as they adapt to the world? Third, how does personality develop over time? To what extent are people consistent; how much do they change? What are the issues that are resolved at each stage of life? How does the social context shape this development?

The study of personality thus encompasses personality *description*, *dynamics*, and *development* (Table 1.2). How would you describe yourself? Why do you behave as you do, whether working hard, overeating, or whatever? What events in your past led you to be as you are, and how will the stages of life yet to come bring change? If we could understand what kind of personality an individual has, why the person behaves one way rather than another, and how the personality came to be, perhaps that would resolve theoretical questions or make them moot. At any rate, these questions are focused on observable phenomena, and that seems a sensible basis for science.

These are interrelated issues, of course. Broad theories emphasize their interrelationships. Psychoanalytic theory, for example, describes one type of personality as "orally fixated," tracing the dynamic explanations for oral behaviors (overeating, smoking, and so on) to salient developmental experiences in infancy. Humanistic theory describes people as more or less self-actualized, dynamically motivated by the need to develop their full potential.

Yet by distinguishing these three D's of personality, we have a framework for asking some of the broader questions not addressed by any single theory and so moving toward a more inclusive paradigm.

SUMMARY

- The field of personality studies the psychological functioning of the individual person, using the scientific method.

- The scientific method emphasizes systematic investigation and verification of observations through hypothesis-testing.

- Personality researchers lack a shared paradigm to guide their research. Instead, many perspectives or theories coexist.

- Two traditions influence personality research: clinical psychology, which focuses on therapy, and academic psychology, which focuses on scientific research.

- The insights stemming from clinical psychology are often difficult to test using the scientific method.

- The method of science demands that independent observers must verify data, that hypotheses must be stated in a form that can be tested, and that these hypotheses must be derived from theory.

- There are diverse viewpoints about the application of the scientific method to research in personality. Two disciplines of scientific psychology have emerged: experimental and correlational.

- Psychometrics is the measurement of personality through many forms of tests.

- Measurement can be qualitative (categorical) or quantitative (gradations in amounts).

- A good test is reliable (consistent) and valid (accurate). Reliability can be assessed by various methods, often using the correlation coefficient (r) statistic, including test-retest, alternate forms, and split half reliability.

- Test validity can be measured by evaluating the correlation of the test with a criterion that occurs in the future (predictive validity) or that is measured at the same time as the test (concurrent validity). Construct validity, in contrast, refers not simply to the test but to the underlying theory, and it requires evidence from many studies.

- Scientific objectivity can be difficult in the study of personality, as illustrated by the debate between determinism and free will and by people's tendency to make errors through confirmation bias.

- Philosophical issues relevant to the study of personality include reductionism, determinism, and the role of subjective experience.

- Scientific theory and research are based upon the philosophy of logical positivism and the hypothetico-deductive method and demand that theories be falsifiable.

• Since no one paradigm, in Kuhn's sense, prevails in the field of personality, the text suggests that research be organized around three fundamental questions: the description, the dynamics, and the development of personality.

GLOSSARY

academic psychology   The branch of psychology that is concerned with research, teaching, and theory-building in various subject areas

alternate forms reliability   The consistency of a test as evaluated by giving two different versions of the test to the same people to see how highly they are correlated

Barnum effect   People's tendency to agree with interpretations that are claimed to be based on personality tests, even if these interpretations are vague and could apply to most people

clinical psychology   The branch of psychology that is concerned with therapy, including therapeutic practice and related theory-building and research

concurrent validity   The accuracy of a test as evaluated by correlating it with a criterion measure that is assessed at the same time as the test

confirmation bias   People's tendency to seek evidence to support what they already believe, rather than seeking evidence that could refute their expectations (as a scientist would do)

construct validity   The value of a theory as established through an accumulation of research from several studies showing that the theory is useful in suggesting hypotheses that are confirmed by research

correlation coefficient (r)   A statistic that measures the relationship between two sets of variables for the same individual, expressed as a number ranging from $+1.00$ to -1.00

correlational psychology   The discipline of scientific psychology that emphasizes careful measurement (rather than the manipulation of variables)

determinism   The assumption that phenomena have causes and that these causes can be discovered through scientific methods

experimental psychology   The discipline of scientific psychology that manipulates variables in controlled situations to examine cause-effect relationships

falsifiability   The capacity of a theory to be shown to be wrong, based on its ability to make precise predictions about what should be observed

free will   The assumption that behavior results from the voluntary, undetermined choices of individuals

hypothesis   A prediction about what will be observed in research

hypothetico-deductive method   Scientific statement of a prediction, derived from theory, and its empirical testing to see whether it withstands the possibility of being disconfirmed

logical positivism   The philosophy that has guided traditional scientific inquiry, emphasizing objective evidence that can be observed rather than subjective evidence that is experienced privately

paradigm   A shared set of assumptions and methodology that guides scientists

personality   The psychological functioning of the individual person and the field of psychology that studies this topic

predictive validity   The accuracy of a test as assessed by correlating it with a criterion measure that occurs at some time after the test is administered

psychometrics   The field of personality that specializes in the measurement of individual differences

reductionism   An explanation of higher order processes, such as the experience or behavior of a person, in terms of lower order processes, such as the functioning of the nervous system

reliability   The dependability of a measuring instrument; reflected, for example, in its consistency in producing similar scores for an individual from one occasion to another

scientific method   Procedures for seeking knowledge by systematic observation and experimentation, using carefully controlled procedures

split half reliability   The consistency of a test as assessed by computing two scores, each from half of the items, to see whether they are highly correlated

test-retest reliability   The consistency of a test in producing similar rank ordering of the same individuals on two different testing occasions

theory   A network of associated propositions about the relationships among concepts that guides research

validity   The accuracy of a test in measuring what it is supposed to measure

THOUGHT QUESTIONS

1. Suggest a possible cause of "happiness." How would you state this in the form of a hypothesis, so that it could be tested using the scientific method?

2. Do you have any beliefs that you would be unwilling to give up, even if a scientific researcher found evidence against them? What kind of evidence would support or refute these beliefs?

3. Discuss the differences among theoretical perspectives in how each would try to understand anxiety. Do you find some of these approaches more appealing than others?

4. How might clinical and academic psychologists differ in their approach to anxiety?

5. Which proposition would be easier to test using an experimental approach: "Firstborn children are more conservative than youngest children" or "People are more generous when they have just experienced a fortunate event"?

6. Why would a graduate school prefer a more reliable admissions test to a less reliable test?

7. Suggest a way of showing the predictive validity of a test that is supposed to measure creativity.

8. How might confirmation bias distort results if a researcher decided to evaluate whether therapy is effective by asking therapists and patients their opinions?

9. Do you think that when scientists study environmental causes of violent behavior they encourage people to excuse their own violent acts? How does this idea relate to the social constructionist position described in this chapter? How does it relate to the determinism versus free will controversy?

10. What questions would you like answered by studying personality? Can you classify these as questions related to description, dynamics, or development?

PART ONE

The Description of Personality

HOW SHALL WE DESCRIBE A PERSON?

Like the allegorical caterpillar walking, it is much easier if we don't give the matter too much thought. People have been describing one another longer than psychologists have done so—indeed, longer than recorded history. It is reasonable, then, that many researchers have based their descriptions of personality on a detailed analysis of the language people use to describe one another. Language does not reflect all the dimensions of individual differences in personality, however (although it does cover many of them). Trait psychologists have devised tests that go beyond the insight of everyday language, as well as those that include it. Many of the tests that are most popular today have been developed with the aid of sophisticated statistical techniques, particularly factor analysis. Whatever their source, tests designed by trait psychologists aim to measure differences in personality among individuals. The vast majority of such tests are self-report measures, so they are limited to aspects of personality about which the individuals being tested have at least some conscious awareness.

With powerful tests to measure personality, it has become possible to investigate some of the popular ideas about group differences. How different are men and women, according to standard measures of personality? (Not so very different after all, we find.) Are differences among racial and ethnic groups as great as we might expect, given the diverse experiences that these social categories bring? (These differences, too, seem to be exaggerated in the public eye.) We can even begin to ask about differences from one nation to another. Questions about group differences, however, are not simple, because our tests are not necessarily valid across all groups. There is no "one size fits all" measure of personality. We will consider some of the methodological problems with comparing groups, returning to group comparisons in Part III, where the discussion will focus on the social context of personality development for the various groups. There is, after all, a limit to the extent to which we can describe personality differences without considering social environmental differences, just as a biologist can only go so far in describing the differences between a chimpanzee and a polar bear without mentioning climate and vegetation.

In the last chapter of this section, we will set aside comparisons of individuals to see how psychologists describe one individual. Comparisons focus attention on the dimensions being compared, but they do not convey the wholeness of a personality. To study individuals, psychologists have gained insights from clinicians and biographers and have attempted to add scientific rigor to these approaches by devising specialized techniques.

The study of personality may well begin with description, but description raises questions of personality dynamics and development that we will investigate in Parts II and III. In studying the individual, for example, clinicians and biographers, and their counterparts in personality research, inevitably ask why a person does one thing rather than another: a question of personality dynamics. Understanding differences between men and women and differences associated with race and ethnicity requires us to consider the social influences on development—the different roles and experiences that accompany gender, race, and ethnicity. To begin, though, let us direct our attention to the more basic question: How can personality can be described and measured?

2

Personality Description

SCIENCE, WE ARE OFTEN TOLD, aims to describe, explain, predict, and control the phenomena within the scope of the particular field of study. At first, it might seem that description would be the simplest of these aims, to be accomplished quickly so that the real investigation can begin. Yet the task is not so simple. There are many ways of describing personality. Some are based on characterizations offered by people who are untrained in psychology and are using everyday language. Others demand specially devised questionnaires and elaborate statistical procedures. As researchers move from description to the "higher" aims of science, to explanation and prediction and (rarely, in this field) to control, they revise their earlier ways of describing personality.

Even though personality description cannot be completed decisively before moving on, it is nonetheless a good place to begin our study of personality. Like the opening chord in a symphony, this theme will be replayed.

Language and Personality Description

People have been talking about personality for countless centuries. Informally, these common sense, lay conceptualizations undoubtedly influence the hunches that theorists and researchers follow. More formally, researchers have developed studies specifically designed to analyze people's language.

Describing Personality in Everyday Language

What are the words that people use, in everyday speech, to describe personality? These words offer a good place for personality researchers to begin their scientific explorations (Funder, 1991). Oliver John and his team of researchers describe the rationale of the **lexical approach** to personality research:

> Those individual differences that are most salient and socially relevant in people's lives will eventually become encoded into their language; the more important such a difference, the more likely it is to become expressed as a single word. *The analysis of the personality vocabulary represented in a natural language should thus yield a finite set of attributes that the people in the language community have generally found to be the most important. (John, Angleitner & Ostendorf, 1988, pp. 174–175 [italics in original])*

Some aspects of personality are described in phrases: "calm in a crisis," "unlucky in love." Other aspects of personality are expressed in a single word: "persistent," "dependable," "shy." Presumably, traits important to those who talk about personality are more often in the single-word category.

The lexical approach has a long history in personality research, beginning with Francis Galton's analysis of a dictionary in 1884 (described by John, Angleitner & Ostendorf, 1988). The best known lexical research was Gordon Allport's compilation of 17,953 terms relevant to personality, culled from Webster's *New International Dictionary* (Allport & Odbert, 1936). Allport suggested that psychological investigation could build on this catalog, although there was no guarantee that all real traits were reflected in language, and Raymond Cattell further built on this analysis of language (Cattell, 1943).

Many decisions about research procedures must be made in such an undertaking. Which words refer to personality, and which don't? Should slang and esoteric words be included? What about words with ambiguous meanings? How shall the words be grouped together? Statistical analysis

How would you describe these kids? The language of everyday life is a starting point for many scientific descriptions of personality.

helps, but empirical procedures can be daunting. Raymond Cattell is reported to have computed a 14-square-foot matrix of 14,535 correlation coefficients during his analysis (John, Angleitner & Ostendorf, 1988)! Nonetheless, computers cannot make personality description a wholly objective process. Human judgment must supplement mathematical analysis, and later researchers have questioned whether Cattell's list of personality dimensions was adequate. See the Research Strategies box for a discussion of how correlation coefficients are used in personality research.

Several other researchers conducted major lexical studies. Emerging from these studies is a consensus among many researchers that personality differences consist of five major dimensions (Digman, 1990; Goldberg, 1981, 1990; Norman, 1963). These **Big Five** dimensions are *Extraversion* (also sometimes called Surgency), *Agreeableness, Conscientiousness* (or Dependability), *Emotional Stability* (low Neuroticism), and *Openness to Experience* (also called Culture or Intellect). (Not all researchers agree on the labels that best summarize the dimensions.)

Studying What People Say

In the case of the Big Five personality traits, the lexical approach culminated in the development of a self-report personality test that could be given to people to assess their personalities. There is, however, another way of using language as a clue to describing personality. This method concentrates on the words the person says, analyzed using one of many procedures. It is a method that is particularly useful when we wish to study the personality of someone who cannot, or will not, take a personality test. Famous people may not cooperate with personality researchers. Dead people can't. If the person has left a written or spoken record, however, that language may be analyzed.

A **content analysis** of verbal material involves coding it for the presence of selected words or meanings. For example, speech can be coded for the presence of words referring to thinking and feeling (Seegmiller & Epperson, 1987). The public speeches and written memoranda of U.S. presidents have been analyzed to determine what motivates them: power, or affiliation, or achievement. David Winter and Leslie Carlson concluded that President Richard Nixon was particularly high in affiliation motivation. What else could have led him to explain the invasion of Cambodia by saying, "We are going to find out who our friends are" (Winter & Carlson, 1988, p. 97)?

As this example shows, content coding enables researchers to study people other than those who are readily available to fill out questionnaires (primarily college undergraduates). It is hard to imagine another way of getting access to data from U.S. presidents. Content coding permits researchers to analyze materials that people produce naturally during their lives (such as letters, speeches, and so forth), rather than in response to psychologists' queries. The technique is also used to analyze certain kinds of data collected from students, clinic patients, and others who respond to researchers' questions, when a simpler coding method (such as multiple-choice questions) is not appropriate. For example, an open-ended interview question might ask, "Describe what you like most about your best friend." A researcher might

RESEARCH STRATEGIES •------------------------------

The Correlation Coefficient in Personality Research

The correlation coefficient, in various forms, is the most widely used statistic in personality research. It is a convenient and versatile way to describe the relationship between two variables. Do people with higher educational degrees earn more money? If so, there will be a "high correlation" between educational status and income. Is the absence of love associated with emotional disturbance? Then there should be a "negative correlation" between love and emotional disturbance. Is your grade in psychology unrelated to the proverbial price of tea in China? Then there should be "zero correlation" between these two variables.

To compute a correlation coefficient, we need to have scores on two variables for several subjects. The most commonly used correlation coefficient is the Pearson product-moment correlation coefficient. The mathematical assumptions of this statistic require that the two variables be measured on an interval scale. That is, a difference (interval) of 5 points is considered to be an identical amount, whether it is a difference between scores of 3 and 8 or between scores of 93 and 98. By convention, psychologists assume that if scores are obtained by adding many items to compute a scale, this criterion is met. For other kinds of variables that do not have interval level measurement, there are other formulas for computing correlation coefficients. For example, rank order variables are correlated using the Spearman correlation coefficient, and nominal level variables can be correlated using the point biserial correlation. In all these cases, the correlation reflects the degree of association between the two variables.

Correlation coefficients can range from +1.00 to −1.00. A correlation of +1.00 occurs only if all scores on the two variables occur exactly on a straight line with a positive slope (that is, high scores on one variable are associated with high scores on the other). For example, the correlation of length measured in inches with length measured in centimeters is exactly +1.00 (unless someone has measured erroneously). Conversely, a correlation of −1.00 occurs only if all scores on the two variables occur exactly on a straight line with a *negative* slope. That is, high scores on one variable are associated with low scores on the other. A correlation of −1.00 would be computed if we correlated the percentage of items students got correct on an exam with the percentage of incorrect items. If, however, there is *no* relationship between the two variables, then the correlation will be zero (0.00) (see the figure on the following page).

Perfect positive and negative correlations are not observed in real data. Such correlations would occur only if no other factors obscured the relationship and if there were no errors of measurement. Correlations over .50 are generally considered to be high correlations. (Negative correlations lower than −.50 would also be considered to be high.) Those between .30 and .50 (or between −.30 and −.50) are considered to be moderate, and those less than .30 (or between −.30 and zero, negative) are considered low.

(continued)

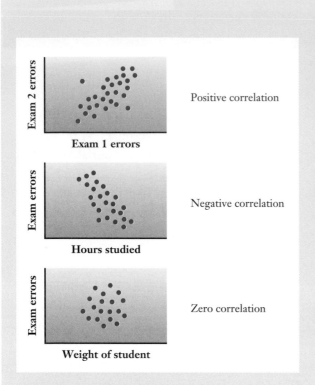

Visualizing correlations: scatterplots illustrating positive, negative, and zero correlations between variables.

Correlations that are *exactly* 0.00 are quite rare. Even if two variables are not related, chance factors that influence scores may lead to a correlation that is a little higher or a little lower than 0.00. When data are analyzed and correlations are computed, how do we know when a correlation is meaningful and when it is just a result of chance? Statistical inference methods help us here. Statisticians have calculated how often various correlations will occur "by chance." A correlation of .33 or higher, for example, will occur once out of every 20 times by chance in a sample of 25 subjects, if there is

no "real" relationship between the variables. For a larger sample, such a large correlation is even more rare by chance. Once in 20 times is 5 percent of the time. By convention, that is accepted as the cutoff for significance. Correlations lower than that are considered "not statistically significant" because they will occur too often (5 percent of the time or more) by chance. Correlations higher than that are considered "statistically significant" because they will occur rarely (less than 5 percent of the time) by chance. Significant correlations are often indicated by asterisks (*) in tables. The footnote "$p < .05$" indicates that a correlation this large would occur less than 5 percent of the time by chance. Even less likely by chance is "$p < .01$"; that is, less than 1 percent of the time.

The correlation coefficient is a convenient statistic for describing the degree of relationship between two variables. The more the correlation differs from zero, the greater the relationship. In one study, David Dunning and Geoffrey Cohen (1992) asked psychology students to rate the studiousness of a hypothetical student, who was described as studying 9 hours per week, on a scale ranging from 1 (not studious) to 7 (very studious). The researchers also obtained self-report measures of the number of hours per week each subject spent studying. The correlation between variable A (subjects' self-reported hours studying) and variable B (the ratings of the hypothetical students) was −.47. This was a statistically significant correlation. There were 54 subjects, and for this sample size, any correlation above .22 is significant. (Notice that when we say "above," we ignore the sign. This seems logical. After all, if the scale had been reversed, labeling "very studious" as 1 rather than 7, the correlation would have been +.47 instead of −.47.)

The relationship can be shown graphically (see the figure below). Subjects who studied many hours per week rated the hypothetical student as much less studious than did those who studied more themselves. Other subjects rated a hypothetical student who studied 36 hours per week. For them, the correlation between rated studiousness and their own hours of study was only −.08. This correlation is not significant because it would occur often by chance. We cannot say, for this group of subjects, that there is any relationship between the two variables. Graphically, this lack of relationship is reflected in a line that is nearly flat.

Fundamentally, the correlation coefficient shows the relationship between two variables.

It is used for many purposes, including assessing the reliability and validity of personality tests, and is the basis for many advanced statistical procedures.

Knowing the fundamentals of the correlation coefficient pays huge dividends in the ability to understand research in personality. These fundamentals, in summary, are as follows:

1. The correlation coefficient measures the degree of relationship between two variables.

2. The correlation coefficient can range from −1.00 (high negative relationship) to 0.00 (no relationship) to +1.00 (high positive relationship).

3. Statistical tests can be used to determine whether a correlation is significant, meaning that it is too large to be expected by chance.

4. Many advanced techniques for data analysis are derived from the correlation coefficient.

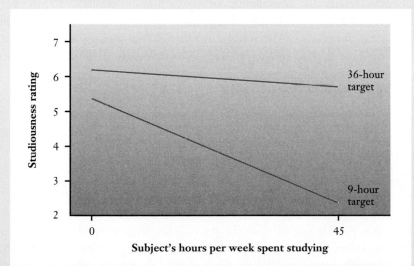

Subjects' rating of the studiousness of targets who studied 9 or 36 hours per week, as a function of subjects' self-reported hours per week spent studying. (Adapted from Dunning & Cohen, 1992, p. 349.)

ask you to make up a story about a picture you are shown, using a projective test such as the Thematic Apperception Test. (A projective test is one that asks people to describe what they see in an ambiguous stimulus, such as a picture or an inkblot.)

Coding procedures have been developed for a variety of dimensions of personality (Smith, 1992; Winter & Carlson, 1988; Zullow et al.,1988). Content coding can be carried out by human judges or by computers (Rosenberg, Schnurr & Oxman, 1990). Despite the different specific things a person may say in one interview or another, the coded scores seem reliable enough to suggest that they indicate enduring personality differences (Schnurr et al., 1986).

Is everyday language adequate for the scientific description of personality? One obvious difficulty is that people speak different languages. Although personality questionnaires can be translated, no translation is perfect. Various languages have words that are not comparable and that cannot convey precisely the same meaning (Angleitner, Ostendorf & John, 1990; Hofstee, 1990). The dictionary translates the Yiddish word *chutzpah* as "brazenness; gall," but the translation misses some of the meaning. Even within a single language community, everyday language has problems that limit its value for science. Scientists strive to describe without passing judgment, but everyday language does this badly. Words that describe people nearly always convey social desirability. How, for example, can we find words to describe one person as "outgoing" and another as "withdrawn" that do not subtly connote more approval of the first person than of the second? Furthermore, there may be dimensions of personality that are not well represented in language. Robert McCrae (1990) finds, for example, that everyday language does not adequately portray a personality factor of "Openness" that has been found in questionnaire studies. These problems and others make everyday language problematic from a scientific point of view (Hofstee, 1990). It is impractical to replace everyday language with an artificial scientific language. At least, though, researchers should consider how language influences their measurements and even, perhaps, their theories.

Experimenting with the Language of Personality

Experimental studies help researchers to understand what influences the language that people use to describe personality. Knowing these influences can help us move from everyday statements about personality to a more refined, scientific language. When, for example, do we describe one another in terms of global traits, such as "friendly" or "serious"? Curt Hoffman, Walter Mischel, and John Baer (1984) found that such global descriptions were more frequent when subjects expected to describe the target person to someone else. Thus, the language of traits facilitates communication about personality to other people. Perhaps when we don't expect to talk about people, we make fewer judgments about their personalities.

Various parts of speech convey different meanings. Adjectives are more abstract and less dependent upon the context of their usage than are verbs. When people hear someone described with an adjective, such as "friendly," they surmise that the person behaves similarly from situation to situation. In contrast, verbs, such as "hug," convey more variation depending upon the context of the behavior (Semin & Fiedler, 1988). Adjectives thus imply more stability in personality than do descriptions of behavior. This finding is of particular interest because theorists have been troubled that behavior varies from one situation to another. That finding seems to contradict the idea that people have stable personality traits that determine behavior. The linguistic research just described makes it clear that, at some level, we knew that all along: behavior (such as "hugging") is more variable from one situation to another than are traits (such as "friendly").

The effects of language can be subtly elegant. Curt Hoffman and Maria Tchir (1990) examined the impact of verbs that have, in the English language, various kinds of associated adjectives. Some verbs have adjectives associated with the subject of the verb. Consider the sentence "Grandma doted on Harry." The adjective "doting" can be used to refer to the subject, Grandma, in that sentence. However there is no corresponding adjective to refer to the object. Harry cannot be described as "dotable." In contrast, for the sentence "Joshua detested liver," we can describe the object, liver, with the adjective "detestable," but there is no adjectival form of the verb to refer to the subject, Joshua. Comparing such verbs, Hoffman and Tchir found that people make different judgments about the cause of behavior, depending upon which kind of verb is presented. The subject, A, who can be "doting," is judged more responsible for what happened in the interaction than B when "A doted on B." In contrast, B is judged to be the cause when "A detested B," corresponding to the possibility of a "detestable" B in the English language. These findings generalize to other verbs that have forms corresponding only to the subject or the object.

Is language determining how we think about causes? Or has language evolved to reflect our assumptions? It is hard to say. In either case, however, the work of personality researchers is complicated by the fact that language has many nonobvious implications. Since so much personality measurement depends upon language, it is wise to examine our measures critically.

Perceptions of Personality

Most words that can be used to describe personality convey evaluation. To what extent does our general liking or disliking of people bias our descriptions of them? Perhaps we are overly generous in describing people we like and more unfavorable about those we dislike. A beloved uncle is "eccentric" whereas a detested one is "crazy," for example, and friends are "efficient" whereas enemies are "compulsive."

This tendency to bias our descriptions of people by our general liking for them is called a **halo effect.** Some researchers have focused on understanding how we decide whether we like others (for example, Pavelchak, 1989). In principle, liking is distinct from perception. Researchers must be cautious when they interpret personality ratings, because descriptions may be distorted by liking or disliking of the person rated and cannot always be taken at face value. On the other hand, it is not certain that the liking is the *cause* of the higher ratings on favorable traits. Perhaps it is the other way around: we like people *because* we perceive them to have desirable traits (Lachman & Bass, 1985).

Do We Naturally Think of Traits?

Researchers often ask subjects to describe themselves and one another. Subjects respond in terms of traits: "I'm shy"; "My sister is an extravert." The ease with which people list traits, and the large number of trait words in natural language, seems to suggest that description by traits is a natural activity. Is it? Do people spontaneously use trait language when they perceive and describe one another, or only when a psychologist hands them a blank form?

The evidence is mixed. Some researchers argue that people spontaneously infer traits when they observe other people's behavior (Newman & Uleman, 1990; Winter & Uleman, 1984). Such inferred traits, even when not conscious, influence later judgments about the person to whom they are applied (Moskowitz & Roman, 1992). Other research suggests that such spontaneous trait inferences are rare (D'Agostino, 1991). Although we sometimes infer that a person who is late for class (behavioral description) is "irresponsible," this inference does not happen automatically. At other times, behavior is assumed to be caused by situational factors, such as a traffic jam.

Social psychologists have been particularly interested in this issue (for example, Jones & Nisbett, 1971). Their theories explain when we make personal attributions; that is, when we say that the behavior was caused by something about the person who behaved, such as the trait of irresponsibility in the example. Their theories also explain when our attributions about the causes of behavior refer to the situation (the traffic jam) instead of to personality. A major finding is that we tend to interpret other people's behavior as reflective of their personalities, whereas we explain our own behavior as determined by the situation. We are more likely to say that our own personality contains complex, apparently contradictory facets or traits that give us flexibility to respond to varying situations, while other people are more predictable (Sande, Goethals & Radloff, 1988).

When do we infer personality from behavior? Social psychologists tell us that individual differences are a significant indicator. When people consistently behave differently from other people, we often interpret this as an indicator of personality. A student who regularly studies on Friday nights rather than socializing with everyone else is assumed to have a studious, introverted personality. Observers do not make inferences about personality, though, if there are clear situational reasons for the behavior. If the student is scheduled to take a final exam Saturday morning, then Friday night studying reveals little about personality. Also, the kind of prior information that we have about a person before observing a specific behavior can prompt either trait or situational attributions (Lupfer, Clark & Hutcherson, 1990). We infer personality traits from behavior, but only sometimes.

The Layman's (Implicit) Personality Theory

When people describe one another, these descriptions are determined only partly by the actual qualities of the person being described. The often unstated assumptions of the perceiver also have an influence. We know, for example, that prejudice may lead some people to rate racial minorities, women, or homosexuals less favorably than they rate other groups. This occurs because of a belief that minority status is associated with negative characteristics. When the basis of distorted judgment is a social category (such as race or gender), the phenomenon is generally studied by social psychologists rather than personality researchers.

Consider a variation. Suppose a person is told that someone else is "warm." The person will tend to expect that other positive traits also characterize the person being described: kind, good, wise, and so forth (Asch, 1946; Asch & Zukier, 1984). Traits are not isolated qualities but are perceived as parts of a unity of personality (Asch & Zukier, 1984). In this case, the basis of the influence is not a social category (such as race) but a personality trait (warmth). This phenomenon is studied by personality psychologists. Assumptions about personality traits and their relationships are often called **implicit personality theory** (Schneider, 1973).

When raters report that people who are "warm" are also "good," "kind," and so forth, they could be reporting real associations in the real people whom they are rating, or they could be leaping to conclusions based on implicit personality theory. An influential study by Frank Passini and Warren Norman (1966) supports the second possibility. The researchers assembled groups of undergraduate students who did not know one another. Groups were composed of six to nine students, with only men or only women in each group. The study was conducted on the first class of the

TABLE **2.1** **Five Dimensions of Personality**

Factor	*Scales*
Extraversion	Talkative versus silent Frank, open versus secretive Adventurous versus cautious Sociable versus reclusive
Agreeableness	Good-natured versus irritable Not jealous versus jealous Mild, gentle versus headstrong Cooperative versus negativistic
Conscientiousness	Fussy, tidy versus careless Responsible versus undependable Scrupulous versus unscrupulous Persevering versus quitting, fickle
Emotional Stability	Poised versus nervous, tense Calm versus anxious Composed versus excitable Not hypochondriacal versus hypochondriacal
Culture	Artistically sensitive versus artistically insensitive Intellectual versus unreflective, narrow Polished, refined versus crude, boorish Imaginative versus simple, direct

Adapted from Norman, 1963, p. 577.

term, and students had been in the room together for less than 15 minutes. They had little basis for making informed ratings about one another. Nonetheless, that is exactly what they were asked to do. The experimenter explained that he needed data to compare with other groups who were acquainted.

Surprisingly, the relationships among personality traits assessed in this study were similar to those found when people rated others whom they knew better. In both cases, people seemed to perceive personality in terms of the Big Five dimensions (Table 2.1). When describing someone we know, such patterns can reflect reality. When judging someone we don't know, the patterning must be something that we impose on a very ambiguous perception. When we "see" elephants and kangaroos in clouds, obviously the images of these animals are in our own minds. By analogy, when we see five dimensions of personality in strangers, these dimensions must belong to our implicit personality theory.

Although we use similar concepts for perceiving strangers and friends, we are not equally accurate in both cases. We become more accurate in perceiving others the longer we know them (Funder & Colvin, 1988; Norman & Goldberg, 1966; Paulhus & Bruce, 1992; Paunonen, 1989). We become more aware that their unique patterns of characteristics may deviate from our implicit personality theory (Vonk & Heiser, 1991). Research confirms that our ratings of strangers are not very well correlated with their self-ratings, but as we get to know people over time, our perceptions come closer to matching their self-perceptions (Funder, 1987). Perhaps when we first meet someone, we are like an imaginary geologist who must categorize rocks by feeling them, blindly, in a paper bag. The types of rocks surmised in this way may not differ from the types assessed when the geologist is permitted to look at the rocks closely. Accuracy, though, is improved by the closer examination.

Even when judging strangers, people's ratings are correlated with the others' self-ratings at greater than a chance level (Funder & Colvin, 1988). Some aspects of personality, especially extraversion, are so obvious that they are conveyed even at first meeting (Borkenau & Liebler, 1992b; Funder & Colvin, 1988; Funder & Dobroth, 1987; Funder & Sneed, 1993; Kenny et al., 1992; Park & Judd, 1989). The rough surface of granite is so different from the smoothness of slate that they are unmistakable even in a paper bag. It would be premature, however, to conclude that perceiving personality is an easy task, done well by almost everyone after even brief encounters. Perhaps most of us are poor at the task, while a few are astute. From a statistical point of view, the significant correlations typically reported in studies of people meeting for the first time could result from combining the judgments of many incompetent judges with a handful of able judges (Paunonen, 1991). In addition, some people are more easily assessed than others. Preliminary work by C. Randall Colvin (1993) indicates that people who are psychologically adjusted, extraverted, agreeable, conscientious, and emotionally stable are more reliably judged than those who are low on these characteristics. Their peers tended to agree with subjects' self-statements and with inferences based on viewing videotaped behavior.

Research on implicit personality theory has most often averaged results across several judges. Using this method, only implicit theories that are shared by many people can be discovered. If most people agree that "good-natured" and "gentle" go together, that will emerge in the data analysis (as it has with the Agreeableness factor of the Big Five). It is possible, however, that people have implicit theories that are idiosyncratic. How can they be found?

Such information can be gleaned from intensive examination of one person's statements. Researchers have analyzed the implicit personality theories of Theodore Dreiser (Rosenberg & Jones, 1972) and of Henry

We perceive people, in part, by comparing them with typical examples of categories of people. What categories (prototypes) of people come to your mind when you consider these people? Prototypes are rich with associations, containing information that goes far beyond what we may have observed in particular individuals.

Kissinger (Swede & Tetlock, 1986). The traits that emerge from analyses of individuals may include some not found in the analysis of group data, particularly when cognitively sophisticated individuals are studied. Henry Kissinger, for example, tended to describe "insecure" political leaders as also "lonely," "private," "unforgetting," and "proud" (Swede & Tetlock, 1986).

Natural Categories of Our Minds

The research described in the previous section has studied implicit personality theory at the level of personality traits. Instead of continuous dimensions (traits), we may think of prototypical examples of a type of person. Archie Bunker, a stereotypical bigot, conveys a richer image than a simple list of traits (for example, "prejudiced" and "loud-mouthed"). Susan Fiske, an expert on social cognition, notes that "compared to traits, stereotypes or person types have richer associations, more visual features, more distinctive characteristics, and operate more efficiently" (Fiske, 1993, p. 165).

This rich detail, though, can lead to overgeneralized and erroneous perceptions of others. Sometimes those who are perceived in stereotyped ways are influenced subtly, acting in ways that confirm the stereotypes. In one experiment, women spoke more warmly on the phone to a man who had been led by the experimenter to believe that they were attractive than to a man who thought them unattractive. This occurred even though the women were unaware of the manipulation, suggesting that the men's expectations changed their behavior in a way that elicited greater warmth from the women who had been randomly labeled as attractive (Snyder, Tanke & Berscheid, 1977). Even when we get to know more about individuals, prior stereotypes can influence the way we interpret information, especially if that information is ambiguous (Kunda & Sherman-Williams, 1993). Stereotypes do not always prevail, however. Sometimes information about the traits or the behavior of individuals can outweigh the effects of stereotypes (Krueger & Rothbart, 1988).

The term *stereotype* has connotations of rigidity and bias. A more neutral term for personality type categories is **prototype** (Cantor & Mischel, 1979a, 1979b). Prototypes are categories that have "fuzzy boundaries." They are defined by typical, clear examples of the category rather than by logical rules that can decisively say whether any particular person is a member of the category or not. A robin, for example, is a prototypical bird, a better example of "birdness" than a penguin. The more an individual deviates from the typical example of the category, the less certain we are that this really is an instance of the category. Prototypes include rich detail about traits and behaviors characteristic of a type of person. Prototypes are more vivid and richer in associations than trait terms (Andersen & Klatzky, 1987), making them particularly useful in forming impressions of people. If we meet a new person who matches a prototype well enough, we use the prototype to fill in the gaps and to create predictions about other aspects of the person that we haven't seen yet in that particular individual.

Prototypes include stereotyped images of such groups as African Americans, businessmen, Jewish mothers (Anderson & Sedikides, 1991), and homosexuals (Abrams, Carter & Hogg, 1989); men and women (Ashmore & Del Boca, 1979); physically attractive men and women (Eagly et al., 1991; Snyder, Tanke & Berscheid, 1977); and African Americans and white Americans (Dovidio, Evans & Tyler, 1986). People also develop prototypes about the interpersonal behaviors of people in different occupations, such as business executive and poet (Broughton, Trapnell & Boyes, 1991). Some prototypes may even be based on people we have known well, significant others such as a parent, a relative, or a best friend (Andersen & Cole, 1990). What do these diverse prototypes have in common? They are all detailed and specific, rather than abstract. In addition, prototypes are categories that have fuzzy boundaries. That is, there are borderline cases in which it is not obvious whether a particular individual should be included in the category or not. The *exemplars* that are clear examples of the category are easy to categorize, but borderline cases (near the fuzzy boundaries) are not.

Are such prototypes accurate? Obviously, any approach that lumps groups of people together produces errors by neglecting individual differences among people within the group. Yet we may still ask whether, on the average, groups differ in the directions that social stereotypes or prototypes suggest. The answer is that, at least sometimes, they do. For example, observers generally expect that babyfaced adults have distinctive personalities. In one study, both males and females with babyfaces were perceived (by undergraduates) as weak, submissive, naive, warm, and honest. These perceptions generally coincided with self-perceptions of the babyfaced adults (Berry & Brownlow, 1989).

The issue of accuracy in person perception (how we form impressions of people) is complicated. To resolve it definitively would require more careful research than typically has been conducted. Reviewers of the existing research conclude that "we actually know relatively little about the accuracy of the content of various social stereotypes" (Judd & Park, 1993, p. 127). Aside from the issue of whether stereotypes are accurate, we may ask the more general question: Do people perceive one another accurately? This question has not been answered adequately by research (Kruglanski, 1989). To resolve it requires a criterion of "true" personality to compare with perceptions. What would that be? A personality test, perhaps? Or the behavior of the target individual? Such behavior would have take into account the other people with whom the person interacts, since behavior depends upon the interacting pair and not only on one personality (Kenny & Albright, 1987). Usually, the research criterion is the individual's self-perception or the perception of a third person. These criteria are themselves suspect. For example, people can present a false image in their self-ratings (Paunonen, 1989). Strictly speaking, researchers generally measure consensus about personality perception, rather than accuracy (Kenny, 1991; Kenny & Albright, 1987).

Methodological and theoretical difficulties preclude easy measurement of the accuracy of interpersonal perception, although some models have been proposed to guide researchers (Cronbach, 1955; Kenny & Albright, 1987). These models suggest that various components of accuracy should be untangled. For example, people can be accurate in perceiving others because they correctly perceive them to be like others in the group being judged. To the extent that the judge has an accurate image of the "generalized other" and describes everyone as like this typical personality, scores will be accurate. This may be called **stereotype accuracy** (Cronbach, 1955). It may occur even if people cannot differentiate among individuals in a group (differential accuracy). To study accuracy, researchers must collect and analyze data in a way that distinguishes among these and other components of overall accuracy.

Ross Broughton (1984) suggests that the concept of prototypes can be used to improve personality tests. Tests generally consist of many self-report items that are answered in terms of numbers and then added together to form a total score. Broughton selected items that were judged, by graduate students in psychology, to be especially prototypical of the traits being measured. The scales composed of these items were compared with tra-

TABLE **2.2 Examples of Behaviors Used to Infer the Big Five Personality Dimensions**

Behaviors that indicate **Extraversion**
- Has high enthusiasm and energy level
- Speaks in a loud voice
- Is talkative

Behaviors that indicate **Neuroticism**
- Shows signs of tension or anxiety
- Expresses guilt
- Seeks reassurance

Behaviors that indicate **Openness**
- Seems interested in what partner says
- "Interviews" partner
- Discusses philosophical issues

Behaviors that indicate **Agreeableness**
- Expresses sympathy to partner
- Seems to enjoy interaction
- Behaves in a cheerful manner

Behaviors that indicate **Conscientiousness**
- Speaks fluently
- Displays ambition
- Exhibits high degree of intelligence

Adapted from Funder & Sneed, 1993.

ditional tests. How well could each predict the way fraternity men were evaluated by their peers on several traits (achievement, dominance, nurturance, affiliation, exhibition, autonomy, aggression, and deference)? The prototype scales were better predictors. Thus, applying the concept of prototypes to psychological measurement can improve formal descriptions of personality, as well as help to explain how people perceive one another in everyday life.

Clues from Behavior

People make inferences about other people's personalities without giving them personality tests. How? They see others and, based on their physical characteristics (such as sex, race, and attractiveness) and their behavior, they make inferences about personality. Trait inferences are facilitated by observations of confirming behaviors; they are discouraged when disconfirming behaviors occur (Borkenau & Müller, 1992). Researchers have identified overt behaviors that people use to make inferences about the Big Five dimensions of personality. In these studies, subjects judge personality after viewing strangers on videotape or listening to them on audiotape (Borkenau & Liebler, 1992a; Funder & Sneed, 1993). Some examples of the behaviors that subjects use to make such judgments are presented in Table 2.2.

People's nonverbal behaviors give important clues. Facial expressions can indicate pleasure or anxiety, tone of speech can indicate confidence or uncertainty, and so forth. We interpret such subtle behaviors to ascertain many things. For example, are people lying or telling the truth? How do they feel about us? A review of several research studies shows that brief observations of expressive behavior (such as facial expressions or tone of voice) lead to perceptions that are just as accurate as those made after longer observations of such behavior (Ambady & Rosenthal, 1992).

Researchers are exploring the various processes by which people infer traits from behaviors. The extent to which a behavior (for example, "setting goals for a group") is prototypical of a trait (for example, "dominant") is one consideration. Implicit theories about the relationships among inferred traits also have an influence; for example, is a person who is "ambitious" likely also to be "arrogant" (Riemann & Angleitner, 1993)? Whatever the process, research suggests that once we have inferred a specific trait from a particular behavior, we make that judgment more quickly in the future. The repeated judgment occurs more quickly when the behavior is presented again in a laboratory experiment, even if the repetition occurs a week later, and even if subjects do not recall that they had seen the cue before (Smith, Stewart & Buttram, 1992).

The fact that we *can* infer personality from behavior does not, of course, indicate that we always do so. We also remember the traits that we have applied in the past, and we can apply them again, without bothering to make behavioral inferences again each time about ourselves (Klein, Loftus & Plog, 1992) or about other people. Once trait labels have been applied, they can modify the impressions that we form from new behavioral information, just as stereotypes and prototypes modify the impact of such observations. In addition, information that we receive is often ambiguous. We must interpret precisely what behavior occurred, in what specific situational context. These interpretations may encourage or discourage trait inferences (Trope, Cohen & Alfieri, 1991), as we interpret the causes of behavior in dispositional or situational terms.

Measuring Behavior   People's understandings of personality traits can lead, as we have seen above, to distortions in their reports of their own personality and that of others. Can personality be measured more directly, in a way that avoids such distortions? One approach is to measure behavior. Richard Shweder (1975) has demonstrated that people's preconceptions about the similarities of certain behaviors distort their reports of behavior. For example, people interpret the two traits "seeks reassurance" and "seeks help" as similar because they are both instances of "dependent" behavior. So, in filling out personality rating forms, they are likely to report that if a person does one, he or she also does the other. Direct behavioral observation, however, produces much less relationship among these items. Therefore, personality may not correspond closely to the social impressions of people that we form based on such generalizations.

One behavioral alternative to trait-based implicit personality theories consists of "action-oriented representations," in which individuals are characterized by their goal-seeking (Trzebinski, 1985). Traits generally imply goals. The goals organize and give meaning to traits, and they aid the perceiver in resolving apparent inconsistencies in behavior (cf. Casselden & Hampson, 1990; Read, Jones & Miller, 1990). The associations among traits, in fact, are not always stable across situations. Dominance and friendliness, for example, are generally uncorrelated. Among male subjects who are interacting with female strangers, however, dominance and friendliness are positively correlated. The males who are dominant (by their own self-reports, by others' ratings, and by behavior counts) are the same ones who are friendly (by the same diverse measures), presumably as they seek flirtatious interactions with the strange females (Moskowitz, 1990). This pattern is not found when males interact with other males.

Situations obviously affect behavior. The fact that we can predict the self-perceived personality traits of people we know well does not necessarily mean that we can predict what they will do in a particular situation. Predicting personality and predicting behavior are different. Without having seen someone, even someone we know well, in a particular situation, our predictions may be poor. On the other hand, if the situation being observed is similar to the one being predicted, strangers who have had only a brief opportunity to observe someone can predict that person's behavior as accurately as close acquaintances can (Colvin & Funder, 1991).

The Act Frequency Approach The **act frequency approach** (Buss & Craik, 1983a) to personality measurement is based on the idea that traits are summary descriptions of behavior. People are said to have a trait of "compulsiveness," for example, if the term seems adequate to describe their behavior over time. Such people may prepare at great lengths for exams, keep very organized records, never let their cars have less than half a tank of gas, and so forth. Rather than measuring personality through self-report questionnaires, why not measure behavior? If a person claims to be gregarious but spends little time with others, would you believe the self-report?

David Buss and Kenneth Craik (1980, 1981, 1983b) have compiled lists of prototypical acts for six traits: aloofness, gregariousness, dominance, submissiveness, quarrelsomeness, and agreeableness. For example, the act "I chose to sit at the head of the table" is a prototypical act for the trait "aloofness." "I insisted on having the last word in the discussion" is prototypical for the trait "quarrelsomeness" (Buss & Craik, 1983b, p. 1086). Such lists can be used to assess personality from behavior, either by self-report or, after changing the pronouns, by the reports of others. The more prototypical acts a person is reported to have done, the higher the person's score on that trait. Besides such retrospective reports of behavior by actors or observers, more direct methods are possible. Observers can be assigned to record responses as they occur, or subjects can carry beepers that sound at random intervals, signaling subjects to record what they were doing at that moment (Buss & Craik, 1983a).

The number of traits that potentially could be investigated in this way is enormous. Buss and Craik suggest that researchers have focused on too few traits, in the interest of simplicity. They argue that personality researchers ought to study many traits rather than prematurely oversimplifying the field (Buss & Craik, 1985). Their approach, though, is not an unstructured, shotgun one. They have suggested that a theoretical model of traits, Wiggins's circumplex model (Wiggins, 1979), helps to predict the relationships to be expected among traits identified through the act frequency approach (Buss & Craik, 1983a, 1983b).

There is not a one-to-one relationship between traits and behavioral acts. Some acts are prototypical of more than one trait. For example, the act "I hit someone who annoyed me" fits two of the traits outlined by Buss and Craik: dominance and quarrelsomeness (Angleitner & Demtröder, 1988). This complication may account for some of the inconsistencies between human judges and more objective recordings of behavior, such as those made from videotapes (Borkenau & Ostendorf, 1987). Human judges "double count" such acts, whereas systematic behavioral observation methods force them into only one category.

The act frequency approach is inherently sensitive to the lives of real people in real situations. The procedure "focus[es] on the actions of persons in everyday life—a critically important source of data for personality psychology" (Buss & Craik, 1989, p. 24). Personality inventories, in contrast, typically assess thoughts and feelings, rather than behavior (Werner & Pervin, 1986). In addition, such questionnaires may ask people about phenomena that have never occurred in their lives, requiring answers based on speculation.

The Eye of the Perceiver

Individual differences occur not only in the targets of our perceptions, but also in the perceivers. Some people tune in to other people's intelligence, others focus on their sense of humor. Why do these differences occur?

For one thing, people's perceptions of others are influenced by their own self-images. Pawel Lewicki (1983) has described a "self-image bias" whereby people pay particular attention to traits on which they themselves are rated favorably and less attention to traits on which they don't score so well. Thus, intelligence is more important to an intelligent person than to one less talented, and a socially skilled individual is more attentive to that dimension in perceiving others. These differential sensitivities bolster self-esteem by emphasizing the importance of our own good points. Defensiveness about our shortcomings can also influence our perceptions of others (Lewicki, 1984).

Many traits have evaluative connotations. To be "mathematically intelligent," for example, is better than to be low in mathematical intelligence. How high an SAT score is necessary before a student is considered to be mathematically intelligent? The answer varies, depending upon one's own standing on the trait (Dunning & Cohen, 1992). Mathematically intelligent undergraduates demand high scores in others whom they are judging before they will consider them to be mathematically intelligent. Lower scoring undergraduates apply the trait more generously to others. Similar biases were found for other traits. These differences serve to enhance the self-esteem of the judges. We define traits from an egocentric viewpoint in ways that are self-serving (see also Dunning, Perie & Story, 1991).

Choosing the Dimensions of Study

Lay perceptions of personality have obvious shortcomings for science. They are distorted by self-serving biases, and lay people too readily see in others what is really in the mind of the perceiver. Some objectivity can be achieved by emphasizing behavior. Even so, personality psychologists ultimately must describe the underlying dimensions of personality. What guides this search?

Chemists describe their observations in terms of the dimensions of physical matter: molecular weight, electrical charge, and so forth. Their choice of descriptive dimensions has changed as the science has developed. What are the analogous dimensions for the study of personality? There is no simple answer to this question. In fact, competing alternatives are fiercely debated. These controversies are part of the struggle for a guiding paradigm in the field, as was discussed in Chapter 1. Many approaches guide personality research. None, though, has been accepted to the exclusion of the other approaches.

To Compare or Not to Compare

One way to describe a person is to compare that individual with other people. Some researchers consider differences among people to be the major phenomenon of personality theory. Jerry Wiggins, for example, defines personality as "that branch of psychology which is concerned with providing a systematic account of the ways in which individuals differ from one another" (Wiggins, 1979, p. 395). This approach, which studies groups of people and describes individuals by comparison with the others, is the

nomothetic approach. It has dominated most personality research. From this perspective, the description of personality consists of a set of dimensions, usually personality traits, that can be used to describe any person. People differ in their scores on these dimensions. For example, some people are more extraverted, others more introverted. The dimension (in this case, introversion-extraversion) is pertinent to all people; that is, each person's score—whether high, middle, or low—is meaningful. In contrast, consider "academic self-confidence." This trait would be meaningful in comparing undergraduates with one another but would be irrelevant in a study of nursing home residents or members of a primitive tribe with no formal schooling.

Traditionally, researchers measure personality by comparing people's scores (the nomothetic approach). But a persistent minority has urged an alternative approach. Traits named and measured by researchers may not apply to everyone. If a person is measured on a trait that is not relevant, the person's score will be inconsistent over time and will not predict behavior (see Baumeister & Tice, 1988; Bem & Allen, 1974; Kenrick & Stringfield, 1980). For some people, on some traits, the best description is not "high," "medium," or "low," or anything in between, but rather "does not apply." Critics of the nomothetic approach argue that we cannot describe everyone with the same list of traits.

The **idiographic** approach tries to understand one individual in his or her own existence. What makes this person "tick"? Perhaps he or she is striving to become a financial success. Perhaps everything in the person's life is inspired by a desire to serve humanity. The idiographic approach focuses on one person. Other people may be similar or different, but that is a side issue. An influential early personality theorist, Gordon Allport (1937), persistently asserted that personality should be studied idiographically. Otherwise, unique aspects of individuals would be overlooked. However, Allport did not succeed in convincing many others of this perspective, and the nomothetic view prevailed instead.

But the idiographic perspective has not entirely disappeared. The issue is intertwined with the question of whether personality traits are appropriate dimensions for describing personality. If they are, then people should behave relatively consistently across situations. If they are not, then situations should produce considerable variability in behavior. In a classic study, Daryl Bem and Andrea Allen (1974) suggested that on a given trait, *some* people will be stable across situations and others will not. The argument that stable traits apply only to some people, not to all, echoes Allport's argument for an idiographic rather than a nomothetic approach to traits.

James Lamiell criticizes the nomothetic approach. He asserts that the study of individual differences investigates the spaces between people rather than the people themselves (Lamiell, 1981, 1987). Although there may be a role for the study of individual differences, this approach should not be the major focus of personality psychology. The field should study personality

TABLE 2.3 **Examples of Personality Typologies**

Ancient Greek personality types
- Sanguine (optimistic, hopeful)
- Melancholic (sad, depressed)
- Choleric (irascible, temperamental)
- Phlegmatic (apathetic, unemotional)

Modern psychetypes (in Jung's theory)
- Introverted thinking (interested in ideas)
- Introverted feeling (sympathetic but not demonstrative)
- Introverted sensation (focuses on inner experiences)
- Introverted intuition (sees possibilities, creative)
- Extraverted thinking (logical)
- Extraverted feeling (interested in people)
- Extraverted sensation (concerned with details)
- Extraverted intuition (adventurer)

description of individuals (not of the spaces between them). Lamiell has offered an alternative, "idiothetic" approach, which will be presented in Chapter 5, where the study of the individual is explored further.

Traits or Types

How many dimensions are needed to describe people? Gordon Allport and H. S. Odbert (1936) listed almost 18,000. Raymond Cattell (Cattell, Eber & Tatsuoka, 1970) identified 16 but conceded that these could be combined into fewer, more general factors. Which is better: a small number of general dimensions, or a large number of very specific ones? Opinions vary. Perhaps we can even have both, if a large number of specific traits are subsumed, in a hierarchical model, under a smaller number of general types.

Can people be grouped into some small number of personality **types?** Several typologies have been suggested, dating back to the ancient Greek list of four personality types: sanguine, melancholic, choleric, and phlegmatic. In modern times, typologies have been developed in clinical settings, based largely on therapeutic experience, and in academic settings, using empirical research methods (Table 2.3).

The major shortcoming of the type approach is that it forces diverse people into too small a set of categories. How can four or five, or even a dozen, groupings adequately describe the diversity of human personality?

Instead, a more favored approach is to describe personality in terms of traits. A trait is more limited in its influence. A trait of achievement motivation, for example, has implications when people are in situations that require skill, such as when trying to do the best double-backflip dive in competition. Outside of competitive and skill-demanding situations, the trait lies dormant. Unlike the type approach, the trait approach permits a large number of dimensions. It avoids oversimplification. Yet the abundance of traits can be unmanageable. How can hundreds, even thousands, of traits be combined into a systematic theory or plan of research?

The question is not whether traits or types exist, but rather which level of generality is most useful for theory and for the measurement of personality. Lee Cronbach and Goldine Gleser (1957) describe a tradeoff between "bandwidth" and "fidelity." Like a radio with a broad bandwidth, a broad, type-oriented psychological test picks up a lot of information but also much static. A narrower bandwidth, like a precisely focused trait-oriented test, has better fidelity but misses a great deal that is outside its scope.

It is possible for both specific traits and more general types to coexist as personality descriptors. They can be thought of as arranged in a hierarchy (see Hampson, John & Goldberg, 1986). A person can be described as an extraverted *type*, with a *trait* of talkativeness, just as Fido is both a dog and a poodle (Fig. 2.1).

People use both broad type statements and more narrow trait statements in perceiving and describing one another. Actually, there are not simply two levels of generality, but a whole continuum. Oliver John and his colleagues investigated people's use of various levels of such trait hierarchies (John, Hampson & Goldberg, 1991). For example, a person may be described with the specific trait, "musical." A more general trait is "artistic." Even more broadly, a person might be described as "talented." Even broader is the term "exceptional." The most descriptive term in a given instance depends upon balancing the precision of the more specific terms against their loss of generality. People tend to prefer a relatively broad term as their "basic level" descriptor (in this example, "talented"), although they vary this choice, depending upon the situation. People tend to use less general trait terms (for example, "unpunctual") when they are describing unfavorable characteristics in people they like. In contrast, they use more general terms to describe unfavorable qualities in people they do not like (for example, "irresponsible"). The reverse occurs when they describe favorable traits. Liked people are given more general favorable traits; disliked people are described in less general terms. Our friends, then, have broad positive qualities and narrow faults, while the opposite is true of those we dislike. For researchers, however, the choice of more or less general trait descriptors must not depend on evaluative factors. Indeed, there is probably no single best level. Different levels may be preferable, depending upon the researcher's purposes and the specific situation (Hampson, John & Goldberg, 1986).

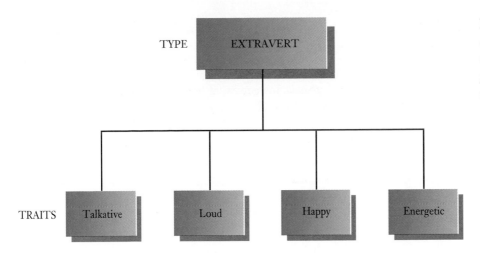

FIGURE 2.1 *Types and traits in hierarchical relationship. A broad personality type has many more specific traits.*

Behavior or Hidden Processes

Should personality theorists study phenomena that can be seen, such as overt behaviors? Or should they postulate processes that cannot be observed directly but that they think describe the way personality functions? The behavioral approach, as we saw in Chapter 1, focuses on observable behaviors. Sometimes these are reported by individuals themselves or by those who know them in everyday life, using the act frequency approach described earlier in this chapter. At other times, and this is preferable from the perspective of behaviorists, trained observers watch subjects and record relevant behaviors as they are actually occurring. This may be done either in natural settings, such as with children on a playground, or in a laboratory environment, such as when subjects are videotaped in a standard setting (for example, Funder & Sneed, 1993).

In one study, observers watched preschool children in class. Observation periods of 4 minutes were selected at various times of day over an 8-week period. Raters noted whether the child behaved in ways that matched predefined categories of dependency or dominance (Table 2.4). The personality traits are valid if they predict the particular corresponding behaviors; for example, if a "dependent" child seeks help and stays near other people.

Other researchers suggest that the external behaviors, or even the trait scores, that differentiate people are less important than the description of personality processes that occur within individuals. In one study, for example, undergraduates filled out daily records every evening for a month. Each day, they rated themselves on 27 pairs of adjectives (for example, worthy-unworthy and valuable-useless). Researchers computed the

TABLE **2.4   Categories of Behavioral Coding in a Study of Preschool Children**

Dependency	1. Seeks instrumental help (e.g., requests someone to tie his or her shoe)
	2. Seeks recognition (e.g., boasting)
	3. Seeks supervision
	4. Touches
	5. Being near (e.g., stays within 6 inches of another person)
Dominance	1. Physical or object placement (e.g., taking another person's toy or play space)
	2. Verbal command
	3. Suggestion
	4. Threat
	5. Direction of an activity (e.g., tells others which role they should play in a game)

Adapted from Moskowitz & Schwarz, 1982, p. 520.

extent to which this measure of self-esteem varied from day to day. Students with labile (variable) self-esteem were found, on another measure, to be more prone to depression than those with less variable self-esteem. The variability of self-esteem from day to day, rather than the level of self-esteem, predicted depression (Butler, Hokanson & Flynn, 1994). This study illustrates the importance of studying personality processes.

Real or Constructed

Does personality consist of components that are real in a physical sense, or do the terms used by personality theorists have no such tangible reality? Undoubtedly, physical phenomena influence personality. When Phineas Gage suffered a brain injury, his personality changed. He became more impulsive and aggressive than before the physical damage. Neurons, hormones, and the like can influence the phenomena studied by personality researchers.

   Realism is an approach wherein researchers look for physical realities that correspond to aspects of personality. What sort of biochemical phenomenon constitutes "aggressiveness"? Where in the brain do we find "shyness"? This approach to personality strives to explain psychological phenomena in terms of physical realities. Assume, for the sake of argument, that personality could be reduced to such physical phenomena as brain structure, hormones, the synaptic changes that occur with learning, and other physical phenomena as yet undiscovered. It does not necessarily follow that a focus on such influences is the most productive way for personality research and theory to be advanced (see Rorer, 1990). The distance from the microlevel physical explanation to the macrolevel psychological phenomena of behavior, thoughts, choices, and so on is so great that we would still have to develop ways of understanding the macrolevel. It is sensible, of course, to study biology, too, and to reconcile higher level processes with biological knowledge.

An alternative approach, **constructivism,** suggests that the concepts of personality theory, like many of the terms that people use in everyday language, do not necessarily correspond to any physical realities. They are, as the name implies, made up or "constructed" for their usefulness. A term such as "shyness" is acceptable if it usefully describes people, quite apart from its possible correspondence to any physical reality. Therefore, rather than expecting to find objectively "real" physical phenomena, the constructivist approach assumes that personality concepts are socially created. Social constructivism has been an explicit perspective in sociology and, to a lesser extent, in social psychology; its impact on the study of personality has been slower (Hampson, 1988). Mindful of the lessons of social constructivism, we must recognize that many traits and other personality terms used by researchers are not real in the same sense that physical objects are real. They are terms whose meaning derives from their usage, in theory and in research.

A trait cannot be "possessed" by a person in the same sense that a person can have a sunburn or a stutter. Yet often, without thinking, we treat these concepts as though they had physical properties. Does a child suffer from too little self-esteem? Give him more! Does a woman "have" depression? Get rid of it! Language tempts us to sloppy thinking because it implies realism, rather than constructivism. Sound theory prevents this confusion.

The constructivist approach describes, more accurately than the approach of realism, what most personality researchers do. Nonetheless, physical reality *does* influence personality. The relationship between the psychological and the physical remains a fascinating research topic. Much research demonstrates that "psychological" variables influence the body. Suzanne Kobasa's work, for example, suggests that psychological "hardiness" produces resistance to physical disease (Kobasa, 1979), and several studies demonstrate that psychological stress affects the functioning of the immune system (Ader & Cohen, 1993). In other cases, the body influences the psychological realm. Stroke victims, for example, may experience personality changes.

Whose Point of View?

As a science, psychology seeks some measure of objectivity. Yet the people we are trying to understand are influenced by thoughts, feelings, and other phenomenological experiences. Perhaps only the research subjects themselves can report phenomena that are crucial for understanding their personalities. (Indeed, it is curious that we call them "subjects" rather than "objects" of study!)

Radical behaviorism disallows subjective experience in its explanations of behavior. This extreme rejection of subjective experience is inconsistent with the field of personality as most workers understand it. Nevertheless, there remain wide differences among the various approaches in how much the person's own experience is explored in personality research.

Approaches may be described as **phenomenological** if they emphasize the importance of the subjective experiences (feelings, thoughts, and so forth) of the people being studied. Phenomenological approaches emphasize the meanings that people ascribe to events, not simply the objective events themselves. Phenomenological approaches attempt to understand an individual in his or her fullness, rather than only selected aspects of the person relevant to a small number of traits or other dimensions. This approach often studies individuals through case histories or accounts.

As with idiographic approaches, it is challenging to translate phenomenological research into systematic science. Each person is unique. An event has one meaning for one individual and another for someone else. Most researchers who acknowledge the importance of subjective experience nonetheless translate that experience into terms defined from an external, scientific perspective. Carl Rogers, for example, listened to his clients in therapy and inferred the extent to which their subjective experience could be characterized by dimensions important to psychological health: openness to experience, existential living, trust in their own feelings, the experience of freedom, and creativity (Rogers, 1961b). These dimensions of experience, which could be measured by a scientific observer, played the major predictive role in his theory.

Don't Overlook the Context

People function in various physical and social contexts. Often, researchers have ignored the impact of the environment on personality, both as a cause of personality and as a context in which personality influences behavior and experience. Without denying the influence of such environmental variables as cultural norms, poverty, and gender roles, they often relegate such factors to other areas of psychology (in particular, to the study of social psychology). Is this approach sound?

Daniel Cervone (1991) describes the field of personality as divided into two competing paths that disagree on "the most basic of questions: the units that one uses to conceptualize personality" (p. 372). One group emphasizes the identification of individual differences: the "trait/dispositional units," as Cervone calls them. The other group emphasizes what Cervone calls "cognitive-affective, person-in-context units." This group describes the adaptive processes of personality, which inherently take the social context into account.

Can we understand an individual personality without attending to the context in which that individual lives? The answer is that we cannot, any more than a biologist can understand a fish without attending to the sea, or a doctor can understand cholera without attending to sanitation. To ignore the environment is to impoverish understanding. For the most part, though, personality has been studied in a limited cultural context, so that we do not know how much our understanding needs to be modified to describe people in other contexts, real or imagined.

The Role of Theory in Description and Measurement

Carefully constructed theory protects researchers from the traps of sloppy thinking and the wastefulness of poorly directed research. Critics have blamed inadequate theoretical development for unproductive controversies in current personality research. Though grand, comprehensive theories are generally out of favor today, even limited theories need to be stated carefully and explicitly.

Theory Guides Description

The descriptions that people make in everyday life offer a good starting place for psychological theory, but they have limits. For example, people are remarkably consistent with one another in judging overt dimensions of introversion and extraversion in others. Yet psychological theory (Eysenck, 1967) identifies aspects of introversion-extraversion that are beyond what people can recognize in everyday life. Specifically, introverts, because of physiological differences from extraverts, are more responsive to stimulation, such as taste and noise (Semin & Krahé, 1987).

Scientific description is guided by theory. Three examples of broad theoretical assumptions will illustrate this point. First, some psychologists, particularly psychoanalysts, have assumed that various experiences in early development are responsible for major personality variations. Second, researchers have often accepted the assumption of stable, global traits, although this assumption has now been challenged. Third, most researchers assume (by their research methods, if not explicitly) that people differ in degree but not in kind.

Consider the psychoanalytic assumption that early childhood experience is important in shaping personality:

> *Certain early life experiences were thought to determine certain personality structures and dispositions, which in turn were thought to determine one's life pattern. There was a limited number of these crucial experiences, and therefore a small number of diagnostic categories. Psychodynamic formulations and the diagnostic system were inextricably intertwined. Given a diagnosis, one could infer a developmental personality pattern, and vice versa. (Rorer, 1990, p. 696)*

This assumption justified such concepts as the "oral personality" and the "anal personality," which have become part of the modern idiom. If early experience is less influential throughout life (or, indeed, if its influence does not focus on the conflicts described by psychoanalytic theory), then these ways of describing personality are faulty.

The assumption of stable, global traits has been the subject of controversy (for example, Mischel, 1990). When psychologists describe an individual's personality in terms of the characteristic traits of that individual, this approach is based on a theoretical assumption that people have stable traits, consistent over time and over a broad spectrum of situations. If this assumption is abandoned, then the description of personality in terms of trait scores is unwarranted.

Our third example of theoretical assumptions is a new twist on an old issue. By giving the same measuring instruments to all people and comparing their scores, researchers implicitly assume that people differ in degree rather than in kind. That is, they make the assumption that traits, rather than types, are the appropriate descriptive category. This assumption seems reasonable, because it permits a large number of more focused concepts (traits) instead of a small number of highly generalized concepts (types). Furthermore, since traits and types were themselves theoretical constructs rather than "real" biological entities, an arbitrary choice seemed perfectly permissible. Recently, however, Paul Meehl has offered a mathematical procedure for determining whether "real" types (he calls them "classes") are being measured by any particular test (Meehl, 1992). If there are any discrete personality types, Meehl proposes that his data-analytic method can verify them, distinguishing them from continuous traits. Yet so long as the theoretical assumption of continuous traits prevails, to the exclusion of discrete types, research based on this alternative way of describing personality will not be conducted.

If "love" and "hate" are opposites (as opposite poles of a unidimensional scale), we have to decide whether this man loves his wife or hates her. It may be more accurate, though, to say that we can both love and hate the same person (a bidimensional scale).

Theory Guides Measurement

Theory guides measurement procedures, too. Although self-report questionnaires come most readily to mind, there are other ways of measuring personality: behavioral assessment, cognitive assessment, projective testing, and others (see Rorer, 1990). Like the proverbial parent, "what I say" (on self-report measures) and "what I do" (assessed by behavioral measures) may be quite different. The choice among these methods of measuring personality should be based on theoretical considerations.

Another aspect of measurement can be guided by theory. This is the issue of dimensionality, the number of independent coordinates needed to specify a measurement mathematically. **Unidimensional** measures assess only one dimension: intelligence, or extraversion, or dominance, for example. Many of these trait measures are **unipolar.** They measure the amount of a trait, ranging from very high to very low. For example, intelligence is a unipolar trait. Other trait measures are theorized to be **bipolar.** Bipolar traits have opposite poles that each have a distinct meaning. For example, until recently, "masculinity versus femininity" has been measured as a bipolar trait. This measure assumes that as a person becomes more masculine, she or he becomes less feminine. Or we could measure the emotions of love and hate on a bipolar scale if we presumed that love and hate are each opposite poles of a single dimension.

Suppose, though, that we can feel ambivalent toward a person: loving and hating that person at the same time (see Rorer, 1990). In the case of masculinity-femininity, suppose that a person can be high on both

FIGURE 2.2
Assumptions underlying personality test scores: dimensionality and polarity of measurement.

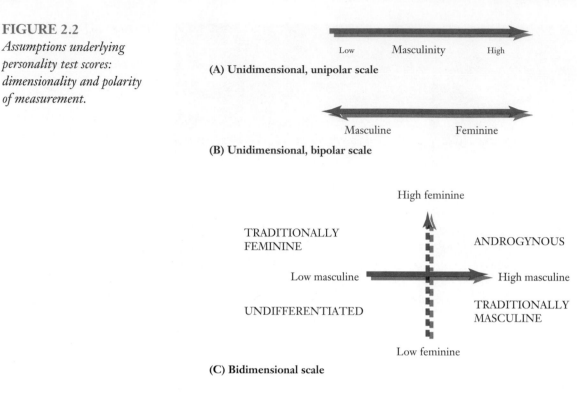

(A) Unidimensional, unipolar scale

(B) Unidimensional, bipolar scale

(C) Bidimensional scale

masculinity and femininity, as Sandra Bem's well-known concept of androgyny asserts (Bem, 1974). In these cases, a unidimensional scale (even though bipolar) is inadequate. Bem's theory suggests that there are two dimensions, not simply two poles. Therefore, **bidimensional** measures are necessary. Measurement must provide two scores: masculinity and femininity. Forcing a bidimensional aspect of personality into a uni-dimensional measure seriously impedes research (Fig. 2.2). As research in an area progresses, measures that were thought to be unidimensional are sometimes found to contain hidden additional dimensions (see, for example, Lennox, 1988). Some scales have three or more dimensions, making them **multidimensional.**

Evaluating Measurement

Personality measures are never perfect. Each measurement method influences the scores obtained. People answering questionnaires may misread questions. They may distort their answers in order to appear better than they would if they answered honestly. They may not remember accurately what they are trying to report. These and other factors produce errors in self-report questionnaires. Other measurement methods are also imperfect.

Peer ratings are subject to biases due to halo effects and implicit personality theories, as we have seen. Peers may also lack sufficient information to make informed ratings. Behavioral observation may err because observers are looking in the wrong direction, are not adequately trained, or make marks in the wrong place on their coding forms.

In effect, each measurement reflects a variety of components. In part, the measure is composed of the *true score*, which would be the perfect, error-free measure of the underlying personality dimension. This true score cannot be seen directly, because a variety of sources of error are also reflected by any measured score. *Random error* sometimes raises and at other times lowers scores, without any systematic pattern. Random error makes measurement less reliable, but unreliability can often be compensated by studying larger numbers of subjects or by aggregating ratings across a larger number of observers, so it is a tolerable problem for researchers (for example, Epstein, 1979, 1980; Moskowitz & Schwarz, 1982). Other errors are *systematic errors* that consistently (rather than randomly) increase scores for some subjects and decrease scores for others. Systematic errors can be a serious problem for researchers. For example, one person taking a self-report questionnaire to measure "anxiety" may consistently underreport his anxiety in order to look better. Another person may consistently report more anxiety whenever in doubt, thereby increasing her score. Thus the measured "anxiety score" in fact reflects both real anxiety (the "true score") plus or minus a "measurement error" due to readiness to report anxiety. Because systematic errors are consistent in their influence on a particular subject, they do not make scores less reliable, and the researcher may have little clue that the scores are invalid.

How, then, can we know who is high in anxiety and who is simply willing to report it? How can we know who is truly low in anxiety, as opposed to denying it in order to appear better? Instead of relying on only one measurement method, such as self-report, researchers may use a variety of techniques. They measure the trait using several different methods that would have different strengths and weaknesses. Self-reports may be biased to form a good impression, but at least they are completed by someone who knows the person well. Observer ratings may be unbiased, but they see only public behavior and miss private information. If all these methods, despite their different sources of error, produce the same results, then we have increased confidence in the scores. For example, Moskowitz and Schwarz (1982) have found that teachers' ratings of dependency in preschool children are significantly correlated with measures of dependency based on behavioral observation. Similarly, ratings of dominance and observations of dominant behavior are significantly correlated. The fact that two different measurement strategies, ratings and observations, tend to agree constitutes evidence of *convergent validity*.

As we have seen, psychologists have many guidelines to help them develop adequate descriptions of personality. The success of research depends upon keeping these guidelines in mind throughout the research enterprise. If our descriptions and measurements are faulty, it will be difficult to develop accurate understandings of the causes and consequences of personality.

SUMMARY

• The lexical approach examines language for its relevance to personality description.

• The Big Five dimensions of personality, suggested by many studies of language, are Extraversion, Agreeableness, Conscientiousness, Emotional Stability, and Openness to Experience.

• Content analysis is a strategy for coding verbal material that can be applied to public material such as speeches, as well as to open-ended questionnaire responses.

• Experimental studies show that language conveys many subtle meanings relevant for measuring personality.

• The halo effect distorts personality measurements when we are overly generous to people whom we like.

• People use traits more often in some situations than others, such as when describing other people's personality (instead of their own). Once made, trait attributions influence later perceptions of the individual.

• Implicit personality theories are people's everyday assumptions about personality traits and their relationships.

• People can be described in terms of prototypes, based on their resemblance to the typical examples that are characteristic of categories with fuzzy boundaries.

• Stereotype accuracy occurs when people agree with a criterion of personality, not because they know the individual being judged, but because their category-based judgments happen to match the criterion.

• The act frequency approach to personality measurement counts the number of times a person does behaviors that typify a trait.

• Trait judgments are sometimes distorted to enhance the self-image of the perceiver.

• Personality can be measured by a nomothetic approach, which describes individual differences among people, or an idiographic approach, which focuses on the study of one individual. The nomothetic approach is more popular.

- Personality can be described by a small number of broad personality types or a larger number of more focused traits.

- Personality researchers can focus on overt behavior or on hidden processes.

- Personality concepts are best regarded as constructed, rather than real in a physical sense; that is, constructivism rather than realism is the usual assumption.

- Phenomenological approaches emphasize the subjective experience of the people being studied.

- The social context should also be of concern to personality psychologists.

- Theory guides the description of personality and the measurement process (suggesting whether measures should be unidimensional, bidimensional, or multidimensional).

- Convergent validity occurs when diverse measures of the same aspect of personality are highly correlated.

GLOSSARY

act frequency approach   a strategy for measuring personality traits by counting instances of behavioral acts that are typical of a trait

bidimensional   having two coordinates or dimensions, as in a test that provides two scores for each individual

Big Five   five major dimensions of personality that have emerged from several lexical studies: Extraversion, Agreeableness, Conscientiousness, Emotional Stability, and Openness to Experience

bipolar   having two anchors, as in a test that measures the standing of a person on some characteristic that ranges between two opposite extremes

constructivism   an approach holding that the concepts of personality theory do not necessarily correspond to any physical realities, but are made up for their usefulness

content analysis   a research procedure that examines verbal material for the presence of selected words or meanings

convergent validity   evidence for the accuracy of a trait that occurs when two or more different ways of measuring the trait are highly correlated

halo effect   the tendency to favorably bias our descriptions of people whom we like

idiographic   an approach that studies one individual, without making comparisons with other people

implicit personality theory   assumptions made by lay people about personality traits and the relationships among them

lexical approach   an approach that studies personality description beginning with the way people use words to describe people in everyday language

multidimensional   having three or more coordinates or dimensions, as in a test that provides three or more scores for an individual

nomothetic   an approach that makes comparisons among individuals, as in comparisons among people's scores on the same personality test

phenomenological   approaches that emphasize the importance of the subjective experiences (feelings, thoughts, and so forth) of the people being studied

prototype   a typical or exemplary instance of a category

realism   an approach whose proponents look for physical realities that correspond to aspects of personality

stereotype accuracy   judging the personality of an individual correctly based simply on the typical personality of the group of which the individual is a member

traits   dimensions of personality that apply to a fairly narrow scope of behavior

types   broad categories of personality, created so that only a few categories are applied to all people

unidimensional   having only one coordinate or dimension, as in a test that provides only one score for an individual

unipolar   having only one anchor, as in a test that measures the amount of some characteristic that a person has

THOUGHT QUESTIONS

1. How would you describe your best friend in words? What are the implications of this description, based on the language of personality traits?

2. What other personality traits are correlated with the words you used to describe your friend in the previous question? Do you think other people would agree with your implicit personality theory?

3. Describe a clear example of a prototypical "A student" (or some other category of your selection). Do real people sometimes fall at the boundaries of this fuzzy category, rather than being clearly in it or out of it?

4. Select a personality trait that interests you. Now list several behaviors you think are prototypical acts that are evidence that a person has that trait.

5. Can you describe a person without making comparisons with other people? Is it difficult to give such an idiographic (rather than nomothetic) description? (Notice that there are hidden comparisons in many descriptions. For example, if a person is "modest," doesn't this imply a comparison with other people?)

6. Look back at your description of your friend in the first question. Does this description illustrate a type of personality, or personality traits?

7. Considering the discussion of realism versus constructivism in the text, do you think that psychologists should study biological science? Why or why not?

8. How do you think the context in which undergraduate students live influences their personality or influences the expression of their personality in behavior?

9. If you have a theory of intelligence that says people vary on two dimensions, verbal intelligence and creative intelligence, how will your measuring instruments be influenced by this theory?

10. Suggest two (or more) measures that could potentially show convergent validity for a trait of creativity.

Personality Traits

IN ITS MOST BASIC SENSE, a personality **trait** is an enduring aspect of individual personality that influences behavior in a particular domain. Personality traits play an important role in personality research and theory; researchers seek to identify and measure important traits and to study their impact on behavior. Some researchers have built upon the language used in ordinary speech to talk about personality traits. Others object to using traits at all as scientific concepts. They argue that the inexact language of everyday life cannot meet the specialized requirements of science. It is certainly true that when a personality theorist describes someone as an "extravert," the implications of this statement are more explicit and conscious than when we make a similar statement in our everyday speech. Controversies over traits have stimulated refinement of the concept, so that the psychological language of traits has become increasingly precise.

Personality Traits: History and Controversies

Historically, Gordon Allport was the most prominent advocate of the trait concept, from his systematic presentation of traits in 1931 until his death in 1967. Since then, critics have attacked trait explanations as overly simplified, while advocates have developed sophisticated ways of measuring what began as a straightforward, common sense idea.

Allport's Concept of Traits

Gordon Allport (1931) was the most conspicuous early theorist to assert the importance of traits as theoretical concepts. He defined a trait as

> *A generalized and focalized neuropsychic system (peculiar to the individual), with the capacity to render many stimuli functionally equivalent, and to initiate and guide consistent (equivalent) forms of adaptive and expressive behavior. (Allport, 1937, p. 295)*

Allport expanded this definition with several theoretical assertions (Table 3.1). He proposed that traits are causes of behavior that are, in principle, unique to each person (that is, *idiographic*). Traits develop as the person learns to adapt to his or her world. Although such adaptations are unique to each individual, there are enough similarities from one person to another to allow research on groups of people (that is, *nomothetic* research).

Traits vary in their scope of influence. Some, called **central traits,** influence a wide range of behavior. For most people, six to eight central traits summarize the major aspects of personality. These central traits are the half dozen or so words you would use to summarize the personality of someone you know well. In one classic study, for example, Allport summarized the personality of a woman, Jenny Grove Masterson. By analyzing letters she had written over 11 years, he concluded that there were eight central traits in her personality: quarrelsome-suspicious, self-centered, independent-autonomous, dramatic-intense, aesthetic-artistic, aggressive, cynical-morbid, and sentimental (Allport, 1965, pp. 193–194).

Occasionally, one trait dominates a personality so much that it influences nearly everything a person does. Most people do not have such a pervasive *cardinal* trait, but those who do are often remembered for this one characteristic. For example, the Marquis de Sade's notoriety stems from his trait of sexual cruelty (Allport, 1937). In addition, everyone has many *secondary traits* that describe the impact of personality in particular limited situations. For example, a person may consistently prefer tea instead of coffee. Secondary traits are irrelevant to behaviors outside their limited area. Although Allport listed three categories of traits—cardinal, central, and

TABLE **3.1 Allport's Eight Assertions about Traits**

1. A trait has more than nominal existence.

2. A trait is more generalized than a habit.

3. A trait is dynamic, or at least determinative, in behavior.

4. A trait may be established empirically.

5. A trait is only relatively independent of other traits.

6. A trait is not synonymous with moral or social judgment.

7. A trait may be viewed either in the light of the personality that contains it or in the light of its distribution in the population at large.

8. Acts, and even habits, that are inconsistent with a trait are not proof of the nonexistence of the trait.

Adapted from Allport, 1966, p. 1.

secondary—he proposed that these exist along a continuum, not as three distinct levels of pervasiveness. Furthermore, traits are only part of a continuum of concepts for describing personality. More specific even than secondary traits are attitudes and habits. More general than even cardinal traits are a person's sense of self and philosophy of life.

Criticisms of Trait Approaches

Allport's theory of traits is richly suggestive, but it has not provided a precise, focused direction for research. It has left researchers to make assumptions about traits based on the vague language of everyday life. Often, these assumptions are not supported by research. Many researchers have become disenchanted with traits as a theoretical approach. Others, on the other hand, have responded to the failures of trait theory by refining and revising the concept of traits and making predictions based on these refinements. This sequence of criticism followed by research has made the study of personality increasingly scientific and less closely tied to lay understandings of traits.

What have investigators criticized about trait theory?

Circular Reasoning: You Can't Have It Both Ways Saying that traits cause behavior is **circular reasoning.** Mike is aggressive. How do we know? We have seen him beating up on people. Why does he? His trait of aggressiveness causes him to beat up on people. The trait explains the

How would you describe this young woman, based on your impressions from this brief glimpse of her?

behavior, and the behavior is the reason that we infer the trait. That is circular reasoning. It does not offer a satisfactory explanation of behavior.

Traits Are Only Weakly Correlated with Behavior
Logic tells us that causes and effects must be correlated. Yet the correlation between measured traits and behavior is generally low. This poses problems for a theory that says traits cause behavior. Walter Mischel (1968) concluded that the correlation between self-reported personality and behavior was limited, not surpassing a ceiling of .30. This **personality coefficient** is too low to justify a theory of personality based primarily on traits, particularly when behavior can be predicted better by knowing the situation than by knowing traits.

The personality coefficient of .30, like the sound barrier in aviation, was a limit that eventually was exceeded. Researchers responded to Mischel's challenge by seeking methods to increase the trait-behavior correlation, and some of them have reported higher correlations (for example, McCrae, 1982). There are several reasons that research might fail to report high trait-behavior correlations even if traits are causes of behavior. Consider these reasons.

Behavior Has Many Causes
It is an oversimplification to expect that one trait will have a high correlation with behavior, because any behavior is determined, jointly, by all the relevant traits that a person possesses. Did you attend the last class in this course? Several aspects of your personality probably influenced this behavior: your motivation to succeed, your general

level of conscientiousness, your liking for classmates, and so on. In addition, situational factors had an impact: whether attendance is required, whether there was an exam, whether it was a sunny day, and so on. This multiple determination of behavior places limits on the correlation that can be found between any *one* trait and a particular behavior (Ahadi & Diener, 1989).

The solution is obvious. Researchers should measure multiple traits if they wish to explain behavior from personality, and they should combine these traits in an appropriate statistical model. In addition, they may wish to include aspects of the situation in their predictions.

Behavior Measures Aren't Perfect, Either   Unreliable measures reduce the correlation of anything with anything else. Researchers are careful to construct reliable measures of personality, but they often settle for any available measure of behavior, without attempting to make them reliable. Just as a one-item test cannot reliably measure a personality trait, a one-act behavioral measure is often unreliable and cannot correlate highly with personality. The strategy for increasing reliability is the same in both cases: consider several items instead of only one. Several questions are added together in a personality test to get a more reliable measure. Similarly, several behaviors can be aggregated to get a more reliable behavioral measure (Epstein, 1979, 1980).

Seymour Epstein (1979) reports, for example, how averaging increases the reliability of self-ratings. Subjects rated themselves on emotions each day for a month. The correlation between ratings on Day 1 and on Day 2 for "energetic" was .36. Another analysis, however, yielded a higher correlation. The researchers averaged all odd-numbered days together to obtain one score and then correlated that with a second score, the average of all even-numbered days. The reliability of these "energetic" ratings rose to .88. Epstein reports such comparisons for many different self-ratings. The general pattern is that averaging many observations increases reliability above that based on single observations. Why? There is more measurement error in single observations than in averaged data. It is more likely, for example, that something could make a usually energetic person less energetic for one day than for many days. This is the principle of **aggregation.**

Aggregated behavioral measures correlate more highly with personality than do single item behaviors (Amelang & Borkenau, 1986). Walter Mischel and Philip Peake (1982; Mischel, 1984), however, warn that aggregation must be done judiciously. Sometimes the situational variability of behavior is important and theoretically interesting. For example, understanding why Daniel talks back to his father but not to his friends would be hampered if an aggregate "talking back" score were computed. Such situational variability should not be lost in overzealous aggregation.

Of *Course* Situations Matter: Who Said They Didn't?   Research supports the conclusion that people's behavior varies greatly from situation to situation. In other words, there is little **cross-situational consistency** of

Some life situations seem overwhelming. While we all know intuitively that situations matter, it is not so simple to know how to include them in theoretical descriptions of personality.

behavior. A person may talk a lot at home but keep quiet in school, or work until the last minute on one class assignment but do another quickly and without much care. Intuitively, though, we expect people to be consistent, as when we call someone "a typical conscientious student" (Mischel, 1984, p. 284). Common sense suggests extensive cross-situational consistency, but research does not support this idea. The conflict between common sense and research evidence of situational variability is termed the **consistency paradox** (Mischel, 1984).

Notice that cross-situational consistency refers to different situations, not to repetitions of the same situation. We are talking about whether a person who is late for psychology class is also late for athletic events: *cross-situational consistency*. We are not considering whether people who are late for psychology class on September 15 are also late for that class on September 17. That would be *temporal stability*, because the variable is time, not situation. Walter Mischel and Philip Peake (1982) claim that temporal stability is higher than cross-situational consistency (although this conclusion is criticized by Conley, 1984c). Temporal stability is not an issue, however, in the debate over traits, because both trait approaches and alternative theories can account for temporal stability.

Theorists have debated the consistency issue at great length, criticizing one another's methods and conclusions (for example, Epstein & O'Brien, 1985; Funder, 1983; Houts, Cook & Shadish, 1986; Mischel & Peake, 1983). Trait theorists have had to explain why behavior isn't entirely consistent. One way is to conceptualize traits in less global terms, focusing on the most prototypical behaviors for a trait, which may show higher levels of cross-situational consistency (Mischel & Peake, 1982). Another way is to postulate moderator variables that predict when there will be consistency and when there will not.

It All Depends on ... Moderator Variables! Sometimes people are consistent. Sometimes they're not. If we can identify when to expect consistency, the consistency paradox may be solved. What does consistency depend on? One important consideration is individual differences: some people are more consistent than others. One professor is always on time for class; another, only sometimes. Another consideration is the type of behavior involved. People tend to be more consistent in their choice of television programs than in their choice of a main dish when eating at a restaurant. The factors that predict the level of consistency are **moderator variables.**

Daryl Bem and Andrea Allen (1974) attempted to resolve the consistency paradox by adopting an idiographic approach. That is, they rejected the nomothetic assumption that all traits are equally relevant for describing everyone's personality. The idiographic alternative begins by determining which traits are relevant to each person. To do this, Bem and Allen asked subjects to report how consistent they were across situations on two dimensions: friendliness and conscientiousness. They assumed that traits are more relevant to consistent individuals. For a person who is consistently friendly or consistently unfriendly, "friendliness" is a relevant trait. For a person who is sometimes friendly and sometimes not, "friendliness" is not such a relevant trait. (Perhaps that person is consistently manipulative, trying to control the situation by friendly behavior at some times and by unfriendly threats at other times.) The results supported Bem and Allen's argument. Personality scores predicted the behavior of those who reported that they were consistent, but not of those who reported that they were less consistent. Thus, while we cannot predict behavior for *all* people very well from their personality tests, we can predict behavior for *some* of the people: the consistent ones.

Bem and Allen urged researchers to become more idiographic in their research; that is, to pay more attention to the personality structure of the individual. Their work challenged nomothetic research, which attempts to understand everyone with the same list of traits. This advice guided Douglas Kenrick and David Stringfield (1980). They found subgroups of subjects whose self-rated personality traits correlated especially highly with criterion measures (ratings by peers and parents). What distinguished the people whose behavior could be predicted from their personality? This time, the moderator variable was that their behavior (according to their own assessment) was not only consistent but also publicly observable.

We can think of the search for moderator variables as the search for people for whom the trait that we are interested in studying is relevant. Such trait relevance is called **traitedness.** It can be measured straightforwardly by asking subjects to rank the influence of traits on their behavior (Zuckerman et al., 1989; Zuckerman, Koestner, et al., 1988). Less directly, traitedness can be inferred from statistical analysis of the personality test (Reise & Waller, 1993). Subjects who respond consistently are considered to possess the trait being measured at whatever level their score indicates, according to Roy Baumeister and Dianne Tice's concept of *metatraits*. Those who respond inconsistently, seeming to have a high level of the trait on some items and a low level on others, are considered to be "untraited" on the item. That is, the trait does not apply to them, and their scores should be disregarded (Baumeister, 1991; Baumeister & Tice, 1988).

Alternatives to Global Traits Without abandoning the notion of traits, we can acknowledge that behavior varies from one situation to another by recognizing that traits do not have to be global. **Global traits** are phrased in quite general terms and are presumed to apply to behavior in many situations. Alternatively, **specific traits** describe behavior in a particular situation. A global trait of "timeliness," for example, would predict that a person will arrive on time for just about any event. What about Joe, who is never late for soccer practice, but who rarely arrives on time for psychology class? For him, a specific trait of "on time for soccer" is more accurate.

Mischel's emphasis on situational determinants of behavior does not mean that individual differences are unimportant (Mischel, 1968, p. 38), although his challenge to global traits has led some researchers to that conclusion. He does argue, though, that traits are "excessively crude, gross units" (Mischel, 1968, p. 301). People interpret and respond to situations in complex and subtle ways. Theorists should describe personality in ways that capture this complexity, as Mischel has done in later work, instead of using the crude units of traits.

Perhaps common sense is more insightful than trait theorists have acknowledged. Trait theorists have assumed that the concept of traits requires extensive cross-situational consistency. When this consistency was not found, perhaps they were too ready to question the theory of traits. Do people really assume such broad consistency when they say that someone has a trait? Apparently not, according to Mischel's later work. When lay people say that a person is aggressive, they mean that the person will hit someone *if threatened*, not regardless of the situation. That is, people apply a "conditional hedge" to the trait-behavior relationship (Wright & Mischel, 1987, 1988).

Interactionism between Traits and Situations Theorists have caught up with this wisdom of common sense by proposing the concept of **interactionism.** This theoretical approach strives to predict behavior from the *joint* effects of personality and situations (Magnusson, 1990). Traits influence behavior, but that influence is contingent upon the situation. Situations influence people, but they do not influence everyone in the same way. Interactionism is the perspective that studies these joint influences of personality (traits) and situations; it requires that both personality and situations be considered in predicting behavior.

From an interactionist perspective, researchers do not seek to identify personality differences that have pervasive effects regardless of situation. Instead, they recognize that a given personality trait may have one impact on behavior in one type of situation and another impact in another. For example, the trait of "altruism" leads to helping in situations where reward is not expected (but not when it is expected), whereas the trait of "receptive giving" predicts helping when reward is expected (Romer, Gruder & Lizzadro, 1986).

A person-situation interactionist approach to aggression takes situations into account in predicting behavior from traits and takes traits into account in predicting behavior from situations. It's not a case of *either* situations *or* behavior, but rather that *both* are necessary to predict behavior. Consider this experiment. Male undergraduate research subjects perform a memory task, and then the experimenter evaluates their performance, saying either it was good or it was poor. Then each subject is asked to play "teacher" and deliver punishment, in the form of electric shock, when a learner makes mistakes in an extrasensory perception task. (Actually, the learner is a confederate of the experimenter and only pretends to receive a shock.) Try to predict the outcome: Will subjects deliver more shock after they have been told their performance was poor, or good? (One psychological postulate, the frustration-aggression hypothesis, predicts that after being frustrated by doing badly, people will deliver more shock; we'll see in a moment whether that happened.) Venture a second prediction: Before this experiment, subjects took a personality test to determine whether they were high or low on authoritarianism, a trait that involves obeying legitimate authority figures. Which subjects will deliver more shock, the high authoritarians or those low on this trait?

Actually, the results do not permit a simple answer to either of these questions. What was found was more complicated. Subjects high on the trait of authoritarianism gave higher levels of electric shock when they had been told they had done well, but lower levels when they had supposedly done badly. Low authoritarians did the opposite, giving higher shocks when they had been told that they did poorly, but lower shocks after success. If being told you have done poorly is a frustration, then low authoritarians did as the frustration-aggression hypothesis predicts: they were aggressive after they had been frustrated. In contrast, the high authoritarians became aggressive not after failure, but after success (Caprara, 1987).

This research illustrates that neither situation nor personality can adequately predict behavior, unless the other is also taken into account. Personality and situations *interact* to determine behavior. It is no wonder that the search for global behavioral effects of traits has been difficult. Personality alone can lead only to limited prediction "in a world populated by person-situation interactions" (Bem & Funder, 1978, p. 499). Much work remains, however, before the possibility of predicting behavior from personality-situation interactions becomes a reality (Epstein & O'Brien, 1985; Kenrick & Dantchik, 1983).

The Situational Challenge in Perspective The controversy over interactionism and situational determinants of behavior has undermined the traditional focus of personality on the individual (Kenrick & Dantchik, 1983). The debate over personality versus situation has been intense and, in the end, neither side is the clear victor. Depending upon how the study is conducted, either factor can be stronger (Buss, 1989).

Situational effects are sometimes overwhelming. When a building catches fire, its occupants try to escape, regardless of the personality differences among them. Situations that have such powerful impacts on behavior are called **strong situations.** When situational pressures are weak, however, personality differences influence behavior. One example of such a **weak situation** is the sight of an elderly person at a street corner. Some will offer to help the old person to cross the street; others will assess the opportunity of stealing some money; others will pass by without even noticing. Personality traits predict behavior best when situations are weak. Researchers who manipulate situations generally select strong situations, and as a consequence they often find little correlation of personality variables with behavior.

Behavioral prediction, though, is not an end in itself. The goal of prediction should be considered in the context of the scientific process. Unlike actuaries, we do not value prediction per se. Rather, accurate prediction is a sign that our theories have described the processes of personality correctly. Investigation of these processes, rather than simple prediction, should be the primary goal, and it is clear that we must understand both personality traits and situations more fully to describe these processes (Funder, 1983; Mischel, 1984b). The trait versus situation controversy has enhanced this understanding by clarifying when traits best predict behavior (Kenrick & Funder, 1988).

Should Traits Be Left for Nonscientists?

As we saw in Chapter 2, traits are well represented in the language of lay people. Can such common sense language serve the purposes of science? If we use everyday language, we may risk repeating the errors of nonscientific understandings of personality.

A specialized language, though, is no guarantee of scientific advance. David Funder has criticized many purported scientific personality variables for being unnecessarily "*esoteric*—they are deliberately nonintuitive or even counterintuitive" (Funder, 1991, p. 31). He defends traits as appropriate concepts for the scientific study of personality. Funder argues that we should study traits that are related to the concepts used by "insightful observers," rather than those that are esoterically scientific (such as "self-regulatory systems" and "encoding strategies," to cite Funder's examples). Intuitively meaningful traits, he says, have many advantages. They have greater social utility, tap a large range of behaviors in people's lives, and make it possible to study how accurately people perceive one another's personalities (Funder, 1991).

If everyday language is suitable for science, then there is probably little to fear from the fact that most personality measurement uses questionnaires. As the field moves away from the language of everyday life, however, our reliance on this measurement technique becomes more troublesome. Some aspects of personality may escape detection by questionnaires. If that is true, even elaborate statistical analyses of questionnaires cannot add these missed dimensions of personality. There is no guarantee that the concepts people use in everyday life to describe one another will be adequate for science. The study of personality may require scientific concepts that, like the neutrons and electrons of physics, were not foreseen in lay understandings, and we may need more sophisticated instruments than questionnaires to measure them.

Can Traits Explain, Or Only Describe?   Traits may describe a person's behaviors at a superficial (topographic) level, but they do not necessarily explain its causes. It would be better, say critics, to focus on the *determinants* of behavior, not simply its *description*. Such determinants may involve motivation, reinforcement, goal-seeking, and other dynamic processes.

Allport, the premier historical advocate of traits, used the concept in two ways: as descriptions of individual differences and as determinants of behavior (Wiggins, 1984). In the second sense, Allport preferred to use the term *personal dispositions* instead of *traits*, although this distinction has not caught on. Allport (1966) considered personal dispositions to be real in a physical sense and thought that they might one day be understood as structures of interconnected neurons (Funder, 1991).

This assertion, however, rings hollow unless we can further describe the relationship between the physical structure and the trait. For some traits, research does point in this direction. Extraversion, for example, has physiological correlates in EEG and other brain activity, brain biochemistry, and reactivity to stimulant and depressive drugs (Eysenck, 1990a). For most traits, however, psychologists have not even suggested a relationship to any specific "neuropsychic" reality, let alone demonstrated such a mechanism by research.

We must hope that description will eventually lead to dynamic understanding. Researchers may discover an underlying physical basis of traits, or at least of some traits. The concepts of introversion-extraversion existed in common language and in psychological theory before scientists investigated their physical correlates. This does not guarantee, however, that all traits have corresponding physical determinants or correlates. Other trait-like consistencies could simply reflect learning experiences. Still, labeling such traits may be a necessary early stage of scientific understanding as we move toward the discovery of biological and experiential determinants. In addition, people describe their own and other people's behavior in trait terms (see Chapter 2), and these understandings probably influence their behavior.

TABLE 3.2 **Examples of Personality Traits in the Research Literature**

Adaptability	Emotional	Insight	Passiveness
Aggressiveness	Immaturity	Instrumentality	Perceptiveness
Altruism	Emotional Inferiority	Internal Locus of	Perfectionism
Androgyny	Emotional Instability	Control	Persistence
Assertiveness	Emotional Maturity	Introversion	Pessimism
Authoritarianism	Emotional Security	Irritability	Psychoticism
Charisma	Emotional Stability	Leadership Style	Repression
Codependency	Emotional	Liberalism	Sensitization
Cognitive Style	Superiority	Likability	Rigidity
Conformity	Emotionality	Loyalty	Risk Taking
Conservatism	Empathy	Machiavellianism	Self-Control
Coronary Prone	External Locus of	Masculinity	Selfishness
Behavior	Control	Misanthropy	Self-Monitoring
Courage	Extraversion	Moodiness	Sensation Seeking
Creativity	Femininity	Narcissism	Sensitivity
Cruelty	Field Dependence	Negativism	Seriousness
Curiosity	Gregariousness	Nervousness	Sexuality
Cynicism	Honesty	Neuroticism	Sincerity
Defensiveness	Hypnotic	Nonconformity	Sociability
Dependency	Susceptibility	Nurturance	Spirituality
Dishonesty	Idealism	Obedience	Suggestibility
Dogmatism	Impulsiveness	Objectivity	Timidity
Egalitarianism	Independence	Openmindedness	Tolerance
Egocentrism	Individuality	Optimism	
Egotism	Initiative	Paranoia	

Adapted from Walker, 1991, p. 159.

Why So Many Traits? Trait approaches risk becoming encyclopedic, listing a very large number of traits without attempting to describe their relationships or rationale. A trait is simply postulated to account for some behavior of interest. When such specific traits are selected, though, it is necessary that there be many of them. This produces another objection to traits as theoretical constructs: so many traits are possible that the catalog becomes unwieldy. Allport and Odbert (1936) listed almost 18,000 traits in their famous study of the dictionary. Researchers have developed measuring instruments for many traits (Table 3.2). How can we understand personality when we are swamped with traits? One solution has involved the search for a systematic description of the relationships among traits. Statistical analysis can simplify the lists. In particular, the technique of **factor analysis** is useful. By systematically considering all the correlations among variables, factor analysis can simplify a large set of data into a smaller number of underlying dimensions called *factors* (see the Appendix).

Theory, Anyone?

It is easy to talk in circles about traits, without getting very far. Trait approaches need to be connected to some theoretical framework if they are to advance the science of personality. A theory will tell us when to expect consistency, how situations come into the picture, and which of the many traits we could list are most important.

Consider, for example, the trait of internal-external locus of control. The trait of internal locus of control means that a person believes he or she is responsible for what happens. Success is a result of effort and ability, and failure is due to one's own shortcomings. On the other hand, external locus of control means that a person believes outcomes are due to causes outside the self. Luck, fate, impersonal social forces, and the like are responsible for one's own good or bad outcomes. This dimension of internal-external locus of control can be measured by a brief self-report questionnaire (Rotter, 1966). A variety of questionnaires have been developed to assess locus of control in specific areas (such as academic success, health outcomes, and so forth).

Locus of control was proposed by Julian Rotter (1966) in the context of an extensive theoretical framework called social learning theory. Much of the research that has measured locus of control, however, ignores the theory on which it is based (Rotter, 1990). Rotter criticizes such neglect of theory. In the case of locus of control, the theory would have prevented the false assumption that people have a consistently high or low locus across time and across situations. Rotter's theory predicts that an individual's locus of control will change with experience. Success makes us more internal, and failure makes us more external. Furthermore, the theory allows a person to have an internal locus of control in some areas and an external locus of control in others. (For example, I took credit for my spelling success in grade school, but when I hit a home run in softball, I knew it was luck. Everyone told me so, and it was a once in a lifetime hit.) Rotter suggests that the intensive research on locus of control over several decades would have been more productive if researchers had been more mindful of theory (Coombs & Schroeder, 1988).

Must theory precede productive research? Perhaps not. Theory may be too abstract at times to focus debate on productive issues. Perhaps theory should emerge from extensive observations, instead of beginning the process (Glaser & Strauss, 1967). Measurement techniques may provide the personality researcher with a tool analogous to a good microscope for the biologist: an instrument for some explorations into new phenomena, beyond the limits of theoretical imagination. We can adopt an empirical approach instead of a theoretical approach.

Empiricism can be systematic if some overview of the structure of traits exists. Can we agree on a list of traits to describe individual differences? This is no trivial issue. Angleitner, Ostendorf, and John (1990) report that judges who coded lists of words for trait relevance disagreed enormously; one judge coded 1600 words as traits, while another judge found only 35 traits in the same list. More consensus would be valuable. If diverse researchers agreed on a set of constructs, they could better coordinate research on a common set of problems in the field. Science, as Thomas Kuhn describes it (see Chapter 1), thrives on such agreement.

How can scientists achieve agreement? Sometimes the lessons of nature are so emphatic that they come through, despite diverse methods. The trait of introversion-extraversion, for example, has emerged in diverse approaches to personality. It is difficult to imagine a comprehensive understanding of personality that ignores this dimension of individual differences. At other times, though, nature is more elusive, teasing scientists along the path of theoretical disagreements and paradigm debates before yielding her knowledge.

Comprehensive Models of Traits

Instead of examining traits one at a time, a comprehensive approach seeks a broad model to organize our understanding of various traits. How are they related to one another? What does personality look like, taken as a whole? Though ambitious, such an undertaking is valuable.

> *It is easy to see why a comprehensive description and classification of personality traits would be useful. It would provide a common language for researchers of different orientations, a basis for comparing and evaluating personality theories, a framework for the convergent and discriminant validation of personality scales, and a guide to comprehensive assessment of the individual. (McCrae, Costa & Busch, 1986, p. 430)*

We will consider several comprehensive models of personality traits that have stimulated much research.

Five-Factor Model

Many researchers enthusiastically endorse the **five-factor model** (the "Big Five" introduced in Chapter 2) as the long-sought comprehensive model for describing personality. This model has a long history. Its roots are in lexical studies, which have been analyzed to determine what dimensions people use when they describe themselves and one another. This research indicates that ordinary people describe personality in terms of five major factors. These are called the "Big Five" (Goldberg, 1981). Although various researchers have used different terms (Table 3.3), similarities across studies

TABLE 3.3   Five-Factor Model of Personality

Investigators	Factor I	Factor II	Factor III	Factor IV	Factor V
Tupes & Christal (1961)	Surgency	Agreeableness	Dependability	Emotional Stability	Culture
Norman (1963)	Surgency	Agreeableness	Conscientiousness	Emotional Stability	Culture
Goldberg (1981, 1989)	Surgency	Agreeableness	Conscientiousness	Emotional Stability	Intellect
McCrae & Costa (1985a)	Extraversion	Agreeableness	Conscientiousness	Neuroticism	Openness to Experience
Conley (1985a)	Social Extraversion	Agreeableness	Impulse Control	Neuroticism	Intellectual Interests
Others	Confident Self-Expression; Assertiveness; Power	Social Adaptability; Likability; Friendly Compliance; Agreeableness vs. Coldheartedness; Agreeable–Stable; Love	Conformity; Task Interest; Will to Achieve; Impulse Control; Work	Emotional Control; Emotionality; Ego Strength (Anxiety); Emotional Instability; Dominant–Assured; Satisfaction; Affect	Inquiring Intellect; Intelligence; Intellectance–Culture

Adapted from John, 1990, p. 72.

suggest underlying agreement. Advocates of the five-factor model claim that it captures the important dimensions of individual differences and can provide an organizing framework for personality research. Oliver John states this claim succinctly:

> *The Big Five structure captures, at a broad level of abstraction, the commonalities among most of the existing systems of personality description, and provides an integrative descriptive model for personality research.* (John, 1990, p. 96)

Analysis of a variety of personality measures, developed for other purposes, has replicated the five-factor model. These include data obtained by peer report and by expert observer ratings (John, 1990). Asking subjects and those who know them to report specific behaviors ("act-report data") also leads to five factors (Botwin & Buss, 1989). In the words of John Digman and Jillian Inouye,

> *A series of research studies of personality traits has led to a finding consistent enough to approach the status of a law. The finding is this: If a large number of rating scales is used and if the scope of the scales is very broad, the domain of personality descriptors is almost completely accounted for by five robust factors. (Digman & Inouye, 1986, p. 116)*

Paul Costa and Robert McCrae have developed a self-report questionnaire, the **NEO Personality Inventory (NEO-PI),** specifically to measure these five factors (Costa & McCrae, 1985, 1992b). Originally, the NEO instrument assessed three factors: Neuroticism, Extraversion, and Openness to Experience. Soon after, two additional factors were added: Agreeableness and Conscientiousness (Costa, McCrae & Dye, 1991; McCrae & Costa, 1987).

The NEO-PI (Form S) consists of 181 items. Subjects indicate how much they agree with each item by marking a 5-point scale. The questionnaire is scored for each of the five factors. Within each factor, subscores measure six more specific traits or "facets." Facets are more specific aspects of the five general factors (Table 3.4). In addition to the self-report form, the NEO-PI has a form suitable for observers to rate others.

Research using the NEO-PI has addressed fundamental questions about personality that we will consider later in this text. Is personality stable over time? Apparently it is, according to a 6-year study using the NEO-PI to assess the self-perceived and spouse-perceived personalities of adults (Costa & McCrae, 1988b). In children, the evidence is not so clear; there may be more personality change in childhood (Digman, 1989). Is personality influenced by genetics? In part, it is (Bergeman et al., 1993; Costa & McCrae, 1992a).

These five personality dimensions are found using a variety of methods, including self-report measures and ratings by peers and spouses (for example, McCrae, Costa & Busch, 1986). When more than one measure is used to measure the personality of the same individual, we would naturally expect the measures to agree. That is, we would expect convergent validity of the measures, as presented in Chapter 2. Peter Borkenau and Fritz Ostendorf (1990) looked for such convergent validity. Their subjects were 256 German adults. (All instruments were translated into German.) They assessed the five factors by three methods. Costa and McCrae's (1985) NEO-PI provided inventory scale scores. The other two scores were based on lists of adjective selected to tap the five factors (Norman, 1963). Subjects rated themselves on these adjectives, and three acquaintances (or relatives)

TABLE 3.4 Facet Scales for the NEO Personality Inventory

Factor	Facet scales	Factor	Facet scales
Neuroticism	N1: Anxiety N2: Hostility N3: Depression N4: Self-Consciousness N5: Impulsiveness N6: Vulnerability	Agreeableness	A1: Trust A2: Straightforwardness A3: Altruism A4: Compliance A5: Modesty A6: Tender-Mindedness
Extraversion	E1: Warmth E2: Gregariousness E3: Assertiveness E4: Activity E5: Excitement Seeking E6: Positive Emotions	Conscientiousness	C1: Competence C2: Order C3: Dutifulness C4: Achievement Striving C5: Self-Discipline C6: Deliberation
Openness	O1: Fantasy O2: Aesthetics O3: Feelings O4: Actions O5: Ideas O6: Values		

Adapted from Costa, McCrae & Dye, 1991.

of each subject provided peer ratings of the subject on the same adjectives. Did these three measures agree in identifying those subjects who were high and low on each of the five factors? That is, was there *convergent validity* across the methods? There was, which supports both the specific measures and the trait concepts as theoretical notions. Details of the way researchers examine such data are presented in the Research Strategies box.

The five factors are not entirely independent of one another. Extraversion and Openness are positively correlated, while Neuroticism and Conscientiousness are negatively correlated (Costa, McCrae & Dye, 1991). Other correlations are small. Studies also support the validity of the five-factor model by showing meaningful correlations with other personality tests (for example, Conn & Ramanaiah, 1990).

Description of the Five Factors What are these five important dimensions of personality? Let us consider each one in turn.

Factor I: Extraversion The first factor, Extraversion, describes people who are rated by peers as "sociable, fun-loving, affectionate, friendly, and

RESEARCH STRATEGIES   ●----------------------------

Do Our Measures Converge? the Multitrait-Multimethod Matrix

When we are looking for something elusive, it makes sense to try a variety of strategies to see whether they agree. In trying to identify a bird you have never seen before, you might take note of its size, color, and distinctive markings to look in a guidebook; ask a friend who knows something about birds; and so on. Of course, if the world ornithology expert makes the identification for you, it would be sensible to assume you have enough information. But if all methods you've tried are a bit uncertain, having several sources of information is sensible. If all methods come up with the same result, you will have much more confidence that you've made the correct identification.

Personality researchers sometimes adopt a similar strategy when they want to confirm the presence of a proposed personality trait. They examine a variety of ways to measure the suggested trait and then look for confirming evidence that these measures agree. To decide who is extraverted, they might administer a self-report questionnaire. Behavioral observation might also be used, in which the subjects are observed by trained research assistants who rate their extraverted behaviors. Friends of the subjects might be asked for their perceptions of the subjects. Each measurement method has different sources of error. To the extent that measures of the same trait, using different measurement methods, correlate highly, we have evidence of **convergent validity** (Campbell & Fiske, 1959).

The correlation coefficient, discussed in Chapter 2, describes the agreement between two measures. Recall that the correlation coefficient indicates how closely two variables agree, ranging from +1.00 (for perfect agreement) to –1.00 (for a perfectly predictable reverse relationship). If we have several ways of measuring a trait, each pair of these measures should have a high positive correlation to provide evidence for convergence of the measures. These correlations could be listed, but it would get rather tedious:

The correlation of the inventory measure of neuroticism with the self-rating measure of neuroticism is .59. The correlation of the inventory measure of neuroticism with the peer rating measure of neuroticism is .25. The correlation of the self-rating measure of neuroticism with the peer rating measure of neuroticism is .27. The correlation of the inventory measure of extraversion with the self-rating measure of extraversion is .66. The correlation of the inventory measure of extraversion with the peer rating measure of extraversion is .40. The correlation of the self-rating measure of extraversion with the peer rating measure of extraversion is .45.

And so on. Such expression may be a fine cure for insomnia, but it doesn't communicate information very effectively. A better way to express that information would be to present it visually as a table.

A *multitrait-multimethod matrix* is a table that presents correlations among several traits, each measured by multiple methods (Campbell & Fiske, 1959). Examine the multi-

(continued)

trait-multimethod matrix in Table B3.1. This table shows the familiar Big Five personality traits measured by three methods: the NEO-PI, self-ratings on adjectives, and ratings on the same adjectives by peers who know the individual.

The correlations that measure the same trait by different methods provide evidence of convergent validity. In the table, these are printed in boldface type. The convergent validity correlations are relatively high, as they should be. These data demonstrate that the five factors can be measured by a variety of methods and that these diverse methods produce similar scores.

The other correlations in the matrix measure different traits (sometimes using the same method and sometimes using different methods). These correlations should be lower than the convergent validity correlations, but they may not be zero. After all, the traits actually might be correlated. Also, there may be correlations due to methodological factors, such as some subjects' distortions of their answers to create a favorable impression. Overall, though, a multitrait-multimethod matrix provides convincing evidence of convergent validity if the highest correlations are those that measure the same trait by various methods, as is the case in this example.

TABLE B3.1 Correlations among Five Personality Factors Assessed by Three Methods (Displayed in a Multitrait-Multimethod Matrix)

		Inventory scales					Self-ratings					Peer ratings				
		N	E	O	A	C	N	E	O	A	C	N	E	O	A	C
Inventory scales	N															
	E	.05														
	O	.28	.31													
	A	−.09	−.06	−.04												
	C	−.38	−.06	−.29	−.23											
Self-ratings	N	**.59**	−.12	.10	−.18	−.15										
	E	−.10	**.66**	.17	.07	−.06	−.23									
	O	−.05	.11	**.39**	−.08	−.03	−.14	.24								
	A	−.23	.08	−.04	**.54**	.06	−.38	.32	.30							
	C	−.39	−.17	−.20	.20	**.70**	−.33	−.05	.09	.28						
Peer ratings	N	**.25**	.12	.14	−.06	−.04	**.27**	.06	−.02	−.08	−.17					
	E	.00	**.40**	.10	−.07	−.12	.00	**.45**	−.02	.04	−.17	−.04				
	O	−.01	−.17	**.20**	−.12	−.11	.09	−.13	**.20**	−.08	−.09	−.21	.14			
	A	−.10	−.14	−.08	**.25**	−.01	−.03	.04	−.09	**.20**	.07	−.55	.17	.26		
	C	−.26	−.32	−.27	.20	**.50**	−.18	−.25	−.06	.05	**.57**	−.47	−.21	.28	.40	

N = Neuroticism   E = Extraversion   O = Openness   A = Agreeableness   C = Conscientiousness

Adapted from Borkenau & Ostendorf, 1990, p. 520.

Is this person an intravert or an extrovert? These traits are well known in everyday language and have appeared in many studies of personality.

talkative" (McCrae & Costa, 1987, p. 87). Extraversion correlates positively with self-esteem (Costa, McCrae & Dye, 1991). Extraversion, although sometimes labeled differently (for example, Surgency), occurs in diverse approaches to personality, attesting to its importance.

Factor II: Agreeableness People high in Agreeableness are forgiving, lenient, sympathetic, agreeable, and softhearted, according to peer ratings (McCrae & Costa, 1987). Peers describe those low in Agreeableness in more negative terms: ruthless, uncooperative, suspicious, and stingy. This low Agreeableness pole is, in a word, "antagonism" (McCrae & Costa, 1987).

Factor III: Conscientiousness Peers describe people high in Conscientiousness as careful, well organized, punctual, ambitious, and persevering (McCrae & Costa, 1987). Conscientiousness "includes both proactive (hardworking, ambitious) and inhibitive (dutiful, scrupulous) aspects"

(McCrae & Costa, 1989c, p. 116). It is sometimes correlated with low erotic interest (McCrae, Costa & Busch, 1986). Conscientious subjects generally have high self-esteem (Costa, McCrae & Dye, 1991).

Studies of children suggest that Conscientiousness can be described as "will to achieve" (Digman, 1989). Teachers describe children high in this factor as "persistent, planful, careful, responsible, neat, and orderly [rather than] lackadaisical, careless, irresponsible, and quitting" (Digman, 1989, p. 209). Conscientiousness predicts who will graduate from high school, and it correlates positively with high-school grade point average (Digman, 1989).

Factor IV: Neuroticism People who score high on Neuroticism typically report negative emotions, such as worry, insecurity, self-consciousness, and temperamentalness (McCrae & Costa, 1987). Neuroticism is negatively correlated with self-esteem (Costa, McCrae & Dye, 1991). The opposite pole of Neuroticism (that is, low Neuroticism) is Emotional Stability.

Factor V: Openness to Experience The final factor in this model is Openness to Experience. Adjectives from lexical studies that describe this factor include "original, imaginative, broad interests, and daring" (McCrae & Costa, 1987, p. 87). McCrae and Costa propose that there are additional aspects of Openness, however, that are not so readily observed by raters. These are not found in studies of adjective descriptions but do emerge from self-report questionnaire data. Costa and McCrae suggest that people high in this factor are "intellectually sensitive, … aesthetically sensitive, high in need for variety, and liberal in their value systems" (Costa & McCrae, 1992a, p. 660).

Various aspects of this factor are conveyed by the labels chosen by past researchers. It has been called "Intellect" (Digman & Takemoto-Chock, 1981; Goldberg, 1981), and it is positively correlated with intelligence, but it is more than simply intelligence. Norman (1963) chose to call this factor "Culture." McCrae and Costa reinterpreted it as "Openness to Experience," a label that captures all of these earlier labels. Perhaps one reason for the difficulty in defining this factor is that openness is not very well represented in natural languages, in contrast to the rich representation of factors such as Extraversion and Agreeableness in our everyday speech (McCrae, 1990). It would appear that the shared lay personality theories that have become encoded in the language do not appreciate this factor, which scientific analysis has revealed.

The Big Five and People's Lives Consensus on the basic dimensions of personality should facilitate research. These five traits of personality have implications for applied issues, including occupational performance (Barrick & Mount, 1991) and therapy (Costa, 1991; Costa, Busch, et al., 1986; Fagan et al., 1991; McCrae, 1991; McCrae & Costa, 1991b; Miller, 1991; Mutén, 1991).

Robert McCrae and Paul Costa have studied the psychological well-being of adults from the perspective of the five-factor model. Married couples completed questionnaires several times in their study. Participants ranged in age from 24 to 81 at the outset of the study in 1979. Their psychological well-being was measured with several questionnaires, and the NEO-PI assessed the five factors of personality. Is personality related to well-being? Decidedly! Whether measured by self-report or by spouse ratings, personality correlated with the various measures of well-being. Those who were happier and more satisfied with life were typically low in Neuroticism and high in Extraversion. To a lesser extent, they were also high in Agreeableness and in Conscientiousness. Openness to Experience had little overall effect. Those high in this factor reported more emotions of all kinds, positive and negative, than those low in the factor, with no overall difference in well-being (McCrae & Costa, 1991a).

Despite enthusiasm for the five-factor model, some cautions are in order. For one thing, some researchers report additional factors beyond these five (for example, Brand & Egan, 1989). Also, other models compete with the five-factor model for the claim of being the comprehensive model to organize trait research. These include Raymond Cattell's sixteen-factor model and Hans Eysenck's three-factor model, which are discussed next.

A Sixteen-Factor Model (Cattell)

Although the five-factor model has gained the attention of many current researchers, "Raymond Cattell will be remembered as the pioneer geometer of the personality realm" (Digman, 1990, p. 428), and his model of personality has generated extensive research for many decades. Cattell developed diverse methods of measuring personality that were systematic and tied to theory (Wiggins, 1984). His extensive research, also using the technique of factor analysis, led him to propose that there are 16 basic dimensions of normal personality, and he devised a questionnaire to measure them, the **16PF**. Once scored, these 16 factors can be diagrammed as a personality *profile* (Fig. 3.1).

Many studies have confirmed the factors described by Cattell. (Several dozen replicating studies are listed in Cattell, 1986). Some studies disagree. Several later researchers have challenged Cattell's model, contending that there are fewer than 16 factors (Barrett & Kline, 1982; Campbell, 1988; Digman, 1989; Gerbing & Tuley, 1991; Matthews, 1989; Meyer et al., 1988). Cattell, however, is adamant that there are no fewer than 16 primary factors, and more in some data sets. "The facts simply do not support a simpler conception of human personality" (Cattell & Krug, 1986, p. 519).

The number of factors can be further reduced by factor analyzing the 16 factors: a secondary factor analysis. Cattell's model includes eight second-order factors: Extraversion, Anxiety, Tough Poise, Independence,

Left Score Meaning	Standard Ten Score (STEN) ➡ Avg. ⬅ 1 2 3 4 5 6 7 8 9 10	Right Score Meaning
Factor **A** COOL Reserved, Impersonal, Detached, Formal, Aloof		Factor **A** WARM Outgoing, Kindly, Easygoing, Participating, Likes People
Factor **B** CONCRETE-THINKING Less Intelligent		Factor **B** ABSTRACT-THINKING More Intelligent, Bright
Factor **C** AFFECTED BY FEELINGS Emotionally Less Stable, Easily Annoyed		Factor **C** EMOTIONALLY STABLE Mature, Faces Reality, Calm
Factor **E** SUBMISSIVE Humble, Mild, Easily Led, Accommodating		Factor **E** DOMINANT Assertive, Aggresive, Stubborn, Competitive, Bossy
Factor **F** SOBER Restrained, Prudent, Taciturn, Serious		Factor **F** ENTHUSIASTIC Spontaneous, Heedless, Expressive, Cheerful
Factor **G** EXPEDIENT Disregards Rules, Self-indulgent		Factor **G** CONSCIENTIOUS Conforming, Moralistic, Staid, Rule-bound
Factor **H** SHY Threat-sensitive, Timid, Hesitant, Intimidated		Factor **H** BOLD Venturesome, Uninhibited, Can Take Stress
Factor **I** TOUGH-MINDED Self-reliant, No-nonsense, Rough, Realistic		Factor **I** TENDER-MINDED Sensitive, Overprotected, Intuitive, Refined
Factor **L** TRUSTING Accepting Conditions, Easy to Get on with		Factor **L** SUSPICIOUS Hard to Fool, Distrustful, Skeptical
Factor **M** PRACTICAL Concerned with "Down-to- Earth" Issues, Steady		Factor **M** IMAGINATIVE Absent-minded, Absorbed in Thought, Impractical
Factor **N** FORTHRIGHT Unpretentious, Open, Genuine, Artless		Factor **N** SHREWD Polished, Socially Aware, Diplomatic, Calculating
Factor **O** SELF-ASSURED Secure, Feels Free of Guilt, Untroubled, Self-satisfied		Factor **O** APPREHENSIVE Self-blaming, Guilt-prone, Insecure, Worrying
Factor Q_1 CONSERVATIVE Respecting Traditional Ideas		Factor Q_1 EXPERIMENTING Liberal, Critical, Open to Change
Factor Q_2 GROUP-ORIENTED A "Joiner" and Sound Follower, Listens to Others		Factor Q_2 SELF-SUFFICIENT Resourceful, Prefers Own Decisions
Factor Q_3 UNDISCIPLINED SELF- CONFLICT Lax, Careless of Social Rules		Factor Q_3 FOLLOWING SELF- IMAGE Socially Precise, Compulsive
Factor Q_4 RELAXED Tranquil, Composed, Has Low Drive, Unfrustrated		Factor Q_4 TENSE Frustrated, Overwrought, Has High Drive

Control, Adjustment, Leadership, and Creativity. The first five of these are generally replicated, while there is less consensus about the last three (Argentero, 1989). Secondary factors are more general than the first-order factors and, according to Cattell, are less useful for predicting behavior. Research confirms his claim (Mershon & Gorsuch, 1988).

Cattell recognized the limitations of questionnaire data and also included other sources of data in his research. In addition to questionnaire data, he analyzed data based on life records and data collected from tests that were not self-report, such as projective tests and performance tests. Analyses of these diverse kinds of data generally yielded the same factors. This approach provides reassurance that the factors are not simply results of personal perception but are more fundamental factors of personality. There is a fascinating difference, however, between self-report data and objective data. The primary factors of Cattell's objective data correspond to the second-order factors of his self-report data.

Cattell's model for the influence of personality on behavior is particularly sophisticated. It recognizes that any particular behavior is influenced by several traits, rather than just one. Such **multivariate prediction** can include the 16 personality factors and also attitudes, sentiments, and other variables. For example, Cattell suggests the following equation to predict school achievement:

> *Achievement = .44 superego − .23 self-assertion + .35 self-sentiment − .15 sex − .24 fear + .21 pugnacity − .33 narcism + .36 constructive erg. (Cattell, 1990, p. 106)*

Although Cattell's 16 personality factors are his best known contribution to the study of personality, he also developed many other measures to assess moods, intelligence, motivation, and so on (Boyle, 1987, 1988; Boyle, Stanley & Start, 1985). Cattell investigated the distribution and causes of personality, including personality differences between men and women and among different nations, the role of heredity in shaping personality, and the development of personality across the life span.

TABLE 3.5   Eysenck's Three Factors of Personality and Traits Constituting Them

Factors	Traits included in each factor	Factors	Traits included in each factor
Extraversion	Sociable Lively Active Assertive Sensation Seeking Carefree Dominant Surgent Venturesome	Psychoticism	Aggressive Cold Egocentric Impersonal Impulsive Antisocial Unempathic Creative Tough-Minded
Neuroticism	Anxious Depressed Guilt Feelings Low Self-Esteem Tense Irrational Shy Moody Emotional		

Adapted from Eysenck & Eysenck, 1985, pp. 14–15.

A Three-Factor Model (Eysenck)

Hans Eysenck has developed one of the most influential and highly researched factor theories of personality. He proposes that there are three major factors of personality: Extraversion, Neuroticism, and Psychoticism. Each of these general factors can be described as a collection of more specific traits (Table 3.5). The three factors are measured by the Eysenck Personality Questionnaire (EPQ) (Eysenck & Eysenck, 1975; Eysenck, Eysenck & Barrett, 1985).

Extraversion and Neuroticism are the two major dimensions for describing variations in normal personality. (These factors correspond to two of the five factors in the five-factor model discussed earlier.) Extraversion is outgoing sociability. Extraverts and introverts behave differently in social situations. For example, extraverts touch other people more during social interactions than do introverts, according to a self-report measure (Lester & Rencher, 1993). Neuroticism corresponds to emotional instability; people high in emotional stability are low in Neuroticism, and their emotional evenness helps them to cope with life's stresses without becoming rattled.

Eysenck's third major factor is Psychoticism. He contends that many forms of social deviance share a common hereditary disposition. These include the major psychoses, criminality, alcoholism, and addiction (Eysenck, 1992b). To avoid the misleading impression that this third factor is specific to psychotic disorders, Marvin Zuckerman, D. Michael Kuhlman, and Curt Camac (1988) suggest that the factor would be better called "social deviance" or "nonconformity." They point out that the factor includes such traits as autonomy, nonconformity, and creativity and that artists score higher than psychotics on this scale. Psychoticism is also negatively associated with religiosity (Francis, 1992).

As is the case with the five-factor model, this three-factor model has also been confirmed by other factor analysts (for example, Zuckerman, Kuhlman & Camac, 1988) and can be linked to other comprehensive personality tests (Eysenck, 1991). Much of Eysenck's research goes beyond the descriptive focus of this chapter. He explores the impact of heredity on these factors and their physiological correlates, topics that we will consider later.

An Interpersonal Trait Model (Wiggins)

Jerry Wiggins (1979; Wiggins & Broughton, 1991) proposed a model of personality to describe aspects of personality that influence interpersonal behavior. He reasoned that research would be facilitated by differentiating

The tendencies to be a nonconformist and social deviate and to be artistically creative are characteristic of people who score high on Eysenck's third personality factor, "Psychoticism."

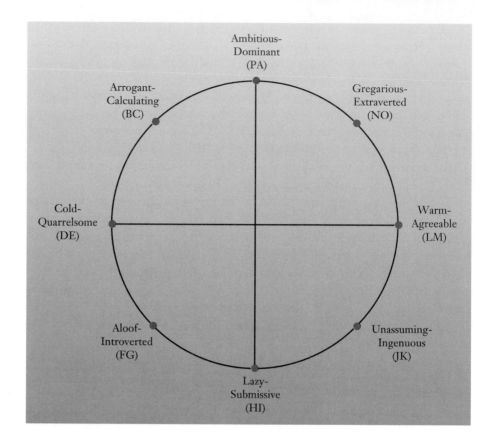

among kinds of traits. On theoretical grounds, he distinguished six trait categories: interpersonal traits (for example, "aggressive"), material traits (for example, "miserly"), temperamental traits (for example, "lively"), social roles (for example, "ceremonious"), character (for example, "dishonest"), and mental predicates (for example, "analytical") (Wiggins, 1979, p. 396). He selected one of these broad categories, interpersonal traits, for further consideration. It is this model of interpersonal traits that will concern us.

Wiggins's approach was more theoretical than the primarily empirical approach of factor analysis. Building on previous theorists (Sullivan, 1953, and others), he proposed that interactions between two people have two kinds of consequences for both self and other: social (status) and emotional (love). Foa and Foa (1974) summarized these consequences in eight interpersonal categories. For example, the category "gregarious-extraverted" describes people who accept both self and other in terms of both love and status. In contrast, the category "aloof-introverted" describes people who reject both self and other in both ways. Wiggins diagrammed these interpersonal variables to define a **circumplex model** (Fig. 3.2). "Circumplex" simply means that the model is diagrammed as a circle. Points around the circle correspond to adjectives. The model makes predictions about the correlations among interpersonal variables (in contrast to factor models, which begin with correlations and infer a model). Points opposite each other on the circumplex—for example, *ambitious-dominant* and *lazy-submissive*— should correlate negatively (–1.00, if there is no measurement error). Those at right angles to each other should not be correlated; some correlation is expected for variables at 45-degree angles to each other (Wiggins, 1979). Obviously, the next step is to collect data to test whether these expected correlations are found. Using the Interpersonal Adjective Scales, Wiggins reported that the correlations found in several samples of subjects closely matched those predicted from his model, and he reinterpreted other personality tests in terms of this model (Wiggins & Broughton, 1991).

Besides Wiggins's interpersonal circumplex, other models have also been proposed to describe complementarity in interpersonal behavior (Kiesler, 1983). The models share the assumption that social aspects of personality involve bipolar descriptions of the roles people play (warm-cold, and so forth). In addition to the measurement of individual personality, there is another important theoretical implication of these interpersonal models: personality is inherently interactive and social. Thus, we can achieve only partial truths when we attempt to describe an individual in isolation (for example, by listing personality traits).

A Model of Psychological Functions (Jung and the Myers-Briggs Type Indicator)

Carl Jung, the Swiss psychoanalyst, proposed that people vary along three important dimensions that correspond to basic psychological processes (Fig. 3.3). In a quite basic sense, this approach promises to be more than simply descriptive. It should be readily integrated with experimental studies of psychological processes such as memory, perception, and so forth (Carlson, 1980).

The first dimension is the familiar *introversion-extraversion* that we have encountered before, and it refers to the tendency to be less or more sociable. Jung argued that psychic energy is directed inward toward the unconscious among introverts and is turned outward toward the world among extraverts. Extraverts are more likely to remember people's names than are introverts (J. Carlson, 1985). They prefer careers that involve public exhibition, such as entertainer, administrator, and marketing manager or agent (Tzeng, Ware & Chen, 1989). In school, ninth-grade students who are extraverts prefer active learning styles such as peer teaching, projects, and simulations, whereas introverts prefer reflective learning styles, including lectures, audiovisual presentations, and learning alone (Fourqurean, Meisgeier & Swank, 1990). Jung described introversion-extraversion as a stable characteristic throughout life, whereas the other important dimensions in his theory describe capacities that can, theoretically, change as personality develops.

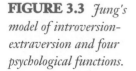

FIGURE 3.3 *Jung's model of introversion-extraversion and four psychological functions.*

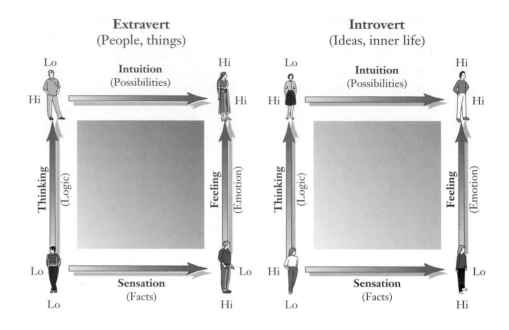

These other two dimensions are what Jung called *psychological functions.* The dimension of *Thinking-Feeling* describes alternate ways of making judgments. Choices can be based on logic (Thinking) or on emotion (Feeling). The dimension of *Sensation-Intuition* describes alternate ways of perceiving. Information can be concrete and detailed, like that which comes through the five senses (Sensation), or it can be global and holistic (Intuition).

Females tend to score higher on feeling and males on thinking (Myers & McCaulley, 1985). The early memories reported by feeling types include more emotional memories of joy, excitement, and shame, compared with thinking types (Carlson, 1980). Thinking types who are also extraverted score high on a measure of assertiveness, the Rathus Assertiveness Schedule (Tucker, 1991).

Intuitive types seem to be in closer touch with the imagination and unconscious than are sensation types. Intuitives recall more archetypal dreams; that is, dreams that use imagery that is highly emotional and mythological (Cann & Donderi, 1986). Psychodramatists, who work professionally with such imagery, are usually Intuitive types (Buchanan & Taylor, 1986). Intuitive types are more open to change in their relationships with their marriage partners (Carlson & Williams, 1984) and are also more accurate than Sensation types when they interpret emotion from facial expression (Carlson & Levy, 1973). Their accuracy in other contexts can be more or less than that of Sensation types, depending upon the task and other dimensions of personality (Hicks, 1985; Ward & Loftus, 1985). Among college freshmen, Intuitive types prefer to be given a broader range of advisement information, whereas Sensation types, who like to work with facts and details, prefer more focused advisement about college programs (Crockett & Crawford, 1989).

The most popular test to measure Jung's model is the **Myers-Briggs Type Indicator (MBTI).** Besides the three dimensions of Introversion-Extraversion, Intuition-Sensation, and Thinking-Feeling, the MBTI provides a fourth score to assess whether the individual is predominantly a judging type (emphasizing either Thinking or Feeling) or a perceiving type (emphasizing either Sensation or Intuition). The judging-perceiving dimension has been interpreted as tapping impulsivity. Ninth-grade students who are Judging types prefer to learn in more structured and quiet environments and through independent study, while Perception type students prefer unstructured, noisy environments and tactile learning (Fourqurean, Meisgeier & Swank, 1990).

Some researchers have questioned how closely the MBTI corresponds to Jung's theory (for example, McCrae and Costa, 1989b). One obvious difference is that Jung proposed distinct *types* (categories) of personality; most researchers have instead analyzed MBTI scores as continuous *traits*. (Recall the discussion of the trait-type difference in Chapter 2.) On theoretical grounds, some researchers prefer to use type categories (which is also possible with the MBTI) instead (J. Carlson, 1989; Hicks, 1984). Despite its theoretical ambiguities, this measure is used extensively, both as a research instrument (Murray, 1990) and as a vehicle for educating and counseling the lay public through books and workshops (for example, Barry, 1991; Kroeger & Thuesen, 1988; McCaulley, 1990). Managers and workers, it is argued, will be more productive if they understand the strengths and limitations of their personality types and learn to work in a complementary rather than combative way with those who differ from them.

Comparison of Models

Overall, the empirical studies surveyed in this chapter show emerging agreement that a relatively small number of major factors can be used to describe people's personalities. Research has demonstrated some convergence among the various measures (Boyle, 1989; Gerbing & Tuley, 1991; John, 1990; McCrae & Costa, 1987, 1989b, 1989d; Noller, Law & Comrey, 1987). Introversion and extraversion, for example, emerge in many studies and are correlated from one measure to the next. Although introversion and extraversion are scales in many tests, including the NEO-PI, the Eysenck Personality Inventory, and the MBTI, there are also differences in these measures. Extraversion consists of several components, including sociability, impulsiveness, and emotion, not all of which are equally represented in every measure (Campbell & Heller, 1987; McCrae & Costa, 1987; Sipps & Alexander, 1987; Sipps & DiCaudo, 1988). The specific tests chosen to measure extraversion and other traits can vary according to the particular interests of the researcher, but we are increasingly confident that the differences simply represent different angles of viewing the same phenomena.

One obvious difference in the models is the number of factors. This is not a serious discrepancy, however. Models will produce more factors if they describe specific traits and fewer factors if they describe broad, general patterns. They can be combined in a hierarchical model with fewer broad, general factors at the top, branching into a larger number of more specific factors at the bottom of the hierarchy (Boyle, 1989; Gerbing & Tuley, 1991; Zuckerman, Kuhlman & Camac, 1988).

Paul Costa and Robert McCrae advocate the five-factor model as a general framework for understanding personality and guiding research. This model offers a systematic approach. In contrast, most earlier approaches seemed to select traits in an arbitrary manner (McCrae & Costa, 1987). Does the five-factor model suggest that we ignore all other research, replacing it by the five factors? No. McCrae and Costa state, "We should make it clear that we do not think of the five-factor model as a replacement for other personality systems, but as a framework for interpreting them" (McCrae & Costa, 1989a, p. 451). Researchers have proposed and measured so many personality traits that it is difficult to grasp how they combine. By showing how each of the diverse traits corresponds to one or more of the Big Five, researchers can bring some conceptual order to a field whose list of traits otherwise reads like an encyclopedia.

SUMMARY

- Traits are enduring aspects of individual personality that influence behavior in particular domains.

- Allport's classic theory of traits described them as physically real, individual (warranting idiographic study), and varying in pervasiveness (cardinal, central, and secondary traits).

- Trait approaches have been criticized as using faulty circular reasoning and predicting higher correlations with behavior than have been found.

- Some explanations for the limited relationship between a trait and behavior (the personality coefficient) are that behavior has many causes and that behavioral measures as well as trait measures have limited reliability. Prediction accuracy can be increased by aggregating across situations.

- The consistency paradox refers to the conflict between the common sense expectation that people will behave consistently across situations in keeping with their traits and research evidence of low cross-situational consistency of behavior.

• Explanations of the limited trait-behavior relationship include moderator variables such as traitedness, the interaction between traits and situations in determining behavior, and the power of strong situations to override the effect of traits.

• Although trait approaches are based on the language of everyday life, a specialized scientific language may be needed to go beyond common sense.

• Traits may describe behavior, but it is less certain that they exist as a determinant of behavior.

• Factor analysis has been used extensively to identify a small number of the most important personality traits.

• Theory must be further developed if it is to guide personality researchers through many of the apparent inconsistencies in trait understandings.

• Comprehensive models of traits have been proposed. The five-factor model describes the Big Five traits (Extraversion, Agreeableness, Conscientiousness, Neuroticism, and Openness to Experience); these traits have been found in many kinds of data and can be measured by the NEO-PI.

• Cattell's sixteen-factor model, measured by the 16PF, describes 16 specific traits that combine for multivariate prediction of behavior.

• Eysenck's three-factor model consists of Extraversion, Neuroticism, and Psychoticism.

• Wiggins's interpersonal trait model is diagrammed as a circumplex to express the theoretical relationships among traits.

• Jung's model describes introversion-extraversion and the psychological functions of sensation-intuition and thinking-feeling. The MBTI measures these dimensions.

• The various models offer alternative ways of describing personality; they can be regarded as different angles on the same phenomenon or different levels in a hierarchy comprising broad traits (or types or factors) and more specific traits.

GLOSSARY

aggregation   the combining of several items to enhance reliability and thus increase the correlation of the combined trait measure with other measures

central traits   traits that influence a wide range of behavior

circular reasoning   the logical flaw of saying that a trait causes a behavior and also using the behavior to infer the trait

circumplex model   a model that can be diagrammed as a circle, such as Wiggins's model of interpersonal variables

consistency paradox   the discrepancy between the common sense idea that personality leads to behavioral consistency and research evidence indicating much variability in behavior from one situation to another

cross-situational consistency the stability of behavior from one situation or environment to another

factor analysis   a statistical technique that systematically considers all the correlations among variables to simplify a large set of data into a smaller number of underlying dimensions

five-factor model   a theoretical model that describes five broad dimensions of personality, often called the Big Five

global traits   traits that are general and apply to behavior in many different situations

interactionism   the theoretical view that personality and situations combine to predict behavior

moderator variables   variables that help to sort out when a finding will occur and when it won't; for example, when behavior is consistent and when it isn't

multivariate prediction   the theoretical recognition that behavior is determined by the combined effects of many variables

Myers-Briggs Type Indicator (MBTI)   a personality test that measures the dimensions suggested by Jung's theory

NEO Personality Inventory (NEO-PI)   a personality test developed to measure the Big Five factors of personality

personality coefficient   the maximum correlation between trait measures and behavior, said to be about .30

specific traits   traits that predict behavior in a particular situation

strong situation   a situation that has powerful determining effects on behavior, regardless of the personality differences among individuals

trait   an enduring aspect of individual personality that influences behavior in a particular domain

traitedness   a moderator variable suggested to explain the observation that a trait predicts behavior better for some people, who are said to possess the trait at some level, than for others, for whom the trait is irrelevant

weak situation   a situation that exerts relatively little influence on behavior, so that the impact of personality differences is not overwhelmed by situational pressures

THOUGHT QUESTIONS

1. List the half dozen or so central traits that you think best describe some-one you know. (You may use any descriptive adjectives or phrases as traits.)

2. Consider the circular reasoning argument against traits. Can you think of any way of knowing that a person has a particular trait besides inferring it from behavior?

3. Identify one personality trait that describes you, and list several behaviors that are consistent with that trait. Now, are there times when your behavior is not consistent with that trait? Explain why you sometimes behave differ-ently.

4. Look at the list of traits in Table 3.2. Are there additional traits that you think psychologists should investigate that are not listed here?

5. Look at the multitrait-multimethod matrix in the Research Strategies box. Explain which correlations show evidence of convergent validity. Why do you suppose these correlations are not higher than they are? How might a researcher try to make them higher?

6. Do you think the Big Five describe the most important dimensions of personality? Think of people you know; are there important aspects of their personalities that are not described by these five factors?

7. Cattell's multivariate prediction can be expressed as an equation, like the one used to predict school achievement. Propose an equation to predict political success, using as many of Cattell's factors as you think appropriate. (You may also add additional terms of your own.)

8. Look at the eight points labeled on Wiggins's Interpersonal Circumplex Model (see Fig. 3.2). Think of someone you know well, and decide which of these points describes that person best. Which other points also describe the person? The model predicts that once you pick a point, the other points that you select should be nearby on the circle. Are they?

9. What do you expect to be doing in 5 years? Do you think you will be more successful if you rely on the Jungian function of Thinking or of Feeling? Of Sensation or of Intuition? Why?

10. Personality traits describe people, but they don't explain why people are the way they are. Identify one or two personality traits that describe some-one you know well. Then go beyond the question of description and beyond the material covered in the chapter, and suggest why the person might behave this way.

Group Differences

ALTHOUGH EVERYONE IS UNIQUE, each individual resembles some people more than others. Folk wisdom tells us that men are different from women and that racial and ethnic groups have distinguishing characteristics. Are these impressions accurate, or are they erroneous stereotypes? Research indicates that the answer is a little bit of each.

Why Study Group Differences?

Why would researchers be interested in testing for group differences? For one thing, differences may offer insights into the causes of personality. In addition, knowing what is characteristic of a group helps us to interpret the scores of an individual who belongs to that group.

Group Differences May Hint at Causes of Personality

Group differences offer a rough sort of natural experiment for personality psychologists and suggest how different experiences in the world affect personality (Kline, 1988). Group differences may be influenced by genetics as well as by experience, and the "natural experiments" of group variations **confound** these two possible causes in ways that we shall not try to untangle in this chapter. "Confounded" variables are those that are correlated. This makes it difficult to be sure which variable is really causing the changes in other variables. For example, men and women differ in both biological characteristics and experiences in society, so that when sex differences are found, it is not immediately obvious whether biology or experience is the real cause of these differences. The same can be said of racial and ethnic differences. Further systematic observations can help untangle the confounded causes. For example, we may ask how widespread such differences are. Are they limited to certain cultures, or are they more extensive around the globe? Have the differences remained throughout changes in society over time, or have they diminished? The more group differences vary from culture to culture and across time, the less likely they are caused by immutable biology.

Group Norms Help Us Interpret Individuals

Knowing what is characteristic of a group helps us to interpret the individual personalities of its members. Consider this illustration. Common lore tells us that males are more aggressive than females. People generally judge a female who gets into physical fights more harshly than they do a male who exhibits similar behavior, because her behavior is more unusual compared to her own group's characteristics. (Whether or not this is fair can be debated, obviously.)

In the formal study of personality, interpreting test scores requires knowing what is typical of other people who have also taken the test. Imagine that you have taken a test of creativity and are told your score is 73. Probably you will ask, "What does that mean?" If most people score lower, the score indicates high creativity; if most people score higher, the score indicates low creativity. In testing, the typical scores that are used as a basis for interpreting an individual's scores are called **norms.**

One set of norms for a test may not be enough, however. Different groups may require the use of different norms. We use different norms in everyday life, though we do not call it by that technical term. For example, if a kindergarten child can read a second grade book, we conclude that the child is very bright. If a fourth grade child can read the same book, we do not draw the same conclusion. In each case, we (implicitly) compare the child with the appropriate comparison group: other kindergartners, or other fourth graders. The comparison group's performance serves as the norm for interpreting an individual's scores.

When inappropriate norms are used to interpret an individual's score, the result is **bias.** Where there is bias, we misjudge the meaning of the test because we compare an individual with a standard that is either too high or too low. Bias is obviously an error. Its results can be harmful if the test is the basis for an important decision. For example, if the instructor in an undergraduate course assigned grades by comparing students' scores on the final exam with norms derived from graduate students, the bias would result in lower grades.

Controversies, even lawsuits, demonstrate that the debate over the use of inappropriate norms is not an esoteric matter that interests only experts. It is not always obvious, however, which norms are appropriate. Suppose, for example, that students in one school score higher on an achievement test than students at a most other schools. Should we conclude that a student with an average score at the first school is "average," based on norms for that school? Or should we conclude that the student is "above average," based on norms for "most schools"? Without further information, the question cannot be answered conclusively. If we knew that students were selectively admitted to the first school based on early academic promise, the second set of norms seems most reasonable, and we should conclude that the student is "above average." If, on the other hand, we knew that the entering students at this school were like other students in their potential, we would draw another conclusion. For example, if students were chosen for the school based on some random process that ensured them to be typical, it might make more sense to call the student "average," and to praise the school for an unusually effective curriculum (Fig. 4.1).

When two groups have different average scores on a test, two interpretations are possible: (1) the groups may really differ on the characteristic, or (2) the groups may really be the same on the characteristic, but the test is biased. In the first case, we should use the same norms for everyone, regardless of group membership. In the second case, we should use different norms for different groups. How can we decide which course to take? We need evidence other than the test to indicate whether the groups are the same or different on whatever it is we're trying to measure.

Consider this research study. At a large university in the U.S. Midwest, 78.8 percent of foreign students failed a competency examination in reading, compared to only 16 percent of students who were raised in the United States. (Similar, but less dramatic, differences were observed in two other tests: writing and math.) Were the foreign students poorer scholars, or was the test biased? (Bias could stem from a variety of factors, including the use of reading topics that were more familiar to those raised in the United States or the use of a test format that was less familiar to foreign students.) The answer to this question was of practical importance at the school,

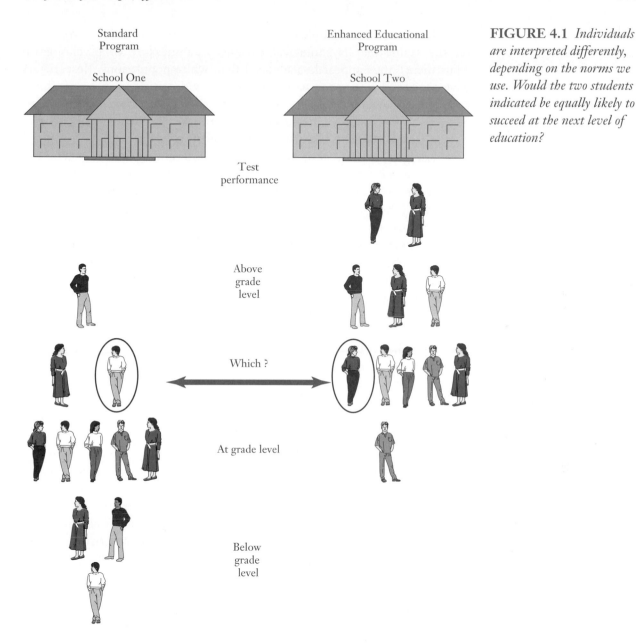

FIGURE 4.1 *Individuals are interpreted differently, depending on the norms we use. Would the two students indicated be equally likely to succeed at the next level of education?*

because students could not graduate until they passed the tests. If the test was biased, foreign students were being unfairly denied graduation. If the test was not biased, the greater failure rate of foreign students was justified on the basis of their lower competence. Which was the case? Other data suggested the answer. The grade point average of the foreign students was not lower than that of United States students; in fact, it was higher (2.86, compared to 2.57). In this case, then, the competency tests were judged to be biased against foreign students (Tompkins & Mehring, 1989).

Here is another example of test bias. When native Americans are tested on the California Psychological Inventory (a measure of psychological adjustment), they appear less adjusted than white populations. Researchers have suggested comparing native Americans with their own norms instead, to avoid bias (Davis, Hoffman & Nelson, 1990). Even better would be to develop a new test that measures native American adjustment in its own right. (Euro-Americans might well score badly on such a test.)

Intelligence tests, too, show group differences; lower scores are obtained by racial minorities in the United States (Brescia & Fortune, 1989; Halpin, Simpson & Martin, 1990; Padilla, 1988). It has been a matter of controversy how much of the difference among racial groups should be attributed to test bias. Some of the difference may reflect real variations, perhaps because of cultural factors that provide unequal opportunities to develop innate potential (Grubb & Ollendick, 1986). The strongest evidence of bias occurs when minorities differ in language and cultural experience from mainstream culture. But even comparisons between two very similar populations, adults from the United States and Canada, are not always justified, because some items are more familiar to one national group than the other (Pugh & Boer, 1989). Test bias is a risk whenever a test is developed in one population and used in another.

Group Differences or Similarities?

Although differences between groups are the focus of this chapter, it would be a mistake to exaggerate these differences. Wide variations occur within any one group. Although the averages may be different from one group to another, there is considerable overlap of the distributions on the personality characteristics considered in this chapter. Differences exist between groups, but the similarities are greater.

Sex Differences

"*Vive la différence*," say the French: "Celebrate the difference" between the sexes. The assumption of sex differences is reflected in literature and philosophy, religion and law. Yet this assumption has come under fire in recent decades, challenged by feminist arguments that differences are exaggerated and misinterpreted to the detriment of women. Researchers who venture into this controversial area must expect their methods to be closely scrutinized and their conclusions vigorously debated. Even the decision to study sex differences is controversial. Why lend scientific weight to the assumption that men and women differ, ask the critics, when differences are interpreted to justify unequal opportunities?

Reluctance to study sex differences stems from fear that differences will be thought of as an inevitable consequence of *biology*. If differences between men and women are biologically determined, they are usually assumed to be inevitable. This assumption tends to undermine attempts to change society so that people are treated equally regardless of sex. If not biology, what could make women different from men? The alternative is *culture*. Situations influence behavior, and experience in a society influences the development of personality traits. Since males and females have different cultural and situational experiences, they could differ because of this experience, rather than because of biology. Perhaps if culture were to change, sex differences would disappear. To emphasize their belief that differences between men and women are due to culture, not biology, many psychologists prefer to use the term **gender** rather than **sex.** *Gender* connotes that differences are due to cultural factors. *Sex* often implies that differences are biological. But because we often do not know to what extent men and women are shaped by biology and to what extent by culture, it is not always possible to know when we should refer to gender (culture) and when to sex (biology). Therefore, the term *sex differences* should be understood to refer to differences between males and females, without certainty about their cause (Eagly, 1987b).

Controversies notwithstanding, researchers have investigated sex differences on many personality variables. Results from one study to the next are sometimes inconsistent. Fortunately, a statistical method called **meta-analysis** has been developed that facilitates the task of finding an overall pattern in a large number of studies with varying outcomes. Using statistics, meta-analysis allows the researcher to examine many studies that test similar hypotheses. For example, many studies test the hypothesis that males are more aggressive than females. Other personality differences can be compared between males and females, or between members of different racial or ethnic groups. The meta-analysis tells the researcher whether, on balance, the groups are different and, if so, how large is the difference. Using meta-analytic procedures and less formal techniques, psychologists are now able to tell us something about *la différence*.

Sex Differences on Widely Used Personality Tests

In Chapter 3, we considered several tests that measure personality traits. On average, males and females are similar on most of the personality traits measured by these tests. There are some sex differences, however.

Cattell's 16PF Cattell (1965) reported sex differences on several of his 16 primary factors of personality. We must keep in mind that these sex differences are more than three decades old; to the extent that they are determined by culture, rather than biology, they may have changed, and they may vary from one cultural group to another. Cattell found that five factors showed the largest sex differences. Men were more dominant and assertive, while women were more submissive and accommodating (Factor E). This difference corresponds to sex differences found using self-report and observer report measures (Moskowitz, 1990). Cattell also reported that women were more tender-minded and sensitive, while men were more tough-minded and self-reliant (Factor I). Women were more imaginative and absent-minded, while men were more practical and concerned with "down to earth" issues (Factor M). Men were more shrewd and calculating in interpersonal situations, while women were more open and genuine (Factor N). Men were more liberal and open to change, while women were more conservative and traditional (Factor Q_1). (Do you believe that these differences apply today, to the people that you know?) Although these differences have not always been replicated (see, for example, Campbell, 1992), it is fair to conclude that on average, men and women have different personality profiles.

The Myers-Briggs Type Indicator On the Myers-Briggs Type Indicator, females are generally more extraverted, intuitive, and feeling; males are more introverted, sensing, and thinking (Furnham & Stringfield, 1993). Of these differences, the most striking is the Thinking-Feeling scale. Because males score higher on Thinking and females higher on Feeling, different norms are used to calculate scores for individual males and females (Myers & McCaulley, 1985).

Wiggins's Interpersonal Adjective Scales Self-report measures often show sex differences. Jerry Wiggins's (1979) interpersonal taxonomy asks respondents to indicate the adjectives that describe themselves. Male and female North American university students respond differently on several scales (Table 4.1). Some of these scales, ambitious-dominant (PA) and warm-agreeable (LM), correspond to masculinity and femininity as measured by the Bem Sex Role Inventory (Bem, 1974), according to Wiggins.

In fact, several scales that measure sex role "masculinity" and "femininity" find similar results. The term **sex role** refers to behaviors expected and approved in society depending upon whether the person is a male or a female. Males are more often "masculine" and females more "feminine" on sex role inventories, but there is a wide range within each sex, so that we can describe some people as more "masculine sex role typed" and others as more "feminine sex role typed," whether we are describing males or females. Femininity scales typically indicate emotional expressiveness, while masculinity scales measure instrumental behaviors (Lippa & Connelly, 1990; Spence & Helmreich, 1978, 1980; Taylor & Hall, 1982).

Other Tests Other standard personality tests, too, report differences between males and females. For example, in a sample of 296 adults ranging

TABLE **4.1** **Wiggin's Interpersonal Adjective Scales, Showing Sex Differences**

Scales on which men score higher	
Scale	*Examples of adjectives*
Ambitious (scale P, success)	Persevering, persistent, industrious
Dominant (scale A, power)	Dominant, assertive, forceful
Arrogant (scale B, narcissism)	Bigheaded, boisterous, conceited
Calculating (scale C, exploitation)	Sly, tricky, wily
Cold (scale D, hate)	Warmthless, unsympathetic, ironhearted
Quarrelsome (scale E, hostility)	Impolite, uncordial, discourteous
Aloof (scale F, disaffiliation)	Antisocial, unneighborly, impersonal
Introverted (scale G, withdrawal)	Silent, shy, introverted

Scales on which women score higher	
Scale	*Examples of adjectives*
Lazy (scale H, failure)	Unproductive, lazy, unthorough
Submissive (scale I, weakness)	Self-doubting, self-effacing, timid
Unassuming (scale J, modesty)	Nonegotistical, undemanding, unvain
Ingenuous (scale K, trust)	Uncunning, uncalculating, uncrafty
Warm (scale L, love)	Tenderhearted, gentlehearted, tender
Agreeable (scale M, collaboration)	Courteous, charitable, well-mannered
Gregarious (scale N, affiliation)	Friendly, genial, neighborly
Extraverted (scale O, outgoingness)	Outgoing, extraverted, vivacious

Based on Wiggins, 1979.

in age from 22 to 90, Paul Costa and Robert McCrae found significant sex differences on more than half of the 20 scales of the Personality Research Form (PRF). Males scored higher on several needs: Achievement, Autonomy, Change, Cognitive Structure, and Endurance. Females scored higher on other needs: Affiliation, Harm Avoidance, Impulsivity, Nurturance, Play, Sentience, and Succorance (Costa & McCrae, 1988a).

Overall, studies indicate that males and females have different average scores on many of the standard scales used to assess personality. Is there any way to make sense of this catalog of differences? The concepts of "individuality" and "social connectedness" provide such an overview.

Individuality and Social Connectedness

Differences between men and women are often described by the concepts of **individuality** and **social connectedness** (for example, Chodorow, 1978;

Gilligan, 1982; Lang-Takac & Osterweil, 1992; Lykes, 1985). According to this description, males typically develop their individuality, emphasizing their separateness from other people, more than females. Males emphasize independence and autonomy, and their self-concept depends on individual accomplishments. In contrast, females emphasize social connectedness, focusing on interpersonal relationships more than on individual achievement. For women, self-concept is influenced by relationships, love, family, and friendships, more than it is for men.

This interpretation is consistent with the sex differences described above on standard personality measures. For example, men's individuality is reflected in their higher scores on measures of autonomy, self-reliance, and dominance. Women's social connectedness is reflected in their higher scores on measures of submissiveness, openness, and affiliation. Other kinds of personality measures portray a similar pattern. Self-ratings and ratings by friends, for example, indicate that males are considered to be more dominant and females to be more friendly (Moskowitz, 1990). Using a projective test, the Thematic Apperception Test (TAT), Dan McAdams and his colleagues found undergraduate females to be higher in intimacy motivation than male students (McAdams, Lester, et al., 1988). One way of indicating the importance of individuality is to overestimate one's uniqueness on valued skills, such as athletic and academic abilities. Someone who can shoot baskets with high accuracy, for example, would estimate that not many others could do so well. This "false uniqueness" perception is characteristic of males with high self-esteem, but not females. In males with high self-esteem, threats to individual uniqueness lead to defensive reactions, but in females it is threats to their connections with others that arouse defensiveness (Josephs, Markus & Tafarodi, 1992).

Several theorists have described variations on this theme of male individuality and female social connectedness (for example, Aries & Olver, 1985; Bakan, 1966; Chodorow, 1974; Lykes, 1985). Other terms used to describe male and female personality characteristics are essentially synonymous with "individuality" and "social connectedness." Alice Eagly and Wendy Wood, using David Bakan's often-cited categories, describe males as "agentic" and females as "communal":

> *Women are expected to possess high levels of communal attributes, including being friendly, unselfish, concerned with others, and emotionally expressive. Men are expected to possess high levels of agentic qualities, including being independent, masterful, assertive, and instrumentally competent. (Eagly & Wood, 1991, p. 309)*

According to Eagly and Wood, social expectations cause males and females to behave differently. For example, dominance in groups can take either a masculine agentic form or a feminine communal form, as research by David Buss (1981) demonstrates. He investigated behaviors of group members that correlated with dominance, as measured by the dominance scales of the California Psychological Inventory (CPI) and the PRF. For women, dominance correlated with such "communal" acts as settling a dispute among group members and taking the lead in organizing a group project. For males, dominance correlated with both communal acts and such "agentic" acts as refusing to compromise and demanding that others run errands for them.

Traits that are characterized as masculine, such as assertiveness and independence, are often highly valued. When females score lower on measures of such traits, we face the issue raised earlier in this chapter: Are females really lower in these traits, or are the tests biased? Carol Gilligan (1982) charged that a popular test of moral development was biased against females. Lawrence Kohlberg (1981) had reported that males scored higher on his measure of moral judgment than did females. Gilligan pointed out that only male subjects were used in the research that developed the measure, and she argued that applying it to females was not warranted. She proposed that there are, in fact, two different types of moral orientations. The first, measured by Kohlberg and more typical of males, is based on abstract principles and individual rights. The second, which Gilligan measured, was more typical of females. It emphasizes the social context of moral decisions and the impact of individual decisions on other people. To evaluate a person's moral development using a measure that does not tap the appropriate orientation is biased. Gilligan and others (for example, Lykes, 1985) have argued that individualism is overvalued in society and by psychologists. They suggest that traditionally feminine values of connectedness should be valued more highly, a sentiment echoed by many others (for example, Green, 1990).

Not all studies confirm the expected sex differences in individuality and social connectedness. In the area of moral judgment and moral development, Peter Lifton's (1985) literature review concludes that "sex differences occur with less frequency and with a less systematic favoring of males than is predicted by several theories of moral development" (p. 306). He suggests that the moral orientations described by Gilligan are related to personality rather than to sex, since each orientation can be found in some males as well as some females. Others also have doubted that the data support Gilligan's theoretical claims about moral development (Friedman, Robinson & Friedman, 1987; Greeno & Maccoby, 1986).

Sally Archer and Alan Waterman (1988) challenged the idea that males are more individualistic than females. They reviewed several dozen studies and concluded that there were no consistent sex differences on variables that assess psychological individualism. These variables include personal identity, self-actualization, internal locus of control, and principled moral reasoning. Furthermore, their review concluded that psychological individualism is equally important for effective functioning in both sexes; the data did not support the idea that a different path toward psychological development exists for females.

Such dissenting voices are to be expected whenever an area of study is as popular and controversial as this. Dissent prompts scientists to clarify their concepts and improve their methods. Despite the disagreements, we can conclude that many psychologists have found it useful to characterize men's personalities as more individualistic and women's personalities as more socially connected. Dissenters remind us that these descriptions are somewhat overstated and that many individuals do not fit the stereotypes.

Altruistic (Helping) Behavior

Psychologists have often studied altruistic behavior by setting up situations in which people need help and then observing how much help is given. An experimental confederate, a research assistant playing the role of a person in need, may stand beside a road with a flat tire, or a shopper may drop packages. Such experimental studies generally find that men are more likely than women to help other people. This finding seems discrepant with the idea that males are individualistic. It also is inconsistent with questionnaire studies that find females to be more altruistic and nurturant than males (Buss & Finn, 1987). Who do you think helps more often, based on your observations of the real world?

One difficulty with experimental studies is that the situations are artificial. Researchers usually set up situations in which people help strangers for a brief time, since these brief encounters permit the researcher to control the situation more completely (Eagly & Crowley, 1986). Researchers usually do not assess situations in which we help the people we know well, such as friends and family. They do not study helping that endures over time, as occurs in ongoing relationships in real life (Greeno & Maccoby, 1986). Perhaps the experimental situations that have been studied favor males, who may be less afraid than females to help a stranger (Ashmore, 1990). For example, males are much more likely than females to help someone with a flat tire, or to stop a fight. Females, on the other hand, are more likely than males to volunteer to spend time with developmentally disabled children (Eagly & Crowley, 1986). Alice Eagly (1987b) interprets such differences as results of the different social roles that females and males occupy. For example, men more often occupy roles that involve physical strength and dangerous situations, and so they are more likely to help in situations that involve risk, such as stopping a fight. Women are more often in the social role of taking care of children, and therefore they are more skilled and willing to help children. Rather than trying to say which sex helps more, it would be more accurate to describe the situations in which each will help.

Sex differences in helping have been observed as early as elementary school. In one observational study of fourth-graders, girls were more often observed "caring" for other children; that is, comforting them when upset, offering sympathy, or taking their side against another. There were no sex differences in helping others or sharing. The pattern of correlations among

When helping other people involves physical danger and the need for strength, men are more likely to help than women. In other kinds of situations, though, there are no sex differences, or women may be more likely to help.

measures of helping behavior was different for boys and girls, suggesting that different patterns of helping were being developed (Larrieu & Mussen, 1986). The researchers suggest that girls' greater caring and empathy, found in other studies also, may be a result of socialization for nurturance and emotionally expressive behaviors.

Empathy and Social Perception

Before helping or comforting others, one must know their needs. The term **empathy** refers to awareness and sensitivity to another person's feelings. Several studies indicate that empathy is higher in females than in males (Buss & Finn, 1987). On self-report inventories, females rate themselves as more empathic and altruistic than males (Eisenberg & Lennon, 1983; Lennon & Eisenberg, 1987). Self-reports, though, can be biased because people's reports may be influenced by what they think is expected of them. Can we find an alternative method?

One way to measure empathy with scientific controls is to use a social perception task. Subjects can be shown films and asked to report what the person in the film was experiencing, or they can be presented with real people who behave in a manner the experimenter has assigned. In such studies, women are generally superior at decoding emotional cues in others (Hall, 1987, 1978). Experiments also indicate that females can more often detect deception by their male dating partners than vice versa (McCornack & Parks, 1990). On aspects of social perception other than emotion, however, sex differences are not found, and males are sometimes more accurate (Gangestad et al., 1992).

Emotions

Stereotypes suggest that women are more emotional than men. Females are regarded as more emotionally warm and more sensitive, likely to suffer from hurt feelings. In contrast, males are stereotyped as emotionally controlled. How accurate are these stereotypes? Several studies confirm their accuracy, but there are exceptions. An analysis of undergraduates who had taken several personality tests showed that females scored higher on a factor of emotionality that emerged from a combined analysis of the various scales (Zuckerman, Kuhlman & Camac, 1988). According to Arnold Buss and Stephen Finn's (1987) review, fear and guilt are higher in females. Another study reports females to be higher on a measure of death anxiety (Dattell & Neimeyer, 1990), and many studies indicate that females suffer from depression more often than males (Nolen-Hokesema, 1987).

Some emotions, however, show the opposite pattern. The emotion of *anger* is more characteristic of males, who are also more rebellious and aggressive than females (Buss & Finn, 1987; Shields, 1987). While females are stereotyped as sensitive to others' emotions and vulnerable to anxiety and hurt, males are seen as possessing "relatively less desirable, self-oriented feelings (e.g., hostility, arrogance, egotism)" (Johnson & Shulman, 1988, p. 68). Based on undergraduates' descriptions of responses of their male and female friends to hypothetical situations, Joel Johnson and Gregory Shulman (1988) conclude that sex differences are more apparent in emotions displayed for others to see than in the subjective experience of emotions. Males and females both experience communal feelings, such as cooperativeness and concern for others, but males are less likely to express them outwardly. Conversely, both genders experience self-oriented feelings, such as ambition and pride, but females are less likely to display them outwardly.

Aggression

Aggression is more frequent in males than in females. Males' greater aggression has been observed in many cultures, and it is seen in crime statistics as well as psychological research (Kenrick, 1987). This sex difference is apparent in observations of young children (Maccoby & Jacklin, 1980), but it decreases with age (Cohn 1991; Hyde, 1984). Based on a meta-analysis of 143 studies, Hyde (1984) concludes that the differences between males and females are reliable, but not large (only about .5 of a standard deviation).

As we observed in the helping literature, situations moderate sex differences. Males and females react differently to various kinds of situations.

While all people experience emotions, there is mounting evidence that depression is more common among women, and anger among men.

Although many situations produce greater aggressive responses in males, some situations that are important and sex-role specific may arouse more aggression in females (Towson & Zanna, 1982). The familiar advice, "Don't get between a mother bear and her cubs" illustrates a situation in which females would be more aggressive. As a result of their meta-analytic review, Alice Eagly and Valerie Steffen (1986) concluded that experimental studies that measure aggression by behaviors causing pain or physical injury (for example, administering electric shocks as punishment in a learning task) show males to be more aggressive. Situations in which aggression is expressed through psychological or social harm show less sex difference. Thus, gender roles shape the expression of aggression.

Conformity

Conformity occurs when people go along with the behavior of others, typically out of a desire to be accepted or approved of. Conformity is studied in the laboratory by exposing subjects to other people's behavior and seeing whether the subjects behave similarly to the models. A classic example of the research situation is the Asch paradigm. Under the cover story that they are participating in an experiment on visual perception, subjects are asked to judge which of three lines is the same length as a standard line. Unbeknownst to them, the other "subjects" are actually confederates, hired to pretend to be subjects and to give the wrong answers sometimes. If the subject chooses the wrong line after observing models make the wrong choice, that choice is scored as "conforming." In such laboratory studies, women conform more than men (Cooper, 1979; Eagly, 1978; Eagly & Carli, 1981). Alice Eagly (1987b) says that these sex differences are produced by social role differences. Managers, for example, exert more influence than lower level employees, and males are more likely to be managers. Because males generally occupy higher status roles in society, and because higher status is associated with less conformity, the sex differences are consistent with her social role analysis. The differences do not appear invariably, however. For example, older females conform more than males; but among younger subjects, there are no sex differences (Eagly & Chrvala, 1986).

By examining many studies together, researchers can see patterns that explain why results sometimes occur as predicted and sometimes don't. An interesting pattern was discovered in a meta-analysis of social influence studies by Alice Eagly and Linda Carli (1981). Although women, overall, were more persuadable and more conforming than men, this sex difference was greater when the researcher was male and was eliminated when the researcher was female. How can the sex of the researcher influence the results of experimental studies? Subtle sex biases may have crept in because male and female subjects respond differently to male and female experimenters, or because the researcher chose topics that males know more about (for example, football). Only when such aspects of the experimental observations are made comparable can we compare the responses of male and female subjects fairly.

Intellectual Abilities

Sex differences have been found in the pattern of intellectual abilities. Males are often reported to be superior in mathematical abilities, especially visual-spatial ability. Females are often reported to be superior in verbal ability. These differences were described as "well-established" sex differences in an influential early review (Maccoby & Jacklin, 1974), and so they are widely accepted, although current evidence has raised doubts (Hyde, 1981). Later, more sophisticated analyses show that these sex differences in verbal and mathematical ability are quite small and inconsistent (Ashmore, 1990; Hyde, Fennema & Lamon, 1990). Changes in research methods and statistical procedures are partially responsible for the disparate results. In addition, sex differences may actually have diminished with the cultural changes that have occurred since Eleanor Maccoby and Carol Jacklin's review.

On mathematics tests, male superiority is greatest on spatial ability tests, particularly those that test the mental rotation of objects (Linn & Petersen, 1985). The mental rotations test has been found to correlate differently with other dimensions of intelligence in males and females (Ozer, 1987), so the sexes may differ in the structure of intellectual abilities, not only in their level.

Janet Shibley Hyde (1981) estimated the size of gender differences in verbal ability and mathematical abilities (including quantitative ability and visual-spatial ability) by reviewing published studies, using meta-analytic techniques. She concluded that these effects were very small. Female superiority on verbal abilities was only about .25 of a standard deviation, and male superiority on mathematical abilities only about .50 of a standard deviation (Fig. 4.2). Hyde and her colleagues later reviewed gender differences in mathematics performance and concluded that gender differences in the general population were small and slightly favored females rather than males. No gender differences were found in elementary and middle school, but in high school and college, males outperformed females in mathematics, particularly on problem-solving items (Hyde, Fennema & Lamon, 1990). These trends suggest that social pressures are causing females to turn away from mathematics, and we may assume that in some cultural contexts there would be no sex differences in these abilities (Eccles, 1989).

Cultural beliefs about sex differences influence the performance of males and females, perhaps creating or exaggerating sex differences as a self-fulfilling prophecy. According to studies described by Carol Jacklin (1989), as scientific accounts of male superiority in mathematics were popularized by the media, parents discouraged their daughters from studying mathematics, which exacerbated the sex difference. More recently, beliefs have changed, and gender differences have declined (Hyde, Fennema & Lamon, 1990). In a recent meta-analysis, Janet Shibley Hyde and colleagues (Hyde, Fennema, et al., 1990) found only small differences between males and females in most mathematics attitudes and affects (such as anxiety). Only one sex difference was large: males held more stereotyped attitudes about mathematics as a masculine activity than did females.

Females have usually scored higher than males on tests of verbal abilities. In addition, the challenge of learning a second language leads to more memory difficulties for males than for females, reflecting males' generally greater weakness in language (Makarec & Persinger, 1993). Verbal abilities, like mathematical abilities, have been influenced by cultural changes. Gender difference in recent studies is less than in studies published in 1973 or earlier, and it is so small as to be of no practical significance. A meta-analysis of 165 studies of verbal ability finds only small differences between males and females (Hyde & Linn, 1988). Furthermore, females no longer score higher than males on the SAT–Verbal test; since 1972, females score lower (Hyde & Linn, 1988).

These findings of very little difference between the sexes in abilities may be surprising to some people; for example, to those who have seen that remedial reading programs are dominated by boys. The apparent incongruity stems from the fact that when we refer to little difference, we are referring to averages; when we focus on special programs for the gifted or the low achievers, we are referring to the extremes of the distribution of abilities. Statistically, it is quite possible to have little average difference between males and females but large sex differences at the extremes of high

FIGURE 4.2 *The personalities of males and females overlap more than they differ. (A) Two normal distributions with means .25 standard deviations apart. This is approximately the magnitude of the gender differences in verbal ability. (B) Two normal distributions with means .50 standard deviations apart. This is approximately the magnitude of the gender differences in quantitative ability, visual-spatial ability, and field articulation. (Adapted from Hyde, 1981, p. 899.)*

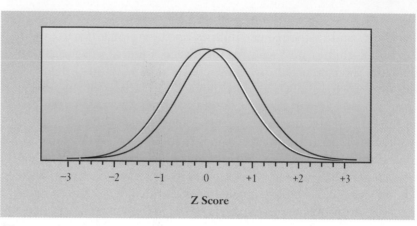

(A)

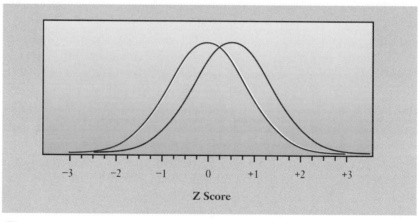

(B)

and low abilities. Michele Wittig notes that despite the small overall average sex differences, "the differences at the ends of the distribution of skill level reflect proportions of three boys to every girl in remedial reading programs . . . and seven or eight junior high school boys to every girl scoring 600 or above on the SAT Math test" (1985, p. 808).

Neuroticism and Other Measures of Mental Well-Being

Turning from intellectual abilities to emotional well-being, we find that sex differences again occur, but not in simple ways. The term *neuroticism* is often used to refer to unhealthy emotional characteristics, such as anxiety. (Such emotionality is often thought to be a sign that people are not coping well with the demands of their lives.) High neuroticism test scores indicate poorer mental health. Males typically score better on mental health inventories, with lower neuroticism scores on several scales (including the Big Five instrument, the NEO-PI) and higher subjective well-being (Costa & McCrae, 1985; Eysenck & Eysenck, 1975; Haring, Stock & Okun, 1984; Jorm, 1987; Trapnell & Wiggins, 1990).

A contradictory finding is reported using a different instrument, the Washington Sentence Completion Test of ego development. Among entering college students, females scored higher (Mabry, 1993). The discrepancy is probably due to the different aspects of mental well-being measured by the two kinds of scales. Neuroticism includes emotionality as one component, and we have seen that females are generally more emotional on self-report measures, so it is not surprising that their self-reports indicate higher neurotic-type emotionality as well. In contrast, ego strength involves cognitive maturity and the ability to think about life choices in a more developed manner. Since neuroticism and ego strength are different theoretical concepts, it is not inconsistent that females would be higher in ego strength although more neurotic than males. Such apparent discrepancies should make us careful about accepting any one approach to measuring "mental health" (or any other concept, for that matter). The truth is often far more complex than our general statements.

How Different Are the Sexes, Overall?

Overall, how different are the sexes? Often, workers conduct their research in a context that assumes significant and substantial sex differences in the strength of personality traits. Repeatedly, literature reviews have found such differences to be less than anticipated (Belle, 1985; Stewart & Chester, 1982). Abigail Stewart and M. Brinton Lykes, commenting on a series of papers on gender that they had edited, summarized a major theme by noting that "sex differences are rather *un*important in the study of personality" (Stewart & Lykes, 1985, p. 5).

When sex differences are found, they often are not due to sex per se but to other variables associated with sex (such as status, employment, or educational background). When these variables are controlled, the sex differences often disappear (Jacklin, 1981; Riger, 1992). In other cases, sex differences may appear in some situations but not in others. For example, females are more friendly and males are more dominant when interacting with friends of the same sex, but these sex differences disappear when the same people interact with strangers of the opposite sex (Moskowitz, 1993).

Simple descriptions of sex differences can be misleading because they eclipse the large overlaps that often exist between groups of men and women. Overall, the sexes are different only a little, and only in some situations. More than they differ, they are similar.

Doubts about the Validity of Sex Differences Research

Since researchers have developed elaborate personality tests to measure traits, it seems natural enough to compare males and females on them. Is this approach conceptually sound? One source of difficulty, easy to understand but difficult to avoid, is that the people who are studied by researchers are not necessarily representative of all males and all females. To measure the personality differences between male and female research subjects, who are mostly college students, and then to assume that these differences also characterize people in the rest of the population, is simply not warranted.

Sexist assumptions can readily distort research, and special precautions may be necessary to avoid this danger (McHugh, Koeske & Frieze, 1986). One precaution would be to report sex differences in all research routinely, even when they are not the question under investigation (Eagly, 1987a). This would counteract a tendency to report selectively only sex differences that confirm prior (stereotyped) expectations and would provide a less distorted body of research. Unfortunately, such an approach also risks focusing attention unduly on sex differences, when they may be relatively minor and when the methodology may not warrant such attention (Baumeister, 1988).

Another difficulty is that trait measures may be the wrong way of comparing males and females. Traits reside within individuals (Ashmore, 1990; Morawski, 1985). To focus on traits ignores the interactions of the person with the social world. Many current theorists and researchers emphasize that gender is a social category and that sex differences should be studied in the context of social processes, rather than described in terms of an individual's traits (for example, Deaux, 1984; Deaux & Major, 1987; Eagly, 1987b; Peplau & Conrad, 1989). To understand sex differences, we must consider more refined theoretical concepts than traits. We must identify the specific ways in which personality is expressed and how situations influence these behaviors. This argument is essentially the position that *personality processes* should be studied instead of simply descriptions of *individual differences.*

One major theoretical development describes the learning of gender roles in a cultural context as the process by which many sex differences are produced. When researchers measure people's acceptance of gender roles, these roles are more closely correlated with a variety of personality traits (including spatial ability, sense of competence, aggressiveness, neuroticism, and several other traits) than is sex (Krampen et al., 1990). Because sex is a biological characteristic, sex differences are often uncritically assumed to be biologically caused. Although biological predispositions could produce the sex differences described in this chapter, cultural learning is an alternative interpretation, even for aggression (Tieger, 1980).

In addition, differences between men and women vary across other social categories, such as race and ethnicity (Amaro, Russo & Pares-Avila, 1987; Vazquez-Nuttall, Romero-Garcia & de Leon, 1987). For example, descriptions of traits that are derived from studying white women may not accurately describe women of color (Stack, 1986). Measures that may be valid for one group are not necessarily valid for another. Differences seem deceptively simple and may lull us into forgetting that many influences interact with gender in determining most characteristics (Fagley & Miller, 1990).

Racial and Ethnic Differences

Despite the diversity of racial and ethnic groups, most psychological research is conducted on white, middle class samples. According to Sandra Graham's review of six major journals, only 3.6 percent of the empirical studies published between 1970 and 1989 reported data collected from African Americans (Graham, 1992). Fewer of these were published in the 1980s than in the 1970s. As poor as this representation is, the attention of researchers to other minorities, including Asian Americans, native Americans, and Hispanic Americans, is no better (Lee, 1993).

Personality in Minority Groups

The reluctance that some psychologists feel about studying sex differences in personality is small compared to reservations about investigating racial and ethnic differences. Similar reasons apply: by documenting differences, we risk perpetuating stereotypes and magnifying small differences into the perception of greater disparities. We also risk the perception that differences are caused solely by biological factors, because the cultural influences that are confounded with race and ethnicity are more complex and less well understood. Historical and current examples of racial conflicts add to our concerns.

Why study such a risky area? Besides a general hope that knowledge will bring a better world, it seems unwise to leave all descriptions of group differences to those whose aims are divisive. Sound scholarship may undermine racist rhetoric. In addition, clinicians and other practitioners who use diagnostic tests in their practices must know how to interpret these tests when they are administered to minority clients. That requires developing norms for appropriate groups and deciding whether the tests are valid for such groups.

African Americans African Americans are probably the most frequently studied minority group in the United States, although the literature on other racial and ethnic minorities is increasing. According to a review of selected major journals of the American Psychological Association, the

Ethnic differences provide many challenges to researchers. Is it sufficient to measure group differences? Or do we need to reconsider the assumptions behind our theories and measures, in order to avoid imposing one set of cultural assumptions on everyone, blinding us to the dimensions of personality that are visible only through other cultural eyes?

study of personality differences between African Americans and white Americans has been seriously limited in scope, focusing primarily on psychopathology (Graham, 1992). Researchers have examined racial differences on several clinical personality tests, including the Defense Mechanisms Inventory (Banks & Juni, 1991), the MMPI (Gynther, 1989; Hutton et al., 1992), the CPI (Davis, Hoffman & Nelson, 1990), and the Rorschach inkblot test (Frank, 1992). In many of the studies reported,

African Americans and other racial minorities appear less well-adjusted than white Americans. Before concluding that psychologists are led by prejudiced expectations to focus on pathology in minority groups, we should keep in mind that these studies are prompted by the concerns of therapists who worry that existing clinical tests, developed in primarily white samples, may be biased when used to diagnose individuals from racial minorities. Documenting group differences in test scores permits more accurate evaluation of individuals from those groups. (See the Research Strategies box for more explanation.)

National survey data are particularly suitable for comparing groups, because they ensure that the samples are representative of the population in society. In a 1980 national survey in the United States, African Americans had lower personal efficacy than white Americans, meaning that they had less confidence that they could accomplish what they wished to do. However, African Americans were not lower in self-esteem; that is, they did not think themselves less worthwhile. Michael Hughes and David Demo (1989) maintain that this finding results from sociological factors in the larger society that undermine the sense of efficacy in African Americans. Society simply presents more obstacles to minorities. Self-esteem does not differ by race, because it is determined primarily by social interactions within the family, not by larger societal influences.

Hispanic Americans The term *Hispanic* encompasses diverse cultural groups, which are not all similar. Few studies discriminate among these groups, so we shall have to settle for some generalized descriptions.

In a sample of United States Navy recruits, Hispanic men responded to surveys with more socially desirable responses. Researchers usually interpret socially desirable responding as a sign of defensiveness, but such an interpretation may not be appropriate in this ethnic group. The tendency to report what is socially desirable may be a result of the Hispanic cultural value of *simpatia*, "a culture-specific Hispanic script that emphasizes the need for behaviors that promote smooth, pleasant, interpersonal relations" (Booth-Kewley, Rosenfeld & Edwards, 1992). This tendency may lead to underreporting of sensitive or unpleasant content on self-report measures, based on an attempt to create a positive impression. Cultural norms that emphasize avoiding disclosure of personal problems can also lead Hispanics to appear more defensive, alienated, and conforming, and less expressive, on the Psychological Screening Inventory (Negy & Woods, 1993).

Steven López and his collaborators have argued for more explicit theoretical analysis of **acculturation,** the cultural change that occurs when a person is in direct contact with a different cultural group. Many things change as people move further from their culture of origin and closer to their new mainstream. Their cultural practices change, and they face the stress of adjustment. Often, measures of adjustment favor those who have become more acculturated to mainstream American culture. For example,

RESEARCH STRATEGIES

Comparing Groups

Much research aims to describe group differences, and such research can offer important insights. Sometimes, however, it can be misleading. An understanding of methodological considerations can help us sort out meaningful studies of group differences from misleading ones.

When researchers refer to "group differences" they are speaking about differences in the mean (average) of one group from another on a trait. They do not assume that all the individuals in one group are different from all the individuals in the other, as a bag of red marbles differs from a bag of blue marbles. There is often considerable overlap between the groups, so that it is not entirely obvious from looking at one member which group the member belongs to. For example, there are more sunny days in California than in New York, but a single photograph of a blue sky does not necessarily come from California, nor a cloudy one from New York. Similarly, limes are generally greener than lemons, but it is possible to find a particular lemon that is greener than a particular lime. When we describe the group differences by saying that "California is sunnier than New York" or "limes are greener than lemons," we are describing characteristics of the group as a whole, the average of each group, rather than characteristics of every member.

This consideration also applies when we make statements about personality traits. If we say that females are more empathic than males or that Americans are more individualistic than the Chinese, we refer to averages, not to all members of a group. Typically, the variability among members of a group is considerably greater than the difference between the averages of two groups. It is quite possible to have group A be higher on the average on a trait than group B and still have many group B members score higher on that trait than the average group A member.

Researchers study two quite distinct kinds of group differences. In experimental research, the groups are constituted by the researcher to be alike in all possible ways. Usually, this goal is achieved by randomly assigning subjects to groups. During experimental research, the groups are treated identically except in one way, by manipulating an independent variable. Any differences between the groups, then, provide the researcher with evidence that the independent variable caused the difference. Experimental research thus creates group differences to provide evidence about independent variables. It does not, however, tell us anything about the differences among groups that already exist in the world.

The second kind of group difference does aim to achieve just that: a description of the differences among groups in the real world. This kind of descriptive research is correlational (not experimental). It tells us what existing groups are like, but it does not explain the causes of those differences. The research described in this chapter is this second, descriptive kind.

When the purpose of research is to describe existing groups, such as racial groups or men and women, good sampling is essential. The researcher could not possibly study all males and all females, or all whites, Hispanics, African Americans, and so on. Yet if the research is intended to say how men and women are different, or how the various racial groups are different, it becomes essential to pick the groups in a reasonable way. Which women are "typical"? Undergraduates at your institution? Those who study introductory psychology? What about women who enroll in noncollegiate institutions, such as beauty schools? Or those who join the military after high school? Should they also be included in a group that is to be used to describe "women in general"? Similar considerations apply to deciding on groups to describe men, racial groups, and so on.

Occasionally, elaborate survey sampling procedures are used to select groups. National surveys, for example, are conducted by randomly sampling people from a variety of areas of the country. These systematic surveys are more trustworthy than most other studies, which may have their own characteristics that make them inadequately representative of "all women," "all men," and so on. In practice, though, many studies are conducted with more limited samples, such as those that compare students at the same undergraduate institution. Replication of results across such studies strengthens confidence that the group differences are reliable. Even with many replications, though, we must be skeptical to the extent that the samples themselves are similar. Even a dozen replications may share a common bias; for example, if they all study college undergraduates only.

In summary, the following points are important to remember in group differences research:

1. "Group differences" refer to differences in the average scores of different groups.

2. Even if two groups have different averages, they often have considerable overlap of individual scores.

3. In experimental research, groups are constituted by randomly assigning individuals to groups. The groups are treated differently on an independent variable, and group differences tell us about the independent variable, not about any preexisting real-world groups.

4. In descriptive research, groups should be constituted by careful sampling. To the extent that this is done, group differences tell us about the characteristics of groups in the real world.

in the study reported above, the apparent lower adaptation of Hispanics on the Psychological Screening Inventory was not found among Hispanics who were highly acculturated to American culture (Negy & Woods, 1993). This is only one of many studies in which Hispanics who are not highly acculturated seem less healthy when evaluated on self-report screening measures (Malgady, Rogler & Constantino, 1987).

Consider one symptom of pathology: hearing voices. Research indicates that "more Mexican-born Latinos reported this symptom (2.3%) than U.S.-born Latinos (1.6%), who reported more such symptoms than Anglos (0.6%)" (Betancourt & López, 1993, p. 635). What is it about the culture of Mexican-born Latinos that would lead more of them to report hearing voices? The researchers suggest that the specific aspect of culture that may account for these group differences is religiosity, since other researchers have found religiosity to be related to reports of hearing voices. To understand cultural effects, researchers should measure aspects of culture more precisely, rather than oversimplifying by interpreting group differences as "cultural."

Asian Americans Images of modest, respectful Asians concur with results of many personality tests. Compared to white Americans, Asian Americans are less narcissistic (Smith, 1990) and less assertive. Asian Canadians, compared with those of Anglo and European descent, are less dominant and more concerned with order and social recognition, among other differences (Dion & Yee, 1987).

In the counseling literature, Asian Americans have sometimes been described as less assertive and less adequate in interpersonal situations. Rather than a global trait, however, the lower assertiveness of Asian Americans compared to Caucasians is found only in situations involving strangers (Zane et al., 1991). Many personality theorists and researchers emphasize the need to consider situations in describing personality, and this caution should be applied to discussions of group differences as well.

Easier Said Than Done: Methods of Comparing Racial, Ethnic, and Cultural Groups

Computing the statistical differences among groups is so easy that we may overlook the distinction between measuring differences and understanding them. Comparing racial, ethnic, and cultural groups is complicated by the same issues that confounded sex differences research, as well as by additional difficulties. We can't assume that the differences we find are true reflections of the underlying characteristics we are measuring; perhaps the test is not valid for one group. We can't simply assume that a small group of research subjects is typical of their racial, ethnic, or cultural group, so general statements based on convenient samples of college students or clinic patients are unwarranted. Let's look at some of these issues.

Social Expectations and Stereotypes May Influence the Measures
Like sex, race is a social category that influences our perception of people (see, for example, Dovidio, Evans & Tyler, 1986; Hewstone, Hantzi & Johnston, 1991; Zeidner, 1989). Therefore, expectations and stereotypes can distort measures based on ratings of other people. Stereotypes may have more subtle effects, too, leading researchers to select traits for comparison that would confirm their prior expectations.

Have We Agreed on Our Categories?
Individuals do not fit so neatly into racial and ethnic groups as they do into the categories of male and female. Psychology has not developed any standard methods for categorizing race, and this lack has impeded research (Yee et al., 1993). The term **ethnicity** emphasizes social and cultural aspects, whereas the term **race** refers to biological differences, yet the two terms have not been differentiated consistently. Many people are best described as mixed race and mixed ethnicity, and even the individuals themselves cannot always accurately report all their background racial and ethnic roots. Furthermore, researchers who ask about racial and ethnic groupings almost universally limit their consideration to a few major categories. They lump together as "white" groups as diverse as the Irish and the English, the French and the Australian. They almost always ignore, under the major heading of "Hispanic," differences among Mexican-Americans, Puerto Ricans, South Americans, and other Hispanic groups. There are many Asian groups that have experienced centuries of cultural distinction and historical conflict. Often, researchers settle for comparisons of only two groups, African Americans and white Americans (Yee et al., 1993).

Has an Adequate Sample of Each Group Been Taken?
Comparisons of groups can easily be misleading. For one thing, inadequate sampling of the populations being compared can bias the results, leaving doubt about whether comparisons between groups would generalize to the whole cultures. Many studies are based on tests of students, who are readily available to researchers. Yet we have no guarantee that the differences among student racial and ethnic groups are the same as the differences in the general population. In fact, since different percentages of various groups attend college, it seems likely that the groups are not comparable.

Racial and ethnic differences can best be evaluated by using carefully sampled populations, such as national surveys. Yet many studies analyze for racial differences without adequate samples. One reviewer criticizes "the emphasis on racial comparison without matching this global and complex endeavor with appropriate methods or sufficient resources commensurate with the massive project" (Bulhan, 1985, p. 374).

What Else Is Different about the Groups? Confounding
Variables Research on variables such as race and sex, which vary in the
world rather than being manipulated by researchers, is complicated by the
confounding of many variables with the dimensions of interest. If enough
data are collected and appropriate statistical analyses are conducted, it is
possible to untangle these naturally occurring variables. Unfortunately
studies of race, even in prestigious journals, often fail to control for such
important variables as **socioeconomic status** (SES) (Graham, 1992), which
is measured by income, education, job level, and similar variables.
Sociologists describe more precisely what we all know more generally:
more whites than minorities occupy high socioeconomic status in the
United States. Since socioeconomic status is confounded with race, studies
showing differences between the races may not be caused by race at all, but
rather by socioeconomic status. This confounding occurs if, for example,
low-SES African Americans are found to differ from middle-SES white
Americans. The white executive may have more confidence in his abilities
than the African American janitor because of his position, rather than his
race. Social class differences may be more important than cultural differences, and they certainly ought to be equated before we can compare racial
and cultural groups (Lanham, 1988; Snarey & Lydens, 1990).

   An adequate sample will be large enough to permit analysis of subgroups. For example, within a racial or ethnic group, there may be important differences between males and females, or between people at different
levels of socioeconomic status. We miss accurate descriptions when we
speak of only one social category, such as race or sex, at a time. Sex differences may vary across racial, ethnic, and socioeconomic groups. Race differences may be different for men and women, and so on.

Should Acculturation Be Measured? Ethnic differences can diminish as groups come into first-hand contact with one another (Negy &
Woods, 1993). When we categorize by racial and ethnic groups alone, we
combine people in the United States who are very close to the cultural
roots of their immigrant ancestors with those who have become largely
assimilated into mainstream culture. Many studies have shown that acculturation modifies the effect of ethnicity. Those who have become more
integrated into the mainstream culture take on personality characteristics
that are less like their ancestors and more like the new culture to which
they have adapted. This acculturation phenomenon occurs among diverse
groups, including Hispanics (Malgady, Rogler & Constantino, 1987; Negy
& Woods, 1993), Chinese (Feldman & Rosenthal, 1990; Lin & Fu, 1990),
and native Americans (Boyer, 1988). Furthermore, individuals can embrace
more than one culture or ethnicity, selecting from among them in different
social situations (Verma & Mallick, 1988). Researchers will be limited in
what they can understand about ethnic differences unless they measure and
analyze the effects of acculturation.

As people whose families originate from other cultures become more and more acculturated to the majority culture, their personality as well as their appearance changes to be like that of the new culture. This process of acculturation does not occur in the same way or at the same rate for everyone, however.

Interpreting the Results of Group Comparisons Once group differences have been described, they require interpretation. Because heredity determines the biological factors of sex and race, it is tempting to conclude that biological factors cause group differences. Arguments that racial differences stem from biology have been hotly debated. J. Philippe Rushton (1985, 1987) proposes that genetic differences are the cause of different social behaviors of various racial groups and also of higher and lower socioeconomic status groups. These behaviors, according to Rushton's arguments, include intelligence, altruism, and criminality. Opponents argue that it is the social context in which people are raised that molds such aspects of personality. Acculturation diminishes such differences, as it could not if they were biological.

The determinants of personality will be considered later in this book. At this point, let us bear in mind that the group differences found by researchers are merely descriptive of observations at the time and in the social context when data were collected. To understand the causes of these differences requires further data and more careful development of theory (Betancourt & López, 1993).

The Validity of Tests across Groups: Challenges and a New Approach

Even if we sample groups carefully, measure other variables including acculturation, and agree to suspend interpretation of the causes of group differences, our comparisons between two groups are flawed if the test itself is not valid in both groups. Unfortunately, it is much easier to state this difficulty than to resolve it. Let's consider the problem of test validity and a new approach that is guiding current researchers.

Testing Has Social Consequences Beyond science and psychology, the existence of group differences poses dilemmas for a society that values equality. Some differences are interpreted as evidence of discrimination, and they trigger remedial social action. Historically, psychological studies of the lower self-esteem of African American children, compared to white Americans, were presented to the U.S. Supreme Court in the 1954 landmark decision that outlawed racial segregation in public schools, *Brown v. Board of Education of Topeka*. More recently, lawsuits have charged racial bias in standardized testing. For example, the fact that minorities disproportionately failed the Illinois insurance licensing exams was the basis of a lawsuit against the Illinois Department of Insurance and the Educational Testing Service, culminating in an out-of-court settlement that changed test construction procedures by requiring that items be dropped if they were much more difficult for some groups than for others (Faggen, 1987; Rooney, 1987; Weiss, 1987). The agreement was controversial. Opponents argued that the problem was not the test, but rather social factors that led whites, on average, to be better prepared (Bond, 1987; Jaeger, 1987). They argued that the *Golden Rule agreement* (as it is called, after the Golden Rule Insurance Company), uses unsound methods for evaluating test bias that will undermine the validity of the test (Linn & Drasgow, 1987). Based on standard practices for evaluating tests, they maintained that group differences were not in themselves evidence against its validity. Test bias should only be claimed if the total test scores did not relate with a criterion measure in the same way across groups (Drasgow, 1987). Defenders of the decision view it as a practical compromise that will reduce racial bias by permitting minorities to become licensed insurance agents, without compromising validity.

What Is Test Validity? A test is valid if it can be shown to measure what it purports to measure. **Test validity** must be established through research. When tests are used to compare groups, they must be shown to have validity in both groups. Experts generally accept correlations between the test and criterion measures as the best evidence of validity.

Some Comparisons Are Meaningless If someone told you that a mouse was bigger than a rattlesnake because the mouse was two inches tall and the rattlesnake only an inch and a half tall, would you be convinced? Probably not. The snake might not be as tall as the mouse, but it is considerably longer and heavier. It's senseless to compare things with a measurement that is not appropriate to both. The same principle applies when we compare the personalities of groups. What measure of personality is appropriate for both groups?

In the ideal case, a test can be found that works for both groups. On such a test, both groups score the same, on the average. Their distribution of high and low scores is similar. Their scores correlate with criterion measures of validity in the same way. The items have similar meanings for both groups. This is the ideal. Reality, though, is often a different case.

Is There Validity Evidence for Both Groups? Does a score of, say, 73 on a test of mental health predict the same level of functioning for an African American and a white American? A man and a woman? This can be determined only by research. Sometimes the raw score itself will have similar predictions across populations. At other times, prediction will be improved by expressing each score in terms of the norms particular to that group. But sometimes a test that is useful in predicting for one population will not be effective for another, with or without adaptation to the norms of the group.

Is the Trait Similar in Both Groups? Traits are measured by adding together many test items to compute a total score. Two individuals can have identical scores even if they get them from answering different items according to the scoring key. When you stop to think about it, though, it may be misleading to say that their personalities are the same on this trait, because they disagree about many items. Some further analysis, beyond the total score, seems necessary. If two groups of people are consistently different in the items that they are scored on, it is misleading to compare their total scores alone. By analogy, comparing the grade point averages of a group of engineers and a group of language majors would be an oversimplified way of expressing their academic abilities, since they probably got higher grades in different courses.

Researchers often tackle this issue by looking at the way items correlate with one another. An advanced statistical procedure, factor analysis, can show whether there is more than one theme or factor suggested by the way items intercorrelate (see the Appendix). These themes or factors are the *factor structure* of the test. The factor structure of the same identical test may be different in different groups. Consider this analogy. A colleague of mine, an English professor, was dismayed upon returning from a vacation to see that her well-intentioned secretary had rearranged all the books in her office, grouping them by size and color! Whereas the professor perceived groups according to topic, the secretary saw the same books in terms of physical characteristics. Similarly, the items in a psychological test may be perceived by one group along dimensions of competitiveness and dominance, while another may see themes of excellence and hard work in the same items. The researcher would be made aware of such differences by looking at group differences in the factor structure of the test, not by looking at the total scores.

Researchers often compare the factor structure of tests in various populations, reasoning that similar factor structures constitute evidence that the tests are measuring similar psychological qualities in the two groups. For example, the PRF shows similar factor structures in diverse samples from the United States, Canada, Holland, Germany, and the Philippines, suggesting that it is an appropriate measuring instrument across many cultures (Stumpf, 1993). Studies have also reported similar factor structures across cultures for the Comrey Personality Scales (CPS) (Caprara, Barbaranelli & Comrey, 1992b; Noller, Law & Comrey, 1988), the Minnesota Multiphasic Personality Inventory (MMPI) (Beck et al., 1989), and other measures. Different factor structures have been reported on the Symptom Checklist (SCL) for Asian Americans and native Hawaiians (Takeuchi et al., 1989). Experts, however, do not always agree whether the evidence of factor similarity is strong enough to warrant comparisons. This issue has been raised with the Eysenck Personality Questionnaire (Bijnen & Poortinga, 1988; Eysenck, 1986b), among others. When the factor structures differ, this suggests that the test or its subscales may be measuring different things in the two populations. Conceptual reconsideration of the trait may be required. It may be the theory, rather than only the measurement, that needs improvement.

A New Strategy: Emic Research If one were to administer an intelligence test developed in the United States or Europe to one of the world's indigenous peoples, the scores obviously would be misleading. It makes no sense to ask hunters and gatherers some of the questions on a standard test of intelligence, such as questions about Western history and government.

A more appropriate approach was reported by John Berry and Jo Bennett (1992). They asked native Cree in northern Ontario to supply words having to do with the concept of competence, and they explored these words by eliciting Cree reactions to them using various methods. This approach produced a depiction of what the Cree mean by competence: a thoughtful, deliberate, attentive, respectful orientation toward nature and others, and distinctly unlike *we-mi-ti-ko-shi-wa-ti-se* (translated, "lives like a white") (Berry & Bennett, 1992, p. 78). Studying concepts within a culture provides insights not available when the dominant culture's theories and measures are imposed. This approach, developing measures within a culture, is the **emic approach.**

An emic approach reported by Ping Chung Cheung and colleagues (1992) studied four different Chinese populations in mainland China, Taiwan, Hong Kong, and the United States. The results showed some common characteristics among these diverse groups, notably self-discipline and moderation, which the researchers attribute to the influence of Confucian tradition in Chinese cultures. There were also substantial differences among these groups. For example, Taiwanese were more tolerant, deliberate, accepting, and obliging than Chinese in Hong Kong and mainland

China. Chinese in the United States were diverse, reflecting their various immigrant roots.

Emic research is particularly time-consuming because it demands that the researcher develop new, culturally based measures rather than importing old ones. There are so many cultures in the world that it seems impossible that we will ever have a comprehensive set of personality tests to apply universally across cultures.

The Goal: Etic (Cross-Cultural) Research

If we had such a set of universally valid personality tests, we could conduct genuine cross-cultural research. Comparisons across cultures are the **etic approach** to research. Typical comparisons of racial and ethnic groups merely document differences on test scores, without sufficient evidence that the tests are valid for diverse groups. Such studies are neither emic (within culture) nor etic (cross-cultural). Rather, they are "pseudoetic" (Triandis, 1972). That is, they masquerade as etic because more than one cultural group is studied, but they are not truly etic because the measuring instruments and theoretical conceptualizations are derived from only one culture. Most often, of course, this one culture is the mainstream culture in the West; that is, white Americans and Europeans. Applying concepts derived from that group to other populations has been criticized as "cultural ethnocentrism" (Verma & Mallick, 1988).

Appropriate cross-cultural research builds on emic research within diverse cultures and integrates these conceptualizations into a more inclusive understanding:

> *The focus of cross-cultural research is not a statistical difference between distinct cultural groups, rather it is the similarity in the data of the different groups. This requires the translation and abstraction of culturally specific constructs into comparable pancultural constructs. (Azibo, 1988, p. 228)*

This line of reasoning would preclude cross-cultural research until each group had been studied separately, developing constructs specifically for that population. For understanding African Americans, Azibo proposes a construct that he calls "the Black personality," or "psychological Blackness." Obviously, such a concept would not emerge in the existing racial and ethnic differences research, which seems increasingly flawed.

Cross-Cultural Personality Research

Cross-cultural researchers have compared personality in several countries. In some cases, measures developed in one culture are administered in other cultures. In other cases, researchers have proposed new concepts based on their observations of other cultures. Some of this research suggests that major personality tests, after careful translation, can be used to measure individual personalities in other cultures. At the same time, cross-cultural research highlights the very different cultural contexts in which personality develops.

On the one hand, how can cultures be compared unless the same instrument is administered to different cultures? On the other hand, how can we be certain that the instrument is valid in various cultures? The answers to these questions are challenging. Some of the principles that guide researchers are listed in Table 4.2.

Cross-Cultural Studies Using Major Personality Tests

Personality tests that claim to measure universal traits have been tested in other cultures. In some cases, the intent of this research is to measure cultural differences (Cattell & Brennan, 1984). For example, Diana Brief and Andrew Comrey report that Russians in St. Petersburg, compared to Americans, are more defensive, lethargic, egocentric, and unstable (Brief & Comrey, 1993). More fundamentally, researchers hope that their work will show the tests to be suitable for measuring individual differences in cultures other than those in which they were developed. They look for similarity of factor structure and evidence of predictive validity to bolster this argument.

Cattell's *16PF* test has been administered in many cultures throughout the world and translated into many foreign languages. Numerous studies have reported that the factor structure of the test and of the High School Personality Questionnaire (designed for younger subjects) is similar, although not necessarily identical, across cultures. Researchers have reported that the factor analysis, originally conducted in England, can be replicated cross-culturally; for example, in Zimbabwe (Wilson et al., 1989). Other reports are more skeptical, citing different factors; for example, in Hawaii (Campbell, 1988, 1991). Cautious use in other cultures may be warranted.

The *Eysenck Personality Questionnaire* has been tested extensively in cross-cultural studies. The three personality factors tapped by this test, Extraversion, Neuroticism, and Psychoticism, are replicated in many cross-cultural studies (Kline, 1988). These factors were originally derived in England but have been replicated in diverse cultures including Russia, Czechoslovakia, Finland, the Netherlands, and Australia (Eysenck & Haapasalo, 1989; Eysenck & Kozeny, 1990; Hanin et al., 1991; O'Gorman & Hattie, 1986; Sanderman, Eysenck & Arrindell, 1991). Sometimes factors vary in different cultures, such as Egypt (Eysenck & Abdel-Khalek, 1989).

The large number of studies that report similar factors suggests that people in many countries are responding to similar themes in the test, and

TABLE   **4.2   Considerations in Cross-Cultural Comparisons**

- Describe each culture's scores in terms of norms appropriate for that culture.

- Evaluate the validity of the test for each culture based on evidence collected in that culture.

- Consider the possibility that the construct itself, not only the test, may be meaningful in one culture but not another.

this finding seems to warrant using the Eysenck Personality Questionnaire to compare the level of traits in various cultures. Comparisons have been made; for example, Neuroticism scores are reported to be higher in England than in several other countries, including Batswana (Maqsud, 1992), Sweden (Eysenck, von Knorring & von Knorring, 1988), and Norway (Eysenck & Tambs, 1990). Factor analysis is a controversial statistical procedure, however, and experts don't always agree that the results warrant comparisons across cultures of average scores (Bijnen, Van der Net & Poortinga, 1986).

The *Myers-Briggs Type Indicator* (MBTI) has also been administered in other countries. In a study of middle and senior managers of an international airline, Chinese and European employees scored differently. The Europeans were extraverted, and the Chinese introverted. According to MBTI scoring, both groups were sensation-thinking-judging types, but the European managers were less extreme on these scores (showing more of the opposite dimensions of intuition, feeling, and perceiving) than the Chinese managers (Furnham & Stringfield, 1993).

The *Big Five* personality factors have also been described in other cultures. Paul Costa and Robert McCrae (1992a) emphasize that the five factors are found in diverse populations: people of different cultural groups, races, and languages, as well as different ages and both sexes. Costa and McCrae acknowledge that there are cultural variations in the five factors, and some cross-cultural researchers emphasize these differences, rather than the similarities. Etic and emic procedures reveal differences. To analyze the dimensions of personality within the Chinese culture (that is, the etic approach), Kuo-shu Yang and Michael Bond (1990) asked more than 2000 Chinese college and university students to rate the personalities of people they knew (father, mother, teacher, neighbor, friend, and self) on bipolar adjectives. The data were factor analyzed to determine the underlying dimensions of personality perception in China. There were five dimensions, which the researchers labeled Social Orientation–Self-Centeredness, Competence–Impotence, Expressiveness–Conservatism, Self-Control–Impulsiveness, and Optimism–Neuroticism. Only two of these factors (Social Orientation and Optimism) corresponded reasonably closely to a particular Big Five factor (Agreeableness and low Neuroticism, respectively). The other factors were not the same in China as in the United States. This sort of cross-cultural comparison shows the inadequacies of using only imported personality tests (referred to above as the "pseudoetic" approach) and the need to develop tests within other cultures (the emic approach).

Translating Personality Tests

Translating statements from one language to another often changes their meaning in subtle ways. When tests developed in one culture are used in another where a different language is spoken, the tests need to be translated. The technique of **back translation** is often used. The test is first translated into the foreign language. Then another group of translators translates the foreign version back into the original language. If the original meaning is recovered, the translation is deemed adequate. If not, the translation is revised.

Even when the translation is adequate, however, some items may not have the same meaning in the two cultures. Ladd Wheeler gives an example. In a test of neuroticism developed in English, one item asked, "Do you allow others to push ahead of you in line?" Respondents who answered yes were given a point on a scale of neuroticism. Chinese students, however, answered yes more frequently than Westerners. Does this mean they are more neurotic? Not necessarily, since the item may be biased against them. In Chinese culture, people do not generally form lines, but simply gather around a location. Thus, their answer is misleading and should not be interpreted in the same way as a "yes" in a culture that lines up (Wheeler, 1988). Some questions are even more inappropriate when removed from their cultural origins. One question in the CPS asks subjects whether they agree with this statement: "If a pay telephone refunded too much money, I would put it back in the phone" (Brief & Comrey, 1993, p. 272). In translating the test for use in Russia, this question had to be changed. Russian pay phones do not give change. In translation, the question asks whether subjects would return excess change to a store clerk, but no translation is entirely adequate. The search for equivalent items can lead to some interesting substitutions. Paul Kline (1988), based on an earlier study by Field (1960), suggests that to ask a Ghanan "Do you visit your shrine regularly?" is equivalent to asking a Californian, "Do you have your own psychoanalyst?" Culture cannot be dismissed, however careful the translation; it is part and parcel of personality.

TABLE **4.3** **Major Characteristics of Individualistic and Collective Cultures**

Major themes of individualistic cultures:

Self-definition as an entity that is distinct and separate from the group(s)

Emphasis on personal goals, even it if inconveniences the group

Less concern for the group

Less emotional attachment to the group

Major themes of collectivistic cultures:

Self-definition as part of the group(s)

Subordination of personal goals to group goals

Concern for the integrity of the group

Intense emotional attachment to the group

Adapted from Triandis et al., 1988, p. 335.

Individualism and Collectivism

Harry Triandis and his collaborators have described cultures as differing in their attitudes toward individualism and collectivism. Typically, people in **individualistic cultures,** such as the United States, Britain, and Australia, define themselves as individuals seeking personal goals. In contrast, people in **collectivistic cultures,** such as China, Africa, and Latin America, emphasize the group above their own welfare and are more likely to care about what others think (Table 4.3). Economic growth is higher in individualistic countries; so is the number of lawsuits (Triandis et al., 1988). People in individualistic cultures tend to value equality, freedom, and enjoying life, in contrast to people in collectivistic cultures, whose values emphasize social order, humility, honoring parents and elders, and preserving one's public image (Triandis, McCusker & Hui, 1990).

People throughout the world care more about those in their immediate families and about close friends than about strangers and mere acquaintances. The general level of caring, though, is higher in collectivist cultures. According to the judgments of researchers in this area, "how an individualist treats a neighbor is similar . . . to how a collectivist would treat a stranger" (Hui & Triandis, 1986, p. 240). The United States is an individualistic culture, while India is more collectivistic. In judging their moral obligations toward others, Americans express less obligation to help strangers than do people in India, and they emphasize individual choices more and social obligations less than do Indians (Miller, Bersoff & Harwood, 1990).

American individualism is reflected in comparisons on personality tests with other countries. For example, students in the southern United States were reported to be more internal on Rotter's Internal-External Locus of Control Scale (Rotter, 1966) than students in Poland (who were also higher in paranormal beliefs than Americans) (Tobacyk & Tobacyk, 1992). In collectivist cultures such as Japan, people define themselves in terms of a specific context, whereas in individualistic countries such as the United States, people are more likely to make abstract, context-free statements. Thus, an American student is more likely to say "I am shy," whereas a Japanese student would state the context: "I am shy *at school*" (Cousins, 1989).

The concepts of individualism and collectivism are enlightening. For example, they help explain why the crime rates are lower in some cultures (collectivist) than in others (individualistic). With individualism comes a decline of social control over the individual. The concepts are, however, more complex when we get down to considering the details. People can be other-oriented in some contexts but self-directed in other situations, for example. Furthermore, some anomalous findings are puzzling. Female undergraduates in Illinois, for example, were found to be more interdependent on friends than were people in collectivist countries in Asia and Latin America (Triandis et al., 1988).

Of course, in every culture, there are some individuals who are more oriented toward their own individual goals, and others who are more community-minded. To make it clear when they are referring to variations within a culture, Harry Triandis and his colleagues use the term **allocentrism** to refer to an individual's tendency to value group goals, corresponding to the term "collectivistic" to refer to the entire culture. Similarly, they use the term **idiocentrism** to refer to an individualism of one person, reserving the term "individualistic" to refer to the entire culture. An allocentric person in a collectivistic culture will experience little conflict between personal values and the culture's norms. Similarly, an idiocentric person in an individualistic culture will feel congruence between self and society. Idiocentric individuals tend to be concerned with achievement and are more lonely than allocentric individuals, who receive much social support (Triandis et al., 1985). Triandis and his colleagues have measured the dimension of idiocentrism versus allocentrism with a self-report scale (Table 4.4). Triandis (1988) suggests that Hispanics and Hawaiians are less individualistic than the mainstream U.S. culture. Among American Navy recruits, Hispanics are more allocentric than others. Hispanics are more concerned than the others with "good interpersonal relationships and harmony, acceptance of authorities, interdependence, loyalty, and reliability" (Hui & Triandis, 1986, p. 228).

TABLE 4.4 **Sample Items to Measure Idiocentrism versus Allocentrism**

1. If the group is slowing down, it is better to leave it and work alone (idiocentrism).

2. Winning is everything (idiocentrism).

3. It is foolish to try to preserve resources for future generations (allocentrism).

4. My parents' opinions are not important in my choice of a spouse (idiocentrism).

5. Even if a child won the Nobel Prize, the parents should not feel honored in any way (allocentrism).

Adapted from Triandis et al., 1998, p. 330. Their measure is analyzed into three factors, which are combined in these sample items.

Some Final Cautions in Interpreting Group Differences

The study of group differences is a sensitive issue. Racial prejudice in society can be fueled by scientific studies that suggest (or that can be misinterpreted to suggest) that one group is superior to another. The frenzy of oversimplified media discussions of race differences in intelligence that followed publication of *The Bell Curve* (Herrnstein & Murray, 1994) illustrates this danger. Marvin Zuckerman (1990b) has warned psychologists that badly conducted science on racial differences supports racism and thus raises ethical issues. He challenges researchers in this area to be more scientifically rigorous. Besides facing all the difficulties of sampling groups appropriately and finding measures that are valid in the various groups, researchers, like the rest of us, are influenced by cultural assumptions. They can be misled by their preconceptions to design studies that perpetuate cultural myths, and they may sometimes misinterpret data to be consistent with those assumptions (Stewart & Lykes, 1985).

When we study race, or sex, or some other group characteristic, we must remember that we are simply describing populations at a particular time. Cultural change is rapid. Such change can make even today's most certain group differences obsolete tomorrow. The research efforts, though, lead to more thoughtful analysis of measurement and more detailed theoretical models of personality.

Should we study racial and ethnic differences, after all? When differences are found, some fear that we run the risk of contributing to beliefs that are used to justify inhumane acts against minority groups. Others counter that objective research can correct misconceptions about racial differences.

SUMMARY

• Studying group differences may provide clues to the causes of personality and provide norms for evaluating individuals from different groups, but it is nonetheless a controversial area.

• In many ways, various groups of people are much more similar than they are different.

• Sex differences may be produced by biological and/or cultural causes. The term *gender* is often used to emphasize the importance of culture.

• Meta-analysis is a statistical technique for combining many studies to see the overall pattern of results.

• Males are considered to be higher in individuality, females in social connectedness.

• Males are more helpful to strangers in situations involving physical strength and danger.

- Females show more caring and empathy to friends.

- Many studies show greater emotionality among females on self-report measures, except that anger is higher among males.

- Males show more aggression in laboratory situations involving pain or physical injury.

- Greater conformity is reported among females in some studies, but this finding is influenced by social status and the sex of the experimenter.

- Intellectual abilities are patterned differently in the two sexes, with males being superior in visual-spatial mathematical ability and females in verbal abilities. These differences are, however, quite small.

- On measures of mental well-being, females score higher (less healthy) on neuroticism, consistent with their greater emotionality, but also higher (more healthy) on ego strength.

- Overall, sex differences are small; they are influenced by cultural factors and therefore may change.

- Research on minority populations is limited and controversial.

- Minority populations often appear less healthy on self-report measures of mental health, but the interpretation of these scores must consider the impact of cultural factors.

- The personality of minority groups is influenced by the extent of their acculturation to mainstream culture.

- Many issues complicate the interpretation of racial, ethnic, and cultural group differences, including the effect of social expectations, difficulty in defining groups, inadequate sampling, confounding variables, and the effects of acculturation.

- To compare groups adequately, a test must have validity for both groups.

- Emic research develops tests within a culture. Etic research makes cross-cultural comparisons, using tests that are known to be valid in the various cultures.

- Much cross-cultural research uses standard personality tests, but the tests must be validated in each culture. Researchers trust tests more if they have similar factors across cultures and if translations from one language to another are confirmed by the back-translation method.

- Cultures are often classified as individualistic or collectivistic, depending upon whether they emphasize the goals and welfare of the individual or the group.

GLOSSARY

acculturation the cultural change that occurs when a person is in direct contact with a different cultural group

allocentrism   an individual's tendency to value group goals

back translation   a method for determining whether a test has been adequately translated into a foreign language by having it retranslated back into the original language to see whether it has the same meaning

bias   misinterpretation of a test, as when it is compared to inappropriate norms

collectivistic cultures cultures that emphasize group goals and welfare over the individual

confound correlate, as in two variables that are correlated, making it difficult to be sure which is really causing changes in other variables

cross-cultural comparing different countries or cultures

emic approach the development of measures within a culture, instead of using existing instruments that were developed in another culture

empathy awareness and sensitivity to another person's feelings

ethnicity social and cultural aspects of social group comparisons

etic approach the use of tests that have been shown to be universally valid across cultures

gender the term used to refer to being masculine or feminine, with the connotation that the differences are due to culture (rather than to biology)

idiocentrism the tendency of an individual to value individual, personal goals rather than group goals

individualistic cultures cultures that value individual, personal goals

individuality an emphasis on separateness from other people

meta-analysis a statistical technique used to combine several studies that test the same hypothesis in order to determine the overall finding

norms typical scores that are used as a basis for interpreting an individual's scores

race biological aspects of differences among populations of people

sex male or female, with the connotation that the differences are due to biology

sex role behaviors expected and approved in society that are different for males and females

social connectedness an emphasis on relationships with other people

socioeconomic status status in society as influenced by income, education, job level, and similar variables

test validity the quality of a test that has been shown to measure what it is intended to measure

THOUGHT QUESTIONS

1. List several variables that you think are probably confounded with differences between two groups (such as males and females, African Americans and white Americans, or any other two groups that you select). Can you think of any way to see whether these confounding variables cause personality differences between the groups?

2. Do you think that different norms should be used when deciding whether to admit applicants from various groups (for example, women or ethnic minorities) to college? Or should everyone be evaluated according to the same cutoff admission test score, regardless of background?

3. Discuss objections to studying sex differences. Do you think psychologists should continue to study the differences between males and females? Why or why not?

4. Summarize the differences that researchers have found between males and females. In your experience, are there individuals who are exceptions to these generalizations? Overall, do you believe the sexes are different in the ways that researchers have described?

5. When most people hear that research has found sex differences, do they assume that the differences are caused by biological factors, rather than culture? What effect does this assumption have on their interpretation of the results?

6. Why do you suppose there has been so little research on minority populations?

7. Do you think that students and psychologists can discuss research on racial and ethnic differences in an unbiased way?

8. Suppose that a psychology student at your school administers personality tests to students and reports the scores of various racial and ethnic groups. What would you expect to find? What cautions would you consider before interpreting these results?

9. What personality traits would be more strongly encouraged in an individualistic than a collectivistic culture? Are these the traits that you, personally, think are most important?

10. What advice would you give to a television or radio program director about reporting sex and race differences?

5

Studying Individuals

ALTHOUGH PERSONALITY RESEARCHERS seek to develop concepts and instruments that can be applied universally, we have seen that this goal is complicated by the diversity of humankind. We saw in the last chapter that we must consider differences in gender, race, and ethnicity if we are to interpret a personality score based on appropriate norms. Certainly if our method is to compare one individual with another, appropriate norms are essential. Are such comparisons sufficient to understand personality, however? Even populations that arc all one gender, all one race, or all one ethnicity have wide variability. Perhaps the challenge to understand an individual personality is even more fundamental than the quest for an appropriate comparison group.

We might try studying only one person at a time. A researcher using the **idiographic** approach studies one individual, making enough observations to describe the person in rich detail. The theorists and researchers described in this chapter advocate getting to know more about the individuals we are describing. This often means abandoning the more popular **nomothetic** tools (which measure individual differences in a group) that we have considered so far. Some of the topics studied from the idiographic approach are presented in Table 5.1.

TABLE 5.1   What Do Researchers Study about Individuals?

- Traits of an individual
- Most relevant traits, selected from a nomothetic list, to study a particular individual
- Central themes in an individual's life
- Various responses that an individual makes, arranged from most likely or most preferred to least likely or least preferred
- Description of the individual's subjective experience, including how events are interpreted by the individual
- Arrangement of variables (or traits) of an individual, including statistical descriptions by factor analysis and correlation
- Causes of an individual's behavior or personality development
- Prediction of what an individual will do in the future

Adapted, with modifications, from Runyan, 1983, p. 415.

The idiographic approach has roots in clinical practice (psychotherapy) and, to a lesser extent, in academic personality study. Clinicians, regardless of their theoretical convictions, have always had to deal with the individuals who are their clients. Sometimes they have been accused of allowing prior theoretical convictions to blind them to the uniqueness of the individual client. Yet it is far easier to overlook the individuality of a research subject answering a questionnaire in a large group, who is often literally anonymous to the researcher.

A Brief History of the Idiographic Perspective

The idiographic perspective has never been a dominant theme in the study of personality, but it has been an enduring minority voice and has recently claimed renewed attention (Pervin, 1985). In the past, critics argued that rigorous scientific methodology was incompatible with the idiographic position. As research methods have become more sophisticated, the idiographic position is gaining methodological credibility.

James Lamiell (1981) asserts that personality must focus on individual personality processes, an approach that he labels "idiothetic." Other *idio* terms have also been used to emphasize the study of individuals, such as "idiodynamics" and "idioverse" (Rosenzweig, 1958), "idiovalidation" (Harris, 1980) and, of course "idiographic." The point of this *idio* emphasis is that we must understand the individual, not only his or her relative standing in a group.

Gordon Allport's "Unique Traits"

Gordon Allport, whose concept of traits was the foundation of the trait approach described in Chapter 3, argued that personality researchers must study individuals as well as groups. He was convinced that no two individuals possess exactly the same traits. A nomothetic researcher "does not measure directly the full-bodied individual trait that alone exists as a neuro-psychic disposition and as the one irreducible unit of personality. What he does is to measure a common *aspect* of this trait, such a portion thereof as takes common forms of cultural expression" (Allport, 1937, p. 298). A researcher might say that two people both have the trait of "conscientiousness," for example, but one person's conscientiousness is different from the other's. One person might be timely and thorough in completing school work; the other might emphasize doing a fair share of the work around the house. All nomothetic research involves some overgeneralized and distorted understanding of individuals.

Implementing his own advice, Allport studied individuals. He often reported individual cases in his lectures as well as in his publications (Lewis, 1985). His analysis of one woman, based on her letters, has become a classic book: *Letters from Jenny* (Allport, 1965).

Despite his conviction, Allport could not persuade mainstream researchers of the importance of an idiographic approach. Perhaps the difficulty was not so much his position, but his inadequate defense of it (according to Lamiell, 1987). It was not Allport's crusade alone, though. Others failed to convince scientists because their emphasis on subjectivity and insight was difficult to reconcile with the objective language of science (Turner, 1967, pp. 288–291). Mainstream researchers continued their work, studying groups and ignoring the individual.

Carlson's Challenge: Find the Lost Person

The call for an alternative to nomothetic comparisons among people was made most pointedly by Rae Carlson, who asked a thought-provoking question: "Where is the person in personality research?" (Carlson, 1971, p. 203). She examined 226 research articles published in two prestigious personality journals (*Journal of Personality* and *Journal of Personality and*

Social Psychology) and found serious inadequacies in the literature. Among her criticisms were these findings:

- Seventy-one percent of studies collected data from undergraduates only.
- Seventy-eight percent of studies collected data in only a single session.
- Seventy-eight percent of studies used experimental research methods (in which subjects responded to a manipulation of the situation).
- Fifty-seven percent of studies deceived subjects in some way.

If personality researchers hoped to understand how adults outside the college setting behave over time in their own worlds (outside the laboratory), they were obviously not seeing a complete picture.

What is the alternative? Carlson (1971, 1982) advocated **personology,** a tradition that studies individuals in their complex social and biological worlds and that emphasizes individuality and striving. Such research, Carlson (1982) argues, requires studying individuals in depth over a span of time. This has been done in a few classic studies, where teams of professionals collected several folders full of data on each individual (for example, Block, 1971; Murray, 1938), and in several later studies. It is not the way most researchers work, however. For one thing, it requires a team of researchers to collect and analyze a huge amount of data, and that is very costly.

Others Join the Search for the Person

An ardent advocate of idiographic methods, William McKinley Runyan stated that "the goal of understanding *individual persons* is one of the most important objectives of personality psychology" (Runyan, 1983, p. 417 [italics added]; see also Runyan, 1990). The call for a holistic individual approach, one that considers the whole person and not just selected traits, has again been made recently (Magnusson & Törestad, 1993).

Why is a study of individuals needed? What is wrong with the trait approach, which measures individual differences? If we know a person's scores on several personality tests, isn't that enough? It is not. Consider this example comparing a typical nomothetic approach that studies a group of people with an idiographic approach that focuses on one individual. Studies of groups show that Neuroticism and Conscientiousness are negatively correlated; people who are high on one variable are usually low on the other (Costa, McCrae & Dye, 1991). In an individual, however, the association could be reversed. As a person reduces his or her neuroticism (perhaps by facing up to sources of anxiety), he or she may become more conscientious than before, rather than less so. Studies of groups measure trait scores. Studies of individuals measure psychological processes; that is, changes within an individual. These are different phenomena. James Lamiell states the difficulty bluntly: *"The empirical evidence generated by individual differences research* [that is, studies of groups] *has no legitimate interpretation whatsoever at the level of the individual"* (Lamiell, 1987, p. 15). Some advocates of the study of individuals go so far as to claim that the study of individual differences (the nomothetic trait approach) is not even central to the field of personality. As Jesse Harris phrases the issue, "It is at least as important to know how [a] trait relates to another trait in the same person as it is to know how that trait relates to the same trait in 1,000 other persons" (1980, p. 742).

The Moderator Variable Approach

Most researchers would not go all the way to idiography, yet many have included some components of an idiographic view in their research. Consider the following approach, suggested by Daryl Bem and Andrea Allen. If you are asked whether you are consistent across situations in displaying a trait (friendliness, for example), you might answer yes, or "no, it depends." If you say that you are consistent on the trait, then that trait predicts your behavior better than traits on which you say that you are less consistent ("it depends") (Bem & Allen, 1974). A variable, such as consistency, that has an impact on the relationship between two other variables is called a **moderator variable.** Consistency is thus one moderator of the trait-behavior relationship. Are there others?

Another moderator variable is the observability of trait behaviors. Traits that others can observe predict behavior better than those that are less observable (Kenrick & Stringfield, 1980). If a person claims to possess the traits of "moodiness" and "ambition" but says that others can observe the moodiness but not the ambition, then moodiness predicts measures of behavior better than ambition does. It seems obvious, doesn't it? Yet this approach is a step forward from the simple nomological method of trying to predict everyone's behavior from the same list of traits. Moderator approaches constitute, in the words of Hubert Hermans and Han Bonarius (1991a), "a shift toward people's individuality" (p. 204).

Modifying Traditional Approaches to Recognize Individuals

Continuing the strategy of Daryl Bem and Andrea Allen, several recent investigations of personality have used idiographic assessment techniques instead of giving exactly the same trait measures to everyone. For example, subjects may be permitted to select their own dimensions for categorizing people in personality perception studies (for example, Pavelchak, 1989). A method for measuring self-esteem has been devised that asks respondents to judge the importance of various areas (task success, social relationships, personal qualities) for their self-esteem (Overholser, 1993). In part, these advances come from theoretical considerations that recognize the uniqueness of individuals. In addition, they are facilitated by developments in computers that have made it possible to translate more complex theories into manageable methods for analyzing data.

All the approaches that we have considered so far, however, still collect data from groups of subjects. Although these methods show how nomothetic approaches have been modified to recognize individuals, they are not full-blown studies of individuals. Let us consider next the ways that people have been studied one individual at a time.

Clinical Case Studies

Therapists and other practitioners report their observations of individual patients or clients in the form of **case studies.** These reports give background information about the individual, describe the personality, and often describe the therapeutic experience. Case studies can be used to describe unusual or interesting phenomena and to develop or confirm theoretical ideas. They are useful sources for training clinicians (Jennings, 1986). Although many researchers discount the case study method, saying that it lacks the appropriate scientific controls, historically it has been the most basic method of clinical research (Runyan, 1982a, 1982b).

Those who write case studies are guided in their analysis by a particular theory, which helps them to decide which details are important and what caused the personality to develop as it did. Psychoanalysis is a psychological theory and form of therapy devised in the late nineteenth and early twentieth centuries by Sigmund Freud. Freud published case histories to illustrate psychoanalytic ideas, in particular the idea that various forms of maladjustment result from childhood experience and unconscious sexual conflict. The case of Dora illustrates his theory that sexual conflicts could lead to hysteria, a form of maladjustment. His analysis of a 5-year-old boy, Little Hans, illustrates the development of a phobia (an irrational fear). According to Freud, Little Hans came to fear horses based upon his childhood sexual conflicts (the Oedipus conflict). In addition, Freud (1963) reported another case of phobia (The Wolf Man), a case study of an obsessional neurosis (The Rat Man), and a paranoid illness (The Schreber case). Freud's analysis of Anna O is his classic statement of therapeutic cure using psychoanalytic methods (Breuer & Freud, 1925/1955; Ellenberger, 1972).

In contrast to Freud, whose case studies traced maladjustment to sexual conflicts and childhood experiences, other theorists reported different origins of personality problems. Among the alternative theoretical interpretations of case studies are humanistic psychology, which emphasizes subjective experience and growth (Rogers, 1961a); social learning theory, which emphasizes situations and how we think about them (Mischel, 1968, pp. 262–272); and personal construct theory, which emphasizes the individual's concepts for understanding the social world (Feixas & Villegas, 1991; Neimeyer, 1992; Viney, 1981).

Case studies provide rich descriptions of personality, but they have shortcomings. Case studies rely on the subjective judgment of the reporter to select relevant information from the extensive observations; perhaps others would judge different information to be relevant, even finding evidence that contradicts the interpretations made by the reporter that the reporter has overlooked. In addition, the clinician who reports the study may have influenced what the client reported, through the choice of questions or by less direct methods such as nonverbal displays of interest or approval. Thus, selective reporting and the observer's influence on the client make case histories less objective than the scientific method requires. Furthermore, because clinical case studies use therapy clients as subjects, we cannot be sure how relevant they are to understanding the general population.

Psychobiography

Can the case study method be applied to people who are not patients? It can. **Psychobiography** consists of the application of psychological theory to the understanding of biographical materials. Biographical materials include a variety of personal documents, such as diaries, letters, memoirs, and autobiographies (Wrightsman, 1981). In the past, psychobiographies were almost always produced from a psychoanalytic perspective, that is, based on Sigmund Freud's theory of psychoanalysis and on revisions of psychoanalytic theory proposed by others. In recent decades, the literature in psychobiography and the related field of psychohistory has increased dramatically (Runyan, 1987, 1988b). Now, diverse theories beyond psychoanalysis also guide psychobiography, and the field has won a wider audience (McAdams, 1988; Runyan, 1982b).

Psychoanalytic Psychobiography

Psychoanalysis and psychobiography have a close affinity. John Mack traces the origins of psychoanalytic interest in biography to 1906–1910, when Freud and his colleagues "sought to find in the lives and works of artists and writers confirmation of the importance of sexuality in the production of psychopathology" (1980, p. 545). In addition to sexuality, psychoanalysis emphasizes development from childhood to adulthood and provides a framework for understanding subjective experience, including emotions and dreams. These themes have become important in psychobiography.

Some psychologists have claimed that only clinicians, preferably those trained as psychoanalysts, are prepared to do psychobiographical analysis (Munter, 1975; Pois, 1990). This precaution stems from the danger that a

TABLE 5.2 Freud's Advice to Psychobiographers

- Avoid arguments built upon a single clue.

- Avoid pathologizing the psychobiographical subject.

- Avoid idealizing the psychobiographical subject.

- Avoid drawing strong conclusions from inadequate data.

Adapted from Elms, 1988a.

biographer will make errors of interpretation because of unresolved personal issues (Falk, 1985). For example, a biographer who has unresolved conflicts with parents may exaggerate the importance of such conflicts in the biography. Psychoanalytic training is supposed to resolve such personal issues, enabling the clinician to be more objective about clients' problems and presumably more objective in analyzing nonpatient psychobiographies as well. In some cases, biographers who were not psychoanalysts have collaborated with psychoanalysts to be able to write more insightful biographies (Baron & Pletsch, 1985).

In addition to case histories of some of his patients, Sigmund Freud wrote analyses of several famous people whom he had never met, notably the artist Leonardo da Vinci (1910/1957) and the Jewish patriarch Moses (1939/1959). Freud traced creativity and other strengths to roots in unconscious aspects of personality (which he believed also provided the source of neurosis). He traced the famous Mona Lisa painting to Leonardo da Vinci's experience with two mothers, a natural mother and a stepmother. Freud based much of his admittedly speculative analysis on Leonardo's report of an early childhood memory. In that memory, a vulture came to Leonardo in his cradle and penetrated his mouth with its tail. Freud interpreted the memory as a homosexual wish. Freud's interpretation was flawed, however, because he based it on an erroneous translation of Leonardo's writing. (The "vulture" was actually a different kind of bird, a kite.)

As Freud's error shows, psychobiography is not an exact method. Freud described guidelines for writing psychobiography (Table 5.2). Nonetheless, he has been criticized for violating his own advice. Alan Elms (1988a) argues that Freud worked through some of his own personal issues while writing the psychobiography and projected onto da Vinci what was really Freud's own personality. Freud also collaborated with William Bullitt, an American diplomat, on a study of the American president Thomas Woodrow Wilson that was published several years after Freud's death (Freud & Bullitt, 1966). Critics suggest that this work was poorly done

What secrets lie behind the Mona Lisa's enigmatic smile? Sigmund Freud believed that Leonardo da Vinci's experience with his mother and stepmother are expressed in his painting.

and that it was primarily the work of Bullitt rather than Freud (Erikson, 1975; Mack, 1971).

Freud's example inspired other psychoanalytic psychobiographies (Loewenberg, 1988). Creative artists, such as Beethoven (Ciardiello, 1985), have been favorite targets of psychoanalytic psychobiography. Leon Edel

(1953–1971) analyzed the writer Henry James from this perspective, interpreting his fictional work as evidence about psychological conflicts. Psychoanalytic interpretations of persons displaying pathologies are abundant, particularly regarding subjects who are historically salient, such as Adolf Hitler (for example, Leavy, 1985).

Criticism of Psychoanalytic Psychobiography Not surprisingly, the bold project of applying psychoanalytic theory to biography has been subjected to much criticism. Although the theory can explain personality after the fact, it does not predict it in advance. If both neurosis and artistic creativity stem from early experience, why does one person suffer pathology and another produce creative works? As John Mack asks, "Why was not Swift with his too early toilet training (speculated) merely obsessive?" (Mack, 1971, p. 152).

William McKinley Runyan (1988a) reviewed criticisms of psychoanalytic psychobiography. He concluded that while they have some merit, they do not discredit psychobiography entirely. What are these shortcomings? First, psychoanalytic psychobiography *builds on inadequate evidence.* After all, the theory proposes that personality is determined largely by the events of infancy and early childhood, for which records are rarely adequate. Psychobiographers typically do not have firsthand information but must rely on reports about their subject that may be distorted in unknown ways (Mack, 1971), such as Freud's reliance on an erroneous translation of Leonardo da Vinci's recollections. Furthermore, psychobiographers often rely on secondary sources, rather than the original records, letters, and other materials, so that even existing information may be neglected (Anderson, 1981). Second, the analysis often *reconstructs events* from childhood, based on theoretical interpretation of clues from the adult record. The subject's memories of childhood are not always available to the biographer, and even when available they are undependable, since research has demonstrated the frailty and plasticity of memory. Third, psychoanalytic psychobiography is accused of *reductionism*, focusing only on those causes that are described in psychoanalytic theory, while neglecting equally important causes that are outside its scope. For example, one analysis of Adolf Hitler's construction of gas chambers to exterminate Jews reduces this act to retaliation for the accidental killing of his mother, overdosed with anesthetic gas during surgery by a Jewish doctor (an interpretation criticized by Loewenberg, 1988). Is it reasonable to reduce explanation of a person's life to intrapsychic factors, to early childhood experiences and one-time events, and to pathology? Freudian psychobiography overemphasizes personality as the cause of events, while neglecting history and the social environment (Table 5.3).

Erikson's Disciplined Subjectivity The term **psychohistory** was used by Erik Erikson (Mack, 1971) to emphasize the interrelationship of the individual personality and the historical setting. His approach to

TABLE 5.3 The Distorted Lens of Psychoanalytic Psychobiography

Psychoanalytic theory emphasizes these aspects	*But neglects these*
Psychological factors (e.g., conflicts over unfulfilled dependency needs)	Social and historical factors
Psychopathological processes ("pathography")	Normal processes and creativity
Critical periods of development (the "critical period fallacy"), especially early childhood experiences (called "originology" by Erikson)	Development throughout life, including experiences in later childhood, adolescence, and adulthood
One-time critical events ("eventism")	The cumulative effects of experience

Adapted from information in Runyan, 1988a, pp. 223–224.

psychobiography (renamed "psychohistory") emphasizes the individual's interrelationships with society, in contrast to the more exclusively individual focus of Freudian psychobiography (Hutton, 1983; Schnell, 1980; Wurgaft, 1976).

Erikson analyzed important historical figures: Adolf Hitler and Maxim Gorky (1950), Martin Luther (1962), and Mahatma Gandhi (1969). His analyses went beyond the individual and showed how the individual's development was intertwined with culture and history; they also showed that the individual both was influenced by society and had the potential to have an impact on it. He explored the search for identity during adolescence in two creative writers, George Bernard Shaw and William James (Erikson, 1968). Erikson described the psychobiographer's method as one of "disciplined subjectivity" (1975, p. 25), a phrase he also used to describe a clinician's stance toward the patient (Erikson, 1958, p. 68). The psychobiographer, like the analyst in therapy, brings personal motivations to the interpretive task that must be recognized so that they do not distort the interpretations (Pois, 1990).

Erikson made many contributions to psychohistorical interpretations. In contrast to Freud's emphasis on pathology, Erikson described the personality strengths of his subjects (Fitzpatrick, 1976). In his interpretation of Mahatma Gandhi, Erikson (1969) described unresolved psychological issues, such as his relationship with his mother. In addition, Erikson described Gandhi's political activities, particularly nonviolent resistance to political oppression. Gandhi's psychological "transformation and redirection of aggression and violence toward creative human and political ends"

(Mack, 1971, p. 172) has implications for history, both in India and beyond (Lorimer, 1976). It is characteristic of Erikson's interest in the mutual influence of the individual and society that he examined this theme in detail.

Erikson's analysis of Martin Luther, the Protestant Reformation theologian, also illustrates the influence of the individual on history:

> *Instead of treating Luther as a patient exhibiting symptoms of depression, paranoia, obsessions, and compulsions that are only incidentally historically relevant, Erikson relates Luther's life history to the historical process in such a way as to emphasize how an extraordinary person like Luther may "lift his individual patienthood to the level of a universal one and to try to solve for all what he could not solve for himself alone." (Fitzpatrick, 1976, p. 303, who quotes Erikson, 1962, p. 67)*

In contrast to Freudian psychoanalysis, which focuses on the individual and does not consider historical change, Erikson emphasized the historical setting and noted that individual development was intertwined with history. Luther, Gandhi, and American youth struggling with identity issues must be understood within the historical context. Furthermore, their personal struggles can shape history, as the adolescent struggles of the hippies of the 1960s influenced America's Vietnam War.

Other Theoretical Perspectives Other theories besides Freudian psychoanalysis and Erikson's modified psychoanalytic theory have guided

Mahatma Gandhi's life of political activism and passive resistance against colonialism was explored by Erik Erikson, using his psychological technique of "disciplined subjectivity."

psychobiography. Most of these alternatives are also variations of psycho-analytic approaches. Marilyn Monroe has been interpreted from the per-spective of Melanie Klein's object relations approach, which is derived from psychoanalysis (Moes, 1990). Alfred Adler's neo-psychoanalytic the-ory has guided psychobiographers (Pozzuto, 1982). From Adler's perspec-tive, power strivings have been interpreted in the biographies of Winston Churchill (Rintala, 1984) and G. Gordon Liddy (Lewis, 1983). Adolf Hitler's pathology can be traced from a pampered childhood to disturbed aspirations and social relationships throughout life (Brink, 1975). Robert Tucker (1985) interpreted Joseph Stalin, using Karen Horney's neo-psy-choanalytic theory to explore how the dictator's inflated self-image played out in the history of Russia. Also using Horney's theory, Joseph Shulim (1977) interpreted the French revolutionary Robespierre.

Although psychoanalytic psychobiography has predominated, many other personality theories can be applied to psychobiography (Cloninger, 1993; Lewis, 1985; Runyan, 1988a), including Raymond Cattell's factor analytic theory (Wright, 1985). Even psychological theories in other areas, such as social and developmental psychology and medicine (Runyan, 1988b), can assist the psychobiographer. In addition, some psychobio-graphical interpretations are not explicitly tied to any theory, although the-oretical perspectives are implicit (for example, Nichtern,1985).

Limitations of Theory-Driven Psychobiography

For all its intrinsic interest and its promise to bridge the gap between psy-chological theory and individuals' lives as they are lived in the real world outside the laboratory, psychobiography has serious limitations from a sci-entific point of view. Like psychoanalytic biography, discussed earlier, psy-chobiography in general rests on the psychobiographer's subjective interpretations and lacks a method for scientific verification, a problem that haunts the clinical uses of psychoanalysis as well (Fitzpatrick, 1976; Rubinstein, 1980). The psychobiographer's emotional feelings about the person being interpreted can distort the analysis (Meyer, 1987; Schepeler, 1990), although subjectivity in psychobiography can also make positive contributions to knowledge (Pletsch, 1985). Furthermore, there is so much material available to psychobiographers that it is easy to select only mater-ial that confirms the guiding theory, overlooking other relevant material. Thus, psychobiography is not a sound method for testing theory.

William McKinley Runyan (1981) underscores the difficulty of making definitive interpretations by listing 13 plausible explanations for the inci-dent in which Vincent van Gogh, the artist, cut off part of his ear and pre-sented it to a prostitute. Alternative accounts seem to be the rule rather than the exception; the lives of Jesus, Shakespeare, and Lincoln can also be interpreted in diverse ways (Runyan, 1982b). So how can psychobiographical explanations be given any credence? Runyan acknowledges that often there is more than a single explanation; after all, many causes interact to determine human behavior. He contends, however, that psychobiographers' alternative explanations are not limitless, nor are they malleable to suit the interpreter's arbitrary theoretical preference. Thorough examination of evidence can rule out some alternative explanations.

At minimum, verification would require agreement between two independent biographers who, dealing with the same materials, would make the same interpretations. This method has not been reported. Even if it were, agreement would establish reliability (consistency) but not necessarily validity (accuracy).

Systematic Analysis of Biographical Materials

Given the difficulties of achieving a scientifically defensible psychobiographical analysis from a psychoanalytic or other personality theory perspective, researchers have suggested alternatives. These alternatives rely less on the subjective, and potentially erroneous, interpretations of analysts by providing systematic methods for analyzing biographical materials.

Tomkins's Script Theory

Silvan Tomkins (1962; 1979a; 1979b; 1987) has proposed a detailed theory for understanding individual lives. Like psychoanalysis, it traces development from the early years through adulthood. Unlike psychoanalysis, it is a theory rooted in psychological processes as they have been described by personality researchers, rather than emerging from clinical work. Tomkins's theory is concerned with affect (emotion) and cognition, two basic psychological processes. He postulates that, influenced by individual experience and cultural learning, a person strives to gain control over positive and negative emotions by developing them into scripts that predict emotion and prescribe appropriate behavior. For example, a "commitment script" may bind a person to a life of hard work for the sake of family. A "sedative script" may mandate reduction of unpleasant emotions through alcohol, eating, or other methods (Tomkins, 1987). Knowing the scripts that a person has developed provides the key to understanding that individual.

Rae Carlson (1988), an enthusiastic supporter of Tomkins's script theory, interpreted two individuals from this theoretical perspective: Nathaniel Hawthorne, the novelist who wrote *The Scarlet Letter*; and

Sometimes people live out unhealthy "scripts," such as overeating to soothe unpleasant emotions. Other scripts, such as working hard for the family, may be more adaptive.

Eleanor Marx, the youngest daughter of the founder of communism, Karl Marx. In addition, she used the theory to interpret an individual who participated in a research project, and she reported that scripts formed in childhood helped to explain this person's adult experience more than 30 years later (Carlson, 1981). She suggests, however, that psychologists should not usually do psychobiography, because they have not been trained in the necessary specialized methods of working with historical material. Rather, psychologists ought to focus their attention on developing psychological theories that psychobiographers can apply and test (Carlson, 1988).

Alexander's Method: Let the Data Reveal Itself

The chief difficulty with psychobiographical research is that it depends so heavily on the subjective judgments of the psychobiographer. In making these judgments, the biographer imposes theory on the data, determining what is important on the basis of preconceived theoretical ideas. Psychoanalysis, for example, assumes that early sexual experience, breast feeding, and toilet training are important, and will seize upon even small bits of evidence about these issues to build an interpretation. In contrast, Irving Alexander (1988, 1990) has developed a systematic method for analyzing biographical data based on the principle of "letting the data reveal itself" (1988, p. 268). This approach focuses attention on the raw data. It can be applied to a variety of types of material, including autobiographical essays, interviews, diaries, dreams, letters, and so on.

Several guidelines help the interpreter decide what is important (Table 5.4). The portions of data on which researchers choose to focus are called *salient extractions.* The researcher then transforms these extractions into *salient units,* each of which is a "microscopic stor[y] with an introduction, an action, and an outcome" (Alexander, 1988, p. 278). For example, Alexander decoded the following salient unit in one young man's description of his attempts to establish intimacy with women: "intimacy → attempts to establish intimacy → success → fear of being controlled and infantalized → withdrawal, disillusionment, reduction of need → renewed emphasis on other sources of gratification [work]" (1990, p. 30). The "salient extractions" (intimacy, attempts to establish intimacy, and so forth) are joined into the "salient unit," which connects all of them in a sequence. Even without reading the raw material upon which this abstraction is based, we can get an impression of the person. Furthermore, since the sequence was derived from the raw materials without the interposition of a theory, the data have been allowed to speak for themselves. Extracted

TABLE 5.4   Clues to Important Details in Biography

1. *Primacy:* What occurs first

2. *Frequency:* What is repeated

3. *Uniqueness:* What the subject says is unusual or unique

4. *Negation:* What the subject denies

5. *Emphasis:* What the subject calls to our attention

6. *Omission:* What is unexpectedly left out

7. *Error:* What is distorted or mistaken

8. *Isolation:* What is kept separate from everything else

9. *Incompletion:* What is ended without reaching closure

Adapted from Alexander, 1990, pp. 15–24.

sequences such as this can then be subjected to further analysis by applying questions or hypotheses to them, perhaps ones suggested by theory. By separating the data extraction from the theory, there is less chance that theoretical expectations will distort observations.

Content Analysis

Content analysis is an approach to data analysis that codes text to describe the frequency with which predefined themes or categories occur. Like Alexander's method, content analysis ensures that researchers will remain close to the materials that they are analyzing, rather than venturing too far into inferences. Some systems of content analysis are guided by theories, but these theories differ from psychoanalysis and its offshoots in that they allow for more diversity of personality. They do not propose universal conflicts or stages that affect everyone. Rather, they assume some global category—such as traits, motives, or emotional processes—that takes diverse forms in each individual's biographical materials. Content analysis then describes the uniqueness of the individual within these general categories.

Gordon Allport developed this method to analyze a series of letters written over an 11-year period by a woman named Jenny Grove Masterson. In his book, *Letters From Jenny*, Allport determined that eight traits prevailed in Jenny's personality: quarrelsome-suspicious, self-centered, independent-autonomous, dramatic-intense, aesthetic-artistic, aggressive, cynical-morbid, and sentimental (Allport, 1965). A variety of systems of content analysis have been developed since this beginning (Krippendorff, 1980; Smith, 1992a).

Computerized Lexical Analysis
Although most coding requires human judgments by trained coders, some researchers have automated the coding procedure by having computers scan text for particular words (Broehl & McGee, 1981; Stone et al., 1966). This **lexical analysis** approach sometimes involves a simple count of words that match those on the predefined list. More sophisticated programs take into account parts of speech and sentence structure. Of course, human coders can also look for specific words without a computer, and this would also constitute a lexical analysis.

Content Analysis to Uncover Implicit Personality Theories
When people write, whether about their own lives or fiction, they reflect their implicit personality theory (as described in Chapter 2). What traits are important to the writer? What traits are correlated? Content analysis can be used to decipher this implicit personality theory.

Seymour Rosenberg and Russell Jones (1972) analyzed the novel *A Gallery of Women*, written by Theodore Dreiser. That work was particularly well-suited for this purpose, because it describes 15 female characters in detail. The researchers searched the book for words and phrases that described stable characteristics of each character (much as Allport and Odbert, discussed in Chapter 2, had searched the dictionary for trait words). Words that were essentially synonymous were grouped together. Then the researchers determined, statistically, which traits tended to occur together in descriptions of the same person. The implicit personality disclosed in this way was congruent with information about Dreiser's own life. For example, characters that were described as nonconformist were also described as suffering and lonely. The results were compared with a theoretical model but did not fit the model. This finding supports the value of being guided by raw data rather than by prior theory.

Rosenberg and Jones's method was later adapted to describe perceptions of political leaders by Henry Kissinger, assistant to the president for national security, then secretary of state under President Nixon (Swede & Tetlock, 1986). Kissinger's published book, *White House Years* (1979), constituted the raw data for this study. Traits were identified, and various ways of clustering them were compared, using alternative statistical models. This analysis resulted in a detailed description of nine types of leaders that Kissinger implicitly distinguished: three individuals (Kissinger himself, Chou En-lai, and Georges Pompidou), a Revolutionary type, a Patriot type, two types of friends (Personal Friend and Professional Friend), and two types of opponents (Able Adversaries and Professional Competitors). The results are specific to Kissinger, of course. Without further evidence, it would not be sensible to assume that others would perceive political leaders along the same dimensions. On the other hand, this kind of highly person-specific information could have obvious value for anyone who wanted to understand Kissinger well (for example, a potential political ally or an opponent). Furthermore, it can be argued that understanding the implicit theory of political types of an expert in this area, such as Kissinger, may teach something to psychologists, who are otherwise too dependent on data from undergraduate subjects and clinic patients.

Coding for Motives

Henry Murray's name is historically important in personality theory as an early advocate of the in-depth study of individuals. At the Harvard Psychological Clinic, he and several colleagues collected a great deal of information from 50 undergraduate men using several data collection techniques, including interviews, psychological tests, and behavioral tests. This study has been published as the classic *Explorations in Personality* (Murray, 1938), and it is regarded as a major work in the intensive study of individuals. Murray and his associates interpreted a thick folder of data on each subject, inferring the man's motives and other psychological characteristics.

TABLE 5.5 Twenty Needs Identified by Henry Murray

Abasement	Defendance	Play
Achievement	Dominance	Rejection
Affiliation	Exhibition	Sentience
Aggression	Harmavoidance	Sex
Autonomy	Infavoidance	Succorance
Counteraction	Nurturance	Understanding
Deference	Order	

Adapted from Murray, 1938, pp. 144–145.

He listed 20 needs or motives that were important to a different extent to various individuals (Table 5.5).

One legacy of this intensive study of individuals has been the development of systematic ways to code motives from a psychological testing technique called the Thematic Apperception Test. Subjects look at pictures and tell creative stories based on these pictures. The researcher codes these stories for imagery related to particular motives. Three motivations have been widely studied: Achievement, Affiliation, and Power. Many studies assess these motives in the usual nomothetic fashion. That is, tests are given to groups of subjects, and their scores compared and correlated with some criterion. (For example, in a large group of students, do those who score highest on need for Achievement earn the highest grades?) In addition, the methods for scoring these motives have been applied to psychobiographical analysis.

David Winter and Leslie Carlson (1988) analyzed President Richard Nixon's 1969 inaugural address for motivation. The profile they found was one of high achievement motivation, high affiliation-intimacy motivation, and average power motivation (compared with other presidents' inaugural speeches). They interpreted biographical details from Nixon's life as consistent with the motivational imagery from the speech. In a later administration, Winter and his colleagues used the motivational analysis, supplemented by other coding techniques, to profile the political leadership of George Bush and Mikhail Gorbachev. They interpreted both leaders as motivated more by achievement and affiliation needs than by power needs and predicted that both would be peacemakers, avoiding war (Winter et al., 1991b). Such predictions are bold, given history's public test; the prognosticators did not foresee all subsequent political develop-

By analyzing the public statements of political leaders, researchers make inferences about their underlying motivations. On this basis, David Winter and his colleagues predicted that peace, rather than war, would prevail under George Bush and Mikhail Gorbachev.

ments, particularly the Persian Gulf War (Winter et al., 1991a). The motivational analysis method has been applied to other American presidents as well, and scores are consistent with the judgments of historians and political scientists (Donley & Winter, 1970). The motivational analysis does not replace analysis of biographical details as in traditional psychobiography, but it is an interesting supplement.

Judgments by Coders: Rating Scales

The idiosyncratic dimensions that emerge from content analysis make it difficult to compare across individuals. A compromise between idiographic aims and nomothetic comparisons can be achieved by having coders evaluate the biographical materials based on a predetermined set of criteria, which can then be compared across individuals. For example, Bernard Bass and Dana Farrow (1977) asked students who read biographies of political leaders to evaluate the materials on several 5-point rating scales measuring aspects of the leaders' relationships with subordinates (for example, "warmth and trust between managers and others").

As these methods show, researchers have developed ways of describing individuals that are more systematic than the subjective judgments of case studies and psychobiography.

Collecting Research Data from the Individual

So far, we have considered descriptions of an individual in which data generally are not collected explicitly for purposes of research. Case studies are secondary to therapy, and psychobiographies rely on existing biographical data. Although the method of analysis may be very subjective (as in psychoanalytic psychobiography) or very systematic (as in content coding), in both cases the data available to the researcher can be distorted by uncontrolled influences.

Can individuals be studied only in such uncontrolled situations? Fortunately not. Researchers have devised new approaches to collect data on individuals. Although we can never control all the influences in a person's life, we can eliminate some sources of error at the time of observation. Like wiping dirt from a window, this elimination of error should give us a clearer vision.

Role Construct Repertory (REP) Test

The **Role Construct Repertory (REP) test** was devised by George Kelly to provide therapists with a more structured assessment method than a clinical interview. Rather than asking his clients to tell about their feelings and their childhood experiences, which required him to evaluate this material subjectively, he devised a written instrument. His theory emphasized the importance of how people interpret other people (similar to the implicit personality theories discussed in Chapter 2). Kelly proposed that each person has a unique set of **personal constructs,** which are concepts for understanding and predicting people by thinking of them in either-or categories. Some common personal constructs that classify people into categories are "warm versus cold," "motivated versus contented," and "mature versus childish." Each person has many personal constructs, and these vary from person to person. If we know a person's personal constructs, argued Kelly, we have the key to that individual's personality.

Kelly measured personal constructs by having people complete a form like the one in Figure 5.1. First, the person being tested lists specific individuals who fit descriptions given by the researcher: a happy person, a successful person, and so on. Then, one row at a time, the subject considers the three people who are indicated by circles: "How are two of these people alike, and how are they different from the third?" Column 1 contains the description of how two people are alike. Column 2 tells how the third is different. Once a construct is defined for each row, the subject goes back and fills in all the boxes without circles, putting a 1 in the box to indicate that the person in that column is like the description in column 1, or a 2 to indicate that the person is like the description in column 2. Although there are many scoring systems for this test, simply looking at the list of con-

Response Sheet

Column 1	Mother	Father	Happy person	Successful person	Andy (self)	Brian (son)	Mike (son)	Sharon (wife)	Beth (lover)	Therapist	Column 2	
1 Someone I love	1	1	1	1	2	1	1	1	1	1	Someone I hate	1
2 Lack sensitivity	1	2	1	2	2	2	2	2	2	2	Sensitive	2
3 Committed to family	1	1	1	1	1	1	2	2	2	2	Independent	3
4 Understanding	2	1	1	1	1	2	1	2	1	1	Impatient	4
5 Bright	1	1	1	1	2	1	1	1	1	1	Just average	5
6 Very inward	1	1	2	1	1	1	1	2	2	1	Very outspoken	6
7 Childlike inside	2	1	2	1	1	1	1	2	1	2	Get what you see	7
8 Have real communication	2	2	2	2	2	2	1	1	1	1	Aloof	8
9 Easy going	2	1	1	1	1	1	1	2	1	1	Emotional	9
10 Unaffectionate	2	2	1	1	2	2	2	1	2	0	Likes to touch	10

FIGURE 5.1   *One person's responses on the Role Construct Repertory (REP) test. Numbers indicate whether the person named in that column fits the construct in column 1 or its opposite pole in column 2. The number 0, as seen in the bottom right corner, indicates that neither column applies. The respondent first names the construct for each row and fills in the circled cells (which should identify two people as column 1 types and one person as a column 2 type, although, as this respondent illustrates, not everyone follows that instruction). (Adapted from R. A. Neimeyer, 1992.)*

structs gives a fairly detailed understanding of the personal constructs of the individual, enabling the clinician (or researcher) to see the world through the eyes of that individual.

Comparing within a Person: Ipsative Assessment

The normative research methods that we have considered in previous chapters give each subject a score based on comparison with other people. On a values survey, for example, a person might get a score of 89 for social service, indicating a high value for social service compared to other people, and a score of 78 for financial rewards, indicating a high value for financial rewards. (Let's assume that an "average" score on each scale is 50.) Does this mean that this person values social service above salary? For example, will he or she take a job that pays poorly in order to feed the homeless? Not necessarily. The difficulty is that each score is compared with the normative population. Perhaps the population as a whole values financial rewards considerably more than social service. In that case, while the individual is *relatively* higher in social service (relative, that is, to the population), he or she is *absolutely* higher in valuing financial rewards. Given a choice, then, between good pay and social service, pay will prevail (Fig. 5.2).

Asking Subjects to Compare Choices   The shortcoming of normative methods is that we cannot compare one trait with another for a particular individual in an absolute sense. Yet such comparisons are essential if we want to predict what individuals will do. An **ipsative** method provides that information. Ipsative methods compare alternatives within an individual. Here is an example of an ipsative question:

> Here are five things to consider in choosing a job. Rank order them in order of importance to you. (Place a 1 in front of the most important, a 2 in front of the next most important, and so on, using the numbers 1 through 5.)
>
> ___ good pay
> ___ job security
> ___ a safe work environment
> ___ good relationships with coworkers
> ___ challenging assignments

Ipsative measures such as this compare the strength of variables (values, traits, and so on) *within the individual.*

Ipsative Judgments by Coders: Q-Sort Method   An innovative coding method was used by Jack Block in his extensive research on children's development from childhood to adulthood (Block, 1971). Extensive files of data were collected for the same set of children at several different ages. Diverse measures had been used over the years, including interviews, parent ratings, tests, and so on. The particular measures varied from one age to another, because it isn't appropriate to give the same measures to young children and to older adolescents. To determine whether individual children changed over time or remained consistent, it was necessary to find a common way of describing these different sets of data. Block achieved this by having coders read each folder and then describe the individual by sorting a deck of cards, each printed with a word or phrase, into various piles to indicate how well that descriptor applied to the individual. The number of cards that could be put into each pile (very much like the per-

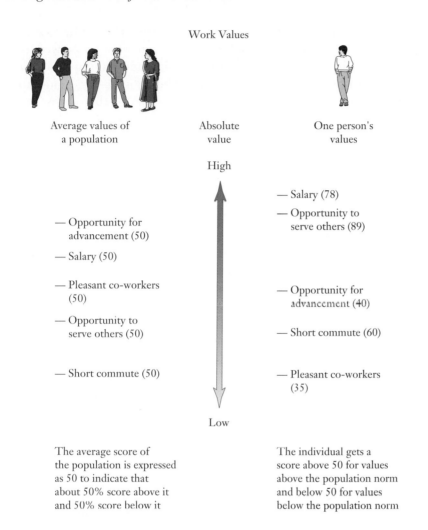

Work Values

Average values of a population

Absolute value

One person's values

High

— Salary (78)
— Opportunity to serve others (89)

— Opportunity for advancement (50)

— Salary (50)

— Pleasant co-workers (50)

— Opportunity to serve others (50)

— Opportunity for advancement (40)

— Short commute (60)

— Short commute (50)

— Pleasant co-workers (35)

Low

The average score of the population is expressed as 50 to indicate that about 50% score above it and 50% score below it

The individual gets a score above 50 for values above the population norm and below 50 for values below the population norm

FIGURE 5.2 *Compared to what? Comparisons with other people don't always mean what they seem to.*

son, somewhat like the person, and so on) was standard for all coders and all individuals described. This method, called the **Q-sort,** allows coders to describe individuals in a way that can be compared across subjects and across time.

In-Depth Individual Interviews

Researchers can study individuals by interviewing them and asking them questions about their lives. The questions may be planned in advance (structured interviews), or they may be modified as the interview proceeds to follow up on material that may not have been anticipated in advance (unstructured or semistructured interviews). In addition to asking questions, the researcher may ask the respondent to fill out questionnaires or take personality tests.

In one study of convicted murderers, researchers began by having each participant write an autobiography. Several interviews followed over a period of months, and participants revised their autobiographies based on interactions with a team of professionals. These "negotiated biographies" provide insights into the subjects' interpretations of their lives and also offer the opportunity to revise those interpretations (DeWaele & Harré, 1979).

The Self-Confrontation Method: Dialog with the Individual

Hubert Hermans (1988, 1991) describes an innovative research method that involves a collaborative interview with the research participants. He calls this method the **self-confrontation method.** He considers the research participant to be an expert in the particulars of his or her life and the researcher to be an expert in the general theory that guides the process and in the interview procedures. The interview begins with general questions about the past, present, and future. One question, for example, is this: "Was there something in your past that has been of major importance or significance for your life and which still plays an important part today?" (Hermans, 1991, p. 222). About the future, one question is, "Is there a goal or object that you expect to play an important role in your future life?" (Hermans, 1991, p. 222). By discussing these questions, the research participant and the researcher develop a list of valuations. A **valuation** is an emotionally charged unit of meaning for the individual. There are many kinds of valuations, including memories, problems, people, dreams, and so on. Consider what your own valuations might be: for example, a memory of winning a competitive event, difficulty with your parents, a nightmare. Each valuation is assessed for its emotional meaning by rating 16 emotions (Table 5.6). Scores are computed by combining related emotions, resulting in four categories: self-enhancement (S), contact and union with others (O), positive affects (P), and negative affects (N). Valuations can change over time, and the participant is generally interviewed again after several weeks or months to assess change. This can provide evidence of change resulting from psychotherapy. While valuations are unique to each person, the patterns of the four category scores can be compared across people (Hermans, 1988).

Behavioral Assessment

Behaviorism is a psychological perspective with a long and respected history in psychology, but it is usually not considered in relationship to personality. Behaviorists, including John Watson and B. F. Skinner, studied

TABLE 5.6 **Emotional Patterns in Herman's Self-Confrontation Method**

Self-enhancement:	Positive affect:
Self-esteem	Joy
Strength	Happiness
Self-confidence	Enjoyment
Pride	Inner calm
Contact and union with others:	Negative affect:
Caring	Worry
Love	Unhappiness
Tenderness	Despondency
Intimacy	Disappointment

Adapted from Hermans, 1991, p. 222.

the external determinants of behavior, especially environmental stimuli and rewards. They argued that psychology is the science of behavior and that behavior is determined by stimuli and reinforcers that are external to the person or, often in their research, to the animal. They explicitly refused to explain behavior in terms of internal determinants, such as personality traits. The theory seems discordant in a text where we are attempting to understand unique human personalities, yet its methods are applicable, especially for studying individuals.

Behavioral assessment techniques study individuals one at a time in a controlled environment to determine how environmental conditions influence behavior. Researchers might observe a problem child, for example, to see what situations instigate misbehavior. The behavioral researcher might establish that placing him in a time-out room away from other children after he has misbehaved has the effect of reducing hitting and other problem behaviors. Even though there is only one subject, rather than the usual group of subjects, it is possible to test such interventions with statistics to determine that they are effective; research designs have been developed specifically for the study of single case experiments (Hersen & Barlow, 1976; Kratochwill, 1978). Although only one individual is studied in each experiment, replications with other individuals can be tested. The series of studies then can establish whether the causes are general or specific to an individual (Bass, 1987).

Behavioral approaches have often been applied in therapy, and they have guided basic research. In addition, a few studies of individual biographies have been guided by this theory, including a reinterpretation of Freud's famous case study, Little Hans, and a brief interpretation of Benjamin Franklin. Such analyses obviously do not have the close environmental control that is essential in behavioral research and treatment. Instead, they speculate about the environmental determinants that have influenced an individual's life. Naturally, the recognized leader of behaviorism, B. F. Skinner, also applied many behavioral principles to understanding his own life (Runyan, 1988a).

Where Should the Person Be in Personality Research?

Let us return to the question posed early in this chapter, Rae Carlson's challenge of a quarter century ago, "Where is the person in personality research?" Although the individual often has been lost in the predominant nomothetic approach of group averages, individuals have been the focus of attention for a surprising diversity of theorists, ranging from Freud with his therapy to Skinner with his animal laboratories. Methods of studying individuals range from subjective descriptions to carefully detailed content analyses. So there is much interest in the study of the individual. How can we place this interest in the context of the study of personality? Let us look at objections to the study of individuals and then consider the contributions of such study to understanding personality.

Scientific Skepticism

Throughout the history of psychology, many critics have expressed doubt that studies of individuals can be scientific (Eysenck, 1954; Skaggs, 1945). To be sure, some have defended the scientific status of this approach (Corsini, 1986), but generally researchers have thought it more scientific to study groups so that the peculiarities of individuals would cancel one another out and idiosyncratic characteristics would not be mistaken for general phenomena. Consider three major objections to studying individuals.

No Predictions   The chief shortcoming of studies of individuals is that they *fail to make predictions in advance* that can be tested by objective observations (Eysenck, 1986a). This failure is a serious violation of the hypothesis testing model of science. In psychoanalytic case studies, the analyst makes interpretations, but they are not systematically tested. Freud and many of his defenders found this method adequate to ensure accurate observations (Rubinstein, 1980), but critics charge that the psychoanalytic method falls short of scientific standards of evidence (Holzman, 1985). All case studies are vulnerable to this criticism.

No Objectivity Virtually all the research methods described in this chapter demand subjective judgments by the researcher to code material. This produces serious methodological difficulties, because others might make different judgments. Unreliable measurement cannot be tolerated in research.

What can be done to ensure reliability? Development of very detailed coding rules is a first step. Next, coders must be trained adequately, and they must practice coding until they can produce results like those of experts. Much of the knowledge about how to code may be conveyed through discussions with the community of other coders and will not necessarily be documented (Mishler, 1990). Finally, researchers can have two coders code the same real data and compute the agreement between them. If it is high enough, the data can be further analyzed and reported. If not, coding must be improved, perhaps through further training. To get a sense of what is involved, see the Research Strategies box.

No General Conclusions Another criticism of idiographic approaches finds fault based on the small number of subjects (*n*), generally only one. Generalizing from one or a few observations to a larger population is seldom warranted. How can we generalize from one? Are we to assume, because the one person we have observed has these characteristics, that all humans have black hair, prefer coffee with cream, and would cheat to save money? These assumptions, of course, are unjustified, because the diversity of human personalities is too great to be sampled adequately by an *n* of 1. Statistical considerations require that the sample be large enough that these generalizations are stable. If people were completely alike, a sample of one would suffice to describe everyone (Dukes, 1965). We also cannot make general statements about causes of personality and behavior from small samples (Lieberson, 1991). There are too many influences on a single case that cloud the picture, making it unclear which influence or combination of influences caused which outcome.

In defense of studying individuals, we may argue that the question of generalizability should not be considered prematurely. Individuals may or may not be similar, but until we understand the personality of one individual, it is premature to ask whether others are similar or not. Once we understand one individual, we can then study other individuals to see whether the same dynamics apply to them (Lamiell, 1991; Rosenzweig, 1958). Conversely, psychologists have no guarantee that relationships discovered in a nomothetic study will also apply at the level of the individual (Lamiell, 1991). Some researchers suggest that there is a reasonable likelihood that nomothetic findings will apply at the level of the individual, although this must verified empirically in each case (Hermans & Bonarius, 1991b).

RESEARCH STRATEGIES

Do Observers Agree about What They See?

One of the most frequent criticisms of studies of individuals is this: There is so much data that the researcher must rely on subjective judgment to interpret it. How can we expect two researchers to make the same sense of the data? The fundamental question is one of *reliability*. If we can show that two researchers would, in fact, interpret the data in the same way, that is a giant step forward in the effort to be scientific.

The fundamental question is: Would two coders reading the same material evaluate it in the same way? Depending upon the nature of the material (a diary, a story, an answer to an interview question, and so on), and depending upon the specific aim of the coding, there are many different ways to compute the agreement between two coders. In some situations, the correlation coefficient (described in Chapter 2) is appropriate. In other situations, other statistics are used.

As an illustration, consider the following brief diary entries by a young adolescent, Sarah. For each entry, decide how Sarah felt, using a scale of 1 to 7. An entry of 1 means "felt horrible," and 7 means "felt wonderful." The middle of the scale, 4, means that Sarah felt neither bad nor good, but something between these extremes. You may use any number from 1 to 7.

a. Today was a great day! I can hardly wait for summer to begin.

b. Not so awful—I had a run-in with my English teacher about homework, but he didn't take off any points.

c. Why bother!!! School is a waste of time! I wish I could get out of here and start LIFE.

d. Got my homework done, and wasn't late for any classes today. A little short of money, but tomorrow I get paid.

e. Sunny day (finally!). And it's Saturday, so no need to study. Just get ready for the big party tonight. What shall I wear?

f. Can't write today. Too overwhelmed!

g. Still aglow over Saturday. . . .

h. I'm never going to take the bus to school again, because too many people who shouldn't be there are there.

i. Can you believe, a B in History? Maybe if I'd studied, I even could have gotten an A. That would sure surprise Mom.

j. I've decided. I want to go to college and I want to do it right after high school. Mary didn't and now she isn't even sure she could get in. Partying is fine, but that's not all there is to life.

After you have written down all your ratings for each of these 10 days, compare them with a classmate's ratings. Did you agree? Disagree? How many of the days were your ratings within 1 point of each other? (If you have studied statistics, you may wish to compute a correlation between the two ratings. Generally, researchers are dissatisfied with correlations of less than .85.) When you disagreed, why did you?

If your ratings are in close agreement with another rater's scores, then the measures are reliable and can be trusted for research. If not, you may wish to consider more detailed rules for coding. For example, should you consider Sarah's explicit statements of emotion as indicating more extreme emotion than descriptions of behavior where emotion must be inferred? Often, subjective ratings need a little extra effort to be made reliable.

Surely a Science of Personality Requires Study of Individuals!

Could we really imagine a science of personality that excluded individuals? Studies of individuals offer strengths that are not shared by traditional research. Although idiographic research can never replace comparisons based on group data, these strengths justify a role within personality psychology for single-subject investigations alongside traditional group studies. Alan Elms (1988b) goes so far as to suggest that biographical psychology ought to be an area of specialization within psychology, in the same way that learning and development are specialties, because it has unique questions and needs specialized methods.

Understanding Unusual People or People in Unusual Situations Personality psychologists do not aim simply to understand the "average" person, but the diversity of people. If we study a large enough population, we are likely to get many unusual cases. But if the aim is to understand an unusual type of personality, it is more efficient to focus on such cases than to collect data on large samples (Dukes, 1965; Marceil, 1977). This is the sort of argument that Abraham Maslow (1987) made when he advocated studying highly developed ("self-actualized") people; they are statistically rare but are theoretically important for understanding mental health.

Maslow studied several people whom he considered to be self-actualized, and others have taken his lead and applied his concepts to understanding such highly developed individuals as Eleanor Roosevelt (Piechowski & Tyska, 1982). Howard Gruber (1989) studied the creative process by investigating biographies of creative individuals such as Sir Isaac Newton and William Wordsworth. By studying the biographies of women who achieved in areas not considered acceptable for women in their time (political and professional, for example), Helen Buss (1990) was able to describe the conflict between private and public lives that these women experienced.

Sometimes One Person Is All That Matters Psychologists study interesting types of people (such as creative individuals), but occasionally one particular person is significant in his or her own right. In 1989, for example, an explosion aboard the USS *Iowa* caused the deaths of 47 sailors. In the highly publicized and controversial investigation that followed, the U.S. Navy attributed the explosion to the suicidal behavior of one sailor, Gunner's Mate Clayton Hartwig. Was this explanation accurate? Opinions vary. One thing is clear: our interpretation of the personality of the one accused sailor is central to the conclusion. Was he suicidal, or not? An investigation to make such determinations is often called a **psychological autopsy.** Unfortunately, even experts have not established that they can make such judgments with reliability and validity (Ault, Hazelwood & Reboussin, 1994; Otto et al., 1993; Poythress et al., 1993; Selkin, 1994; Shneidman, 1994).

Suggesting Theoretical Revisions The application of a theory to a particular person not only helps us to understand the individual, but also sheds light on the theory. Particularities of the individual's life may suggest modifications of the theory. For example, researchers applied Erik Erikson's theory of development to Vera Brittain, an early twentieth century British writer and feminist. On the basis of the biographical analysis, they suggested some changes in the theory: for example, that it should take external events into account more than it does (Stewart, Franz & Layton, 1988). Analysis of Richard Nixon from a humanistic perspective suggested, after his political downfall, that humanistic theory had not adequately distinguished self-actualization from public success (Anderson, 1975).

Putting the Person in Context People are profoundly influenced by their social environments, which provide the incentives and reactions that shape behavior and which teach the meanings that the person learns to apply to experience. Studies of individuals open the investigator to more complete knowledge of the situational context in which the person functions (Bromley, 1990). Appreciating the context in which the subject lives can suggest gaps or changes of emphasis in our theories. For example, studies of artists, like Freud's study of Leonardo, are often studies of male artists. Studying female artists, as Eunice Lipton (1990) has done, highlights the importance of gender as the context for the artist's life. Lipton describes the unwillingness of the artistic community to accept the personal life and sexuality of female artists in a way parallel to its acceptance of male artists and examines the impact of this social reaction on the lives of two women artists (Suzanne Valadon and Victorine Meurent).

Appreciating the Complexity of Personality In contrast to nomothetic approaches that reduce personality to one or a few variables, idiographic approaches inherently recognize the complexity of the person. This complexity overwhelms the traditional scientist, who seeks to make predictions from a manageable number of variables. When, as in studies of individuals, the number of variables (or dimensions of personality) greatly exceeds the number of people studied, prediction in the usual scientific sense is not possible. This fact may prevent misleading and oversimplified prediction, however, while "push[ing] the personality system to a new, more complex level of order and coherence, which can then be examined for its specific regularities and features" (Hermans & Bonarius, 1991a, p. 214).

Understanding Personality Change and Development Unlike traditional research, which most often observes people on one occasion only, psychobiography introduces the dimension of time into the materials. Thus, psychobiography fosters the awareness of development over time as an important theoretical issue for personality psychologists, which permits the study of the process of aging (Cole & Premo, 1987; Weiland, 1989). William McKinley Runyan (1982b), for example, suggests a theoretical model orientation that he calls "the life course," which emphasizes interactions of the person, behavior, and situations over time.

Emphasis on Personality Processes The study of individuals highlights the *processes* of personality. What are the patterns of behavior? How does a person behave in response to external situations and inner motivations? These are questions of personality dynamics (which will be our concern in the next several chapters). Advocates of the idiographic approach claim that these questions are central and that, logically, the answers must be discovered in individuals. Consider this analogy: studies of individual brain-damaged patients play an important role in research to discover the specific parts of the brain responsible for cognitive functions (Bub & Bub, 1988). Similarly, studies of individuals' personalities provide an in-depth look at the complexities of the whole person that so much of psychology has dissected into abstract processes.

The study of individuals makes important contributions to the field of personality. Although it cannot replace nomothetic research (Marceil, 1977), it contributes alternative methods to a science whose subject matter eludes any single methodology.

● -

SUMMARY

- Idiographic research studies one individual. Nomothetic research, which is conducted more often, studies groups of people.

- Gordon Allport called attention to the unique traits of individuals, and Rae Carlson criticized researchers for ignoring the person. Current researchers have modified traditional research methods to recognize individuals.

- Clinicians report individual personalities through case studies.

- Psychobiography has been dominated by psychoanalytic theory and its derivatives. It emphasizes some issues (such as early experience) but neglects others (such as the social context), and it is criticized for building on inadequate evidence.

- Erik Erikson described "disciplined subjectivity" as the psychohistorian's method.

- A problem with psychobiography is that many interpretations of the same observations can be made.

- Methods have been proposed to analyze biographical materials more systematically, including Tomkins's script approach, Alexander's method of extracting salient units, and content analysis.

- A person's motives can be coded from responses to creative stories or from material produced outside a research setting (such as presidential speeches).

- The Role Construct Repertory (REP) test measures the personal constructs that individuals use to understand people.

- Ipsative assessment methods make comparisons within a person, rather than between people; for example, a person judges preferences in rank order.

- Individuals can be studied through in-depth interviews. The self-confrontation method engages the individual in a dialog with the interviewer to analyze emotional units called "valuations."

- Behavioral assessment studies individuals to determine how environmental factors influence behavior.

- Scientific skepticism has raised many arguments against the study of individuals, including its failure to make prior predictions, its lack of objectivity, and its difficulties in reaching conclusions that can be generalized to other people.

- Despite these criticisms, the study of individuals is essential to the field of personality. For example, the study of individuals helps us to understand individuals who are particularly important for some reason and extends theoretical developments.

GLOSSARY

case studies reports of the personalities of individual patients or clients

content analysis an approach to data analysis that codes text in order to describe the frequency with which predefined themes or categories occur

idiographic an approach that studies one individual at a time

ipsative an approach to measurement that compares alternatives or traits within an individual; for example, having the subject rank various choices in order of preference

lexical analysis the analysis of text for specific words or phrases, usually by computer

moderator variable a variable that has an impact on the relationship between two other variables

nomothetic an approach that studies people by comparing them to others

personal constructs concepts for understanding and predicting people by thinking of them in either-or categories; said by George Kelly to be important cognitive dimensions of personality

personology an approach that studies individuals in their complex social and biological worlds and that emphasizes individuality and striving

psychobiography the study of biography from the perspective of psychological theory

psychohistory the study of the interrelationships of the individual personality and the historical setting

psychological autopsy a psychological analysis of a person who has died, conducted to determine whether the person was psychologically likely to have committed suicide

Q-sort a method for coding data in which coders sort statements into a standard distribution to indicate how well the statements describe the person being coded, based on their reading of the available materials

Role Construct Repertory (REP) test a test devised by George Kelly to assess personal constructs by having people describe the ways that individuals they know are similar to and different from other individuals they know

self-confrontation method a procedure for interviewing subjects in a collaborative way by identifying valuations and revising them through discussion between the researcher and the subject

valuation an emotionally charged unit of meaning for an individual, important in the self-confrontation interview method

THOUGHT QUESTIONS

1. Do you think someone could get to know you better by giving you a large number of written personality tests or by talking with you in an interview?

2. Evidence obtained from interviews, including interviews in therapy, has been criticized for being influenced by the expectations of the interviewer. Based on your everyday experience talking to people, do you believe that expectations are that important?

3. Look at the biased interpretations alleged for psychoanalytic psychobiography summarized in Table 5.3. If your life (or that of someone you know well) were interpreted from a psychoanalytic perspective, what would be given exaggerated importance, and what would be neglected?

4. The text mentions two of Tomkins's scripts, a "commitment script" and a "sedative script." What other scripts can you imagine? (Hint: Thinking of story lines that are popular on televisions and movies may provide some ideas.) Do you think that some scripts are healthier than others?

5. If you were taking the Role Construct Repertory (REP) test, what are some of the constructs that you would use to describe people?

6. If you wanted to know what choices an individual would make in selecting a job, would you prefer to have ipsative (within individual) or normative (between individual) information? Why?

7. Think of an important memory in your life. From the categories considered in the self-confrontation method, does this memory have emotions that are best described as self-enhancement, contact and union with others, positive affects, or negative affects?

8. Consider your studying habits from a behavioral point of view. What environmental factors influence whether you study or not? How is this interpretation different from a trait interpretation of your studying?

9. Do you believe that the study of an individual can be scientific, or should the study of individuals be left to nonscientific fields?

10. Is there one person in history or in current culture whom you would particularly like to understand? Why?

PART TWO

The Dynamics of Personality

As we turn from the *description* of personality to the *dynamics* of personality, we ask *why* people behave as they do. The answers to *why* are more abstract than the answers to *what*, and we encounter theories that are often equivocal. These theories lead to interpretations that are acceptable to some researchers but seem too unscientific to others. *Why* may be an inherently more difficult question than *what*. (Those who converse with young children can attest to this observation.)

In science, the philosophical assumptions necessary to specify *why* are more complicated than those needed to describe shared and unique features. Causes, even in the physical sciences, are often proposed in abstract terms that cannot be observed directly: for example, gravity, magnetism, radiation. The proposed causes must be consistent with observations made to date. Further, these hypotheses suggest new observations, and making these observations may demand the development of new techniques. Scientists in the physical sciences have progressed further in validating their proposed causes of motion, energy release, and so on, than have psychologists, who often disagree about which answers to *why* questions are even worthy of investigation.

In Part II, we will consider personality as a cause of behavior. The term *personality dynamics* refers to the way a person functions—the internal forces or motivations that determine what the person does. Broadly and generally, most psychologists would agree that people do what they find rewarding and avoid what they find not rewarding or even punishing. This assumption, however, is not very enlightening, because it quickly reduces to circular reasoning. Why does Joe run a marathon? He must enjoy it. Why does Jake sit in front of the television all day? He must enjoy it. This simplistic explanation adds little or nothing to our understanding of behavior. The challenge is to develop theories that are detailed enough to be tested and to provide strategies for influencing personality. Researchers have had considerable success in meeting this challenge.

First, in Chapter 6, we will consider psychodynamic theory. Based on the psychoanalytic approach to personality, psychodynamic theory proposes that people are motivated by unconscious forces. Sigmund Freud proposed psychoanalytic theory and emphasized its relationship to biological motivations (sex and aggression). Later psychoanalysts suggested that interpersonal and cultural factors are also significant in shaping personality dynamics. Throughout these modifications, psychodynamic approaches have maintained that the answers to why we behave as we do are to be found in a dynamic unconscious, knowable through such indirect methods as dreams, hypnosis, and the famous Rorschach inkblot test.

In Chapter 7, we will consider motivational theories that were influenced, historically, by psychoanalytic theory, especially as they were brought out of the clinic and into the research laboratory through the work of Henry Murray and his collaborators. This research is based on the idea that motivations or goals influence perceptions. Have you ever driven down a road when you're famished? You're likely to have noticed many more restaurants, fast-food establishments, and convenience markets than when you were in the same place but not hungry. Because motivations influence perception, we can test for motivation by presenting people with ambiguous stimuli and asking them to report what they see. Murray and researchers influenced by his work typically present people with ambiguous pictures, often a standard set of pictures called the Thematic Apperception Test. People who make up stories about winning races are assumed to be concerned with achievement, those whose stories report the making and breaking of friendships are said to be motivated by a need for affiliation, and so on.

The individual always functions in a social environment, which requires adaptation. Chapter 8 considers processes by which we adapt or cope with the environment. Some people tackle their problems by direct action, seeking to change the situation that is problematic; for example, finding a quiet place to study to conquer the problem of distracting roommates. Other people focus on the emotional aspects of problems; for example, talking things through with a friend to overcome anger. Some coping strategies are labeled healthy and others unhealthy, although researchers find that coping strategies that work in one situation may not work in another. We do know that unsuccessful coping not only produces discontent and stress but also contributes to physical diseases, including cardiovascular disorders and cancer.

People look outward at situations to which they adapt and in which they satisfy their motivations. In addition, they also look inward, at who they are. Many researchers have proposed personality dynamics based on this capacity for reflection upon the self, and we will discuss these theories in Chapter 9. We are motivated to think highly of ourselves (self-esteem), to get others to do the same (self-presentation), and to live up to our potential (self-actualization). We reflect upon ourselves, and we choose tasks and life commitments to enact a vision of ourselves. The understanding of "the self" in personality is a productive and active area of research, which many psychologists consider to be central to personality dynamics and development.

6

Psychodynamics

As our focus changes from description to dynamics, we will be discussing psychodynamic approaches, which developed from the clinical work of Sigmund Freud and his colleagues. Psychodynamic explanations began in a clinical setting, and psychoanalysis has been closely allied with psychological treatment ever since, even though Freud claimed it to be a more general theory of personality. Psychology has had an ambivalent relationship with psychoanalysis throughout its history, criticizing the lack of scientific rigor that typifies psychoanalysis, yet incorporating many of its ideas (Hornstein, 1992).

When he failed to find physical causes for the symptoms of some of his patients, the Viennese neurologist Sigmund Freud proposed **psychodynamic** causes. He postulated that psychological forces alone, in the absence of physical damage, can produce symptoms such as tics, anxiety, and even paralysis of parts of the body. He believed that these forces exist in the unconscious parts of personality, the legacy of conflicts in childhood that have been resolved only partially. These conflicts center around impulses that are not acceptable, such as impulses to seek sexual pleasures or to express aggressive feelings in unacceptable ways. Many other impulses may also stem from such conflicts, including impulses to overeat, to drink to excess, to be generous to a fault, to be overly rigid and excessively orderly, and so on. People with poorer conflict resolution, owing to traumas that produced greater conflicts, are less well adjusted as adults.

Freud developed **psychoanalysis** as a method for diagnosing and treating these disorders that stem from unconscious causes. In psychoanalytic treatment, the therapist (the "analyst") encourages the patient to say whatever comes to mind, even if it seems irrelevant or senseless. This method of **free association** permits the patient's own impulses to be observed, because he or she is not given clear directions or social expectations about what to say. Ordinarily, people do not allow their real impulses to be observed. For example, how often have you thought something that would be socially inappropriate to say or do, yet successfully hidden these embarrassing impulses from others? Free association would reveal them, and it would probably uncover even deeper tendencies of which you yourself are unaware.

Freud's theory contained many assumptions that have been revised by modern psychoanalytic theorists. The history of psychoanalysis is a fascinating saga of bold theoretical proposals that have been vigorously debated. These debates have raised questions about the kind of evidence that science demands to validate theories, as well as whether an analyst's observations during clinical treatment can provide evidence that meets scientific criteria. The history of psychoanalysis and its theoretical debates, however, are too long a tale to be reported here. We will focus on a few of the phenomena described by this theory that researchers have tested. Can we be influenced by unconscious thoughts? How shall we understand dreams? Is hypnosis real? Is therapy effective? These and other questions have been brought to our attention by psychoanalytic theory. We will also consider the contributions to these areas of theorists and researchers outside of psychoanalysis. Cognitive theories, for example, can account for many of the same phenomena as psychoanalytic theory (Kihlstrom, 1990).

Many therapists accept Freud's assertion that evidence gathered in the clinical treatment of individuals provides adequate validation of the theory, but others are troubled that there are few controls in clinical settings to guarantee that observations are accurate (Meissner, 1990; Rubinstein, 1980). Observations may be distorted by the therapist's theoretical expectations, especially when the therapist is the sole observer. To help overcome this problem, some researchers have systematically recorded therapy sessions and then have transcribed this information to have it coded by independent observers (for example, Horowitz et al., 1975; Weiss, 1988). In addition, many researchers have looked for evidence of psychodynamics in laboratory settings, which offer more rigorous controls than are possible in therapeutic treatment sessions.

The Unconscious

Humans have traditionally prided ourselves on our consciousness. We claim to be superior to other species because of our ability to reason and to think. To describe psychological growth, people sometimes refer to a "higher consciousness," and we are cautioned to avoid the dangers of unconsciousness or unawareness (Langer, 1989). Freud offered a model of the mind that included, along with **conscious** experience (that is, experience of which we are aware at any given moment), two other levels: the preconscious and the unconscious. The **preconscious** consists of information that can be readily brought to awareness when needed, such as our middle name and phone number. The **unconscious** consists of material that is not readily made conscious. Indeed, most of it never will become conscious.

Psychodynamic approaches assert that behavior is influenced by motivations of which individuals are unaware. These motivations reside in a dynamic unconscious. The unconscious consists of primitive motivations that are concerned (according to Freud) with sex and aggression. Later theorists (for example, Fairbairn, 1952; Sullivan, 1953) have expanded the list to include interpersonal attachments, such as love and caring.

Childhood Origins of the Unconscious

However theorists construe the motivations of the unconscious, they agree that experiences in childhood are very important in shaping the motivations that impel an individual for a lifetime. In particular, stress or trauma in childhood can produce **fixation,** dooming the adult to continue to seek the satisfactions that were denied in childhood. Fixation occurs when experiences or thoughts at one stage of life are overwhelming and anxiety-provoking. To defend against this anxiety, the thoughts are not permitted to be known consciously. Instead they are "repressed." **Repression** eradicates these thoughts, with their accompanying anxiety, from consciousness. Unfortunately, repression sets up a habit that becomes characteristic of personality and that requires an adult to reenact the defensive patterns established in childhood. For example, a child who is not permitted to express criticism of parents may repress even thinking critical thoughts and may become an adult who remains unaware of the errors of authority figures, even when such knowledge might be important and would even be welcomed by a boss who values suggestions from employees.

Freud described three stages of childhood development that risk such fixation. In the *oral stage,* from birth to age one year, the infant seeks oral

Childhood experiences are crucial to personality development. Abuse, whether physical, sexual, or psychological, has a negative impact on later personality and well-being.

pleasure through breast feeding. If the infant is denied oral satisfaction, fixation can result in later oral symptoms such as overeating, smoking, or (more symbolically) dependency upon others. In the *anal stage*, from age one to three years, the toddler seeks self-control. Fixation can result in later anal symptoms such as rigid concern with cleanliness and orderliness. In the *phallic stage*, from age three to five, a love affair with the parent of the opposite sex (the Oedipus complex). Fixation can result in such phallic symptoms as vanity, sex role confusion, and lack of conscience. Some research confirms that there are personality types corresponding to these theoretical stages (Fisher & Greenberg, 1977), although Freud's idea that the types are specifically linked to these early developmental periods has been challenged by those who have studied infant development (Zeanah et al., 1989).

Other psychoanalytic theorists have suggested that childhood development does not need to be described in terms of these biological zones (oral, anal, and phallic). We are social creatures as well as physical ones. Interpersonal relationships, beginning with the development of attachment to the mother, provide an alternative model (for example, Barends et al., 1990; Chodorow, 1978; Fairbairn, 1952; Kernberg, 1976; Rendon, 1987; Sullivan, 1953). In either case, though, childhood patterns form the basis of adult personality dynamics, and these dynamics have their motivational source in the repressed contents of the unconscious.

The unconscious was originally proposed by Freud to explain the causes of psychiatric symptoms, such as paralysis that did not correspond to any possible nerve damage, or unusual tics. In place of physical determinism, Freud postulated "psychic determinism" of such symptoms. Since Freud, other clinicians have described many individuals whose case histories are consistent with the theory that unconscious conflicts lead to symptoms. Case studies are suggestive, but they do not provide unambiguous proof of unconscious causation. In any case history, too many influences are uncontrolled. For that reason, researchers have sought experimental verification of the unconscious in the laboratory.

From the Clinic to the Experimental Laboratory

Traditional scientific methods require that a **true experiment** be conducted to demonstrate causes. In a true experiment, the influence that is thought to be the cause is systematically manipulated by the experimenter while everything else is kept constant. This provides a clear-cut test of the hypothesized cause. (See the Research Strategies box for a more complete explanation.)

An image from popular psychology illustrates a form of unconscious motivation that is the basis of one simple experiment. It has been claimed that liquor advertisements appeal to unconscious motivations by disguising sexual images in their pictures. Unconsciously, the audience is told that purchasing that particular alcoholic beverage will bring sexual satisfaction. In one experimental study, college undergraduates looked at liquor advertisements that contained symbolically sexual images and advertisements for competing brands with nonsexual images. Although they were unaware of the sexual symbolism, the subjects reported that they were more likely to purchase the brands with the symbolically sexual images (Ruth, Mosatche & Kramer, 1989). This study is consistent with an interpretation in terms of unconscious sexual motivation, but it does not provide clear proof. Other aspects of the images, such as their color and size, might have caused the different preferences.

The interpretation that unconscious sexual motivation caused the different preferences is only one possible interpretation of this experiment and thus is not clearly established by this one study. Can more direct connections somehow be forged between experimental manipulations and the elusive unconscious? An experimenter would aim to influence behaviors, ranging from the psychiatric symptoms described by Freud and other clinicians to the purchasing habits of consumers such as those described in the advertising study, by bringing about changes in the unconscious. How could this be done? At first, the task seems impossible. Psychoanalytic theory suggests that the unconscious is formed by early experience. Do we start with a group of infants and raise them from birth in some standardized way to produce known unconscious conflicts? Only in science fiction.

The key to solving this dilemma is that the unconscious responds to stimuli in the environment. It may lie inactive without appropriate triggering stimuli, just as the body's stress system is relatively inactive in non-threatening circumstances. When a threatening event occurs, however, such as the sight of a car headed straight toward you, the body's stress

RESEARCH STRATEGIES ●---

Expectancy Effects

Have you ever felt the pressure of people's expectations for your behavior? Friends expect you to join them in some activity that you would not choose on your own; teachers expect you to spend your time one way, while your job demands something different. Living up (or down) to people's expectations is a fact of everyday life.

This phenomenon, however, can undermine research. Consider a simple example, a study to assess the pain-relieving properties of a new medication. The researcher who administers the medication is convinced that it works. (Perhaps visions of research grants, fame, and wealth are somewhere in the background.) Being a well-trained scientist, our researcher designs a classic two-group experiment, recalling from a research methods course that this design can provide data to demonstrate that there is a cause-effect relationship between one variable and another. In this study, the cause ("independent variable") is the new pain medication, and the effect ("dependent variable") is pain reduction. All the researcher needs to do is to divide the subjects participating in the study randomly into two groups. An experimental group will receive the pain medication. A control group will not. Everything else must be kept equal between the two groups. (Random assignment ensures that the groups will be equal on any preexisting variables: sex, degree of pain, age, and so on.)

After the medication has been given and sufficient time has elapsed for it to take effect, all subjects are asked to report their levels of pain. Let's assume that the researcher's hypothesis is confirmed. The experimental group reports less pain than the control group. It would appear that the new medica-

tion is effective, since everything else about the two groups is the same.

Or is it? What could possibly be wrong with such a study? **Expectancy,** that's what! The experimental group took the medication, *and they knew that they were taking the medication.* Probably, they expected it to help them. The control group, on the other hand, did not take the medication, *and they knew that they were not getting any medication.* They had no reason to expect the headaches to subside. Unfortunately, then, the experimental group and the control group differed in *two* ways: (1) taking the medication or not, and (2) expecting to get better or not. Without further evidence, we have no way of knowing whether the effective treatment was (1) the medication, or (2) the expectancy (see Rosenthal, 1966).

How could this experiment be improved? There is a way to eliminate expectation as an alternative explanation for the pain reduction. The experimental group and the control group should be "treated" with equal expectations. Prepare a **placebo,** an inert pill ("sugar pill," perhaps) that looks, tastes, and smells like the medicine and in all other ways is indistinguishable from the medicine. Give it to the control group with exactly the same instructions and nonverbal communications as the medicine is given to the experimental group. This requires, not incidentally, that the experimenter giving the medication must not know which subjects are receiving the medication and which the placebo. Otherwise, the experimenter could inadvertently convey this expectation to the subjects, through a tone of voice, facial expression, or whatever. So long as the experimenter does not have this information, no expectation can be created in one group that is different from that in the other group: that is, "everything else" (besides the medication) is equal between the two groups. This precaution is termed a **double-blind** procedure. Two parties are "blind" as to the drug (or placebo): the experimenter and the subject. (Obviously, somewhere there must be records kept of who got what, or it won't be possible to analyze the data. The person interacting with the subjects, though, should not have this information.) Now, if the study is conducted and the experimental group reports less pain than the control group, the cause of this reduction must be the medication, since everything else, including expectancy, is equal between the two groups.

It is easy to imagine a double-blind technique in a drug study. The placebo control technique is not limited to drug studies, however. In Silverman's studies of subliminal activation of unconscious conflicts, for example, we could refer to subjects receiving neutral stimuli as a placebo control group, while the experimental group is shown the stimuli that are thought to have an effect (for example, "Mommy and I are one"). As in the drug study, it is important that the experimenter not know which slide is shown to which sub-

jects, lest expectancies be created and contaminate the study. Silverman effected such a double-blind procedure by having research assistants prepare the stimuli in advance; the experimenter did not know which stimulus was experimental and which was control (Hardaway, 1990).

By similar reasoning, in hypnosis studies, if the subject is asked to recall something not usually known, it is important that the hypnotist also not know the correct answer. In one study, if the subject was asked what was the day of the week of his or her birthday at age 4, or 7, or 10, or the previous Christmas, hypnotized subjects were unable to answer correctly if the hypnotist did not know the correct answer. If the hypnotist knew the correct answer, however, 81 percent of subjects knew the correct answer (True, 1949, cited in Nash, 1987). Similar tests of hypnotically recalled memories were reviewed by Michael Nash (1987), and on the basis of these many studies, we can conclude that much of the research evidence that seems to support hypnotic recall is flawed by failure to control for expectancy or by inadequate control groups (the figure below).

Studies supporting hypnotic improvement

Studies *not* supporting hypnotic improvement

Studies without adequate controls

Studies with adequate controls

7 of 14 studies support hypnotic improvement

0 of 10 studies support hypnotic improvement

When proper experimental controls are used, hypothesis does not improve memory. (From data presented in Nash, 1987.)

system springs into action, causing an increase in heart rate and a burst of energy to deal with the situation. In the same way, a patient with an unresolved oral conflict may not be motivated by it until circumstances arouse the conflict. The experimenter's task, then, is to stimulate dormant conflicts into an aroused state and to see what effect this manipulation has on behavior. In addition, the conflicts must remain unconscious. If they become conscious, the theory predicts that they will not have the same effect on symptoms, because then the mature coping mechanisms of our conscious life take over, replacing the immature coping mechanisms that constitute symptoms. Research evidence supports this claim that making conflicts conscious reduces symptoms (Shulman, 1990).

Perceiving without Awareness   The technique of **subliminal perception** has been proposed to activate unconscious material. In subliminal perception, an individual responds to a stimulus at some level but does not know consciously what the stimulus was and is unable to report it. Generally, stimuli are presented visually, using a **tachistoscope.** This device consists of a slide projector with a cameralike shutter on the end that can be set to control the projection for very brief periods of time, about 4 milliseconds. Alternatively, brief images can be spliced into film or videotape that is then played. Today, computers can be programmed to present stimuli for such brief exposures.

In the tachistoscopic method, the subject is first presented with such brief exposures that nothing is seen. The exposures are repeated for increasing durations. When the exposure is seen as a brief flicker of light, the person cannot report what is pictured or written on the screen. Yet at some level, the person has perceived the stimulus, and behavior can be influenced. If the exposure duration is increased even more, ultimately the stimulus is perceived consciously and can be reported verbally. At this longer duration, though, the unconscious effects generally disappear (Geisler, 1985).

Consider the following experiment. Undergraduate subjects watched 2-minute videotapes of computer-generated graphics. Unknown to them, subliminal stimuli were spliced into the tapes every 7 seconds for a duration of $\frac{1}{60}$ of a second or less. Each subject saw only one version of subliminal presentation. For one group, the subliminal images were smiling cartoon characters (positive condition). For a second, the subliminal images were a threatening and violent scene (negative condition). A third, control group was presented with subliminal blank gray inserts (neutral condition). Subjects could not report the stimuli consciously. In fact, they were surprised when told, after the experiment, that there had been subliminal inserts. Nonetheless, they were affected by the brief images. On questionnaire measures of mood, those who had been exposed to the positive condition reported that they were less anxious, and those exposed to the negative condition reported that they were more anxious, compared to subjects exposed to the neutral condition. Reports of their usual levels of anxiety were not affected, because those questions did not ask for reports for the mood of the moment. Thus, it was shown that subliminal exposures can influence moods (Robles et al., 1987; see also Shulman & Ferguson, 1988).

In a Flash: Silverman's Studies   Lloyd Silverman has reported a program of research to test the psychoanalytic model of unconscious motivation using experimental procedures. Silverman's method is called **subliminal psychodynamic activation.** Using a tachistoscope, the experimenter displays to the subjects stimuli that, according to psychoanalytic theory, should either increase or decrease unconscious conflict. Stimuli that should increase unconscious conflict are those that arouse unconscious wishes. Stimuli that suggest the wishes have been fulfilled, in contrast, should reduce unconscious conflict. These stimuli are displayed briefly (4 milliseconds), so that they cannot be recognized consciously; they appear only as flickers of light. Silverman reasoned that at these brief exposures, the unconscious mind perceives the stimulus and responds to it, even though the conscious mind cannot recognize the stimulus.

Unlike the study of college undergraduates reported above, Silverman used psychiatric patients as subjects in most of his research. Patients with different diagnoses have different unconscious conflicts, according to psychoanalytic theory. Schizophrenics are theorized to have serious unresolved conflicts stemming from the first year of life and an unconscious wish to return to a symbiotic merger with the mother. Conflict originating in the second and third years is theorized to produce a variety of symptoms, including stuttering.

Silverman reported several studies in which subliminal stimuli that aroused unconscious conflicts resulted in increased symptoms. For schizophrenics, symptoms were increased when the stimulus "I am losing Mommy" was presented subliminally. In contrast, "Mommy and I are one" reduced symptoms. Stuttering was increased by subliminal activation of anal conflict by presenting phrases ("Go shit") or pictures (of a person or a dog defecating) (Silverman, 1983). These studies suggested that the subliminal message needed to match the specific unconscious conflict to influence symptoms.

In his later work, however, Silverman found that one stimulus ("Mommy and I are one") had a therapeutic effect for patients with a variety of diagnoses. This wish for pre-Oedipal union with the mother seemed ubiquitous, and satisfying it had broad therapeutic implications. Silverman reasoned that the wish for oneness or symbiosis with the mother originated in early infancy, which psychoanalysts describe as a period of symbiosis with a nurturing good mother (Silverman & Weinberger, 1985).

Silverman's technique has also been used with college students to see whether unconscious conflict influences performance on academic tasks and laboratory tasks. College men were more accurate on a dart-throwing task after being told, by means of subliminal exposure, that "beating Dad is

OK" (Silverman, Ross, et al., 1978). Swedish students performed better on a motor task (tracing a line with a pen) after exposure to the subliminal message "Mamma och jag är ett" (Swedish for "Mommy and I are one"), compared to a control message ("Folk promenerar"; that is, "People are walking") (Gustafson & Källmén, 1990). Studies even report that grades can be improved by this method! Among Israeli students, the Hebrew translation of "Mommy and I are one" improved grades in a mathematics course (Ariam & Siller, 1982). In another study, American graduate students in classes in probability and statistics and in measurement and evaluation were exposed to repeated subliminal stimuli throughout the course. By random assignment, some students were presented with the ubiquitous "Mommy and I are one." A second group was exposed to either "I understand measurement" or "I understand statistics" (depending upon the course they were taking). A control group was presented with "People are walking." As in previous studies, the "Mommy and I are one" stimulus had a positive effect, increasing grades significantly above the control stimulus. The course-specific "I understand measurement" (or statistics) produced intermediate results (Cook, 1985) (Fig. 6.1).

The use of experimental procedures to validate the psychoanalytic idea that the unconscious can produce symptomatic behaviors is indeed a major step in validating the theory of the unconscious. Still, science demands skepticism. Critics argue that such subliminal effects may not be genuine; for example, there may be some uncontrolled aspects of the experiment that are producing these effects. Most of the replications have occurred in Silverman's own laboratory or in studies conducted by his students; perhaps the experimenters are unintentionally conveying some expectations to their subjects or, in the studies of psychiatric patients, are biased in their evaluation of symptoms. Evaluation of symptoms is subjective, and research reports should clearly indicate the extent to which different raters have agreed in making those judgments (that is, interrater reliability). Furthermore, the specific measures that Silverman reports as significant vary from one study to another: sometimes responses to psychological tests, sometimes the nonverbal behaviors of the patients, sometimes their word associations, and so on. Data collected but not found significant are deemphasized or not reported. Therefore, critics suggest that Silverman may be unfairly selective in reporting only those few of many statistical tests that are in the expected direction, which means that they could be due to chance (Balay & Shevrin, 1988).

Some reviewers have been more positive about Silverman's work (for example, Weinberger, 1986). Richard Hardaway (1990) concluded that these subliminal effects were small but real and that the basic question had been settled beyond the need for further research. Most reviewers, though, have tempered their positive responses with methodological cautions, requiring further replications before wholeheartedly accepting Silverman's bold claims (for example, Brody, 1987; Fudin, 1986).

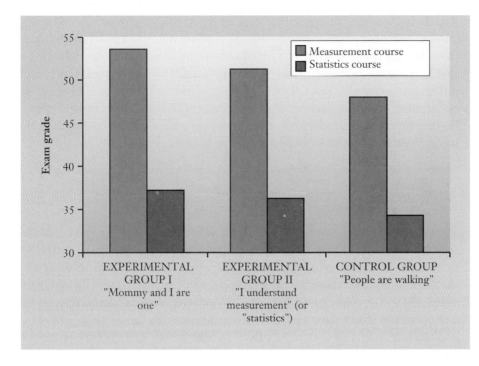

FIGURE 6.1 *Subliminal exposure improves objective final examination grades for graduate students in statistics classes and measurement classes. (From data presented in Cook, 1985.)*

Consciousness Reconsidered

Whatever the final judgment may be about the psychodynamic notion of a dynamic unconscious, the debate has focused attention on our often unstated assumptions about consciousness. Many people assume, without much thought, that consciousness is king and directs, or ought to direct, behavior and experience. The unconscious is thought to be less mature, less civilized, less moral. This was Freud's attitude, and it caused him to advocate replacing the unconscious with consciousness for better mental health.

It is an attitude shared by other psychologists, even those outside the psychoanalytic perspective. Ellen Langer (1989) advocates "mindfulness" to replace the potentially maladaptive "mindlessness" that often dominates our thought. Mindlessness is not the dynamic motivated unconsciousness described by Freud, but simple neglect to pay attention to material that could be made conscious. Thomas Natsoulas, whose scholarly review of the literature demonstrates that even consciousness is hard to define, let alone the unconscious, lists "explicit consciousness" as one usage of the term *conscious*. By explicit consciousness, Natsoulas means being more fully aware of oneself and one's situation. This is the sort of "consciousness raising" that psychoanalytic therapy strives to achieve, beyond simple insight into the past (Natsoulas, 1981).

Distrust of the unconscious has been a major theme in Western thought, but other views exist. Among psychoanalysts, Carl Jung is best known for his more respectful attitude toward the unconscious, which, he argued, contains positive growth potentials and not only pathology and conflict (for example, Jung, 1959). This positive orientation is shared by some humanists and non-Western philosophers (Nitis, 1989; Smith, 1985). They agree with psychodynamic theorists, however, that the unconscious is a force to be considered in a psychology of human personality.

Creativity

Lest we consider the unconscious only a source of pathology and maladjustment, let us note that psychoanalytic theory also describes **creativity.** Creative people produce original, unusual, and adaptive solutions to problems. Generally, we think of creativity as applying to people in the arts (music, theater, painting, and so on). Creativity also is characteristic of those in other areas who approach their tasks with originality and who solve problems in new ways. Creative people score high on measures of playfulness and tolerance of ambiguity. They are high on Myers-Briggs scales for Intuition and Perception (Tegano, 1990).

A classic study by Cynthia Wild illustrates that creative people have closer contact with their unconscious than most people, without the pathology that unconscious material sometimes produces. She found that creative artists, compared to a control group of high school and elementary teachers, were more able to suspend controlled thinking when instructed to do so, based on a Word Association test and an Object Sorting test. In this way, they are like psychotic individuals. Unlike the psychotic subjects, though, the creative artists could respond with more regulated thinking when instructed to do so. Thus, creative artists have access to both primary and secondary thinking processes and are able, in psychoanalytic terms, to "regress in the service of the ego" (Wild, 1965). We might say that, rather than being stuck entirely in either the unconscious or conscious mode of thinking, creative people are those who can freely navigate both.

The Cognitive Unconscious: A Modern Alternative

Freud's model of the mind presumes that material is made unconscious to protect the individual from anxiety, because conscious experience of this material would be too threatening. This traditional Freudian depiction is often called the **dynamic unconscious.** It is difficult, however, to understand how the material is kept unconscious. Is there a part of the personality that serves as a gatekeeper, knowing what is in the unconscious before

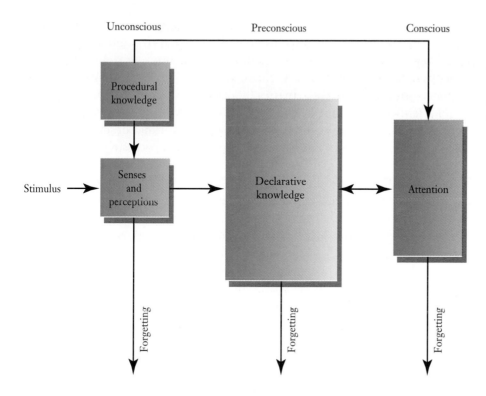

Unconscious   Preconscious   Conscious

Procedural knowledge

Senses and perceptions

Stimulus →

Declarative knowledge

Attention

Forgetting   Forgetting   Forgetting

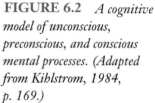

FIGURE 6.2 *A cognitive model of unconscious, preconscious, and conscious mental processes. (Adapted from Kihlstrom, 1984, p. 169.)*

we know it consciously and deciding whether it may be allowed consciousness or not? The image is an intriguing metaphor, but it raises the logical question of how we can know what we do not know.

Although the dynamic unconscious proposed by Freud has theoretical shortcomings, it is possible to posit an unconscious that is not the Freudian unconscious, to "liberate" the concept of the unconscious from psychoanalytic theory (Kihlstrom, 1984). The alternative model advocated by John Kihlstrom and others is the **cognitive unconscious.** It describes cognitive processes that are outside of conscious awareness, some of which were never conscious and others of which are not retrievable or have been forgotten. Material is conscious when we are paying *attention* to it (roughly corresponding to what many memory models call "short term memory"). Much material that is not currently conscious can be made conscious by attending to it; this potentially conscious material (which Freud would call "preconscious") is *declarative knowledge*. It includes names of people and places, memories of past experiences, goals, and many other aspects of our mental life that we can reflect upon or think about consciously. Other aspects of mind are unconscious (Fig. 6.2). In this cognitive model, there is no need to assume that repression or anxiety forces material to be unconscious. The *sensory and perceptual systems*, such as touch, hearing, and vision, are unconscious inherently, although when they combine with our internal images of what we see or hear (located in the declarative knowledge area), we can become conscious of what we perceive. *Procedural knowledge* consists of our abilities to do various skilled acts; it too is unconscious. We type, play the piano, ride a bicycle, and so on without awareness, once we know how to do these things. We can, as the arrow in the diagram shows, become conscious of those activities by paying attention to them, but ordinarily attention is occupied elsewhere (Bowers, 1984).

Research supports cognitive models of the mind that describe a limited role for consciousness. Humans are capable of processing much more information than they can describe consciously (Kihlstrom, 1990; Nisbett & Wilson, 1977). For example, in some studies, subjects listen to two different messages, one presented to each ear. They can consciously report only the one message that they are paying attention to. (Perhaps you have experienced something like this when more than one person is talking to you at the same time.) Nonetheless, the information presented to the nonattended ear influences what is reported. For example, in one study, subjects paid attention to sentences presented to one ear while a list of words was presented to the other ear (which was not the focus of attention). Some subjects were presented with the unattended word *river,* while others were presented with the word *money.* Afterward, even though they had not paid attention to the individual words, the subjects had been influenced by them in their interpretation of the ambiguous sentence that was presented to the attended ear: "They threw stones toward the bank yesterday." In the one case, the sentence was interpreted as throwing stones at a river; in the other, at a building (Bowers, 1984, describing research by MacKay, 1973).

Although there are theoretical disagreements about what constitutes consciousness and what is evidence of conscious and unconscious thought (Natsoulas, 1981; White, 1980, 1988), it is clear that people cannot verbally report all of their mental processes. In that sense, there is certainly an "unconscious." Some behavior is simply automatic, such as riding a bicycle or driving a familiar road. Such automatic behaviors are done without much conscious thought. Even when behavior is consciously willed, neurological studies show that conscious reports of making a choice to behave lag behind neurological activity in other, "unconscious," parts of the brain. Subjects in an experiment are told to move their fingers whenever they feel like it and to tell the experimenter when they decide to move; by monitoring brain activities, the experimenter can see evidence of an "unconscious" decision to move the fingers before the subject is consciously aware of making the choice (Ornstein, 1991). These phenomena support the psychoanalytic challenge to our everyday belief that consciousness controls behavior, but they can also be explained in terms of newer cognitive models of the mind that allow information to be processed in unconscious as well as conscious systems.

Freud's dynamic unconscious, however, has an added feature: conflict over anxiety-provoking ideas. Can a cognitive model account for emotional aspects of the unconscious? It can, by proposing that there is a **dis-**

sociation of various components of mental experiences, a lack of connection between processes that would usually be associated. At the moment an emotional event occurs, the emotions and the awareness of the event are ordinarily both present and thus seem to be unified in content. They are not, however. The memory for the events and the memory for the emotional experience are represented in different parts of the mind, and it is possible for them to be recalled together or separately, or for one to be recalled and the other forgotten. As an analogy, imagine that you have videotaped a party. Although both the visual images and the sound occurred at the same time and seem to belong together, it would be possible to play back the videotape on a machine with a defective audio component and thus see but not hear the event. Or, the machine could have a broken visual system, and you might hear the sounds but not see the pictures. Although the mind is more complicated than a videotape machine, it too can fail to combine aspects of an event that seem to belong together.

Consider the following case studies (among others described by Kihlstrom, 1990). An amnesic patient who is a rape victim cannot recall her identity or address but when presented with personally relevant stimuli (including the name of the road where she lived as a child and her own name) shows electrodermal responses; that is, emotional responses recorded by a polygraph-type machine (Gudjonsson, 1979). A patient is suffering fugue, a disorder in which there is amnesia for the past, including forgetting personal identity. Yet when asked to dial random digits on the telephone, she phones her mother (Lyon, 1985). Classic psychodynamic theory would explain these events as motivated repression: the memory of the rape, or of one's personal identity, would produce excessive anxiety if recalled, so it is repressed. The classic psychodynamic theory of repression has more difficulty, however, in explaining why some of the experience, such as the telephone number, is recalled. The cognitive concept of dissociation accounts for the partial recall by postulating that events are not stored as a unified experience in memory.

Developments in cognitive science have led to more specific models of the mind, which can guide specific research that is more compatible with the scientific method than are psychoanalytic case studies. Systematic research with controlled exposures to stimuli has demonstrated that emotional reactions can be triggered by stimuli that do not become conscious (Bowers, 1984; Mandler & Nakamura, 1987; Zajonc, 1980). Subliminal exposure to stimuli that produce positive or negative emotions (for example, smiling people versus a bucket of snakes) influences the attitudes formed by subjects toward people they viewed at readily perceived (2-second) slide exposure intervals; this experiment demonstrates that subliminal conditioning can occur (Krosnick et al., 1992). In addition to such evidence of subliminal perception, other studies show that people selectively attend to information that is particularly relevant to them, seeming to sift through more visual or auditory information than can be processed consciously to attend to what is most relevant. Such broad-ranging studies have led to interest in an unconscious that has no necessary connection, except historical, with psychoanalytic theory. The psychological unconscious, in the words of Howard Shevrin and Scott Dickman, may be a "necessary assumption for all psychological theory" (1980, p. 421).

For Freud, the unconscious is revealed by dreams, which he called "the royal road to the unconscious." Although not all modern psychologists agree with Freud's assessment, many of them consider dreams worthy of further investigation.

Dreams

According to dream laboratory studies, dreams occur several times every night. Whether the images presented in dreams are meaningful or simply curious, however, is controversial.

Freud's Theory of Dreams

Freud believed that dreams present in symbolic form the core unconscious conflicts of an individual (Freud, 1900/1953). His theory says that dreams reveal the contents of an individual's unconscious through symbols that can be interpreted as disguised expressions of unfulfilled wishes and conflicts. The overt content (*manifest content*) of the dream is thought to be a symbolic expression of unconscious meanings (*latent content*).

Dreams often are bizarre, portraying movements and images impossible in the real world. In dreams, as in the unconscious generally, the **primary process** mode of functioning prevails. Primary process is primitive: illogical, emotional, nonadaptive. It permits magical transformations of one object into another and even allows an object's simultaneous existence as two objects. ("It might be my mother, or it might be my friend," says one dreamer, trying to convey the ambiguity of the primary process experience of a dream.) In contrast, waking life operates according to **secondary process** thinking. Secondary process is mature: logical, rational, and adaptive to the real world.

Physiological Perspectives on Dreaming

Although psychodynamic approaches emphasize the psychological, symbolic interpretation of dreams, Freud's theory is not universally accepted. Much is known about dreaming as a biological phenomenon. Dreaming occurs during REM sleep, a period characterized by rapid eye movements and distinctive brain wave patterns. Sleepers awakened during this stage of

What causes the severe mental illness called schizophrenia? One theory, proposed by Crick and Mitchison, is that the brain cannot function normally when dreams do not fulfill their intended function, which is to edit out the erroneous learning that inevitably occurs as a result of experience. From this point of view, dreams do not have symbolic meaning.

sleep are far more likely to recall dreaming than those awakened during non-REM sleep.

Neurologists emphasize the physiological processes that occur during dreaming, rather than any meaning of the content of dreams. (For a review, see Miller, 1989). Some have described meaning as an illusion produced by random physiological activity. Some types of dreams have been associated with brain abnormalities (Epstein, 1982). Dreams are unlike waking life, which is controlled by the more recently evolved frontal lobes of the brain that control "ego" processes (Epstein, 1987). Francis Crick and Graeme Mitchison (1983) suggest that the function of dreaming is to remove unnecessary, faulty neural connections from the cerebral cortex of the brain, a sort of reverse learning or garbage-removal system. It is an elegant biological theory that accounts for phenomena beyond the scope of Freud's dream theory, such as the existence of REM sleep in fetuses and various nonhuman animals. Crick and Mitchison speculate that failures of this reverse learning mechanism could produce severe disturbances, such as the symptoms of schizophrenia. They advise against seeking symbolic meanings in dreams and warn that remembering dreams interferes with this housekeeping activity.

Others, although not placing dream interpretation on the pedestal created by Freud, do accept that the experiences of dreams are instructive as we attempt to develop models of cognitive processes more generally. With external reality largely (though not completely) tuned out, the experiences of the dreamer reflect the mental processes structured by the mind itself. John Antrobus has studied these processes carefully to develop a computer simulation of imagery and thought that he calls "DREAMIT:S" (Antrobus, 1991). Models such as these may help forge connections between the largely metaphorical approach to dreaming that psychoanalysis presents and the new understandings of the brain that come from neurological research. Although physiological studies and dream interpretation seem to be two irreconcilably different approaches, efforts to merge the two approaches are being made. This is a promising direction for research and theory, according to J. Allan Hobson (1988), who urges physiological approaches to become more integrative and psychological interpretations to become more precise, so that the two can join.

Dream Interpretation: A Challenge for Science

Symbolic interpretation of dreams varies according to the particular version of psychoanalytic theory being applied. Freudian interpretation emphasizes sexuality. Interpretation inspired by Carl Jung's analytical psychology emphasizes the creative and developmental potentials of the unconscious (Jung, 1974). In addition to theory, the dream analyst relies considerably upon subjective judgment to decipher the meanings of dream images. When the interpretation is communicated to the dreamer, the accuracy of interpretation may be verified by the dreamer's acceptance of the interpretation or by changes in conscious thought that result. This verification is fraught with potential error, however. Even a correct interpretation may be rejected if the person is not willing to accept the troublesome unconscious contents, the material that is being repressed. On the other hand, an incorrect or arbitrary interpretation may be accepted because the suggestion of an expert is powerful. These are some of the considerations that make dream interpretation difficult to verify from an objective stance.

Researchers have described systematic methods for analyzing dreams (for example, Hermans, 1987; Živković, 1982). Nonetheless, the interpretations must depend upon subjective human judgments.

Empirical Studies of Recalled Dreams

The content of people's dreams varies with the sex, cultural background (for example, Munroe & Munroe, 1992), and personality of the dreamer. People also vary in their recall of dreams. These differences probably have less to do with defensiveness or repression than with cognitive functioning, such as having a good short-term memory. People can probably learn to recall dreams through practice (Martinetti, 1985).

The types of dreams recalled vary with personality. Jungian intuitive types are more likely to recall dreams that are from the deeper ("archetypal") levels of the unconscious, reflecting highly symbolic images such as those also found in the world's myths and religions. Those scoring high on Neuroticism on the Eysenck Personality Inventory (EPI) had fewer archetypal dreams, as would be expected from Carl Jung's suggestion that neurotic people are more concerned with their individual conflicts and less with the human condition at large (Cann & Donderi, 1986).

Although we cannot elicit dreams on demand, an alternative method permits tapping of the unconscious on cue: the method of projective tests.

Projective Tests

Since people cannot know their unconscious, much less report it to researchers, how can it be measured? For this purpose, **projective tests** have been developed. Projective tests require people to describe what they see in an ambiguous stimulus. The **Rorschach inkblot test** consists of cards containing ambiguous visual stimuli (Pichot, 1984). The respondent is required to describe what he or she sees in the inkblot. Presumably, because the conscious mind is at a loss to know what "should" be there, the unconscious takes over, so that responses provide clues to what is in the unconscious. Clinical interpretation of the Rorschach and other projective tests is an art that is substantially influenced by theory (Lerner, 1990). It is also guided by standardized scoring procedures. The most popular of these is the Exner system, which counts various categories of responses, such as references to the form or color of the inkblot and mention of animals or human movement perceived in the stimuli (Acklin, 1993; Exner, 1986; Viglione, Brager & Haller, 1991). Clinicians consider these scores along with other information when they diagnose patients.

Another popular projective test is the Thematic Apperception Test (TAT), which requires subjects to make up a story for each of several pictures. The TAT was originally developed by Henry Murray and Christiana Morgan, and in its original form it consisted of a standard set of pictures (Morgan & Murray, 1938/1962). Other pictures are frequently substituted, however, often on the assumption that certain pictures will elicit particular psychological issues. It is often assumed that respondents will identify more easily with pictures of people who are like them; for example, of the same sex. Many scoring systems have been developed for the TAT. Some of these systems concern motivation outside of the psychoanalytic and clinical realms and will be described in Chapter 7. Of clinical interest, a Personal Problem-Solving System has been developed to assess the problem-solving skills of clients based on responses to the TAT (Ronan, Colavito & Hammontree, 1993).

Projective tests are widely used by clinicians. The responses of an individual client are interpreted by the examiner, who looks for unusual responses or responses indicative of particular psychological patterns and then considers these in the context of all else that is known about the respondent (Jaffe, 1990). To be sure, the face validity of the measures is not high; that is, they do not seem, based on appearance to the casual observer, to be measuring what they claim to measure. Interpreting the Rorschach test, for example, involves counting responses that describe categories such as animals, human movement, and parts of objects. This lack of face validity would not be a problem if there were adequate evidence of predictive validity (as described in Chapter 1). For the most part, only those researchers who are already sympathetic to psychodynamic theorizing readily accept projective tests as measures of the unconscious (Kline, 1987a).

Compared to objective (for example, multiple-choice) tests, projective tests have low reliability. People who take the test more than once are likely to change their responses from one time to the next, in contrast to self-report tests, in which people generally choose the same answers. Even for the same set of responses, interscorer reliability is surprisingly low (for example, Ritzler, Zillmer & Belevich, 1993). It has long been documented that scores are influenced by situational and interpersonal variables, such as the examiner's behavior and instructions (Masling, 1960/1992). Reliability can be improved to some extent by standardizing administrative procedures (Keiser & Prather, 1990) and by improving scoring procedures on the basis of statistical evaluations (Kline, 1987a).

The Rorschach test is widely used as part of a diagnostic evaluation. It has served as a criterion measure for research that evaluates the effectiveness of therapy. Furthermore, it describes particular kinds of personality conflicts and defense mechanisms, both for individuals in psychotherapy and in clinical research. What are these conflicts and defense mechanisms?

Defense Mechanisms

Although all people, according to psychoanalytic theory, experience unconscious motivations, individuals differ in the specific content of this unconscious and in how they resolve the conflicts between this unconscious and their conscious lives. Late in his life, Freud formulated his *structural hypothesis*, which proposes three main structures in personality. The *id* is the source of psychic motivations, particularly the biologically based motivations of sex and aggression. The *superego* is the inner voice of conscience and morality, although it remains forever childish, seeing moral issues as a child understands parental rules. The *ego* is the most mature of the three structures, representing rationality and reality, in contrast to the less mature id and superego. The ego uses specific strategies to resolve the

TABLE **6.1** **Major Defense Mechanisms**

Denial	Not accepting the reality of unpleasant facts or feelings
Projection	Perceiving unaccepted impulses or characteristics as belonging to other people, when in fact they belong to the self
Repression	Not permitting unpleasant material to be perceived consciously
Reaction formation	Doing or experiencing something that is the opposite of what is actually felt but unacceptable
Isolation	Not permitting conscious recognition of unaccepted feelings that accompany thoughts
Regression	Returning to earlier, more primitive ways of coping

conflict between conscious and unconscious aspects of personality. These strategies are called **defense mechanisms** (Table 6.1).

According to psychodynamic theory, defense mechanisms are formed in childhood. Some mechanisms, those used earliest in life, are immature and less successful in achieving the task of adapting to reality. For example, *denial* is an immature defense mechanism. Others, such as rationalization, are formed when the ego is more developed and are considered more mature defense mechanisms (Cramer, 1987; Schibuk, Bond & Bouffard, 1989).

Freud never satisfactorily resolved the relationship between this structural hypothesis and his *topographic hypothesis*, which described the three levels of consciousness (conscious, preconscious, and unconscious) discussed earlier in this chapter (Kihlstrom, 1990). However, we can say that the id and superego are generally unconscious. The ego is the structure that is most conscious, although its defense mechanisms are unconscious.

Clues in Projective Tests

To assess unconscious material, researchers cannot count on the direct reports of subjects, any more than therapists can expect their patients to

Threatening events may trigger immature defense mechanisms, such as denial, in which we do not face unpleasant reality. More mature mechanisms develop in childhood and adulthood, preparing us to face life's conflicts more realistically.

explain clearly the personality flaws that contribute to their suffering. Assessment by projective tests exploits the tendency of the unconscious to express itself indirectly when given the opportunity.

Projective tests, including the Rorschach, are used for clinical assessment (for example, Eyman & Eyman, 1991) and, in personality research, to assess character types and defense mechanisms. The Rorschach test can be scored for several kinds of psychological defenses. Lower defense mechanisms are found in more seriously disturbed clinical groups (Cooper, Perry & Arnow, 1988). Defense scores predict future mental status among young adults. Some defense mechanisms are "higher" than others and predict better mental health (Cooper, Perry & O'Connell, 1991). Rorschach *oral imagery* is scored from a variety of obviously oral responses, such as seeing a mouth or food in the inkblot, and responses theoretically related to early life, such as baby talk ("a bunny rabbit") or passivity and helplessness (seeing a "confused" person). Oral imagery indicates oral fixation and therefore concerns with nurturance and dependency, and it is negatively correlated with undergraduates' tendency to idealize their parents. This finding suggests that for some young people, a defensive pattern includes an inability to criticize their parents and an inability to express the need to be nurtured (Duberstein & Talbot, 1992).

The Rorschach was administered to Nuremberg war criminals who had participated in the Nazi atrocities of World War II. Later analysis of these records revealed that the war criminals, although not seriously disturbed according to the Rorschach, had rigid authoritarian personalities that explained their participation in the Nazi organization (Resnick & Nunno, 1991). To understand people, we need to consider their styles of relationships with other people, and not only the internal conflict that tra-ditional psychoanalytic theory emphasizes.

Modern psychoanalysts often focus on the capacity for healthy rela-tionships with others. Can we genuinely love others and recognize their needs, rather than regarding them only as potential satisfiers of our own desires? The **object relations** approach of modern psychoanalysis con-siders such interpersonal capacities. It derives its name from the fact that psychoanalysis describes other people as "objects" of libidinal desire. Drew Westen and his colleagues have developed a method for scoring TAT responses on dimensions of object relations. Healthier responses reflect more complex thinking about people and more positive and committed emotional relationships (Table 6.2). The researchers have demonstrated that diagnosed borderline and major depressive patients score lower than normal subjects (Barends et al., 1990; Westen et al., 1990).

Can Questionnaires Reveal Defenses?

Despite the elusiveness of the unconscious, researchers have also devel-oped questionnaires that require subjects to answer multiple-choice ques-tions, in an attempt to measure defense mechanisms more reliably than through projective tests. One such measure is the Defense Mechanism Inventory (DMI), a multiple-choice test based on responses to hypothetical

---

TABLE 6.2 Healthy Personality from an Object Relations Perspective, Coded from Thematic Apperception Tests (TAT)

Scale 1: **Complexity of representations of people**
Complex understandings of personality and social interactions

Scale 2: **Affect-tone relationship paradigms**
Positive emotional representations of relationships

Scale 3: **Capacity for emotional investment**
Ability to be concerned for and committed to others

Scale 4: **Understanding of social causality**
Complex understandings of mental processes and of unconscious motivations

Adapted from Westen et al., 1990, p. 359.

conflict situations (Banks & Juni, 1991; Cramer, 1988; Gleser & Ihilevich, 1969; Ihilevich & Gleser, 1986). As research has accumulated using these scales, some evidence supports their validity; for example, the finding of more defenses in clinical samples and of improvement following therapy on some scales. Other research using self-report measures has found that immature defenses are associated with lower adjustment (Brems, 1990; Tennen & Affleck, 1990; Vaillant & Drake, 1985). Some results, however, are inconsistent with the concept of defensiveness, including the finding of higher Projection scores on the DMI following psychotherapy (Juni, 1982). The scales, which are more reliably scored than clinical judgments, are a valuable tool for research on psychodynamic defenses, but they are not flawless.

Sex differences have been reported in the use of defense mechanisms. Females use more internalizing defenses, such as turning against the self. Males use more externalizing defenses, such as projection and aggressive acting out (Brems, 1990; Levit, 1991). In classic Freudian theory, this sex difference is a consequence of anatomical differences in the genital apparatus, which projects outward for males and is internal for females. Contrary to this "anatomy is destiny" interpretation, however, current research indicates that it is learned sex role orientations that correlate with the use of various defense mechanisms. Regardless of their biological sex, people who score as "masculine" on sex role inventories, such as the Bem Sex Role Inventory, use externalizing defenses, whereas those who score as "feminine" use internalizing defenses (Brems, 1990; Evans, 1982; Levit, 1991; Lobel & Winch, 1986).

Defense mechanisms influence the perception of other people. In one study, undergraduate women were presented with hypothetical scenarios describing sexual assault. Those subjects classified as "repressors" (who minimized their awareness of threatening stimuli) were less likely than "sensitizers" to say that the hypothetical victims of sexual assault had behaved in ways that caused their victimization. Sensitizers, who experience more threat, presumably defend against this threat by blaming the victim (Thornton, 1992). This study had some experimental controls, because it provided the situation about which defenses were assessed. The situations, though, were simply hypothetical. Other studies, which we consider next, go even further by putting subjects in uncomfortable situations designed to arouse conflict and then assess their use of defense mechanisms.

Experimental Studies of Defense Mechanisms

Phebe Cramer asked undergraduates to tell stories about eight TAT pictures. For some of the subjects, the experimenter voiced criticism after the fourth, fifth, sixth, and seventh stories. Imagine lying on a cot, making up creative stories to pictures, and having the experimenter say to you, "These stories are about the worst I have ever heard. Could you try to get some better ones?" (Cramer, 1991, p. 42). Compared to control subjects who were not criticized, the experimental subjects reported that their feelings had become more negative during the experiment. In particular, they reported that they were angry. Their TAT stories contained more aggression and included more defense mechanisms. In another study, children also increased their use of defense mechanisms when criticized. Children, not surprisingly, used less mature defense mechanisms than the college students (Cramer & Gaul, 1988).

Defense mechanisms should not be dismissed as mere immature remnants from childhood. In the psychoanalytic view of personality, they are the way that we cope with internal conflict and external threats. Psychoanalysts seek not to eradicate them but to make them as mature and adaptive as possible.

Hypnosis

Since the beginning of psychoanalysis, hypnosis has been explored as a technique that provides access to the unconscious. Popular images of hypnosis describe the hypnotized individual as being under the spell of the hypnotist, having lost free will over action. Experts are skeptical that hypnotic behavior is as involuntary as popular images suggest, and they stress that the hypnotized individual is trying to behave according to his or her understanding of appropriate hypnotic behavior (Lynn, Rhue & Weekes, 1990). In either popular or expert interpretation, however, **hypnosis** puts a person into a state of enhanced suggestibility, making him or her particularly receptive to instructions from the hypnotist. Instructions may influence memory, perception, or behavior. The individual may remember or forget selected past events; may perceive things that are not there or fail to see what others see; or may do strange things, such as touching the forehead every time the word "behavior" is uttered.

Hypnosis and Recovered Memories

Can unconscious memories be retrieved through hypnosis? Such a possibility has intriguing applications, ranging from the hope of solving crimes by enhancing the testimony of eyewitnesses to the possibility of accessing the unconscious to facilitate psychotherapeutic treatment for traumatic events.

Some of the claims that have been made for hypnosis have not withstood scientific scrutiny. One example is **hypnotic age regression.** It has been claimed that under hypnotic suggestion, individuals can return to earlier periods of their lives, reexperiencing and recalling phenomena that have since been forgotten. Although such enactments can appear highly convincing to observers and to the subjects themselves, a review of the empirical literature suggests that the age regression is not genuine. In adequately controlled studies, people retain adult cognitive skills such as adult moral reasoning, and they are inaccurate about details that they would know if the regression were genuine (Nash, 1987, 1988).

Hypnosis does produce cognitive changes that resemble childlike states. Michael Nash indicates that hypnotized subjects "elicit more imagistic, primary process material, display more spontaneous and intense affect, are more likely to experience unusual body sensations, and may often displace core attitudes about important others onto the hypnotist" (1988, p. 396). Such phenomena appear childlike, but they are not genuine age regression. Others have argued, however, that age regression as explored in experimental studies underestimates the age regression produced in clinical settings, where there is more intensive interaction with the patient (Spinhoven & Van Wijk, 1992).

It is commonly believed that hypnosis enhances memory for adult events too, such as those that an eyewitness may have observed when a crime is committed. Testimony collected under hypnosis is particularly convincing to jurors in a simulated criminal trial, although experimental research indicates that such evidence does not live up to its claim of greater accuracy (Wagstaff, Vella & Perfect, 1992). In one case, the suggestions produced during a hypnotic-like state caused a highly suggestible man to develop "memories" for crimes that had never been committed (Ofshe, 1992). The possibility that hypnosis can produce false memories, **pseudomemories,** certainly suggests caution about believing hypnotically retrieved memories. Elizabeth Loftus, an eminent researcher on the (in)accuracy of eyewitness testimony, warns that many cases of recovered memories may be inaccurate and may be produced sometimes by therapists' misguided suggestions (Loftus, 1993). Her research on memory has demonstrated that misleading questions can produce false memories in controlled laboratory settings, even without hypnosis. Subjects questioned in a misleading manner often report that they saw broken glass or stop signs on videos of a car accident that had no such details, or a cap on a bareheaded robber. Hypnotized subjects fill in details, embellishing a suggestion made to them, and they later report these pseudomemories with more confidence than subjects who were not hypnotized (Weekes et al., 1992). This confidence makes them more believable, even though they are not accurate.

The social pressure to produce particular memories contributes substantially to these errors. It leads to reporting bias, whereby subjects describe what they think the experimenter wants to hear (Spanos et al., 1992). Pseudomemories can be reversed by changing the subjects' expectations and interpretation of the situation. When they are instructed that they have a *hidden observer* that can distinguish true from false memories, most subjects correctly report that pseudomemories were really fantasy (Spanos & McLean, 1986). Providing hypnotized experimental subjects with a monetary reward for distinguishing between true and false memories also reduces the number of pseudomemories (Murrey, Cross & Whipple, 1992).

Elizabeth Loftus cautions that therapists who are convinced that sexual abuse is widespread can ask misleading questions and even blatantly suggest to their clients that they have been sexually abused. These experiences in therapy, with or without hypnosis, can lead to the construction of pseudomemories and ultimately to false accusations against parents or other alleged perpetrators. These issues have reached popular attention with television personality Rosanne Barr Arnold's controversial accusations that her father abused her. Lawsuits have been filed against alleged perpetrators and against therapists accused of creating false memories. Obviously, the accuracy of recalled childhood events is a controversial matter.

Can Everyone Be Hypnotized?

Individuals vary in their responsiveness to hypnosis. Some can be trained easily to enter a hypnotic trance. Others need more instruction. There are also individuals who seem not to be hypnotizable. Are we able to predict who can be hypnotized? Expectation is one predictor; subjects who expect to respond to hypnotic instructions are more likely to do so (Spanos, Burnley & Cross, 1993). Individual differences in hypnotizability can also be predicted using self-report questionnaires or performance measures to assess suggestibility (Hilgard, 1965; Lynn & Rhue, 1988; Shor & Orne, 1962; Spanos et al., 1983).

People who are easily hypnotizable report, on self-report measures, that they readily become absorbed in imagination (Hilgard, 1965). This includes reports of a variety of imaginative or absorbing activities, such as drama, reading, religious experiences, and psychic experiences. Similar characteristics are described by other researchers: a capacity for absorption (Tellegen & Atkinson, 1974) and being fantasy-prone (Wilson & Barber, 1983) and capable of vivid mental imagery (Silverstein, 1993; Spanos et al., 1987). In some cases, the tendency to engage in fantasy is part of a maladaptive, even seriously maladjusted personality, which may originate as a defensive reaction to abuse in childhood. Usually, though, fantasy-prone people are psychologically healthy (Lynn & Rhue, 1988).

Models of Hypnosis

Although much is known about hypnosis, disagreements remain over fundamental explanations of the phenomenon. In hypnosis, do people enter a separate state of consciousness, in the sense that sleeping and waking are separate states with different physiological patterns? Or is hypnosis more analogous to the changes that take place when an actor dons a costume and changes character? Even the experts disagree (Singer & Bonanno, 1990). If hypnosis is a separate state of consciousness, it would have to be rather subtle physiologically, because physiological measures, such as EEG (electroencephalograph) brain wave recordings, do not differ between hypnotized subjects and nonhypnotized subjects (Silverstein, 1993).

Ernest Hilgard (1976), an eminent researcher on hypnosis, describes hypnosis as a state of dissociation among aspects of the mind, analogous to dissociations that occur in amnesia and split personality. The mind requires a great deal of communication among its parts to coordinate the processes that are occurring in separate parts of the brain (as presented earlier in this chapter, in the discussion of the cognitive unconscious). Like the earlier videotape analogy, these parts can play separately, producing the dissociations of amnesia or of hypnosis. Through such dissociation, hypnosis can be used to control pain by dissociating the sensory perception of a toothache or other pain from the higher awareness of suffering. Hypnotic suggestibility does not, however, relate to people's capacity to divide their attention between two performance tasks while *not* hypnotized; for example, copying digits while listening to a tape-recorded story (Stava & Jaffa, 1988).

One explanation of hypnosis is that language can be processed automatically, dissociated from the rest of the mind in a similar way to the dissociation from consciousness of the details of bicycle riding (to one who knows how to ride). Some people process verbal information more automatically than others and so respond more automatically to the verbal instructions of the hypnotist (Nadon, Laurence & Perry, 1991). The Stroop color-naming task illustrates automatic verbal processing. Try reading a list of words:

BLUE
RED
GREEN
BLUE
YELLOW
RED
GREEN
BLUE

You can probably read the list rather quickly. Now, try reading such a list with the words printed in colored ink, but colors not corresponding to the word. BLUE is printed in red, for example, and YELLOW in green. You can read the list, but much more slowly, because of the conflict between reading the word (BLUE) and naming the color of the ink (red).

Hypnotizable people have particular difficulty with this task, presumably because they process language more automatically and are less able to suspend this automatic processing for the more conscious thought required by the Stroop task (Dixon, Brunet & Laurence, 1990). This "verbal automaticity" makes them more likely to be influenced by hypnotic suggestions, which are given verbally.

Martin Orne (1959) is perhaps the best known skeptic of the view that hypnosis represents an altered state of consciousness. He has certainly demonstrated some thought-provoking phenomena. Once he showed a rigged demonstration to students in a lecture class, leading them to believe that hypnotized individuals experience an unusual tendency for their dominant hand to remain wherever it is placed ("catalepsy"). This is not really a characteristic of hypnosis, but it sounds plausible enough to be believed. When later hypnotized, those who had viewed the lecture demonstrated this phenomenon. A control group, which were not so deceived, did not (Orne, 1971). Orne argues that hypnotic induction does not produce a separate state of consciousness but rather enactment of a *role*, the role of hypnotized subject, that has been learned from culture. This does not mean that subjects are consciously faking, but that hypnotic behavior is shaped by social expectations and not simply determined by a physiologically separate state of consciousness. An experiment, whether on hypnosis or on any other topic, presents subjects with certain **demand characteristics** that convey, perhaps subtly, what is expected (Orne, 1971). These demand characteristics influence behavior. This explains why pseudomemories can be both created and reversed by changing the demand characteristics of the experiment or, in the real world, of the interaction with a therapist or anyone else in an authoritative position.

Hypnosis in Clinical Treatment

Hypnosis permits access to the unconscious, which can be given instructions. Many types of pain have been treated effectively with hypnosis. Burn patients treated by hypnosis report less pain than control subjects (Patterson et al., 1992; Van der Does & Van Dyck, 1989). Hypnosis has been used to treat the pain of cancer (Kraft, 1992). Patients recover more quickly after surgery when treated by hypnosis (Blankfield, 1991). Hypnosis can reduce headaches, although biofeedback and relaxation training are equally effective (Primavera & Kaiser, 1992).

The technique is used in therapy to encourage the unconscious to cooperate in individuals' efforts to stop smoking, lose weight, recover from eating disorders, and make other life-style changes (for example, Fairfield, 1990). Nonhypnotic treatments may be equally effective, however, for life-style changes such as quitting smoking (Spanos et al., 1992–1993).

Smoking is one of the maladaptive behaviors that is sometimes treated with hypnosis.

Hypnosis in Experimental Studies of Psychodynamic Hypotheses

Researchers have used hypnosis as an experimental procedure in the study of psychodynamic hypotheses. By permitting control over the contents of the unconscious, hypnosis permits the systematic observations that science requires. Gerald Blum (1989) has used hypnosis in conjunction with subliminal perception to reduce some of the uncertainties of the latter procedure. He works with a small number of subjects who are trained, under hypnosis, to respond to selected stimuli with specific emotions. The stimuli have been selected on the basis of psychoanalytic theory to represent common sources of unconscious conflict. These stimuli portray a cartoon figure of a dog named Blacky doing various things. A picture of Blacky nursing from his mother, for example, is related to oral anxiety, while a picture of Blacky burying feces is related to anal anxiety. By hypnotically instructing subjects to feel various levels of anxiety (or the absence of anxiety) in response to particular pictures, the experimenter has enhanced control over these emotions.

Anxiety, according to Blum's model of psychoanalytic theory, interferes with thinking. It slows down reactions when subjects are required to name pictures (for example, of a carrot, a banana, or a hat). (Students may have observed this adverse effect of anxiety when taking exams. If overly anxious, a person cannot solve, or is slower to solve, problems that seem much easier when one is relaxed.) Blum has tested these ideas by exposing subjects to tachistoscopic presentations of stimuli that (as a result of hypnotic training) produce anxiety and then measuring their reaction time on cognitive tasks. Picture-naming reactions are slower following anxiety-producing subliminal stimuli (Blum, 1989). He reports similar studies in which the task is to solve an anagram rather than to name a picture. The results were not so straightforward; pleasure slowed down reaction times, and anxiety sometimes had no effect and sometimes actually improved performance. Although the results were not simple, Blum concluded that anxiety, under some conditions, inhibits cognitive processing of stimuli, as psychoanalytic theory suggests. Blum has developed a cognitive model that describes psychodynamics in a computer model of neural inhibition. This computer model suggests new hypotheses for further human research. In fact, the phenomenon of hypnosis, however it will finally be understood, has promise for enlightening researchers about psychological phenomena beyond those suggested by psychoanalysis, including in particular the nature of cognition and the relationship between the mind and the body (see Holroyd, 1985–1986).

Sexuality

Freud's theory emphasized sexuality as the core motivation for all behavior and anxiety over sexuality as the fundamental conflict of personality. To motivate "civilized" behavior, sexual impulses must be transformed, through a process he called **sublimation.** In its raw form, "it is not possible for the claims of the sexual instinct to be reconciled with the demands of culture" (Freud, 1925/1958, p. 186).

Normal, healthy development succeeds in transforming primitive and childish sexual impulses into socially acceptable expressions, but one of the legacies of Freudian theory has been our heightened awareness of the failures of such transformation.

Freud's Theory of Childhood Sexuality

Freud's description of childhood sexuality has always been rejected by more people than have accepted it. Despite this inhospitable reception to his formal theory, the issues he raised about sexual experience in childhood have continued to guide researchers. Let us briefly review Freud's classic theory, as a historical introduction, before turning to current research findings.

According to Freud, personality is formed during the first five years of life, as the child learns how to deal with physical impulses. He suggested that all personality dynamics are based on sexual motivation, although he defined "sexual" in broad terms. The term **libido** refers to this broadly defined sexual motivation, including not only the sexual drives of adults, but also their childhood precursors, which are not focused on the body parts that we usually refer to as "sexual." During the first year of life, the **oral period,** the libido is concerned with obtaining pleasure through feeding. During the second and third years of life, the **anal period,** the libido is focused on control over the bowels, and the toddler resists restrictive toilet training. While the oral and anal phases, called "pre-Oedipal," are characterized by a libido that is not focused in the sexual organs, this changes during the **Oedipal period.** From age three to five (or a bit later), eroticism is focused on the genitals. According to Freud, the young child masturbates and fantasizes a sexual union with the opposite-sex parent. A boy's love for his mother is accompanied by the wish that he, like Oedipus of the tragic Greek play, will be able to marry her and to remove his father as a rival for his mother's love. A girl's love for her father is accompanied by a parallel wish to become her father's sexual partner.

According to Freud, these wishes arouse conflict. The boy fears that he will be punished by his father for this wish. The feared punishment is castration ("castration anxiety"). The boy resolves this conflict by giving up his mother as a sexual object, instead identifying with his father and with the male sex role, and internalizing the prohibition against incest to develop a superego, the inner voice of conscience.

Freud suggested that girls' development is hampered by their anatomical difference from males. Lacking a penis, they are not motivated by castration anxiety. Instead, they experience "penis envy." In the absence of castration anxiety, girls have less motivation to develop a superego and less incentive to accept the female sex role. Their psychological development, argued Freud, is less mature than that of males for these reasons. Nonetheless, both sexes emerge from the Oedipal period having achieved the major personality developments of their lives, ready to set childhood sexual impulses aside and to wait (through a "latency period") for the biological urging of puberty to experience adult sexual impulses.

Needless to say, Freud's formulations have aroused much criticism. Psychoanalysts themselves have offered theoretical revisions of the description of early childhood development, particularly of girls' development (for example, Chehrazi, 1986; Chodorow, 1978). Many revisions of the classic theory have stressed alternatives to the emphasis on sexual urges.

Although the classic Freudian theory is rarely accepted without revision, it focused attention on childhood sexual experience, and that issue still concerns therapists and researchers. In particular, sexual abuse in childhood impedes normal development. Freud proposed, to a shocked medical community, that many of his female patients had developed their psychiatric disturbances because they were the victims of childhood sexual abuse, most often incest by their fathers; this theory is termed the **seduction hypothesis.** Later, he rescinded this theory, instead proposing that no

In early childhood, boys fantasize about their sexual potential and fear punishment, according to Freud's controversial theory of childhood sexuality.

actual incest was necessary for the psychiatric disturbance to develop. His revised theory postulates that the young girl's *wish* for an incestuous relationship with her father is the cause of later neurosis, without any misconduct on the father's part.

Even this revised theory, though, has provoked controversy. Its most well known critic, Jeffrey Masson, accuses Freud of intellectual cowardice, of publicly disavowing his seduction hypothesis to appease the powerful men who did not wish to endure close examination of their sexual misbehavior (Masson, 1984, 1990). According to Masson, Freud's private letters reveal that he continued to believe that incest was a widespread problem, even after he publicly proclaimed that girls' fantasies were the problem. Masson's challenge has provoked controversy. On one side, critics have joined his attack on Freud and on the establishment's resistance to claims of child abuse (for example, deMause, 1988). On the other side, defenders of psychoanalysis have questioned Masson's evidence and his motives (for example, Paul, 1985; Rosenman, 1989).

Masson's argument leads us to a historical question: What did Freud truly believe? More important to psychologists, however, are the substantive questions, some of which are difficult to observe scientifically. How can we know what are the unconscious wishes of young children? Other questions are more objective: How widespread is sexual abuse? What are its consequences for personality development? Several researchers have collected relevant data to answer these questions.

Studies of Sexual Abuse

Because many empirical studies of sexual abuse have been reported in recent years, the topic can now be examined on the basis of accumulating scientific evidence. Earlier studies, biased by psychoanalytic assumptions, described the victim as provoking the incest through seductive behavior (reviewed by Vander Mey & Neff, 1982). More recent studies focus on the prevalence of sexual abuse and the adverse consequences of the victimization.

Methodological difficulties challenge researchers. Questionnaire and interview studies may underestimate the frequency of sexual abuse because respondents choose to not disclose the material, perhaps to avoid confronting it themselves. Amnesia may prevent recall. On the other hand, suggestive questioning may lead to reports of abuse where there was none. Studies that select respondents from clinical samples or from legal records are questionable, because the majority of cases of sexual abuse go unreported (Finkelhor, 1979; Vander Mey & Neff, 1982). Many studies suggest that sexual abuse of children, including incest, is not rare (Alter-Reid et al., 1986; Finkelhor et al., 1990; Vander Mey, 1988).

Sexual abuse has been linked to a variety of symptoms, both in children and in adults (Barnard & Hirsch, 1985; Browne & Finkelhor, 1986; Haugaard & Emery, 1989; Kendall-Tackett, Williams & Finkelhor, 1993; Silon, 1992). Multiple personality is a very rare but serious disturbance that is thought to be more common among victims of incest (Saltman & Solomon, 1982; Trickett & Putnam, 1993). Considerable data now support Freud's early claim that understanding the adjustment problems of adulthood may require examining the sexual traumas of childhood.

Psychotherapy

If psychodynamic explanations are accurate, we may expect psychoanalytic therapy to relieve symptoms. Is it effective? In 1952, Hans Eysenck claimed that the studies then available did not provide evidence that psychotherapy was effective. (He was indicting all forms of therapy, not only psychoanalysis.) Such studies had methodological problems, however. Eysenck observed that the statistics "do not necessarily disprove the possibility of therapeutic effectiveness" (Eysenck, 1952/1992, p. 661) and suggested the need for better research. Although Eysenck remained skeptical about the effectiveness of psychoanalytic therapy (Erwin, 1980), studies done in the decades since his challenge have provided more convincing evidence that therapy works.

Therapeutic effectiveness is not easy to measure. For one thing, the goals of therapy are not always clearly defined. Patients may seek relief from acute symptoms, such as anxiety and depression, but often therapy aims at more extensive personality restructuring as well: changes in patterns of thought, and **insight;** that is, understanding the cause of the problem. Furthermore, the variety of complaints that patients bring to the therapist makes it difficult to agree upon an assessment method that fits everyone. How shall we evaluate techniques that may seek to treat depressive people who have attempted suicide, anxious people too fearful to leave the house, and successful individuals who have vague feelings that something is missing from their lives? There is no "one size fits all" criterion of improvement.

Nonetheless, the effort has been made, for a variety of reasons. Knowing what works and what doesn't can help practitioners choose, from the variety of therapies available, the appropriate ones for particular patients. Knowing what doesn't work can prompt improvements in therapeutic practice. Insurance companies may demand evidence that therapy is effective before agreeing to pay for it. In addition, since therapy is an intervention to change personality, its effectiveness has implications for theoretical understandings about the nature of personality.

Since projective tests are used for clinical diagnosis by psychoanalytic therapists, it is reasonable to ask whether these tests provide evidence of improvement after treatment. They do, according to some studies. For example, defense mechanisms scored from the TAT were reduced in young adults treated with intensive psychoanalytic therapy as inpatients (Cramer & Blatt, 1990).

In addition to comparing psychoanalytic treatment to no therapy, we can compare psychoanalytic treatment to other forms of therapy. If psychoanalytic treatment is effective, but no more effective than other modes of psychotherapy, this would suggest that it is not the unconscious dynamics that account for change. Perhaps other factors, such as the interpersonal relationship with the therapist or changes in the patient's self-image, could be responsible.

A major long-term (30-year) study to assess the effectiveness of psychoanalysis, launched in the early 1950s, was the Psychotherapy Research Project of the Menninger Foundation (Wallerstein, 1989). This research compared psychoanalysis with other forms of therapy, expressive psychotherapy and supportive psychotherapy, which do not probe the unconscious dynamics identified by psychoanalytic theory as requiring therapeutic work. The researchers predicted that psychoanalysis would be superior to these other therapy methods, but that was not found to be the case. These results suggest that therapy can be effective without focusing on unconscious material.

Overall, the evidence indicates to some reviewers that these different forms of psychotherapy are similar in their effectiveness (Stiles, Shapiro & Elliott, 1986). Psychoanalysis is no more effective than other forms of therapy that do not aim to probe the unconscious. On the other hand, it is also not less effective, overall, although it may be more lengthy and expensive. Other reviewers are convinced that for certain problems, other methods are better. For treating phobias (irrational fears) and other anxieties, behavioral treatments are often reported to be more effective than alternative therapies, including psychoanalysis (for example, Goisman, 1983; Goldfried, Greenberg & Marmar, 1990). Behavioral treatments are also more effective than other interventions for treating children and adolescents (Weisz et al., 1987). For severe depression, drug therapy adds to the effectiveness of psychotherapy (Goldfried, Greenberg & Marmar, 1990).

The factors that make therapy effective may not be closely tied to the theoretical model guiding the therapist. Other factors may include the therapist's personality; the match between the therapist and the client; and changes in the client's beliefs beyond those described by the particular therapeutic orientation, such as the expectation of getting better (Norcross, 1991; Stiles, Shapiro & Elliott, 1986). Recent research has considered many aspects of the therapeutic process to determine the effects of each. For example, what kinds of interpretations should be made, and when? What is the nature of the bond between the therapist and the client (Goldfried, Greenberg & Marmar, 1990)? Such investigations may improve therapy.

Cultural Issues and Psychodynamic Theory

Psychodynamic theory focuses on the internal dynamics of the individual and largely overlooks external influences from the social environment. Case histories of Jewish patients published at the time of the Holocaust contained no reference to those events or to their impact on the people who were undergoing in-depth analysis (Masson, 1990, pp. 154–155). Is an unconscious that excludes such cultural factors complete? Can it guide therapists adequately in their task of facilitating the mental health of their clients?

As proposed by Freud, psychodynamic theory posits an unconscious, formed in early childhood, that is universal. Freud claimed that his developmental stages, including the Oedipus conflict, applied to all cultures. This assertion of universality has been challenged. Critics maintain that Freud's ideas presume a cultural background in which males have disproportionate power: that is, *patriarchy*. Only in such a culture would the young boy's competition with his father be so central to development and girls and women be so often the victims of sexual exploitation. Only in such a culture would a theory assert that females are psychologically less developed than males as a consequence of anatomy (deChesnay, 1985; Herman, 1981).

In addition to the accusations of sex bias and insensitivity to racial and ethnic prejudice, psychoanalytic theory can be criticized for neglecting many cultural issues that affect psychological well-being. It espouses a model of health that esteems the autonomous individual, inadequately considering relationships and interpersonal connectedness (for example, Green, 1990). Some of these accusations, to be sure, can be made against other psychological perspectives as well. Whatever its shortcomings, psychoanalysis encouraged psychologists to look beyond the obvious, to be skeptical about taking self-report statements as correct reports of personality, and to consider the roles of childhood and of sexuality in personality.

SUMMARY

- Sigmund Freud proposed that psychodynamic causes, which are unconscious conflicts originating in childhood, motivate personality.

- The therapeutic technique of psychoanalysis reveals unconscious material through free association.

- Traumatic experiences in the oral, anal, and phallic periods produce fixation, in which repression forces the conflict into the unconscious, where it remains unchanged.

- Researchers have found support for psychodynamic theory using experimental methods, especially techniques of subliminal perception and Silverman's subliminal psychodynamic activation.

- It is widely assumed that conscious thought is superior to unconsciousness, although the unconscious plays an important role in creativity.

- In contrast to Freud's dynamic unconscious, modern theorists have proposed a cognitive unconscious, emphasizing information processing instead of conflict.

- Dreams were described by Freud as "the royal road to the unconscious," which portray unconscious material in symbolic form.

- Physiological studies show that dreams occur during REM sleep and are related to brain functioning.

- Projective tests assess the contents of the unconscious by examining people's reactions to ambiguous stimuli, such as the Rorschach inkblots.

- Defense mechanisms are used by the ego to avoid the anxiety that would result if unconscious conflicts were recognized consciously. They are assessed by projective tests and by questionnaires.

- Hypnosis is a state of heightened suggestibility. Memories retrieved under hypnosis are often erroneous and influenced by suggestion.

- Not everyone can be hypnotized. Hypnotizability is associated with imaginativeness.

• Many experts doubt that hypnosis is a separate state of consciousness, citing evidence that subjects' expectations influence their behavior under hypnosis.

• Controversies over the role of childhood sexuality in adult adjustment have raged since Freud's time. Modern studies support the claim that sexual abuse contributes to various symptoms.

• Psychoanalytic treatment is no more effective than other forms of treatment, but treatment in general is more effective than no treatment.

• Psychoanalytic approaches have been criticized for neglecting cultural issues, such as racial and ethnic prejudice and sex roles.

GLOSSARY

anal period the second and third years of life, when the libido is invested in obtaining pleasure through control of bowel functions

cognitive unconscious a modern model of the unconscious, emphasizing knowledge and attention (that is, information processing)

conscious experience of which we are aware at any given moment

creativity the capacity to produce original, unusual, and adaptive solutions to problems

defense mechanisms strategies used by the ego to resolve the conflict between unconscious and conscious aspects of personality

demand characteristics expectations conveyed to subjects about what is expected of them in an experiment or while under hypnosis, which can influence behavior and lead to apparent confirmation of the researcher's expectations

dissociation a lack of connection among mental experiences that ordinarily would be connected

double-blind a procedure for controlling for expectancy effects by taking precautions that neither the subjects nor the experimenter knows who is receiving the treatment and who is receiving the placebo control

dynamic unconscious Freud's view of the unconscious; it includes needs and conflicts that influence experience and behavior

expectancy belief about what will happen in an experiment, which may produce the anticipated effect

fixation continued seeking of unconsciously motivated needs because earlier satisfactions were denied, often because of childhood stress or trauma

free association a technique used in psychoanalysis for revealing the unconscious by having the patient say whatever comes to mind, even if it seems irrelevant

hypnosis a state of enhanced suggestibility, thought by some to be a separate state of consciousness

hypnotic age regression apparent access to memories and experiences from earlier periods of life that occurs while under hypnosis

insight understanding the psychodynamic causes of one's symptoms or problems

libido motivation that, in Freud's theory, is fundamentally sexual

object relations an alternative approach in modern psychoanalysis that emphasizes relationships with other people

Oedipal period the period from ages three to five (or a bit later), when libido is concerned with genital pleasure and a fantasized sexual relationship with the opposite-sex parent

oral period the first year of life, when the libido is invested in obtaining pleasure through feeding

placebo an inert pill or an innocuous treatment that is administered to a control group to control for expectancy effects

preconscious material that can be readily brought to awareness when needed, although it is not in awareness at the moment

primary process primitive psychological dynamics, such as occurs during dreaming

projective tests tests that assess unconscious material by asking people to describe what they see in an ambiguous stimulus

pseudomemories false memories, such as those that seem to be retrieved while under hypnosis or in therapy

psychoanalysis Freud's method for diagnosing and treating disorders that stem from unconscious causes; also, Freud's theory of personality

psychodynamic referring to the power of psychological forces to influence symptoms and other behavioral effects

repression forcing thoughts to remain unconscious, thus avoiding the anxiety that would result if they were conscious

Rorschach inkblot test a well-known projective test that elicits responses to cards containing inkblot patterns, given to assess unconscious aspects of personality

secondary process logical, rational, adaptive psychological functioning

seduction hypothesis Freud's proposal, which he later abandoned, that many female patients had developed their psychiatric disturbances because they had been victims of childhood sexual abuse, most often incest by their fathers

sublimation transformation of sexual impulses into culturally acceptable forms so that civilized behavior can occur

subliminal perception unconscious awareness of a stimulus, evidenced by response at some level, without conscious awareness of the stimulus

subliminal psychodynamic activation Silverman's research technique of arousing unconscious motivation by tachistoscopic presentation of a stimulus that is related to unconscious needs

tachistoscope a device for presenting a stimulus very briefly, so that a person perceives the stimulus only unconsciously

true experiment a research method in which the alleged cause is systematically manipulated by the experimenter, while other influences are kept constant; used to test cause-effect relationships

unconscious material that is not readily made conscious

THOUGHT QUESTIONS

1. Can you provide an example of a childhood fixation that interferes with optimal adult functioning?

2. Does focusing on the childhood origins of neurosis run the risk of blaming parents excessively for our problems?

3. Have you noticed that advertisers seem to associate sexual messages with their products? Are these conscious or unconscious messages?

4. Do you think that creativity is a product of the unconscious? What else might be involved?

5. How is dissociation different from simply forgetting?

6. Do you believe that dreams have significant meaning? How would you go about validating your opinion scientifically?

7. Look at the list of defense mechanisms in Table 6.1. Can you give examples of these mechanisms (real or hypothetical)? How might using these defense mechanisms prevent people from functioning optimally?

8. How would you test whether a person who seems to be hypnotized is genuinely hypnotized or is simply faking or playing a role?

9. What do you think would be a reasonable criterion for saying whether or not therapy has been effective? (That is, what should people expect to achieve through psychotherapy?)

10. Do you believe that personality theory should be concerned with social issues such as prejudice and gender, or should these topics be left for social psychologists and others?

Motivation in Personality

PSYCHODYNAMIC THEORY, as we saw in Chapter 6, offers one model of the dynamics or motivation of personality. Because the theory originated in the treatment of psychotherapy patients, it historically has been linked to issues of maladjustment and irrationality and to the study of individuals (in contrast to nomothetic research). Other models of motivation, to which we now turn, have been developed from studying groups rather than individuals and normal populations rather than clinic patients. These models explain behavior that is widely observed in the population at large, rather than symptoms that drive people to therapy. Like psychodynamic approaches, these models generally assume that the experiences of childhood influence adult motivation and that people vary in their stable trait-like motivational patterns.

The term **motivation** refers to the energy or drive that impels a person to make choices and to seek goals actively. The concept shares a metaphor of psychodynamic approaches—that "energy" or "drive" energizes and directs behavior—but it offers alternatives to the libido (sexual energy) of psychoanalysis. Hunger, thirst, and other bodily motivations are of less concern to personality psychologists than the social motivations we will consider, including achievement, affiliation, and power motivation.

Motivational intensity is presumed to increase and decrease. Hearing a challenge or a pep talk may increase motivation, for example, while learning that an expected reward for finishing a task has been cancelled is likely to decrease motivation. Motivation impels a person to strive toward goals and to seek satisfaction of unmet needs. When a need is satisfied or a goal reached, motivation decreases, and the individual turns to other activities. This rise and fall of motivation explains why we do one thing for a while and then change to something else. We eat until we are satiated; then we do something else.

Because motivation rises and falls, it is not a term that can be used to describe a traitlike characteristic of a person. How can we take note of the fact that after eating, one person characteristically does homework and another talks to friends? To indicate these traitlike characteristics of a person, we use the term **motive,** which refers to the stable or recurring patterns of motivation within a person. We could say that Joe, who does homework after dinner, has a motive for academic achievement, whereas his roommate, who spends time with friends, has a motive for friendship. Level of motivation is influenced by an individual's motives as well as by external circumstances, such as the threat of an exam, which may prompt studying in people with a low academic achievement motive as well as in those high on this motive.

The Legacy of Henry Murray

Motivational studies in current personality research have developed from the influential work of Henry Murray and his colleagues at the Harvard Psychological Clinic (Murray, 1938). That work created a bridge from the psychoanalytic model to modern motivational theory. Murray had studied psychoanalysis and had been analyzed himself. He accepted parts of psychoanalytic theory as he developed his own approach, which he called *personology.* In particular, Murray was attracted to the greater depth with which psychoanalysis described individuals, compared to the more superficial approach he saw in academic psychology at that time (Murray, 1940).

The Murray research team administered a variety of tests to 50 college men. These included written questionnaires, biographical interviews, tests of abilities, and tests of reactions to situations provoking frustration or tempting cheating, among other measures. Erik Erikson, a pioneer child psychoanalyst, presented the young men with toy figures with which to construct dramatic scenes, a procedure similar to one he used in observations of children. The team administered several projective tests, including the Rorschach inkblot test. They also used the Thematic Apperception Test (TAT), which requires the respondent to make up a story based on a picture (Murray, 1938). This test is important in the development of motivational theory.

The Murray team conferred to pool their insights about each of these 50 extensive case studies. Their emphasis was on understanding individuals (idiographic research), rather than on testing hypotheses in a group (nomothetic research). They found evidence supporting some psychoanalytic ideas, including concerns over sexuality and evidence of an Oedipus complex in some subjects. They extended personality study considerably beyond psychoanalytic issues, however. The Murray team proposed an extensive list of "needs" or motives, such as achievement and dominance (see Table 5.5). In addition to needs, which exist *within* individuals, they recognized the importance of factors in the external situation, which they termed *press*. Combining the two dimensions, Murray's theory is sometimes referred to as a **needs-press theory.**

It is not surprising, given most researchers' preference for nomothetic research, that Murray's approach has been adapted from the clinic to the subject pool; that is, to the more usual practice of collecting data on a few variables from groups of people. In this tradition, three motives have received the greatest attention: achievement, affiliation, and power. An extensive research tradition has provided much information about these motives.

Measuring Motives: Thematic Apperception

The tradition of thematic apperception, derived from Murray's work at the Harvard Psychological Clinic, measures motives by analyzing fantasy stories that subjects write. These stories often seem to reflect both inner needs and environmental press. When both needs and press were described by Murray's subjects on projective test stories, the combination was called a **thema.** That term is the reason for naming the testing approach the method of *thematic* apperception (see Smith, 1992b, p. 4).

Imagine that two people have written stories about a picture often used in this research, a boy with a violin. One story describes the boy as depressed that he has been told to practice. He would prefer to be playing baseball with his friends and is afraid he will be called a sissy. The other person writes a story about a boy who has always aspired to be the best violinist in the country, and who is wondering whether his favorite uncle is going to give him a better violin for his birthday, since he has been studying the instrument for five years and has won a local competition because of his hard work. It seems obvious that the writer of the second story is more achievement motivated than the writer of the first story. For research, however, it is desirable to be able to describe how we arrived at this conclusion, so that we can apply our method of making such judgments in a standard way.

How can we know which details in a story constitute evidence of a particular need or motive? A general model of motivation provides a frame-

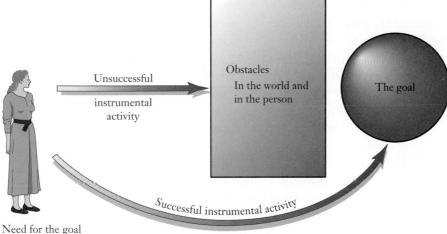

Need for the goal
Positive (and negative) expectations about success (and failure)
Positive (and negative) emotions about goal attainment (and nonattainment)

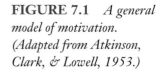

FIGURE 7.1 *A general model of motivation. (Adapted from Atkinson, Clark, & Lowell, 1953.)*

work for coding a variety of motives (Fig. 7.1) This model describes a person seeking a goal by efforts that require overcoming obstacles. It suggests several kinds of imagery that may be elaborated in a motivational story. The story may explicitly describe the goal (to be the best violinist in the country). The story may describe instrumental activities toward the goal, such as practicing long hours. These instrumental activities may be successful (I+), unsuccessful (I−), or have a doubtful outcome (I?). The story may say explicitly that the person has a need (N) or desire to achieve the goal (wanting to be the best). Positive emotions, such as pride and happiness, may be described when the goal is reached (G+) or anticipated (Ga+). Negative emotions, such as disappointment, may be described when failure occurs (G−) or is contemplated (Ga−). Obstacles may be described in the world (Bw), such as not having an adequate violin, or within the person (Bp), such as lack of ability. Someone in the environment may help the individual; for example, the uncle who may give him a better violin, providing "nurturant press" in Murray's sense of environmental "press" (Nup). Each of these images is worth one point on a motive score. In addition, if a story is clearly focused on the motive being scored, without other subplots, an additional point is scored for "thema" (Th). The more elaborate the description of a motive, then, the more points are scored.

Next, researchers test the validity of this coding scheme for the specific motive. Validation procedures are based on the assumption that motives vary not only between individuals but also within individuals, because circumstances sometimes arouse a need and sometimes permit its satisfaction.

Motives are like biological drives; they direct and energize behavior toward a particular goal, and when that goal is reached, the motive decreases because it is satisfied. Hunger, for example, increases with food deprivation and diminishes when a person eats. Jack Atkinson and David McClelland (1948) showed that depriving subjects of food led to changes in their TAT stories, thus confirming in principle the validity of projective tests as measures of motivation.

How can we know whether measures based on TAT stories are valid for motives other than food? The strategy that researchers have adopted is to treat an experimental group in a way that arouses the particular motive. For example, to arouse achievement motivation, subjects were told that the tests they were taking assessed intelligence and career potential (Atkinson, 1958). Their thematic stories were compared with those of a control group tested under neutral conditions. Coding categories were retained in the scoring system only if they differed between these two groups. The scoring system was then used to evaluate stories written by subjects under standard test administration procedures to determine their motives. If a person wrote a story under neutral conditions that was like those produced by achievement-aroused subjects, that subject was considered to be high in the personality trait of the achievement motive. Similar reasoning applies to other motives, such as affiliation and power.

Evidence of the validity of thematic measures of motivation comes from many studies that show correlations between motive scores and behavioral criteria. Achievement motive scores, for example, predict successful achievement in business careers, and power motive scores predict leadership in student government. Tests must be administered under standard conditions for such validity to occur. Standard instructions are neutral; that is, they do not particularly stimulate the motive being measured. A projective measure of achievement motivation given under achievement-aroused conditions (for example, telling subjects that their intelligence is being measured) would produce higher scores, but these scores would not predict achievement behaviors as well as the scores obtained under standard, neutral conditions (Lundy, 1988). This temporary arousal would mask the differences between those low and high on the motive. Measures administered under neutral conditions are better indicators of the level of motivation that people experience in their everyday lives.

Reliability of Coding

Reliable measures, by definition, are measures that produce similar scores when a test is taken again. On objective tests, unreliability occurs if subjects give different answers the second time a test is taken. On thematic apperception tests and other projective tests, unreliability has an additional source. Stories must be coded to translate them into numbers for research.

Two coders may code the same story differently. If you read a story describing a man who wanted to impress his boss in order to get a raise to provide better for his children, would you code it as achievement motivation, because of the job concern? Or power motivation, because of the desire to impress someone? Or affiliation motivation, because of the nurturant attitude toward the family? Such coding decisions are not always easy. Careful instructions and training minimize discrepancies among coders, but disagreements cannot be eliminated entirely. The extent of this disagreement is assessed by having two coders score the same materials independently and then evaluating their agreement. This **intercoder reliability** is usually expressed as a correlation coefficient; sometimes it is computed as a percentage agreement score. The higher the intercoder reliability, the better. Using standard coding instructions, experienced coders typically obtain reliabilities of $r = .85$ or higher.

Traditionally, psychological tests are expected to have high reliability from one item to the next (called *interitem reliability*) and from one testing session to the next (called *test-retest reliability*). Both kinds of reliability are generally lower with projective tests than with objective tests, and this fact has discouraged some researchers from using projective tests. With multiple-choice tests, items that do not correlate highly with other items are dropped, so that the test as a whole has high interitem reliability. This is not a suitable technique for projective tests, however. The subject responds to pictures rather than questions, and regardless of the pictures used, it is unusual for a subject to score consistently high on a given motive (such as achievement) for all pictures. Critics point out the low interitem reliability of thematically scored motives (Entwistle, 1972) and warn that such unreliable measures are not of much use, because test construction theory assumes that unreliability stems from measurement error.

Defenders of the technique have devised explanations of the unreliability, arguing that a different theory of testing is required for projective tests (Lundy, 1985). For one thing, research subjects try to vary their stories, assuming that doing so is better, in contrast to their attempts to be consistent on multiple-choice and true-false questions. (Wouldn't you vary your stories, too, when the researcher presents the test as a measure of "creative imagination"?) In addition, motivation is probably less stable across time than the beliefs about ourselves that are measured by most self-report questionnaires. Jack Atkinson and David Birch propose, as part of a more general mathematical model of motivation, that the motivations being measured actually do vary from one moment to the next, influenced by the storytelling procedure itself. Nonetheless, a person with a high achievement motive will be in a highly motivated state more often both in real life and in the assessment period. The number of achievement images in the pictures, therefore, is a good estimate of the person's achievement motive, despite variation from picture to picture (Atkinson & Birch, 1978). This sort of unreliability is not measurement error, any more than variations in your response to the question "How hungry are you?" throughout the day would suggest that your answers were erroneous (Atkinson, 1982; Smith, 1992c).

Why Not Use Self-Report Measures?

Self-report measures, generally in the form of multiple-choice tests, are usually more reliable than projective tests. In addition, they are easier to score. Coding stories for motives is time-consuming, which adds to the cost of research. Only with extensive training do coders achieve adequate reliability. Some time can be saved by simplifying the coding method (Chusmir, 1985) or even by computerizing the coding (Stone et al., 1966), but coding stories still requires more time than objective tests. Why not use a multiple-choice test? Although such tests have been devised to measure motives (Moser & Gerth, 1986; Ray, 1986; see also Piedmont, 1989), projective and objective measures are not interchangeable. The correlations between the corresponding two types of measures of achievement, power, and affiliation motivation are essentially zero (McClelland, Koestner & Weinberger, 1989). This means that even though both projective and objective tests are labeled similarly, they do not measure the same thing.

David McClelland (1980) argues that objective tests do not measure motives at all. According to theory, motives must rise and fall as they are aroused and satisfied. Researchers need to demonstrate this variation with arousal studies, analogous to the hunger study mentioned earlier. Projective measures do this; objective (multiple-choice) measures do not. Thus, while projective measures tap motives, objective measures reflect something else, perhaps values or self-image or cognitive "schemas." McClelland speculates that projective measures tap psychological processes associated with the right cerebral hemisphere, which is involved in dreaming and imagination, whereas self-report measures tap the more rational and logical thought of the left cerebral hemisphere (McClelland, 1986). He also suggests that projective measures tap into prelanguage personality developments, whereas self-report measures tap the later developments that can be coded in language (McClelland, Koestner & Weinberger, 1989).

Of the two methods, the thematic (or projective) method, although more tedious, seems to work better. William Spangler (1992), on the basis of a systematic review of published research, concluded that TAT measures of achievement motivation are more highly correlated with outcomes than are questionnaire measures. The two types of measures are not interchangeable; they predict different behaviors. Spangler's review shows that motives predict spontaneous behaviors, such as spending time with friends (need for affiliation) or working at job-related activities (need for achievement). In contrast, questionnaire measures predict more conscious choices, such as saying how free time would be spent or saying what goal would be selected. They can predict, for example, whether achievement motivation will be channeled into career success or successful interpersonal relationships (French & Lesser, 1964; McClelland, Koestner & Weinberger, 1989).

A considerable body of research has accumulated using thematic measures of affiliation, achievement, and power. Let us consider each of these in turn.

The Affiliation Motive: Seeking Friendship

Motivations to maintain friendly relationships with other people represent an important dimension, and researchers have studied them. The first **affiliation motive** scoring system in the TAT tradition (Shipley & Veroff, 1958) coded the need for affiliation (*n*Affiliation), which was defined as "a motive to establish, maintain, or restore positive affective relations with another person or persons" (Smith, 1992b, p. 11).

Behaviors Associated with Affiliation Motivation

The TAT measure of affiliation motivation predicts behaviors in the real world. People scoring high in *n*Affiliation have been reported to keep in closer contact with friends through letters, phone calls, and visits. They pay attention to information that will facilitate social interactions. For example, they master social networks more quickly, learning who is friends with whom, and they pay more attention to people's faces than do those low in need for affiliation. They accommodate to other people's wishes and dislike conflict, and they are attracted to careers that involve other people. Given a choice of work partners, they pick friends, even if they aren't as good at the task as others who could be chosen (Koestner & McClelland, 1992; McClelland, 1985).

Given all this friendship-seeking behavior, we might expect that affiliation-motivated people would be especially popular. Surprisingly, they are not; in fact, they may be less popular than those with low affiliation motivation. This odd result can be explained, however. The scoring system for *n*Affiliation was developed by comparing fraternity members whose affiliation needs had been aroused by having them rate one another on several adjectives (for example, "aggressive," "cooperative," "self-assured") with a control group of fraternity members. As you might imagine, having a group of close friends fill out questionnaires evaluating one another arouses anxiety or fear of rejection, as well as friendship. So the *n*Affiliation measure reflects anxiety about the loss of friendship, as well as positive motivations of enjoying warm relationships. A more straightforward measure seemed desirable.

An Alternative Measure: Intimacy Motivation

Dan McAdams developed a measure of the **intimacy motive,** which he defined as a motive to experience "a warm, close, and communicative exchange with another person" (McAdams, 1980, p. 413). He contrasts it with the need for affiliation. According to McAdams, the need for affiliation is an active goal-seeking orientation, with personal relationships as the goal. In contrast, intimacy motivation is not active striving, but rather a preoccupation with the state of relationship: being there, rather than getting there. He compares it to the secure relationship of an infant with its mother, which various theories have described as the basis for good interpersonal relationships later in life (McAdams, 1982). Although intimacy motivation is not identical to affiliation motivation, the two measures partially overlap, and so they are positively correlated (McAdams & Powers, 1981).

The intimacy measure was developed using both male and female subjects, carefully devising several arousal procedures that did not elicit fear of rejection. For example, fraternity and sorority members were tested following their initiation ceremonies or after attending a party, and steadily dating couples were compared with a control group. As a result, intimacy motive scores correlate with more positive qualities, compared to *n*Affiliation scores. Peers rate subjects with high intimacy motive as warmer, more sincere, and more loving than those who score low; *n*Affiliation is not related to these peer ratings (McAdams, 1980). When observed in a laboratory, those who score high on intimacy motivation also laugh, smile, and make eye contact more often than others (McAdams, Jackson & Kirshnit, 1984). When asked to report what they were doing in everyday life when a pager sounded at random intervals (an experience-sampling procedure), they reported thinking about and talking to other people more often than did students with low intimacy motivation (McAdams & Constantian, 1983). In impromptu dramatic skits, college students high in intimacy motivation stand closer to others and more often refer to "we"; affiliation motivation also shows these correlations, although somewhat less strongly (McAdams & Powers, 1981).

Intimacy motivation is negatively correlated with narcissism, a more selfish and exploitative mode of seeking interpersonal relationships (Carroll, 1987). Intimacy motivation in a sample of 30-year-old men predicted positive adjustment 17 years later (McAdams & Vaillant, 1982). Intimacy motivation is positively correlated with health and well-being for

What motivates Mother Teresa's loving acts of charity toward the poorest of the poor? Her actions are the opposite of narcissistic self-love, and they appeal to our affiliation and intimacy motives, even improving the immune system functioning of those who think of such acts (as research reported later in this chapter indicates).

women as well as men. Different aspects of well-being are related to intimacy in the two sexes. For women, intimacy seems to be central to overall happiness and satisfaction with life roles. For men, intimacy seems to provide psychological security; it is related to more certainty and less strain and psychophysical symptoms (McAdams & Bryant, 1987). There is some evidence that females score higher than males on intimacy motivation, although many studies report no sex differences; with age, women's intimacy scores decrease (McAdams & Bryant, 1987; McAdams, Lester, et al., 1988).

The Achievement Motive: Seeking Excellence

The **achievement motive,** abbreviated "*n*Achievement" or "*n*Ach," is the tendency to seek excellence. This is the motive that energizes striving toward success, whether measured by competitive achievements such as winning in sports or by other accomplishments, such as reaching a long-sought career goal. To be scored for this motive, a story must include one of three kinds of achievement imagery. Most often, achievement stories describe a character who seeks to perform well in comparison to a *standard of excellence:* to get a high grade, to run a fast race, to dance well, and so on. A second kind of achievement imagery is a *unique accomplishment*, such as discovering a cure for a dreaded disease or winning the Pulitzer Prize. The third kind of achievement imagery is *long-term involvement* toward some achievement goal: studying the violin for 15 years, or working for several years to earn a college degree.

If a story contains any of these three kinds of achievement imagery, additional points may be scored for elaboration of the achievement theme. For example, additional points are scored for describing the positive emotions (pride, joy) of achievement success or the negative emotions (disappointment, sadness) of failure, anticipating these positive or negative outcomes, describing obstacles to achievement (such as lack of money to pay tuition), or mentioning helpful people (such as an anonymous benefactor) (McClelland et al., 1953).

Behaviors Associated with Achievement Motivation

Researchers have identified several behaviors that are more characteristic of people who score high on the achievement motive than of those who score low. They seek opportunities to test their abilities, whether in the real world or in the experimental laboratory. In laboratory settings, achievement-motivated people choose tasks that provide opportunities to test their abilities. In the real world, they choose careers that provide challenges and feedback about success, and they are particularly attracted to careers as business entrepreneurs.

Achievement-motivated people do not show higher achievement on all tasks. For example, they do not consistently get higher grades than those low in achievement motivation (McClelland, 1980). Why not? For the answer, we must understand the nature of the achievement motive more precisely.

Choice of Moderately Difficult Tasks To achieve our goals, we generally must risk failure. Runners don't win every race; business entrepreneurs don't make a profit on every transaction. In the long run, success depends on picking tasks that are difficult enough to be meaningful and challenging, but not so hard that we have no chance of succeeding. That, according to laboratory studies, is what people with a high achievement motive do. Individuals who score high on *n*Achievement choose tasks of *intermediate difficulty*. In classic experiments that present subjects with a game of ring toss, such individuals choose to stand at a distance where they

How far back will these basketball players stand when they shoot? Research suggests that those high in achievement motivation will take shots from moderately difficult distances, avoiding long shots and getting more satisfaction from moderately difficult shots than from easy ones.

can successfully toss the ring onto the peg about half the time. Others, less motivated for achievement, may stand so close that they toss ringers almost every time, or so far away that, although they seldom succeed, there is little shame in failing (Atkinson, 1966).

If the achievement motive predicted only ring-toss choices, its value would be seriously limited. Like all good laboratory research, though, it provides an opportunity to observe behavior with more precise controls than the real world allows. Findings can then be generalized to the real world; thus, we have the answer to the puzzle that students high in the achievement motive don't consistently get better grades. They are optimally motivated only on tasks of moderate difficulty. They are not particularly attracted to courses that are too easy and so don't seek the easy A. High *n*Achievement individuals select moderately difficult college majors and careers (McClelland & Koestner, 1992). In business, they take reasonable risks. In the real world, a preference for intermediate risk pays off.

These are the choices that challenge the development of skills, without being so difficult that failure is likely. The choices are also not so easy that success is trivial. What about the grade point average, though, and the risk of a lower grade? It is apparently a risk worth taking. According to David McClelland, research indicates that "there is surprisingly little evidence that how well one does in school is related to any other life outcomes of importance" (McClelland, 1980, p. 18).

Other variables also influence the preference for various levels of risk. Subjects who score high on a thematically assessed measure of *need for uncertainty* prefer moderate risks to safe situations. Gender also plays a role; men select riskier distances in a ring-toss game than do women (Sorrentino, Hewitt & Raso-Knott, 1992; Sorrentino, Short & Raynor, 1984).

Don't Stop Until It's Done   Achievement requires not only choosing challenging tasks, but also persisting until they are completed. Do you know the pull of a half-finished game? The tendency to return to incomplete tasks is called the **Zeigarnik effect,** after the researcher who described it. Achievement-motivated individuals are more likely to recall achievement tasks that were interrupted before completion, such as unsolved puzzles (Atkinson, 1953; Moot, Teevan & Greenfeld, 1988). Like the choice of intermediate risk, this tendency to resume partially completed tasks gives achievement-motivated people an edge in the real world. It increases persistence at achievement tasks, such as partially completed homework assignments.

Careers: The Entrepreneur   Making money in business is a prototype of success in Western capitalist countries. Many studies in the United States, India, and other countries have found that achievement-motivated individuals are particularly likely to choose careers in business and to be successful in business (McClelland, 1961, 1965; McClelland & Winter, 1969; Singh, 1990). Achievement-motivated management students are attracted to hypothetical jobs where pay is based on performance rather than seniority (Turban & Keon, 1993). Achievement-motivated managers value professional fulfillment above security (Ruf & Chusmir, 1991). In business careers, financial gains and losses provide clear feedback about competence, appealing to the achievement-motivated person's desire for feedback about performance. Leonard Chusmir and Ana Azevedo analyzed the letters to stockholders written by the chief executive officers of the 50 largest industrial firms in the United States. They found that letters containing high levels of achievement imagery were associated with sales growth of the companies. Profits, on the other hand, were associated with high need for power (Chusmir & Azevedo, 1992). Various occupations require different activities, and achievement motivation is not always relevant to success. In jobs that require management of other people, power motivation is more important for success than achievement motivation (McClelland & Boyatzis, 1982; McClelland & Burnham, 1976).

David McClelland and his associates have undertaken extensive training programs in which they have demonstrated that teaching entrepreneurs to think in terms of achievement motivation improves their business productivity (McClelland & Winter, 1969). Such programs constitute strong evidence that the motive to achieve not only is associated with success in business, but causes such success.

Achievement motivation has implications beyond individual personality; the impact of this motivation is felt in society. As the achievement motivation of a society increases, its economy grows (McClelland, 1961). This effect is well documented with the TAT measure of the achievement motive, but it does not necessarily hold when self-report measures are used (Lynn, Yamauchi & Tachibana, 1991). This further supports the predictive validity of the projective measures of motives.

Sex and Gender Differences: Limits of a Simple Theory

Although women generally score as high as men on *n*Achievement, for many years it was reported that the motive did not predict their behavior as clearly as it did men's. Women's achievement motivation was reported to be aroused by experimental instructions that emphasized social acceptance, rather than more traditional career and academic success (Alper, 1974). In a critical review of this literature, Abigail Stewart and Nia Chester argue that these conclusions are not justified by the research. Inconsistencies are not unusual in research. When evidence is mixed (as it often is), researchers may misinterpret results on the basis of their own prior stereotypes. Stewart and Chester accuse researchers of "an intellectual and cultural climate of unconscious sexism" (Stewart & Chester, 1982, p. 184) for being so ready to conclude that women's achievement motivation is problematic, rather than recognizing flaws in the experimental procedures and a perhaps excessively stereotyped male definition of achievement.

Rather than regarding females as a problem, then, the challenge is to develop a theory of achievement motivation that is complex enough to describe the phenomena observed. The theory must say more about the nature of achievement goals. Research indicates that some achievement-motivated women channel their efforts into marriage and child-rearing, rather than into occupations outside the home (Elder & MacInnis, 1983). For many women, however, career success is related to the need for achievement (Stewart & Chester, 1982). The careers chosen by achievement-motivated women differ somewhat from those chosen by men. In addition to entrepreneurial occupations, achievement-motivated women are attracted to such careers as teaching, probably because it offers achievement satisfactions within a traditional occupational role for women (Jenkins, 1987).

Current thinking emphasizes the similarity of the sexes (McClelland & Koestner, 1992) and recognizes that although there are sex differences, the extent of these differences has been exaggerated by past researchers. In understanding these differences, theorists have moved from an earlier phase that focused on women's failure to fit a model that had been developed to explain male achievement. In later research, sex differences have acted as a springboard to a more detailed understanding of achievement motivation for both sexes.

Explaining Women: The Birth and Maturation of the Fear of Success Concept

How should sex differences in achievement be explained? One line of thinking might be called the "female deficit model." It describes the (exaggerated, according to Stewart and Chester) anomalies of women's achievement as stemming from a psychological deficiency in women. What might such a deficiency be? Some candidates are low self-confidence about achievement (Lenney, 1977; Maccoby & Jacklin, 1974) and anxiety or fear about success (Horner, 1972). Let's consider the best known alleged deficiency, the **fear of success** trait.

Matina Horner, building on the earlier observations of the therapist Karen Horney, proposed that females fear success and that this fear interferes with achievement striving. Success sometimes has negative outcomes. Friends may be jealous of achievement or may resent the time that achievement striving takes away from social interactions. When achievement leads to social mobility (moving up to a higher status in society), family and friends may be left behind. These outcomes are negative, and the more one contemplates them, the more one will "fear success." Matina Horner argued that these costs are more salient for females than for males because achievement conflicts with the traditional female role. She found that female undergraduates at the University of Michigan scored higher than their male classmates on her measure of fear of success, scored from TAT verbal cues that described successful situations. For example, subjects wrote stories in response to the cue "After first term finals, Anne finds herself at the top of her medical school class." Some stories described negative outcomes for Anne because of her success; for example, she became unpopular, or she was so stressed that she committed suicide. Other stories were bizarre or denied Anne's success; for example, Anne was captured by an alien spaceship for study, or there was no such person as Anne but rather the male students wrote exams all semester under this fictional name. Such stories indicate fear of success. Revisions in the scoring manual have been made based on further research. In the revised coding, insufficient effort (instrumental activity) toward success often indicates fear of success (Fleming, 1982; Horner & Fleming, 1992) (Table 7.1).

Fear of success scores are higher when women face situations in which they must compete against men (Fleming, 1982). Fear of success, when aroused by such situations, undermines performance. Horner's female undergraduates did not achieve as highly as men on a competitive task

TABLE **7.1** **Examples of Fear of Success Stories**

1. **Negative consequences caused by external forces**

A student has carefully written a major paper, but her dog ate it before she could turn it in.

2. **Absence of instrumental activity toward success**

Judy's application to graduate school is due next week. There is a knock at the door. Her friend invites her to a movie, and she decides to go.

3. **A sudden, almost magical relief of tension occurring without effort**

Sally's exam is on the desk. She has been worried sick about her grade, which may determine whether she makes the Dean's list. She looks at it. Miraculously, she got an A.

These examples are based on the scoring manual described by Horner & Fleming, 1992.

when they were tested in a mixed-sex situation, with performance made public. Presumably, this situation aroused sex role conflicts, and the women held back to avoid appearing too competent in the presence of males (Fleming & Horner, 1992). Outside the laboratory, women's colleges have traditionally provided an environment where women can achieve without the need to avoid success in order to appear feminine to men.

These findings supported Horner's (and Horney's) description of a conflict between femininity and achievement, and they inspired much more research. Later studies reported that women with high fear of success sometimes avoided success conflicts by putting marriage and child-rearing ahead of careers or by avoiding careers often chosen by men (Fleming & Horner, 1992). As these studies accumulated, however, it became clear that the predicted results were not always found. Females usually, but not always, score higher than males on fear of success, and the results vary widely from one study to another (Alper, 1974; Fleming & Horner, 1992; Paludi, 1984). Some researchers speculated that Horner's findings reflected a phase of traditional sex roles that was disappearing from American culture; since her research in the 1960s, sex differences have decreased, with males now scoring higher on fear of success than before (Pedersen & Conlin, 1987). Others lamented that the fear of success explanation had become popular among researchers and the press without a sufficient empirical foundation (Mednick, 1989; Tresemer, 1974).

Ralph Piedmont (1988) points out that many of the studies of fear of success have oversimplified the concept. As proposed originally by Matina Horner, fear of success is only one of several achievement-related motives that combine to determine behavior. High fear of success will undermine a woman's achievement behavior only if she also has a high achievement motive. Most of the studies of fear of success do not even measure the achievement motive and so cannot adequately test the theory. Based on Piedmont's analysis, it is no wonder that inconsistent results have been found.

As originally proposed by Horner, the fear of success is a stable motive learned early in life, like other motives in the thematic coding tradition. The assumption was that fear of success is a motive in the personality of the subject telling the story, projected onto the stimulus (a character in the story or in the picture, such as Anne in medical school). As the concept evolved, however, researchers suggested cultural interpretations, focusing on society's messages about what women and men should be like. Perhaps when women wrote stories to a cue describing a successful woman (such as Anne at the top of her medical school class), they were not project-ing internal conflicts at all, but simply describing the cultural messages about what is acceptable for females such as Anne. The cues usually used to assess fear of success portray situations in which success is achieved in an area that is unusual or inappropriate for the person described in the cue (Hyland, Curtis & Mason, 1985). In a culture where more men than women attend medical school, it is not a fair comparison to have male sub-jects write about John in medical school and compare their stories to those of women writing about Anne in medical school. The cues, as well as the sex of the subjects, are different. When men are given cues describing suc-cessful females, such as Anne in medical school, they too write stories high in fear of success. Similarly, when women write stories in response to cues about successful males, their stories are low in fear of success. These find-ings support the conclusion that fear of success stories are reflections of cultural learning about the acceptability of success. Michele Paludi (1984, p. 774) concluded from this evidence that "FOS [fear of success] is not deep-seated in women's personality, but situationally determined" in the context of culture.

Is fear of success more likely to be expressed when success is portrayed in unusual or unfamiliar settings? A study of college men is consistent with that hypothesis. Male college freshmen whose parents had not attended college had higher fear of success than those whose parents had also attended college (Balkin, 1986). These students wrote to the cue "At grad-uation from college John is first in his class," so the issue was not sex role conflict. Instead, the first-generation college students presumably feared that their education would alienate them from their friends or family. Similarly, fear of success was higher in female first-year students whose friends were not attending college (Balkin, 1987). Michael Hyland (1989) proposed another alternative to the motive interpretation: that what appears to be fear of success is actually a result of compromises that an individual makes among competing goals, forgoing a particular achievement goal to pursue another goal that is more important for that individual.

Because fear of success has often been attributed to a conflict between being successful and being feminine, it seemed natural to look for an association between measures of feminine sex role orientation and the fear of success. The Bem Sex Role Inventory (BSRI) measures the extent to which subjects' self-descriptions on a standard set of adjectives are similar to descriptions of a traditionally feminine person. The test also measures similarity to a traditionally masculine person (Bem, 1974). We would expect traditionally feminine females to show the fear of success effect most clearly, but inconsistent results have been reported. Confirming expectation, many studies find that women who score as "feminine" on various measures of sex roles have higher levels of fear of success (Davis, Ray & Burt, 1987), but there are many exceptions, and Michele Paludi (1984) concluded from her review that fear of success was unrelated to sex role orientation. Surprisingly, Brenda Major (1979) found that females who scored high on masculinity but low on femininity had the highest levels of fear of success. This result could be explained by hypothesizing either greater anxiety about loss of femininity in this group or life choices that exposed them to more anxiety-producing situations, but the result was not anticipated, and any after-the-fact interpretation is speculative. Nor does fear of success correlate with the need for affiliation, as it might if loss of affiliation were the primary source of anxiety (Hyland & Mancini, 1985).

Sex roles have been studied in relation to both achievement motivation and affiliation motivation. Achievement and affiliation motives are correlated for females but are independent for males (Schroth, 1985). Traditional sex roles encourage men to achieve more highly than women. The more a person accepts the traditionally male sex role (that is, scores high on measures of "psychological masculinity"), the higher the person's achievement motivation. This association holds for women as well as men (Adams, Priest & Prince, 1985).

Like the achievement motive, the fear of success motive does not manifest itself in a simple way. Perhaps one difficulty is that thematic apperception measures are influenced by many factors, both stable characteristics within the individual and more transitory situational factors, which may not be entirely comparable from one study to the next. Or there may be more than one type of fear of success. Michael Hyland and Peter Dann suggest four dimensions: negative social consequences of success, denial of success, pressures consequent on success, and ego-based success anxiety (Hyland & Dann, 1988). Although achievement can bring conflict as well as pride, there does not seem to be a simple formula for predicting achievement-related conflict. The attempt to explain achievement behavior in terms of one motive, ignoring other personality and situational factors, does not provide a model adequate to more complicated social realities.

Varieties of Achievement Motivation   Another way of looking at the inconsistencies in predicting behavior from the TAT measure of achievement motivation is to reject the conceptualization of achievement motivation as a single trait and think of it as multidimensional. Men and women, and other populations too, may differ in their configuration of the components of achievement motivation. Sometimes achievement is associated with social dominance or competition with other people; at other times, it is more individual and task-focused. Such differences can explain why one situation arouses achievement aspirations in some people but not others, while other situations inspire different people. (See the Research Strategies box for how researchers study the combined effects of situations and personality.)

For example, in a survey of a cross section of people in the United States, Joseph Veroff and his colleagues factor-analyzed several measures related to achievement. They concluded that men were higher than women in an Assertive Competence factor and in Fear of Failure, while women were higher in Hope of Success (Veroff, McClelland & Ruhland, 1975). Such multidimensional models can help explain sex differences; more important, they enhance our understanding of the variety of ways that individuals, both male and female, can be motivated for achievement.

Thoughts Also Matter: Attributions about Success

People's behavior is not driven by unconscious motives alone. The way we think about things consciously is also important. Achievement motivation researchers have always included *expectancies* about the probability of success in their theory. When they expect that they can succeed with significant effort (that is, when the task presents an intermediate risk), people with a high achievement motive are most highly motivated. Expecting easy success or extraordinary difficulty reduces their motivation. In addition, many researchers have studied the **attributions** that people make about achievement: their explanations for why they succeed or fail. Ask five people why they got a good grade on an exam and notice the diversity of answers: "I studied very hard." "The test was easy." "I was lucky." "The professor likes me." "I'm brilliant; what more can I say?" These attributions influence achievement behaviors. Only if we believe that our own efforts matter will we try to achieve.

Julian Rotter (1966, 1975) proposed that individuals differ in their locus of control; that is, the reasons they give for succeeding or failing. People with an **internal locus of control** believe that whether they succeed or fail depends primarily on factors within themselves, such as their effort and ability. In contrast, people with an **external locus of control** believe that forces outside themselves are responsible for their outcomes: luck, fate, and social forces, for example. Internal locus of control

RESEARCH STRATEGIES ●- - - - - - - - - - - - - - - - - - - -

Main Effects and Interactions in Experiments

How do we know what causes behavior? From the perspective of scientific methodology, the answer is clear: conduct an experiment to test whether a suspected cause really has the effect you anticipate. Experimental research is conducted to determine whether some variable that the experimenter can manipulate causes a change in another variable. The manipulated cause is called the independent variable. The effect is observed in the dependent variable. For example, the arousal studies of motivation are based on this principle. Subjects are placed in a situation that is designed to arouse a particular need. Achievement needs are aroused by telling students that the test they are taking predicts future success. A control group is given neutral instructions; the test is presented as a questionnaire that is being developed, so that achievement needs can be presumed not to be aroused. Then the dependent variable is measured; in this case, having subjects write stories to projective stimuli. Differences between the experimental and control groups' stories are caused by the experimenter's manipulation of the subjects' achievement motivation.

When an independent variable has a significant effect on the group of subjects tested, as in the achievement arousal study just described, this effect is referred to as a **main effect.** People differ, however, and sometimes an independent variable influences some people in one way and other people in another way. Saying that "the next problem will be more difficult" will probably challenge achievement-motivated people to greater effort but dishearten low-achievement-motivated people into less effort. In this case, we can say that the independent variable (the instructions) *interacts with* the subjects' motivation. This is an example of an **interaction effect.** In this case, a manipulated independent variable interacts with a subject variable (a pre-existing characteristic of the subject). It is also

possible for two independent variables to interact with each other, regardless of subject variables. For example, announcing that the next problem will be more difficult will have one effect when accompanied by a statement that the next problem is solved correctly by most freshmen, and another effect when accompanied by a statement that typically only experienced nuclear physicists can solve it. Interactions between manipulated independent variables and subject variables are of particular interest to the personality psychologist, because they demonstrate that people respond differently to similar situations, which is a core reason for trying to understand personality.

Here are some statements related to material covered in this chapter. Can you identify which statements describe a main effect and which describe an interaction?

1. Offering extrinsic incentives such as money decreases intrinsic motivation.

2. Achievement-motivated people work harder on intermediate-difficulty tasks than on easy ones; people with low achievement motivation work harder on easy tasks.

3. Watching an affiliative film, such as one that portrays Mother Teresa's charitable acts toward the poor, improves immune system functioning.

4. Power-motivated subjects are more likely than subjects with low power motive to get sick when confronted with stressful power situations.

When a statement describes an average effect on a group of subjects, it describes a main effect. When a statement describes an effect that is different for one group than for another, it describes an interaction. Thus, statements 1 and 3 describe main effects; statements 2 and 4 describe interactions.

promotes more adaptive behavior. For example, employees in a community mental health facility who had an internal locus of control responded to frustrations at work in a more productive way than those with an external locus of control. Externals were more likely to respond to frustration with such counterproductive behavior as withdrawal, sabotage, aggression, or the intention to quit (Storms & Spector, 1987). Rotter did not propose locus of control simply as a personality trait, but rather as one aspect of a more inclusive model based on learning theory (Rotter, 1990). The reinforcement (success or failure) achieved in a particular situation was also important and could modify locus of control expectations for similar situations. The mental health facility employees just described would be expected to respond to continued failure with decreasing internal locus of control (and job burnout), whereas success should increase their confidence that they could be effective at work.

Bernard Weiner (1991) expanded Rotter's concept, focusing particularly on attributions for achievement outcomes. Why do we succeed? Why do we fail? In addition to internal versus external locus of control (or, as Weiner preferred to call it, **locus of causality**), Weiner and his colleagues (Weiner et al., 1971) called attention to a second dimension of achievement attributions: **stability** or change. Some internal causes of success or failure are stable: ability, for example. Others, such as motivation, may fluctuate. If you believe you failed because of lack of ability, you will be less likely to try a second time than if you blame your lack of motivation. Motivations can be enhanced; ability is generally fixed, although Weiner later noted that learning can sometimes change ability (Weiner, 1985). Similarly, external causes can be either stable or unstable. A person who completes a five-page paper in an evening because "it's easy" (task difficulty, a stable external cause) has a different attribution than someone who finished the assignment because "the computer just happened to be free when I needed it" (luck, an unstable external cause). A third dimension can also be considered: **controllability** (Weiner, 1985). Some factors are controllable, including some internal causes and some external causes. We can take a course to improve our ability or go to the library to remove distractions. Other factors, both internal and external, are uncontrollable, such as genetically determined aptitude and the cost of tuition.

All three dimensions—locus of causality, stability, and controllability—have implications for our behavior and our emotions (Weiner, 1985, 1991). We can take pride in success that is attributed to internal causes. After failure, we will be hopeful only if we attribute the failure to an unstable cause, and our self-esteem will be threatened if the attribution is to an internal cause. It is obvious that children who are told "You failed because you are stupid" (an internal, stable, uncontrollable attribution) will think less well of themselves and will give up more quickly than those who are told "You failed because you didn't try hard enough" (an internal, unstable, controllable attribution). (What attribution is implied by the oft-stated advice, "If at first you don't succeed, try, try again"?) Differences in their attributions can explain why one student who fails an exam drops out of school, while another works harder and gets a tutor (Weiner, 1990). Research shows that achievement can be promoted through training programs to change attributions to be adaptive and realistic (Försterling, 1985, 1986).

Attributions are not entirely logical. They are influenced by forces that, like psychoanalytic defense mechanisms, protect the individual from psychological pain. The **hedonic bias** refers to people's tendency to take credit for their successes by attributing them to internal causes and to avoid blame for their failures by attributing them to external causes (Weiner, 1990). Many students, for example, attribute their high grades to intelligence and hard work but their low grades to difficult exams and professors.

Although these attributional biases protect self-esteem and avoid anxiety, they sometimes impede achievement. A person who expects to fail may be tempted to behave in a way that provides a ready excuse for failure, rather than putting self-esteem on the line by trying very hard to succeed. Before an exam, for example, a student who fears doing badly may go to a party and become intoxicated instead of studying. That way, failure can be blamed on the party rather than on lack of ability. Self-esteem is protected, but a real world failure has been made more probable. This sort of self-defeating behavior is called the **self-handicapping strategy** (Jones & Berglas, 1978).

Some researchers have reported that men and women make different attributions for achievement outcomes. Men say that they succeed because of their ability; women say that they succeed because of effort and luck (Levine, Gillman & Reis, 1982). In theory, such differences in attributions would explain why the sexes don't always behave similarly in achievement situations, even if their level of achievement motivation is the same. In fact, however, the overall evidence for sex differences in attributions is not very strong (Sohn, 1982).

Enjoying the Task: Intrinsic Motivation

Edward Deci and Richard Ryan define **intrinsic motivation** as occurring "when a person does the activity in the absence of a reward contingency or control" (Deci & Ryan, 1985, p. 34). The concept is a modern statement of a theme that has recurred in personality: that the causes of behavior are to be found within the person, who is motivated by curiosity and strives for competence (White, 1959). Researchers have found that people spend more of their free time working on puzzles that have been presented as games rather than as tasks to be done for money; the enjoyable game format provides subjects with intrinsic motivation to solve the puzzles. Richard Koestner and his colleagues report that presenting a hidden-figure task with gamelike instructions results in more intrinsic motivation than presenting the same task as a test (Koestner, Zuckerman & Koestner,

1987). In contrast, money is an example of an **extrinsic incentive,** a reward that is external to the task itself. Other extrinsic incentives and controls, including praise, grades, deadlines, and surveillance, also undermine intrinsic motivation.

In classrooms and other learning environments, students learn more when their intrinsic motivations are engaged; for example, when they enjoy the material that they are learning (Rigby et al., 1992). The perception that teachers are motivated by extrinsic incentives can also undermine students' interest in learning, according to a laboratory study (Wild, Enzle & Hawkins, 1992). In many situations, providing extrinsic incentives for performance has a negative effect; it impedes performance. Paying people to do something leads them to do it for the money, rather than for the intrinsic satisfaction of the task. Other extrinsic incentives can also undermine intrinsic motivation.

Teresa Amabile and her colleagues (Amabile et al., 1994) have developed a self-report test to assess the intrinsic and extrinsic motivations of workers and students (Table 7.2). The dimensions are related to other measures of personality. Extrinsically motivated individuals generally score as ESTJ types on the Myers-Briggs Type Inventory, indicating that they are high on extraversion, sensation, thinking, and judging. Intrinsically motivated people score high on creativity (Amabile et al., 1994). Amabile and her colleagues suggest, however, that intrinsic and extrinsic motivations are not necessarily in conflict. Some people are motivated both by intrinsic motivations, such as the love of the work, and by extrinsic motivations, such as money.

Despite the general belief among researchers that rewards interfere with intrinsic motivation and creativity, experimental studies show that this is not always the case. If rewards are not too large and not too conspicuous, they can increase creativity among schoolchildren (Eisenberger & Selbst, 1994). Such small and inconspicuous rewards may serve more as feedback about competence than as extrinsic motivators. David McClelland and his colleagues explain that extrinsic incentives undermine intrinsic motivation when people's own motivations are different from those emphasized by the incentives. When the experimenter's instructions emphasize achievement incentives in a situation, people high in power motivation actually do worse than without incentives, presumably because the irrelevant incentives make the situation seem less worthwhile to them (McClelland, Koestner & Weinberger, 1989). Environmental incentives that match the individual's motives, however, should not undermine intrinsic motivation. It would be more motivating to tell people high in the power motive that success on a task predicts their influence over other people than to tell them that it predicts their competence.

Achievement motivation and intrinsic motivation are related, although they are not identical. Research on achievement motivation has emphasized personality differences, measuring the achievement motive and its correlations with behaviors on laboratory tasks and in the real world.

TABLE 7.2 **Examples of Items from the Work Preference Inventory that Measure Intrinsic and Extrinsic Motivation**

Intrinsic items

The more difficult the problem, the more I enjoy trying to solve it.

Curiosity is the driving force behind much of what I do.

It is important for me to have an outlet for self-expression.

Extrinsic items

I am keenly aware of the GPA (grade point average) goals I have set for myself. [Note: Workers are asked instead about promotion goals.]

I'm less concerned with what work I do than with what I get for it.

I prefer having someone set clear goals for me in my work.

Adapted from Amabile et al., 1994, p. 956

Research on intrinsic motivation has focused instead on situational effects that emphasize intrinsic or extrinsic sources of motivation, such as the effect of offering rewards for performance (Strickland, 1989). A more complete picture can be achieved by bringing the two concepts together. Studies indicate that people who are high in achievement motivation expect to do better on experimental tasks than those who are low in achievement motivation, even when presented with the same objective information. Because intrinsic motivation is higher when we feel competent at a task, this positively biased expectancy has the effect of enhancing the intrinsic motivation of those high in achievement motivation (Reeve, Olson & Cole, 1987). Based on these findings, we would expect that teachers would need to give more encouragement to students who are low on the achievement motive to engage their intrinsic motivation for schoolwork.

Some people perform best when they are competing, others when they are cooperating (Eisenberger, Kuhlman & Cotterell, 1992). Would you be more interested in a word-puzzle task if you were competing against others or if you were not competing? Undergraduates who are high in achievement motivation, measured by the Personality Research Form (PRF), a multiple-choice measure, enjoy the competitive situation more (Epstein & Harackiewicz, 1992). On a pinball machine, would you be more motivated if you were comparing your performance to that of other people or to your own previous performance? Researchers report that competing with others is more motivating for those high in achievement motivation on the PRF, whereas those low in achievement motivation are more motivated when goals are set relative to their own prior performance (Elliot & Harackiewicz, 1994; Harackiewicz & Elliot, 1993). (As noted earlier, though, such self-report measures often yield results different from those obtained using TAT measures.)

Research by Carol Dweck and her colleagues shows that even young children, when presented with problems to solve, respond with anxiety and behavioral disruption if the experimenter emphasizes performance goals. In contrast, instructions that emphasize increasing mastery (learning) produce more persistent and effective achievement efforts. These two orientations, toward performance or toward learning, can be influenced by experimental situations. In addition, children characteristically display one or the other orientation in achievement settings (Dweck, 1991; Dweck & Leggett, 1988).

Research on intrinsic motivation suggests that trying to influence behavior by providing rewards is likely to backfire. Thus, such research challenges a major perspective in psychology—the behavioral perspective, which advocates influencing behavior by providing rewards for desired behavior. Behaviorists, in direct opposition to intrinsic motivation theorists, hold the view that all behavior is controlled by rewards and punishments provided by the environment. Based on behavioral theory, many programs in schools, psychiatric hospitals, prisons, and other settings involve a system of rewards and punishments that attempt to "shape" behavior. Behaviorists regard "intrinsic motivation" and other motives as erroneous theoretical ideas. They point out that extrinsic rewards do not always decrease behavior, and when they do so the effect is transient and can be explained within a behavioral framework, without proposing the concept of intrinsic motivation (Dickinson, 1989; Flora, 1990). From a practical point of view, too, the implication that employers do not need to pay workers much when the work is intrinsically interesting is not justified based on research (Wiersma, 1992). Although intrinsic and extrinsic motivations do sometimes conflict, we can best understand highly motivated behavior by trying to understand how the individual's intrinsic pattern of motivation can be enhanced by the environment.

The Power Motive: Seeking Influence

The third important social motive that has inspired much research is the **power motive.** The power motive, also called the need for power (abbreviated *n*Pow), is the desire to control the means of influencing others (Veroff, 1958). Many kinds of power are exerted in social living. Some are based on the institutionalized influence that comes from occupying certain social roles, such as political offices. Other power comes from more personal characteristics, such as personal charm and charisma, whether used to guide or to exploit others. Weapons bring yet another kind of power. Perhaps it should be no surprise that humans, who live in complex social settings, have found numerous ways to influence one another. Like achievement motivation, power motivation takes a variety of forms.

The original scoring method for the thematic measure of power motivation was developed by Joseph Veroff (1958) and validated by comparing the stories written by male undergraduate candidates for offices in student government with a control group of students in the classroom. This measure was discovered to reflect anxieties associated with fear of weakness, and so it emphasizes the avoidance of being powerless. Another measure, developed by David Winter, emphasizes the positive or "approach" aspects of power (Winter, 1973). Other scoring systems distinguish whether power is sought for personal benefit or used for social contributions (McClelland et al., 1972).

Behaviors Associated with Power Motivation

Power motivation has implications for political behavior and for reactions to authority figures. Undergraduates who are high in the power motive hold offices in student government more often than those who are low in this motive (Winter, 1973). What about national government? Although no one has reported a study in which national political figures have agreed to take projective tests for the sake of research, their public speeches have been scrutinized by psychologists who have coded them for motivation, and these motivational measures correlate with their public political behaviors (Donley & Winter, 1970; Winter & Carlson, 1988; Winter et al., 1991a, 1991b). Historically, American presidents who are high in power motivation, as scored from their first inaugural addresses, have been in office when the country entered a war (Winter, 1987). Recent examples include John Kennedy (the Vietnam War) and Harry Truman (the Korean War). The relationship between power motivation and war has been confirmed in historical records of government communications in British history, World War I, and the Cuban missile crisis; a pattern of high power motivation and low affiliation motivation reliably predicts war, and wars end only when power motivation declines (Winter, 1993). Power-motivated presidents also are rated as greater presidents by historians (McCann, 1990b).

Authoritarianism involves respect for legitimate authority, and it has been found in other research to predispose people to be concerned with having power. Canadian undergraduates who scored high on a measure of authoritarianism indicated that in the 1988 U.S. election, they favored

Power motivation is expressed in a variety of different forms, including the power of aggressive criminal acts and the power of a legitimate authority such as this arresting officer.

the candidate, Bush or Dukakis, whom they perceived to be higher on the power motive (McCann, 1990a). An experimental study confirms that undergraduate men who score high in power motivation are especially positively affected by social status when they form impressions of people (Assor, 1989).

Outside the political realm, power motivation predicts a variety of behaviors. One way to have an influence on others is to make yourself visible, and power-motivated undergraduates do so: by writing letters to the college newspaper and putting their names on their dormitory room doors. They also decorate their rooms with more prestigious possessions, including stereos, carpets, framed pictures, and wall hangings; and power-motivated women are more concerned about clothes (Winter, 1973). We would expect the particular behaviors to change to reflect the different values of various times and groups. The point is that power-motivated people are concerned with their impact on others.

Power sometimes takes the form of influence that is responsible and contributes to the welfare of others, such as the impact of an effective political leader or the guidance of a caring teacher. At other times, power takes uncontrolled and selfish forms, as in overt aggression. To make more specific predictions, some researchers have combined power motivation with other measures that suggest the form power will take. Impulsive displays of power, including drinking, aggression, and sexual exploitation, are predicted by a motive profile that David McClelland (1975) described as a *conquistador motive pattern*, characterized by high power motivation, low affiliation motivation, and low inhibition. Power-motivated men with low inhibition are especially likely to become problem drinkers (McClelland et al., 1972). Elements of this conquistador pattern predict wife abuse. Men high in power motivation are more likely to abuse women in intimate relationships (Mason & Blankenship, 1987). In a cross-cultural study, David Lester (1987) found that low need for affiliation predicted wife abuse.

Impulsive and antisocial behaviors are correlated with power motivation in men but not in women, although the sexes are similar in their level of power motivation and in many of its other correlates. Some researchers speculate that the difference between the sexes reflects the greater responsibility training usually given to females; women are more likely to channel their power motivation in socially positive ways, such as nurturing children, than to live a life of wild abandon. Women high in power motivation show more responsible, less selfish expressions of power if they had younger siblings when they were growing up and if they have children as adults; presumably, these factors channel their power strivings into more nurturing, responsible directions. Among male undergraduates, a similar effect is found. Power-motivated male undergraduates with younger siblings are more likely to hold office in student government, whereas those without younger siblings are more likely to get into fights (Winter, 1988). Power motivation seems to have adverse outcomes if it is not combined with responsibility.

One configuration of motives that produces desirable manifestations of power motivation is the *leadership motive profile*, which combines high power motivation with high activity inhibition and a lower affiliation motivation (McClelland & Boyatzis, 1982). *Activity inhibition* is coded from thematic tests by counting the number of times the word *not* is used. Presumably, people who use the word *not* are also able to inhibit their overt behavior, to control undesirable expressions of power motivation. That is, they have a high degree of self-control. High-level managers often have this leadership motive profile (McClelland & Boyatzis, 1982; McClelland & Burnham, 1976). So, too, do American presidents who have been rated as great by historians and who show other evidence of presidential effectiveness (Spangler & House, 1991).

Careers

Power motivation influences career choice for both men and women. The ideal job for a power-motivated person provides opportunities to influence people. Some of the careers that attract those seeking power are teacher, psychotherapist, clergy, journalist, and business executive (Jenkins, 1994; Winter, 1988). In a longitudinal study of managers at AT&T, David Winter (1991) found that managers rose to higher levels in the company after 16 years if they showed a pattern of "responsible power" (power motivation combined with a projective measure of responsibility). The power motive can set a person up for disappointment, though. Sometimes jobs seem to offer opportunities to exert power, but then thwart influence.

This sort of job is particularly dissatisfying for people high in the need for power (Jenkins, 1994). For example, a job may give a manager responsibility to direct other people, but the workers may not be responsive to their manager.

Physiological Effects of Motivation: The Mind and the Body

The social motives that we have been considering are not only mental. Research has made it clear that when social motives are aroused, there are measurable effects on the body. Moreover, these effects are different depending upon which motive is aroused. Research has focused primarily on the power and affiliation motives.

Power motivation is associated with changes in biochemicals measured in blood and urine. These changes indicate increased arousal and decreased immune system functioning, leaving power-motivated people vulnerable to illness when faced with stress. Power-motivated individuals respond to stress by releasing more of the stress hormone epinephrine than do individuals low in power motivation (McClelland et al., 1980). Robert Steele (1977) reports that subjects whose power motivation was increased by listening to inspirational speeches also showed increases in epinephrine measured in their urine. Epinephrine stimulates the autonomic nervous system, so this finding shows that the inspiring speeches aroused the body as well as the mind. Other studies indicate that power motivation can have adverse effects on the body when power needs are aroused but blocked; this is called a **stressed power syndrome.** In such cases, various measures of immune system activity are significantly decreased (Jemmott et al., 1990; McClelland, Alexander & Marks, 1982; McClelland & Krishnit, 1988). Presumably, this leaves the individual more vulnerable to disease, including respiratory infections. Indeed, power-motivated people do have greater rates of physical illnesses, including minor disorders such as headaches and potentially life-threatening diseases, especially hypertension (Jemmott, 1987; McClelland, 1979; McClelland et al., 1980). Illness is especially likely when power-motivated individuals face stress that is related to power issues, such as difficulties with a boss or detention in jail (McClelland & Jemmott, 1980). Such illness may be a result of a drop in the level of salivary immunoglobulin A (S-IgA), a part of the immune system that protects the mouth and nose from infections. Even the stress of taking an examination produced a brief increase and then a significant drop in S-IgA in power-motivated students (McClelland, Ross & Patel, 1985) (Fig. 7.2).

Affiliation motivation, at least when it can be satisfied, has effects opposite to those of power motivation. In contrast to the immune system impairments of stressed power motivation, unstressed affiliation motiva-

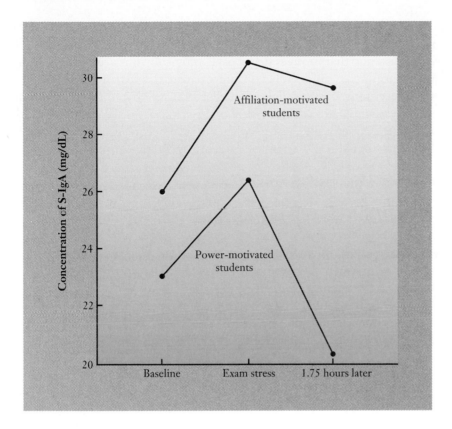

FIGURE 7.2 *The stress of an exam stimulates students' immune systems. After the exam, the immune reaction is still present in those high in the affiliation motive but has worn off in power-motivated students. (Adapted from McClelland, Ross, & Patel, 1985, p. 56.)*

tion is associated with a more effective immune system and less susceptibility to disease (Jemmott, 1987; Jemmott et al., 1990). When college students watched a film that aroused affiliation motivation by depicting Mother Teresa ministering to the needs of the poor, their levels of S-IgA increased (McClelland & Krishnit, 1988). A revised affiliation coding system, which scores for *affiliative trust-mistrust*, is correlated with another indicator of improved immune system functioning: a higher ratio of helper to suppressor T cells (McKay, 1992). Could such effects of affiliation or love be the mechanism responsible for the increased death rate among those who are widowed, or the healing power of social support?

College students who watch films of affiliative themes show increased dopamine concentration in their saliva and blood (McClelland et al., 1987), which should help the immune system. Affiliation motivation is not a guarantee of good health, of course. In fact, David McClelland reports that diabetics who are high in affiliation motivation are less successful in controlling their blood sugar, in part because they are less careful about following their prescribed diet and in part because they have higher levels of the neurotransmitter dopamine, which leads to elevated blood sugar levels (McClelland, 1989).

One of the most exciting implications of these studies is that the body is more fully involved in social motives than was previously thought. Past theories assumed that motives differ psychologically but are similar physiologically, producing a generalized state of arousal. Now we have evidence that "different motive systems may be subserved by different neuroendocrine systems" (McClelland et al., 1987, p. 65)—affiliation with the dopaminergic system and power with the adrenergic system. Potentially, such findings could lead to new medical or psychological treatments.

Can Motives Be Changed?

Achievement aspirations are influenced by factors other than motives; sociological influences, such as religion and economic opportunities, also play a role (Spenner & Featherman, 1978). Individual motives are powerful influences, however. Can these motives, which influence achievement and other important social behaviors, be changed? In the case of the achievement motive, the answer is decidedly yes. David McClelland has conducted workshops designed to increase the level of achievement motivation in entrepreneurs, to provide them with the motivational style that has proved effective in business. The programs work. They increase need for achievement, and business profits subsequently also rise (McClelland & Winter, 1969). The idea of using training programs to change motivations strategically has been generalized to other populations. Patricia Ashton (1986) reports a program modeled after McClelland's workshops that trained high school students to increase their level of internal locus of control, an important variable that predicts school achievement. Wouldn't it be splendid to be able to program people's motives to ensure their optimal psychological and physiological functioning and to make a more peaceful and productive world as well?

SUMMARY

• Motivation refers to the energy or drive that directs choices and goal-seeking. It is influenced by trait-like motives within the individual and by external circumstances.

• Henry Murray's needs-press theory influenced motivational research and the development of the Thematic Apperception Test, used to score various motives.

- Projective tests must be shown to have adequate intercoder reliability.

- Self-report measures are not correlated with projective measures and do not predict behaviors as well as the more time-consuming projective tests.

- The affiliation motive includes fear of rejection as well as desire for friendship. The alternative intimacy motive measures only the positive concerns with interpersonal closeness and communication.

- The achievement motive involves a need to seek excellence through competitive achievements or other accomplishments, such as long-term achievement goals. This motive predicts preference for intermediate risks and choice of entrepreneurial careers.

- The fear of success has been proposed as a motive to explain sex differences in levels of achievement, although research evidence is mixed and has caused researchers to consider cultural factors more critically.

- People's thoughts about the reasons for success influence their behavior, particularly whether they attribute success to internal or to external factors and whether they believe the causes are stable and controllable.

- Intrinsic motivation refers to behavior that is undertaken for its own sake; extrinsic motivation refers to behavior that is determined by external incentives.

- The power motive is the desire to control the means of influencing others; it predicts diverse behaviors including politics, violence, and leadership.

- Motivation has physiological effects on the immune system, which is impeded by a stressed power syndrome but enhanced by unstressed affiliation motivation.

- Although generally considered to be a stable trait, the achievement motive can be increased by training programs.

GLOSSARY

achievement motive the need to seek excellence and success

affiliation motive the need for friendship or other positive affective relationships with another person or persons

attributions explanations for why things turned out as they did; for example, reasons given to explain success and failure

controllability whether the causes of behavior (which may be internal or external) can be changed or controlled by the individual

external locus of control the belief that success and failure are caused by forces outside the individual, such as luck, fate, and social forces

extrinsic incentive a reward that is external to the task itself, such as money or praise

fear of success the trait of a motive to avoid success, often thought to explain the lower achievement of women in situations where success conflicts with the traditional female role

hedonic bias people's tendency to take credit for their successes by attributing them to internal causes or to avoid blame for their failures by attributing them to external causes

intercoder reliability the extent of agreement between two independent coders evaluating TAT stories or other data; usually expressed as a correlation coefficient, or sometimes as a percentage agreement score

interaction effect in an experiment, the combined effect of two independent variables, or of an independent variable and a subject variable, in producing an effect on the dependent variable beyond what would be expected from the sum of the two effects considered separately; that is, the effect of one independent variable is different depending upon the level of the other variable

internal locus of control the belief that success or failure depends upon factors within the individual, such as effort and ability

intimacy motive the need for warm, close, and communicative exchange with another person; similar to affiliation motivation except that the emphasis is on positive goal-seeking without negative imagery (for example, avoidance of rejection)

intrinsic motivation doing an activity for its own sake, without an external reward or control

locus of causality location of the causes of success and failure outcomes; specifically, whether internal or external to the individual

main effect in an experiment, the effect of an independent variable, considered alone, on the dependent variable

motivation the energy or drive that impels a person to make choices and to seek goals actively

motive the stable or recurring patterns of motivation within a person; that is, a motivational trait of a person

needs-press theory a theory that explains motivation in terms of both internal factors (motives) and external factors (such as incentives in the environment)

power motive the need to control the means of influencing other people

self-handicapping strategy self-defeating behavior that provides an excuse for failure, but only by accepting circumstances that reduce the probability of success

stability the extent to which causes of success or failure remain constant and unchanging

stressed power syndrome a situation that occurs when power needs are aroused but blocked

thema the combination of needs of a person and press of the environment that appears in a projective test story

Zeigarnik effect people's tendency to return to incomplete tasks

THOUGHT QUESTIONS

1. Could motivation be explained in terms of individual traits only (motives)? In terms of external circumstances only? Give examples to illustrate why both are necessary or, if that is your conclusion, why only one is necessary.

2. If you could rewrite the history of psychology, would you have the study of motivation begin with several dozen male Harvard undergraduates, or would you study a different group of people? Why?

3. Research shows that self-report questionnaire measures of motives often disagree with projective test measures. Does this finding have implications for the role of the unconscious in personality?

4. Researchers may choose either the original affiliation motive scoring method or the alternative intimacy motive scoring method. Based on the text descriptions, suggest some specific criteria that are likely to be better correlated with one of these measures than the other. (For example, which measure would you expect to predict the winner of a popularity contest?)

5. Based on the research reported in the text, do you think that the need for achievement would be different among students in different majors? If so, which majors do you think would score high, and which low? (Might there be other kinds of achievement that are not measured by the *n*Achievement method?)

6. Do you believe that the fear of success explains why some people are more successful than others? Does it explain sex differences adequately? Why or why not?

7. Based on your own experience, give an example of an attribution about success that led to sustained effort and an example of an attribution that discouraged effort.

8. Do you recommend that students be paid for good grades? Why or why not? (Consider the concepts of intrinsic motivation and extrinsic motivation.)

9. How would you use the research on motivation to improve people's immunity to disease?

10. If you had access to an effective method for changing people's motives, what motives would you try to increase? Why?

Adaptation to the Environment

THE WORLD IN WHICH WE LIVE provides opportunities for satisfaction of our motives: goals to achieve, friends to cherish, people to influence. The world also makes demands and poses threats, however. Unless we adapt, it can overwhelm us. We may fail to do the things required of us and suffer setbacks in our jobs and personal lives. Or we may behave as needed but pay a toll on a physical level, becoming vulnerable to one of many stress-related diseases. Observers of the human condition have commented that we are a highly adaptable species, inhabiting a variety of physical environments on this planet and exhibiting diverse social arrangements. How do we do this? Can we learn to adapt in ways that produce both mental and physical health?

The process of **adaptation** refers to a person's efforts to adjust to the challenges and demands of the environment in a way that achieves or maintains well-being. Adaptation takes many forms. Sometimes we change the environment; for example, by closing the door to keep out unwanted noise. At other times, we think about the environment in a different way; for example, a student who is terrified of a course that requires oral reports may come to think of these reports as valuable practice for a later career. Both examples involve conscious thought, but other adaptive behaviors are so automatic that they are hard to detect, such as when someone reflexively pulls a hand from a hot plate or habitually avoids places where unpleasant people are likely to be met.

Understanding how people adapt to the current demands of their lives is a central issue in the field of personality. Adaptation involves many levels of psychological functioning, from physical to cognitive to social. It affects the body, influencing physical health and disease. Cognitive approaches to understanding adaptation and coping identify the ways of thinking that foster healthy adaptation and those that impede it. A person's social interactions must be taken into account as well, because support from other people facilitates adaptation, and aggressive behavior toward others may result from failed adaptation. Consider, for example, a new parent. Adapting to this new role affects the body, as parents who have experienced many weeks of interrupted sleep can attest. The new parent's thoughts about the situation may be more or less adaptive; for example, whether he or she deems it necessary to maintain the same level of housekeeping and social activities as before. Social interactions also play a role in adaptation, providing the positive benefits of supportive others or the increased stress that arises when other people offer criticism instead.

Our emotions are closely tied to these adaptive processes. As we seek to avoid anxiety and other unpleasant emotions, we find ways to cope with stress; when coping fails, negative emotions, such as anxiety and depression, often result.

Stress

You turn a corner and see a car racing straight toward you. A friend with whom you have spent a great deal of time is diagnosed as having a serious and highly infectious disease. You need a course to graduate on time, but the registrar's office informs you that the class is closed. What do these events have in common? They are all *stressful.* They all threaten well-being and don't have easy and automatic solutions.

When our usual adaptive behaviors fail, or when the environment presents a new difficulty that cannot be readily solved, we experience **stress.** Stress is the state of tension that occurs when a person is presented with problems or challenges that have not been resolved or that require resources that interfere with what the person would otherwise do. Stress can result from a wide range of causes, from the threat of nuclear annihilation to the irritation of a slow traffic signal.

Stressors: Sources of Stress

A condition that produces stress is called a **stressor.** Often stressors are events that impinge upon us from the outside, such as deadlines, traffic

Traumatic events such as fires are very stressful and challenge our capacities to adapt. What advice would you give to this man to help him cope with this disaster?

jams, insults, and crime. We may call these environmental circumstances that require adaptation **environmental stressors,** to distinguish them from internal sources of stress such as physical illness.

Traumatic Events Hurricanes, earthquakes, floods, and other natural disasters are obviously stressful. When war forces people to leave their homes, they experience stress that often manifests itself emotionally in the form of depression and physiologically in the form of elevated serum cortisol levels (Roglić et al., 1993). Traumatic events can also occur on a personal level that affects the individual alone, such as being victimized by crime, losing a loved one, or suffering illness or injury.

Although traumatic events seem obvious as causes of stress, the relationship between such traumas and the appearance of symptoms is not uniform. Studies have found that people's symptoms do not always worsen when disaster falls. Some children in Northern Ireland do not succumb to depression despite living in an area of high political violence (Joseph, Cairns & McCollam, 1993). Some people endure bereavement or spinal cord injury without becoming depressed (Wortman & Silver, 1989).

Illness, Injury, and Medical Treatment Physical illness and injury cause stress. (As we shall see later, they also can be results of stress.) Suffering an injury or illness disrupts life's usual routines and calls for new coping behaviors. This is particularly obvious in the case of AIDS, cancer, and other deadly diseases (Schulz & Schlarb, 1987–1988; Weitz, 1989). Many psychologists have helped devise patient education programs to help those experiencing illness or undergoing operations to deal effectively with their stress.

Life Changes and Daily Hassles Even without illness and major trauma, life's changes present stressors. In often-cited research, Thomas Holmes and Richard Rahe measured recent life event changes that had occurred recently in people's lives. They reasoned that any event involving change would require adaptation, even if the event itself were positive, such as getting a new job. Their Social Readjustment Rating Scale counts the number of life changes that a person is undergoing, giving more weight to those that involve major changes (such as marriage, mortgages, and graduation). Research shows that people experiencing much life change are more likely to become ill (Holmes & Rahe, 1967; see also Holmes & Masuda, 1974).

Life presents everyday hassles as well as major changes. Items are lost or misplaced, traffic is snarled, we feel too fat or unattractive. The overall toll taken by life's minor hassles, which require continual adaptation, can be as stressful as major life changes (Kanner et al., 1981). Bruce Compas and his colleagues found that major upheavals in our lives lead to symptoms of distress through the mediating step of daily hassles. That is, major upheavals disrupt the smooth flow of daily events, and this increase in daily hassles, in turn, leads to psychological symptoms of stress. Having one's home destroyed by a hurricane or flood, for example, is debilitating because of all the little things: no place to cook, no pure water, no telephone, and so on. This relationship—life events leading to hassles leading in turn to symptoms—has been replicated by a number of researchers (Aldwin et al., 1989).

Other Environmental Sources of Stress The world around us presents constant sources of stress. Stressors in the workplace range from financial to status to interpersonal issues (Locke & Taylor, 1991). Urban environments bombard people with noise and demands for attention. The temperature outside may be too hot or too cold. For minority group members, racism and prejudice are stressful. African American college students show elevated blood pressure when they view excerpts of commercial films that contain racist situations involving African Americans (Armstead et al., 1989). A catalog of sources of life stress would be enormous. Our major concern, though, is not the external world, but what goes on inside the individual.

Is Stress Determined Only by External Events? The preceding approaches, whether based on major life changes or daily hassles, are *stimulus* approaches to stress: they define stress in terms of the outside stimuli that trigger it, without referring to what is going on within the person. Such approaches do not provide a full picture of stress. For example, many people enjoy listening to the rock group Nirvana in their workout rooms and consider it a pleasant addition to their physical exercise; others, with different musical tastes, find the bombardment of electric guitar to be stressful. These are individual differences; no stimulus definition of stress can capture the idea that one person's stressor might well soothe another person. To understand this aspect of stress, we need an alternative approach.

The Lazarus Model of Stress Appraisal

Richard Lazarus has developed a theoretical model of stress that emphasizes the individual's evaluation of the situation, taking into account both situational threats and the person's coping resources. This is a *transactional* definition of stress, because it takes into account the transactions or interactions between the person and the environment (Singer & Davidson, 1991). Richard Lazarus and Susan Folkman define **psychological stress** as "a particular relationship between the person and the environment that is appraised by the person as taxing or exceeding his or her resources and endangering his or her well-being" (Lazarus & Folkman, 1984, p. 19).

When people experience stress, they try to understand why (Friedland & Keinan, 1991). The particular understandings that they develop influence the ways in which they try to cope. Lazarus's approach emphasizes the individual's *interpretation* ("appraisal") of the situation, rather than the objective situation, as the source of stress. The objective situation (perhaps a roller coaster, or an exam) may be stressful for one person but not another, depending upon what the individual thinks of the situation and how he or she evaluates personal coping abilities in the situation.

The process of appraising stress is multifaceted and consists of three steps. First, we make our **primary appraisal.** We judge whether the situation is of any concern, whether it is potentially harmful or even, conversely, helpful. A variety of judgments are possible (Table 8.1). These judgments are not necessarily mutually exclusive. For example, an athlete who has suffered an injury may appraise the situation as having caused harm and also as threatening additional loss (such as the loss of an athletic scholarship).

Following primary appraisal, we make a second judgment. (It is second in order, but not in importance, according to Lazarus.) The **secondary appraisal** involves judging what can be done to deal with the situation. What options for coping are available, given the realities of the situation and of one's own resources? What would be the likely outcome of each option? An injured athlete, for example, might consider many possible ways of coping: asking the coach or friends for advice, trying to heal the injury through special treatments, or engaging in some distracting activity to forget about the problem.

A third step of the stress appraisal process may occur later. With time, new information may become available or we may come to think

TABLE **8.1**   **Lazarus's Model of Categories for Primary Appraisal of Events**

An athlete who has been injured makes an appraisal of the situation. Here are some possible appraisals.

Nonstressful appraisals

> **Irrelevant:** The person judges that the situation has no implications for the individual's well-being.
>
> > *"The injury is of no consequence because the sports season has ended."*
>
> **Benign-positive:** The person judges that the situation has the potential to preserve or enhance the individual's well-being.
>
> > *"No big games are coming up anyway, and now I'll have something to brag about."*

Stressful appraisals

> **Harm/loss:** The person has already been harmed in some way.
>
> > *"This injury will certainly make me miss the rest of the season—and a chance to win an athletic scholarship."*
>
> **Threat:** The person anticipates harm or loss, but it has not yet occurred. Typically, negative emotions are experienced, such as fear, anger, or anxiety.
>
> > *"I might miss the rest of the season, but I don't know yet."*
>
> **Challenge:** The person anticipates that there is some potential for gain or growth. Typically, positive emotions are experienced, such as eagerness, excitement, or exhilaration.
>
> > *"The injury is minor and will offer an opportunity to consult with a highly knowledgeable physician in the area of sports medicine, which may lead to important training ideas."*

Adapted from information in Lazarus & Folkman, 1984, pp. 31–35.

differently about the situation after mulling it over. This is **reappraisal,** a changed appraisal of the situation. An injured athlete whose earlier appraisal was of harm and loss may discover a new career interest: physical therapy.

The Folkman and Lazarus model of appraisal has inspired much research, but it is not without critics. Robert Croyle (1992) suggests that the model falls short when applied to health and illness because it focuses only on environmental events, neglecting the role of *symptoms* in appraising health and illness. Don't people also appraise symptoms such as chest pain and fatigue? In addition, the model does not incorporate social psychological processes such as social comparison, in which people compare themselves with other people in appraising their condition. Instead, other people are described only as potential sources of social support. Such considerations can be added to the stress appraisal model, of course, and that sort of modification is commonplace in the development of psychological theories.

Coping: Dealing with Stress

When times are tough, what do you do? Perhaps you talk to friends, asking for advice or just for understanding. Going for a run or the distraction of a game of basketball may help. Or do you tackle the problem head-on, dealing with the problem more directly? These are some of the coping methods that people often use to overcome stress.

The term **coping** refers to thought and behavior that is adopted to reduce stress and avoid threatened adverse outcomes. Coping aims to reduce stress by overcoming environmental and psychological threats. Needless to say, researchers would like to understand effective coping and to identify ineffective coping so that they could offer practical advice. To this end, they have studied coping in a variety of populations, including the ubiquitous college student population, patients with a variety of medical diseases, and those suffering personal traumas and surviving natural disasters. Measures of coping are different from measures of defense mechanisms (as considered in Chapter 6). Defense mechanisms, in the psychoanalytic model, are considered only from an intrapsychic point of view, so they are assessed without taking the situation into account. In contrast, coping methods are context-specific; coping measures refer to the contexts or situations with which the individual must cope (Aldwin & Revenson, 1987).

Alternative Ways of Coping: Problem-Focused or Emotion-Focused

Richard Lazarus distinguishes coping methods as either trying to change the environment, **problem-focused coping,** or trying to change the individual's emotional reactions to the difficulty, **emotion-focused coping.** Imagine that you oversleep and miss the bus for a ski trip. One problem-focused way of coping would be to look for alternative transportation to the slopes. An emotion-focused coping method would be to find someone to comfort you to alleviate your distress. (Can you think of additional problem-focused and emotion-focused ways of coping with this situation?)

Problem-focused coping includes a variety of strategies such as trying to analyze the problem, working harder, and applying the lessons learned from past experiences. Emotion-focused coping includes expressing feelings, making light of the situation, and keeping a stiff upper lip (Lazarus & Folkman, 1984). The Ways of Coping Checklist (WCCL) asks subjects to identify a negative stressor they have experienced in the past year and to rate their use of a variety of coping responses to that stressor on a 4-point scale (from "not used" to "used a great deal"). It isn't always obvious whether a particular coping technique should be considered emotion-focused or problem-focused. (What does it mean, for example, to seek professional advice?) Researchers have not agreed on a single standard way for combining items into scales. They have also developed alternative measures (Amirkhan, 1990, 1994; Carver, Scheier & Weintraub, 1989; Vitaliano et al., 1985).

Problem-Focused Coping Techniques   Direct *instrumental action* to solve the problem is evidenced when people report, "I knew what had to be done, so I doubled my efforts to make things work." A student who stays up all night to study for an exam is taking such direct instrumental action. Other problem-focused techniques include exercising caution (for example, not taking more courses than you can handle) and negotiation (for example, requesting an extension to complete an assignment) (Aldwin & Revenson, 1987). Problem-focused coping is generally considered to be good coping (presuming, of course, that the problem has a solution). Undergraduate students who report that they use problem-focused coping techniques judge themselves to be more effective problem solvers than do those who use emotion-focused coping techniques (MacNair & Elliott, 1992).

Emotion-Focused Coping Techniques   Like a person allergic to cats who takes antihistamines rather than getting rid of the family pet, people sometimes cope by altering their own emotional reactions rather than by changing the external problem. This approach risks allowing external problems to continue by neglecting them. Some emotion-focused coping methods are clearly ineffective. Sometimes people avoid confronting their negative emotions through *escapism*, for example: daydreaming, sleeping excessively, or using drugs or alcohol. Other emotion-focused techniques are self-blame, minimization, and seeking meaning in a bad situation (Aldwin & Revenson, 1987).

On the other hand, emotion-focused techniques can be beneficial. People turn to friends or others for **social support,** emotional and/or instrumental help with their problems. Good sources of social support are associated with better well-being and with improved coping in a variety of circumstances (Kalimo & Vuori, 1990). Palestinians injured during the *intifada*, the Palestinian uprising to protest Israeli occupation, were better adjusted if they reported more satisfying social support (Khamis, 1993). Turning to others for support improves women's adjustment when undergoing an abortion by increasing their confidence in being able to cope with

When you have problems, do you turn to friends or family for comfort or guidance? Researchers have found that such social support is often a beneficial coping strategy.

the event (self-efficacy), provided the others are perceived as completely supportive (Major et al., 1990). Support from friends seems more helpful than that from family members in this situation, and also for divorced mothers coping with single parenthood (Holloway & Machida, 1991).

Researchers have often found sex differences in the use of social support. Women cope through social support more often than men (for example, Butler, Giordano & Neren, 1985). Social support is related to lower blood pressure in female students. A device recorded their blood pressure every 20 minutes for 8 to 12 hours. High social support, based on a self-report scale, was associated with lower blood pressure (averaged across the day) for women, although not for men (Linden et al., 1993). Could women's more frequent use of social support be a reason for their greater cardiovascular health? We do know that coronary-prone individuals (Type A personalities) have less effective social support resources. Among men, those classified as the coronary-prone Type A personalities are particularly unlikely to turn to others for social support. Type A women report feeling inadequately cared for or loved (Vroege & Aaronson, 1994). When they do receive social support, though, Type A individuals benefit, just as others do. A laboratory study compared Type A females who did cognitive tasks either alone or in the presence of a friend. Type A individuals typically show increased blood pressure in such experiments, but this physiological sign of stress was significantly reduced in the presence of the friend (Kamarck, Manuck & Jennings, 1990).

What Determines the Choice of Coping Technique?

Different individuals are likely to cope with the same problem in different ways. Coping styles can vary from one person to another, as do personality traits. Like stress, coping can be understood as involving a transaction between the individual and the environment, and coping strategies vary from one situation to another, according to Richard Lazarus. In general, problem-focused coping occurs when people believe that something can be done about the situation. If they conclude that nothing can be done, people turn to emotion-focused coping (Lazarus, 1993). By emphasizing the need to take the situation into account, Lazarus disagrees with a *trait approach* that would simply label each person according to his or her typical coping technique.

Personal resources and family support influence the choice of coping strategy. Charles Holahan and Rudolf Moos compared patients treated for depression with a carefully selected community control group and analyzed their coping strategies. For this study, three broad categories of coping strategies were considered: active-cognitive, active-behavioral, and avoidance. (Table 8.2 gives examples of these coping strategies.) In many ways, the patients were similar to the healthy control group (Fig. 8.1). Both groups reported about equal levels of active-cognitive and active-behavioral coping, and in both groups these active coping strategies were positively correlated with self-confidence and family support. Patients did report higher levels of avoidance than the healthy control group. In both groups, avoidance coping could be predicted from similar variables. Avoidance was negatively correlated with self-confidence, an easygoing disposition, family support, and education and family income. Thus, people with more personal resources and support use more active coping techniques and fewer avoidance techniques.

The type of stressful event that has occurred also influences choice of coping strategy. In a study of adults in the Baltimore area ranging in age from 24 to 91 years, Robert McCrae (1984) found that people respond differently to three kinds of stressful events. Typical "challenging" events

TABLE 8.2 Examples of Active–Cognitive, Active–Behavioral, and Avoidance Coping Strategies

Examples of active-cognitive coping strategies

Prayed for guidance and/or strength

Considered several alternatives for handling the situation

Tried to see the positive side of the situation

Examples of active-behavioral coping strategies

Talked with a friend about the problem

Made a plan of action and followed it

Tried to reduce tension by exercising more

Examples of avoidance coping strategies

Kept my feelings to myself

Refused to believe that it happened

Tried to reduce tension by drinking more

Adapted from Holahan & Moos, 1987, p. 949.

include starting school, getting married, or being promoted. Typical "loss" events include the death of a relative or friend, divorce, or being robbed. Typical "threat" events include illness, unemployment, and being sued. Challenging events mobilize the most adaptive coping responses, such as rational action, restraint, and humor. In contrast, loss and threatening events elicit less active responses, including fatalism, faith, and wishful thinking.

Coping is triggered when there is a threat to our sense of identity. Michael Berzonsky found that among undergraduates, their style of coping was consistent with the manner in which they reported maintaining their identity. Those who used problem-focused coping methods reported maintaining their identity through an informational style, such as thinking about options. Those who used avoidance coping strategies had less mature methods of maintaining their identity, such as a diffuse identity style, in which they put off action, or a normative identity style, in which they relied on social norms to define themselves (Berzonsky, 1992). Some of these coping methods would appear to be more adaptive than others.

FIGURE 8.1 *Coping strategies of patients and controls. (Adapted from Holahan & Moos, 1987, p. 950.)*

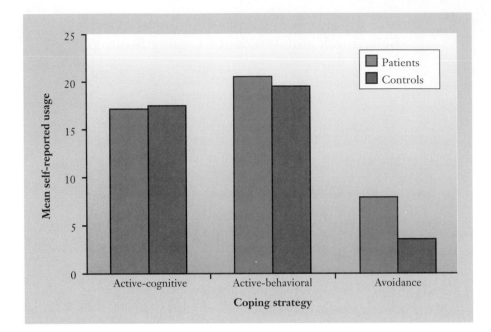

Do Coping Techniques Work?

It seems reasonable to ask how effective coping techniques are and whether some coping techniques are more effective than others. Unfortunately, there is no simple answer to these questions (Aldwin & Revenson, 1987). Some coping techniques are generally considered to be more effective and more mature than others, but effectiveness depends in part on the particular problem.

Emotion-focused strategies, unlike problem-focused techniques, do not deal with the problematic situation. In general, emotion-focused strategies are considered to be less effective than problem-focused techniques, but either is better than avoidance of the problem (Aldwin & Revenson, 1987; Bhagat, Allie & Ford, 1991; Headey & Wearing, 1990). A student who does poorly on an exam, for example, copes more effectively by learning better study techniques and getting tutoring (problem-focused coping) than by learning to accept poor performance without distress (emotion-focused coping). Avoidance, such as dropping out of school, would be worse than either of these.

Nonetheless, emotion-focused techniques are sometimes effective. For example, among premedical students preparing for the demanding Medical College Admissions Test (MCAT), those who used wishful thinking (an emotion-focused coping technique) became more anxious, but so did those who coped by using problem-focused methods. Distancing (another emotion-focused technique) reduced anxiety. None of these techniques, incidentally, predicted MCAT scores (Bolger, 1990). Another study of students coping with exams also reports that problem-focused coping increases the negative emotions of threat and harm (Carver & Scheier, 1994). Exams, it seems, bring anxiety and threat regardless of how a student copes. The negative feelings can be averted temporarily by avoiding the issue (for example, by drinking alcohol), but low grades will ultimately bring regret. Actively confronting the imminent exam by studying means experiencing the anxiety, but the successful result brings relief.

Some emotion-focused coping techniques, such as denial, may improve emotions temporarily but not succeed in the long run because they do not improve the problematic situation. Based on retrospective reports of married couples, Susan Folkman and Richard Lazarus (1991) suggest that planful problem-solving (a problem-focused coping technique) and positive reappraisal (an emotion-focused coping technique) can both lead to an improved emotional state. Faced with too little leisure time together, a couple might either plan a vacation or decide that the financial security that comes from working long hours is more important; either technique may be effective. Attempts to deal with emotions by distancing, however, failed, leading instead to a worsened emotional state. It may be that these categories of coping are only partial descriptions of people's actual behaviors. It seems plausible that associated behaviors, such as a cool demeanor toward the spouse by someone who reports "distancing" compared to friendlier behavior by someone who reports "positive reappraisal," may produce the different outcomes. Without more detailed observations about what people are actually doing, beyond their reports, we can only speculate about why certain coping strategies work better than others in various situations.

What should a person do when a situation causes distress? Is it better to avoid the situation to feel better, or to pay attention to it to try to change it? Jerry Suls and Barbara Fletcher (1985) reviewed research in order to compare the effectiveness of avoidant coping strategies with non-avoidant (attention) strategies. They concluded that avoidant strategies generally were superior at alleviating stress in the short term, but non-avoidant strategies were better in the longer run. When the stressful event first occurs, the individual may not have the resources to cope effectively, so paying attention to the situation increases anxiety. (If the person did have adequate coping resources, the event would, by definition, not be stressful.) Later, attention helps the person to develop effective coping techniques.

If an effective problem-solving method is available, it should be used. If the problem is genuinely insolvable, however, ineffective problem-focused techniques may ironically increase distress. In such circumstances, emotion-focused techniques, such as putting the problem in perspective, may be more effective. ("When all else fails, become philosophical" has some merit.)

There are many ways to describe coping strategies besides the problem-focused versus emotion-focused comparison, and researchers continue to explore the consequences of adopting various strategies. Students who use *self-focused coping* strategies—who blame themselves for problems, hold in feelings (including anger), and avoid people—show higher blood pressure on exam days than other students (Dolan, Sherwood & Light, 1992). *Cognitive coping* strategies involve controlling one's thoughts, such as thinking of pleasant things and focusing attention on external events instead of on oneself. These strategies have been shown to reduce pain and are taught to patients with headaches and other pain (Fernandez & Turk, 1989). Some people turn to *religion* to cope with traumatic events, such as the death of an infant. More active religious participants and those who regard religion as important have been found to perceive more social support, to think more about the dead child, and to find more meaning in the event (McIntosh, Silver & Wortman, 1993).

Can Coping Skills Be Improved?

Can we teach people to cope more effectively with life's stressors? Certainly this effort has been a major goal of psychotherapists for many decades. Using self-report measures of coping, researchers have shown that therapists' interventions can improve coping skills. James Amirkhan (1994) reports that students who took a course in critical thinking showed increases in problem-solving coping, whereas those who studied introductory psychology showed very little improvement. Outside of the classroom, people who had been in treatment for alcohol and drug addiction for a longer time showed better coping than did newcomers: more problem solving and seeking support and less avoidance (Amirkhan, 1994). Other research shows that men who drop out of treatment for cocaine abuse are more likely to use a confrontive coping style, whereas those who complete treatment report a self-controlling coping style on the WCCL (McMahon, Kelley & Kouzekanani, 1993). These studies are suggestive and support the idea that people can learn more effective ways of coping, but there is still much to be learned.

Emotions, Coping, and Health

Whether we use an emotion-focused or a problem-focused coping strategy, we would doubt that coping was effective if negative emotions, such as anxiety or depression, were not alleviated. Emotions have both physiological and cognitive components. Besides thinking "I am afraid," a person feels a pounding pulse and sweaty hands. (How would you describe the physical aspects of other emotions, such as joy or anger?) This dual aspect

Emotions, such as depression, influence the body as well as the mind. Emotions have been implicated as risk factors for disease.

of emotions provides a bridge between the mind and the body, a link that helps explain how coping and stress can bolster health or lead to illness.

Inadequate coping with stress leaves us with troublesome emotions, including depression, anxiety, and anger. These emotions are not simply psychologically unpleasant. They also are related to physical disease. Based on a comprehensive review of research relating personality to physical disease, Howard Friedman and Stephanie Booth-Kewley conclude that "states of depression, and anger and hostility, seem to be implicated in a wide variety of diseases" (1987a). Many diseases have characteristic emotional patterns. The emotional profiles that typify two major life-threatening diseases, coronary heart disease and cancer, will be described in detail later in this chapter: hostility or anger with heart disease, and depression with cancer. Diseases that are heavily influenced by psychological factors such as stress are called **psychosomatic** disorders. They are real physical illnesses, in contrast to *hypochondriacal* disorders, which exist in the mind but not the body. The list of psychosomatic disorders is long, including asthma, coronary heart disease, headaches, hypertension, and ulcers, among other diseases.

Emotional suppression is no solution. The term *alexithymia* refers to difficulty in describing feelings and a tendency to turn attention to external events rather than inner feelings and fantasies. In many health-related studies, alexithymia is measured by the self-report Toronto Alexithymia Scale (Taylor et al., 1988). Lack of emotional expression is thought to contribute to a variety of psychosomatic disorders (Abramson et al., 1991; Kirmayer & Robbins, 1993). Other researchers, however, point out that the key to illness is not simply lack of expressiveness but rather conflict over emotional expression. According to this view, low expressiveness contributes to illness only if emotion is being suppressed (King & Emmons, 1990, 1991).

Suspicions of a relationship among personality, emotion, and disease can be traced back to ancient Greek medicine. Modern research confirms that there is a relationship, but it struggles with fundamental questions. Is emotional upheaval a general factor related to many diseases? Or are there specific relationships between certain aspects of personality and particular diseases?

The General Adaptation Syndrome

Hans Selye proposed that many different kinds of stress produce essentially the same set of responses. He described a general mobilization of defensive activity in the body, which he called the **General Adaptation Syndrome** (Selye, 1946, 1991). This defensive activity prepares the body to fight or to flee by mobilizing energy for muscle activity, increasing blood pressure and heart rate. It involves activation of the adrenal cortex. Such activation may provide a life-saving extra edge for immediate dangers that can be overcome by physical activity, such as the dangerous animals that our remote ancestors confronted. It is, however, an archaic response in the context of the stressors of modern life, which seldom can be relieved by brief physical exertion. In fact, chronic activation, in response to chronic stress, may lead to disease.

Life Events and Risk of Illness

The early studies of life event stress indicated that people who experience more life change are at greater risk of becoming ill than those whose lives are more stable (Dohrenwend & Dohrenwend, 1974; Holmes & Masuda, 1974; Holmes & Rahe, 1967). Subsequently, many studies have investigated the stress-illness relationship, and both physical illness and psychological or emotional maladjustment have been found to follow high levels of life event stress (for example, Compas, Howell, Phares, Williams & Giunta, 1989). One person's stressors may affect others, too; Bruce Compas and his colleagues found that young adolescents' stressors also predicted symptoms in their parents (Compas, Howell, Phares, Williams & Ledoux, 1989).

A review of published research supports the conclusion that stress increases the incidence of infectious disease, such as upper respiratory infections and reactivation of herpesvirus infections. The mechanisms that produce the relationship are not clearly established. For example, stress could predispose a person to disease by bringing about changes in the immune system, by disrupting health practices (lack of sleep or poor diet), or by leading to behaviors that increase exposure to infectious agents (for example, being around ill people) (Cohen & Williamson, 1991).

A meta-analysis of the relationship between stress and immunity confirms that stress does impair cellular immune function according to laboratory tests of white blood cells. Specifically, stress is associated with decreased proliferation of lymphocytes to phytohemagglutinin (PHA) and concanavalin A (Con A) and with decreased natural killer (NK) cell activity. Stress is also associated with higher levels of herpesvirus antibodies, consistent with the observation that stress can produce a flare-up of this latent virus in those infected (Herbert & Cohen, 1993). See the Research Strategies box for a further discussion of meta-analysis.

Personality and the Stress-Illness Relationship

Despite the frequent reports of a relationship between life event stress and physical illness, questions have been raised about this finding. Could it be an artifact, produced by inaccurate reports of life events? Perhaps the finding results from biased measurement, since illness, neuroticism, and other factors may lead subjects to distort their reports of life events (Schroeder & Costa, 1984). Research is complicated by the fact that people are not all at equal risk for experiencing stressful events (Headey & Wearing, 1989). The logic of research tells us that differences between groups who have experienced more stress and those who have experienced less stress might be due to the effects of stress; on the other hand, the differences might have preexisted before the stress. What might such preexisting differences be?

Increased Risk Factors Two characteristics seem to predispose people to illness in general: introversion and neuroticism. In several studies,

RESEARCH STRATEGIES   ●--

Combining Studies with Meta-Analysis

Many of the questions that researchers exam-ine have been tested repeatedly. Popular questions have been tested dozens or in some cases hundreds of times: "Does stress lead to illness?" "Are women more emotional than men?" "Are some coping techniques more effective than others?" From one study to another, many differences exist: the subjects, the particular questionnaires or other obser-vations, and so on (Table B8.1). Not surpris-ingly, the results of these repeated tests are not always consistent. Some researchers will find a relationship that others do not find. Many studies have tested whether stress makes people more susceptible to infection by impairing their immune systems, for example; some find that it does and others

that it doesn't. How can we make sense of all these studies and come to reasonable overall conclusions despite the contradic-tions? It will not suffice to let everyone pick and choose to find those studies that sup-port their preferred conclusions, because that contradicts the scientific aim of finding truth through unbiased empirical observa-tions. Fortunately, a technique for combining studies has been devised: the technique of **meta-analysis** (Rosenthal, 1984). How is this done?

First, consider some of the issues. If we test a hypothesis, even an incorrect hypothe-sis, often enough, it is likely that some of the results will seem to confirm it, by chance. For example, consider the hypothesis, "If I

TABLE B8.1   Variables Affecting Research Results That Can Be Determined by Meta-Analysis

Age of subjects
Sex of subjects
Subject population (parents, college students, children, working adults, etc.)
Specific tests or questionnaires
Physical measurements (physiological tests such as S-IgA, etc.)
Self-report or observer measures
Sex of experimenter
Year of study (current, 1980s, 1970s, etc.)
Duration of observation

concentrate hard enough, I can toss a penny to land heads up five times in a row." Try it once. Unlikely you'll succeed. Try it 100 times. Odds of a confirmation increase. On any one toss, there is a 50 percent chance of heads. The chance of two consecutive heads is 25 percent ($\frac{1}{2}$ times $\frac{1}{2}$). On five consecutive tosses, the odds are $(\frac{1}{2})^5$ or 1/32, which is just a little less than 3 percent. By chance, then, if you try for five consecutive heads 100 times, you'll succeed about 3 times. To say that those three "successes" occurred because of better concentration on those tosses would be a logical error.

How does this imagined coin-tossing relate to research? Imagine that 100 psychologists each test the same hypothesis which, for this illustration, has no merit. By chance, some of them will get confirmatory results (like the five consecutive heads). If they publish their results, while the failures do not (a reasonable outcome, given the preference of journals for significant findings), the literature will reflect confirmation of the hypothesis. The nonconfirmations are still in the file drawers of the researchers who couldn't publish. The term **file-drawer problem** refers to the difficulty of knowing how many replications have not confirmed a hypothesis, because they are unpublished (Rosenthal, 1979). Usually, of course, we know what has been published and can only guess what researchers' file drawers may contain. Statistical estimates can be made, however. In one case, for example, Nalina Ambady and Robert Rosenthal conducted a meta-analysis of 44 published studies that tested whether people could perceive others accurately based on brief observations of expressive behavior; for example, could they tell who was telling the truth and who was being deceptive by observing a film showing their facial expressions? The researchers concluded that, yes, such brief observations do permit accurate judgments. They estimated that for the published findings to have occurred by chance, there would have to be 7110 nonsignificant studies in file drawers (Ambady & Rosenthal, 1992). Such an improbably large number makes it more convincing that the published results describe true confirmation, not chance.

Throughout this chapter, many of the questions that interest us have been studied by multiple research projects, including studies of the relationships between personality and heart disease, cancer, and immunity. Typically, the reviewer of such large numbers of studies faces difficulties in addition to the file-drawer problem. In particular, some of the studies will support the hypothesis, while others do not. How can these be combined? Early researchers sometimes reported a *tally* of the number of studies that supported the hypothesis and the number that did not. It seems reasonable that if the majority of studies support the hypothesis, it should be accepted. Other considerations are also relevant, however. If the effect being studied is a weak one and the studies are not particularly powerful (because they use small numbers of subjects or not very reliable measures, for example), many studies may fail to support

(continued)

the hypothesis, not because it is wrong but because it is elusive. By analogy, if a deer is hiding in the woods, only a minority of observers may see it, but we don't require that the majority of those who look see it before we accept that it is there. If only three people in a busload of observers see the deer, wouldn't you still conclude that the deer was there?

Robert Rosenthal (1978, 1984) has described methods for combining independent studies through meta-analysis. Although the statistics are complicated, the rationale is not. First, each published study contains more than simply a yes-no answer to the question being tested. It also contains information about the size of the difference between groups (the *effect size*). For example, how much more likely are Type A people to have coronary disease than those who are not Type A? Are they twice as likely to suffer from coronary heart disease (as Booth-Kewley & Friedman, 1987, report)? That is a stronger effect than an increase of merely 10 percent would be.

In addition, some studies are more credible because of their methodology: they have larger numbers of subjects, more reliable measures, better experimental procedures, and so on. These studies ought to be given more weight than studies with methodological flaws.

Finally, even by chance, it is expected that there will be some variation in the results of studies that replicate the same investigation. These variations can be predicted in advance, based on statistical assumptions. To oversimplify: if Type A increases coronary risk to twice what others experience (or 100 percent increase), some studies will find less

than 100 percent increase, some none, and some more. If, however, we find that a large number of studies show no increase, and the rest are clustered around a high increase, we begin to suspect that this variation is not simply due to chance. Perhaps there are really two groups that have been reported, one group whose risk is increased by Type A, and another group whose risk is unaffected. By looking at the studies in each group, researchers may be able to find systematic differences. Perhaps those researchers reporting increased risk have investigated different kinds of subjects than those who find that Type A doesn't matter. Perhaps the studies differ in which measure they have used to identify Type A behavior. Such differences are important, and they may well have been overlooked by reviewers of research who have not used the systematic statistical review method of meta-analysis.

Meta-analysis is a powerful research tool:

- Meta-analysis is a technique for examining many research studies that investigate the same hypothesis, even if they use various methods.

- Meta-analysis yields a summary conclusion about whether or not the hypothesis is supported.

- By taking into account the file-drawer problem, meta-analysis helps researchers to judge whether the hypothesis is really false but seems true because disconfirming studies are not published.

- Meta-analysis can reveal what other variables (subjects, methods, and so on) cause the hypothesis to be supported in some studies and rejected in others.

greater illness has been reported among introverts and among people lacking social skills (Cohen & Williamson, 1991). One possible explanation of this finding is that these individuals are less successful in mustering social support, which has been found to help people to cope with stress.

People who score high on the trait of neuroticism (measured by the Eysenck Personality Inventory) report a greater number of adverse life events than those who score low (Headey & Wearing, 1989). Whether their reports are biased or they are in fact at greater risk for life's stressors, the empirical result is that the trait of neuroticism is a better predictor of subsequent depression than are life events (Horwood & Fergusson, 1986). Neuroticism is a personality trait that involves emotional reactivity. Emotionality, like neuroticism, predicts stress; that is, people who score higher on emotionality report more stressful life events and more hassles than do those who are lower on emotionality (Aldwin et al., 1989). The greater emotional responsiveness of neurotic individuals makes them more susceptible to anxiety and places a greater burden on their coping mechanisms. Furthermore, neurotic individuals use relatively ineffective coping techniques, including wishful thinking and self-blame, that do not alleviate their distress (Bolger, 1990; McCrae & Costa, 1986). When Iraq invaded Kuwait on August 2, 1990, Kuwaiti citizens were subjected to a clearly stressful event. Those who scored higher on Neuroticism (on an Arabic translation of the Eysenck Personality Inventory) reported more physical symptoms related to stress than those who scored low, both during the invasion and after their country had been liberated. These included dry mouth, tense neck or back, nervous stomach, fatigue, difficulty sleeping, palpitations, and a variety of other symptoms (Torki, 1994).

Personality and Resistance to Illness   Characteristics of the individual can offer protection from stress-induced illness. Does it come as a surprise that *coping ability* is one such beneficial personality characteristic? The more effectively people cope with their problems, the less likely they are to become ill (McCrae, 1984).

Personality can influence the stress-illness relationship in many ways. For one thing, personality influences the meaning of an event and thus determines whether a particular event will produce stress, with its potentially unhealthy consequences. As David McClelland's research (described in Chapter 7) shows, people with inhibited power motivation show more impaired immune system responses and higher blood pressure (McClelland, 1979) than do others. Personality can have less direct effects, too. Some people have the sort of personality that leads them to live a reasonably healthy life-style even when events are stressful: eating well, exercising, getting enough sleep, and so on. There is considerable evidence that people who are aerobically fit are less affected by psychosocial stress than other people, presumably because of the physiological changes (in the sympathetic nervous system or in cardiovascular functioning, for instance) that occur as a result of exercise (Crews & Landers, 1987). Other people's health habits deteriorate under stress, and this makes their bodies more vulnerable to illness.

Hardiness In an influential study of the relationship between stressful life events and illness, Suzanne Kobasa (1979) proposed that a personality trait she called **hardiness** could protect stressed people from becoming ill. She compared 75 middle and upper level male business executives who had become ill following an accumulation of stressful life events with 86 executives who had endured similar stress without becoming ill. Hardy people face life actively. They have three distinctive characteristics:

> *(a) the belief that they can control or influence the events of their experience,*
>
> *(b) an ability to feel deeply involved in or committed to the activities of their lives, and*
>
> *(c) the anticipation of change as an exciting challenge to further development. (Kobasa, 1979, p. 3)*

Subsequent studies further reported the health-protective effects of hardiness in this group of men (Kobasa, Maddi & Courington, 1981; Kobasa, Maddi & Kahn, 1982; Kobasa, Maddi & Puccetti, 1982). Other researchers have also reported that hardiness moderates the effects of stress for men. For example, male undergraduates who expected to tape a lecture for an evaluative audience of professors (a stressful laboratory task) had elevated heart rates, but the elevation was less for hardy students (Wiebe, 1991). Hardiness does not have similar effects for women, however, suggesting that the measure might apply well only to males (Schmied & Lawler, 1986; Wiebe, 1991), and perhaps only to those who are similar to the middle-class executives studied in developing the measure.

Despite its appeal and popularity, the concept of hardiness has been criticized. Most seriously, it is not a unitary trait, but rather the sum of different characteristics. One alternative is to consider each of the components separately. Two of them, commitment and control, do relate to better health, perhaps because people who lack commitment and perceive that they have little control are, in fact, subjectively experiencing greater levels of stress in response to situations. Evidence is less convincing for the third component, challenge; perhaps it is not measured adequately (Hull, Van Treuren & Virnelli, 1987).

Optimism Several investigators have observed that optimistic people generally remain healthy, whereas pessimistic people are more susceptible to a variety of illnesses (for example, Peterson & Seligman, 1987; Peterson, Seligman & Vaillant, 1988). In a 15-year longitudinal study of 500 older male and female Americans, those with a suspicious attitude (measured by Factor L from Cattell's 16PF inventory) had poorer health and were more likely to die. This relationship remained even when health-related behaviors and physicians' ratings of earlier health were taken into account (Barefoot et al., 1987).

It seems reasonable to expect that unrealistic optimism may at times lead people to take risks and to neglect healthy behaviors, but overall the evidence is on the other side. Among men tested for AIDS, Shelley Taylor and her colleagues found that optimism was unrelated to risky sexual behavior and seemed to help those who tested HIV-positive to adapt psychologically to their risk of developing the disease (Taylor et al., 1992). Shelley Taylor and Jonathon Brown proposed that unrealistic optimism and other positive illusions help maintain psychological well-being (Taylor & Brown, 1988, 1994; but see Colvin & Block, 1994, for a dissenting view). Of course, our view of the world must not be grossly inaccurate, but thinking ourselves a little better than we are, and external threats a little less serious, may provide us with a helpful boost of motivation and self-confidence.

Self-Efficacy Personality can influence disease indirectly, by influencing whether people behave in healthy or unhealthy ways. Decisions to smoke, to engage in risky sexual behaviors, to eat too much fat and salt, to take illegal drugs, or to abuse legal ones, are all influenced by personality. What makes people engage in unhealthy behaviors, or in healthy ones? Obviously there is no one answer to this complex question. Researchers have found insights from a variety of theoretical perspectives. Consider smoking, for example. From a physiological point of view, the nicotine in cigarette smoke, or administered through IV drug injection in laboratory animals, is a reinforcer (Goldberg & Henningfield, 1988), which makes continued use of the drug likely. From a cognitive point of view, people who are trying to quit smoking develop a set of beliefs, labeled *self-efficacy*, that describe whether they expect that they will be able to refrain from smoking in various situations (Garcia, Schmitz & Doerfler, 1990).

Beliefs about efficacy and locus of control influence many health-related behaviors. People who have an *internal locus of control*, by definition, believe that their own behavior determines what happens to them in life (Rotter, 1966). Efficacy beliefs are similar to locus of control beliefs, except that they focus on whether the individual can actually do the behavior (for example, can I avoid smoking for 24 hours?), whereas locus of control beliefs refer to more remote outcomes (for example, can I keep healthy by something that I can do myself?). An internal locus of control and high efficacy beliefs contribute to healthy living, including such behaviors as quitting smoking, using seat belts, taking better care of teeth, and exercising, at least when locus of control is measured specifically for these health-related behaviors (Carlisle-Frank, 1991; Desharnais, Bouillon & Godin, 1986; Dzewaltowski, 1989; Hofstetter, Sallis & Hovell, 1990; O'Leary, 1985; Taylor & Cooper, 1989). In addition to promoting healthy behaviors, self-efficacy contributes to health in a second way through its beneficial effects on the physiological stress response. High efficacy is associated with favorable levels of various immune responses including catecholamines, helper and suppressor T-cells, and lymphocyte response to mitogens (O'Leary, 1990).

Personality Profiles of Specific Diseases

Researchers have sought to determine whether, and how, personality may predispose people to particular diseases. Aside from purely biological influences, are certain personality types more susceptible than others to certain diseases? Although the details and mechanisms are still under investigation, the answer is a confident yes: there is a relationship between personality and the risk of certain illnesses.

Type A Personality and Coronary Heart Disease

For decades, the popular press as well as professional journals have described the relationship between the **Type A** behavior pattern (TABP) and coronary heart disease (CHD). The elevated coronary risk of Type A's was demonstrated in the prospective Western Collaborative Group Study (Rosenman et al., 1975) and has been replicated several times since then. A meta-analysis estimates that about twice as many Type A as other individuals suffer from coronary heart disease (Booth-Kewley & Friedman, 1987).

The Type A syndrome was first described by Meyer Friedman and Ray Rosenman (1974) on the basis of their clinical work as cardiologists. The Type A behavior pattern can be described as "the behavior of an individual who is involved in an aggressive and incessant struggle to achieve more and more in less and less time: the idea of hurry sickness" (Friedman & Booth-Kewley, 1987b, p. 783). The hurried behavior of coronary-prone people is reflected in an anecdote told by Friedman and Rosenman (1974). An upholsterer, fixing the chairs in their waiting room, wanted to know what kind of practice they had, since "it's so peculiar that only the front edge of your chair seats are worn out" (p. 71). Their patients, characteristically Type A individuals, did not sit back and relax. Type A individuals are impatient, hostile, competitive, and achievement-oriented (Table 8.3). Their own self-ratings reflect these characteristics. Type A's (assessed by the Eysenck A/B Type Measure) describe themselves as demanding, dominating, outspoken, forceful, aggressive, and argumentative, and not calm, patient, or relaxed (Henley & Furnham, 1989). It is particularly interesting, in view of this list of traits and because of the parallel with the coping literature, that Type A is defined in a transactional way, as a predisposition to respond to particular situations in a particular way (Rosenman, 1990; Thoresen & Powell, 1992). Research shows that Type A people estimate time to pass more quickly; respond more aggressively when provoked; endure longer at achievement tasks despite fatigue; and perceive themselves as more intellectually able, competent, moral, and higher in self-

TABLE 8.3   Type A Personality Characteristics, Indicating Increased Risk of Coronary Heart Disease

Behavioral dispositions   Emotional responses
    Ambitiousness   Irritation
    Aggressiveness   Hostility
    Competitiveness   Anger
    Impatience

Specific behaviors
    Muscle tenseness
    Alertness
    Rapid and emphatic speech
    Quick movements

Adapted from Rosenman, 1990, p. ?

worth (McGregor et al., 1991). Type A students spend more hours studying and get higher grades (Matthews, 1982; Ovcharchyn, Johnson & Petzel, 1981).

The primary method for measuring Type A behavior is the Structured Interview. In this technique, the interviewer intentionally behaves in ways that can provoke impatience or anger; for example, by being unnecessarily slow or by seeming to doubt answers. Type A is coded from the style of response, such as interrupting the interviewer or acting annoyed, as well as the content of answers. In addition to the Structured Interview, a self-report measure, the Jenkins Activity Survey (JAS) (Jenkins, Zyzanski & Rosenman, 1979), is often used to measure Type A. This self-report measure, however, does not correlate highly with the Structured Interview measure, and it is less predictive of heart disease than the Structured Interview (Booth-Kewley & Friedman, 1987; Matthews, 1982). Most seriously, Rosenman and Friedman criticize the JAS because it does not assess hostility, a particularly important component of the Type A behavior pattern. Perhaps it should not be surprising that an interviewer would be sensitive to aspects of a person's behavior that are not accessible through a self-report instrument.

Of the several aspects of Type A, the one generally considered most predictive of illness is *hostility* (Contrada, Leventhal & O'Leary, 1990; MacDougall et al., 1985). Being a "workaholic" is not, in itself, a factor leading to heart disease risk; rather, negative emotions, such as aggressive competitiveness, are the disease-prone component of Type A. For example, in one study, borderline hypertensive students were recruited on the basis of elevated blood pressure readings during college registration. They were

taught to monitor their blood pressure at home. The researchers found
that those who maintained higher blood pressure throughout their routine
days reported more intense anger, particularly when under time pressure,
and they tended to hold in this anger rather than expressing it openly. In
contrast, those who dropped to lower blood pressure at home reported less
anger (Schneider et al., 1986).

   In addition to hostility or anger, other negative emotions have been
implicated as cardiovascular risk components, including emotional distress,
frustration, anxiety, nervousness, negative mood, and stress (Booth-Kewley
& Friedman, 1987; Byrne, 1987; Friedman & Booth-Kewley, 1987b;
Thoresen & Low, 1990). The negative emotions associated with Type A
should be interpreted with caution, though. They are probably not global
traits of personality, but rather results of the transactions between the individual and his or her particular social world, emerging when this transaction does not proceed smoothly.

Cardiovascular Reactions to Emotion   Cardiovascular reactivity has long
been thought to be the mechanism by which Type A leads to illness (Taylor
& Cooper, 1989). Stress affects everyone by arousing the sympathetic nervous system, the "fight or flight" response, which leads to increased heart
rate and blood pressure. Cardiovascular reactivity, if sustained, ultimately
takes its toll in wear and tear on the cardiovascular system and the kidneys
(Schmieder et al., 1993), resulting in disease. Many studies have found that
Type A individuals show more cardiovascular reactivity than do their Type
B counterparts when confronted with stressful laboratory situations or
while playing video games (Lyness, 1993; Rosenman, 1990). This is true of
women as well as men (Baker et al., 1984). These cardiovascular reactions
are particularly pronounced in certain situations: those providing evaluative feedback about performance and those involving social stresses such as
harassment or criticism.

   Experimental studies demonstrate that presenting subjects with stressful coping tasks can lead to elevated blood pressure. Researchers have suggested that this cardiovascular reactivity is especially likely among people
who suppress their anger (Hodapp, Heiligtag & Störmer, 1990; Houston,
Smith & Cates, 1989). But the stressful coping tasks typically used in such
experimental studies involve performance tasks (such as mental subtrac-
tion), rather than social situations. These findings may not apply to the
many social stresses that occur in everyday life. In men and boys, cardiovascular reactivity to social stressors is uncorrelated with reactivity to simple performance tasks. Women, on the other hand, show similar reactivity
to the asocial performance tasks and to the social task of resolving a family
disagreement (Lassner, Matthews & Stoney, 1994).

   The effect of situations that produce anger depends in part on how
people express their anger. Some people prefer to express their anger
overtly while others hold it in. Karen Matthews and her colleagues manipulated the expression of anger by asking male undergraduates who had

been annoyed by a confederate to write either positive (anger-in manipulation) or negative (anger-out manipulation) evaluations of the confederate as a work partner. The subjects' blood pressure, which had been elevated by the confederate's annoying criticisms during a collaborative maze task, dropped more when they were assigned to the anger-in or anger-out condition that matched their preferred style of expressing anger, which had earlier been measured by a questionnaire. Thus, holding in anger has greater cardiovascular consequences for those who prefer to express it. Conversely, those who prefer to hold in anger show greater blood pressure elevation when they must express their anger (Engebretson, Matthews & Scheier, 1989).

Emotions play an important role in this cardiovascular reactivity. Among high school students, those who tend to suppress anger, according to a self-report measure, had higher blood pressure. This relationship occurred for both white and African American students, although the latter reported more suppression of anger than whites and also had higher blood pressure (Johnson, 1989). Other researchers also suggest that anger suppression contributes to elevated blood pressure among both African Americans and whites but propose that the situations that elicit blood pressure reactivity in the laboratory as well as the real world may vary by race and by sex (Durel, et al., 1989). In a nationally representative sample of African American adults, anger was significantly related to hypertension and other health problems, once demographic variables, smoking, and drinking were statistically controlled (Johnson & Broman, 1987). Although the realities of the social world may contribute to racial differences in cardiovascular reactivity, there is also evidence that the physiological reasons for elevated blood pressure vary by race. Blacks more often develop high blood pressure because of vasoconstriction in the peripheral blood vessels, whereas white hypertensives more often have problems because of the heart itself (Anderson, McNeilly & Myers, 1993).

Most of the research on the personality precursors of cardiovascular disease has been conducted on white men. There are some studies of women and of minorities, but not the extensive prospective studies, which assess risk factors and then track people over several years to monitor health outcomes, that have been carried out with white males (Thoresen & Powell, 1992). The available evidence suggests that Type A is at least as strongly related to heart disease in women as it is in men (Booth-Kewley & Friedman, 1987), and the incidence of Type A is similar in the two sexes when socioeconomic status is controlled (Baker et al., 1984).

Biological and Developmental Roots What causes Type A behavior? Biological factors have been implicated. In particular, the greater reactivity of Type A persons suggests greater activity of the sympathetic nervous system. Many studies have shown that, when stressed, Type A subjects have different levels of various neuroendocrine hormones, especially catecholamines, than others (Fava, Littman & Halperin, 1987).

Type A behavior is manifested long before adulthood; Type A personality traits have even been found in children, particularly in boys (Compas, 1987). Correlations with other personality measures indicate that Type A children (grades 5, 7, and 9) experience higher levels of anger, anxiety, and depression than other children and also report more behavioral symptoms of stress (Heft et al., 1988). Furthermore, there is evidence from a longitudinal study of Swedish males and females from age 13 to 27 that Type A behavior is stable over time (Bergman & Magnusson, 1986).

Although we generally think of personality and of disease as characteristics of individuals, there is also some value in considering the contribution of *culture* to both. Studies have often found that immigrants who assimilate to the diet and cultural practices of their new country take on the disease risk of that new country. Aside from dietary risk, the American cultural context of "rugged individualism" may encourage the Type A pattern (Thoresen & Powell, 1992) more than the environments of more collectivist societies. Type A behavior facilitates hard work and economic productivity (Ivancevich & Matteson, 1988). The Protestant work ethic and the Type A pattern have some overlap, to the extent that both are correlated with the need for achievement (Mudrack, 1993).

Can changing Type A behavior reduce the risk of cardiovascular disease? Studies suggest that it can (Nunes, Frank & Kornfeld, 1987; Thoresen & Powell, 1992). Interventions to teach Type A individuals to change their angry and hostile thoughts seem to reduce their health risk. In addition, stress management techniques that do not explicitly refer to Type A characteristics have also been shown to reduce Type A behavior, as well as the associated coronary risk factors of hypertension and elevated cholesterol levels (Bennett & Carroll, 1990).

Understanding the role of personality in one of the major life-threatening diseases has offered some new treatment strategies. What about another killer: cancer?

Type C Personality and Cancer   Is there a cancer-prone personality type, a **Type C?** The idea has been around at least since the second century, when it was described by the Greek physician Galen (Greer & Watson, 1985). Although the evidence is less complete than that for the coronary-prone personality, considerable research suggests that personality can predispose people to cancer. The cancer-prone personality is inclined toward depression, has a hopeless or helpless attitude, and displays little emotion, particularly negative emotion. Suppression of anger is particularly characteristic of people who develop cancer. In many ways, this pattern is opposite to the coronary-prone Type A personality (Contrada, Leventhal & O'Leary, 1990; Greer & Watson, 1985; Temoshok, 1987) (Table 8.4).

The Type C personality is emotionally contained, especially when confronted with stress (Greer & Watson, 1985; Morris & Greer, 1980). According to one reviewer, studies show that the cancer-prone personality

TABLE 8.4 Type C Personality Characteristics, Indicating Increased Risk of Cancer

Depression
Hopeless or helpless attitude
Holding in emotion, especially negative emotions such as anger
Perfectionistic
Conventional

has traits of "stoicism, niceness, industriousness, perfectionism, sociability, conventionality and more rigid defensive controls" (Temoshok, 1987, p. 547). People who cannot express emotion, particularly negative emotion, are at increased risk of cancer (Cox & McCay, 1982). Depression, measured by the Minnesota Multiphasic Personality Inventory (MMPI), predicted death from cancer in a 20-year follow-up study of men employed in the late 1950s at a company that manufactured telephone equipment, even when a variety of risk factors such as age, smoking, and family history were taken into account (Persky, Kempthorne-Rawson & Shekelle, 1987). A meta-analysis of seven longitudinal studies confirms that depression is associated with the subsequent development of cancer, although the overall effect was small (McGee, Williams & Elwood, 1994). Thus, there is impressive evidence that emotions play a role in the development of cancer, despite the need for clearer measures of emotion (Gross, 1989).

We might expect that measures of personality would be different for cancer patients than for those without cancer, and they are. Cancer patients have lower Neuroticism scores on the Eysenck Personality Inventory; low scores are obtained by denying that one experiences much anxiety (Temoshok, 1987). Cancer patients express less anxiety and other emotions than those without cancer, even when the situation seems to call for emotional expression. If an experimenter shows subjects derogatory comments, such as "No one loves you" or "You have only yourself to blame," we would expect that subjects exposed to these statements would experience some stress or anxiety. One way of measuring emotional repression is to look for people who say, on self-report measures, that they are not anxious but who show physiological arousal (increased skin conductance) when exposed to such stimuli. This pattern is characteristic of patients suffering malignant melanoma (one form of cancer), compared with cardiovascular patients and healthy control subjects (Kneier & Temoshok, 1984). Once diagnosed, cancer patients who continue to hold in their emotions have a poorer prognosis (Temoshok, 1987).

One difficulty with studies of cancer patients is that having cancer might itself produce psychological changes. Characteristics of cancer patients don't necessarily indicate what personality was like before the cancer was diagnosed, and so they are ambiguous as potential causes of the disease. To get around this problem, several researchers have studied patients before they are diagnosed, sometimes literally in the waiting room. At this stage, too, there is evidence of avoidant coping. For example, women waiting to have a breast lump examined were interviewed and asked to describe the three problems they had experienced in the past 3 months that had been of greatest subjective concern. Surprisingly, only 26 of the 100 patients listed the breast lump, and those who did not mention the lump described their other problems in ways that evidenced denial as a coping mechanism (Styrax et al., 1993).

Such waiting room studies, however, are less convincing than truly prospective studies; that is, studies that assess personality before the onset of the disease and follow subjects over time to see who becomes ill. Waiting room studies may capture only personality at a moment of great stress, rather than stable personality characteristics, and they often do not have adequate control groups (Hiller, 1989). A prospective study of physicians, the Precursors Study, examined the relationship between psychological tests taken while in medical school at Johns Hopkins and health outcomes two decades or more later. Those subsequently diagnosed with cancer had been characterized as "loners" on the basis of their earlier personality tests, and they probably suppressed their emotions (although there was no direct measurement of this characteristic). On the other hand, those least likely to come down with cancer had expressed more emotion and acted out their impulses. The "loner" group was 16 times more likely to get cancer than the "acting out-emotional" group (Shaffer et al., 1987). In a different analysis of this same longitudinal study, Caroline Thomas, the director of the Precursors Study, described medical students who later came down with cancer as lacking a close relationship to their parents and having "an ambivalent attitude toward life and human relationships" (Thomas, 1988).

Other prospective studies have also demonstrated that personality measures predict cancer many years later. Hans Eysenck (1988) summarized three such longitudinal studies that confirm the existence of a cancer-prone personality. (In fact, he regards personality as a more powerful predictor of cancer than cigarette smoking!) In one study, Ronald Grossarth-Maticek measured personality and other variables in a sample of 1353 representative older residents in a small town in Yugoslavia. After 10 years, he found that those who had contracted cancer were distinctive in several ways. Those who approached life with a highly rational, antiemotional attitude were far more likely to contract cancer, which is consistent with the findings cited above about avoidance of emotion. Experiencing traumatic life events that provoked hopelessness also was highly predictive of cancer. Further work confirms that cancer patients score higher on rationality and antiemotionality than healthy controls and supports the suspicion that suppressing feelings, especially anger, is characteristic of cancer patients (van der Ploeg et al., 1989).

Another analysis of these data by Grossarth-Maticek produced a typology in which cancer-prone people are described as understimulated by stress, in contrast to those prone to cardiovascular diseases, who become overaroused by stress (Eysenck, 1988). This typology was applied to two additional samples of people, this time in Heidelberg, Germany. The cross-validation was successful; the typologies predicted cancer and cardiovascular disease as expected, while two non-disease-prone personality types were relatively free of these major killers.

If only we could all develop the right personality type! In Eysenck's theory, personality is substantially influenced by heredity and physiology. The physiological factors, including hormones, influence both personality and disease, thus producing the correlation (Eysenck, 1988). Even so, when people's personalities change, the risk of cancer and coronary disease also changes, according to Eysenck and Grossarth-Maticek's ongoing longitudinal study. Among a group of their subjects whose personality tests indicated cancer risk, those whose tests 6 months later had changed to a healthier profile, with freer expression of emotion, reduced their risk of dying of cancer over the next 13 years from 43 percent (in the group that had not changed or had become more cancer-prone) to 4 percent. Similarly, improvements on the scale measuring proneness to coronary disease reduced the risk of death from that disorder from 47 percent to 12 percent. Those whose tests indicated a healthy profile died at much lower rates (Grossarth-Maticek & Eysenck, 1990). Even though this study is continuing, there is clearly a basis for believing not only that personality predicts specific diseases, but even more, that change in personality may alter the disease risk.

Can therapy reduce the risk of cancer for cancer-prone individuals, as it can for those prone to coronary heart disease? Although much research remains to be done, there is some evidence that psychotherapy can reduce the risk of cancer by teaching people to express feelings and needs that had been repressed and to develop better social interactions. This therapy increases survival among cancer patients somewhat more than does chemotherapy. Combining psychotherapy with chemotherapy improves the outcome more than either alone. Perhaps the benefit comes from providing hope to a hopeless, depressed patient (Temoshok, 1987). Once again, as with heart disease, we see that taking personality into account offers the potential for more effective therapies.

Personality and the Immune System Under healthy conditions, the body is capable of defending itself against many diseases. The immune system fights infectious diseases, ranging from the common cold to deadly AIDS and cancer, though it is doomed to lose some of these battles. A well-functioning immune system, however, wins more of the battles, and research shows that the functioning of the immune system is influenced by personality. The field of **psychoneuroimmunology** studies the relationships among behavior, neural and endocrine function, and immune

*Watching a stressful movie
can have immediate,
measurable effects on the
immune system, according to
research. Nonetheless, many
people choose to be frightened
by horror films such as those
featuring Freddie Krueger.*

processes (Ader & Cohen, 1993). Traditionally, we have thought of diseases as caused by either physical agents (such as viruses) or mental factors (such as the psychological losses thought to produce depression). For example, traditional African American hoodoo, a system of folk beliefs, holds that a disease called "white liver" can be caused by someone casting a spell on another. It is not considered treatable by medical intervention. Its symptoms are strikingly similar to those of AIDS, for which medical treatment rather than hoodoo is considered appropriate, because the cause of AIDS is regarded as physical rather than magical (Kerr, 1993). The separation of mind and body has a long tradition in Western thought, but is called into question by advances in psychoneuroimmunology (Vollhardt, 1991).

The effects of stress on immune function occur quickly enough to be assessed in a brief laboratory session, appearing as soon as 15 minutes after the stress manipulation. Watching an emotional film increased the level of salivary immunoglobulin A (S-IgA), an immune response in many female subjects, especially those who did not cry or have tears in their eyes (Martin, Guthrie & Pitts, 1993). In one study, healthy men watched a stress-inducing videotape that depicted combat surgery in Vietnam. Compared to a control group that viewed landscape scenes, their blood samples showed decreased immune functioning, specifically decreased lymphocyte proliferation to the mitogen Con A, especially among subjects whose blood pressure rose more during the film (Zakowski et al., 1992). In the laboratory, then, the immune system responds to emotional stimuli, and people vary in their immune responsiveness. In Chapter 7, we saw that people with a stressed power motive typically show impaired immune functioning and are more likely to become ill as a result. James Pennebaker and his colleagues (Pennebaker, Colder & Sharp, 1990) suggest that inhibited power motivation is only one of several unhealthy patterns of inhibiting stressful experiences. Other unhealthy inhibitions include keeping secrets, inhibiting personal strivings, and using repressive coping strategies.

Fortunately, immune functioning can also be improved by psychological techniques. James Pennebaker and his colleagues have studied the effects of writing about personal traumatic experiences and the emotions about these events. College students who wrote about such experiences showed improved cellular immune system function and fewer visits to the campus health center than did control subjects who wrote about emotionally neutral topics (Pennebaker & Beall, 1986; Pennebaker, Kiecolt-Glaser & Glaser, 1988). In a follow-up study, freshmen wrote about their current transition to college. This, too, reduced health center visits compared to a control group, and the effect lasted for 4 months (Pennebaker, Colder & Sharp, 1990).

Immune system responses can be learned, according to the principles of classical conditioning described by Pavlov. This conditioning has been demonstrated in controlled studies using laboratory animals, so that previously neutral stimuli, such as certain tastes or odors, can become the conditioned stimuli for immune responses. Allergic release of histamine can also be conditioned to a previously neutral stimulus (Ader & Cohen, 1993). It is not yet known how these mechanisms influence human immune functioning in the real world, but the likelihood of a relationship between psychological experience and immune functioning is strengthened by such findings.

Research on the immune system is very much in the public eye, because of the attention brought by the AIDS epidemic. Immune disorders, like heart disease, cancer, and other diseases, illustrate the interrelationships of the body's adaptations and the mind's coping. Personality psychologists may focus on the mind, but we must recognize that the boundaries between mind and body are not clearly marked.

SUMMARY

• People adapt to environmental challenges and demands to maintain physical and mental well-being.

• Stressful events threaten well-being and require adaptation. Stressors come from many sources, such as traumatic events, illness, life change, daily hassles.

• According to Lazarus's transaction model of stress, a person first evaluates whether a situation is potentially harmful (primary appraisal) and then decides what can be done about it (secondary appraisal). Later, the situation may appear different upon reconsideration (reappraisal).

- Problem-focused coping techniques attempt to change the situation. Emotion-focused coping techniques attempt to change the person's emotional reaction to it. Each approach is effective sometimes.

- Psychological factors, particularly stress, contribute to psychosomatic disorders such as coronary heart disease and ulcers.

- Stressful life events increase the risk of illness.

- Personality can predispose people to illness or, through the traits of hardiness, optimism, and self-efficacy, can offer protection from illness.

- Type A personality, characterized by hostility and time pressure, puts people at increased risk of coronary heart disease.

- Type C personality, characterized by depression, hopelessness, and suppression of anger and other emotions, increases people's risk of cancer.

- Immune system responses are influenced by stress and by personality factors such as inhibiting emotional responses to stressful experiences.

GLOSSARY

adaptation a person's efforts to adjust to environmental challenges and demands in a way that achieves or maintains well-being

coping thought and behavior that is adopted to reduce stress and avoid adverse outcomes

emotion-focused coping adaptation by techniques that try to change the individual's emotional reactions to the difficulty

environmental stressors sources of stress that arise from external situations, rather than from internal sources

file-drawer problem the difficulty of knowing whether apparent replications of a hypothesized result in the published literature are misleading, because of the possibility that publication biases have overlooked a large number of unpublished failures to replicate the finding; such biases make chance results appear to be significant

General Adaptation Syndrome a generalized response to many forms of stress, in which the body mobilizes a "fight or flight" response, regardless of the nature of the threat

hardiness a personality trait that is characteristic of people who experience stress without becoming ill, characterized by control, commitment, and challenge

meta-analysis a statistical technique for reviewing a large number of research investigations of the same hypothesis to determine whether, taken as a whole, they are significant, and to what extent

primary appraisal the first stage of evaluating a potential stressor, in which a person judges whether the situation is potentially harmful

problem-focused coping adaptation by techniques that try to change the environment

psychological stress a particular relationship between the person and the environment that is appraised by the person as taxing or exceeding his or her resources and endangering his or her well-being

psychoneuroimmunology the study of the relationships among behavior, neural and endocrine function, and immune processes

psychosomatic disorders illnesses that involve physical components and that also are heavily influenced by psychological factors

reappraisal the third stage of evaluating a potential stressor, involving a changed interpretation of the situation

secondary appraisal the second stage of evaluating a potential stressor, in which a person judges what can be done to deal with the situation

social support a type of emotion-focused coping that involves turning to friends or other people for emotional and/or instrumental help with the problem

stress uncomfortable experience that occurs when a person is presented with problems or challenges that require adaptation

stressor a situation or event that produces stress

Type C cancer-prone personality, characterized by depression, hopelessness, and suppression of anger and other emotions

Type A a characteristic behavioral pattern of people at increased risk of coronary heart disease, characterized by hostility and time pressure

THOUGHT QUESTIONS

1. What are some of the environmental circumstances that have required adaptation in your recent experience?

2. Consider one event in your life that has been stressful. Apply Lazarus's model of stress appraisal to it; that is, identify how you appraised the event. Would any other appraisals have been reasonable?

3. For the stressful event that you have identified in the preceding question, list some coping methods that could have been used. Include both problem-focused and emotion-focused methods. Considering the situation, which technique do you judge to be most effective?

4. Why might some people use social support as a coping technique more often than other people do?

5. Can you describe stressful situations for which emotion-focused coping would be appropriate? Can you describe other situations for which problem-focused coping would be more effective?

6. How do emotions contribute to illness? What advice would you give to people who aren't sure whether to express emotions or not?

7. Stress is one of many factors that contribute to disease. What precautions could a person take during times of high stress to reduce the chances of getting sick?

8. How might learning more effective techniques of dealing with emotion, including hostility and anger, influence health? What might you do to teach people to deal with such emotions?

9. Based on what we know about personality and the immune system, can you give advice to students to increase their resistance to infections? Would it be important to consider exposure to infection, as well as psychological effects on the immune system?

10. Does it surprise you that the mind and the body seem to be closely related, according to the research reported in this chapter?

9

The Self

ONE OF THE DISTINGUISHING CHARACTERISTICS of the human species is our capacity for consciousness of self. We can be aware of our individuality, our differences from other people that make us unique, and our hopes and plans. Only a few closely related species have anything even approaching the human capacity for self-recognition. Gordon Gallup (1970, 1977; Povinelli, 1993) reports that chimpanzees and orangutans can recognize their physical images reflected in a mirror as themselves. They will touch their foreheads if they see a strange mark on the mirror reflection of themselves in that spot (just as humans who see a smudge of dirt on their faces in a mirror will touch themselves). Lower species do not recognize themselves in their mirror reflections. Cats, for example, may arch their backs and hiss at the "other cat" they see in the mirror or explore behind the mirror to find it.

In humans, the capacity for self-recognition is well developed, and consciousness of self extends considerably beyond awareness of our physical bodies. Tradition teaches us to "know thyself" and "to thine own self be true," and many people seek to "find themselves" through the experiences of life. On the other hand, both traditional teachings and some modern critics have warned against the dangers of excessive concern for the self,

We look into mirrors as a way of checking our appearance. Though we take this physical self-recognition for granted, in fact only a few other species are capable of recognizing themselves in their mirror reflection.

which can put "selfishness" ahead of social connections and responsibility. The self is not simply a scientific concept, obviously.

Theorists often describe the self in metaphorical terms (Knowles & Sibicky, 1990; Pratkanis & Greenwald, 1985). The self has been likened to an actor on the stage of life (a theatrical metaphor) or to an inner center of personality beneath more superficial layers (a "core" metaphor). Or the emphasis can be on growth, analogous to the growth of a plant toward its mature form (an organic metaphor). Such metaphors underlie more explicit theories and systematic research. The concept of self has been used to understand many of people's central motivations and higher functions. In psychoanalytic approaches, individuals are theorized to form a self early in life, based on interaction with the mother as the traditional primary caretaker. Interpersonal experiences in this early period become unconscious patterns directing later relationships that define the self, which continues to be shaped by social experience. Classic personality theorist Gordon Allport (1968) described the self as a holistic or integrative concept, of a higher order than learned habits or motives, which it integrates or unifies in a healthy personality. Modern personality approaches are again emphasizing this organizing function of the self, according to Walter Mischel (1992). For instance, humanistic theorists refer to the healthy tendency to develop (or "actualize") the self fully, sometimes despite social forces that work against healthy development.

It may be more appropriate to speak of *selves* than of *self,* because the self has been cast in many forms by various theorists (Table 9.1). Some theories of the self emphasize the motivation to value ourselves positively,

TABLE 9.1 **Examples of Diverse Theories of the Self**

Theorist	*Postulated "self"*	*Explanation*
William James (1890/1950)	Material self	Body, family, and perceptions
	Social self	Perception of other people's perceptions and expectations of us
	Spiritual self	Emotions and desires
Charles Cooley (1902)	Looking-glass self	Individual's perceptions of others' perceptions of him or her
George Herbert Mead (1934)	Social self	Self as perceived by the "generalized other" (other people in general), or by others who see one in a particular social role
Carl Rogers (1959)	Ideal self	What a person would like to be
	Real self	What a person truly is or can become
Gordon Allport (1955)	*Proprium*	All aspects of a person that make for inward unity

both privately and in our public self-presentation. Some theories approach the self from a cognitive point of view, emphasizing various kinds of self-knowledge. Some consider the self as it develops over time and strive to understand how people can attain their highest potentials. Recently, several critics have pointed out that psychological descriptions of the self reflect the limited insights of our traditional Western thinking. According to the critics, there is an overemphasis on individualism and rationalism, with not enough attention paid to connections among people and to larger social issues (Cushman, 1990; Hermans, Kempen & van Loon, 1992; Smith, 1994).

An overall definition of the **self** would have to be very general, given the disparate emphases in the field. Perhaps the definition suggested by Constantine Sedikides is as suitable as any: "A person's self is the person's mental representation of information pertaining to him or her" (Sedikides, 1992, p. 273). The self is not simply cognitive, however. Other researchers (for example, Pratkanis & Greenwald, 1985) point out that emotion is also relevant; we have positive and/or negative feelings about the self.

Valuing One's Self

The mental representations we have about ourselves are rarely neutral. **Self-esteem** is the sense of positive self-worth, and it can be measured by several self-report questionnaires. The questions on these scales are not subtle. Consider these items (quoted by Overholser, 1993):

> *"On the whole, I am satisfied with myself."*
> *"Taking everything into account, I would rate myself fairly highly."*
> *"I am very confident of myself."*

Compared to the subtleties of a projective test, or even the ambiguities of many multiple-choice questions, these items are obvious in their intended meaning.

In addition to overall, or global, self-esteem, researchers have also measured people's self-esteem in various areas, such as sexual self-esteem (Wiederman & Allgeier, 1993), social self-esteem, and academic self-esteem. James Overholser reports that, among undergraduate psychology students, males' self-esteem was more influenced by task success, and females' self-esteem depended more on social relationships and personal qualities (Overholser, 1993). Similar sex differences have been reported in other studies, which also often find that global self-esteem is higher among males (Skaalvik, 1986). Despite these sex differences, self-esteem among gifted and talented female adolescents is enhanced by both traditionally feminine abilities, such as ability in the performing arts, and activities that are traditionally masculine, such as athletic and mechanical ability (Hollinger & Fleming, 1985, 1988). Self-esteem, then, can have different bases in different people. It is somewhat oversimplified to speak of self-esteem in general terms only, without considering its foundation in specific activities.

High scores on a self-esteem test don't always mean the same thing. Some people score high because of genuinely high self-regard. Others are choosing high self-esteem responses to defend themselves against the self-doubts that they don't want to face. Still others score high because of narcissism, a grandiose but unrealistic view of the self (Raskin, Novacek & Hogan, 1991). Only genuinely high self-esteem corresponds to a mentally healthy personality; defensive and narcissistic efforts are unhealthy. These patterns are not easy to differentiate when using self-report questionnaires alone, but we may be able to recognize defensive reactions by observing sweaty palms, blushing, and other evidence of emotion. Defensively high self-esteem is often accompanied by physiological reactivity, whereas people with nondefensively high self-esteem generally appear more calm (Epstein, 1985).

Maintaining Self-Esteem

We learn to evaluate ourselves positively or negatively as a result of social experience (see Leary et al., 1995). When others think well or ill of us, these messages often become internalized aspects of our own sense of self. In addition, we often strive to make a positive impression on others, putting our "best foot forward" in an attempt to create positive impressions on others, which in turn enhances our own sense of self-worth. People who are uncertain of their self-esteem may strive especially hard to bolster their self-worth in the situations they encounter (Kernis et al., 1993).

Success enhances self-esteem. William James (1890/1950), whose thinking about the self has influenced psychologists for many decades, described self-esteem with a now-classic equation:

$$\text{Self-esteem} = \frac{\text{Success}}{\text{Pretensions}}$$

This equation states that self-esteem can be achieved by increasing success or by lowering aspirations, or "pretensions." James gives the example of people who would be happier if they did not have to keep up the pretense of enjoying classical music just to impress others. Can you think of an example from your own experience in which your self-esteem was reduced because of pretensions and unrealistic aspirations?

Modern psychologists would add that we can also maintain self-esteem by positive thinking. We use *self-enhancement* strategies: seeking positive information about ourselves and interpreting ambiguous information in the most favorable light (Markus & Wurf, 1987; Sedikides, 1993; Taylor & Brown, 1988). Researchers find that most people remember their successes better than their failures and give self-serving reasons for their successes and failures. We take credit for our successes, saying that they are caused by our own skills and efforts, while we avoid accepting blame for our failures, attributing them instead to other people's unfairness or to bad luck.

The Benefits of High Self-Esteem

Mood and self-evaluation influence each other. When people evaluate themselves negatively, they experience unpleasant emotions, such as shame, embarrassment, and feelings of inferiority. The reverse is also true; when our mood is momentarily decreased, we recall more negative memories, judgments, and other information about the self (Sedikides, 1992). High self-esteem and the self-serving attributions that maintain it contribute to emotional well-being and protect us against depression and anxiety (Greenberg et al., 1992; Haaga, Dyck & Ernst, 1991; Luthar & Blatt, 1993). When people with low self-esteem are in a negative mood, they are more likely to criticize themselves than are people with high self-esteem, which may put them at increased risk for depression (Brown & Mankowski, 1993). Low self-esteem influences social interactions in various ways. Jealousy is more common among people with low self-esteem (Stewart & Beatty, 1985), and they are also more swayed by messages aimed at influencing them (Rhodes & Wood, 1992).

Positive views of the self are generally adaptive, even though they are often not wholly realistic (Taylor & Brown, 1988, 1994). Most people have positive illusions about the self, believing that they are better off than others—healthier, happier, more likely to succeed, and so on—even when they aren't. Positive illusions are adaptive in many ways. When they expect to succeed, people are more persistent in working toward goals when they encounter obstacles, and they are more effective without the distractions of self-doubt. How many aspiring athletes would continue to work toward the major leagues, or undergraduates toward graduate programs, if they didn't believe their chances of success were better than average? People with low self-esteem are less likely to use benign illusions (Brown & Mankowski, 1993). Of course, having unrealistic, exceptionally high and inflexible expectations may also be maladaptive (Dweck, 1991). After a sufficient accumulation of disconfirming experience, the would-be professional athlete or Ph.D. ought to change aspirations, which William James called "pretensions", bowing to reality.

Under most circumstances, people with high self-esteem set appropriate goals and are effective at meeting their goals. Imagine, though, that you are in an experiment and hear the experimenter describe the goal you have thought about setting as a level that reflects "playing it safe to avoid choking under pressure." Under this condition, people with high self-esteem often increase their goals to levels that are too high, and they actually perform worse under this added pressure (Baumeister, Heatherton & Tice, 1993). Jennifer Crocker (1993) reports that subjects with high self-esteem who experienced failure on a rigged social sensitivity test recalled more negative behaviors of other people. That is, when trying to remember two dozen separate statements about people on a memory test, they were more likely to remember negative statements ("Mary was placed on academic probation last quarter") than positive ones ("Joe got the highest score on the midterm in his chemistry test"). Subjects who were moderate or low in self-esteem did not show this pattern, suggesting that people with high self-esteem are particularly likely to defend their self-esteem by comparing themselves with others who have negative characteristics. Roy Baumeister and his colleagues (Baumeister, Tice & Hutton, 1989) suggest that people with high self-esteem are especially concerned with presenting an enhanced, successful self-image. In contrast, those with low self-esteem are more concerned with protecting themselves against the threat of failure.

Self-Esteem of Various Groups

Self-esteem, like many personality traits, is not evenly distributed across the diverse groups that make up our world. By considering the patterns of self-esteem across race and gender, we can begin to understand the processes by which self-esteem influences us.

Minority Groups We might expect that people who are members of privileged groups would have higher self-esteem, applying to themselves the positive images of their group in society, but that is not the case. Contrary to expectation, research does not show that the self-esteem of less privileged groups is any lower than that of the general population (Crocker & Major, 1989). Jennifer Crocker and Brenda Major (1989) propose several self-protective mechanisms to explain why most research studies find that members of stigmatized groups, such as racial minorities, disabled people, and homosexuals, do not have low self-esteem. For one thing, they may compare their own successes or failures with the lower levels attained by their group, rather than the higher levels of society at large. In this way, identification with the devalued, stigmatized group protects individual self-esteem. In addition, when stigmatized people receive negative feedback, they may attribute it to prejudice against their group, rather than assuming that it signifies personal shortcomings. These and other mechanisms can protect individual self-esteem.

Although the self-esteem of African Americans is as high as that of white Americans (higher in some studies), the experiences that seem to contribute to self-esteem vary in the two groups. In one study of middle school students, self-descriptions of physical appearance are more closely associated with self-esteem among white adolescents, while perceived control seems more important for African-American boys, and popularity for African-American girls (Tashakkori, 1993). Although these specific associations may vary in other samples, the general message seems clear: the basis for self-esteem may vary from one group to another, just as it varies from one person to another.

Gender What makes a man feel good about himself is often different from what makes a woman feel good about herself. Although it is easy to exaggerate the differences between the sexes, the currently popular view that males are more individualistic and females more connected has also been applied to understanding sex differences in self-esteem (Josephs, Markus & Tafarodi, 1992). If society evaluates males according to their individual accomplishments, they will be socially approved on this basis and will learn to think well of themselves for their individual accomplishments. In contrast, by expecting females to be more involved in shared efforts, society teaches them to base their self-esteem on interdependence and interpersonal connectedness. Self-esteem depends, in part, on living up to the gender norms of one's society.

These ideas are confirmed by laboratory studies showing that males, but not females, with high self-esteem think themselves to have unique abilities; they exaggerate the rarity of their athletic or academic strengths. Given a memory task, women with high self-esteem showed improved memory by associating the words with a best friend, supporting the importance of interpersonal relationships for them (Josephs, Markus & Tafarodi, 1992).

Presenting Ourselves to Others

The term **self-presentation** refers to efforts to appear in a way that will create a desired impression on others. The metaphor of theater is sometimes applied to this concept: we are actors, and the others whom we are trying to impress are our audience. Some actors' self-presentations not only convince others but also can change the actors' own self-perceptions (McKillop, Berzonsky & Schlenker, 1992; Tice, 1992). Thus, we may become the roles we play. Sometimes we convince our audience, and sometimes we learn the roles that the audience expects. This dual possibility is confirmed in research indicating that college students come to match their roommate's perception of them over time, both because they change and because their roommate's perception changes to reduce the discrepancy (McNulty & Swann, 1994). Public criticism or negative feedback may cut through our defenses, however, forcing us to be more honest with ourselves (Baumeister & Cairns, 1992).

Self-presentations activate a variety of emotions. Barry Schlenker and Mark Leary (1982) propose that *social anxiety* occurs when we are motivated to impress others but don't expect to succeed. According to sociologist Erving Goffman (1967), *embarrassment* results when we are aware that our intended presentations of the self are flawed. Embarrassment is related to social anxiety but is not identical to it (Miller & Leary, 1992). Of course, positive emotions, such as pride, can also result from self-presentation.

People use a variety of strategies to present themselves effectively. Overt behavior is easier to control than subtle nonverbal behaviors—the facial expressions and body movements that accompany emotion. Those who can control the more subtle signs, such as politicians and experienced salespeople, have a strategic advantage in conveying their desired image to others (DePaulo, 1992).

Two personality traits have been widely used to measure differences among individuals in their emphasis on the self as a social object. These traits, self-monitoring and public self-consciousness, typify people who are self-conscious in the sense of an actor on the stage of life.

Self-Monitoring

When my son was in kindergarten, I was in the midst of reprimanding him in an angry voice. The phone rang, and I answered it. After the conversation was finished, my son looked at me in astonishment and said, "I thought you were mad." He couldn't understand my sudden switch from anger to a friendly voice. As an adult, of course I knew that it would be inappropriate to yell into the phone instead of saying "hello," however angry I might feel, because adults control their emotional expressions depending upon the audience. (My son did not know, either, that my anger was strategically exaggerated to make an impression on him.)

To convey a particular impression strategically, a person must be aware of how others perceive him or her. Mark Snyder (1974) proposes that people vary in the trait of **self-monitoring.** This trait refers to self-observation and self-control of expressive behavior and to self-presentation. People high in self-monitoring are sensitive to social cues about what is appropriate behavior in a given situation. They are aware of how they appear to others, and they modify their behavior based on knowing what is appropriate in the particular situation to create a desired impression. This leads high self-monitors to behave differently in various situations, depending upon the audience. High self-monitors are more effective than low self-monitors when they try to deceive others (DePaulo, 1992). They conceal expressions of happiness when it would be socially inappropriate to express the emotion; for example, in the presence of other experimental subjects who were doing worse than they were on a competitive complex reasoning task (Friedman & Miller-Herringer, 1991). In contrast, low self-monitors behave more consistently from one situation to another, and their behavior is a more accurate reflection of their actual feelings. One researcher describes people's impressions of the high self-monitor as "a very social creature, skilled in interpersonal communication and adept at managing self-presentation," in contrast to the low self-monitor, who is seen as "the internally consistent individual who relates to others in a straightforward way that reflects the inner self" (Larkin, 1991, p. 19).

Self-monitoring can be a highly adaptive trait when it enables strategic self-presentation. Consider the act of buying a car: presenting oneself as excited about one car, put off by the cost of another, and so on, can influence the outcome of a negotiation. Unfortunately, the high self-monitor is also influenced by image more than by quality in advertising (Zuckerman,

TABLE **9.2   Characteristics of Potential Dating Partners Preferred by Subjects High and Low in Self-Monitoring**

High self-monitors	*Low self-monitors*
Financial resources	Faithful and loyal
Physical attractiveness	Honest
Recreational interests	Kind and considerate
Sex appeal	Responsible
Social status	Similar educational level
	Similar values and beliefs

Based on information in Jones, 1993.

Gioioso & Tellini, 1988) and so may weigh options based on superficial considerations. The car salesperson also becomes more effective if he or she is able to control expression of emotions and presentation of the self as knowledgeable, honest, and so on. Beyond such business negotiations, self-monitoring contributes to self-esteem and friendship, at least among boys, whose childhood friendships typically involve larger groups and therefore demand more self-presentation skills than do the friendships of girls (Musser & Browne, 1991). Among college undergraduates, high self-monitors select their dating relationships based upon extrinsic motivations such as the image their partner projects, whereas low self-monitors are more influenced by intrinsic motivations such as shared values and beliefs (Jones, 1993) (Table 9.2).

Individual differences in self-monitoring are measured by a true-false self-report questionnaire developed by Mark Snyder (Table 9.3), as well as by revisions of this scale (Gangestad & Snyder, 1985; Lennox & Wolfe, 1984; Shuptrine, Bearden & Teel, 1990). Average scores of various groups confirm Snyder's description of self-monitoring. Actors must monitor their impact on an audience. Not surprisingly, stage actors score high on the Self-Monitoring Scale, 18.4 out of 25 possible points. Hospitalized psychiatric patients, who are unsuccessful in their social self-presentations, averaged only 10.19 out of 25. Stanford University undergraduates scored between these two groups (Snyder, 1974).

Several researchers have subjected the Self-Monitoring Scale to factor analysis to determine whether it is a one-dimensional scale or whether (as they have found) it contains more than one dimension (or factor).

Three factors often reported are Acting Ability, Extraversion, and Other-Directedness (for example, Briggs, Cheek & Buss, 1980). Richard Lennox (1988) emphasizes that self-monitoring can either help people work toward positive goals or serve a defensive function, so he distinguishes two independent factors. One factor, which he calls Acquisitive Self-Monitoring, reflects a confident, approach-oriented style, in which a person seeks to impress others in a way that will gain interpersonal rewards. People with this style are extraverted and say they that have the ability to act (as in a theatrical role). The other factor, which Lennox calls Protective Self-Monitoring, is oriented to avoiding social disapproval. People with the protective style are socially anxious and low in self-esteem. Most researchers doubt that self-monitoring is a simple, one-dimensional trait. High self-monitors don't all monitor their behavior in the same way or for the same reasons. Clarifying these various processes is an ongoing challenge for researchers.

Public Self-Consciousness

The trait of **public self-consciousness** refers to awareness of the self as a social object (Fenigstein, Scheier & Buss, 1975). To score high on this scale, people describe themselves as concerned with their appearance and with making a good impression. As a temporary state, virtually everyone feels publicly self-conscious when performing in front of an audience or when being filmed (Buss, 1980). As a trait, the measure assesses the extent to which an individual is high in public self-consciousness even outside of these special situations.

TABLE 9.3 **Examples of Items Measuring the Trait of Self-Monitoring**

1. I would probably make a good actor.

2. At parties, I let others keep the jokes and stories going. [reverse scored]

3. When I am uncertain how to act in social situations, I look to the behavior of others for cues.

From Snyder, 1974. These items illustrate three factors often reported in factor analysis studies of self-monitoring: the Acting, Extraversion, and Other-Directedness factors, respectively.

TABLE 9.4   Examples of Items That Measure Three Factors of Self-Consciousness

Public self-consciousness
>   I usually worry about making a good impression.
>   I'm concerned about what other people think of me.

Social anxiety
>   I get embarrassed very easily.
>   I feel anxious when I speak in front of a group.

Private self-consciousness
>   I reflect about myself a lot.
>   I'm generally attentive to my inner feelings.

Adapted from Fenigstein, Scheier & Buss, 1975.

Public self-consciousness was first described as one factor in a larger questionnaire to measure self-consciousness more generally. Allan Fenigstein, Michael Scheier, and Arnold Buss (1975) set out to develop a measure of self-consciousness, the sort of self-awareness that is characteristic of insightful people and that psychotherapy aims to develop. The 38-item measure that they created, the Self-Consciousness Scale, was found to contain three factors (Table 9.4). In addition to the factor of *public self-consciousness* just described, they also found a *social anxiety* factor, which included questions about shyness and nervousness in social situations and which can be thought of as anxiety-laden public self-consciousness (see Bruch, Hamer & Heimberg, 1995). The third factor, *private self-consciousness*, taps a quite different dimension, which we will now consider.

Knowing Oneself

How do we know about ourselves? What kind of information about ourselves do we seek? Theoretical answers vary: we want information that is accurate, or that is enhancing to our self-image, reflecting the complexity of our motivations for knowing ourselves (Strube, 1990). How do we get that information? For the most part, psychologists describe social interactions with others as a major source of information about the self. People treat us well or badly, reflecting (presumably) our worth, and we gain further information by comparing ourselves with others, a process called *social comparison*. What about the direct experience of inner processes, through introspection? Although such experiential self-knowledge (which some would call "soul-searching") is less discussed in mainstream psychology, it has always been part of the literature on the self. Some writers go so far as to refer to a "spiritual self" that can be known directly by experience (Tloczynski, 1993).

Although self-knowledge is often advocated as a key to wisdom, do we really know ourselves? Most of us have a positive bias, viewing ourselves as somewhat better than others do. There are important individual differences in accuracy, however, so we may think either better or worse of ourselves than others do (John & Robins, 1994). Researchers report that people who have a clear image of who they are (what personality traits they possess) also tend to have higher self-esteem (Baumgardner, 1990; Campbell, 1990). In experimental studies, the clear self-image of undergraduates with high self-esteem directs their choices according to a prototype matching strategy. When making hypothetical choices among cars or restaurants, they are more likely to select those that have been described as preferred by people with a personality profile that matches their own. Subjects with low self-esteem are less likely to do this, presumably (according to the researchers) because they are less clear in their own self-image (Setterlund & Niedenthal, 1993).

Private Self-Consciousness

In contrast to the self that can be known to others, some parts of the self can be known only directly by the individual. These aspects are the *private self*, and awareness of them is termed **private self-consciousness.** All of us experience increases in the temporary state of private self-consciousness when we are engaged in introspective activities such as writing in a diary, just as our public self-consciousness increases when we are performing on stage (Buss, 1980). There are individual differences in the extent to which people feel private self-consciousness, with or without such special conditions. That is, private self-consciousness is a trait as well as a state. Typical questions to assess private self-consciousness ask about awareness of fantasies and moods.

Private self-consciousness involves more than introspection, however. It is correlated with belief in paranormal phenomena, such as mental telepathy (Davies, 1985) and with psychoticism on the Eysenck Personality Scale (Darvill, Johnson & Danko, 1992), which has also been shown to relate to paranormal reports. While it may appear that privately self-conscious people are absorbed in their own worlds, oblivious to social reality, that is not generally the case. Private and public self-consciousness are positively correlated, so that many people who are high on private self-consciousness are also high on public self-consciousness. (They are, after all, separate dimensions, rather than alternative poles of one dimension.) Experimental evidence shows that privately self-conscious people do change their behavior to present a particular image to an audience: the image of being autonomous and nonconforming (Schlenker & Weigold, 1990).

Does private self-consciousness give us more accurate self-knowledge? Some researchers think so. Subjects with high private self-consciousness respond to self-report measures more reliably (Hjelle & Bernard, 1994), and questionnaires predict behavior better for them than for people low in private self-consciousness (Underwood & Moore, 1981). Before giving too much credence to the claim that private self-consciousness is accurate self-consciousness, though, we should ask whether we really know what is accurate for an individual. Unfortunately, researchers too often rely on self-reports of behavior rather than on actual behavior (Osborne, Maguire & Angus, 1987). It is possible that private self-consciousness predicts consistent *reports* of behavior but not actual behavior, since self-reports are not always accurate. For example, college women high in private self-consciousness report that they disclosed more personal information to unacquainted others in a laboratory experiment, but this was not confirmed when the partners assessed the level of self-disclosure they had received (Reno & Kenny, 1992). Nonetheless, it is intriguing to ponder whether some of us know our "true self" better than others.

The Self-Concept

The term **self-concept** refers to a person's cognitions that describe the self. In contrast to self-esteem, which is evaluative, the self-concept is descriptive. How would you answer the question, "Who am I?" Typical answers that have been given to researchers reflect a variety of dimensions of the self-concept. Some answers reflect the impact of social roles on the self concept: "I am a student"; "I am a parent." Other answers reflect the more private aspects of the self: "I am in conflict"; "I am happy." Researchers have developed a variety of coding schemes for categorizing answers to this simple question, "Who am I?" (Gordon, 1968). More recently, cognitive psychologists have described the self-concept as a prototype (a category that is detailed and describes what is typical; see Chapter 2). A person's self-concept is an important anchor point for thinking (Markus & Wurf, 1987). You probably perk up when a reading or lecture topic strikes a self-relevant chord, and you find it easier to recall what someone has said about you than about a less personally relevant topic.

A View from Cognitive Psychology   Hazel Markus (1977) has contributed extensively to cognitive theories of the self. Her concept of the **self-schema** (*plural:* self-schemata) describes the self-concept as a cognitive structure. Markus defines self-schemata as "cognitive generalizations about the self, derived from past experience, that organize and guide the processing of the self-related information contained in an individual's social experiences" (Markus, 1977, p. 64). For example, if you have been criticized in the past for voicing your opinions, you may think of yourself as someone who is likely to have a wrong or unpopular opinion, and you will probably hesitate to offer an opinion in later situations. This self-doubt about your opinions is one self-schema. You will have other schemata in other areas. Perhaps you also think of yourself as a good athlete, as a loyal friend, and as tone-deaf musically.

Markus calls people "schematic" if they have some kind of self-schema in a particular area that is of interest to the researcher. A researcher interested in independence, for example, may find it useful to look at people who are schematic on this trait, who think of themselves as "independent." People who haven't given it much thought are not schematic (we may call them "aschematic") on this trait. Because they don't think of themselves as independent, aschematic individuals have a harder time thinking of examples of times when they have been independent, and they respond more slowly when asked questions about independence. Schematic individuals respond more quickly and readily come up with examples of their independent behavior (Markus, 1977). Of course, researchers may be interested in comparing people who are schematic with those who are aschematic on any other trait, such as friendliness, powerfulness, and so on.

Because self-schemata are based on social experience, people are likely to have a diversity of such cognitive structures. After all, we interact with different people in diverse ways, and it is unlikely that they would be unanimous in their messages about who we are. This raises a central question that scientists have asked since the early psychological discussions of the self: is the self a unified entity or a collection of various "selves"?

One Self or Many?   Do we think of ourselves as one unified whole? Or do we imagine ourselves to be composed of diverse components that are not wholly integrated? More than 100 years ago, in his classic work *The Principles of Psychology*, William James (1890/1950) discussed what has been called the "one-in-many-selves paradox" (Knowles & Sibicky, 1990). On the one hand, we present different selves to different groups of people. The self known to our friends is not the same self known to our family. On the other hand, we feel a sameness and continuity of the self in our stream of consciousness.

Many Selves   Theorists have recognized that the self varies from one interaction to another. This happens because the **social self** is created through social interaction, and each different interaction creates a different social self. William James (1890/1950) voiced the classic statement on this issue:

> *Properly speaking, a man has as many social selves as there are individuals who recognize him and carry an image of him in their mind. . . . But as the individuals who carry the images fall naturally into classes, we may*

practically say that he has as many different social selves as there are distinct groups of persons about whose opinion he cares. He generally shows a different side of himself to each of these different groups. Many a youth who is demure enough before his parents and teachers, swears and swaggers like a pirate among his "tough" young friends. We do not show ourselves to our children as to our club-companions, to our customers as to the laborers we employ, to our own masters and employers as to our intimate friends. From this there results what practically is a division of the man into several selves. (James, 1890/1950, p. 294)

This theoretical position has been elaborated by others. Erving Goffman (1959) compared people's various selves with the many roles that actors play. George Herbert Mead (1934), according to his symbolic interactionist point of view, described the self as constructed through social interactions that he compared to games. We may call them scripts, such as the "restaurant script" that describes the standard interaction involved in ordering food, paying, and so on. Modern psychological theories describe *interpersonal scripts* as social contexts for understanding the self (Baldwin, 1992). People have both culturally shared and individualized scripts that define their social interactions and personal meanings (for example, Abelson, 1981; Lewis, 1989; Tomkins, 1979b). Like players in a small theater company, we play roles in a variety of scripts.

Hubert Hermans and his colleagues (Hermans, 1991; Hermans, Rijks & Kempen, 1993) have developed a method for studying self-narratives that builds on the idea that self consists of multiple perspectives. They ask people to describe their lives, from past to future, from their own perspective and also from the perspective of an imagined other with whom they have carried on an internal dialog for many years. The imagined other is a part of the self, evidence that we are not entirely unified. Although an elaborate experience of an imagined other is not characteristic of everyone, Hermans argues that the self is better described as a collection of "I's" in dialog, rather than as one unitary "I."

The Unified Self Despite the reasonableness of the multiple-self argument, it is somewhat disconcerting. Don't we expect people to be consistent, to be "like themselves"? Inconsistency is disturbing. When we tell someone, "I wasn't myself yesterday," it is with an apologetic tone. Extreme splits, such as multiple personalities, are unquestionably unhealthy. Perhaps the theories of multiple or disunified selves offer inadequate descriptions of healthy personality. Some theorists, holding firmly to the theory of a unified self, oppose theoretical emphasis on multiple selves. A few even doubt the diagnosis of multiple personalities (Dell, 1988a, 1988b; Fadiman, 1993; Frick, 1993).

Theorists, notably Gordon Allport (1937), have often described unity of personality as a mark of mental health. Colloquially, people approve of "getting it together." Psychoanalysts regard split-off parts of the personality as the products of defenses. Psychoanalyst Carl Jung described the Self (capitalized in his theory) as the achievement of psychic wholeness that is produced when conscious and unconscious aspects of the personality are ultimately united, a goal achieved by only a few highly developed personalities. The unity of personality has been described in metaphors of sameness across time: the continuity of the stream of consciousness (James, 1890/ 1950) and the cohesiveness of the life story (Gergen & Gergen, 1988; McAdams, 1990), among other metaphors (Knowles & Sibicky, 1990).

Research provides evidence for both many selves and a unified self. Women who had graduated from college 30 years earlier were asked to describe themselves in four roles: daughter, friend, worker, and partner. Self-concept varied depending on the role; for example, the women described themselves as more competent as workers than as daughters. At the same time, though, consistency across roles also was found. Those women who rated themselves high on the traits measured for one role (positive affect, competence, and dependability) also tended to rate themselves high on that trait in other roles (Roberts & Donahue, 1994). Thus, the self does vary with social roles but at the same time is consistent. We are more likely to notice inconsistency if we compare roles or situations, and consistency if we compare people.

It may be unrealistic, though, to think of unity as a lasting attainment. Carl Rogers (for example, Rogers, 1961) described people who are psychologically healthy as fully open in each moment to the experience of the changing self. Michael Bütz (1992) has offered a contemporary revision of the unified self using the metaphor of fractal theory from mathematics. He describes a *transitory self* that is stable only temporarily, always remaining open to change from outside influences. Such a self is not a "closed system," which theoretically could be stable, but rather an "open system" that can be disrupted by outside influences. Think of the outside influences that can have a disruptive effect on apparently stable selves: natural disasters, illness, even unexpected reactions from others. Such realities suggest exchanging the image of a stable, unified self for the image of the self as a meaningful process.

The Complex Self: Integrating One and Many Selves Both ideas have merit: one self and many selves. Theory can guide us to having it both ways. The personal construct approach, building on the theory proposed by George Kelly (1955), has led to an emphasis on *cognitive complexity* measures. Such measures assess a person's ability to use many different concepts to understand the self and other people. Personal construct theorists postulate that cognitions about the self are arranged hierarchically and that a healthy pattern includes a complex diversity of concepts that are integrated at a higher level in the hierarchy; for example, "proud" and "emotionally needy" are aspects of the higher level concept "a genuine human being." Diversity of concepts offers flexibility, and unity at the top provides the cohesiveness necessary for health.

From a cognitive point of view, having a complex self-schema offers more flexibility for processing incoming information. Cognitive complexity permits more accurate judgments. For example, more cognitively complex counselors made fewer diagnostic errors on a hypothetical case of a patient who actually had two diagnosable disorders. Less complex counselors overlooked the second diagnosis of schizophrenia in a client whose IQ score indicated mental retardation (Spengler & Strohmer, 1994). Complexity is helpful when applied to the self as well as to other people. When feedback suggests that our self-concepts have been inaccurate, those with simple images of themselves may reject the feedback and assert that their positive views were correct. Those with more complex self-schemata can incorporate the negative feedback into their images of themselves and thus profit from experience (Stein, 1994). Self-complexity provides a buffer against the disquieting effects of stressful life events (Kalthoff & Neimeyer, 1993; Linville, 1987). Having a complex self-concept also seems to moderate emotional reactions to feedback about the likelihood of attaining present and future goals; this prevents emotionally extreme reactions (Niedenthal, Setterlund & Wherry, 1992) and helps to protect against depression (Evans, 1994). Not only are people high in cognitive complexity less distressed by failure, but they may even be stimulated to better performance because failure is less globally threatening to them than to those with simpler self-concepts (Dixon & Baumeister, 1991).

The key to optimal mental health may be to have a self that is unified without being oversimplified and diverse without being fragmented. But what about those unpleasant areas of the self—are they compartmentalized into categories that may be thought about rarely, or are they interspersed among categories that are accessed frequently (Showers, 1992)? The fragmented, compartmentalized pattern may seem to encapsulate conflict, but it does not resolve it. One resolution to the one-in-many-selves paradox is suggested by William James's (1890/1950) distinction between the "I" and the "me." As suggested by their grammatical forms, the "I" is the self as an active executive in personality, while the "me" is the self as object of reflection. Diversity of the "me" is desirable as a reflection of our ability to relate to various groups and types of people. Continuity or unity of the "I" is desirable because this executive of personality (comparable to the Freudian *ego*) would otherwise be handicapped by conflict and indecision.

Life Stories

The eminent psychiatrist Robert Coles, who has studied the lives of children in the context of American historical changes in race relations over several decades, suggests that people cannot be understood with theoretical abstractions alone. It is also necessary to hear their life stories (Coles, 1989). He describes the pedagogical function of narratives, which teach his psychiatry students to see beyond diagnostic labels. Theorists, too, are now discovering the power of narrative understandings of the self (for example, Malm, 1993).

Although people's reports of earlier life events are often biased (Ross, 1989), such memories are significant aspects of personality. Our memory for information about ourselves during past events in life may be termed **autobiographical memory.** Alfred Adler (1950), one of the first psychoanalysts to offer modifications of Freud's theory, suggested that early memories provide key insights to the unique personality of an individual and give direction to later striving toward goals. Arnold Bruhn says that autobiographical memory "provides an identity to the self, especially the self in relation to others and to the world" (1990, p. 95). He has developed a method for systematically measuring early memories as a diagnostic procedure for therapy clients (Bruhn, 1992a, 1992b).

Autobiographical memory, like memory in general, is not always accurate; rather, it is reconstructed at the time of remembering. It is influenced or, in effect, reconstructed by ongoing factors such as mood and beliefs about personality. Students who are depressed, for example, recall more details of negative events than do their nondepressed classmates (McAdams, Lensky, Daple & Allen, 1988). Among Vietnam veterans suffering from posttraumatic stress disorder (PTSD), traumatic memories intrude on everyday life, whereas positive memories are difficult to recall (McNally et al., 1994). As personality changes, whether through psychotherapy or otherwise, memories often change. Some therapies focus specifically on memories. A program of life review for elderly people, designed to revise autobiographical memories in an effort to help resolve conflicts, has been reported to improve psychological health, as measured by the Personal Orientation Inventory (POI) measure of self-actualization (Giltinan, 1990).

According to Dan McAdams, formulating a personal life story provides individuals with an identity (McAdams, 1985; McAdams, Lensky, Daple & Allen, 1988). These life stories, like narratives in general, describe the scripts that unite past, present, and future into one coherent account. College students who are more advanced on a measure of identity (based on the theory of Erik Erikson) recall more early memories and recall them more quickly than those with less developed identities (Neimeyer & Rareshide, 1991). Events that disrupt our established identities, such as injury to an athlete, can cause depression (Brewer, 1993).

Developing an identity involves developing one's individual life story, from childhood onward, with a sense of cohesiveness and meaning. When parents talk to children, they influence the formation of these autobiographical memories (Nelson, 1993). Parents talk more with firstborns and with girls, which explains why these children usually report earlier memories (Mullen, 1994). Autobiographical memory is also earlier among Caucasian than among Asian college students in America. Why might this be? One explanation is that the greater emphasis on individuality in American culture encourages more storytelling with the individual child

Recalling memories from earlier in life helps maintain the sense of self throughout life.

featured. Among Asian Americans, the influence of their more collectivist Asian ethnic background encourages stories that feature the family group rather than the individual (Mullen, 1994), as has been clearly demonstrated in cross-cultural research (Triandis, 1989). The selves that we become are, in large part, products of our life stories.

Knowing through Feelings

Seymour Epstein (1985, 1990, 1994), in his *cognitive-experiential self-theory*, provides a systematic framework for thinking about broad issues in personality theory. In this system, narratives or life stories, in contrast to abstract logical discourse, have particular appeal (Epstein, 1994). Drawing on the work of others, including George Kelly (who developed personal construct theory; see Chapter 5), Epstein suggests that people have personal theories about the self and about the world. These theories influence experience, including vaguely felt emotions ("vibes") as well as stronger emotions and behavior. A person's theory of the self is only part of a broader personal theory of reality, a theory that describes the individual's beliefs about four basic issues (see Epstein, 1990, p. 167):

1. Is the world benign or harmful?

2. Is the world meaningful (predictable, controllable, and just) or not?

3. Are people worth relating to?

4. Is the self worthy (competent, good, and lovable)?

These beliefs are "experiential," meaning that they are felt emotionally, rather than thought rationally. In fact, the experiential system may conflict with a person's rational system of beliefs. For example, we sometimes think we should do something but do not feel like doing it. Many people feel safer driving than flying, although they know that accident statistics show that flying is actually safer. Common irrational judgments that people make can often be understood as consequences of the experiential system rather than the rational system (Epstein et al., 1992).

Much of what we know about the self is experiential, rather than rational. Certainly this is true of those parts of the self that reach back to early life, before rational thought has developed very far. Even among college students, Peter Salovey has demonstrated that experimentally produced changes in mood achieved through imagery, both happy and sad, caused undergraduates to focus attention more on themselves (Salovey, 1992). Experiential beliefs are often not conscious. Epstein notes that people with a history of trauma, including accidents, parental death, illness, and rape, often have formed a basic belief that the self is not worthy (Janoff-Bulman, 1989). Despite these adverse forces, people are motivated to enhance their self-esteem, as well as to experience pleasure, to maintain a stable and coherent conceptual system, and to maintain favorable relationships with others (Epstein, 1985).

Developing One's Potential

Development toward higher levels of psychological health has long been an interest of psychologists who study the self. Humanistic psychologists, in particular, have focused attention on the development of the highest potential self. Such discussions often emphasize an individual's *will*, in contrast to external determinants. Goal-seeking or willful behavior has been considered since the classic discussion of the self by William James, who wrote that the self is the source of the will (Cross & Markus, 1990).

Setting Goals

People strive for goals, trying to become a self that is first imagined. While sometimes we have a clear, conscious image of our goals (such as graduating from college), at other times the goals are not verbalized or conscious. These goals have been given various descriptions by psychologists.

The Ideal Self The term **ideal self** refers to what a person would like to be: good-looking, rich, popular, and so on. While some characteristics valued by our society have an impact on most of our ideal images, the ideal self that motivates each person is unique. Classic theorist Alfred Adler proposed that people develop fantasized goals to compensate for the disappointments of early life and suggested that these ideals motivate personality throughout life (Ansbacher & Ansbacher, 1956). Whatever the source of the ideal self, the experience of a discrepancy between what is and what we would like to be is a widely shared human experience.

It might seem that development would be enhanced by keeping the ideal self in mind and constantly striving to reduce the discrepancy between the self you perceive you are at the moment and the ideal self to which you aspire. This simple formulation, regrettably, does not explain psychological growth very well. When people focus on the discrepancy between the **actual self,** who we really are at the moment, and the ideal self, the result is often depression rather than motivation. A large discrepancy between the ideal self and the self that *others* see results in another unpleasant emotion: social anxiety (Sánchez-Bernardos & Sanz, 1992).

Carl Rogers (1961), the well-known humanistic psychologist, examined the discrepancy between the actual self and the ideal self and found that this discrepancy was reduced after psychotherapy. Had clients changed to become more like their ideal selves? They had not. Instead, their ideal selves had changed, becoming more like their actual selves. In other words, they had come to accept themselves.

Whose Ideal? Individualized Self-Guides E. Tory Higgins points out that there are many possibilities when people start to compare themselves with some more desirable standard. Do we compare ourselves with the self that others (parents or teachers, for example) think we should be? Do we compare ourselves with the self that is our own personal goal, even if that is different from others' views? And are these images based on what we "should" be or on a hope or aspiration?

Higgins distinguishes what he terms three "domains" of the self: the *actual* self (what you are really thought to be), the *ideal* self (what you ideally would be, based on hopes and wishes), and the *ought* self (what you ought to be, based on duty or obligations). For example, a student who really gets by with average study habits and grades (actual self), while harboring a desire to drop everything but creative writing and produce a novel

A child's experience of being criticized leaves its legacy in personality in the form of self-guides that influence emotional reactions and striving later in life.

(the ideal self), still recognizes the necessity of facing the curriculum with its required courses and minimum grades (the ought self).

In addition, Higgins distinguishes whether we are considering the person's own point of view or looking from the standpoint of another person. Both of these "standpoints on the self" may have an actual, ideal, and ought component. The hypothetical student may have a parent who believes the student is a failure (actual self) and would have been better off majoring in business to ensure a job after graduation (ideal self), but because doing so would now take extra semesters, he should simply plod through the declared major and work hard to graduate on schedule (the ought self). If the student focuses on the discrepancy between what he is and what his parent holds as the ideal, he will experience different emotions and motivations than he would if comparing himself with his own creative writing aspirations. Higgins's theory points out the impact of these different **self-guides,** the ideal self and the ought self, as defined by the individual or by some other person. Discrepancies between the actual self and the ought self produce anxiety. Discrepancies between the actual self and the ideal self produce depression (Higgins, 1987).

People vary both in the specific content of these standpoints on the self as viewed by self and significant others and in the extent to which each component is salient. Higgins and his colleagues suggested that firstborns would have stronger "other"-standpoint self-guides, based on the greater influence of parents on the first child. They expected, and found, that firstborns and only children had fewer discrepancies between their actual self and their ought and ideal selves, probably because they had been more strongly influenced to behave according to parental standpoints. Firstborns and only children were also more emotionally distressed by such discrepancies than were those who came later in birth order (Newman, Higgins & Vookles, 1992). Although firstborns were not more depressed or anxious than later-born children, their depression was more closely tied to discrepancies from parental ideal selves, and their anxiety was more closely tied to discrepancies from parental ought selves.

Other research indicates that self-guide cues lead to quicker retrieval of childhood memories and more frequent recall of memories associated with negative emotion. These findings support the idea that self-guides originate in childhood experiences, particularly experiences of being criticized (Strauman, 1990). Researchers theorize that children learn the basis for parental criticism in order to avoid it and that this becomes the basis of the self-guides that continue to influence behavior and emotion throughout life. Failure to live up to self-guides carries the added implication of loss of the affection and approval of others, based on early experiences with the parents or others who were influential in the development of these self-guides.

Ideal and ought self-guides influence behavior in somewhat different ways. The ideal self-guide provides a goal that we strive toward (an approach orientation), as we seek pleasure and nurturance. The ought self-guide, in contrast, tells us what to avoid. We avoid discrepancies from the ought self-guide, as we seek to avoid pain and danger. For example, the ideal self-guide may direct a person to "be smart," whereas the ought self-guide says "don't be stupid." In an experiment, Higgins and his colleagues demonstrated that activating the ideal self-guide by having subjects write about their hopes and goals led them to recall more approach incidents in a story they read; for example, someone getting up early to go to an enjoyable morning class. In contrast, subjects whose ought self-guide was activated by writing about their duty and obligation recalled more avoidance incidents from the same story; for example, avoiding registering for a class that conflicts with another that is preferred. When they described friendships, subjects who were more oriented toward the ideal self-guide, as assessed by the Selves Questionnaire (Higgins et al., 1986), were more likely to select approach-type strategies, such as being emotionally supportive. Those who were more oriented toward the ought self-guide selected more avoidance-type strategies, such as not losing contact with friends (Higgins et al., 1994).

Higgins's theory provides a theoretical framework for understanding why life events have sometimes surprising emotional repercussions. Self-discrepancy theory predicts that when events call attention to self-discrepancies or increase such discrepancies, the result is anxiety (for self-ought discrepancies) or depression (for self-ideal discrepancies). If events decrease self-discrepancies, they bring emotional relief. Mary Jane

Alexander and E. Tory Higgins applied the theory to the transition of becoming parents, setting out to answer the question, "Why do some people suffer from becoming a parent, whereas others do not?" (Alexander & Higgins, 1993, p. 1259). They studied couples who were expecting their first child, assessing their own actual, ideal, and ought selves and their perceptions of what their spouses would wish for them (ideal and ought selves). The expectant parents' emotions at this time were also measured. Once they had become parents, the couples completed more questionnaires.

The results indicated that the theory was, indeed, helpful in predicting which people responded to parenthood with positive emotions and which experienced more negative emotions. Parenthood increased sadness for those new mothers and fathers who had higher actual (own)–ideal (own) discrepancies before birth. Parenthood, with its demands, seems to have made their personal hopes and wishes even more remote. On the other hand, mothers who had large actual (own)–ought (spouse) discrepancies before birth showed a decrease in anxiety with parenthood. The researchers interpreted this result to mean that the pressures of parenthood decreased the attention paid to the spouse's demands for the ought self, such as impeccable housekeeping and home-cooked meals, bringing some relief. Becoming a mother provided distraction and escape from the anxieties of not living up to the husband's standards. (The effect was not observed among fathers.) If the baby was more difficult, the mothers' anxiety reduction, paradoxically—but as predicted by the theory—was greater (Alexander & Higgins, 1993).

Possible Selves   Our self-concept is not limited to the present. We can also imagine our future selves. Hazel Markus and Paula Nurius define **possible selves** as "individuals' ideas of what they might become, what they would like to become, and what they are afraid of becoming" (Markus & Nurius, 1986, p. 954). These include both the ideal self (which we hope for) and negative images of possible selves (which we fear). Markus and Nurius suggest that negative possible selves, images of failure and worthlessness, are associated with depression and are more common among those who suffered a major loss or death of a loved one early in life.

Possible selves are motivating. They direct action. One reason proposed to explain the fact that women do not attain high-status, high-paying jobs in as great numbers as men is that they do not entertain the necessary images among their possible selves (Curry et al., 1994). Similarly, researchers find that unlike their nondelinquent age-mates, delinquent adolescents seldom describe possible selves that are successful in school or work, instead turning to delinquent paths to achieve possibilities (Oyserman & Markus, 1990; Oyserman & Saltz, 1993). If possible selves are elaborated and specific, rather than general, they are more likely to move from thought to reality. Those delinquents who can formulate detailed images of positive possible selves that do not involve delinquent activities are more likely to escape from their delinquent paths (Oyserman & Markus, 1990).

Optimists and pessimists have equally positive hopes (hoped-for selves) and equally negative fears (feared selves), differing only in their expected selves (Carver, Reynolds & Scheier, 1994). Similarly, depression is more strongly correlated with possible selves that are rated "probable" than with possible selves that have been simply considered (Markus & Nurius, 1986).

Current life events may activate possible selves—either positive, as when we are successful or experience other desirable events, or negative, as when we fail or are rejected. Thus, life's setbacks will activate more dismal possibilities for people whose possible selves include images of failure than for those who have only positive, successful possible selves. Therapy and other interventions may help shape new possible selves. Guided imagery can also help develop a more successful positive self; videotape edited to portray us performing successfully, with mistakes edited out, can shape our possible selves. We are well advised to select our fantasies carefully, since we may be rehearsing new possible selves!

Striving toward Our Individual Goals

The selves that we wish to become are associated with individual goals. Researchers have studied people's real life goals in many ways. Let us sample some of these approaches.

Life Tasks Nancy Cantor (1990) urges personality psychologists to look beyond the traits that people *have* to the things that people *do* based on their personality. This can be accomplished by asking people to describe their **life tasks.** A life task is "the problem(s) that individuals see themselves as working on in a particular life period or life transition"(Cantor & Zirkel, 1990, p.150; see Cantor & Kihlstrom, 1987). These self-chosen projects or goals vary in importance and scope. Some of them are universal for all humans or within a given culture. All people need to find food. All children in our culture must go to school. More interesting to the personality researcher are the tasks that are individualized. One person may wish to spend a lot of time with friends, while another wants to gain the highest possible status at work, for example. Our more important life tasks are reflected most often in the activities of daily life and are most emotionally involving (Cantor et al., 1991).

Even when two people seem to be pursuing the same task, they may construe it in different ways. College students vary in their descriptions of the task of "becoming independent." For many of them, the task is defined by a long list of routine daily activities, such as doing laundry, managing money, and getting meals. Others express abstract concerns such as "not having Mom and Dad to run to" and "dealing with competition on my own" (Cantor, 1990, p. 741). These abstract ways of defining the life task made it less easily managed and were predictive of more stress. Individuals' understandings about their life tasks, then, offer important insights into their behaviors and coping. As psychologists learn more about which understandings are adaptive, they will be better able to apply this knowledge in therapy.

Personal Strivings To be a particular kind of self, people strive to achieve goals that represent parts of this intended self. Robert Emmons defines **personal strivings** as "what individuals are characteristically aiming to accomplish through their behavior or the purpose or purposes that a person is trying to carry out" (Emmons, 1986, p. 1059). They are higher order goals. Emmons (1986) uses the example of a person with a personal striving to be physically attractive, which organizes the subordinate goals of exercising, dressing attractively, and wearing a particular hairstyle. As this example shows, personal strivings organize our goals and help us to set priorities. These goals relate to the self and make personal strivings the "motivational aspects of self-representation" (Emmons & King, 1989, p. 479).

Personal strivings are uniquely individual motivations. For research purposes, they can be evaluated to see how much they correspond to shared motives, such as achievement, power, and affiliation or intimacy. When Emmons evaluated his undergraduate sample in this way, he found that those who reported more affiliation-related personal strivings also reported more positive emotions. Those who reported more power-related personal strivings reported more negative emotions (Emmons, 1991). This finding replicates research using the more customary TAT measures of motivation (Zeldow, Daughtery & McAdams, 1988). When statistical analyses were conducted to examine the relationship between emotion and the events of daily life over a 3-week period, Emmons found that subjects responded differently to life events depending upon their personal strivings. Those with achievement strivings felt positive or negative depending upon whether they were making progress toward their goals or suffering setbacks. Those with affiliation strivings felt positive or negative depending upon the outcome of their interpersonal events. So life events are especially likely to affect us emotionally when they correspond to our personal strivings (Emmons, 1991). Our responses to early memories, too, are emotionally positive or negative depending upon whether they are memories consistent with attaining our personal strivings or not attaining them (Moffitt & Singer, 1994).

Robert Emmons suggests that people experience a sense of well-being based upon their efforts to achieve personal goals. Those who have important goals and who are attaining them are likely to feel good about themselves. This approach regards happiness not as a trait but as a product of goal-seeking.

Personal Projects Brian Little's concept of **personal projects** takes the notion of personal strivings one step further and addresses the many behaviors required to attain a goal. A personal project consists of the "interrelated sequence of actions intended to achieve some personal goal" (Palys & Little, 1983, p. 1222). Although theoretically distinguished from personal strivings, those who research personal projects may elicit essentially the same information from subjects; namely, a list of a dozen or so projects or goals that are personally relevant to the subject (Omodei & Wearing, 1990). The personal project approach provides an alternative way of eliciting issues that may have clinical relevance. For example, college women whose Eating Attitudes Test scores suggested dysfunctional attitudes toward eating generally listed more food-related personal projects (Barris, 1987).

Involvement in personal projects, like involvement in personal strivings, is associated with positive emotions and well-being (Omodei & Wearing, 1990). To produce benefits, the strivings must be realistic and sufficiently elaborate. Detailed descriptions by Canadian university students revealed that those who were focused on shorter term important goals were more satisfied with their lives than those whose goals were more distant; a second sample of nonstudent adults replicated this finding (Palys & Little, 1983). Depression and anxiety, assessed by self-report questionnaires, were greater among undergraduates who reported stressful, difficult goals about which they did not feel confident of success (Lecci et al., 1994).

Researchers' interest in personal projects has not replaced their interest in personality traits. In fact, several studies find that trait measures are related to undergraduates' descriptions of their personal projects in ways that make sense. For example, in one study, female undergraduates who scored particularly high on the MMPI Hypochondriasis scale listed more health-related personal projects, such as losing weight and stopping smoking, than those who scored low (Karoly & Lecci, 1993). Brian Little and his colleagues suggest that personal projects may be thought of as the way that personality traits are expressed in people's behavior (Little, Lecci & Watkinson, 1992). Their research explored relationships between personal projects reported by undergraduates and their scores on the Big Five personality factors. Many significant relationships were found (Table 9.5). Subjects who scored high on Neuroticism, for example, reported that they did not enjoy their projects as much as others did, found them more difficult and stressful, and were making less progress on them. High scores on Conscientiousness, on the other hand, were associated with greater enjoyment and progress. People who scored high on Openness were more likely to have initiated their projects, as opposed to having them thrust upon them or assigned.

It is clear from these various approaches that the self is expressed through tasks, projects, and goals—whatever we wish to call them—in the real, external world. Researchers have found that to achieve our goals, we must believe in ourselves.

TABLE 9.5 **Selected Correlations between Personal Project Dimensions and the Big Five Personality Factors**

Project dimensions	Big Five personality factors				
	Neuroticism	*Extraversion*	*Openness*	*Agreeableness*	*Conscientiousness*
Enjoyment	**−.27**	**.15**	**.18**	.08	**.23**
Initiation	−.11	.04	**.17**	−.02	.04
Progress	**−.32**	**.28**	.05	**.13**	**.33**
Difficulty	**.23**	−.12	**−.18**	**−.20**	−.10

Adapted from Little, Lecci & Watkinson, 1992. Correlation coefficients printed in boldface are statistically significant, indicating that they are unlikely to have occurred by chance. Those in lightface are small enough that they may have arisen by chance.

Believing We Can Do It

Cognitive approaches emphasize the importance of beliefs about our ability to perform various behaviors and to achieve desired results. Overall, they suggest that confident belief in ourselves contributes to successful attainment of our goals.

Self-Efficacy and Self-Regulation Perhaps you have heard of "the power of positive thinking." Popular psychology promotes this concept, which asserts that having confidence in your ability to reach goals will help you to attain them. Although this popular message is oversimplified, it is consistent with psychological research.

When people try to "think positive," they generally believe they'll be rewarded with a desirable outcome: a school paper will get a high mark, a traffic jam will not prevent them from reaching the airport before the plane departs, and so on. Albert Bandura's theory is more precise. He distinguishes between a desirable outcome and the behavior that contributes to it. In his theory, an **outcome expectancy** is "a person's estimate that a given behavior will lead to certain outcomes" (Bandura, 1977, p. 193). Will exercising every day lead to a more attractive body? Will taking statistics lower your grade point average? These are examples of outcome expectancies, and they influence our everyday decisions.

In addition, Bandura calls attention to *efficacy expectancies*, which he defines as "the conviction that one can successfully execute the behavior required to produce the outcomes" (Bandura, 1977, p. 193). Such efficacy expectancies are usually called self-efficacy expectancies or, more simply, **self-efficacy.** If you do not believe that you can exercise every day because of time constraints or for other reasons, the positive outcome expectancy associated with this behavior will not be sufficient to make you do it. First, you must believe that you can. (It is also true, though, that efficacy expectancies alone will not be sufficient to produce the behavior. They must be accompanied by desirable outcome expectancies, which we may call *incentives.*) For example, both outcome expectancies and self-efficacy expectancies must be considered when developing programs to discourage behaviors that risk AIDS infection. A program suggested by Bandura (1990a) provides information about the disease and its causes (outcome expectancy). It also teaches specific behaviors, including how to clean intravenous needles used for drugs and how to negotiate sexual behaviors with a partner. These behaviors are modeled and practiced to increase self-efficacy expectancies for them.

Albert Bandura and other researchers testing his ideas have reported an enormous list of the effects of self-efficacy. These include lower levels of depression, higher tolerance of pain, greater success at efforts to lose weight and stop smoking, better health, better athletic performance, and higher grades, among other desirable effects. Many studies attest to a positive effect of self-efficacy on health (Holden, 1991; see also Chapter 8). Self-efficacy contributes to health in part by causing people to engage in healthier behaviors, such as controlling weight and giving up smoking (O'Leary, 1985, 1992). People with high self-efficacy are more successful when they try to lose weight (Weinberg et al., 1984). In addition, self-efficacy can influence physical conditions directly, contributing to activation of the body's pain-controlling mechanisms (Bandura et al., 1988) and to physiological stress reactions (Bandura et al., 1985). Self-efficacy beliefs enhance academic performance and persistence toward academic goals (Multon, Brown & Lent, 1991); for example, undergraduates studying to be teachers did more extra credit homework if they were high in self-efficacy for doing the assignments (Tuckman & Sexton, 1990). Effects of self-efficacy on academic behavior and performance probably influence subsequent careers (Lent & Hackett, 1987). Although traditional behaviorists try to explain behavior without resorting to cognitive processes, Bandura has argued persuasively for the greater explanatory power of cognitive theory, and his detailed analyses of interventions to increase self-efficacy support his views. (See the Research Strategies box for an example.)

Should we think of self-efficacy as a global belief that we apply to all aspects of life, ranging from studying to sociability? Or do we have separate self-efficacies in various areas, believing there are some things we can do and others we can't? Albert Bandura's cognitive social learning theory proposes that self-efficacy should be measured for the specific behavior that is to be predicted. Believing that you can complete a paper before falling asleep keeps you working; believing you can resist forbidden foods

RESESARCH STRATEGIES   ●---

Close-up Observation of Cause-Effect Relationships

Does a person's thinking about the self *cause* that person to behave differently? Or are these internal thoughts about the self simply incidental mental processes that accompany change without really being the *cause* of the change? This constitutes a core question in psychology, one that deserves the most thoughtful empirical strategies to answer. Cognitive theories accept thoughts as important causes of our behavior, and they are very popular in current psychology. Change the way people think, and you will change their behavior, according to this view. On the other hand, thoughts are elusive to the rigorous scientist, because they are hidden and private rather than open and public phenomena. How can theorized cognitive causes be tested with scientific rigor? Let's consider two of the strategies devised by researchers: experimental manipulation and microanalysis.

Traditionally, experimental manipulation has been accepted as the standard method for testing hypotheses about what factors cause particular behaviors. For instance, let's say you want to see how overcrowding a room affects behavior. The hypothesized cause (the number of people in a small room) is manipulated by the experimenter as the independent variable, and then its effects on the dependent variable (the level of irritability of people in that room) are measured. When the suspected cause is an environmental variable that can be directly manipulated, like crowding, this method is most straightforward.

When the suspected cause is a variable that cannot be directly manipulated and observed, however, such as a person's thoughts, the experimental method is somewhat less straightforward. The experimenter can manipulate a situation in which that thought is likely to occur, thus indirectly manipulating the thought. Sometimes the manipulation is easy. If I say, "Think about white elephants," chances are very good that you will do so. Other times the manipulation will not work. If I say, "Do not think about white elephants," chances are my instruction will backfire. In either case, though, you will be aware that someone has told you what to think, and that fact may have some effect on you. Perhaps you will feel resentment at the intrusion. For this reason, researchers are usually more subtle. To manipulate thoughts about being successful, for example, the researcher might have the subject participate in a rigged test and then tell the subject that his or her score was outstanding. To be certain that the manipulation worked, the researcher often performs a **manipulation check.** The subject is asked to report his or her thoughts, generally on a multiple-choice or true-false questionnaire. The subject in this hypothetical example might be asked, "How successful did you feel on the test just completed?" and be asked to rate these feelings on a numerical scale. If subjects report high levels of success, the manipulation check is taken as evidence that the manipulation of the covert cognitions was successful.

There is, however, a complication with this strategy of manipulating people's cognitions experimentally. The difficulty is that along with the intended cognition, other variables may also change. If you had been told, for example, that you had done very poorly on a test (intended to put you in the "unsuccessful" cognition group), you might also conclude that the test was poorly designed or that the researcher was disappointed in you. You might spend time worrying and therefore less time focusing on subsequent problems. These variables are likely

(continued)

to occur more or less together; that is, they are *confounded.* How can we know which variables are the important ones that influence later behavior? If you do worse later, is it because of your lowered expectations, your lowered motivation to perform on a test you think poorly designed, or your decreased time working on later problems? Although we may be able to report an overall effect of the manipulation, these ambiguities leave doubts about the exact processes involved, and we cannot identify the cognitive cause unequivocally. This makes it more difficult to anticipate when the real world will show results similar to those found in this contrived experimental situation.

A second approach to establishing causality of mental processes is to conduct a **microanalysis.** In this approach, the researcher tries to measure both the suspected causes and their effects over time, to see whether they change together. If two (or more) causes are being compared, they should both (or all) be measured. To illustrate, imagine that you want to discover why people have fun at parties. Is it the interaction with other people? The food? If we watch people throughout the party and record whether they are interacting with other people and whether they are eating, and also ask them frequently how much fun they are having, we may be able to answer the question. The evidence is the co-occurrence over time of changes in the variables. Do increases in "fun" occur at the times that our subjects are with other people, or when they are eating? This approach is called a *micro*analysis to point out that we are examining detailed processes, not simply the global (*macro*) effect of the party taken as a whole. A microanalysis may well uncover processes that would be masked by the macro approach.

In studies of cognitions about the self, the cognition that we believe to be the cause is measured at several points in a process that occurs over time. The relationship between

this changing cognition and the effect being tested is then examined. If the effect occurs in close relationship with the changing cognition, this is strong evidence that the two are causally linked. In one microanalysis, Albert Bandura and his colleagues (Bandura, Reese & Adams, 1982) examined changes in self-efficacy among patients receiving behavioral treatment for snake phobia. Patients observed a model handle a snake, then individualized treatments enabled each patient to gradually approach, touch, and hold a boa constrictor. After treatment, they were given a posttest to see whether they could tolerate a corn snake and to measure how much fear this induced.

Throughout treatment, the subjects answered questions that measured their self-efficacy at that stage. As the behaviors of the subjects brought them into increasing interaction with the snake, their self-efficacy beliefs also changed (Fig. B9.1). There was not a perfect match between the behaviors that the patients had accomplished and their changing beliefs; sometimes they judged they could do more than they had accomplished so far, sometimes the same, and sometimes even less. Did these cognitions add anything to the accuracy with which their posttest coping could be predicted? Or was it enough to know what behaviors the patients had actually accomplished with the training snake? The results showed that cognition was important. The posttest performance with the corn snake matched self-efficacy cognitions (88 percent matching) better than it matched performance with the training snake (77 percent matching). Efficacy beliefs are more than simple summaries of past performance.

Admittedly, there is some disagreement about which statistical assumptions are most appropriate for microanalytic studies (Bandura, 1980; Kirsch, 1980). Such is often the case when theories develop to suggest new ways of looking at data. These minor controversies cannot eclipse the main point, however, which is to measure both the theorized cognitive cause and the proposed alternative cause and to judge whether each is a cause by seeing how closely each is related to the outcome.

To summarize, researchers have considered the difficulties of testing whether hidden cognitive variables are causes of behavior and have developed various strategies for testing such hypotheses.

• The experimental method is best suited to test causes that can be manipulated directly, such as environmental variables.

• The experimental method can be used to test whether cognitions are causes by indirectly arousing cognitions through environmental manipulations. In this case, a manipulation check can be used to be sure the manipulation worked as intended.

• Experimental manipulations often have unintended effects on cognition that cannot be ruled out as alternative causes.

• Microanalysis tests whether cognitions are causes, by carefully tracking the co-occurrence of cognition and its hypothesized effect at frequent points in time.

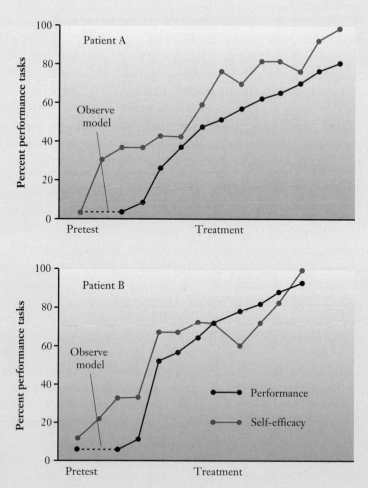

Increasing behavorial performance and self-efficacy beliefs of two people treated for snake phobia. (Adapted from Bandura, Reese & Adams, 1982, p. 10.)

gives you the strength to stay on a diet. Nonetheless, it is possible to think of a more global self-efficacy (see Shelton, 1990) that would influence a broad variety of behaviors. The development of a basic sense of efficacy has been described as "the core of the developing sense of self" in infancy (Broucek, 1979, p. 315). At that age, efficacy is based on the discovery that the infant's own behavior influences external events. For example, crying makes parents appear.

People's self-efficacy is influenced by their life experiences, as well as by race, ethnicity, social class, and other social factors (Gecas, 1989). Therapy and other intervention programs can increase self-efficacy. For example, women participating in a self-defense course demonstrated increased self-efficacy to control threats, to defend themselves, and to engage in various activities in the community that might otherwise seem too dangerous. This intervention was powerful enough to eliminate the sense of vulnerability that had developed in women who had been sexually assaulted before taking the self-defense course (Ozer & Bandura, 1990). The researchers describe the intervention as having an effect of "empowerment."

Bandura suggests several ways to increase self-efficacy. One way is through actual behavior; in Bandura's terminology, self-efficacy is enhanced through *performance accomplishments*. To illustrate his theory, Bandura applied his method to the treatment of patients with phobias. The self-efficacy of phobic patients was enhanced by using behavioral techniques to change their outward behavior. During treatment, those afraid of snakes gradually approached and then touched a harmless snake (Bandura et al., 1980). Second, self-efficacy can be increased by *vicarious experience*. Seeing someone else model the desired behavior can increase self-efficacy, if we feel we are like the model. Third, *verbal persuasion* is sometimes effective, whether in the form of pep talks or psychotherapy. Finally, *emotional arousal* influences self-efficacy. If a person can be made to feel calm rather than fearful in the presence of a snake, self-efficacy for confronting snakes is increased. Relaxation training and other therapy techniques can reduce unwanted emotions or change their interpretation and thus increase self-efficacy.

Many of these strategies are used by athletic coaches to improve their players' performance by enhancing the self-confidence that high self-efficacy provides. A survey of 124 elite coaches in Olympic sports found that they most often used instruction and drilling to increase self-efficacy, and they rated this the most effective technique (Gould et al., 1989). This approach illustrates Bandura's category of performance accomplishments, which Bandura suggested was generally more effective than the other techniques. Additional techniques used by the coaches correspond to other ways of increasing self-efficacy in Bandura's model (Table 9.6).

Reciprocal Determinism   The importance of self-efficacy illustrates that the individual's thinking influences the course of life, but that is only

TABLE 9.6   **How Coaches Apply Psychology: Sources of Efficacy Expectations in Bandura's Theory**

Sources of efficacy expectations	Ways of inducing these expectations	Examples of coaches' behavior
Performance accomplishments	Participant modeling Performance desensitization Performance exposure Self-instructed performance	Instruction and drilling Emphasize technique improvement, downplay outcome Set specific goals Employ hard physical conditioning
Vicarious experience	Live modeling Symbolic modeling (e.g., films)	Act confident yourself Identify similar athletes who have achieved
Verbal persuasion	Suggestion Exhortation Self-instruction Interpretive treatments	Encourage positive talk Verbally persuade
Emotional arousal	Attribution Relaxation, biofeedback Symbolic desensitization Symbolic exposure	Emphasize that anxiety is not fear but readiness Emphasize lack of effort, not lack of ability, as source of failure Reduce anxiety by using relaxation training Liberal use of reward statements Imagine success

Adapted from Bandura, 1977, and Gould, Hodge, Peterson & Giannini, 1989.

part of the story. Other factors also have an influence. What if an athlete is seriously injured in a random act of violence? Athletic behavior will surely be affected. In his model of **reciprocal determinism,** Bandura theorized that the person, the external environment, and behavior all influence one another.

Through processes of self-regulation, people can take control of their own behavior, rather than allowing it to be influenced primarily by external forces (Bandura, 1978). Self-regulation includes many interrelated processes. By *self-observation,* we attend to our behavior, noticing whatever is relevant. How fast did I run the race? Did I say something original?

Based on standards that may be personal or may be based on comparison with others, our *judgmental process* rates the adequacy of our performance, decides whether it was worthwhile, and evaluates who gets the credit or blame. Performance and self-efficacy are enhanced if we do not wait until the end of a project to judge our performance. For long, difficult tasks, setting intermediate subgoals increases both persistence and self-efficacy (Stock & Cervone, 1990). We may also provide some rewarding or punishing *self-response*, such as treating ourselves to a night on the town or deciding that overindulgence requires running an extra mile.

The particular processes of self-regulation vary from one individual to another and from one behavior to another. The same strategy that works in one situation may not be effective in another. For example, subgoals enhance performance when people are working on difficult tasks or have little intrinsic interest in the work. When the overall goals are more readily attainable and people are more highly motivated, subgoals are not necessary and may even detract from performance (Markus & Wurf, 1987). Flexibility distinguishes the human species. Whatever self-regulation processes are developed do empower individuals and protect them from the power of external forces.

The processes that help us attain our own selfish individual goals have parallels in our ethical behavior toward others. Ethical behavior, too, requires self-regulation. When we stop evaluating our own behavior and lose touch with ethical standards, immoral behavior can result (Bandura, 1978, 1990b). People are not always able to maintain ethical standards, however, and instead of holding ourselves accountable, we may be tempted to disengage our moral controls. Because of this, Bandura suggests that we cannot rely on individuals alone to produce a humane society. We must also consider the social level, which can enforce behavior through threats of punishment, and be sure that social safeguards are in place to prevent moral disengagement (Bandura, 1990b). This approach suggests than an individual trait explanation of morality is inadequate. The reciprocal determinism model helps us to understand individual selves in relationship to a larger perspective.

Undercutting Our Own Potential: Self-Handicapping If life presented us with only simple choices, perhaps it would be easy to understand the self. Given the choice between improving or staying the same, we would choose improvement. Life, though, gives multiple choices that make any instructor's exam questions look simple. Life presents us with opportunities to improve but, along with that, a substantial risk of knowing our limitations. Consider these examples. You get an A on your first exam in a class outside your field, where you expected to be an average student at best. Before the second exam, you find it difficult to settle down to serious studying, so you spend the time with friends instead. Or you take a test in a psychological experiment and do very well on it. You're given another, similar test, but you choose to do that under distracting conditions that virtually ensure poor performance. Why don't you try under optimal conditions that would make success more likely? Why do you subject yourself to such a handicap?

The concept of **self-handicapping** explains acts that undermine our potential for success. Steven Berglas and Edward Jones define self-handicapping strategies as "any action or choice of performance setting that enhances the opportunity to externalize (or excuse) failure and to internalize (reasonably accept credit for) success" (Berglas & Jones, 1978, p. 406). According to this concept, when circumstances present us with challenging tasks that we fear we cannot achieve, we have two choices. We can genuinely try but risk possible failure. Or we can not try, or try without adequate practice or under extenuating circumstances that can readily be blamed if we fail. If we do not try, we cannot succeed and therefore cannot gain the rewards that success would offer, but neither can we fail. Self-handicapping is not the same as procrastination. A procrastinator may get off to a delayed start but ultimately try hard; a self-handicapper does not genuinely engage the task (Lay, Knish & Zanatta, 1992).

When would a person choose to "pass" when opportunity knocks? Researchers have found that such a choice is especially appealing when we have succeeded at similar tasks in the past but doubt that we can continue such high achievement. If, for example, you were surprised to receive an A on your first exam in a course, you might feel especially reluctant to risk losing the positive self-image with another exam. If you find excuses not to study before the second exam (for example, by partying or working so long on other classes that there is not time to study adequately), you will probably not receive another A, but you can believe that you "could have" earned such a grade, if you had been able to try your hardest. Thus, self-handicapping permits us to maintain a positive but fragile self-image by preventing real effort. This strategy is obviously defensive, and it is more likely to be chosen by people with low self-esteem, who also avoid comparing themselves with others whom they believe to have performed better than they did (Wood et al., 1994). Those with higher self-esteem more actively seek to repeat their successes, risking the possibility of failure but also making possible the rewards that require sustained success and not simply promise (Baumeister, Tice & Hutton, 1989).

Fulfilling Our Human Potential

We have been considering people's own individually chosen goals. What if a person aims too low or in the wrong direction? Is there another standard, one for comparing the person against his or her own highest potential? Humanistic theorists, especially Carl Rogers and Abraham Maslow, urged psychologists to focus attention on the growth and inner direction of the healthy personality (Maslow, 1954/1987; Rogers, 1961). They describe **self-actualization** as the full development of an individual's potential

(Maslow, 1968). This potential is neither so arbitrary nor so external as the self described by social interaction theories. It comes from an individual's true nature, which contains the potential for growth when it is recognized and nurtured rather than ignored to pursue goals that don't really come from within the individual. This genuine and healthy self is often referred to as the **real self,** as distinguished from the *social self* (Wilson, 1988).

Whether a person has such a core "real self" or whether the self is better regarded as a social construction is a matter of theoretical debate. Unstated disagreements over values underlie this debate. According to Roy Baumeister (1987), self-actualization has emerged, historically, in the late twentieth century as a way of describing human fulfillment, supplanting earlier emphasis on work and family. So the real-self concept carries with it the idea that humans are fulfilled by individual growth. This idea has been criticized for reflecting Western values rather than encompassing the more universal view that is deemed desirable for a scientific theory.

Many researchers have studied self-actualization using self-report measures, the most popular of which is the Personal Orientation Inventory (POI) (Shostrom, 1964). It consists of several subscales. Two subscales indicate the primary dimensions of self-actualization. The *Time Competence* subscale assesses the extent to which a person reports living in the present (rather than in the past or the future), and the *Inner Support* subscale measures the extent to which a person is autonomous rather than dependent on other people. The POI has been widely used as a measure of mental health (Hattie & Cooksey, 1984). More recently developed, the Feelings, Reactions, and Beliefs Survey (FRBS) assesses six aspects of the self-actualized or fully functioning person, as described by Carl Rogers and other humanists (Cartwright & Mori, 1988).

Researchers have found, as predicted by humanistic theorists, that subjects scoring high on self-actualization are more creative than those who score low (Runco, Ebersole & Mraz, 1991). Self-actualization is also correlated with assertiveness (Ramanaiah, Heerboth & Jinkerson, 1985) and with low boredom proneness (McLeod & Vodanovich, 1991). Groups of people who have been trained to become counselors, among them trainees in a variety of counseling methods, increase their self-actualization scores (Duncan, Konefal & Spechler, 1990; Elizabeth, 1983).

Self-actualization is partially reflected in how people think about themselves. Those scoring high on self-actualization show less discrepancy between their ideal self and their self-concept, or who they think they really are (Rogers, 1961). In addition, Abraham Maslow and others have described self-actualization as associated with noncognitive aspects of experience. Maslow's well-known **peak experiences,** which he theorized are more frequent among self-actualized people, are visionary states of consciousness in which the individual is filled with a sense of meaning and awe, a connection with something larger than the self. Researchers have asked people to describe peak experiences on questionnaires. They report that the types of peak experiences reported by artists, social science students, and other adults are all similar (Yeagle, Privette & Dunham, 1989), and they may be evoked by a variety of circumstances, including the beauty of nature, creating a painting, making love, meditation, and athletic activities. For some people, physical self-confidence contributes to self-actualization (as Maslow expected), but different paths to self-actualization are effective for different people (Ryckman et al., 1985).

Mihaly Csikszentmihalyi describes the absorption people feel when engaged in *flow experiences*. Intense concentration on a task brings happiness; for example, when artists are absorbed in their work. Activities that produce flow have certain characteristics (Csikszentmihalyi, 1993, p. xiv):

> *(1) They have concrete goals and manageable rules,*
> *(2) they make it possible to adjust opportunities for action to our capacities,*
> *(3) they provide clear information about how well we are doing, and*
> *(4) they screen out distractions and make concentration possible.*

This concept of flow captures the subjective experiences of people whom humanists would call self-actualized. It also reflects the self-management ideas of Bandura's cognitive approach, thus integrating two major approaches to the self. No concept, however, has integrated all the theoretical descriptions of a multifaceted self, from the social self to the private self, the self of aspiration to the real self. Although the self has not been wholly captured in our theoretical net, it has left traces in theory and data that add to the partial understandings that experience itself provides.

SUMMARY

• Awareness of the self is a uniquely human capacity, made possible by our capacity for self-reflection.

• Self-esteem is a sense of positive self-worth; it may be considered globally or in specific areas, such as academic and social self-esteem.

• Self-esteem is maintained in various ways including lowering aspirations, seeking positive information, and interpreting events in ways favorable to ourselves.

• Low self-esteem is associated with depression. High self-esteem is associated with persistent efforts to reach goals.

• Research indicates that the self-esteem of minority and majority group members is equally high. Some research indicates that men are more likely to base their self-esteem on individual accomplishments and women on interpersonal connectedness.

• Self-presentation processes involve the self as a social object, like an actor before an audience.

• People vary in the trait of self-monitoring; that is, their tendency to observe and control their expressive behavior and self-presentation.

• Public self-consciousness is a trait that involves awareness of the self as a social object.

• Private self-consciousness is a trait that involves awareness of inner thoughts and feelings.

• Self-concept refers to people's ideas about who they are. It is a descriptive rather than evaluative dimension (in contrast to self-esteem).

• The self-concept may be described as a cognitive category called a self-schema. People may be schematic or aschematic on a particular trait, indicating whether it is part of their self-schema.

• The paradox of the one-in-many-selves can be resolved by suggesting that we have many selves created through social interaction and that we strive for a healthy unity by developing complex cognitive self-concepts arranged in a hierarchy.

• The self is reflected in the life stories that people tell and in their autobiographical memories.

• Cognitive experiential self-theory studies emotional experience related to beliefs about the world, other people, and the self.

• Self-actualization, a high level of personality development, is characterized by little discrepancy between who we are (the actual self) and who we wish to be (the ideal self).

• Individualized self-guides are a person's images of the actual self, ideal self, and ought self, described from the person's own point of view and from the standpoint of a significant other person.

• People imagine future selves, called possible selves, that may be desirable or not.

• Several concepts have been proposed to study people's striving: life tasks, personal strivings, and personal projects.

• Self-efficacy beliefs refer to people's conviction that they can do the behavior required to reach some goal; these beliefs increase persistence.

• Reciprocal determinism refers to the mutual influences among the person, the environment, and behavior. All are both causes and effects.

• People sometimes engage in self-handicapping behavior, compromising accomplishment to defend their self-image.

• Self-actualization is the full development of the potentials of the real self, and it is sometimes at odds with the socially defined self.

GLOSSARY

actual self who we really are at the present time

autobiographical memory memory for information about ourselves during past events in life

ideal self what a person would like to be

life task a problem (or project or goal) that a person regards himself or herself to be working on during a particular period of life

manipulation check a precaution taken by a researcher to ensure that an experimental manipulation has had the intended effect on subjects

microanalysis a research strategy to study cause-effect relationships by measuring both cause and effect several times over a period of time to see whether they change together, as expected if one causes the other

outcome expectancy a person's estimate that a given behavior will lead to certain outcomes, assuming that the behavior is accomplished

peak experiences visionary states of consciousness in which the individual is filled with a sense of meaning and awe, a connection with something larger than the self

personal strivings what individuals are trying to accomplish; their purposes

personal projects interrelated sequences of actions intended to achieve a personal goal

possible selves individuals' ideas of what they might become, including positive ideas of what they would like to become and negative ideas of what they are afraid of becoming

private self-consciousness the awareness of aspects of the self that are known directly by personal experience, such as through introspection

public self-consciousness awareness of the self as a social object

real self the genuine core self that contains the potential for healthy growth or self-actualization

reciprocal determinism a model asserting that the person, the environment, and behavior all have mutual influences upon one another

self the mental representation of information about one's own being, and associated feelings

self-actualization the full development of an individual's potential

self-concept a person's cognitions that describe the self

self-efficacy the belief or expectancy that one will be able to do a particular behavior

self-esteem a sense of positive self-worth

self-guides individualized representations of the ideal self or of the self that one ought to be, which may be defined by the individual or by another person

self-handicapping actions that undermine the chances of success but that give plausible reasons for failure in order to avoid blame

self-monitoring self-observation and self-control of expressive behavior and of self-presentation

self-presentation efforts to appear in a way that creates a desired impression on others

self-regulation processes that enable people to have control over their own behavior, rather than being controlled by external forces only

self-schema the self-concept viewed as a cognitive structure

social self the self that is created through interactions with other people

THOUGHT QUESTIONS

1. Have you ever observed behavior by a member of a nonhuman species that made you think it possesses a "self"? If so, describe it.

2. Do you think that lowering your aspirations is a desirable way to maintain self-esteem? Why or why not?

3. Why do you suppose that the self-esteem of minority groups and the majority population is equally high? Do you think that minority or majority status has any bearing on the factors that maintain self-esteem?

4. Based on the text discussion and your own experience, what are the advantages of being a high self-monitor? What are the disadvantages?

5. Research shows that people with high self-esteem make choices similar to those of people they believe to be like themselves. As the text mentions, researchers interpret this finding as a result of their clearer self-images, compared to those of individuals with low self-esteem. Can you suggest any alternative interpretations of this finding?

6. Do you believe that privately self-conscious people attain more accurate self-knowledge through introspection? Or are they simply tuned in to dimensions of the self that are different from those for whom public self-consciousness is higher?

7. Do you think it is possible to study self-concept as a nonevaluative aspect of the self, separate from self-esteem? Or do our ideas about who we are always have implications for our sense of self-worth?

8. Which side of the one-in-many-selves paradox seems more accurate to you: the idea that people have many selves, or the idea that there is one self?

9. Have self-efficacy beliefs ever made a significant difference in your own efforts toward some goal?

10. Do you believe that the socially defined self gets in the way of self-actualization? Or do our social roles provide opportunities for fulfillment?

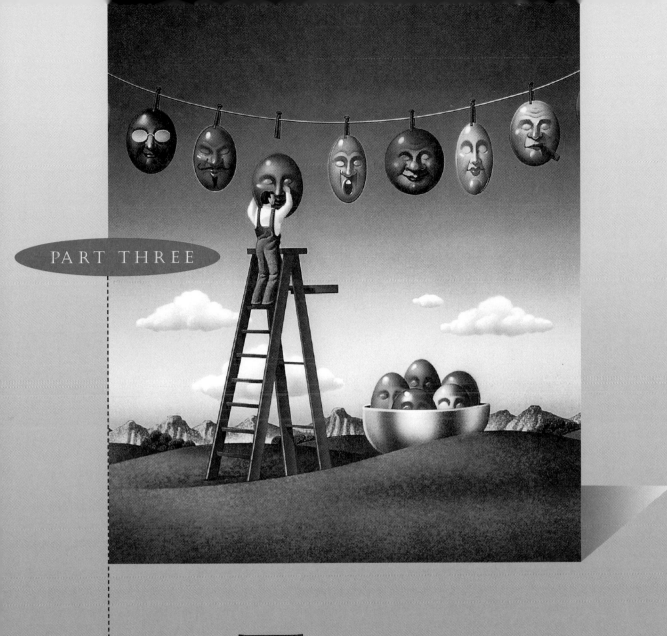

PART THREE

The Development of Personality

PERSONALITY, AS WE SAW IN PART II, is dynamic, not fixed or static. In the next chapters we will consider how personality develops over time, and how society and culture influence this development. Common wisdom tells us that "as the twig is bent, the tree grows," leading us to expect that knowing how early experience influences children will help us to predict their adult personalities. Personality is expressed in somewhat different ways throughout the life span. Aggressiveness, for example, takes different forms, from the temper tantrums of a child to the verbal or physical aggression of an adult, to perhaps the angry demands of an elderly person. An adult's achievement-striving, too, leads to different behaviors than that of a child, but we might expect that behavior on the child's ball field will have something to do will career competitiveness in adulthood.

Personality is influenced by environmental conditions that are close at hand (the family) and by those broader in scope (the culture). Studying these influences scientifically is, however, a daunting task. Practical and ethical considerations do not permit conducting true experimental manipulations of such influences. Just think what a true experiment would entail! Randomly assigning children to parents, or manipulating who is exposed to traumatic events or economic stressors, would obviously be unethical and impractical, however desirable it is in an abstract sense to establish cause-effect relationships. In reality, though, people's lives cannot be studied by techniques of experimental manipulation, any more than astronomers could learn about the cosmos through manipulation. We are humble observers in both contexts. Yet if we observe attentively, there is much to be learned.

New research methods have been developed to meet the challenge of studying personality development. Longitudinal research, which studies the same individuals across a long time span, is the preferred method for developmental studies. It demands considerably more commitment by researchers than the usual one-time data collections that have predominated in the studies we have examined so far. The researcher must maintain contact with subjects, which means maintaining records of addresses and phone numbers, while maintaining the confidentiality of subjects' disclosures. Some participants inevitably move or lose interest, and so leave a study in progress. Jack Block (1993), whose longitudinal research on ego development is among the best known in the field, maintains subjects' motivation for participation by such innovative strategies as sending them birthday cards, even in years when no data collection occurs.

Studying the developmental unfolding of personality is essential if we are to fully understand personality and its potential. Classic theorists have almost always included a discussion of personality development in their theories. For Sigmund Freud, Alfred Adler, Karen Horney, and other psychoanalysts, it was the child's relationships with the parents and, to a lesser extent, with sisters and brothers, that mattered most. Occasionally theorists (e.g., Karen Horney and Raymond Cattell) called attention to the importance of cultural factors in shaping personality, but until recent researchers tackled the problem systematically, such statements remained ungrounded theoretical abstractions. The traditional division between personality and social psychology has further shackled the investigation of personality in its cultural context. While personality psychologists have studied the individual out of context, social psychologists have focused largely on the effects of situations and on processes that are observed in people generally, ignoring individual differences. Now, though, the two perspectives are coming together again, and personality psychologists are exploring social tasks (such as work and marriage) and culture (including nationality and ethnicity). After all, it is through participation in culture that we become fully human. A person without cultural learning is like a computer with no software—an unnatural and nonfunctional mockery of the real thing. In these chapters, we see that the development of personality can be enlightened by studying all levels from biological to cultural. If it is a daunting task to understand this multilevel development, we can be heartened by realizing that every adult has developed through such a multifaceted process to become a unique person.

Continuity and Change across Time

MOST PERSONALITY RESEARCH TESTS subjects only once or, at most, at a few times that are close together. This approach can reveal a cross section of personality, but it ignores questions related to time. How much do people change over time, or do they stay the same? What can we say about our potential to influence change and produce beneficial effects on personality development? Do the same theories that have been used to understand adults, especially the college age populations that are so prevalent in our research, also apply to children and the elderly? Understanding these questions about personality across time requires a different approach.

Longitudinal Studies of Personality

Researchers use **longitudinal research designs** to answer questions of personality continuity and change over time. In this approach, researchers collect data periodically from the same subjects over a long span of time, often for several decades. (This contrasts with **cross-sectional research**

designs, in which subjects are studied at only one point in time and any comparisons of one age with another are based on different groups of subjects for each age.) By definition, longitudinal research designs require collecting data on the same people for at least two time periods (Menard, 1991), but in practice, researchers often make many more observations than that.

Longitudinal data can answer questions about *continuity of personality.* Are young children with certain characteristics likely to grow up to be certain kinds of adults—do impulsive children grow up to be criminals, for example? Which characteristics are most important in making these predictions? Furthermore, we can use such data sets to provide insight about *personality change.* Can we identify the factors, such as environmental influences, that cause changes over time? Such information might help us to alter the predicted life course of children who seem headed toward maladaptive personality development. These are some of the most significant questions about personality (Funder et al., 1993; Menard, 1991). If we could answer them, we could divert the flow of people to our prisons and unemployment lines and fill our classrooms with eager students and our workplaces with productive workers.

Designing a Study of Lives

The simplest kind of longitudinal research begins with a group of subjects at one time—for example, a class of nursery school students—and investigates them repeatedly over many years. By looking at the measures taken at various years, it is possible to describe how these children changed as they grew into adolescence and adulthood: nursery school innocence, childhood friendships, adolescent self-consciousness, adult responsibilities. We may find that they have no political opinions in childhood, become politically liberal during adolescence, and then become conservative in middle adulthood. What do these changes mean? Unfortunately, there is more than one possible answer to that question, and a simple one-group longitudinal study cannot indicate which answer is correct. It is possible that these changes represent **age effects;** that is, the developmental changes that are caused by the increasing age of individuals. It makes sense that during adolescence, as part of the process of becoming an individual separate from parents, people would rebel against the established political attitudes, and then as they become adults with the associated responsibilities, they would turn conservative.

It is also possible, however, that these changes have nothing to do with age. Perhaps when these subjects were adolescents, the whole country was experiencing a liberal political climate, and young and old alike shifted toward that political pole. Then, a few decades later, when these subjects were studied again, the country could have shifted toward a conserva-

People who grow up in different historical times are influenced by the unique experiences of their birth cohort. The generation of the Great Depression, for example, encountered far different experiences in childhood than those who grew up in the 1970s.

tive stance. This hypothetical situation is called a **period effect;** that is, the effect of a time in history. Conceivably, age could have nothing to do with it.

The truth may be more complicated than either age or period effects. Sometimes history affects people of a particular age differently from those of another age. Changes in school systems, for example, would affect school-age children, whereas changes in pension funds would affect those who are older. Thus, we often need to consider not simply age but the point in history when a group of people were that age. That is, we need to consider **cohort** effects. A cohort is a group of people who experienced the same events when they were the same age. Usually, researchers have in mind a *birth cohort,* a group of people who were all born in the same year. Occasionally, they may refer to other types of *event cohorts;* for example, all people who got married in 1990 or all people who retired in 1995 (Menard, 1991).

History brings different life circumstances to different cohorts. Some people, born in years when fewer births occurred, find more job prospects when they reach adulthood. Some enter adulthood when the country is at war, and this circumstance influences their work and marriage patterns. The Great Depression, the Vietnam War, AIDS, technological advances, and other social phenomena have each influenced some cohorts but not others. Thus, cohorts differ in the social context within which their personalities develop. National survey data suggest some of the effects of social context that make cohorts distinctive. American women who were adolescents or young adults during World War II, when many women worked outside the home while men who otherwise would have taken those jobs were at war, became higher in achievement motivation, and this heightened drive to succeed lasted during later years. Men who were too old to be drafted during this era also had high achievement motivation, perhaps because they, like the younger women, had better job prospects (Veroff, Reuman & Feld, 1984). We must be careful about generalizing the life course patterns of one cohort to other cohorts. Because researchers are typically interested in more than one generation or cohort, they have devised variations on the simple longitudinal design that provide more information.

Lives, the Computerized Codes: Analyzing Longitudinal Data

It is common to make informal judgments about personality changes over the course of life. We say that "Joe's the same in college as he was as a child" or "Judy has really changed." We identify experiences, such as going to college, that we think made a difference in a person's life. Perhaps our judgments are right; perhaps not. How can we get beyond such informal judgments to make systematic scientific statements that can stand up to critical scrutiny? In other words, how do we analyze longitudinal data?

Perhaps you have kept diaries or journals for some years of your life or have old scrapbooks and photograph albums. A lot of information accumulates! Now imagine adding several interviews, some objective tests, some imaginative stories, and records of observers' impressions of you over the years. Multiply this by dozens or hundreds of people, and you can begin to grasp the mountain of data that confronts a longitudinal researcher. How can one analyze such a huge data set? Where does one begin? One problem is that if you simply try to analyze every hunch that occurs to you, there may be hundreds of statistical tests that will need to be done. With modern computers there is time to do this, but after testing many relationships, you can expect that some of the "significant" results are really just due to chance. (The logic of statistics produces 5 "significant" results for every 100 tests on random data. The more tests you conduct, the less willing a statistically educated person will be to believe that your significant results reflect truth instead of chance.) To focus our analysis, we turn to theory, which guides us to be more selective in testing relationships and so makes our results more meaningful.

A second problem in analyzing longitudinal data is that the measures are quite different throughout the life span. How can we compare a preschool child with an adult to see whether personality has changed or remained similar? For this, the Q-sort method is helpful.

Comparing Apples and Oranges: The Q-Sort Method One of the challenges of analyzing longitudinal data is that measures collected at one age often do not correspond to measures collected at a different age. How can we compare observations of a preschool child at play with the personality questionnaire test scores of an adult? Direct comparison of the two ages is difficult, like comparing the proverbial apples and oranges. To resolve this difficulty, Jack Block (1961) used the **Q-sort** method. He has gathered data over the years and now has research assistants who examine the materials. For a young child, the material might consist of parents' answers to various questions about the child, observers' descriptions of the child's behavior with other children, and so on. For older children and adults, the material might include self-descriptions and questionnaires. The research assistants have the task of expressing these diverse sets of materials in a common language that can be used to compare the same person at different ages (for example, preschool Tommy with adolescent Tommy). To do this, they rate a set of materials, a folder of data collected for one person at one age, using a standard rating method. Raters consider a standard set of 100 cards, each printed with a word or phrase that can be used to describe a person. The rater considers all the material that has been examined and sorts these cards into piles to indicate how descriptive each card is of that individual, making an informed subjective coding. Jack Block's standard California Q-sort consists of 100 items that are sorted into 9 categories, with fewer numbers of items permitted at the ends of the distribution and more in the middle categories (Fig. 10.1). The process can be repeated for the folders of data collected for that individual at a different age. Since the same cards are used at various ages, it is possible to compare the individual at two different ages. This solves the "apples and oranges" problem. We can determine whether a young child who is judged "calm" grows up to be an adult who is rated "calm" without worrying too much about the disparate information available at each age, assuming that the rater's subjective assessment was reasonable.

Notice that the Q-sort method is ipsative (as described in Chapter 5). That is, it examines one individual only. It cannot be used to compare one person with another, because there is no uniform scale that applies to all people. Mary, for whom "outgoing" is in the seventh pile, might be more or less outgoing than Jerry, for whom that item is in the sixth pile. Such comparisons would require nomothetic measures, which evaluate everyone on the same scale of outgoingness, rather than comparing that trait with other personality characteristics. Just as a car mechanic does not expect the same tool to serve all purposes, the psychological researcher selects tools for particular purposes. If the purpose is to compare personality from one age to another, despite the differences in methods of observation across the ages, the Q-sort is a very useful tool.

FIGURE 10.1 *In the Q-sort method, judges sort 100 descriptive phrases, each written on a small card, into piles based on how well that phrase describes the person they are evaluating. Here is an example of a partially completed Q-sort.*

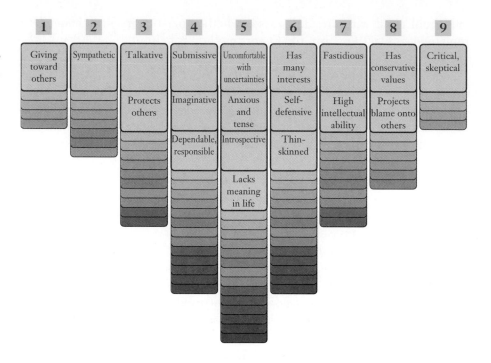

Recycling Data Longitudinal research is costly. It requires extensive effort to maintain contact with subjects over a period of time. Typically, the repeated contacts result in extensive records for each subject. The sheer amount of this data is greater than a single researcher or even a small team of researchers can fully examine. After the data have been analyzed sufficiently to answer the questions that originally prompted the research, there remains information that could be gleaned from the records. To avoid wasting data, longitudinal data sets may be made available to later researchers, who often analyze them for purposes not originally imagined at the time the data were collected. This later analysis of data originally collected for other purposes is called *secondary analysis.* Specialized techniques have been developed for extracting information from such data sets (James & Paul, 1993).

Stability or Change?

Is personality fixed early in life, as psychoanalytic theorists and many trait theorists (for example, Allport, 1937) have traditionally maintained? Or does it change as a result of experience, as learning theorists and those more concerned with social influences assert? This question can be tested empirically with longitudinal research. Not surprisingly, there is evidence to support both sides of this theoretical question. Some traits, such as intelligence, neuroticism, and extraversion, are more consistent than others, such as self-esteem and life satisfaction (Conley, 1984a, 1984b). In addition, some people change and others stay the same, whether in an unhealthy or a more adaptive mode (Lerner & Tubman, 1989; Ozer & Gjerde, 1989).

Evidence for Stability (or Continuity) Think over your past. Was your personality similar to what it is today? Researchers sometimes adopt a *retrospective* method, asking subjects to report about past experiences. For example, college students might be asked to describe their experiences in elementary school. In one retrospective study, elderly people recalled their personality at age 40 as having been much the same as it was at age 65 or older (Gold, Andres & Schwartzman, 1987).

When people recall their earlier personality, however, it is always possible that their memory is distorted. We may not realize how much we have changed, or we may overestimate the changes. People sometimes overestimate change when they have undertaken a program to learn a desired skill (such as study techniques), and afterward they retrospectively report inflated numbers of earlier problems. This makes the program seem more effective than it really was. This is not done consciously, but it serves to justify the effort and expense that went into the effort to change.

A better approach is to examine longitudinal data, waiting for many years between one administration of a test and a later retest to compare similarity without the possibility of biased retrospective reporting. This approach, too, yields evidence of stability. Type A behavior, which puts people at risk for coronary heart disease, is reasonably stable from ages 13 to 27 among men and women (Bergman & Magnusson, 1986). Paul Costa, Jr., and Robert McCrae (1988b), for example, found considerable stability on the Big Five factors of personality among adults over a 6-year period and so concluded "that personality is stable after age 30" (p. 853). In the opinion of Robert McCrae (1993), when researchers find change in adult personality, it is likely to be a result of measurement error rather than actual personality change. Considerable stability has also been reported for aggressive behavior from ages 8 to 30, however disconcerting it may be to realize that adult criminal behavior and physical aggression can be predicted from classmates' responses to such questions as "Who pushes or shoves children?" (Huesmann et al., 1984) (see the Research Strategies box).

Jack Block (1971, 1993) has reported many analyses of his ongoing longitudinal study of subjects from the Berkeley, California, area. He has assessed these subjects frequently from nursery school until their early 20s, and the research continues. Block has repeatedly found evidence of continuity. For example, preschoolers who were aggressive and did not cope well with stress were more likely to use drugs by age 14. Levels of ego control, whether a person is undercontrolled and acts impulsively or is overcontrolled and suppresses most impulses, showed consistency over the years, particularly for boys. Block prefers to refer to such findings as "continuity" rather than "stability," because that language recognizes that people do indeed change; even consistently undercontrolled individuals

RESEARCH STRATEGIES   ●--

Changes across Time: Why Longitudinal Studies are Better

Imagine that you are working on a research project to determine whether attending college increases people's self-esteem. You want to document the changes that occur in college students from the beginning of the first year until graduation 4 years later. At first, such a study doesn't seem to pose any particular difficulties. Simply administer your questionnaires to a group of first-year students and to another group of graduating seniors and compare their scores. If self-esteem differs, you've proven your hypothesis, right? Wrong! Maybe this year's first-year students are simply an insecure group, exposed to new admissions requirements and changes in society that have filled them with self-doubt. Maybe this year's seniors were higher in self-esteem all along, even when they arrived on campus 4 years earlier. It would be easier to assume that every class is just like every other class at the beginning, but without evidence, this is an unwarranted assumption. So the first research design, a *cross-sectional design*, is not adequate to measure change (see figure on facing page).

We need to compare the same people as first-year students and again as seniors, so let's administer the self-esteem tests during freshman orientation and then wait and administer them again as students are waiting for graduation rehearsal to begin. This *simple longitudinal design* will tell us how that particular group of students changed over time. Perhaps they increased their self-esteem by 20 points on a scale. This is an improvement over the first design, because we know that people changed (which we did not know when we measured two different groups of people). Can we be sure that this change reflects personality development; that is, age-related or experi-

ence-related changes in personality? That is what our research question proposes, and the data are certainly consistent with this idea. There is another possibility, though. Perhaps the difference reflects differences in the *period in history* between the first and second assessment, instead of differences in the subjects' personality. These students may be graduating at a time when prospects for jobs and graduate school admissions are at an all-time high. That effect, due to the year rather than their own personality development, may have produced the boost in self-esteem. The next class might not be so fortunate and could even show a decrease in self-esteem if there is a downturn in the job market by the time they finish their undergraduate education. So the second research design, while an improvement, still does not offer a definitive answer to our question.

How can researchers untangle these alternative interpretations? The basic idea is to determine what additional information would be enlightening and to collect the necessary data. In this case, we could try a third plan that combines elements of the cross-sectional design and the longitudinal design. In effect, we could conduct several longitudinal designs, each beginning in a different year and following a different group of subjects over the college years. If attending college truly produces the increase in self-esteem, we will see this pattern replicated in each group of subjects. This design, called a *panel design*, allows us to untangle the effects of different entering classes of college students (cohort effect) and the effects of the time in history when measurement occurs (period effect) from the developmental change in which we are interested. As even more research questions are proposed, longitudinal designs and their analysis can become much more complicated than this (Kenny & Campbell, 1989; Menard, 1991), but the fundamental idea is simple. Consider all the factors that may influence your observations and make comparisons that allow you to evaluate which factors are having an influence on your data.

In a *cross-sectional design*, subjects are studied only once. Two or more groups may be compared, as in this comparison of first-year students and seniors.

Group 1

First-year students

Group 2

Seniors

Time 1

In a *longitudinal design*, one group of subjects is studied on more than one occasion. In this case, the same group of subjects is studied as first-year students and again four years later.

All subjects

First-year students   Seniors

Time 1   Time 2

In a *panel design*, which is a variety of longitudinal design, two (or more) groups of subjects are studied on more than one occasion. There are many types of panel designs. In this example, two groups of subjects are studied, both as first-year students and as seniors. During the second data collection, one group is seniors and the other is first-year students.

Group 1

First-year students   Seniors

Group 2

First-year students   Seniors

Time 1   Time 2   Time 3

Research designs used to compare people at different ages and to study developmental change.

gain considerable ego control in the decades that follow nursery school. Longitudinal researchers look for consistency across the life span: do people keep their relative position compared to others across time? They do not expect strict stability, which would mean that people do not change (Block, 1993).

Avshalom Caspi has found many instances of continuity in his longitudinal analyses of data from the Berkeley Guidance Study. Children who were described as shy, or dependent, or ill-tempered at ages 8 to 10 had different lives in the decades that followed (Caspi, Bem & Elder, 1989). These distinct life courses support an interpretation of personality continuity. Shy children showed less sociability throughout life. They were described on adolescent and adult Q-sorts as "aloof, lacking social poise, bothered by demands, withdrawing when frustrated, and showing a reluctance to act" (Caspi, Bem & Elder, 1989, p. 390). Shy boys (but not girls) waited an average of 3 years longer before marriage and 4 years longer before becoming fathers, compared to their less shy peers (Caspi, Elder & Bem, 1988). Shy boys took longer to establish their careers, and shy girls were less likely to work outside the home.

What about the children classified as dependent? This early characteristic predicted earlier marriage and parenthood for females and less chance of divorce for males. Descriptions of dependent children in adolescence and adulthood suggest that the girls suffered from self-absorption and a lack of assertiveness, whereas the boys became warm, sympathetic, and socially poised (Caspi, Bem & Elder, 1989). It appears that early dependency has different outcomes for males and females, perhaps because of the social effects of sex role expectations.

Children were identified as explosive and undercontrolled at ages 8 to 10 if their mothers reported frequent and severe temper tantrums. Boys with this pattern had poorer outcomes as adults, attaining less formal schooling, having lower status jobs at age 40, and having more than double the chance of divorce of their more controlled peers. Girls with this pattern married men of lower occupational status, were more often divorced, and were perceived as less adequate mothers by their husbands and children (Caspi, 1987; Caspi, Elder & Bem, 1987).

To the extent that people's lives are stable or continuous, why is this so? There are many answers to this question, and each is at least partially true. One answer is that individual differences are caused in part by inherited biological differences and that heredity has continuous effects throughout life. Biological differences influence psychological traits that can be measured by diverse strategies, including written personality tests and teacher ratings in childhood, and they also influence behaviors, such as subsequent alcohol abuse (Cloninger, Sigvardsson & Bohman, 1988). The predisposition to experience anxiety is another effect of biological differences that has profound implications for personality throughout life (Eysenck, 1990a). We will consider biological influences in more detail in Chapter 11.

Usually, psychologists think of the environment as providing stimuli that produce change, but the environment can also contribute to personality stability (see Caspi, 1993). Individuals differ in the kind of environment they are exposed to, and these differences persist across the years. Spending childhood and adolescence in a crime-infested and impoverished environment, for example, may support personality continuity because of the consistently adverse environmental effects. As an additional twist, personality itself may interact with situations to produce consistency. For example, some troubled youths might interpret certain situations as justifying an aggressive response, even though other people would interpret the same situations differently. If a car drives onto your street in the middle of the night, is this a situation that justifies shooting the people in the car? Aggressive youths have done so; most of us would not consider this event to be a reason for violent action. The interpretation of such events as reasons for retaliation is a cognitive aspect of personality that may lead to consistently aggressive interactions with the environment.

In considering whether personality is stable across the decades of a life, we must recognize that all people change. Remember that it is more accurate to discuss the *continuity* of personality than its stability. That is, we should be asking whether the changes that occur in all people reflect underlying systematic processes. Does time take us further along our individual life paths, or are people influenced by environmental factors to switch from one path to another along the way? Are we "building on" rather than "erasing" or "undoing" earlier personality developments? If so, the early building blocks are all the more significant.

Evidence for Change Although personality psychologists are most inclined to emphasize personality continuity, development also brings substantial change. The longer the time between measures, and the younger in life that people are studied, the more change is found (Caspi & Bem, 1990; Ozer & Gjerde, 1989; Schuerger, Zarrella & Hotz, 1989). Infancy, in particular, has little relationship to later personality, probably because of the powerful effects of thinking and self-awareness that are not yet developed (Caspi & Bem, 1990). Even in the two decades or so from college to middle adulthood, considerable change occurs (Siegler et al., 1990).

Sometimes events in a person's life can produce personality change. Among these potentially transformative events are marriage, military service, and work (Caspi, 1993). The onset of adulthood, often with the new roles of (full-time) worker and spouse, brings particular personality change to the individual (Haan, Millsap & Hartka, 1986). Such changes, however, are often similar for most members of a group or cohort. That is, people may still maintain their relative position on various personality traits compared to other people in their research sample. Marriage to a spouse whose personality is similar to one's own (termed homogamy) contributes to personality continuity rather than change, and some researchers report that people usually do marry similar others (Caspi & Herbener, 1990).

When we find change, though, we should take careful note of what is changing. Are the fundamental underlying dimensions of personality changing? Or are they stable, but finding new expressions in changed behaviors or ways of thinking? One way of accounting for both stability and change is to reason that the most basic underlying dimensions are probably stable, whether because of constant biological forces or the relatively basic strategies of adaptation and self-concept that are formed early in life. On the other hand, as we adopt new roles and try new activities, we may develop new behaviors, adapting our basic personalities to changing situations. Robert McCrae (1993) supports this view by suggesting that people who score high on the trait of openness to experience, one of the Big Five personality traits, are more likely to experience change through such experimentation.

Identifying Paths and Forks in Life's Road   Longitudinal research can help us to identify the points along the road of life when critical events or decisions influence the future. Robert Frost, the poet, conveyed the image of such critical points when he reflected upon his choice of which fork to take when "Two paths diverged in a yellow wood." Where are these forks? Which path is the better one? If researchers can answer these questions, we may be able to identify which people have chosen the wrong path and focus our intervention efforts to redirecting them. Many children identified as "ill-tempered" get into trouble later, but many do not. Knowing when ill-tempered children confront that life fork may permit intervention before we must simply hire more police and build more jails.

Longitudinal data can tell us when it is very likely that we can predict a later outcome from an earlier measure, because in such cases the two variables are highly correlated. Such data can also sometimes reveal the intermediate steps along the path from an earlier measure to a later outcome. Researchers systematically examine the links between earlier events and those that occur later. These links can be expressed as correlation coefficients and as more advanced statistics. Consider the Berkeley Guidance Study (Fig. 10.2). Positive correlations in the diagram indicate that high scores on measures collected earlier in life (on the left) predict high scores on later measures (on the right). For example, boys with more childhood temper tantrums had more erratic worklife patterns (more breaks in employment) in adulthood ($r = .45$). Negative correlations indicate that high scores on early measures predict low scores on later measures. For example, more childhood temper tantrums predicted lower education ($r = -.34$). By midlife, it was clear that those who had attained more education also achieved higher occupational status ($r = .59$). Furthermore, higher occupational status predicted a less erratic worklife ($r = -.35$). Childhood temper tantrums also predict erratic worklife directly, presumably because of the remaining ill temper in adulthood. Such a *path analysis* helps researchers to identify the important links and turning points that explain

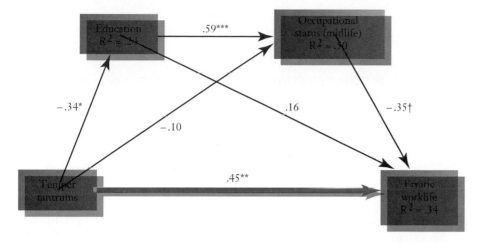

FIGURE 10.2 *Longitudinal data permit researchers to determine the paths by which early characteristics, such as temper tantrums in late childhood, influence adult life. In this path diagram summarizing 87 male subjects from the Berkeley Guidance Study, arrows indicate paths between earlier (left) and later (right) measures, which are significant at the indicated levels if the correlation coefficient on the path is marked with a note (*p < .10; **p < .05; ***p < .01; †p < .001). The R^2 statistics summarize how well the variable in each box can be predicted from all of the variables earlier in the path, plus intelligence; higher values indicate better prediction. (From Caspi, Elder & Bem, 1987, p. 312.)*

continuity and change in personality. This particular study suggests that educational attainment is a crucial link in determining the occupational status children will eventually attain. If we were to intervene in the life of an ill-tempered boy to improve his job prospects, it would make sense to focus on helping him to continue his education.

The importance of schooling in this example illustrates an important lesson from longitudinal studies. Understanding the *life course*, a term that describes personality through its changes over a lifetime, requires considering the social context of development, not simply psychological variables within a person (Caspi, 1987; Caspi & Bem, 1990; Levinson, 1986). People change settings and social roles as they go through life; for example, leaving the student role and becoming workers and parents. Many of these role changes are guided, more or less, by a *social clock* that conveys society's expectations about the age at which a person should graduate, begin a career, become a parent, and make other role changes. Of course, we all know that despite the social clock, there are wide variations in the age at which such role changes occur. Studies of the life course examine the specific situations in which a person is functioning. They also look at specific ages of a person's life. Both of these characteristics distinguish life course studies from trait models of personality.

Theories of Development

Theories of personality development guide our thinking about what is developed, and how. That may seem like a simple statement, but there are so many aspects of personality upon which we might focus that we are wise to recognize that our search is selective. A theory is to the researcher what a guidebook is to the traveler in a foreign land. It directs the expenditure of precious time (and money) so that the most important experiences can be selected. An outdated theory or one designed for another purpose will cause researchers to waste resources and miss relevant observations with a blindness analogous to that of tourists who do not visit the magnificent cathedral at Pisa because they are looking only at the more famous Leaning Tower.

Theories of development contain important assumptions (see Lerner & Tubman, 1989). Some theories are based on the assumption that people develop through a predetermined sequence of stages, confronting developmental issues in a particular time frame that is similar for everyone. Psychoanalytic theories, such as those of Sigmund Freud or (more widely accepted) of Erik Erikson, offer such assumptions about life stages. Other theories, in stark contrast, suggest that people develop in response to environmental influences that have no necessary stage sequencing. Learning theories illustrate this second alternative.

Effects of Experience: Learning Theory

Learning theory approaches, which are used to explain a broad variety of psychological phenomena, have been applied to understanding personality development. These theories emphasize the impact of experience and the consequences of behavior. From this perspective, people are malleable and can develop in a variety of ways, depending upon the experiences they undergo. Learning theory in its simplest form, based upon the reinforcement principles described by B. F. Skinner, suggests that people will become aggressive if their aggressive behavior is reinforced (by getting attention or other rewards). If reinforcement is instead given for cooperation, achievement, or some other behavior, that will become the characteristic behavior of a person, defining his or her personality. Behavior that is punished, in contrast, will be suppressed. If all a child's statements in class are criticized, we should expect silence.

If personality develops by the selective strengthening of some behaviors, varying from person to person depending upon experience, then personality can be measured by assessing the frequency of various behaviors. This approach constitutes the *act frequency approach* to personality measurement (Buss & Craik, 1980), described in Chapter 2. The act frequency approach has its critics, however, including Jack Block (1989). Block argues that the self-report inventories used to measure behaviors in the act frequency approach are not an adequate replacement for more direct observation of behavior and that researchers need to consider the situation in which behavior occurs. Do you know someone who often spends three or four hours in the evening without speaking to anyone? Does it make a difference whether this occurs in the library or in the student center? Of course it does.

John Dollard and Neal Miller (1950) applied learning principles to understanding how psychological disorders develop. They believe that people develop such disorders when they avoid behaving in ways that would lead them to experience anxiety and when this avoidance prevents them from engaging in the healthy, adaptive behaviors of life. For example, people who avoid speaking in public because of anxiety may be considered to suffer a disorder (called "neurosis" in earlier terminology) if such speaking would be helpful in their jobs. Since then, many psychologists have expanded the idea that maladaptive learning is the basis for psychological difficulties and that therapeutic relearning can provide relief.

Although learning theory emphasizes experience, some learning theories also take into account the biological variations among people. Hans Eysenck (1979) added consideration of individual differences that result from some people's greater biological predisposition to anxiety. Some people, because of the effects of genetic predispositions, experience great anxiety over the same events that leave other people feeling only mildly anxious. Anxiety-prone individuals are more likely to avoid behaving in ways that they have learned would lead to arousal of their excessive anxiety. For example, they may avoid attending parties or taking classes that require giving oral reports. These patterns of avoidance constitute "neurosis" or psychological dysfunction. Thus, the principles described by learning theorists can be combined with biological determinants of personality to explain different developmental paths.

Anxiety and other emotions, however, are not central to all learning approaches (see Crick & Dodge, 1994). Most current learning interpretations of personality emphasize cognition; that is, the thoughts that accompany behavior and help to determine what a person will do in a given situation. Self-efficacy expectations and self-regulatory plans, described by Albert Bandura (which we discussed in Chapter 9), are developed through learning in childhood and contribute to effective performance on cognitive tasks, such as measures of memory and intelligence (Berry, 1989; Chapman & Skinner, 1989; Chapman, Skinner & Baltes, 1990). Some of the most important learning in childhood is learning about the social world: learning to make realistic judgments about other people's intentions and dispositions, their likely responses to one's own behavior, and so on (Crick & Dodge, 1994; Rholes, Jones & Wade, 1988). Childhood is also a time for learning to have empathy and to be concerned about other people's feelings (Zahn-Waxler & Radke-Yarrow, 1990; Zahn-Waxler et al., 1992).

It seems reasonable that many of these important lessons for personality need to be learned in childhood. Stage approaches to personality development focus our attention on the sequencing of such life lessons.

Stages of Life

In contrast to learning theory approaches, stage approaches describe development through a sequence of stages that occur in the same order for everyone. Thus, not only what experiences a person has, but when they occur, is important, because the implications of experience are different depending upon the maturity of the individual. Losing a limb at age 5 is a far different experience from losing one at age 50. Further, some lessons of personality are easier to master at one age than another. Common lore asserts that it is hard to teach an old dog new tricks, which suggests that some of our basic personality lessons, such as how to relate to other people, are difficult to relearn.

Many stage theories have been offered, each emphasizing somewhat different aspects of personality. Let us consider some of these approaches.

Implications of Cognitive Development for Personality
A shortcoming of learning theory is that it does not take into account the increasing mental capacities a person develops over time. Cognitive development, besides permitting mastery of mathematical, logical, and other intellectual problems, has implications for personality. For one thing, it is the basis for the more sophisticated moral reasoning of adults, compared to that of children. According to Lawrence Kohlberg's (1981) theory of moral development, people make moral judgments according to different decision rules as they develop through three levels (six stages) of moral judgment (Table 10.1). Young children judge something to be wrong if it brings punishment or other negative outcomes. They reason that it is wrong to steal because you could be spanked or put into prison. By early adulthood, most people have moved far beyond this level and judge moral right and wrong on the basis of less immediate outcomes, such as the implications of behavior for relationships between people or the extent to which the behavior is consistent with general principles of right and wrong. Thus, they consider stealing to be wrong because of the harm it does to others or the violation of their principles or ethics.

E. Tory Higgins (1989) has considered how discrepancies from the ought-self and the ideal-self (as presented in Chapter 9) develop as the child matures cognitively. Over time, the child becomes increasingly able to take other people's perspectives into account. Children become aware of the consequences of their own behavior in terms of other people's reactions and approval, and this is a stage that prepares them to evaluate them-

TABLE 10.1 Kohlberg's Model of the Development of Moral Judgment

Self-centered thinking: **the preconventional level**	
Stage 1: Punishment and obedience orientation	Would I be punished?
Stage 2: Naive hedonistic orientation	Would I enjoy it?
Getting along with others: **the conventional level**	
Stage 3: Good boy–good girl orientation	Is this what people expect?
Stage 4: Social order orientation	Is this behavior the sort that makes society function in an orderly way? (What if everyone did this?)
Internal judgments: **the postconventional level**	
Stage 5: Legalistic orientation	Do people have a right to do this?
Stage 6: Universal ethical principle orientation	Does this behavior follow the rules that I personally believe in?

Adapted from Kohlberg, 1981.

selves more accurately. Parental behavior toward the child also influences the development of internal guides to behavior, which Higgins called self-guides. These develop more fully if parents are highly involved with their children, are consistent in their reactions, and are clear in conveying to their children what is expected and that their behaviors are significant. Cognitive development thus provides the possibility for new developments in personality.

Stages of the Life Cycle: Levinson's Model Daniel Levinson (1986) has proposed an influential model of adult development through the life course. He suggests that we consider the *life cycle*, a metaphor invoking images of the cycle of the seasons, and states that "the life course evolves through a sequence of definable forms" (p. 4). Levinson proposes that these forms or seasons of life include three major periods, each occupying 20 years or more: preadulthood, adulthood, and old age. In turn, each of these seasons is divided into several eras that describe the life structures attained at that phase of life or that offer transition periods between one structure and another (Table 10.2). Although the theory is most appropriately applied to understanding individuals, it can be illustrated in looking at changes in a group of women as they matured during the two decades following college graduation. During their late 20s, these women typically

TABLE **10.2   Levinson's Model of the Adult Life Cycle**

Age	Transition	Structure
17–22	Early adult transition	
22–28		Entry early adult structure
28–33	Age 30 transition	
33–40		Culminating early adult structure
40–45	Midlife transition	
45–50		Entry middle adult structure
50–55	Age 50 transition	
55–60		Culminating middle adult structure
60–65	Late adult transition	

Adapted from Levinson, 1986

increased their traditionally feminine sex role characteristics as they were involved in the marriage and parenting activities of this age. In their 30s and early 40s, feminine sex role characteristics decreased as the women took on more varied responsibilities (Helson & Moane, 1987).

As Levinson's model suggests, structures are formed and then modified during the life cycle changes of adulthood. Consider a hypothetical adult whose early adult transition is marriage, leading to the early adult structure of a dual-income home. At age 30 another transition occurs when a child is born, leading to a revised structure of a larger household. Another major transition occurs at midlife: a divorce. The middle adult structure takes the form of a single-parent household, until the age 50 transition, when children leave for college. The culminating middle adult structure for this hypothetical person is an enhanced position at work. Retirement constitutes the late adult transition. Structures, in Levinson's model, are often interrupted by transitions.

The idea that adult life follows such age-graded sequences is controversial. If, as most psychologists believe, the personality changes of adulthood are driven by social forces rather than biological ones, why would people fall into a standard series of stages? Despite these questions, Levinson's theory provides a framework for considering personality development in adulthood, and it emphasizes the social context within which structures and transitions occur. In those senses it is similar to the ego development theory of Erik Erikson.

Ego Development Theory

Learning theory focuses researchers' attention on behaviors that are relatively easily observed, with less attention on the hidden psychological processes that underlie these behaviors. In fact, behaviorists have tradition-ally discouraged scientifically minded psychologists from basing their work on unobservable processes. In contrast, other psychologists believe that behaviors are only the surface manifestations of personality. From this point of view, the underlying causes, though hidden, are the primary con-cern. It may come as a surprise to learn that Sigmund Freud, the founder of psychoanalysis, at first attempted to locate the causes of his patients' symptomatic behavior in damaged neurons. Only when that effort failed did he propose that there could be psychological, nonphysical causes for such symptoms as memory lapses, obsessive thoughts, and compulsive acts. Whereas behaviorists dismiss Freud's proposal as a nonscientific conclu-sion, those who favor **ego developmental stage theories** accept the fun-damental premise that hidden psychological causes develop over time and cumulatively provide each personality with the means to adapt to its envi-ronment. Psychoanalysts since Freud have referred to such adaptive capac-ities as *ego* capacities, and so we may think of personality development as the development of a mature, competent ego.

Longitudinal researchers have often observed that children who develop ego strengths are more likely to thrive in later life. Ego strengths constitute a repertoire of adaptive coping strategies. One important ele-ment of ego strength is the ability to delay gratification. In children, the capacity to delay gratification can be assessed by observing a child who has been told that he or she will receive a present after completing a difficult puzzle, but who is confronted by an experimenter who seems to have for-gotten this promise. Those who tolerated this delay at age 4 were rated as more independent and socially mature by teachers and researchers throughout childhood, although the specific items varied for boys and girls (Funder, Block & Block, 1983). Among 14-year-old children, those who chose a larger delayed payment of money over a smaller immediate amount were rated more positively on Q-sort items for a number of traits (respon-sibility, productiveness, ethical consistency, interest in intellectual matters) than those who chose the smaller payment (Funder & Block, 1989). Walter Mischel and his colleagues found that some nursery school children can delay gratification, waiting to obtain a larger reward rather than settling for an immediate smaller one. Children who could delay gratification became more competent and better able to tolerate stress in adolescence (Mischel & Mischel, 1983; Mischel, Shoda & Peake, 1988; Mischel, Shoda & Rodriguez, 1989). The ability to delay gratification and to control impulses (to hold back rage instead of having a tantrum, for example) is adaptive beyond early childhood, of course. For instance, poor impulse control is associated with frequent drug use at age 18 in the longitudinal sample studied by Jack Block and his colleagues (Shedler & Block, 1990).

Ego skills include not only holding the lid on impulses and waiting for gratification but also knowing how to plan and achieve our goals. Such abilities are sometimes called *competence*. John Clausen (1991) studied ado-lescent competence in a longitudinal study. Competent adolescents are described as dependable, intellectually invested, and self-confident on a Q-sort measure, and adolescent competence is predictive of stable careers and marriages. Clausen notes, from his sociological perspective, that the ego strength of competence is particularly important in modern society, since "rationality and functionality have replaced tradition as determinants of individual choices in the transition to adulthood" (p. 805). If that observation, which seems reasonable, is correct, then understanding such ego strengths will be essential in developing a view of personality that will continue to have merit as cultural change moves society even further away from tradition.

Loevinger's Stages of Ego Development   Jane Loevinger (1966) has offered a model that describes seven stages of increasing maturity of ego development, which she calls a "master trait" of personality because of its importance. These stages describe the progression of a person from an infantile obliviousness to selfhood, through childish stages of impulsiveness and expediency, to a capacity to conform to society and to obey internal rules of conduct, and finally to the most mature stages of mastering inner conflict (Table 10.3).

Those adults who have achieved high levels of ego development, as assessed by a sentence completion measure developed by Jane Loevinger (1966, 1985), score higher on tests of personal adjustment (White, 1985) and report commitment to a greater variety of future goals (McAdams, Ruetzel & Foley, 1986). Longitudinal research supports the importance in adulthood of early ego development. Lea Pulkkinen (1992) found that the ability to control impulses was consistent in the lives of Finnish boys as they matured from ages 8 to 26. Those with less impulse control were more antisocial; they had more behavioral problems in school and were more likely to be arrested as adults. In contrast, a group that became more highly educated in adulthood showed evidence of greater ego strength throughout life, with fewer injuries and accidents and far fewer problems with alcohol. As early as age 8, these groups were viewed differently by their teachers, with the antisocial group showing more aggression and less concentration and the educated group behaving more constructively and more submissively. As in the study described earlier in this chapter, educational attainment is a key link between childhood and a successful adulthood.

What can parents do to facilitate good ego development in their children? Obviously, they should avoid physically abusing their children. Physical abuse has been related to a variety of subsequent adverse outcomes, including violence, criminal behavior, emotional problems, and suicidal behavior (Malinosky-Rummell & Hansen, 1993). Longitudinal research suggests that children who were treated with acceptance, were disciplined in a nonauthoritarian manner, and who seemed to identify with their parents manifested higher levels of ego development on the Loevinger Sentence Completion Test of Ego Development 22 years later

TABLE **10.3** **Loevinger's Model of the Increasing Maturity of Ego Development**

Stage	Ego functioning
1. Presocial	Unaware of distinction between self and nonself
2. Impulse-ridden	Impulsive; afraid of retaliation
3. Opportunistic	Expedient; afraid of being caught
4. Conformist	Conforms to external rules; shame
5. Conscientious	Follows internal rules; guilt
6. Autonomous	Copes with inner conflict; tolerates differences
7. Integrated	Reconciles inner conflicts; renounces what can't be attained

Adapted from Loevinger, 1966.

(Dubow, Huesmann & Eron, 1987). Although researchers have most often focused on the role of the mother, fathers also play an important role in producing psychologically healthy children (Phares & Compas, 1992).

Studies such as these suggest that the development of a strong ego, which we may think of as a repertoire of adaptive coping strategies, is a major accomplishment of childhood that has implications throughout life. Erik Erikson has offered a theory that describes ego development in considerable detail.

Erikson's Psychosocial Theory Erik Erikson was a psychoanalyst trained in the Freudian tradition. He extended Freud's theory, however, by providing a model of development in which significant growth occurs throughout the life span, and not only in the first 5 years of life as Freud had theorized. Erikson (1959) proposed that people develop through eight stages, which he called **psychosocial stages** to emphasize the relationship between the psychological development of the individual and the social context in which this development occurs (Table 10.4).

Erikson's theory describes the aspect of a healthy ego that is developed at each stage of life. In infancy, the task is to achieve a sense of *trust* that the mother or other caretaker will meet one's needs. This trust provides the basis for trusting relationships throughout life and so is an essential component of a healthy ego. In the second and third stages, the preschool child attains a sense of *autonomy*, the confidence that he or she can be separate and act independently, and a sense of *initiative*, which permits making choices and decisions. During the school years, a sense of *industry* develops as the child works on projects and attains a sense of accomplishment.

TABLE **10.4   Erikson's Eight Stages of Psychosocial Development**

Psychological stage	Age
1. Trust versus mistrust	Infancy
2. Autonomy versus shame, doubt	Early childhood
3. Initiative versus guilt	Play age
4. Industry versus inferiority	School age
5. Identity versus identity diffusion	Adolescence
6. Intimacy versus isolation	Young adulthood
7. Generativity versus self-absorption	Adulthood
8. Integrity versus despair	Old age

Adapted from Erikson, 1982.

Adolescence brings the crisis of *identity*, as the teenager struggles to attain an individual sense of who he or she is in relationship to society. This often involves the choice of a career, but it may also involve political or social activism. *Intimacy* is attained as the young adult develops the capacity for mature love, and *generativity* develops as the mature adult cares for children and for the next generation in other contexts, such as work. Even the elderly continue to achieve new ego strengths, as they look back over what has been accomplished in their individual lives and what has been left undone, forging a sense of *integrity* from this life review.

At each stage, the developing ego strength is in conflict with its opposite: trust with mistrust, autonomy with shame, initiative with guilt, and so on. We achieve a healthy balance if our strengths prevail over their opposites. It is best not to extinguish mistrust, shame, and other negative characteristics, however, because we need them to keep a realistic equilibrium: the person who trusts everyone or who never feels ashamed cannot function optimally in the real world.

Erikson's theory provides therapists with a framework for understanding the age-appropriate developmental issues of their clients and for recognizing how past difficulties have an adverse effect on certain aspects of current ego functioning. Adolescents, for example, are struggling with the task of attaining an identity and so may be especially concerned with society's recognition (or lack of recognition) of their unique characteristics. People with a history of trauma at age 4 or so would be expected to have lasting problems with excessive guilt and to have difficulty taking initiative. Outside the therapeutic setting, researchers have measured these various ego strengths by self-report questionnaires. For example, agreement with the statement "I can usually depend on others" is interpreted as evidence of trust, and people who have attained intimacy are unlikely to agree with the statement "I often feel lonely even when there are others around me" (Domino & Affonso, 1990, p. 580).

Infancy: The Early Basis of Personality

Erikson and other ego development theorists propose that ego strengths develop throughout the stages of life. Obviously, the lessons of each stage are different. We will now consider the personality attainments of various stages of life, beginning with infancy. Infants seem so different from adults that it is difficult to imagine that the experiences of infancy could shape adult personality. Many theorists, however, consider infancy to be a time for the most basic and influential developments in personality.

Perhaps the most important contribution of infancy to later personality comes through the process of attachment. By experiencing a reliable relationship with a nurturing caretaker (usually the mother), the infant develops the basis for positive relationships with other people throughout life. If maternal care is inadequate, later relationships are compromised. This foundation corresponds to Erik Erikson's concept of "basic trust."

Mary Ainsworth (Ainsworth et al., 1978; Ainsworth, 1989), building on the work of John Bowlby (1969), has pioneered theory and research about infant attachment. Infants soon learn to love their mother or other primary caretaker. Infant **attachment** to the caretaker is the bond of the infant to the caretaker that is evidenced by distress when the caretaker leaves and by security when the caretaker is present. John Bowlby describes **secure attachment** as attachment

> *in which individuals are confident that their parent (or parent figure) will be available, responsive, and helpful should they encounter adverse or frightening situations. With this assurance, they feel bold in their explorations of the world and also competent in dealing with it. This pattern is found to be promoted by a parent (in the early years, especially by the mother) being readily available, sensitive to her child's signals, and lovingly responsive when he or she seeks protection and/or comfort and/or assistance. (Bowlby, 1988, p. 4)*

The presence of the caretaker provides the attached infant with security, so that the infant does not show distress, or at least not so much distress, at otherwise fearsome stimuli when the caretaker is present. With the mother or father nearby, the baby will be able to cope with otherwise frightening people or objects. From a secure attachment base, the infant will begin to explore new aspects of the environment, seeking the attachment figure again if the new experience provokes distress. The baby who looks curiously at other people from the security of a parent's arms and the toddler whose new mobility permits walking to new places are building on their secure attachment. Their security permits them to seek new experiences rather than to defend against fear, and this exploration contributes to the growth of intelligence.

Ainsworth believes that attachment behavior is rooted in biology. It is adaptive for survival because it ensures that the infant and young child will remain close to the caregiver, whose nurturance is essential for survival. In humans, crying and other behaviors summon the caretaker to come near and attend to the child's needs. Other species have somewhat similar mechanisms. In geese and ducks, attachment takes the form of imprinting, and the baby geese follow their parent, waddling on land or paddling in the water to stay nearby. Perhaps you have seen pictures of baby geese following Konrad Lorenz, who showed that if the parent goose is not around, the goslings may adopt a human as their attachment object. Such aberrant behavior illustrates the strength of the drive for attachment, which in humans produces the puzzle of children's attachment even to abusive parents.

Ainsworth and her colleagues (Ainsworth et al., 1978) studied infant attachment to the mother by observing infants' responses to strangers in a standardized laboratory situation. In the **strange-situation procedure,** the baby is left alone with a stranger for a few minutes, with the mother out of view. Based on the infant's response to the absence of the mother and to the mother's return, he or she is judged to be *securely attached, anxious-avoidant,* or *anxious-resistant.* Securely attached children show evidence of distress when the mother departs and of comfort when she returns; this is the most healthy pattern. Anxious-avoidant children expect that they will be rejected if they seek comfort and so try to make do without love and support. Anxious-resistant children, because of inconsistent parental responsiveness, are uncertain whether the parent will be responsive when needed and so tend to be clinging and distressed (Bowlby, 1988).

Mothers who are responsive to their infants' distress produce securely attached children. Children typically cry and show facial expressions of anger when separated from their mothers under the conditions just described. Some (in the anxious-resistant group) also show sadness (Shiller, Izard & Hembree, 1986). Secure attachment provides a means for this important relationship to orchestrate the baby's emotions in an adaptive way. When attachment is not secure, the foundation of an emotionally healthy relationship pattern is flawed.

Infant attachment to the caregiver is the primary and basic human bond. It is the basis for later affectional bonds that people develop throughout their lives, including the parents' bond to their growing child and our affectional bonds to friends and lovers. Mary Ainsworth defines an *affectional bond* as "a relatively long-enduring tie in which the partner is important as a unique individual and is interchangeable with none other"

(Ainsworth, 1989, p. 711). Ainsworth says that we seek to remain close to those with whom we have affectional bonds and that we experience distress when apart, joy when together, and grief when the bond is broken. Affectional bonds, however, do not provide a sense of security comparable to that of an attachment bond, so the infant's experience is unique.

Longitudinal studies suggest that early attachment has momentous implications for later development. Although the evidence is still incomplete (Paterson & Moran, 1988), several studies support the prediction that difficulties with infant attachment bode ill for later relationships and adjustment. Infants who were not securely attached as infants are at greater risk for adverse outcomes in childhood and beyond. Their nursery school teachers approximately 3 years later rate them as excessively dependent compared to securely attached children (Sroufe, Fox & Pancake, 1983). Children can tease mercilessly, and insecurely attached infants were more likely than securely attached infants to be victimized or victimizers in childhood; they were also judged to be less competent and less socially skilled by their camp counselors and had less mature friendships (Sroufe, Carlson & Shulman, 1993).

These interpersonal difficulties also are reflected in tasks that are not interpersonal. When researchers assessed 7-year-olds using observations along with a storytelling task, they found that attachment was associated with higher performance on standard tests of cognitive development for the next decade (Jacobsen, Edelstein & Hofmann, 1994). This is what Erikson's theory would predict: inadequate achievement of an earlier ego developmental task (attachment) leads to less success in accomplishing later tasks as well (industry).

The consequences of the attachment process can be inferred from the memories that people recall as adults. Marvin Acklin studied undergraduates whose early childhood memories included themes of lack of control or difficulties with relationships, such as an unsatisfied need to be nurtured or defeat in sibling rivalry situations. Those with such memories, among other predictors, were likely to score high on a questionnaire measure of depression (Acklin et al., 1989). In a sample of psychiatric outpatients, inadequate relationships in early memories were associated with greater pathology on various clinical scales (Acklin et al., 1991). We may add an optimistic note: psychotherapy can help to move people back to a healthy track (Bowlby, 1988; Zeanah et al., 1989).

The impact of infant attachment on later personality is widely accepted. Cautionary warnings have been voiced, however. Michael Lamb (1987) points out that it may not be the infant attachment alone that produces favorable development later. Infants who show positive attachment are also usually raised in homes that continue to have desirable parental treatment for many years. Likewise, infants who show insecure attachment are likely to receive less adequate parenting later. How can we say that it is the early attachment rather than the later parental practices that influences behavior later in childhood? Lamb believes that we can't. Results from studies of infants in the United States were not replicated when similar studies were conducted in Japan, and for some unexplained reason, secure attachment occurs less frequently in countries other than the United States. Such findings suggest that the attachment process is more complicated than we have yet understood (Nakagawa, Lamb & Miyaki, 1992; Sternberg & Lamb, 1992). In addition, the outcome of the attachment process is not so wholly determined by parental behavior as many researchers have assumed. The child's temperament, a biologically determined characteristic, is also an important contributor (Goldsmith & Alansky, 1987). Some infants are predisposed to be more easily distressed; others are more calm. Mothers vary, too, and the match between infant temperament and maternal personality may influence the outcome of the attachment process (Chess, 1986; Mangelsdorf et al., 1990). The emotionality of infants is not entirely determined biologically, though; parental behavior influences it as well (Belsky, Fish & Isabella, 1991). It is the interaction of these two processes that directs (or should direct) future research.

Although emotionality and attachment are the most readily observed developments of infancy, even at this young age a child begins to learn that he or she has some impact on the world. This early sense of efficacy (Broucek, 1979) is a beginning upon which important childhood developments are built.

Childhood: Personality Molded in the Family

Building on the foundation of attachment, personality is further molded in the family. Theorists have long believed that how parents treat their children influences the developing personality. Longitudinal research suggests, for example, that parents who provide their children with psychological safety and freedom foster their children's creativity, as Carl Rogers's theory of self-actualization proposes (Harrington, Block & Block, 1987). Researchers have often found, however, that the associations between parental behavior and child personality are weaker than might be expected (McCrae & Costa, 1988). It isn't always a simple matter to interpret such associations. For one thing, the idea that parental behavior is the cause and child personality is the effect is obviously an oversimplification. Parent-child interaction is reciprocal (Rothbaum & Weisz, 1994). Parents respond to their children, so how can we be sure that parents who are very loving, for example, are *producing* a child with a good-natured personality rather than vice versa? In addition, parents and children are responding to their shared social context; neighborhoods and other social variables may influence both parents and children, making comparisons with other parent-child units misleading. Furthermore, the effects of parents' behavior on their children's personality may not be observable for many years. Using retrospective reports—recollections by adults of their earlier experiences—

Each stage of life teaches lessons of increasing maturity. The impulsive and aggressive behavior of children facing such problems as sibling rivalry, is usually transformed into more civilized behavior by adulthood. Could this be why oldest children often become higher achievers?

Robert McCrae and Paul Costa, Jr. (1988), found that adults' personality scores were related to the childhood relationships they recalled with their parents. The associations were less striking than might be expected, however, which suggests that parents have less impact on children's development than many people believe. The associations they found seem reasonable. Loving parents had children who, as adults, were lower in Neuroticism and higher in Extraversion, Openness to Experience, Agreeableness, and Conscientiousness. Demanding parents raised children who became higher in Extraversion and Conscientiousness and lower in Openness to Experience. Attentive (spoiling) parents raised children who were high in Extraversion and low in Agreeableness; that is, "confident but self-centered," (p. 430). Of course, with retrospective reports, there is always the possibility of biased recall.

To address this shortcoming, researchers have undertaken several longitudinal studies that are not subject to the shortcomings of retrospective reports. These studies have also found that the way parents behave toward their children during childhood predicts outcomes years later. For example, several parenting behaviors at age 5 predict the empathic concern of these children when they reached age 31. Those who described themselves in empathic ways (generous, helpful, sympathetic, and so on) on an adjective checklist in adulthood had, at age 5, higher involvement by their fathers in child care and mothers who were more satisfied with their role as mother and more tolerant of the child's dependency but less tolerant of their aggression (Koestner, Franz & Weinberger, 1990).

Sisters and brothers, as well as parents, influence personality development. Since Alfred Adler (1921/1927) called attention to the importance of birth order in personality formation, many investigations have tested whether personality is influenced by the fact of being an oldest child, a middle child, a youngest child, or an only child. These investigations generally show that the firstborn child is a higher achiever and more conservative than his or her younger siblings. Only children are also generally high achievers (Falbo & Polit, 1986; Polit & Falbo, 1987). Parents treat children differently, depending on birth order. For example, they have more time to spend with the oldest child before the birth of siblings, at which time the oldest child no longer receives so much attention (Hoffman, 1991).

Although the family is very important in childhood development, successful relationships with peers are also important. Children who are less successful with peers because of shyness, aggressiveness, or lack of acceptance are at greater risk of adverse outcomes in later life: dropping out of school, criminal behavior, and psychopathology (Parker & Asher, 1987). It will take further research to establish the causes more definitively. Is lack of success with peers a direct cause of later problems, or an early symptom?

Adolescence: Forging a Personal Identity

During the next stage of life, the arena for an individual's personality development increasingly moves beyond the family to the world at large. Erik Erikson's (1959, 1968) description of the adolescent's struggle to attain a sense of **identity** has inspired considerable research. He describes identity as a sense that one's style of individuality is recognized by significant others in a way that matches one's own sense of self. If this does not occur, the person is said to have *identity confusion*. Because the task of achieving identity is not easy, particularly in a society that offers diverse options, development is enhanced by taking the time to explore possible identities. For college students, trying out new courses of study and exploring different majors is part of this task. Society can foster this exploration by providing a *moratorium* period in which the adolescent is not required to undertake adult responsibilities (for example, earning a living and raising a family) but remains free to explore identity issues. In other societies, where identity is constrained by tradition or economic constraints, identity issues are less salient.

James Marcia (1966) has developed the *identity status paradigm* for measuring the extent to which an individual has attained a sense of identity, based upon interviews. He reasons, based on Erikson's description, that a person who has completed this stage satisfactorily (such a person may be called **identity achieved**) will report explorations that have been undertaken and that have culminated in a commitment. For example, a college student may report exploring a variety of potential majors (psychology, business, mathematics) before selecting one. A person who is actively exploring options but has still not made a commitment to one is said to be in **moratorium.** With continued exploration, individuals in moratorium are likely to make the transition to identity achievement and thus to resolve this developmental stage satisfactorily. In contrast, people who report that they have not ever doubted what they wished to become and so have not explored other options are considered not to have undertaken the necessary exploration for healthy resolution of this stage and so are called **identity foreclosed.** For example, a person who has always wanted to be an accountant and has never considered another career would be considered identity foreclosed. This is not a healthy resolution, because it commits a person to an identity that may be unsuitable, and the commitment precludes the uncertainty that could motivate exploration. **Identity diffusion** status describes the final possibility: no evidence of exploration and no commitment to an identity. A college student who hasn't any idea what to choose as a major or how to explore the possibilities exemplifies identity diffusion. Individuals categorized in this way may well experience exploration and commitment in the future (Kroger & Haslett, 1988; Waterman, 1982; Waterman, Geary & Waterman, 1974).

As predicted theoretically, adolescents who are classified as in moratorium are less committed to an occupation, and exploration of career options is high in both moratorium and identity achievement statuses (Blustein, Devenis & Kidney, 1989). Of these four identity statuses, achievement and moratorium statuses are most desirable. Individuals in these statuses use the most mature strategies for coping with problems, in contrast to individuals in diffusion status, who tend to avoid coping, and individuals in foreclosure status, who are rigid and unwilling to accept ambiguity (Berzonsky, Rice & Neimeyer, 1990).

In addition to interview measures, which are time-consuming, questionnaire measures of identity status have been developed that can be administered to groups of subjects (Côté, 1986; Grotevant & Adams, 1984). Unfortunately, self-report and interview measures do not correlate highly (Craig-Bray & Adams, 1986). In addition, although identity is usually considered as an overall concept, some researchers have measured identity separately in various areas, such as occupation, religion, family, and politics (Kroger, 1986). Besides exploring career options, adolescents make choices about their religious beliefs and commitments, their desire to marry or have children, and so on, and a person may explore one area in depth while not considering others.

Erikson's description of identity (like all of his psychosocial stages) emphasizes society's involvement in the process. Society provides the various adult roles toward which an individual may aspire or rebel. In societies where there is little social mobility—that is, where adult roles follow family lines rather than individual attainment—identity is not such a salient developmental issue. James Côté and Charles Levine have argued that researchers should be more attentive to the societal dimension of identity. For example, from a social point of view, all "university students of the normal attending age" are experiencing an institutionalized moratorium, free from the commitments that will be required when they leave school (1988a, p. 161). Moratorium is a social phase, not a state of mind or of individual psychological development only. Identity is not simply a concept for personality development; it is also a social psychological concept (Côté & Levine, 1988b; Greenwood, 1994). Struggles over identity can have significance for the larger society as well as the individual. The generation that grappled with identity during the antiwar protests of the 1960s in the United States changed society. Some individuals, such as Mahatma Gandhi (Erikson, 1969; Nichtern,1985), have also had a political impact as their individual struggles with identity are played out on the stage of history.

There are variations in the extent to which identity exploration is encouraged even within the college environment. Those students majoring in the technological fields generally experience a less severe identity crisis than students in the humanities (Côté & Levine, 1989, 1992). This is not necessarily desirable, because the technological values that are adopted focus on external accomplishments and preclude the individual introspective exploration that Erikson described as desirable for optimal identity resolution.

Although society is changing, opportunities for adult women traditionally have been different from those for men. As a result, according to many researchers, young women experience the identity-formation process differently from how young men experience it. At the time when young men are working on identity issues, many young women may be more concerned with intimacy rather than individual identity, believing that decisions about marriage are more central to their identity than decisions about work (Schiedel & Marcia, 1985; Streitmatter, 1993). Other women turn away from the traditional definition of a woman's status through marriage. Some young women whose mothers have not worked outside the home, for example, may rebel against this model to achieve an identity that includes a career (Cella, DeWolfe & Fitzgibbon, 1987).

Adulthood: The Mature Personality

A person who has consolidated a healthy identity in adolescence is better prepared for the tasks of adulthood. Those who have not done so are less able to achieve adequate resolution of adult tasks. Instead of a healthy and mutual intimacy, they may cling to an idealized image of their love partner in a way that Michael Sperling (1987) calls "desperate love." He proposes that inadequate development of attachment in infancy also contributes to adult difficulties with adult attachment and love (Sperling & Berman, 1991; Sperling, Berman & Fagen, 1992). Attaining a capacity for intimacy leads to security and better coping with separation or loss of loved ones (Levitz-Jones & Orlofsky, 1985). Because difficulties with intimacy are obstacles to adult development, it is not surprising that men who score high on intimacy motivation at age 30 show better adjustment during the following 17 years (McAdams & Vaillant, 1982).

The midlife task that Erikson calls "generativity" involves nurturing and fostering the next generation, whether one's own children or others, such as those in the community or in one's field of work. Generativity can be expressed by volunteering at a grade school or by serving as a mentor to a new employee at work. People who have high levels of the trait of nurturance score higher on measures of generativity as well (Van De Water & McAdams, 1989). A motivational analysis suggests that both power and intimacy motives (as described in Chapter 7) contribute to generativity (McAdams, Ruetzel & Folcy, 1986). This makes sense if generativity involves a loving influence over others.

Most research does not support the popular idea that adults experience a "midlife crisis" (Costa & McCrae, 1989). Instead, adults continue to build on the strengths developed in earlier life and respond to the age-specific tasks of adulthood. This pattern continues into old age.

Old Age

In recent years, partly as a result of demographic changes that have made us all more cognizant of the elderly, researchers have studied this last stage of life. The elderly become increasingly aware of their declining control over their own lives and of their increasing dependence on others (Lachman & Leff, 1989; Lumpkin, 1985). It would be incorrect, however, to look only at the losses of old age. The elderly still have important life goals that contribute to their health and psychological well-being (Holahan, 1988). Erikson's theory has helped turn attention to the ego developments of this age, rather than only to the physical declines that accompany aging. The developmental task of the elderly is to achieve a sense of *ego integrity*, the conviction that life has been meaningful, considering all that they have done and all that has not been done, given the brevity of life and other restrictions. Based on questionnaire assessment of ego integrity, researchers report that the elderly who have developed this strength have less fear of death (Goebel & Boeck, 1987). In their effort to achieve ego integrity, many people turn to religion and religious issues (Koenig, 1990).

Personality development lasts a lifetime. From the infant's first lessons in love and trust to the philosophical reflections of the old about the meanings of life and of death, we all are still learning.

The social clock conveys society's expectations about the age when marriage, graduation, and other life tasks are accomplished, but people sometimes follow a different timetable.

A *Humbling Lesson: The Complexity of Personality*

Too often, personality research has sought simple correlations between one or two personality characteristics and behavior (or even simply between two personality characteristics). With longitudinal research has come a humbling lesson for those who would settle for simple prediction: such prediction doesn't fit the data. Instead, the meaningful patterns that emerge involve complex interplays among personality characteristics and the social context, which develop over time. These patterns are often described as different for the two sexes (for example, Cohn, 1991; Gjerde, 1993) and for people born in different historical periods (for example, Helson, 1993). This does not necessarily mean that the developmental processes are different, although differences in the intercorrelations among variables, such as those noticed often by Jack Block (1993) between males and females, raise this possibility. We do know that sex differences in development are reported frequently. For example, the predictors of depression at age 18 from childhood personality at age 7 are different for boys and girls (Block, Gjerde & Block, 1991).

Although one might expect race and ethnicity to have a major impact on development, David Rowe and his colleagues argue against that view, at least for the development of intelligence, achievement, and social adjustment. They acknowledge differences among ethnic and racial groups in the average levels of these variables but argue that the developmental *processes* that produce these different outcomes are similar when evaluated statistically (Rowe, Vazsonyi & Flannery, 1994). Rowe and colleagues used statistical techniques different from those used by researchers who argue for differences based on sex and history. Would similar developmental processes also be found across these dimensions, using different statistical methods? Such questions guide ongoing research.

In any case, developmental patterns reflect the combined influence of many variables. These patterns are often difficult to predict in advance, and they emerge only when several variables are considered. A change in only one variable, whether an event or a family influence or another social influence, can drastically change the pattern that emerges in the complex interplay of forces that determines personality development. The death of a parent, a fire that destroys a home, the admission or rejection of a student to a chosen college—these and many other influences can have a major impact on personality development. How could such incidents possibly be factored into the mathematical models that researchers devise? The impact of isolated events on later developments may require a new model, perhaps chaos theory, which was devised to understand weather patterns (Gleick, 1987). If the force of one butterfly's wings can influence the development of a powerful weather system thousands of miles away by providing a critical nudge that changes the emergent patterns, so can a subtle change in one developmental variable alter the course of personality development. The more we study the diversity of personalities as they develop over time, the more likely we are to gain an understanding of just where such effects will probably occur.

SUMMARY

- Longitudinal studies of personality study the same people over a long span of time. In contrast, cross-sectional studies investigate different groups of people at one time.

- Differences between groups of people at different ages in cross-sectional studies may be caused by age effects, period effects, or cohort effects.

- Longitudinal designs produce large quantities of data, which are analyzed with the guidance of a theory. The Q-sort procedure permits comparisons across ages with diverse measures.

• Longitudinal studies are better suited to evaluating personality stability or change than are retrospective studies. Continuity across the life span has been found for various characteristics, including ego control, shyness, dependency, and ill temper. Change occurs, too, especially when life roles change or when education breaks maladaptive patterns.

• Learning theories emphasize change and the impact of situations, and they can take into account biological variables and/or cognitive learning.

• Stage theories, including Kohlberg's approach to moral development and Levinson's model of the life cycle, emphasize the different developments of particular ages of life.

• Ego development theories, including Loevinger's model of ego development and Erikson's psychosocial theory, describe increased adaptive capacities at various stages through the life span.

• During infancy, secure attachment to the parent becomes the basis for later social relationships.

• During childhood, parental behavior, as well as relationships with siblings and peers, contributes to ego development.

• During adolescence, the major developmental task is achieving a sense of identity through exploring career and other options.

• During adulthood, intimacy and generativity develop.

• In old age, a sense of ego integrity reflects the belief that one has led a meaningful life.

• Throughout the life span, many influences interact in complex ways, which makes outcomes difficult to predict but also provides the hope of intervention.

GLOSSARY

age effects developmental changes caused by the increasing age of individuals

attachment the bond that the infant develops with his or her caretaker

cohort a group of people who experience the same events when they are the same age (for example, who are born in the same year)

cross-sectional research designs research designs that study people at one point in time, comparing people of different ages

ego development stage theories theories that describe the development of adaptive capacities over the various periods of life

identity adolescent development in which a sense of individuality is attained, with a good fit between the individual's sense of self and the self that is recognized by significant others

identity achieved the successful attainment of adolescent identity

identity foreclosed premature solution to the task of attaining an identity

identity diffusion uncertainty about identity without active effort to explore options

longitudinal research designs research designs that study the same individuals over a long span of time

moratorium a period of exploration of identity options

period effect the effect of a time in history that influences subjects at the time of data collection

psychosocial stages Erikson's term for the periods of life, which emphasizes that psychological development occurs in a social context

Q-sort a method for analyzing data by having raters evaluate diverse materials describing a person, using a common set of descriptions that are presented as a deck of cards to be sorted

secure attachment the healthy bond of the infant for the caretaker that provides security for exploration and further development

strange-situation procedure a laboratory method for assessing infant attachment

THOUGHT QUESTIONS

1. Do you think that a cross-sectional study that compares today's adolescents with today's middle-aged adults would be helpful in predicting what those adolescents will be like when they are middle-aged? Why or why not?

2. What, in your opinion, are the most important factors that influenced your birth cohort, in contrast with other cohorts?

3. If you were to devise a Q-sort deck of cards to describe personality, what statements would you put on the cards?

4. Do you believe that people are mostly stable throughout life or that they change? Which characteristics do you think are most likely to be stable, and which to change?

5. What influences besides education would you suggest to help change the life course of children who seem headed down the wrong path?

6. Levinson's model of the life cycle suggests that adults spend as much time in transition as in stable structures. Based on your observations, do you agree?

7. Ego development approaches emphasize control of impulses as an important ego skill. How would lack of impulse control be observed in children? In adolescents? In adults?

8. Review Erikson's eight stages of ego development (see Table 10.4). Give an example of behavior at each stage that illustrates the ego development of that part of the life span.

9. Attachment of the infant to the caretaker is suggested as important for later interpersonal relationships. Do you think it matters whether the primary caretaker is the child's mother? Would a father have a different effect? What about someone who is not a member of the family?

10. How does society help or hinder adolescents as they strive to attain a sense of identity? Are there any groups of adolescents that you think would have particular difficulty with this stage of life in current society?

Biological Aspects of Personality

PERSONALITY IS NOT SIMPLY a mental phenomenon. Since at least 400 B.C., many thinkers have suggested that personality and the body are interrelated (Merenda, 1987). The Greek physician Hippocrates claimed that each person's temperament reflects the balance of the body's fluids—a large amount of blood makes a person optimistic, an excess of black bile produces depression, and so on (Table 11.1). More than 50 years ago, William Sheldon (1942) suggested that body build was associated with personality, observing that more muscular people (mesomorphs) tend to be more adventurous, thinner people (ectomorphs) more sensitive and intellectual, and heavier people (endomorphs) more sociable. Sheldon's theory today seems oversimplified because it does not specify the mechanisms of the association, although his proposal has some empirical support (Lester, 1986).

There is now ample evidence to support the general claim that personality is related to physical factors, although the particular mechanisms claimed by Hippocrates seem quaint and Sheldon's theory oversimplified. Today we would find an explanation in terms of neurotransmitters more

TABLE **11.1** **The Relationship between Body Fluids and Personality Temperaments, According to Hippocrates**

Body fluid ("humor")	Temperament
Blood	Sanguine (optimistic, hopeful)
Black bile	Melancholic (sad, depressed)
Yellow bile	Choleric (irascible, angry)
Phlegm	Phlegmatic (apathetic, unemotional)

Adapted from Merenda, 1987.

acceptable than one based on bodily fluids. Modern categories of biologically based personality types have replaced the older models, and sometimes researchers have explored the relationships between the ancient and the new models (Howarth & Zumbo, 1989). Although researchers have discovered some of the physical bases of personality, there is still much to be learned about the details of the mind-body relationship as it influences personality.

Some Intriguing Relationships between Personality and Biology

Mapping the relationship between the psychological experiences of personality and the physiological happenings in the body is a daunting enterprise and will not be completed soon. Still, we have come a long way in the more than 2000 years since Hippocrates proposed his humoral theory. We know that some of the experiences that have been described as psychologically caused are related to particular brain sites or particular hormones. It is reasonable to speculate that variations in brain and hormonal functioning contribute to personality differences.

The brain, the organ that we credit with directing personality, is a complicated system of anatomical circuits and biochemical neurosynaptic transmitters. Various circuits and neurotransmitters have specific functions, and depending upon how the various systems are balanced, the result may correspond to many personality variations, such as impulsiveness, easy arousal, emotionality, and so on (Derryberry & Tucker, 1991; Lester, 1989). From what we know about the functioning of various parts of the brain, it is tempting to speculate that neural differences predispose people to develop personality differences, just as a person with a genetically muscular body is more likely to develop athletic abilities. Unusual functioning of the temporal lobe of the brain has been associated with a variety of experiences that are more frequent among introverted intuitive types as described by Carl Jung: paranormal phenomena, mystical experiences, and dreams (Dewhurst & Beard, 1970; Epstein, 1982; Geschwind, 1979; Huot, Makarec & Persinger, 1989; Persinger, 1983, 1984; Persinger & Valliant, 1985). Could it be that biological variations in the temporal lobe predispose people to these experiences? Does a dominant right cerebral hemisphere, which is more involved in nonverbal functioning and dreaming than the left hemisphere, predispose some people to have more access to the unconscious (Martindale, Covello & West, 1986; Miller, 1989)? Could more effective functioning of the frontal lobe, widely described as responsible for higher mental functions, be the basis for the Freudian ego and the experience of self (Epstein, 1987; Frick, 1982)?

Or are these parts of the brain essentially similar in everyone, waiting for solely psychological factors to activate them? Is the body's involvement in personality more like the difference between a sports car and a station wagon or like two identical cars with much different drivers? Although evidence of abnormalities in the frontal lobe and other areas of the brain is well documented in the serious psychotic disorder schizophrenia, we cannot be certain that brain differences cause variations in normal personality. Any such differences in the brain may be results, rather than causes, of personality differences. Brain functioning has also been linked to some of the attributes we will consider more fully later in this chapter, including emotion and temperament.

Important as the brain is, it is not the entire story. Personality and behavior have also been associated with hormones, the messengers of the endocrine system. Who will be violent? Charming? Stressed? Part of the answer lies in the endocrine system, although there is no simple relationship between hormones and personality. Diminished activity of the neurotransmitter serotonin contributes to impulsive violence, and drug treatment with lithium to enhance serotonin functioning decreases aggressive behavior among prisoners. This biochemical mechanism may underlie the inheritance of impulsiveness, aggression, and suicidal behavior, although learning also plays an important role (Coccaro, 1995; Coccaro, Bergeman & McClearn, 1993). The hormone testosterone has been implicated in violent behavior and other characteristics. In one study, prison inmates who had been convicted of violent crimes had higher levels of testosterone, on average, than those whose crimes were not violent (Dabbs et al., 1987). Among undergraduate men, levels of testosterone were correlated with self-report measures of personality. Those with higher

388 Chapter 11 Biological Aspects of Personality

testosterone described themselves on the Adjective Check List as high on a factor that the researchers labeled "Handsome Devil," including such adjectives as sociable, friendly, handsome, sexy, and charming (Dabbs & Ruback, 1988). Other studies show that endocrine activity is influenced by the stress of an exam (Rauste-von Wright & Frankenhaeuser, 1989) and by the perception of having self-efficacy that is adequate to confront a feared object (Bandura et al., 1985).

As described in Chapter 8, personality is linked with such diseases as coronary heart disease, cancer, and immune disorders, although it is not entirely clear what mechanisms are involved. In part, these associations may reflect the impact of lifestyle on exposure to risk factors, such as lack of exercise or a poor diet. In part, they may signal that some underlying inherited physiological pattern has effects on both the body and personality.

Biology Influences Personality Traits

If biological variations such as different levels of neurotransmitters or different brain anatomy cause personality differences, they would be expected to have broad effects on personality. The details of their influence can be understood in terms of learning; an impulsive child still is influenced by learning, which may determine whether he becomes an aggressive prisoner or a class clown (Nelson, 1992). The broad features, though, should be observable across the spectrum of ways that the biological influence can be manifested. It seems logical to expect that such features would correspond to the broad traits described by factor models of personality (Chapter 3).

Researchers have investigated Raymond Cattell's 16 source traits of personality to determine the extent to which heredity influences these factors. Does genetics play a role in our personalities? Some factors are greatly influenced by heredity, according to Cattell (1960, 1973), whereas other factors have little or no hereditary influence. He based this conclusion on studies of twins and other genetic relatives, using statistical procedures to estimate how much of the total variance of a trait in a population could be explained by shared heredity (Table 11.2). It seems reasonable to conclude that biology influences some, but not all, of these personality traits. Although these findings are enlightening, they do not tell us as much about biological influence as we might wish to understand. The studies do not clearly isolate hereditary effects from other influences, and the biological mechanisms are not described. Such findings encourage us, however, to pursue the biological approach.

Let us turn our attention to those factor models that have been explicitly tied to biological underpinnings.

TABLE 11.2   Heritability of Cattell's Sixteen Personality Factors

Factor	Description of the factor	Heritability
A	Cool–warm	.50
B	Concrete thinking–abstract thinking	.75
C	Affected by feelings–emotionally stable	.40
E	Submissive–dominant	.25
F	Serious, restrained–enthusiastic	.60
G	Self-indulgent–conscientious	.40
H	Shy–uninhibited	.40
I	Realistic–sensitive	.50
L	Trusting–suspicious	.50
M	Practical–imaginative	.40
N	Open–shrewd	.25
O	Self-assured–apprehensive	.25
Q_1	Conservative–liberal	.10
Q_2	Group-oriented–self-sufficient	.25
Q_3	Undisciplined–controlled	.40
Q_4	Relaxed–tense	.10

Adapted from Cattell, 1973.

Eysenck's Model

Hans Eysenck (1990a, 1990b) has proposed that there are three major factors of personality: Neuroticism versus Emotional Stability (N), Extraversion versus Introversion (E), and Psychoticism versus Super-Ego Control (P). These dimensions, he argues, are biological. They exist in animals (rhesus monkeys and even rats) and are found in people in many countries with greatly diverse cultures, which supports the idea that they are caused by a fundamental biological variability. These dimensions are influenced by heredity, and people tend to be stable on these traits throughout their lives. This biological foundation, of course, does not preclude people's being shaped in particular directions by experience.

Extraversion is related to many physiological measures that indicate a biological basis for the trait. By definition, extraverts are more sociable than introverts. Hans Eysenck proposes that introverts and extraverts

Some people are more sensitive than others to the sedating effects of alcohol. Research shows that introverts don't become drowsy as quickly as extraverts do when they are drinking.

Intro vrs contrc
differin
(actical
orcusal

differ in cortical arousal. Introverts generally have higher levels of cortical arousal than extraverts, as evidenced by such physiological observations as larger pupils in the eyes, greater electrodermal skin conductance, and EEG data (Eysenck, 1990a; Matthews & Amelang, 1993; Stelmack, 1990). As a consequence, they can tolerate higher doses of sedatives before becoming drowsy. Extraverts are less arousable than introverts. Extraversion corresponds to a "strong nervous system" and introversion to a "weak nervous system" in the sense that a strong nervous system can endure high levels of stimulation without becoming overstimulated, while a weak nervous system is more readily overloaded and so inhibits neural activity. Stimulants such as caffeine and nicotine affect introverts and extraverts differently (Stelmack, 1990): tobacco smokers tend to score high on Extraversion (Patton, Barnes & Murray, 1993).

Neuroticism corresponds to high emotional arousal and reactivity. People who are high on this dimension readily develop conditioned emotional reactions as a result of learning (Eysenck, 1979). For instance, someone high on Neuroticism whose plane encounters turbulence might be likely to develop a fear of flying. Such learning can produce various symptoms, including phobias and increased blood pressure in response to stimuli. Eysenck (1990a) remarks that Type A behavior, which we have seen (in Chapter 8) is a risk factor for cardiovascular disease, is related to Neuroticism.

Psychoticism is the third major dimension of personality in Eysenck's model, and by his own account is less well understood than the other two.

The term *psychoticism* has been criticized because it gives the misleading impression that people high in this trait are psychotic. Perhaps *impulsiveness* would be a better term. Eysenck (1990a) suggests that in people high in Psychoticism, whether they are actually psychotic or, much more often, not, the emotions are less adequately controlled by the central nervous system than they are in other people. These differences can lead to more aggressive and/or impulsive behavior. Psychoticism scores of males are generally higher than those of females, which is consistent with the fact that men are more likely to engage in aggressive and impulsive behaviors.

Creative artists and professors who are productive researchers tend to score high on Psychoticism (Eysenck, 1993). What do creative people and schizophrenics have in common, besides a common hereditary element? Cognitively, both groups tend to make associations that seem remote to others. Salvador Dali, the surrealist painter, imagined birth to be like the cracking of an egg. Such "overinclusiveness" can lead to adaptive and original ideas, or it can simply seem mad. Whatever the neurological mechanisms behind this cognitive overinclusiveness, we cannot know their effect on the individual in the absence of other information.

Gray's Model

Progress in neurology since Eysenck's formulation has prompted revisions of his model in an attempt to portray the relationship between neurological functioning and personality more accurately (for example, Rammsayer, Netter & Vogel, 1993). One influential modification of Eysenck's theory of Extraversion-Introversion has been proposed by J. A. Gray (1987). In place of a biological mechanism of cortical arousal, Gray proposes a Behavioral Activation System (BAS) or "reward mechanism" and a Behavioral Inhibition System (BIS) or "punishment mechanism." The BAS emphasizes response to reward and the BIS to punishment. According to Gray's theory, some people are more responsive to the BAS; they are more readily conditioned by reward in learning experiments, and they become extraverts. Others are more responsive to the BIS; they are more readily conditioned by punishment, and they become introverts. Consider the mixture of rewards and punishments that occurs when you interact with others at a party. The rewards, such as people's friendly conversation, would have more impact on BAS-dominant extraverts, and the punishments, such as other people's rebuffs, would have more impact on the BIS-dominant introverts. Gray suggests that there are neurological mechanisms underlying these two systems, and he describes the specific brain structures and neurosynaptic transmitters that he believes to be involved (Gray, 1987). He suggests that Eysenck's Extraversion-Introversion reflects the balance of the BAS and BIS systems, with extraverts being more sensitive to reward and introverts to punishment. If these sensitivities are very great, then the individual is classified as neurotic, either anxious (if the BIS system predominates, as it does in introverts) or impulsive (if the BAS system predominates, as it does in extraverts).

The different responsiveness of introverts and extraverts to reward and punishment can be monitored by an EEG while subjects play a game in which they win or lose money. The researchers interpret one particular EEG measure as an index of the emotional significance of a stimulus. For instance, the happy event of winning and the sad event of losing a game are revealed in the EEG pattern. Extraverts responded more strongly to winning these games and introverts to losing (Bartussek et al., 1993).

Arousal in response to pleasant and unpleasant stimuli can influence subsequent experiences that happen before the arousal fades completely. The glow of getting a much-wanted invitation makes all that happens afterward a little happier. This **excitation transfer** may lead people to mislabel experiences, because people subjectively believe that they return to "normal" much more quickly than physiological measures show they do. Arousal produced by physical exercise, for example, can continue through subsequent experimental situations and, by excitation transfer, increase aggressive behavior (Zillman & Bryant, 1974). Physically fit individuals, who recover more quickly from exercise, are less subject to such excitation transfer. Furthermore, according to Scott Bunce and his colleagues, people are less likely to experience excitation transfer for emotions that are more familiar to them. This suggests that extraverts would be less likely to transfer pleasant emotions to subsequent situations and that neurotics (introverted neurotics, in Gray's typology) would be less likely to transfer unpleasant emotions. The researchers tested female college students, who rode a stationary bicycle to achieve physiological arousal and then sat quietly until they indicated that they had returned to normal levels of arousal. At this point, they rated various slides on a scale from "extremely pleasant" to "extremely unpleasant." Compared to their own ratings on another occasion, when they were not recovering from exercise, extraverts rated negative slides, such as those depicting a terrorist bombing, as more negative. Neurotics rated positive slides, such as smiling children, as more positive. Thus, the excitation transfer from exercise had a greater effect for the less familiar emotions (Bunce, Larsen & Cruz, 1993). Based on this idea, postexercise periods would be especially effective times for bringing good news to an otherwise anxious person (neurotic) or for getting an extravert to realize how unpleasant some situation is.

Cloninger's Biosocial Theory

C. Robert Cloninger (1986, 1987b) has proposed three dimensions of personality that are based on inherited biological differences. The dimension of *novelty seeking* (NS) is expressed in exploratory activity. People high in this dimension experience excitement in response to novel stimuli. The dimension of *harm avoidance* (HA) is expressed by avoiding punishing and nonrewarding situations and also by avoiding novelty (which can potentially bring punishment). People high in this dimension respond greatly to aversive stimuli. Finally, the dimension of *reward dependence* (RD) is expressed by continuing to engage in rewarded behavior. People high in this dimension respond more intensely to reward. Each of these three dimensions corresponds to a specific neurotransmitter: dopamine (in low levels, for novelty seeking), serotonin (in high levels, for harm avoidance), and norepinephrine (in low levels, for reward dependence).

These three personality dimensions can be measured by the Tridimensional Personality Questionnaire (Cloninger, Przybeck & Svrakic, 1991). In cross-cultural research, the three dimensions of the Tridimensional Personality Questionnaire have been confirmed in Yugoslavia (Svrakic, Przybeck & Cloninger, 1991). The model applies to the population at large and to people with specific psychiatric diagnoses, such as anxiety disorders. For understanding alcoholism, Cloninger proposes that there are two types of alcoholics (Cloninger, 1987a). Type I alcoholics are low in novelty seeking but high in harm avoidance and reward dependence. These people, including many female alcoholics, usually do not become alcoholics unless there are environmental pressures. Type II alcoholics have the opposite pattern: high novelty seeking and low harm avoidance and reward dependence. These alcoholics, usually men, typically begin drinking earlier and get into trouble because of impulsive and aggressive behavior. Longitudinal investigation over a 17-year period, in which personality was assessed by interviewing the 10- or 11-year-old child's school teacher, showed that boys with high novelty seeking and low harm avoidance were 20 times more likely to abuse alcohol by age 27 (Cloninger, Sigvardsson & Bohman, 1988). The drugs that psychiatrists use to treat various disorders have biological effects that fit the tridimensional model. These proposals, however, have been challenged by other researchers, whose data do not fit the model (Nixon & Parsons, 1990; Peterson et al., 1991). Further research may explain such discrepancies.

Personality builds on each person's biological base, and individuals have different beginning points because of their different heredity. Personality is more than simply physical, however, and social and learning influences are also important in this unified biosocial model (Cloninger, 1986).

Heredity and Personality

How much of the variability in personality from one individual to another is caused by heredity? The field of **behavioral genetics** studies the impact of heredity on personality and other behavior. Evidence has been accumulating that heredity plays a large role in determining personality. According to Sandra Scarr (1987), in a review of the evidence, behavior geneticists have agreed that 25 to 40 percent of the total variance stems from heredity. This is an astonishing finding, considering that traditional personality theories have largely ignored heredity and have instead emphasized experience, especially how a child is treated in the family, as the primary determinant of personality. Recent genetic evidence, according to Hans Eysenck, "necessitates a revolution in current thinking about the development of personality" (1990b, p. 251).

The term **heritability** refers to the extent to which genetic inheritance is responsible for the variability of a trait in a population. For example, how much of the variability in scores on an intelligence test given to students in a school is caused by their inherited differences in intelligence? Notice that heritability does not refer simply to whether genetics influences a characteristic. If genetics determines a characteristic but influences everyone similarly (for example, humans have two eyes) and does not influence individual differences, then the trait is not heritable. Likewise, heritability does not refer to only one individual; researchers do not attempt to describe the extent to which a trait in one person is either inherited or caused by environment, although in everyday discussions we can do so. For example, we can describe one person as unintelligent because of the misfortune of having unintelligent parents who passed on those genes, while another person may be unintelligent because of brain damage caused by an automobile accident. In such everyday description, we are not systematic in our analysis, because we are looking for an explanation that may use different sources of information for each case. The data available for systematic analysis, however, permit researchers to describe the heritability of a trait only within a population. They do so by examining the correlations on a trait between twins and among other close relatives (see the Research Strategies box).

Many twin studies have been conducted to estimate the extent to which personality is influenced by heredity. John Loehlin (1992) reports the heritability of the Big Five personality traits; that is, the proportion of variability that can be accounted for by heredity. Genetics accounted for approximately 28 to 46 percent of the variability of these traits using one model for estimating heritability (Table 11.3). Auke Tellegen and his collaborators report heritabilities of .39 to .58 for the Multidimensional Personality Questionnaire (MPQ) (Tellegen et al., 1988). Genetic variation accounts for about 50 percent of the variance of scores on the California Psychological Inventory (CPI), an often-used personality test, based on studies of identical twins reared together and apart (Bouchard & McGue, 1990). For intelligence, heritability is estimated at about 50 to 70 percent, with the heritability increasing with the age of the sample (Bouchard et al., 1990). The similar heritabilities of self-report measures such as these may occur because all of them reflect the same major underlying dimensions of personality (Tellegen et al., 1988). Diagnosable personality disorders, too, are influenced by heredity (Nigg & Goldsmith, 1994).

TABLE **11.3** **Heritabilities of the Big Five Personality Factors**

Personality factor	Heritability
Extraversion	.36
Agreeableness	.28
Conscientiousness	.28
Neuroticism	.31
Openness	.46

Adapted from Loehlin, 1992, p. 67.

For some personality traits, it is not difficult to understand why heredity would play an important role in their development. Consider the trait of neuroticism that appears in many models of personality. This trait involves excessive emotional reactions, and genes can influence the readiness of an individual to respond with a surge of emotional reaction caused by sympathetic nervous system activity. For other personality traits, though, it is more surprising that heredity plays such an important role. Consider altruism and aggression. Given the care with which parents teach children to share, or not to hit, it is surprising that these traits have heritabilities of about .50 but no environmental influence (in the usual sense of shared family environments) (Rushton et al., 1986). Raymond Cattell and his colleagues report that heredity influences three personality traits that permit control of impulses: ego strength, superego strength, and the self sentiment (Cattell, Rao & Schuerger, 1985; Cattell, Schuerger & Klein, 1982). Traditional personality theories describe these characteristics as learned, not inherited. Even many attitudes show the impact of heritability, including attitudes toward the death penalty, divorce, euthanasia, religion, and many others. Although, presumably, there are not specific genes for such attitudes, a variety of biological mechanisms could ultimately affect these attitudes. These may include the senses, hormones, intelligence, temperament, and emotionality (Tesser, 1993). Only by describing such mechanisms and the traits we are trying to explain more precisely can we make sense of some genetic effects, such as a significant heritability for time spent watching television (Prescott, Johnson & McArdle, 1991) or for the risk that marriage will end in divorce (McGue & Lykken, 1992). Genetic effects reach deeply into our social behavior.

RESEARCH STRATEGIES ●--

How Do We Know What Is Inherited?

The folk saying, "The apple does not fall far from the tree," expresses the view that children tend to be like their parents. The similarity of parents and children supports the idea that personality is inherited—or does it? In the usual family, children not only inherit their parents' genes but also grow up in an environment that is largely defined in terms of parental behavior. If Johnny is aggressive like his father, does this mean that his genetic predisposition is the cause? Couldn't it also be that growing up in a household with an aggressive parent taught him to be a bully?

The key to research in this area is to untangle genetic and environmental effects. If we can compare two groups that share heredity but not environment, or environment but not heredity, we can estimate these effects. Adoption studies offer useful information. Children who are adopted in infancy by parents who are not biologically related to them will be similar to their adoptive parents because of environment, not heredity. They will be similar to their biological parents because of heredity, not environment. (We are making some methodological assumptions in this research. We assume, for example, that the adoptive parents are not biologically related to the child or to the child's parents; adoption by grandparents would confuse the analysis. Further-more, we assume that the environment in which the child is raised is not similar to the one their biological parents would have provided, except by chance.)

It is difficult, however, to get sufficient information from enough adoptees and their biological and adoptive parents to know all we would wish to know about heredity. In some countries, the required information is kept secret by law. Another strategy, one that has many advantages, is to study twins. Twins provide a "natural experiment" in the effects of genetics, and they are often motivated to participate in research because of curiosity and the perception that they are special. Researchers compare two kinds of twins. Identical twins, or more formally *monozygotic twins* (MZ), develop from the same egg and sperm and share all of the same genetic material. This means that they must be both male or both female. *Dizygotic twins* (DZ), on the other hand, develop from different eggs and sperm, although they share the womb at the same time. (We might call the "wombmates," although most people would call them fraternal twins.) Dizygotic twins may be the same sex or one may be female and the other male. They often look different, as different as any two siblings.

A variety of mathematical models are used to estimate heritability from twin data. The simplest model compares monozygotic twins, who have all identical genes, with dizygotic twins, who share half their genes, on the average, just as nontwin siblings do. Then correlation coefficients are computed to see how similar MZ twins are on a trait and how similar DZ twins are. If heredity matters at all, both sets of twins will tend to be more similar than unrelated people chosen at random. (The correlation coefficients, therefore, will be greater than zero.) In addition, the MZ twins will be more similar than the DZ twins. The extent of this difference between MZ and DZ twins corresponds to 50 percent of the effect of heredity (because DZ twins share 50 percent of their genes and MZ twins 100 percent). In addition, environmental effects contribute to the trait. The environment that the twins share, the *common environment*, influences both of them equally. It corresponds to the general climate in the family, including parents' style of child rearing. In addition, it is possible that there are effects of their *unshared environment*; for example, if one twin takes music lessons and the other plays sports, or if one spends summers at camp and the other visits relatives. Similarities between twins come from shared genetics and their common environment. Differences come from their different genetics (only if they are not identical twins), from their unshared environment, and from such random factors as errors in measuring the trait (see the figure on the next page).

This model is straightforward, and it is based on several assumptions, including the assumption that the environment influences each twin equally and that the trait being measured shows no correlation in the fathers and mothers of the twins. Such assumptions seem reasonable if not certain; researchers have examined these assumptions in analyzing the heritability of various traits, and they have developed alternative models based on different assumptions where that seemed appropriate (Loehlin, 1992).

Studies of the impact of heredity on personality do not need to be limited to studies of twins. Other relatives, too, share genes: parents and children, siblings, cousins, and so on. Mathematical analysis of the similarity of all such relatives can be made. Raymond Cattell (1960) developed one influential model for the analysis of all relatives, the Multiple Abstract Variance Analysis (MAVA). Other methods have been developed since then. Each model must make assumptions about how much genetic sharing there is between pairs (a simple assumption) and how much environmental sharing there is (a much more difficult assumption). It is more difficult to measure environmental sharing because of uncertainty about what "environment" is. Does it mean being in the same home? Or does it require that people within the family treat the two individuals in the same way? Some aspects of environment,

(continued)

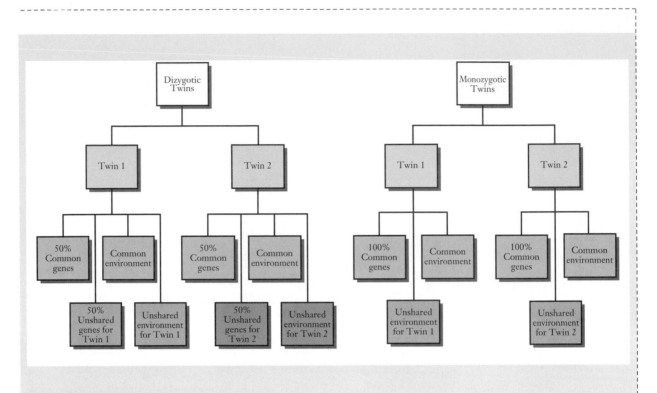

Monozygotic and dizygotic twins are similar because of the effects of shared and unshared genes and environments.

such as being treated differently because a child looks like a favorite uncle, elude mathematical models because they are not measured systematically.

Although twin studies seem convincing, they are not consistent with studies of other family relationships, which generally give lower estimates of heritability (Eysenck, 1990b). Robert Plomin and his colleagues (Plomin et al., 1991), for example, report that adoption studies of non-twin siblings show much lower effects of heredity on temperament in infancy and childhood than do twin studies. Such findings call into question the methods that are used to estimate the effects of heredity. One weakness is that parents' ratings of their children may be biased; parents may overestimate the similarity of identical twins and emphasize differences among fraternal twins and other siblings. Or the genes may have combined effects that do not fit the additive model that is typically used in the mathematical equations. Other models are available, and they are being explored by behavioral geneticists.

Misconceptions about Heredity

Heredity is easily misunderstood. Although it is a powerful force in personality, to be discussed accurately it needs to be considered in the context of the environment and other factors. We are all products of the interrelationships between genetics and the environment. Consider the following misconceptions.

Myth: Heredity means that a person will not change. In fact, people do change. Sometimes the effects of heredity change with age. In the case of intelligence, heredity exerts a stronger effect as children get older (Loehlin, 1992). In other cases, the impact of heredity may be reduced as environmental influences outweigh it.

Myth: It is a waste of effort to try to influence a trait that has a strong hereditary component. In fact, the impact of heredity may vary from one environment to another. Researchers can only describe the relative contribution of heredity in the environments that have been studied. If other environments, perhaps some that have not yet been devised, are considered instead, the inherited trait may no longer influence behavior. In the case of fruit flies (the subjects of much genetic research), some traits are temperature-sensitive; they may produce paralysis at some temperatures but have no observable effect at others. Some human personality traits may be like that: ineffectual in some environments. As we look for the environments that will eradicate the effects of traits deemed undesirable, we should consider that these environments may not influence people who do not have the inherited predisposition in the same way as they will influence those who do; thus, we need to study various environments in the population whose traits we wish to influence.

Myth: If the heritability of a trait is high, it shows that society has had little influence on the trait. Surprisingly, the opposite is true. The more pressure society exerts on everyone regarding a specific trait, the less environmental variability there is (because the same environmental effect of high pressure occurs for everyone), and the higher the heritability of the trait will be in that culture. For example, because U.S. culture provides opportunities for virtually all boys to play baseball, the variability in baseball performance is due primarily to heredity rather than environment (Bouchard et al., 1990). In contrast, we would expect soccer performance in the United States to be influenced more by environmental effects. Of course, the opposite would be true in cultures that encourage soccer rather than baseball, which illustrates that a researcher's estimate of the heritability of a trait does not describe a human universal, but is very much affected by the variations in environment (and heredity) within the population studied.

Myth: If a trait is inherited, it will have similar effects in the various people who inherit it. To see why this statement is wrong, we need to consider the difference between the gene that is inherited and the way the gene is manifested in an individual, in combination with other genes and with environmental effects. Researchers have established that the severe psychotic disorder schizophrenia is partly genetic (Eysenck, 1993). Offspring of schizophrenics have an increased probability of themselves becoming schizophrenic. However, they also have an increased probability of becoming creative, if they are not schizophrenic. Whatever the genetic contribution is to schizophrenia, it also contributes to creativity. The creative physicist Albert Einstein had a schizophrenic child, to give one famous example. There is no one-to-one relationship between what is inherited and the form in which this characteristic is displayed.

   Myth: If a trait is inherited, it is responsible for differences that are observed between men and women and among various racial groups. This myth is wrong because it ignores the fact that the sexes and races experience different environmental influences that make it impossible to know whether differences are caused by heredity or environment.

The Role of Environment

What about environment? The heredity studies that we have been considering also permit an estimation of the effect of environment by examining how much more alike twins (or other siblings) are when they grow up in the same family than when they are raised in different adoptive families. The shared family environment influences some areas more than others. Relatively strong influences are found for conservatism and religiosity (Loehlin, 1987). Family environment also influences whether siblings develop common interests, such as an interest in music (Hoffman, 1991). Other personality characteristics, however, show the opposite tendency: that is, siblings who grow up together tend to be more different from one another than those who do not share an environment. Dependency is one such characteristic; a variety of factors, including birth order and illness, work to make one sibling the dependent one and to prevent the expression of dependency in the others (Hoffman, 1991).

   Often, when we ask how much heredity contributes to personality, we are thinking that heredity and environment (or experience) are two opposing determinants of personality. It's easy to think of contributions in either-or terms, but it is not accurate. The environment of a child is not independent of the child's genetics, even when we consider children who are raised by adoptive parents not genetically related to them. As a child develops, under the influence of heredity, the child's characteristics can elicit certain reactions from the environment, particularly from the parents. This can help to explain why studies of twins show that identical twins who are raised together in the same family are not any more alike than identical twins who are raised apart (Bouchard et al., 1990; Eysenck, 1990b; Plomin et al., 1988). The same can be said of fraternal twins and other biological relatives (Bouchard & McGue, 1990; Tellegen et al.,

1988). The contribution of the child-rearing environment to many dimensions of adult personality is low, perhaps as low as 1 to 9 percent of the variance in adult personality (Bouchard & McGue, 1990). Most of us probably think our parents had more effect on us than that!

There could be methodological problems, however, that lead to an underestimation of environmental effects. Characteristics that are inherited may not show high heritabilities by usual research methods when the observable behaviors depend upon both genetics and environmental conditions (Crawford & Anderson, 1989). Environment is, after all, more difficult to quantify than genetic relationship. Is it simply being raised in the same household? Does it also include how parents and other family members treat a child? If so, what behaviors from these family members are important, and how shall we measure them? Researchers cannot estimate the impact of environment unless they can measure it, and for the most part they have settled for simply identifying the household in which children grow up, reasoning that if they grow up in the same household, whatever is an important environmental effect (such as parents' style of raising children) will be shared by all children in the family. If parents don't treat different children in the household alike, this assumption about the environment is wrong and means that the measure of the environment is inadequate. To the extent that researchers have not found good measures of the influential aspects of environment, their analyses will underestimate the impact of the environment on development. Many psychologists have suspected that it is not the shared environment in the family that is most influential, but the environmental effects that vary from one child to another, and such effects are not included in the usual estimates of shared family environmental effects.

Another problem is that the usual statistical analyses estimate environmental effects by looking at similarity between parents and children (or other family members) after statistically removing the effects of shared heredity. Lois Hoffman (1991) criticizes this method. She argues: "Environmental influences do not produce clones of the parent. To explain dependency in a child, one would not expect to find a dependent parent but rather an overprotective one. Anxiety might develop from having an anxious parent, but it might also result because the parent creates a frightening world" (p. 189). So, environments may really have the powerful effects that most personality theories suggest, and the lower environmental estimates that researchers report may result from inadequate empirical testing of this idea, based on inadequate measures of the environment and erroneous hypotheses about the specific traits affected by the environment.

Sandra Scarr (1987) notes that heredity and environment can combine in various ways. Sometimes heredity influences people to select or pay attention to certain kinds of environments. In effect, people are selectively attracted to environments that are most suitable for their inherited personality predispositions (Scarr & McCartney, 1983). The effects of these selected environments can then accentuate the effects of heredity, as when an introverted person chooses to spend time alone and thus becomes even more introverted. For researchers, the effect of this selection is to increase the effects of heredity among older samples, where this amplification has occurred to a greater extent (McCall, 1990). Thus, as we become older, we become more and more our genetic selves.

Environmental effects on personality may vary for two people who seem to be sharing the same environment. The most striking instance occurs when identical twins are raised together. Surprisingly, such twins, though highly similar, have personalities that are *less* similar than identical twins who are reared apart! How can this be? Apparently, being reared together influences twins so that they become different, one more dominant and one more submissive, for example. Perhaps their parents and family encourage these differences (McCartney, Harris & Bernieri, 1990; Scarr, 1987). Still, our common sense expectation that parents treat twins in much the same way holds true, when compared with how they treat two nontwin children. Children's descriptions indicate that parents treat twins more similarly than they treat other siblings; fraternal twins fall between these two groups (Baker & Daniels, 1990). Once they grow up and leave the family, however, twins are exposed to different environments, and they become less similar to each other than they were when they were younger (McCartney, Harris & Bernieri, 1990).

All siblings, not only twins, are influenced by family tendencies to treat children differently (Hoffman, 1991). One obvious influence is the different expectations for the firstborn and for youngest children. Parents are younger and generally more uncertain and anxious about parenting when raising their first child, and these uncertainties influence their treatment of the child. Additionally, they may be more restrictive and demand more responsible behavior with the oldest child. Other factors also contribute to different treatment of children within the same family. Parental health, finances, changes in work responsibilities, divorce, and so on, can affect parent-child interactions differently for children depending upon when they occur in the child's development. Children's desires to be seen as individuals, distinct from their siblings, can accentuate this different treatment.

Temperament

Temperament in Infancy

Anyone who has spent time with several infants can attest that, even before there has been time for them to be influenced by learning, there are considerable differences among them. One fusses and cries. Another is quieter, rarely expressing discontent. Such apparently innate differences in the style

TABLE **11.4** **Examples of Behaviors Observed in Assessing Infant Temperament**

Smiling (at the mother, at other people, at no one in particular)

Vocalizing

Fussing and/or crying

Frowning

Kicking

Reaching for objects

Putting objects in the mouth

Banging an object on the floor

Adapted from Bornstein, Gaughran & Segui, 1991

of a person's behavior are called **temperament.** Temperament is important to personality researchers because it provides a basis upon which later personality is built. It describes the early appearance of characteristics that will endure for a lifetime. In addition, temperament influences the interactions of the child with parents and others and so shapes the learning experiences that influence personality development.

Researchers have developed a variety of theoretical models to describe temperament (Goldsmith et al., 1987). The themes of emotionality and heredity are prevalent in most of these models. Biological and hereditary influences determine temperament. Studies of twins show high heritability of temperament (Cyphers et al., 1990; Saudino & Eaton, 1991).

Researchers consider several dimensions of infant behavior when they are assessing temperament (Table 11.4). One statistical analysis suggests that two major factors can be used to describe temperament: whether the baby is easy or difficult, and whether the baby is sociable or shy (Bagley, 1991).

Temperament is evidenced in children's reactions to novel stimuli. In fact, Arnold Buss and Robert Plomin consider reactions to stimuli to be a defining feature of temperament. In a roundtable discussion of the issue, they said: "Temperament is always expressed as a response to an external stimulus, opportunity, expectation, or demand. It can be considered a dynamic factor that mediates and shapes the influence of the environment on the individual's psychological structure" (Goldsmith et al., 1987, p. 509). For researchers, this means that temperament should be measured when infants (or older children and adults) are presented with stimuli from the world around them. Theoretically, this position highlights the importance of temperament in contributing to the individual's development of adaptation skills.

Some children are readily frightened, whereas others tolerate novelty with little distress. When a toy jack-in-the-box opens, one child is overcome with fear and cries; another laughs and inspects the toy. The easily frightened children are predisposed to shyness, according to observations by Jerome Kagan and his colleagues (Kagan, Reznick & Snidman, 1988; Kagan & Snidman, 1991a). In new situations, these children experience greater arousal of anxiety. At younger ages, they cling to the mother, are quiet, and avoid the new situation if possible. In preschool and early school years, they do not talk with an experimenter as much as do less inhibited children. Physiologically, inhibited children have more reactive sympathetic nervous systems, evidenced by such measures as faster heart rate, higher blood pressure, and high levels of the neurotransmitter norepinephrine and the stress hormone cortisol. The researchers suggest that these inhibited children have a lower threshold for limbic-hypothalamic arousal than others. Individual differences in such reactions have been observed in animals, which supports the interpretation that shyness is produced by biological differences, although stressful environmental pressures also contribute to its development.

Fear and shyness are not all there is to temperament. John Bates summarizes three major dimensions to temperament. *Negative emotionality* includes the fearfulness and inhibition or shyness that we have been considering. *Positive emotionality*, in contrast, includes "enthusiasm, excitement, and happiness" (Bates, 1994, p. 4). The third dimension is *impulsiveness or sensation seeking* (Zuckerman, 1990a), the desire for stimulation that motivates people to seek thrills through dangerous sports and other adventures.

The infant's emotional activity shows considerable stability from an assessment in the first 4 days of life to a second observation at 9 months. The newborn who is irritable and difficult to soothe is likely to become an irritable 9-month-old and 24-month-old (Matheny, Riese & Wilson, 1985; Riese, 1987). In fact, temperament is remarkably stable through age 12 (Guerin & Gottfried, 1994) and beyond.

Temperament involves other components besides emotional reactivity. Douglas Derryberry and Mary Rothbart suggest that temperament also includes differences in the capacity for self-regulation, such as the ability to calm down after anger or distress. Infants, of course, cannot use the mature strategies of self-regulation that have been described in adults (see Chapter 9). They can, however, pay attention to an unpleasant stimulus or turn away from it, and individual differences in this capacity exist in infancy (Derryberry & Rothbart, 1988).

A difficult temperament influences interactions with the mother or other caretaker and thus has a tremendous potential to alter the infant's course of social development. Parents may become frustrated around fussy babies and therefore behave differently toward them than they would toward temperamentally happy babies. It seems reasonable that an infant's temperament would influence the course of attachment. Several researchers have investigated this relationship. Recall from Chapter 10 that infants' attachment to their mothers is measured by their behavior when she leaves. It is intriguing that this behavior can be predicted from a measure of brain activity. Richard Davidson and Nathan Fox (1989) measured the resting EEG activity of the frontal lobe of the brains of normal 10-month-old baby girls. Then they observed the children's reactions when their mothers left them alone, seated at a feeding table, for 60 seconds. Those infants who cried more when their mothers departed showed more EEG activity on the right side of the brain, while those who did not cry showed more activity on the left side. This finding is consistent with adult studies, described shortly, that show the right hemisphere to be associated with negative emotions. Physiological correlates of attachment have also been reported that may represent the physiological effects of distress during testing. Babies who are more distressed when their mothers leave them, based on observations in the strange-situation procedure, show higher adrenocortical activity and somewhat elevated levels of cortisol (Gunnar et al., 1990).

There is a relationship, albeit a small one, between infant distress and resistant behavior in the strange-situation procedure (Goldsmith & Alansky, 1987). It would be an exaggeration, however, to conclude that babies who are less prone to distress automatically become more securely attached than those who are more distressed. Attachment is an interactive process between caretaker and baby, and it is the match between the baby's temperament and the caretaker's behavior and personality that is critical for attachment. Infants with temperaments more prone to distress are particularly in need of more flexible and responsive caretaking if they are to become securely attached, although the specific maternal behaviors that constitute this optimal caretaking are not well defined (Mangelsdorf et al., 1990). In addition to the mother, the father and family dynamics contribute to the baby's emotionality and attachment (Belsky, Fish & Isabella, 1991).

Temperament beyond Infancy

Temperament describes the consistent styles of behavior that persist throughout life. In infancy, temperament can be observed more directly because there has been less learning to shape its expression, and this may be why those interested in the role of temperament in personality have often concentrated on infancy (Goldsmith et al., 1987). Temperament among adults is generally studied by self-report questionnaires, which in turn are correlated with the personality measures of neuroticism and extraversion (Windle, 1989b). Arnold Buss and Robert Plomin (1984) identify the three temperament dimensions of emotionality, activity level, and sociability as the most important and heritable dimensions of personality.

Although temperament influences behavior throughout life, the particular ways it is expressed change with age. Obviously, an infant has limited physical and verbal abilities, compared with a child's capacity for activity and an adult's ability to speak with a sophisticated repertoire of emotional tones. In addition, some of the early influences on infant behavior, such as painful colic resulting from the disturbances of an immature digestive system, may be so powerful that they may temporarily override the effects of temperament. As time passes, however, the effects of temperament become more apparent, and researchers find continuity in temperament across time. In one study, in fact, identical twins were rated more similar in temperament at age 15 years than they were in infancy and at age 6 years (Torgersen, 1987).

Temperament contributes to important social learning in childhood, much as it contributes to the development of attachment in infancy. Conscience is developed as parents teach children what is right and what is wrong, and this teaching is especially influential among children with a fear-prone temperament (Kochanska, 1991). Temperament is associated with teachers' ratings of academic competence in the sixth grade of school (Talwar, Schwab & Lerner, 1989).

Among college students, temperament is related to several aspects of social experience, influencing the adjustments that students made when they first entered college. Some dimensions of temperament were associated with establishing friendships more quickly: high approach tendencies, positive mood, and flexibility (Klein, 1987). Temperament contributes to mental health in late adolescence and early adulthood. Emotional stability is conducive to mental health (Windle, 1989a).

Emotions

Emotion, or "affect," is a key component of temperament (Strelau, 1987). H. Hill Goldsmith, in fact, defines infant temperament as "individual differences in the expression of primary emotions" (Goldsmith et al., 1987). Personality traits are often correlated with emotions. Positive emotions are more typical of extraverts and impulsive individuals, negative emotions of anxious and neurotic persons (Strelau, 1987; Watson & Clark, 1984). A better understanding of the role of emotions in personality can help us to understand the development of personality from its early beginnings in infancy.

Emotions serve many functions in personality. They direct motivated behavior, in general pulling us toward pleasant outcomes and pushing us away from unpleasant ones. They are an important facet of unconscious

Unlike the Vulcan Mr. Spock, humans experience a wide variety of emotions that play important roles in personality.

experience, translating only partially into the more logical language of conscious life. Conversely, although our thoughts clearly can influence our emotional experiences, as when we decide whether or not we can achieve an important goal and feel happy or not as a result of that appraisal, there are other, noncognitive bases for emotions as well. Most of the brain—more primitive brain centers, the amygdala and the hypothalamus, as well as the higher cortical areas—influences emotion (Izard, 1993). It may not be too great a stretch to suggest that emotions are the basic ground of our personality. Insight is not all there is to life, and mind is not independent of body.

Positive and Negative Emotions

The brain, as well as common sense, distinguishes between positive and negative emotions. Brain studies indicate that emotions are accompanied by asymmetrical activation of the left and right cerebral hemispheres (Tomarken, Davidson & Henriques, 1990). Happy emotions are accompanied by activation of the left anterior temporal region of the cerebral hemisphere, whereas disgust is accompanied by activation on the right frontal and anterior temporal region (Davidson et al., 1990).

David Watson and Auke Tellegen (1985) propose a simple model of emotions, one that has two factors: positive moods and negative moods. Other emotions can be fit within this two-factor structure. The two factors are not opposite but orthogonal; that is, a mood can consist of any combination of positive and negative emotion, rather than having to be one or the other. Some emotions consist of mixtures of positive and negative emotions ("astonished" and "surprised," for example). Others have low levels of both ("quiet" and "still"). Still other emotions can be described as simply consisting of positive (for example, "elated") or negative (for example, "nervous") emotions (Fig. 11.1). Evidence supporting this model comes from factor analyses of words that people use to describe emotion, from people's self-ratings of emotion, and from studies of facial expressions.

These emotions can be measured more directly by a self-report scale, the Positive and Negative Affect Schedule (PANAS). Subjects describe their moods by indicating, on a 5-point scale, how much various mood descriptions, such as "enthusiastic" or "distressed," apply to them at the moment, in the past few days, or at some particular time. Summary scores are computed to indicate overall Positive Affect and Negative Affect. As one might expect, the Negative Affect scale is higher in people who perceive themselves to be under stress and who complain about health problems. The Positive Affect scale is higher among those who report spending more time with friends (Watson, Clark & Tellegen, 1988; Watson & Pennebaker, 1989).

Anxiety

Considerable evidence indicates that people differ in their anxiety proneness and that this variation is greatly influenced by genetic inheritance. Activity of the autonomic nervous system produces symptoms of anxiety, including rapid heart beat, sweating, and feelings of nervousness. Raymond Cattell and his colleagues assert that anxiety is highly heritable (Cattell, Vaughn, et al., 1982). They do not assert, however, that people who are genetically predisposed to high levels of anxiety are doomed to this emotion. Fortunate childhood experiences in the family can "desensitize" such individuals to some extent, and the researchers suggest that educators and clinicians should attempt to learn how best to deal with anxiety-prone individuals. Under less optimal circumstances, though, people's efforts to avoid anxiety and other unpleasant emotions lead to maladaptive behavior. People who are emotionally reactive are more likely to develop anxiety disorders.

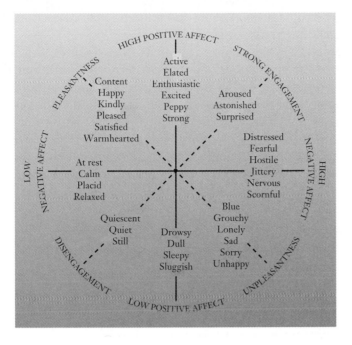

FIGURE 11.1 *A two-factor theory of affect, showing different mixtures of positive and negative emotions. (From Watson & Tellegen, 1985, p. 221.)*

Emotional reactivity can serve as the basis for desirable personality developments, too. Albert Mehrabian and his colleagues (Mehrabian, Young & Sato, 1988) report that emotional reactivity is characteristic of those who are empathic, in the sense that they respond vicariously to the emotional reactions of others. Thus, the emotionally reactive person is likely to feel saddened by others' misery and joyous at their elation.

Affect Intensity

Randy Larsen and Ed Diener have suggested that **affect intensity** is an important trait that varies from one individual to another (Larsen & Diener, 1987). Affect intensity refers to the intensity of emotions that are experienced. Some people typically have mild experiences of emotions, whereas others are more strongly affected. These researchers suggest that people who experience positive emotions such as joy intensely also experience negative emotions such as fear and depression intensely. Evidence for this conclusion comes from various sources. On a self-report measure of affect intensity, the Affect Intensity Measure (Larsen & Diener, 1987), agreement with statements describing positive emotions is correlated with agreement with statements describing negative emotions. People who say "Sad movies deeply touch me" also tend to say "When I'm happy I bubble over with energy." Similar agreement between positive and negative emotions is found when subjects report the emotions they experience on a day-by-day basis (Larsen, Diener & Emmons, 1986). Reactions of subjects to emotional movies also are correlated.

Larsen and Diener suggest that affect intensity is an important aspect of temperament in adults. It is positively correlated with four dimensions that they consider to be the fundamental dimensions of temperament in adults: activity, sociability, arousability/reactivity, and emotionality (Larsen & Diener, 1987). (The term *emotionality* is often used to refer to negative emotions only, in contrast to *affect intensity*, which refers to both positive and negative emotions.) People high in affect intensity are more likely to suffer from bodily symptoms such as headaches and neurotic symptoms such as irritability and panic. On average, women score higher than men on affect intensity.

Sensation Seeking

Although anxious individuals seem to be overly aroused and attempt, through behavior or sometimes through drugs, to reduce their arousal, there are others who seem to crave more arousal. They become **sensation seekers,** according to Marvin Zuckerman (1990a). Why do some people crave more stimulation, while others want less? Why do some people prefer vacation activities of sky diving or bungee jumping, while others prefer to read a book quietly on a beach? A theoretical idea that helps to explain this apparent contradiction is the idea of an optimal level of arousal. Too much arousal is unpleasant; it is experienced as anxiety and other negative emotions. Too little arousal is unpleasant; it is experienced as boredom. But people don't all agree about what is the happy medium. Some people's optimal level of arousal is particularly high, and so they become sensation seekers. To achieve their comparatively high optimal level of arousal, sensation seekers engage in thrilling activities, such as skiing and sky diving. They prefer such arousal and can concentrate at high arousal levels that would distract (and sometimes distress) others.

It is apparent that humans display a diversity of emotional patterns. Unlike Mr. Spock of the TV series "Star Trek," we experience emotions, but in ways that may cause us to be as puzzled with others' emotional reactions as the Vulcan is when observing humans.

Facial Displays of Emotion

Charles Darwin (1872), the famous biologist who proposed the theory of evolution, suggested that facial and behavioral expressions of emotion serve essential functions among animals. Anger (as we might label it), signaled by the dog's bared teeth and growl, is a claim of dominance and thus plays an important role in the maintenance of the social hierarchy that reg-

Some people seem to crave stimulation, choosing thrilling activities over the tame pastimes that are preferred by those who are lower in the trait of sensation-seeking.

ulates survival and reproduction. In humans, it is reasonable to assume that emotion would play a similarly important role and that communication of emotion from one person to another must occur.

Paul Ekman (1993) and Carroll Izard (1994) have studied the facial expression of emotions. A central issue is this: are emotions expressed in some universal way, so that people throughout the world will be able to look at a face and agree whether the person is happy, angry, depressed, or whatever? If there is such a universal language for emotional expression, this finding would support the interpretation that emotional displays are influenced largely by innate determinants, rather than being learned. If expressions vary from culture to culture, that finding would support an interpretation that culture-specific learning has shaped the display patterns. To a large extent, the evidence supports the argument of universality. People throughout the world agree when they have seen a picture of a face whether the person is happy, sad, afraid, disgusted, angry, or surprised (Ekman, 1993). Despite scholars' debates over methodological details (Ekman, 1994; Izard, 1994; Russell, 1994), emotion seems to be a universal language. For example, few native English speakers know what is being said when they hear someone speak Japanese. When they see a Japanese person smile or frown, however, the message is as accurately received as if it were emitted by someone from their own culture (Ekman, 1994). This universality extends to preliterate cultures as well. Further supporting the conclusion that facial expressions of emotions are innate and universal is the observation that these expressions are observed in infants only 2 to 3 months old, and in a variety of cultures (Izard, 1994).

Can people fake emotional displays? For example, can we "put on a happy face" to try to convey enjoyment when privately we are not happy? To an extent, of course, people do so, and this effort can help to make social interactions run smoothly. It can also improve the mood of the person pretending to be happy. People who make the facial expressions usually associated with happiness, even if they do so only in obedience to an experimenter's directions, show an increase in actual reported happiness. Apparently, our bodies interpret our own facial expressions, which we feel because of feedback from the muscles involved, as unconscious indicators of our moods (Izard, 1994; Laird, 1974). Biology, however, limits our powers of pretense. In the case of happiness, genuine emotional displays involve activation of the muscle that orbits the eye. Fake happy faces lack such involvement. Genuine and fake smiles also differ in the EEG patterns with which they are associated (Ekman, Davidson & Friesen, 1990). Other emotions, such as disgust and surprise, are easier to control voluntarily.

It would do little good to display emotions if there were no one to "read" them. It has been argued, based on observations of infants, that the ability to interpret other people's facial displays of emotions is innate (for example, Collins & Gunnar, 1990). We do learn cultural messages about emotions, however. We learn **display rules** that tell us which emotions can be safely expressed and which must be hidden. To grimace when presented with a disappointing gift, for example, is unacceptable. Anecdotally, many Europeans have observed that Americans smile all the time.

Although emotions and their expression do have an innate basis, we require social experience to learn the culturally acceptable ways of expressing them and interpreting their expression by others. Observations of rhesus monkeys show that those deprived of normal social experience were less able than those raised with other monkeys to interpret other monkeys' expressions of fear and distress (Geen, 1992). Just because emotion is built on an innate foundation does not mean that it can unfold effectively without nurturing.

The Evolutionary Approach

Emotionality and other phenomena of interest to personality psychologists are part of "human nature" in the sense that our genetic codes determine our development. The **evolutionary approach** takes a very long view of human nature and asks why these particular genetic codes, of all those that have been produced in the variation that is part of nature, should have been selected. The basic premise of evolutionary theory is that nature will

select for those traits that are adaptive; that is, that lead to successful reproduction and survival. Over the hundreds of thousands (if not millions) of
years that humans have lived, reproduced, and died on this planet, nature
has slowly but surely molded our genetic codes, as certainly but even more
slowly than the waters of the Colorado River molded the Grand Canyon
of the American Southwest. Each time a baby is born, and each time a person dies, some genetic combinations are added to and some subtracted
from the total human population. What is added and what is subtracted are
not identical, because death and birth, for all their uncertainties, are not
entirely random. In the remote past, we may assume that people with
slower than average reflexes were more likely to die at the hand (or tooth
or claw) of a predator before replacing their genes through successful
reproduction, and so over time, the human population contained more and
more individuals with quick reflexes. Dietary preferences for fatty, salty,
and sweet foods are understandable advantages for ancestors who lived in
environments where these nutrients were scarcer than they are today, and
when indulgence in times of plenty could prepare for health and even
survival in times of scarcity. More central to personality concerns, evolutionary psychologists have agreed with psychoanalyst Sigmund Freud that
sex and aggression are major themes that echo from the ancient past.
People who reproduce and leave offspring that survive, and people who
can prevail in aggressive encounters with opponents, have the advantage in
the genetic competition of evolution. Over hundreds of thousands of years,
by the selective evolutionary pressures that favored the fittest, the human
population, like all other species, developed characteristics that enhanced
their survival chances in the environment that they faced generation after
generation.

We can speculate, based on observations of humans today, about what
traits evolutionary forces selected long ago: perhaps aggressiveness, to
allow our ancestors to fight off predators and to eliminate their human
rivals, their genetic competitors; perhaps sexual aggressiveness, because
rape can increase some men's chance of fathering children. Pervasive
human concern with social status may reflect the struggle for dominance
that is fundamental to evolutionary explanations. Depression, it is speculated, may be an adaptive response by those who suffer defeat in such social
competition; the inactivity that typically accompanies depression could
protect the individual from further harm (Price et al., 1994). Traits, such as
beauty and strength, that lead to reproduction with the most genetically
desirable reproductive partner and that ensure the maximum number of
offspring that themselves survive and reproduce will prevail in evolution.
Nurturance toward children and relatives has obvious survival value for
these carriers of one's genes to future generations.

Evolutionary selective pressures operated on Earth as it existed for our
ancestors. These pressures would not adapt humans to life on another
planet or, more pointedly, to life on Earth in another time. Look around
you. Chances are that you see an Earth very different from those portrayed

in museum recreations of ancient times: asphalt instead of open space, buildings and automobiles instead of wild vegetation and animals. How likely is it that our genetic predispositions, so exquisitely selected for survival in prehistoric times, are also optimal for today's world? That match seems highly unlikely. Some observers blame modern problems of "human nature" on the selection of traits that are now obsolete because our environment has changed much too quickly for genetic selection to be able to keep up. The quick reflexes that saved our ancestors from predators simply make us chronically "on edge" in an era when stresses come by the minute and are rarely solved by physical action, and so the same trait that saved the prehistoric human threatens the twentieth century human with cardiovascular disorders. The aggressive trait that fostered survival in the remote past may, in modern times, be expressed with missiles and bombs instead of clubs and stones, thus threatening the survival of our entire species. At minimum, aggressiveness undermines our quality of life and is especially devastating to those who live in high crime areas. The appetite for fat and salt that prepared our hunter-gatherer ancestors for cycles of plenty and famine is maladaptive for many twentieth century humans who gorge themselves on foods that evolution never contended with in chronic abundance, in a time when food came on trees and hooves but not in supermarkets. Human intelligence, which is largely responsible for these environmental transformations, may be a mixed gift, after all.

Lest the list of speculations loom too dismal and explain our problems but not our strengths, let us add cooperativeness, which enhanced the survival and reproductive chances of our ancestors who could band together to do what they could not do as individuals. Our ancestors were also shaped by evolutionary selective pressures to share their food and to help others in distress, as well as to fight. They must have known when to share and when to fight. Could it be that modern social conditions send signals that tell our primitive evolutionary legacy that it is time to fight, even when our more evolved minds think not, and that the environmental signals that stimulated sharing and helping in our ancestors are infrequent in modern culture?

Human Differences from an Evolutionary Perspective

Evolutionary approaches have been devised to explain differences between males and females and among human racial groups. These are controversial ideas, and they are untestable because we cannot observe what happened long ago. The world is different today. We can assume that our remote ancestors were more likely to remain in one location, so that different racial groups developed with distinct genetic patterns, presumably shaped to optimize survival in their locality. It is a far leap from that reasoning to a conclusion that current racial and ethnic characteristics are determined by evolution. Most psychologists believe that the effects of culture and environment are so much more potent than biological tendencies that locally distinctive genetic tendencies by our remote ancestors have no relevance for understanding current racial and ethnic differences. Sex differences, too, are so influenced by cultural lessons that it is impossible to isolate the effects of heredity. The predominant viewpoint in current psychology emphasizes cognition and experience, not biology. In addition, the political repercussions of claiming that sex and race predispose personality differences because of ancient evolutionary forces are frightening. Biological arguments have been used to persecute and even to exterminate groups of people throughout history, and such atrocities continue today. Nonetheless, some theorists have ventured into this controversial area; they confront critics who claim that science is being misused to support prejudice, but they hope that sensible analysis will distinguish between truth and propaganda.

A key to understanding these controversial ideas is the biological concept of reproductive strategies. Successful reproduction is essential for success in the evolutionary competition, but that does not always mean having as many children as possible as soon as possible. Alternative **reproductive strategies** exist in other species and presumably in humans, too. One can try to maximize the number of surviving offspring either by having many children or by having fewer children but investing more effort in their safety so that more of them survive. (Modern conditions make the death of infants and children less frequent than in the harsh environment that our ancestors faced.)

There are sex differences in the availability of these strategies because females must invest more time in each child. Thus, evolutionary theory has been used to explain sex differences in sexual behavior, particularly the double standard that permits more sexual license to males than to females. The argument is that males can specialize in impregnating the maximum number of females, since doing so requires relatively little effort. The more children, the greater the chances that at least a few will survive to adulthood. Other species, such as fish and insects, produce huge numbers of offspring. In humans and in other species with a long gestation and one birth or a few births for each pregnancy, males can father many more babies than an individual female can bear. Some evolutionists argue that males, therefore, are by nature sexually unfaithful, in order to reproduce more children. (Whether or not a man consciously has this desire is irrelevant, because instincts do not require conscious thought; in fact, as Freud pointed out, they are often in conflict with consciousness.) Rape has even been described as a reproductive strategy designed to maximize a man's offspring (Thornhill & Thornhill, 1992). For females, the number of offspring is limited, since each pregnancy requires 9 months, plus a few years to nurse the young. Females, in other words, have more **parental investment** in each child (Feingold, 1992; Trivers, 1972, 1985). With more of their genetic heritage at risk with each baby, there has been more evolutionary pressure to select females who nurture their young successfully, and for females to be more selective about the male who will father their children so that the genetic endowment of the child is enhanced. This reproductive argument has been offered to explain why males are "naturally" more promiscuous and intolerant of sexual infidelity in their partners and females more nurturant and selective about their sexual partners (Buss, 1991).

J. Philippe Rushton (1985, 1987) makes the controversial assertion that the various human races differ in the extent to which they use these reproductive strategies, depending upon environmental factors that influence the offspring's chances of survival. He suggests that the modern choice between strategies of high parental investment and high number of offspring depends upon heredity (including race) and environmental circumstances (including socioeconomic status and childhood stress). Numerous critics, however, have disagreed with the logic of Rushton's arguments and have stated that remote evolutionary causes of racial differences are unimportant, compared to immediate social conditions (Belsky, Steinberg & Draper, 1991a, 1991b; Buss & Schmitt, 1993; Maccoby, 1991).

Sexual fidelity and infidelity may represent alternative strategies for reproductive success (whether or not these follow the racial lines posited by Rushton's controversial theory). It is a bad investment of parental resources to bear children in extremely harsh times; for example, when famine threatens survival. Mechanisms for controlling reproduction in such times have been proposed. It has been suggested that anorexia nervosa, a serious eating disorder that reduces women's fertility as well as threatening their health, may be such a mechanism (Voland & Voland, 1989). Even the abuse of children, and especially of stepchildren, may reflect the harsh impulses of our evolutionary past: today's children may be seen as less promising than those that might be conceived tomorrow. The impulse to reproduce in times when children could survive and to restrict reproduction in times of adversity was a mandate deep in our genetic code that sometimes was served by eliminating the weakest and youngest in times too harsh to permit everyone to survive.

The fact that males are more aggressive than females has also been traced to evolutionary selection and biological mechanisms. Males who are aggressive become more dominant, thus securing access to mates and more effectively protecting mates and offspring against danger. The evolutionary argument, however, is not universally accepted for a number of reasons. Aggression has many causes, including learning and social cues, which makes evolutionary explanations seem oversimplified to some critics (Maccoby & Jacklin, 1974, 1980; Tieger, 1980).

What about cooperation? Counterintuitively, evolution recognizes the value of cooperation, which is not simply a triumph of civilization over our animal nature. Evolution favors cooperation when it helps those who share our genes—our relatives. Like other animals, we show greater altruism toward genetic relatives than toward strangers. Our relatives share our genes; therefore, *kin altruism* is encouraged by evolution because relatives can pass on some of the genes that they share with us. It is easy to understand that helping our children, siblings, and other relatives to survive is a reasonable evolutionary strategy, but what about helping nonrelatives? Why help the competition? In some cases this behavior, too, has survival value, according to the concept of *reciprocal altruism* (Trivers, 1992). Altruism toward nonrelatives has evolutionary advantage when it is reciprocated, provided that the risks incurred by helping others are more than outweighed by the advantages of being helped. For example, if you take a small risk to rescue a drowning person, that will be a good bet if your own survival chances are sufficiently increased by the benefit of being rescued if you yourself are in danger of drowning. However, greater survival advantage goes to those who cheat the system and receive help from nonrelatives without themselves helping in a dangerous crisis. Therefore, nature may have produced some individuals who, when the situation becomes dangerous, place their own interests ahead of others.

Evolutionary explanations are consistent with psychoanalytic explanations of the unconscious in many important respects. The primitive impulses to compete and to reproduce (aggression and love) correspond to Freud's concept of the id. The alternative strategy of surviving through social cooperation corresponds to Freud's ego. These two strategies are in conflict, like the unconscious struggles between id and superego that Freud described (Leak & Christopher, 1982). Far from being a triumph of spirit over nature, the conscience and morality upon which humans pride themselves is understandable as a product of evolution (Wright, 1994).

Still, even with all these implications of evolution for key issues in personality, it is a fallacy to believe that evolutionary biological predispositions are manifested automatically. They depend on context, more than is usually acknowledged, and they can take different forms depending on context (Crawford & Anderson, 1989; DeKay & Buss, 1992). The description of the effects of the environment on development is central to a modern understanding of evolution. A biological understanding of evolution also supports explanations of individual differences, an obvious area of interest to personality psychologists that has not been sufficiently explored (Buss, 1984). Although more detailed descriptions of current personality development must supplement statements about evolution, some strong basic impulses from our evolutionary past cannot simply be ignored. These are sex and aggression (Freud's basic id impulses), nurturance and altruism. Because dominance in human societies brings not only privilege but also leadership, it does not seem too far-fetched to speculate that a tendency to obey authority figures (dominant members of a group) may have evolutionary origins, which would be consistent with the strength and prevalence of this tendency that is evidenced by Stanley Milgram's (1974) classic studies of obedience to authority. For all the changes in modern society, a propensity to place males and females in different social roles may also be partly a product of evolution. Yet the human species also has a highly evolved capacity to profit from the experience of individual lives in new environments, so the most important evolutionary heritage of all may be our adaptability and our ability to supplement biological evolution with culture. But culture only supplements, and does not supplant, biology. Personality psychologists need to include biological phenomena in their theories and to develop a better understanding of biological mechanisms, going beyond the usual preference for explaining behavior only at higher levels such as social experience (Steklis & Walter, 1991).

SUMMARY

- Relationships between personality and biology have been suggested since ancient Greek times, when Hippocrates proposed his humoral theory. Current theories emphasize the brain and neurotransmitters.

- Biological mechanisms are proposed as the basis for broad factors of personality such as those described by Eysenck (Neuroticism, Extraversion, and Psychoticism), Gray (BAS reward system and BIS punishment system), and Cloninger (novelty seeking, harm avoidance, and reward dependence).

- The field of behavioral genetics studies the impact of heredity on personality and other behavior. It assesses the heritability of traits; that is, the extent to which they are genetically determined. Heritabilities of 25 to 50 percent for personality traits are commonly reported.

- Even if heredity influences traits, they can change and they do not necessarily appear the same on the surface in all people who share the same heredity. Even if a trait is inherited, heredity does not necessarily account for differences between the sexes or among various racial and ethnic groups.

- Heredity must be considered in its environmental context, as it combines with environmental variables to influence personality. For example, heredity influences people's choice of environments, especially as they become older.

- Environmental effects include different parental treatment of children in the same family, even if they are identical twins.

- Temperament refers to innate differences in style of behavior that are apparent from infancy onward, such as whether a baby is easy or difficult. It is especially evident when children respond to new stimuli, showing varying amounts of fear or shyness, and it is thought to influence attachment.

- Beyond infancy, temperament is manifested as emotionality, activity level, and sociability, and it continues to influence social experience throughout life.

- Positive and negative emotions and the intensity of emotions vary from person to person.

- Emotions are displayed in facial expressions, which have a biological basis and which are largely universal worldwide.

- People also vary in the extent to which they are prone to anxiety and the extent to which they are sensation seekers who crave high levels of stimulation.

- The evolutionary approach views personality as based on evolutionary selection, emphasizing sex (reproductive strategies), aggression, and altruism.

GLOSSARY

affect intensity the trait of typically experiencing mild or strong emotions

behavioral genetics the field that studies the impact of heredity on personality and other behavior

display rules cultural messages about the appropriateness of expressing various emotions or of hiding them

evolutionary approach a perspective that studies inheritance based on the assumption that what was adaptive for our ancestors in the remote past has been passed down to us genetically because of natural selection

excitation transfer the tendency of emotional arousal to linger after the event has passed, with the potential of influencing our interpretation of subsequent events

Extraversion Eysenck's factor describing a person's tendency to be outgoing or shy

heritability the extent to which genetic inheritance is responsible for the variability of a trait in a population

Neuroticism Eysenck's factor describing a person's tendency for high levels of emotional arousal and reactivity (or, conversely, for low levels)

parental investment the cost, in time and energy, of each child, based on the number of children that a male or female is capable of producing

Psychoticism Eysenck's factor describing a person's tendency to be impulsive, perhaps aggressive, and to have uncontrolled emotions

reproductive strategies the biological alternatives of having more offspring or of having fewer that are then protected more carefully by parents

sensation seeker a person who seeks high levels of stimulation to achieve his or her optimal level of arousal

temperament apparently innate differences in the style of a person's behavior, evident from infancy throughout life, including emotionality and activity level

--●

THOUGHT QUESTIONS

1. What personality characteristics do *you* think are most influenced by heredity and biology?

2. The names given to Eysenck's personality factors (Neuroticism, Extraversion, and Psychoticism) are not neutral in their connotation. Can you think of alternative labels that don't seem so clearly desirable or undesirable?

3. Give an example, real or hypothetical, of excitation transfer in the real world.

4. Assuming that Cloninger's biosocial model is accurate in identifying specific neurotransmitters for the three dimensions of personality that he describes, speculate how this knowledge could be used to treat people who seem "out of balance."

5. Do you believe that discovering the genetic basis of personality should be a high priority? Should these efforts be abandoned? If we were able to conduct a simple and inexpensive laboratory test to evaluate the genetics of real people's personality, should we do it, and who should have access to this information?

6. Many models of heredity are based on the assumption that children in the same family are treated similarly by their parents. Do you believe that this is the case?

7. How would you argue that we should still pay attention to the environments in which children are raised, even if personality is determined to a large extent by heredity?

8. How would you describe the temperaments of several people you know well? If these people are related to one another, do these observations cause you to believe that temperament is inherited, or not?

9. If you could change your emotions, increasing or decreasing their intensity and increasing or decreasing the number of positive and negative emotions, would you do so? Why or why not? What might be some of unexpected effects of making these hypothetical changes?

10. Do you feel offended by the evolutionary approach to personality? Why or why not?

Social Tasks and Personality

PERSONALITY DEVELOPS IN A SOCIAL CONTEXT, and it finds expression in social tasks. As we saw in Chapter 7, the person who needs a sense of achievement may be attracted to entrepreneurial work and excel in that context, whereas someone who is motivated by affiliation needs may prefer friendship. What personality motives or characteristics make a successful athlete, a devoted parent, or a good marriage partner? What social tasks will provide each of us with the niche that fits our unique style of being human?

The life-span approach to development emphasizes that some of these tasks are particularly important at certain stages of life and provide a focus for continued personality growth, as well as revealing the personality formed so far. Formal schooling, marriage, and parenthood each have their usual time at the forefront. Yet, as Erik Erikson (1959) pointed out, the personality developments that reach crisis proportions at a certain point in the life cycle have many preliminary developments that prepare the way, and they continue to impact a person throughout life. Sometimes we can even return to an earlier stage to redo what was incomplete or now needs revision. The sense of competence that derives from school experience, for example, can be bolstered by continuing education in adulthood (or perhaps even by learning to program a VCR).

James Côté (1993) has extended Erikson's model of a relationship between personality and cultural institutions. He proposes that social institutions (such as a police force) and psychic structures (such as the superego) often are mirror images of one another, or mutually reproducing patterns. However we ultimately come to understand the relationship between inner personality and outer cultural institutions, there is no question that personality cannot be understood without such awareness of its social context. The more we understand about the relationship between personality and the tasks of society, the better able we will be to guide people into the tasks for which they are most suited. It may also be possible to modify some of these social tasks so that they become more suited to our personalities, both in the aspects that are similar among most of us and in those that are unique to each individual.

Education

Education is a key to adult career opportunities and a key variable when socioeconomic status is measured. Children spend a major portion of their lives in school, and college and other advanced education extends into early adulthood. Obviously, such a major investment of time and money (by the individual and by society) may be expected to have major implications for personality. Erik Erikson described the school-age years as a time for attaining a sense of competence. School projects provide an opportunity to envision a task and to work on it until it is completed, whether it is a picture, a paper, or some other project. Feedback in the form of grades provides clear evaluation of the worth of the product. Furthermore, the curriculum educates the child in the values, as well as the information, deemed important in that culture. You may have noticed from news reports that boards of education often encounter disagreements over such values.

Intelligence

Education provides opportunities to test and develop a person's **intelligence.** What is intelligence? Fundamentally, it is a person's ability to learn, to process information. Most theoretical models of intelligence have traditionally focused on a *general factor* of intelligence that influences a wide variety of kinds of learning, such as the diverse courses that students take in school (Spearman, 1927). Simply referring to some students as "very bright," others as "average," and others as "slow learners" does tell us a considerable amount about them, but it clearly is not the whole story.

Is the ability to dance a talent, or a form of intelligence? If you ask an expert, you will get different answers, depending upon which expert you choose.

Other models of intelligence focus on specific factors of intelligence (Thurstone, 1938): verbal intelligence and mathematical intelligence can be distinguished, for example. Even more varieties of intelligence are identified by Howard Gardner (1983) in his theory of *multiple intelligences*. His model includes seven distinct kinds of intelligence. Some of them—such as linguistic intelligence, logical-mathematical intelligence, and spatial intelligence—correspond to the sorts of intelligence that have traditionally been recognized and measured by those who devise intelligence tests. Others, however, are more controversial. Musical intelligence, for example, is dismissed by other experts (for example, Herrnstein & Murray, 1994) as a talent, not a form of intelligence. The same controversy exists for kinesthetic intelligence; is the ability to dance and excel at sports a form of intelligence? Interpersonal intelligence in Gardner's model refers to social skills and intrapersonal intelligence to insight into oneself. These qualities are far different from those that traditionally have been termed "intelligence," and they can be hard to measure.

The debate might seem to be merely a matter of semantics. What does it matter whether we call these abilities "talents" or "intelligence" or whatever? However the debate is resolved, we are faced with decisions about how to deal with these various abilities when people are educated. Verbal and mathematical intelligences are more entrenched in school systems, receiving time and support that is less compromised by the obstacles of budget cuts and curriculum changes than other of Gardner's proposed intelligences.

Personality in Education

Advocates of *humanistic education* strive to foster the development of the student as a well-rounded person. The foremost spokesperson for humanistic education was Carl Rogers (1969, 1974), whose humanistic approach is based on the assumption that each person's own subjective experience is the best guide to healthy development, if that experience is not overshadowed by the demands imposed by parents and by society. Self-esteem, feelings, subjective experience, and individual choice are among the values given high priority by humanistic educators (Table 12.1).

There are many students these days who are breaking new ground within their families by attending college. They tend to be vulnerable to conflict that stems from this social mobility. Research by Joseph Balkin (1986, 1987) indicates that first-year college students whose parents had not attended college, and who have friends who are not attending college, show higher levels of fear of success on projective tests than those students whose parents and friends have also attended college. Balkin believes that this fear of success reflects a fear of rejection and disapproval by significant others, an interpretation in line with arguments set forth by traditional researchers into fear of success (Horner, 1972). This speculation, however, has not been tested by asking subjects to report their expectations about others' rejection or acceptance of their academic efforts. Another possibility is that, lacking detailed information about the requirements of college life, first-generation college students face more uncertainty about what is required to master the situation. This interpretation would be consistent with other evidence, to which we now turn, indicating that cognitive confidence is associated with college success.

Self-efficacy (Bandura, 1977) is the belief that we can accomplish what we are trying to do (see Chapter 9). This attribute contributes to success in school, particularly in high school and college but also to a lesser extent in elementary school (Multon, Brown & Lent, 1991). Sometimes it gives us the extra edge to do optional assignments. Researchers have found that students who have high self-efficacy about being able to perform a task, in this case writing exam questions to earn extra points, were more successful at the task than those with low expectations (Tuckman & Sexton, 1990). Self-efficacy is particularly important when students are making choices

TABLE **12.1** **Humanist Values in Education**

Process orientation (instead of facts only)

Self-direction and self-evaluation

Connectedness, relationships, and empathy

Relevance to the individual

Integration of class material with life activities and feelings

Awareness of social and environmental context

Emotional and experiential focus

Innovation and social change instead of authority

Democratic values and equity

Personal growth emphasis

People-oriented

Individualistic

Reality-oriented and pragmatic

Evaluation to guide growth instead of judging final worth

Creative

Adapted from Shapiro, 1985.

about their academic courses. Those with a low self-efficacy for mathematics, for example, are likely to avoid math courses (Sexton & Tuckman, 1991).

Self-efficacy expectations change as experience at a task provides concrete feedback about how we are doing. School assignments provide frequent feedback, and so they are a powerful mechanism for changing expectations about what we can accomplish. If efficacy is very low and a course of study is optional, of course, students generally will elect not to take it, and their beliefs about having little ability in the avoided area are not likely to be challenged by evidence to the contrary. Accurate feedback is essential, because students with high self-efficacy may persist with incorrect problem-solving methods in the absence of feedback from teachers (Schunk, 1989).

School consists of more than academic work. Elementary school provides opportunities for children to learn social skills as well as academic skills (Schunk, 1989). By the end of the first year of college, according to one survey, students who have an external locus of control—that is, who believe that the outcomes in their lives depend on factors other than their own effort—are less involved in school organizations, such as clubs and student activities, than those with an internal locus of control. They also perceived themselves as making less progress toward developing academic skills and preparing for careers (Clarke, 1988). This is not simply a first-year phenomenon. Juniors, too, are more active in student activities if they reveal an internal locus of control by agreeing with items such as this: "I am very committed to my career, and I will do what I need to succeed in it" (Trice, Haire & Elliott, 1989). In a study of students taking correspondence courses, those with an external locus of control were less likely to complete the course on time (Trice & Milton, 1987).

School experiences teach powerful lessons about how to relate to other people. Because grades in most schools are based on individual accomplishments in a competitive atmosphere, children from their elementary years onward learn that rewards are based on their skill as individual competitors. Cooperation is subtly discouraged, although special class exercises can be added to change this. Elliot Aronson (1978, 1982) has developed cooperative assignments for elementary students, which he calls the **jigsaw classroom,** to teach cooperation. This approach is especially useful as a way to promote better interracial relationships in desegregated classrooms, because it teaches children to rely upon one another to complete their work. We may think of it as a method for overcoming some of the limitations of an overly individualistic approach to education.

Educational experiences provide entry into career paths. Particularly among those who attend college, the choice of curriculum is a key to a job in a chosen field (although not necessarily a guarantee). Many observers are concerned that for women, this key doesn't unlock as many doors as it does for men. Women earn more than half of the college degrees in the United States, but professional and doctoral programs enroll more men than women, and high-paying jobs that offer opportunities for advancement are more often attained by men (Mickelson, 1989). The reasons for this discrepancy are debatable and may include components of individual choice and opportunity as well as discrimination. The path from education to work may be rocky and unevenly accessible, but it is still a major route for the attainment of career as a major component of identity for most men and women.

Work

Work is the role that defines social identity for most adults in North America. When developmental researchers are assessing adolescents' progress in attaining an identity, they often focus their questions around the issues of career exploration and commitment (Blustein, Devenis & Kidney, 1989). Commitment to a particular career path is, in effect, an indicator of having entered psychological adulthood. Of course, adults

Women and men choose careers based, in part, on their feelings of self-efficacy. What sorts of earlier life experiences do you suppose created the confidence to aspire to a career such as this.

have many commitments besides work, but none so publicly defines a person's status in our society. For wives who do not work outside the home, it is the husband's work that researchers have generally used to define social status.

How do we decide what career to pursue? Of course, our choices are limited to some extent. Not everyone has the personal abilities necessary to become a professional athlete or a rocket scientist. Furthermore, our vision of future possible career attainments may be enhanced by positive models and opportunities or limited by lack of such social backing. Career is also determined largely by each individual's personality.

Self-Efficacy and Careers

Self-efficacy, which we have already seen is an important predictor of school performance, also predicts interest in pursuing particular careers (Schunk, 1989). In a study of students studying for their high school equivalency certificate, self-efficacy was associated with consideration of a variety of occupational activities (Bores-Rangel et al., 1990). People generally choose careers for which they have a high sense of self-efficacy. To the extent that past life experiences lead men and women to have different expectations about careers that are traditionally sex-typed, they will make different occupational choices. To encourage women to enter scientific and technical occupations in greater numbers, for instance, it is helpful to provide experiences to bolster their self-efficacy in these areas. School courses in math and science can do this. Self-efficacy expectations are also useful in understanding the career development of those who face discrimination and other barriers to occupational entry, including racial and ethnic minorities and disabled people (Lent & Hackett, 1987).

Cognitive Complexity

How do we know which careers might suit us best, of the thousands of jobs that people do? Many factors need to be considered, including aspects of the job itself as well as our own interests, abilities, and values. To make an optimal choice requires complex thinking. From the perspective of George Kelly's theory of personal constructs, Greg Neimeyer (1988) has reviewed how two aspects of complex thinking, cognitive integration and differentiation, relate to vocational behavior. Kelly's (1955) theory, which has guided many researchers interested in vocational issues, counseling, and other areas, proposes that people think in terms of a uniquely individual set of constructs, which are concepts that they use to understand and evaluate people. Each construct, or concept, that people consider consists of two opposite poles (so, in the theory, all constructs are *dichotomous* constructs). For example, "People are either diligent or lazy." "People either are friends or enemies." The two poles do not need to be logical opposites, if they are viewed as being in opposition by the individual. A workaholic, for example, may construe people as "either hard-working or bad people." A person's constructs are the key to personality in Kelly's personal construct approach because they determine how we perceive reality and what choices we make in life.

People who have a large number of constructs, who consider each idea or situation from more viewpoints, are said to have a high level of **cognitive differentiation.** It seems reasonable to predict that a rich repertoire of constructs would enable a person to see the world more accurately. In the career area, one college sophomore described several constructs as part of a counseling assessment. For example, he described careers as either "helping individuals or helping society," "practical or not vital," "people oriented or paperwork oriented," and so on. His preference for one of the two poles in each instance was helpful in guiding his career choice (Neimeyer, 1989). In choosing a career, a person with a differentiated set of constructs ought to be able to match career opportunities with individual preferences more precisely and thus make a better choice. Career counselors can help individuals to identify their career interests more precisely by eliciting career constructs using a test such as the Vocational Reptest (Fig. 12.1).

A second aspect of cognitive complexity is **cognitive integration,** which refers to the organization of constructs, generally in hierarchical arrangements. As people develop more highly integrated thinking about careers, their thoughts may become orderly and correspond to the types of

Farmer	Machine Operator	Architect	Physicist	Physician	Social Worker	Public School Teacher	Accountant	Office Worker	Lawyer	Life Insurance Salesman	Artist	Positive Side				Negative Side		
												+3 +2 +1 0				−1 −2 −3		
−3	−3	+2	+3	+3	+1	+3	+3	+3	+3	+3	0	Indoors a lot				Outdoors a lot		
+2	+2	−3	−3	−3	+1	−2	−3	−1	−3	−2	+3	Don't need much education				Need a lot of education		
+1	−2	+2	−2	−3	+3	+2	−3	−1	+3	−2	+3	More freedom				A lot of rules & regulations		
+3	−2	+2	−2	−3	+3	+1	−3	−2	0	−2	+3	Non-restricted job				Restricted job		
−2	−2	+1	+2	+3	−2	−2	+3	0	+3	+2	−3	A lot of money				Little money		
−2	−2	−2	−2	−3	−3	+3	−2	−2	−3	−2	0	Teaches more				Helps more		
−2	−3	+2	+2	+3	+3	+3	−3	−3	+3	−2	+3	Interesting (something new every day)				Boring (same stuff every day)		
−3	−3	−3	+3	+1	+3	+2	−2	−2	+3	−3	−3	Investigative				Not investigative		
−2	−2	−2	−2	+3	+3	+3	−2	−2	+3	+3	+1	Works with many people				Doesn't work with many people		
+2	+3	+3	+3	−3	−3	−2	+3	+3	+1	−3	−1	Doesn't deal with families				Deals with families		
−2	−3	+3	−2	−3	+1	+2	−3	−3	+2	−3	+3	Creativity involved				Not much creativity involved		
−3	−3	−3	+3	+3	+3	+3	+3	+3	+3	+3	+2	Not much manual labor				Involves manual labor		

FIGURE 12.1 *What advice would you give to Jean, who filled out this Vocational Reptest? Constructs in the left column indicate her preferences; constructs in the right column indicate things she doesn't like. (Adapted from Neimeyer, 1992, p. 167.)*

careers that are available (for example, service industries, technological careers, and so forth). In the case of the college sophomore just described, some constructs were well integrated. For example, he saw jobs that earned high salaries as also requiring college. In other cases, however, we find conflict: he preferred jobs helping individuals to those that help society and jobs involving creating over jobs that didn't involve creating, but he also thought that jobs helping individuals were very seldom creative. This conflict would need to be resolved if he were to choose a satisfying career (Neimeyer, 1989). Cognitive differentiation and integration both contribute to more satisfying career choices (Neimeyer, 1988).

Personality Traits and Career Choice

As people think about their career choices, they strive to find careers that match their personality and interests. Someone who enjoys being with people is unlikely to choose a job that demands solitary work or to be happy if that is all that is available. Do you like to figure out problems? To be outdoors? To negotiate? Such preferences are relevant to selecting your career. Tests that have been devised to guide career choice assess such preferences systematically and provide scores that describe the test-taker's level of interest in various types of careers. One often-used test, the Vocational Preference Inventory (Holland, 1985), assesses interest in six categories of careers: Realistic, Investigative, Social, Artistic, Enterprising, and Conventional. The theory behind this test, Holland's **congruence model,** is that people will be happier if they work in settings where their own interests and values are shared by others. Research indicates that clients who have received career counseling, whether individually or in groups, show improvement on vocational search activities and other measures compared to those who never received counseling (Osipow, 1986).

Not surprisingly, career preference inventories are correlated with other measures of personality. For example, the Strong-Campbell Interest Inventory scale of introversion-extraversion correlates with the introversion-extraversion measure of the Myers-Briggs Type Indicator, which we covered in Chapter 3 (Apostal & Marks, 1990). Extraversion is high among people working in sales (Kline & Lapham, 1992). Career interests are also closely related to Wiggins's model of interpersonal traits; for example, a dominant individual is likely to prefer the occupation of business executive and a quarrelsome person to express interest in being a credit investigator (Broughton, Trapnell & Boyes, 1991).

The Protestant Work Ethic

Work is more central to some people's lives than others, even if we compare only people who are working full time. Although work is a central life role for most adults, some people subscribe more than others to the Protestant work ethic, which was described by sociologist Max Weber (1958). The ethic is called Protestant because of its historical association with Protestant teachings about the value of hard work, but it is not limited to any particular religious group. Researchers measure the extent to which individuals subscribe to the Protestant work ethic by asking questions about their willingness to work hard, respect of others who work hard, disdain for leisure, and preference for saving money rather than spending it on pleasures. The hard work that this work ethic fosters has consequences for society, leading to economic growth (Baguma & Furnham, 1993; Furnham, et al., 1993; Tang, 1993).

People who endorse statements associated with the Protestant ethic also are generally high in the need for achievement and have an internal locus of control. It has been well documented by researchers that the need for achievement is associated with choice of entrepreneurial business careers and success in such careers (McClelland, 1965). Achievement-motivated students (assessed by a self-report measure), when considering hypothetical job offers, preferred jobs in which rewards depend upon performance, not seniority (Turban & Keon, 1993). Achievement-motivated individuals also tend to accept the traditional values of their culture, and this motivation may dissuade many women from entering careers that are not traditional for women. Women often express achievement motivation by choosing teaching careers. Those who become entrepreneurs and college teachers become even more achievement motivated as their careers progress. Other achievement-motivated women, perhaps also responding to the expectations of their culture, opt for careers that are less individualistic and more nurturing of others' achievement and become social workers and therapists (Jenkins, 1987).

Business managers, whose jobs require extensive dealing with people, typically have high power motivation. Other power-relevant jobs include teacher, psychotherapist, journalist, and clergy (Jenkins, 1994; McClelland & Boyatzis, 1982). Sharon Jenkins reports, however, that women high in power motivation were not attracted to teaching at the elementary and secondary level, and those college women who planned to teach at this level often changed their plans, perhaps because societal changes at the time of this study (the 1970s) were making other careers more readily available to them (Jenkins, 1994). People are attracted to jobs that provide frequent opportunities to satisfy their motivations, whether the pursuit of excellence (achievement motivation) or the pursuit of interpersonal influence (power motivation). The same job may offer a variety of potential satisfactions. Teaching, for example, can satisfy achievement motivation when a lesson is well done or power motivation when the teacher has an influence over students or moves up in the professional ranks. According to the **sensitization principle,** people are particularly likely to perceive those demands, frustrations, and gratifications at work that are relevant to their own motivations (Veroff & Feld, 1970). Sensitization can lead to dissatisfaction when motive-relevant cues are perceived but it is not possible to satisfy the motivation, as when one can imagine writing a great paper but does not have the time to do so.

Personality and Work Performance

Once a career is launched, personality continues to influence the manner in which the work is performed. Entrepreneurial success is associated with the achievement motive (McClelland, 1961, 1965) and its correlated work ethic; this motive directs productive business decisions. Harry Levinson (1994) charges that many of the failures of American corporations should be blamed on psychological causes, including "narcissism, unconscious recapitulation of family dynamics in the organization, exacerbating dependency, psychologically illogical organization structure and compensation schemes, inadequate management of change, and inability to recognize and manage cognitive complexity" (p. 428). According to this indictment, if personality issues could be better understood and taken into account in the workplace, the benefits would be felt at the corporate as well as the individual level. Executives, like parents, sometimes need to take decisive action; are they psychologically prepared to do so? Workers, like members of families and all groups, form bonds with one another; do these bonds work against productivity? In the complicated business world, as in the world at large, cognitive complexity is essential for those who must plan strategically for the future.

Among those who advise managers about how best to use their workers, some consultants base their understandings on the Jungian model of personality types (described in Chapter 3). This model suggests that some people, Intuitive types, are particularly skilled at seeing the big picture and planning for the long term, whereas others, Sensation types, have the ability to attend to the necessary details that their intuitive colleagues often neglect (Davis, Grove & Knowles, 1990). The full model also considers other Jungian dimensions (introversion and extraversion, thinking and feeling, judging and perceiving). Some jobs are filled predominantly by one type of personality; for example, the majority of accountants are sensing-thinkers. (See Chapter 3; sensing-thinkers are oriented to details instead of the whole picture and emphasize thought over emotion in making decisions.) Complex organizations, however, are best served by a variety of types because each can contribute something unique: innovation, attention to detail, skills with people, and so on. By making sure that the contributions of each type are recognized and implemented, managers can enhance organizational effectiveness (Barry, 1991; Rideout & Richardson, 1989).

In the motivational literature, researchers report that a high need for achievement predicts higher wages, and high "socialized" need for power predicts working at a higher occupational level; that is, a more prestigious or high status job (McClelland & Franz, 1992). A similar measure of "responsible power," or power motivation combined with a sense of responsibility, predicted success among managers at a major corporation over a 16-year period (Winter, 1991).

Obviously, different jobs make different demands, so there is no one personality type that is best for all jobs. The job performance of managers and sales people is higher if they are extraverted, but that trait does not predict success in many other careers (Davis, Grove & Knowles, 1990): it would be a handicap for a job requiring extensive time alone, such as a lighthouse watchman. Similarly, an introverted salesperson might find herself at a disadvantage.

Work and Life Satisfaction

Work occupies many hours of each day, and it can be an important source of satisfaction or dissatisfaction with life. Our jobs can be a basis of self-esteem; women who work outside the home have, on the average, higher self-esteem than those who do not (Baruch & Barnett, 1986). Studies show that favorable job conditions contribute to life satisfaction. People who work without too many external constraints and who have the opportunity to achieve and to have an influence at work are most competent and satisfied with their lives; these jobs, of course, are generally high status and relatively well paid (Kalimo & Vuori, 1990).

Work can be a source of stress as well as satisfaction. A **workaholic** is a person who is highly involved in work and is driven to work to perfection, but displays high levels of stress and low levels of satisfaction. If work is enjoyable despite high drive, the term *work enthusiast* is used instead of workaholic (Spence & Robbins, 1992). Certain jobs may be conducive to unhealthy lifestyles, such as the drinking that is said to explain writers' relatively short life expectancy (Kaun, 1991). Careers can present workers with demands that exceed their perceived self-efficacy, which can lead to stress. Such stressors include demands that cause a person to think "*I* cannot do that" or "*We* cannot do that"; that is, both individual and collective self-efficacy are relevant to work stress (Jex & Gudanowski, 1992).

Work stress, like stress in general, requires people to develop methods of coping; they adopt the emotion-focused and problem-focused techniques that we considered in Chapter 8 (Dewe, Cox & Ferguson, 1993). For example, workers can learn to express their distress to colleagues or to plan and prioritize work tasks more effectively (Latack & Havlovic, 1992). Obviously, some coping strategies are more effective than others. The most effective coping methods for a particular work situation may be unique, because coping is, to a considerable extent, situation specific. In keeping with current models that describe stress in terms of a transaction between the person and the environment, these strategies are best understood by considering factors beyond the individual; for example, the available social support at work and elsewhere. Special programs can be offered at the workplace to help employees learn effective methods of stress reduction (Goodspeed & DeLucia, 1990). Organizations can go beyond stress reduction workshops and offer such concrete assistance as adequate maternity leave, which helps to protect employees from depression after childbirth (Hyde et al., 1995).

When stress continues to exceed coping resources, workers risk **burnout,** a response to long-term stress that involves decreased work motivation and accomplishment and increased emotional difficulties and cynicism (Pines & Aronson, 1988). Burnout can occur in almost any job, but it has been of particular interest to researchers in health care professions, where it can result in an increasingly impersonal and uncaring attitude toward patients.

Job stress does not automatically produce burnout. Some people, because of their personalities, are far more susceptible than others. In a study of occupational therapists, those who scored high on Neuroticism on the NEO-PI were especially susceptible to burnout, expressing emotional exhaustion and impersonal and cynical attitudes toward clients. Burnout is more likely when people are in jobs that aren't congruent with their personality, as when a health care worker does not have the high level of interpersonal caring, reflected in high Agreeableness scores, required by the profession (Piedmont, 1993). This vulnerability to burnout that stems from a poor person-job match makes the importance of an appropriate career choice even more obvious.

Love and Marriage

If life itself does not provide adequate evidence, one needs only to listen to popular music and watch movies to note the prevalence of the search for love. Researchers have analyzed those aspects of love and marriage that are amenable to empirical study. They report that married people are, on the average, healthier and happier than those who are not married (Kalimo & Vuori, 1990). Averages do not tell the whole story, though. With half of North American marriages ending in divorce and many adults opting to remain unmarried, there is ample evidence that love is not always easy.

Various types of love have been described by researchers. One popular typology proposes that, at least among the U.S. college students studied, there are six categories of love. *Eros*, erotic love, involves intense emotion and strong physical preferences; love is a high priority in life and the Eros-type lover is committed to the partner. *Ludus*, in contrast, sees love as a game, without intense feeling or commitment to the partner, which permits manipulation and deception. *Storge* is friendship, not passionate but enduring. *Pragma* is pragmatic love, rational and planned. *Mania* is highly emotional love, leading to the inability to concentrate and to physical symptoms such as sleeplessness and stomach upset. *Agape* is self-sacrificing, undemanding love (Hendrick & Hendrick, 1986). These love styles can be measured by questionnaire (Table 12.2).

Undergraduate psychology students who scored high on Eros were more likely to report that they were in love, and they had high self-esteem. Those high on Mania generally had low self-esteem. Those high on Ludus had been in love many times or, if the relationships were thought of as games or casual affairs, had never been in love; Ludus was found more often among men than women (Hendrick & Hendrick, 1986). Strength of religious belief is also related to the love scales. Students who reported that they are very religious scored higher on Storge, Pragma, and Agape, and lower on Ludus, than other students (Hendrick & Hendrick, 1987).

A person's ability to develop satisfying romantic relationships in adulthood is influenced by childhood relationship experiences. Based on early attachment relationships, adults develop a variety of attachment patterns in their romantic relationships. They may be *secure*, comfortable with relationships. They may be *anxious/ambivalent*, concerned that the partner may

Love does not always endure. Psychologists hope that understanding various styles of love will change the odds. Perhaps we should ask these people for their advice.

not be as committed to a close relationship as they are. Or they may be *avoidant*, uncomfortable about a close, committed relationship and the dependency it would involve (Hazan & Shaver, 1987). This attachment model suggests that adult intimacy is not a new task but one that builds on childhood relationships, especially with parents. A retrospective study of young adults suggests that those who reported a history of cold parents, family problems, and lower social self-esteem tended to avoid romantic attachments (Bringle & Bagby, 1992). Such attachment difficulties and avoidance of romantic relationships are often accompanied by depression (Carnelley, Pietromonaco & Jaffe, 1994). Depression and other evidence of demoralization increase over time as a consequence of deteriorating marital relationships (Schaefer & Burnett, 1987). So the problem of parents' marital difficulties is, as a vicious circle, recreated in the next generation.

In addition to the three categories of adult attachment just described, Michael Sperling and his colleagues describe a category of *desperate love*. This style of love "incorporates the behavioral and affective dimensions of passionate love with an extraordinary need for fusional interdependence as well as the intrapsychic dynamic of much anxiety around attachment" (Sperling & Berman, 1991, p. 47). More mature love would require that the individual has attained a sense of individual identity, as Erik Erikson described, rather than bringing to the relationship this extraordinary neediness that is reminiscent of the infant's needs to be nurtured by an adult (Sperling, 1987). When a person who is "in love" needs to be with the loved one constantly and becomes suspicious and jealous if he or she imagines any signs of interest in someone else, we must ask ourselves whether this is a case of desperate love. The film *Fatal Attraction* depicts a woman

TABLE 12.2   **Sample Items to Measure Six Love Styles**

Love style	Sample item
Eros	I feel that my lover and I were meant for each other.
Ludus	I try to keep my lover a little uncertain about my commitment to him/her.
Storge	It is hard to say exactly when my lover and I fell in love. (Our friendship merged gradually into love over time.)
Pragma	I consider what a person is going to become in life before I commit myself to him/her.
Mania	When my lover doesn't pay attention to me, I feel sick all over.
Agape	I am usually willing to sacrifice my own wishes to let my lover achieve his/hers.

Adapted from Hendrick & Hendrick, 1986.

whose desperate love led her to murder. Women are less often aggressive and destructive, even when driven by desperate love, than men, based on Sperling's studies of college students (Sperling & Berman, 1991). Other research, which studied couples longitudinally from engagement onward, shows that the husband's lack of impulse control is a major predictor of divorce (Kelly & Conley, 1987).

It is not easy for people to develop constructive relationships. Ironically, people who have negative self-concepts are more committed to spouses who think poorly of them and less committed to spouses who think more highly of them (Swann, Hixon & De La Ronde, 1992). The comfort derived from knowing that their partners agree with their poor self-image outweighs the quest for an approving partner. Such counterintuitive evidence attests to the importance of the self-concept as a powerful force in personality. Fortunately, the self can also support healthier behavior. Active coping with the stresses of marriage is associated with a sense of self-efficacy (Wells-Parker, Miller & Topping, 1990).

Not all love relationships involve a man and a woman. Some researchers have suggested that the intimacy that can develop in homosexual couples is as psychologically valuable as that in traditional heterosexual couples (Sohier, 1985–1986). There can be no question, however, that society presents greater obstacles to such couples and to those who are developing their identity and intimacy as gay and lesbian people (Sullivan & Schneider, 1987).

A popular myth alleges that two people who marry become increasingly similar over the years. According to Avshalom Caspi and his colleagues' study of married couples, this is not true. Spouses are no more similar or different after 20 years than at the beginning of their marriage (Caspi, Herbener & Ozer, 1992).

Although both common lore and some psychological theory (Jung, 1954) tell us that "opposites attract," evidence is stronger for the conclusion that romantic and marital partners are usually similar to one another in personality, as well as in physical characteristics and intelligence (Caspi & Herbener, 1990). On Jungian dimensions of personality, couples tend particularly to be similar on the intuition-sensation dimension, but not on introversion-extraversion (Carlson & Williams, 1984; Vinacke et al., 1988). Not all personality characteristics show this tendency for couples to be similar, however, and despite widespread acceptance of the similarity hypothesis, some recent researchers offer surprising evidence that our choice of partners is essentially random; height and physical attractiveness seem more important than personality (Lykken & Tellegen, 1993). Hans Eysenck (1990b) states that couples are essentially randomly matched on the personality traits in his model, but they do tend to be similar in intelligence.

Similarity of personality seems to be associated with marital happiness, perhaps because it permits both partners to see issues in much the same way (Carlson & Williams, 1984). In addition, personality traits of individual partners contribute to marital happiness. When one partner in a marriage scores high on Neuroticism, the relationship is generally unhappy and divorce is more likely (Cramer, 1993; Kelly & Conley, 1987; Russell & Wells, 1994). It seems reasonable to conclude that neurotic individuals are unable to offer their partners the acceptance, empathy, and emotionally honest communication that contribute to a healthy relationship and enhance the well-being of their partners (Cramer, 1990a, 1990b). It is tempting to think of success in relationships as entirely a matter of such psychological explanations. Surprisingly, Matt McGue and David Lykken's genetic studies of twins show that the risk of divorce is strongly influenced by genetic factors (McGue & Lykken, 1992)! This is not to say that there is a gene for marital stability, of course. Neuroticism, which we know contributes to the risk of divorce, is influenced by heredity, and such personality traits may be the mechanisms by which genetics influences marital stability.

Ultimately, analyzing relationships requires us to consider the development of people's shared and unshared understandings of their relationship and perceptions of one another (Duck, 1993; Kirchler, 1989). We can no longer look only at the individual personality, either as the cause of relationship outcomes or as the target of influence from the relationship. Love relationships, so central to personality from infancy onward, force us to acknowledge that the study of individual personalities can only be a starting point. To complete the picture, we also need to consider the social context in which the couple functions; for example, what are the social forces that yield higher average marital happiness among couples with higher incomes and among white couples as opposed to black couples in the United States (Oggins, Veroff & Leber, 1993)? Perhaps then we will know how to predict or even increase marital happiness, a worthy goal for the individuals involved and for their children.

Parenting

Parenting continues the theme of the interrelationship of the individual personality with others. The old view that parental behavior alone causes desirable or adverse outcomes in children has been rejected as a partial truth; it has been recognized that child behavior also shapes parental responses.

When a couple has its first child, the marital relationship changes. These changes are transformative, and they often seem different at the moment than after time, when memory rewrites past events from a more distant perspective (Smith, 1994). A longitudinal study found that most women expected their husbands to do more of the housework and child care than they actually did after the baby was born, and this unmet expectation led to some negative feelings about their husbands (Ruble et al., 1988). Other studies suggest that the demands of parenthood are more difficult for women than for men. Survey data examining depression in residents of the Los Angeles area show that parenting has different implications for the depression levels of men and women. Among couples living with children, men were significantly lower in depression than women. Women who were single parents were particularly depressed (Aneshensel, Frerichs & Clark, 1981).

In the now rare traditional family, the husband works outside the home and the wife does not; the wife takes care of the house and children. Each partner in that model of the family had one role, either breadwinner or homemaker. Now most married adults follow a *dual-role* model, filling both roles: wage-earner and caretaker of the children. Despite the stresses of these extra responsibilities, the expansion of roles has advantages for both men and women, offering some protection against the threats to mental health that occur when one role is dissatisfying (Barnett et al., 1994). Increasingly, fathers have become involved in housework and in the care of their children, with many positive results. Fathers develop better relationships with their children and greater satisfaction as parents; children have enhanced self-esteem and less rigid sex role stereotypes; mothers are less depressed and have time to develop their professional identities. The extent to which the father contributes is influenced by the mother's

Increasing numbers of dual role couples, where both parents work outside the home as well as in it, are changing the modern family, challenging people to find new creative solutions to the work-family conflict.

occupational prestige, income, and work hours, and by the father's sex role attitudes (Deutsch, Lussier & Servis, 1993).

One parental task is discipline, and parents exert authority in a variety of ways (Baumrind, 1971; Buri, 1991). *Authoritative* parents provide direction to children and enforce their requirements, but with warmth and flexibility. This pattern helps children to learn the rules without being taught that they are unworthy. *Permissive* parents provide less direction and make few demands. In the extreme, they may be neglectful. *Authoritarian* parents provide considerable direction and demand obedience by children, who are not permitted to challenge their authority. Unlike authoritative parents, authoritarian parents do not encourage discussion of the rules. What about the extreme of discipline: child abuse? Jay Belsky (1993) acknowledges that some personality traits, such as low self-esteem and neuroticism (including depression and anxiety), predict abuse in many studies, but he suggests that the environmental context must also be considered. Child abuse is more likely to occur when a parent experiences too many stressors and too few supports. The cumulative effect of financial strains, job loss or setback, marital difficulty, and so on pushes some parents beyond their limits of self-control. This finding suggests that the problem can be reduced by increasing supports and reducing stressors for parents through a variety of strategies such as those that improve economic well-being or increase supportive relationships.

Parental divorce often has adverse effects on children, although these are probably no more severe than the negative impact of serious parental conflict (Hoffman, 1986). Among problems reported to be more common in children of divorced parents are aggression, impulsive behavior, depression, anxiety, difficulties with social interactions, and academic problems. When divorce occurs, parents can minimize the adverse effects on children by cooperation, consistency, and good relationships with the children. Providing a stable environment and adequate financial support also helps (Grych & Fincham, 1992).

As society changes, it is increasingly important to understand which varieties of parenting can be healthy for both parents and children. Some lessons are available from experiences with a collective living arrangement, the *kibbutz*, in Israel. Since the early 1900s, several kibbutzim have been established as planned utopian communities. Children are raised in group settings and have frequent contact with their parents, but they do not live in the parental home. By most reports, the children grow to be psychologically healthy, although there are reports of difficulties with intimate relationships. These difficulties may indicate interference with the development of healthy attachment because of the decreased contact with their parents or the inadequacy of the substitute group care setting. More recent changes, in which the children sleep with their families and are in group care only during the day, have produced more secure attachment (Aviezer et al., 1994).

Important as family is to personality and personality is to family life, people also function in a wider social world, a world in which political events can have profound effects at virtually all levels of our lives. What do we know about the relationship of personality to political life?

Political Life

Can we understand enough about the relationship of personality to politics to attract and elect wise and honorable leaders to government? Can we recognize a demagogue in time to avoid reliving the atrocities of history? These aims can provide direction to our inquiry (in addition to the simple curiosity of how personality relates to politics).

Attitudes about political issues are influenced, at least in part, by personality. The Big Five factor called Openness to Experience, for example, is negatively correlated with conservative political attitudes (Riemann et al., 1993): the more open we are to experience, the more liberal our political views, it seems. Political liberalism and conservatism can be understood by considering how we judge other people. Liberals tend to believe that people who are poor are in that condition for reasons that are caused by society, rather than of their own making. Conservatives more often believe that people's own behavior and choices affect their economic well-being. These internal and external attributions are consistent with the more favorable attitudes of liberals toward expansion of social programs and aid for those in need, as well as with conservatives' concern about such aid (Skitka & Tetlock, 1993).

Integrative complexity of thinking varies among those who express different political persuasions. During the pre–Civil War period in the United States, those who favored the abolition of slavery and those who favored its continuation were less cognitively complex in their political writings than those who argued for an intermediate position: restricting slavery to certain areas of the country (Tetlock, Armor & Peterson, 1994). We can't be sure, of course, that the cognitive complexity of the *individuals* was adequately measured by their political writings. Some very complex thinkers may present a message, such as abolition, in a simple and straightforward way. Conversely, when conflicting principles (such as slavery and states' rights) need to be reconciled, the communication may inherently require more intricate statements. In modern times, when Israeli prime ministers have argued for peace, their speeches are more cognitively complex than when they have argued for war (Maoz & Shayer, 1987). Philip Tetlock and his colleagues caution us that more complex thinking is not necessarily morally superior (Tetlock, Armor & Peterson, 1994). It may offer an edge in planning, though. The military success of Robert E. Lee during the Civil War is credited in part to his greater integrative complexity, compared to that of his opponents, based on analysis of historical documents (Suedfeld, Corteen & McCormick, 1986).

Personality influences political participation. Among undergraduates and nonstudents, those higher in political efficacy (the belief that one has the skills to influence the political system) were more often members of political organizations (Zimmerman, 1989). Efficacy beliefs that are specific to a situation, such as the efficacy of voting or of participating in demonstrations, are better predictors of specific behavior (Wollman & Stouder, 1991). There is a converse relationship between personality and political events, too: political events can change personalities. When Poland became a democratic country in 1988, Polish university students began to shift significantly from an external to an internal locus of control on a Political Control subscale of Rotter's Internal-External Locus of Control Scale (Tobacyk, 1992). This subscale contains such items as "The average citizen can influence government." Nonpolitical items on the scale did not change. Sometimes personality reflects reality. This is consistent with Albert Bandura's (1978) model of an interrelationship among personality, behavior, and the environment (discussed in Chapter 9).

Major changes in government are relatively infrequent, but the level of threat experienced within a country rises and falls periodically, depending upon such factors as economic conditions and crime rates. In difficult times, more people turn to strong leaders, who promise to maintain social order and to solve society's problems with their power and authority. During times of threat in the United States, the attitudes of its citizens become more authoritarian, a syndrome characterized by an emphasis on powerful authority figures, dominance-submission, cynicism, and aggression. These authoritarian attitudes, which stem in part from social conditions and in part from personality predispositions, influence many political behaviors. Politically conservative groups, such as the Moral Majority, become more popular, and conservative candidates fare well in elections. Violent pornography increases. Incidents of ethnic and racial violence increase (Doty, Peterson & Winter, 1991). Authoritarianism is associated with prejudiced attitudes toward racial and ethnic minorities, homophobia, religious fundamentalism, and punitiveness (Wylie & Forest, 1992). Understanding the personality dynamics behind the authoritarian personality (Adorno et al., 1950) can make political changes more understandable and predictable.

Citizens perceive political candidates in terms of their own personality concepts and scripts, not purely in terms of political issues. Just before the U.S. presidential election of 1984, college students and adults in the community were asked to cast the major parties' presidential and vice-presidential candidates in imaginary television dramas that had been devised to represent particular themes deemed important in Tomkins's (1987) script theory. The first (humanistic) theme was concerned with the emotions of joy, distress, and shame; the second (normative) theme was concerned with the emotions of excitement, anger, and contempt. As the researchers predicted, the Republican candidates Ronald Reagan and George Bush were cast more often in the imaginary dramas involving normative themes (such as sports competition and punishment), while the Democratic candidates Walter Mondale and Geraldine Ferraro were cast in humanistic roles, such as class reunions and caring for flood victims (Carlson & Brincka, 1987).

Can we predict who will win an election, using personality concepts? David Winter (1987) analyzed the achievement, affiliation, and power motives of American presidents based on their inaugural speeches and found that when their motive profile matched the prevailing mood in the country at the time (as coded from cultural documents), they won the election by a wider margin. They were not necessarily more popular with the electorate, although people with authoritarian personalities prefer more power motivated candidates.

Presidential behavior in office could also be predicted from motives: presidents with high power motive were more likely to be in office when the country entered a war, and they were rated by historians as more effective presidents (McCann, 1990a, 1990b; Winter, 1987, 1993). Would the United States have become involved in the war in Bosnia earlier under a more power motivated president? Perhaps. Researchers speculate that if George Bush and Mikhail Gorbachev had been higher on the power motive, the world could have experienced greater military escalation during the Persian Gulf War of 1991 (Winter et al., 1991a, 1991b). Even

TABLE 12.3 **Types of Political Personalities among World Leaders**

1. Active-independent (forceful/aggressive) pattern
   Need for power and dominance
   Examples: Winston Churchill, Saddam Hussein

2. Active-dependent (social/histrionic) pattern
   Need for affiliation, impulsiveness, low resistance to corrupting influences
   Examples: Ronald Reagan, Bill Clinton

3. Passive-independent (confident/narcissistic) pattern
   Exploitative, macho, hardball politics
   Example: Muammar Qaddafi

4. Passive-ambivalent (respectful/conforming) pattern
   Conventional, authoritarian
   Examples: P. W. Botha, George Bush

5. Paranoid
   Severely disorganized, narcissistic
   Example: Adolf Hitler

Adapted from Immelman, 1993, who suggests all the examples except Hitler.

Richard Nixon, who presided over a controversial invasion of Cambodia in 1970, was only moderate in the power motive, which can partially explain his ambivalence over that action (Winter & Carlson, 1988). A higher power motive was evidenced in the inaugural speech of John Fitzgerald Kennedy (Donley & Winter, 1970), which helps to explain the attempted U.S. invasion of Cuba in 1961. Power can, of course, be exercised in a variety of ways, and more detailed models help predict whether a president will take personal charge of decisions or will exercise power through Congress and ambassadors. Motives, of course, are not the only predictor of presidential action, but they are a significant component (House, Spangler & Woycke, 1991; Spangler & House, 1991).

Political leaders can drastically affect the course of world events. Several approaches to understanding them by applying concepts from personality and from psychopathology have been proposed. One approach applies Theodore Millon's model of personality types and personality disorders to political figures (Immelman, 1993) (Table 12.3). It is a mistake, however, to exaggerate the role of the leader's personality in determining political outcomes. The domestic and international situations interact with any leader's personality to determine these outcomes (Simonton, 1990).

In addition to political leaders, the personalities of those who play important supportive roles in the political events of an era are worthy of study. Many people have wondered about the atrocities of German concentration camps in World War II. Even if the behavior of Hitler can be understood—such as by analyzing his psychopathology (for example, Waite, 1977)—how can we explain the fact that thousands of German citizens cooperated in the well-coordinated behaviors that were necessary to effect mass exterminations? Were they all disturbed? Were they all motivated by hatred? Or could it be that, as the defense claimed at the Nuremberg war trials, they were simply following orders (Milgram, 1974)? Based on an analysis of Rorschach inkblot tests, researchers have concluded that high-level Nazi leaders were not psychotic. Although they may have been somewhat compulsive and mildly paranoid, they were similar to many other people who, but for the luck of history, were leading uneventful lives in other countries (Resnick & Nunno, 1991).

It would be oversimplistic, of course, to explain political events only in terms of personality. That would be analogous to trying to explain personality only in terms of biological variables. Yet we would miss important insights into political events if we were to ignore the personalities of our leaders, the personality dynamics aroused by political upheavals, and the personalities of citizens.

Religion

Gordon Allport (1950) criticized the psychologists of his day for largely neglecting to investigate religion, despite its importance for many people. He offered one of the most influential conceptualizations of religious orientation, one that has generated considerable research. He proposed that there are two kinds of religious orientation: intrinsic and extrinsic. People with an **intrinsic religious orientation** truly believe the teachings of their religion, and their practice of religion stems from heartfelt inner conviction. In contrast, people with an **extrinsic religious orientation** are simply putting on a show of religious behavior to gain some selfish advantage for themselves: perhaps to increase their status in the community or to meet business contacts, for example (Allport & Ross, 1967). According to one reviewer, this distinction between intrinsic and extrinsic religiousness is "the single greatest contribution to the empirical study of religion" (Van Wicklin, 1990).

Allport claimed that, because intrinsically religious people had internalized the teachings of their religion, they would be tolerant of other people. After all, virtually all world religions teach us to love our neighbors. He proposed that racial prejudice would be low among those who are intrinsically religious, and research supported this claim by showing that racial prejudice was low among those who were scored as intrinsically religious on a written measure and high among those scored as extrinsically religious (Herek, 1987). Intrinsically religious people seem to have higher levels of empathy for others, which may motivate their tolerance and also their helpful behavior toward others (Watson et al., 1984).

There are, however, other forms of prejudice besides those based on race. Recently, attention has turned to prejudice based on sexual orientation. Does prejudice against homosexuals show the same pattern as that against racial minorities? Research on Christians indicates that it does not. In fact, intrinsically oriented individuals are *more* prejudiced against gays and lesbians than are those who are not religious. Why would this be? One explanation, proposed by Gregory Herek, is that religious teachings explicitly warn against homosexuality, so that antihomosexual attitudes are part of the religious teachings (Herek, 1987; Kirkpatrick, 1993). Those Christians whose religious attitudes are fundamentalist—that is, who accept the Bible as a literal and infallible authority—are also more likely to be prejudiced against a variety of groups: blacks, women, homosexuals, and communists.

If we are to understand the implications of religious belief for social behavior, such as prejudice and altruism (Batson, 1990), we must consider the particular teachings of the religion. Albert Bandura noted that moral behavior cannot be maintained by individual personality alone but requires the supports and constraints of social institutions (Bandura, 1990b). It is important to examine those social institutions critically and to evaluate individuals within that context.

Several studies have indicated that those with high scores on intrinsic religiousness also score high on measures of social desirability and impression management, which suggests that perhaps people were only reporting that they were religious to give answers that they thought would be approved by the experimenter (Leak & Fish, 1989; Richards, 1994). This may be an overly pessimistic interpretation, however. Social desirability is measured by asking people whether they do things that many people consider desirable but that they don't always do, such as obeying the speed limit. Perhaps highly religious people say yes to items like this not to deceive themselves and others by appearing better than they really are, but because they do, in fact, behave in the ways they report. If that is the case, they should not be said to be managing their impressions, any more than a person who claims to have won an Oscar should be accused of lying if he or she has, in fact, won that prize (see the Research Strategies box).

Besides Allport's distinction between intrinsic and extrinsic religiousness, other categories have been proposed. An extension of Allport and Ross's categories describes three orientations: Religion as a Means, Religion as an End, and Religion as a Quest (Batson & Ventis, 1982).

RESEARCH STRATEGIES ●---------------------------------

Can Our Research Subjects Represent the Public at Large?

When we read research reports, it is tempting to skim over many of the details of the method, including the detailed descriptions of subjects, to get to the conclusion of the study. That may leave us with misleading impressions, however. Suppose a study concludes that people who score high on a measure of intrinsic religiousness are less racially prejudiced than those who score low. Does it matter whether our subjects are chosen from the general population or from those who attend a particular church or religiously affiliated school? Does the racial composition of the sample matter, whether it consists of all whites or a racial mixture more representative of the general population? Does it matter whether they have had extensive interactions with other racial groups or not? Or whether the study was conducted recently or decades ago? The correlation of any two measures can vary from one data collection to another, and we ought not to assume that a relationship found in any one study can be expected to be replicated in all circumstances, or even in any other circumstances.

A general principle of research says that we can generalize the results of a research study only to populations and settings similar to those we have actually observed. Ideally, we should randomly sample our subjects from the group we wish to understand as, for example, voters are randomly selected before an election by professional pollsters who wish to predict the results accurately. More practically, because random sampling is too time-consuming and expensive for most research studies, we should at least look at the particulars of our research sample and make sensible judgments about what other groups may be regarded as similar. For example, if you asked 10 high school students to name their favorite musical group, and their top choices were Pearl Jam, Cypress Hill, and R.E.M., you would hardly expect their judgments to predict the choices of graduate students, professors, or the general population.

To practice this kind of judgment about the generalizability of research results, read these brief descriptions of research results and the subjects upon which they are based. Then consider the other potential subject populations and say whether you would expect the results to be similar or different, and why.

1. Personality tests given to a group of college seniors are found to correlate with type of occupation 20 years later. Those who scored high in the need for achievement were more likely to be working as businessmen. Subjects were all male, and they attended Harvard University in the 1960s.

What aspects of the group studied might affect the outcome? For example, would you expect these results to be similar if female subjects were studied? Suppose the research were carried out at an inexpensive state university in the American Midwest or at a prestigious European or Asian university. Suppose the students were seniors in the late 1990s instead of the 1960s. Suppose they were members of racial minority groups.

2. Couples who did not have sexual relationships before marriage were found to have a lower divorce rate than those who engaged in premarital sex. Subjects were married in the 1950s and came from a white, middle class population.

Would you expect these results to be similar if the study were conducted among people getting married today? Would you predict any differences if the subjects were African American? Asian? Hispanic? Would it matter if you studied people from large cities or from rural areas, or if the subjects came from a lower socioeconomic level?

Not all groups of people are the same, obviously. In addition, we might wish to look at the impact of a variety of personality measures to see whether they add to our understanding: Openness to Experience or any of the other five personality factors, religious attitudes, and so on. These personality traits are fascinating, but we must always remember that they are traits that describe particular people, in particular social contexts.

Now that you have thought about the limitations of any particular research that result from the choice of a particular subject population, look back at the studies summarized in this chapter. (You may wish to look at other chapters, too.) Consider whether the results seem to you to be likely to be true of humans in general or limited to particular groups based on sex, race or ethnicity, country, age, historical time, sexual orientation, socioeconomic status, or other characteristics that you think are significant. Remember, though: there is no way to be sure that results can be generalized unless other populations are, in fact, studied.

Another approach distinguishes religious orientations in which people have come to accept religious teaching internally (Identification) and orientations that remain dependent on others' approval (Introjection) (Ryan, Rigby & King, 1993). Clearly, what one person means by religiousness is not always the same as what another person means. This is theoretically sensible, because religiousness is not a separate, isolated feature but is integrated with the rest of the unique personality of an individual. Gordon Allport (1950) described religion as a unifying philosophy of life, and each of us has different components to unify, so it is not surprising that each style of religious thought would have an individual mark. Among undergraduates, for example, religious experiences tend to be described more often in terms of love and friendship by those motivated by intimacy, but in terms of strength and uplift by those motivated by power (McAdams, Booth & Selvik, 1981).

Hans Eysenck's personality dimension of Psychoticism has often been reported to be negatively correlated with religiousness. That is, highly religious people score low on psychoticism (Francis, 1991, 1992; Francis & Pearson, 1993). In Eysenck's model, the personality dimension of Psychoticism includes a high level of impulsiveness, which contrasts with the learned self-control that is inherent in religiousness. This is not to say that religious individuals have nothing in common with psychotics. Some psychotic people have religious delusions as major symptoms; for example, occasional schizophrenics who believe that they are Christ (Rokeach, 1981). Some religious mystics have been thought mad. An empirical study of members of contemplative or mystical religious groups found that they were similar to a group of psychotics in having high scores on the Hood Mysticism Scale. They differed on other personality measures, of course, especially a measure of ego control, on which the religious mystics were similar to the normal population (Stifler et al., 1993). Even a group with a highly unusual religious practice in the United States, cult followers of an Eastern mystic residing on a commune in Oregon, seemed quite similar to more mainstream populations according to psychological tests (Sundberg et al., 1992).

Most studies of religion rely upon self-report measures to decide who is religious and in what way (Van Wicklin, 1990). Although it may seem inadequate, the questionnaire method has produced meaningful results, and questionnaires may actually be more effective in measuring religious convictions than in measuring some of the other areas studied by psychologists, because this is a private matter known best to the individual. As with all the social tasks we have considered, we must keep in mind that religious experience develops over a lifetime (Allport, 1950; Baird, 1990) and that it may be different if studied in a young population, such as the undergraduate students so often surveyed, rather than in a more mature group. In fact, religion seems to be particularly important in the coping and mental health of older people (Koenig, 1990).

*O*ur Multiple Social Tasks

Although we have considered these social tasks one at a time, we all somehow combine most of them—education, work, love and marriage, parenting, politics, and religion—into one life. They are not independent. The work role, for example, has a different significance for the individual and for those who know her or him, depending upon the marriage relationship and parenting roles. Sometimes multiple roles enhance one another, as when the positive self-esteem that successful work can bring leads to more positive interactions in the family. At other times, roles conflict, as when scarcity of time or energy prevents us from performing each task to the level we otherwise could accomplish (Hoffman, 1986; Moos, 1986).

Culture provides messages about how these roles should be combined and about how different people (particularly men and women) or people at different stages of life should configure the mix. For example, when shoppers at a U.S. shopping mall were asked to describe hypothetical people, they evaluated mothers of young children differently depending upon whether or not they worked outside the home and whether or not they were married. Knowing that the hypothetical mother was employed led subjects to judge her as less dedicated to her family than if she stayed at home, and divorced mothers were judged less nurturant and less adjusted than those who were married (Etaugh & Nekolny, 1990). Such a result, of course, may depend upon whom you ask. Women and men, divorced and married people, modern respondents or people living in the 1950s, people with money to hire good child care or people of more modest means, may well make different judgments about such social roles and how they should be combined.

SUMMARY

• People develop and express their personalities through social tasks, including education, work, love and marriage, parenting, political life, and religion.

• Education enhances a child's sense of competence and develops the child's intelligence. Experts disagree whether intelligence consists of a general factor or several factors (multiple intelligences).

• Humanistic education fosters the development of the whole person. Educational success depends on personality, such as self-efficacy expectations, as well as on intelligence, and education provides a setting for learning inter-personal skills, such as the cooperation fostered by the jigsaw classroom.

• Career choice and performance are influenced by personality variables, including self-efficacy, cognitive complexity, interests, the so-called Protestant work ethic, and motives. Work provides satisfaction, but at risk of stress and burnout.

• There are several love styles, ranging from the playful (Ludus) to the self-sacrificing (Agape), and attachment styles (secure, anxious/avoidant, and ambivalent). Desperate love is a maladaptive style.

• Couples may tend to have similar personalities, although some evidence suggests that couples are matched more randomly. Similarity of personality and absence of neuroticism contribute to marital happiness.

• Parenting produces stress. Various forms of parenting include the increasingly popular dual-role model, in which both parents are actively involved in child care, and group child care such as the Israeli kibbutz. Parental discipline and authority styles and the stability of the parental marriage influence children's development.

• Political views are influenced by personality traits, including Openness to Experience and integrative complexity. The personality of political leaders is related to their action; for example, power motivation is predictive of war.

• Intrinsic religious attitudes predict racial tolerance but prejudice against homosexuals. A variety of self-report measures of religious orientation have been developed, but these may be limited, and religiousness is intertwined with other aspects of personality.

• Culture influences all these social tasks.

GLOSSARY

burnout decreased work motivation and accomplishments, with increased emotional difficulties and cynicism, produced by long-term stress

cognitive integration a cognitive trait in which a person has constructs that are organized in hierarchical arrangements

cognitive differentiation a cognitive trait in which a person has many constructs and can adopt many viewpoints toward a situation

congruence model the theory that people will be happier in work settings if their own interests and values are shared by others in the work setting

extrinsic religious orientation the trait of religious involvement based on external advantages of being religious, such as increased status and social contacts

intelligence a person's ability to learn

intrinsic religious orientation the trait of religious conviction and true belief

jigsaw classroom a strategy of using cooperative assignments in elementary school to promote cooperation and to improve interracial harmony

sensitization principle the postulate that people are especially likely to perceive demands, frustrations, and gratifications at work that are relevant to their own motivations

workaholic a person who is highly involved in work and seeks perfection, but who is also highly stressed and dissatisfied

THOUGHT QUESTIONS

1. What changes would you suggest in the educational system to make it more conducive to personality development or more effective for people with a variety of personalities?

2. Do you favor the idea that intelligence is best described as one general trait or as multiple intelligences?

3. From the point of view of personality (for example, efficacy), do you believe that schools should require many courses or allow more electives? Why?

4. What, in your opinion, should be the role of work for adults? That is, should it be a central task requiring many hours and defining the adult's identity, or should it be less central?

5. Based on your experience and observation, how do people decide what careers to enter? Do the models described in this chapter seem to fit these observations?

6. What style or styles of love and attachment would you prefer in your partner in a relationship?

7. Considering cultural changes in the family, how has parenting changed? What suggestions would you offer to improve parenting?

8. Do you believe that the personality of a political leader contributes to his or her political actions and success? What traits are important, and what effect do they have?

9. Do you believe that religion contributes to tolerance or to prejudice? Consider the research results in this chapter but, more importantly, your own observations.

10. Would you add any social tasks to those discussed in this chapter? Which ones?

13

The Cultural Context of Personality

THE WORD *CULTURE* CONJURES UP IMAGES of opera performances, place settings with enough forks and spoons to confuse all but the most well-bred, and literature that many people know only from the questions asked on television game shows. This is not the culture we will be concerned with here, but considering these connotations does make the point that people learn a great deal through social experience. These cultural lessons are pervasive and shape our personalities profoundly.

As the term is used in psychology, **culture** consists of the socially transmitted beliefs and practices that influence our behavior and personality. These beliefs and practices vary from one country to another and among groups within a country.

The field of **cross-cultural psychology** compares cultures and ethnic groups and examines similarities and differences in psychological functioning of the members of these groups (Kagitçibaşi & Berry, 1989). In many cases, researchers expect to find similarities across cultures. Personality traits, for example, are thought to be similar when they constitute basic individual differences determined by biological processes, such as variations in the levels of neurotransmitters and hormones (see Chapter 11). Many studies find similarities in such traits; for example, in the structure of Extraversion, Neuroticism, and other major personality factors (Angleitner, Buss & Demtröder, 1990; Eysenck, 1986c; Paunonen et al., 1992). Of course, such cross-cultural comparisons are meaningful only if the tests used to measure the traits have validity in all the cultures being compared (Harrington, 1986; see Chapter 4).

In contrast to cross-cultural psychology, the emerging field of **cultural psychology** studies the processes by which cultural practices and traditions influence personality and other psychological phenomena (Shweder, 1990). Rather than simply describing differences, cultural psychology weaves the thread of culture through all of personality. It is closely connected with the fields of anthropology and linguistics, which also investigate the impact of culture on individuals (Shweder & Sullivan, 1993). The learning of language depends upon culture. Children learn to speak the language that surrounds them, but more than that, they are born with an innate ability to learn to utter many sounds. Those that are not used in the language of a particular culture are lost from the child's repertoire and can be learned later in life only with great difficulty, as native English speakers discover when they struggle to pronounce a French trilling *r*. The way that we learn language may be a metaphor for the many potentials we all have, only some of which are developed in each culture.

Personality is thoroughly cultural, especially because culture influences the meanings that we accept about ourselves and our world. Culture teaches us whether our sexuality is a shameful reminder of evil or a vibrant sign of life. Culture teaches us whether ambition is a moral virtue or evidence of sinful pride. A student doing homework is not simply doing homework but seeking a culturally valued college degree and a career that has cultural meaning. Our worlds, in the language of Richard Shweder (1990), are not passive but are defined by our goals and strivings; they are "intentional worlds" that guide our striving within the context of culture. The sense of self and the experience of emotion are influenced by culture (Shweder & Sullivan, 1993). How do you feel about your racial and ethnic background, your religious heritage, your family's socioeconomic status? Does your physical appearance give you pleasure or grief? Does anger make you feel strong or ashamed? All these values, and more, are learned.

Cross-cultural comparisons help to reveal the impact of culture, but according to Richard Shweder (1990), they underestimate the centrality of culture by looking for an underlying similarity based on the assumption that culture shapes the expression of personality without changing its core. Cultural psychology, in contrast, assumes that culture helps to create personality, not simply to shape it. There is no context-free personality. Studying cultural differences is a good place to begin, because it can make us aware of our own cultural shortsightedness.

National Differences

From one country to another, people learn not only different languages and customs but also different ways of thinking about themselves and relating to other people. Their personalities are molded to the patterns characteristic of their nation. As global communications have increased contact among nations, the general personality differences we observe intrigue us and show us some of our potentials. By seeing the diversity of personalities across nations, we can understand one another better. We can begin to appreciate some of the potential forms that human personality can take.

Psychologists, understandably, build theories based on their experiences. Unless the cultural component of personality is considered, however, theories are biased by unconscious cultural assumptions that the theorists assume are universal. Among these assumptions are ideas about the separate individual self. In Western cultural tradition, the individual is honored for his or her independence, and the assumption that individuality is desirable is reflected in many descriptions of the healthy personality. The cultural emphasis on the independent self explains why self-enhancing behaviors, such as describing an athletic triumph, occur among Westerners. People in many Eastern cultures, including Japan, behave with greater humility, following the self-effacing norms of their cultures (Kitayama & Markus, 1992). Concern for the well-being of others is a higher priority in moral decisions in India than in the United States (Miller & Bersoff, 1992).

Cultural psychologists have observed that the understanding of the self depends upon cultural lessons and that it varies from one culture to another. For example, Westerners accept the statement "I am sociable" as a meaningful way of describing the self. The Japanese, however, would not make such a statement and would find it overly simplified. The specific social context in which the trait occurs would need to be stated, because the notion that the self shows the same traits across settings assumes a separate, autonomous self, independent instead of interdependent, which is a Western concept not shared in Eastern cultures (Cousins, 1989; Kitayama & Markus, 1992; Rhee et al., 1995). A person from an Eastern culture would not say "I am sociable" but instead would describe sociability with a friend, with a school acquaintance, and with other specific people. Sociability in non-Western cultures is a characteristic of a person in a particular social context that must be specified; it is not a characteristic of an individual alone. The sense of self, and self-esteem, are culturally shaped.

Different cultural practices that contribute to personality provide "natural experiments" to learn how personalities are shaped: different child-rearing practices, rituals, or social expectations might result in different expressions of personality. Keep in mind that both cultural practices and genetic variations from one group of people to another may contribute to resulting personality differences (Greenfield & Childs, 1991). As some people move from one country to another, however, there is an opportunity to observe how much this cultural change produces personality change. Such observations allow us to untangle confounded biological and cultural variables. This information may have practical as well as theoretical significance, as we consider how to apply this knowledge to influence the direction of cultural change.

Because so much of personality results from our learning experiences and not only our biological inheritance, the circumstances of learning must be considered if we wish to understand personality. Culture provides the context for learning and determines whether a child will be encouraged to be obedient or assertive, autonomous or cooperative. Thus, the different cultural practices of various nations would naturally be expected to produce different effects on the personalities of their members. The social tasks that we considered in Chapter 12 are enacted in a variety of ways around the world.

Some of the most basic differences in cultural practices occur within the family. The division of responsibilities between parents and family relationships with other relatives are two examples. The variation in the typical number of children in each family, from large numbers of children to the one-child official policy of modern China, influences children's (and parents') development. Some psychologists believe that only children are less likely to develop such interpersonal skills as the ability to cooperate, so a whole nation of only children would be expected to influence the interpersonal climate of a country (Chen & Goldsmith, 1991).

Some cultural institutions and traditions relate to education and the selection of various kinds of intelligence. The particular tasks that a child is expected to master vary cross-culturally, such as the age at which an infant is expected to sleep through the night, reading, and making pottery (Best & Ruther, 1994). Culture, in essence, sets the curriculum for learning to be a person.

Many processes that were thought to be universal are not, according to cultural psychologists. For example, culture influences the development of intelligence. Like a college student who might take any course but has time for relatively few, a person may develop specific abilities and neglect others, depending upon the selections encouraged within his or her cultural setting. Abilities, then, are not only determined biologically but are patterned by culture, according to the "law of Cultural Differentiation" (Irvine & Berry, 1988; Kagitçibaşi & Berry, 1989). Native Cree of Canada, for example, are encouraged to learn a wealth of specific information about the physical world to prepare them for the traditional life of hunting and trapping, but the decontextualized, abstract ways of thinking that are required by nonnative schools are not part of their culture (Berry &

Bennett, 1992). Cross-cultural studies of cognition find that people who have been educated in schools do better than unschooled people on many cognitive tasks because unschooled people are less willing to consider matters about which they do not have direct personal experience. A specific experience, such as the use of an abacus, improves memory for related material, in this case for numbers (Rogoff & Chavajay, 1995). Such cultural effects mean that we cannot interpret differences between groups in measured intelligence, which demands such abstract thinking, as differences in innate potential intelligence.

Culture shapes the values that cause some people to spend many hours reading and writing, ignoring sunny weather, while others play ball until every muscle aches. Culture influences attitudes toward work, as reflected in studies of the Protestant work ethic (Furnham et al., 1993; Lynn, Yamauchi & Tachibana, 1991). The work ethic varies from country to country and from one historical period to another. It is theorized that such differences account for variations in economic productivity among nations and explain the recent economic prosperity of Japan and Hong Kong and the historical rise in wealth of northern Europe and the United States.

Love and marriage take different forms around the world, ranging from arranged marriages to romantic individual choice. Interactions with other people are more open in some cultures and more constrained in others. Ladd Wheeler (1988) notes that, compared to university students in the United States, Chinese students in Hong Kong have more restricted social lives; the heterosexual relationships of Chinese females are especially constrained.

Religious practices vary, too, as history tells us repeatedly when religious conflict leads to war. Even setting that aside, religious practices influence people differently from the biological level to the level of social consciousness. In Tibet, the meditation practices of Buddhist monks have produced dramatic effects on brain activity and body metabolism (Benson et al., 1990). The traditional Sun Dance of the Lakota Sioux of the American Midwest celebrates the strength and unity of those who participate. People who bear the scars of painful body piercing performed during the celebration bear a mark of honor. Those who celebrate the Sun Dance do not all agree about whether nonnative people should be allowed to participate or it should be limited to natives as a way of enhancing ethnic pride (Lincoln, 1994). Within the United States, the psychological function of religion seems to vary by race. In a study of university students, psychological well-being was higher among African American students who reported that religious beliefs were important to them, but this relationship was not observed among white students (Blaine & Crocker, 1995). From one study, we cannot be sure that this finding would apply to African Americans and whites generally, but it seems reasonable to conclude that the role of religion in people's lives can vary among groups within the same country as well as among different countries.

Japanese Amae

As we saw in Chapter 10, a child's attachment to the primary caretaker is the basis for social relationships throughout life. Children depend upon adults for physical care and emotional support. As we mature, we take on more responsibility for self-care, but we do not completely outgrow our dependency on others. The availability of emotional support, as we saw in Chapter 8, is an important source of psychological well-being. How much can we depend upon others, and how do we seek that nurturance from them? Different cultures give very different messages about this important issue.

Takeo Doi (1971/1973) describes the traditional Japanese cultural expression of *amae,* a much more explicitly dependent stance toward others than is expressed by any English word. Japanese culture permits adults to adopt a passive dependent stance in which they expect another to take care of their needs—to serve them food without asking first whether they are hungry or what they wish to eat, for example. Such dependency is reminiscent of the infant's need for the mother. Doi says that Americans, including psychiatrists, are very slow to perceive *amae* needs, at least in part because there is no English word that describes this attitude. The needs still exist, but without cultural recognition, they remain unfulfilled, neglected in favor of the more active, independent stance that is encouraged in American culture. Because Japanese culture recognizes these needs, it provides individuals with considerable guidance about their expression: toward whom such dependency can be expressed and how these needs can be fulfilled without placing such extraordinary expectations on the caretaker that nurturance is exhausted. The closest equivalent in the United States is to say "I'm sorry" when receiving such nurturance, but that does not have the same connotations as Japanese cultural expressions. Understanding Japanese culture offers increased insight for Westerners into their own unrecognized *amae* needs.

If dependency relationships, which are so important from infancy onward, are as influenced by culture as Doi's analysis suggests, we must be particularly cautious when we make comparisons across cultures about dependency and independence. Even research methods that seem well standardized, such as the strange-situation procedure for assessing infant attachment to the caretaker (presented in Chapter 10), may not be equally appropriate in all cultures. In fact, the correlations of infant strange-situation behaviors with other measures of maternal and infant behaviors that are typically found in American babies are not found when Japanese babies are studied, which suggests that the strange-situation procedure may not be an appropriate method for studying their development. Japanese babies may find the situation more stressful than American babies do (Nakagawa, Lamb & Miyaki, 1992), which is certainly consistent with Doi's suggestion that Americans are taught early not to expect indulgence of their dependency needs. In fact, Western theories of infant and child development have traditionally emphasized individuality; it has been only recently that attention has turned to interpersonal mutuality, an area in which the concept of *amae* articulated by Doi may provide insights into those aspects of the phenomenon that are not specific to Japan (Emde, 1992). *Amae* psychology also interests feminist psychologists, who have argued that women's personalities are typically more interpersonal than men's and are less well represented in the individualistic models of personality that have predominated (Bradshaw, 1990). If, as seems likely, all humans can experience the same emotions but in actuality are not often aware of experiencing those that are not recognized and labeled in their culture (Mauro, Sato & Tucker, 1992), then the cross-cultural investigation of emotion promises to enrich everyone's emotional life and to help bring nonverbalized experiences into awareness—a result that should raise consciousness and enhance mental health.

Cultural Context of Individuality: Individualist and Collectivist Cultures

Humans display two contradictory impulses: on the one hand, we cooperate in interdependent, mutually supportive ways; on the other, we separate from one another as autonomous individuals. Cultures vary in the balance of these impulses. Cultures are called **individualistic** if each person is expected to place personal goals ahead of the group and **collectivist** if group goals and welfare are a higher priority (see Chapter 4). Western thought, including the psychological views with which we are familiar, is firmly entrenched in the individualistic mode. Seventy percent of the world, in contrast, lives in collectivist cultures (Triandis, 1990).

Western models of development emphasize the importance of the development of a separate ego; Eastern traditions, including Buddhism, do not advocate such strong differentiation of the ego from the unconscious (Nitis, 1989) or of self from nonself (Landrine, 1992). One description of an African approach to the person describes a "community" of selves within each person, rather than a single unified self. These selves include ancestral components and animal souls (Ogbonnaya, 1994). Both of these traditions challenge the Western assumption of a self-contained, unified individual. In Western culture, a serious breakdown in such unity may be called multiple personality disorder (MPD). MPD is a controversial disorder thought to be influenced by cultural beliefs; it is defined as a disease in our culture but not in all cultures (Spanos, 1994). The African belief in a community of selves demonstrates the availability of an alternative cultural interpretation of this phenomenon.

Culture provides shared meanings that guide individuals through their lives. Those who do not share the meanings, values, and interpretations of their culture are deviant—perhaps criminal or mentally disturbed, depending upon the nature of their deviant stories (Howard, 1991). Stories vary from one culture to another; for example, witchcraft and modern medicine are "stories" or narrative explanations that have been accepted only in some cultures. Personality disturbances vary from one part of the world to another. Eating disorders, for example, are widely believed to be produced by the cultural expectations for thinness that prevail in Western cultures. Eating disorders are reported only infrequently in third world countries and in nonwhite populations (Davis & Yager, 1992; Dolan, 1991).

Collectivist cultures emphasize interpersonal harmony and responsibility, in contrast to the competitive emphasis of individualist cultures. People from collectivist cultures are more likely to share rewards equally, while those from individualist cultures prefer to allocate rewards according to the perceived contribution of each person to the successful outcome (Triandis, 1988). In a traditional hunting environment, the collectivist strategy would help protect everyone against starvation. Harry Triandis (1988) suggests that smaller families, lower population density, social and geographic mobility, and hedonism—all of which are circumstances that are less facilitated by group efforts—are some of the factors that lead to individualism in society. This list certainly may help explain why the United States is ranked high in individualism.

In the United States, some ethnic minorities have, as part of their cultural heritage, a more collectivist orientation than the highly individualist majority culture. Hispanics, for example, have a traditional emphasis on family solidarity and the extended family (Segura & Pierce, 1993). So do Hawaiians (Triandis, 1988). Such values have been largely neglected by researchers and devalued by mainstream culture. African Americans, too, have a cultural tradition that emphasizes collective strivings (Gaines & Reed, 1995). The collective orientations of these groups may subtly influence their reactions to social phenomena that we all encounter. An interesting study demonstrates that the collectivism of Hispanics in the United States has an effect on a controversial social issue: smoking. Non-Hispanic Americans considered smoking from an individualist perspective, considering such issues as the physiological symptoms of their own withdrawal if they stopped smoking. In contrast, the more collectivist Hispanic group described concern about smoking's effect on others, with its potential to harm children, set a bad example, annoy others, and so on (Marin et al., 1987, cited in Triandis, 1989). Clearly, the individualism-collectivism dimension of culture is not an isolated issue but a cultural orientation that pervades our life experiences.

Individualism and collectivism are part of the cultural context that shapes the expression of personality traits. Many of the aspects of personality that we have considered in previous chapters take different forms, depending upon whether they are expressed in an individualist or a collectivist culture. Consider achievement motivation. A person may strive to achieve as an individual, working alone for individual glory, or as part of a team, combining efforts with the work of others to achieve a collective goal. The individual pattern is more descriptive of the United States, the collective pattern more descriptive of Japan and Iran. In one study, Americans take more credit for their successes, even distorting their perceptions in a self-enhancing way, than do Japanese college students (Markus & Kitayama, 1991). Because the original studies of achievement motivation were conceived in an individualist culture, the motive has been described in ways that may be culturally biased (Torney-Purta, 1984) and that do not help us understand shared efforts toward group goals.

Psychological understandings of the self may be similarly biased, suitable for "white, middle-class men with a Western European ethnic background" but not for everyone (Markus & Kitayama, 1991, p. 225). Psychological understandings of an independent, separate self do not accurately describe the selves of women and non-European ethnic groups. Different understandings of the self are so fundamental that they are reflected in language. The Japanese word for self, *jibun*, is translated as "one's share of the shared life space" (Hamaguchi, 1985, cited in Markus & Kitayama, 1991, p. 228). Imagine the difficulties that such language differences pose to the researcher who attempts to translate a personality questionnaire for use in a different culture! There are even cultures in which, if a researcher inquires about an individual's health, it is not considered culturally appropriate to say that one is healthy if there are others to whom one is attached who are not healthy. So the assumptions that guide psychological researchers, based on their background in an individualist society, do not prepare them even to ask questions of people in a collectivist culture.

The concepts of individualism and collectivism are useful ways of thinking about cultures, but we should be careful not to overgeneralize them. Much current cultural research builds on ideas that were originally derived from a study of work-related values (Hofstede, 1980). There is considerable evidence that individualism and collectivism are meaningful ways of thinking about values beyond the realm of work, but this does not mean that they are all-pervasive or that collectivist cultures are evenly collectivist in all areas of life. Cultures can manifest *contextual collectivism*, displaying collective orientations in some areas or contexts but not others (collective health care but individual housing, for example). Furthermore, the others with whom we share goals need to be defined. Who is a member of our group and who is not? Perhaps in tribal cultures, loyalty to others means only those who live in the same tribe. In modern life, the "other" can range from members of our household to those we see often at work and school to members of the community to strangers we see only once to people in distant parts of the globe. Which of these belong to our collective interest? In language used by social psychologists, who is a member of our *ingroup*, to whom we are bound by loyalty and solidarity, and who belongs to the *outgroup*, those who do not share our common interest?

The answers can and do vary, which makes the "individual versus collective" distinction a concept that needs further refinement. In times of war, we feel ingroup loyalty to others in our country who would be members of the outgroup in times of peace. The phrase "war on poverty" in the United States attempts to elicit this feeling of community. Researcher Harry Triandis describes Italians as "family collectivists and outside the family basic individualists" (Triandis, 1988, p. 82)—the family context is one of cooperation and mutual support, but the outside world is a place of competition. In Israel, food is collectively grown in the kibbutz, but some kibbutzim practice collective child-rearing while others do not (Aviezer et al., 1994).

Perhaps we can all provide illustrations of contexts in which we expect collective interests to prevail and other contexts in which we expect individual self-interest to prevail. If people disagree about whether a particular context should be one of collectivist or individualist norms, there is a risk of misunderstanding or conflict. It is also possible, though, that we overstate the conflict between individuality and collectivity. Perhaps they are better understood as two themes that interact in a dialectical relationship because both are necessary for people to become mature (Guisinger & Blatt, 1994). Although certain cultures and certain groups within a culture may emphasize one theme over the other, both themes are intrinsic to the human condition.

Race and Ethnicity

The term **race** refers to a group of people who are distinct in their genetic makeup as a result of a history of inbreeding in a local geographic area. Those who study race as a determinant of personality believe that personality is influenced by genetic causes and that the genetic differences from one race to another contribute to personality differences among groups. It is virtually impossible, however, to consider race by itself, because genetic differences work in conjunction with cultural differences. The term **ethnicity** refers to a shared cultural heritage.

Although it is commonly supposed that the races are biologically distinct genetic groups, the term is generally used to refer to people who are not really very genetically distinct. Many people have mixed ancestry; they are descended from different groups of ancestors who may have been genetically distinct inbred groups in the remote past. Culture, rather than biology, defines race today. Even these definitions are not consistent. Marvin Zuckerman (1990b) notes that in the United States prior to the Civil War, any person who had $\frac{1}{32}$ black genetic ancestry (one ancestor five generations earlier) was defined as black. In Brazil, in contrast, any hint of Caucasian appearance suffices for the person to be called white. Race is

When Martin Luther King, Jr. was leading protests in the 1960s, African Americans were called Negroes. Since then, social change in America has brought substantial changes in racial identity and self-esteem, reminding us that personality must be understood in its social context.

thus a social category, not a biological one. Even on biological DNA measures described by Zuckerman, the differences within racial groups are far greater than the differences between groups. This is also true of personality measures (Zuckerman, 1990b).

Race functions as a social category, and one that is associated with various indicators of social advantage. Although a proper discussion of the higher rates of poverty and crime among racial minorities in the United States is the province of sociology, not psychology, we cannot understand the psychological implications of race without acknowledging that, in the main, social advantage goes to those who are white. The conditions of poverty subject disproportionate numbers of minority children to social stresses, such as crime and educational disadvantage, and to physical afflictions, such as exposure to lead and other toxins and less than optimal health care. It is difficult to estimate the extent to which such living conditions contribute to personality breakdown or shape personality, but it is unreasonable to think that the confounding of social disadvantage with minority status is inconsequential for personality. At the same time, to focus only on the disadvantages of minority status without understanding the strengths that exist (for example, in minority families) presents a distorted picture (Greene, 1992).

Race and Mental Health

Many psychologists who study mental health have expressed concern that racial minorities, especially African Americans, are diagnosed as having severe mental disorders more frequently than whites (Bulhan, 1985; Lindsey & Paul, 1989). A number of explanations have been suggested. The more stressful life circumstances experienced by the less privileged in society may propel them to more frequent breakdown. Another possible explanation is that the expectations of mental health professionals lead them to make biased diagnoses, judging the problems reported by those whose racial and socioeconomic background is similar to their own as less severe and diagnosing serious disturbances such as schizophrenia more often among minorities (Pavkov, Lewis & Lyons, 1989). The psychological tests that are sometimes used to help make diagnoses may also be biased (Choca et al., 1990). Tests do seem to favor those who are more "mainstream" in their cultural identification. For example, Mexican-American college students who are more closely identified with Hispanic culture have less healthy profiles on the Psychological Screening Inventory than do those who are more identified with mainstream Anglo culture. Traditional Mexican norms that encourage presenting a favorable public image and keeping personal and family problems to oneself presumably contribute to the higher scores on Alienation and Defensiveness and lower scores on Social Nonconformity and Expression subscales of the more traditionally identified Mexican students (Negy & Woods, 1993). Although tests seem "objective," they are not free of bias and must be evaluated critically to be sure that validity and comparisons for various groups are fair. Otherwise, tests may be used inappropriately to substantiate the belief that minorities are psychologically deficient (Greene, 1994b).

White therapists must be taught to understand minority cultures adequately, including their clients' expectations about treatment, motivations for work and achievement, and the strengths of their family and religious support systems (Jones, 1990; Sue, 1988). Without understanding a patient's cultural background, it is not possible to evaluate his or her behavior accurately. When the therapist comes from a culture different from that of the client, it is also important to be sure that racist assumptions in a variety of forms do not impede therapy (Greene, 1985). Sensitivity to ethnicity is important for therapeutic effectiveness, but the available evidence does not suggest that therapists and patients must be members of the same ethnic group for therapy to be successful (Sue, 1988). Furthermore, the importance of cultural issues to the presenting problems of patients is variable. For some, such issues are central. For others, the core issues may have little to do with culture (Jones, 1985).

Racial/Ethnic Identity

Most of us have, from time to time, filled out surveys in which we are asked to indicate our ethnicity. Categories vary, but often include white (or Caucasian), black (or African American), Hispanic, Asian, and so on. Some people, of course, find such categorizations offensive. (During the 1960s, some of us checked the "Other" box on school registration forms and defiantly filled in the blank with the word "human," thinking it politically savvy to indicate only that we were members of the human race. I've always wondered whether this well-intended rebellion undermined affirmative admission policies.) With history, the particular designations have changed. "African American" displaced "Black," which in turn substituted for "Negro" and before that, "Colored" (Philogene, 1994; Smith, 1992). Each changed designation reflected an attempt to claim a more positive social identity. Many Hispanic individuals prefer to be called "Latino" (or the feminine form, "Latina") to emphasize their ties with Latin America instead of with Spain.

The term **ethnic identity** refers to accepting as part of one's self-concept the culture of an ethnic group. A variety of measures of ethnic and racial identity are possible, because the concept can be considered from several points of view: the development of the racial or ethnic identity in the individual, the acceptance of a non-European world view, affiliation with others belonging to the same group, or acceptance of cultural stereotypes about the group (Burlew & Smith, 1961; Thompson, 1995). Strong racial or ethnic identity is usually associated with feelings of belonging and commitment to the group and is reflected in participation in its cultural practices and traditions. People with the same objective background may vary considerably in their ethnic identity. Those with a strong ethnic identity feel a close association with the ethnic group and are involved in its activities and practices. People with a weak ethnic identity have little such involvement or interest (Table 13.1).

Those with a strong ethnic identity are likely to evaluate the group more positively than those with a weak ethnic identity, and for them, the group may contribute to a positive individual self-esteem. The relationship is not a simple one, though. When a person's ethnic group is evaluated negatively by members of majority ethnic groups, many studies show no relationship between identifying with that group and self-esteem (Phinney, 1991). If the group is evaluated negatively, this social fact may help to protect individual self-esteem, because insults and mistreatment by others can be dismissed as based on prejudice against the group rather than taken as evidence of individual inadequacy (Crocker & Major, 1989). Societal prejudice may not harm personal self-esteem, which depends more on relationships with family, friends, and such community groups as churches. This does not imply, however, that prejudice is innocuous. A sense of efficacy is impaired if a group faces discrimination, as do African Americans (Hughes & Demo, 1989). Because efficacy is an important predictor of effective behavior (see Chapter 9), losing a sense of efficacy is a cause, as well as an effect, of lower achievement by African Americans. Interventions to enhance a sense of efficacy among minorities would probably be more important than attention to self-esteem as a way of breaking cycles of low achievement and poverty.

TABLE **13.1** **Some Indicators of Ethnic Identification Assessed by Researchers**

Language:	Speaking the language of the ethnic group
Friendship:	Having friends who share the ethnic background
Religion:	Participating in religious activities associated with the ethnic group
Social groups:	Participating in formal social groups oriented toward the ethnic group
Politics:	Engaging in political activities and embracing political beliefs to further the ethnic group
Housing:	Living in areas where large numbers of the ethnic group live

Adapted from Phinney, 1990.

People do not fit neatly into discrete categories; a variety of ethnic identifications are possible (Table 13.2). Consider a person whose parents are of two different races or cultures and who identifies with both. For such **bicultural** individuals, developing an ethnic identity (or repertoire of identities) may be a complicated process. Identity development always takes place in the context of social attitudes, but for children of mixed race, the social attitudes of racism are particularly salient as they develop a cultural identity (Root, 1990). Many theorists believe that resolving ethnic identity issues is part of the ego development process that occurs during adolescent identity development, and that acceptance rather than rejection of ethnicity is conducive to good adjustment (Spencer & Markstrom-Adams, 1990).

It may seem that only ethnic minorities face issues of ethnic identity. Certainly the experience of being different from the majority raises unique identity issues not felt by those who blend in. There are instances in which a majority identity does become an issue, however. In North America, for example, white counselors who treat members of minority groups may need to examine their own ethnic identity as whites to ensure that unexamined issues do not undermine counseling effectiveness (Helms, 1984).

TABLE 13.2   **Alternatives Adopted by Individuals Who Are Caught Between Two Cultures**

	Strong identification with majority culture	*Weak identification with majority culture*
Strong identification with ethnic group	Biculturalism	Separation
Weak identification with ethnic group	Assimilation	Marginalization

Based on Berry et al., 1989.

Adapting to a New Culture

Sometimes people are caught between two cultures. This situation may occur because they are members of a group that immigrated to another land; because another culture has taken over their land; or because they are temporarily living in another country as students, refugees, or tourists. Whatever the reason, if individuals from two cultures come into direct contact, their traditions and psychological characteristics will be changed; this process is called **acculturation.** The process of acculturation is affected by the kind of contact: the effects are likely to be different if a person immigrates in search of a better life than if that person's country is overtaken by a conquering power or if someone is kidnapped into slavery (Berry, 1990).

When people immigrate to a new culture, they experience a discontinuity between the cultural expectations of their culture of origin and those of the new culture. This may be stressful and may lead to the experience of "culture shock." Mismatches between old cultural expectations and new cultural practices may be trivial. Years ago, when I (an American) waited for a store clerk in England to place my one purchase, a box of laundry detergent, into a bag, it soon became apparent that she expected me simply to take it unwrapped. Sensible, but a culture shock for me. Mismatches may be far more critical, however. A Japanese student in the United States was shot to death when he accidentally tried to enter the wrong home for a Halloween party, not understanding (because of both language and culture) that the homeowner's reactions signaled threat.

Over time, immigrants and their children usually change their behavior and expectations, becoming more like the members of the new culture.

A more acculturated Japanese person will eat hot dogs instead of sushi and speak English instead of Japanese. Unfortunately, a more acculturated Japanese American also is more susceptible to heart attacks than a less acculturated Japanese American who eats more traditionally (Marmot & Syme, 1976, cited in Triandis et al., 1988). Acculturation involves giving up one's native language, associating with friends who are not members of one's cultural group, eating foods that are typical of the new culture rather than one's culture of origin, and so on (Suinn, Ahana & Khoo, 1992). In the past, the "melting-pot" model urged immigrants to give up vestiges of their past culture, including its language and customs. (My mother tells of being punished when, in the 1920s and 1930s, she spoke her family's language, Finnish, at school in Minnesota.) Today, the goal of multiculturalism is espoused, and people are urged to maintain their old culture while adding the new.

A person can acquire a second culture in more than one way. Teresa LaFromboise and her colleagues distinguish five forms of acquiring a second culture (LaFromboise, Coleman & Gerton, 1993). In the *assimilation model*, the former culture is given up as a new cultural identity is formed. Historically, this was the melting-pot model in which many immigrants to the United States gave up the language and customs of the "old country" in order to become Americanized. In the *acculturation model*, identification with the minority culture remains as the new culture is assumed. The individual, although learning to function in the new culture, remains an identifiable minority member. This identification may result in the person being treated as a second-class citizen. In the third model, the *alternation model*, the individual can fully participate in two separate cultures, perhaps in different situations. Unlike the assimilation and acculturation models, the alternation model does not assume that one culture is of higher status than the other. Some American Indian tribes have provided traditional tribal education in early grades and Anglo-American education later in an attempt to provide both cultural experiences to their children. The *multicultural model* extends the notion of equally valuable cultures to more than two, making it especially applicable to schools, businesses, and other institutional environments in which several cultural groups interact. Such interaction, though, is likely to transform the participants, rather than permitting the multiple cultures to coexist unchanged, and the final *fusion model* describes the formation of a new, shared culture through the interaction of various cultures that are in contact. The fusion model differs from the melting-pot model in that there is not one culture regarded as superior; each transforms the other. Although these models can be distinguished theoretically, individuals may experience elements of more than one model. LaFromboise and her colleagues suggest that the alternation model is most consistent with the desirable outcome of bicultural competence, in which both cultures are respected and known, without (as in the multicultural model) being lost over time.

These models are not simply academic, of course. Historically, dominant colonial cultures have suppressed native cultures. In the past, Native American children were forced by whites to attend board schools that did not permit maintenance of native language and traditions, a practice that has been labeled "cultural genocide." Eventually, this model was abandoned, and more institutions today espouse the multicultural model.

Cultural differences can be more influential in some situations than others. Asian and Caucasian college students in the United States are about equally assertive in their families, but with strangers they differ; Asians report more anxiety and guilt (Zane et al., 1991). This may occur because with strangers, Asian Americans experience cultural conflict. Outside their homes, both their Asian heritage and the American mainstream compete for attention, whereas in the family, Asian students do not necessarily have to deal with both cultures. Conflict between the values and practices of two cultures often produces anxiety (Sue, 1983).

Studies indicate that there is not a simple relationship between acculturation and adjustment. Other factors need to be taken into account, such as economic status. For those with lower socioeconomic status, acculturation is associated with increased conflict and psychological symptoms; for those with higher socioeconomic status, acculturation is associated with healthy adjustment (Moyerman & Forman, 1992). In addition to measures of adjustment, standard personality tests find differences between members of an ethnic minority who are less acculturated to the majority culture and those who are more acculturated. A study compared Mexican-American students who chose to take a personality test (Cattell's 16PF) in either English or Spanish, reflecting their preferred language and, by implication, their degree of acculturation to U.S. culture. The two groups scored differently on several scales, and the more acculturated (English language) group was much more similar to Anglo-American students than the Spanish-speaking group (Whitworth & Perry, 1990). Although it is possible that the translation of the test was imperfect, the likely meaning of this result is that acculturation influences personality as well as language and other behaviors.

For many European Americans, the process of acculturation was sufficiently complete among their ancestors that they do not now think of themselves in terms of ethnicity, unless they choose to do so, and so they may have difficulty understanding the importance of ethnic identity for others. This option of forgetting about ethnicity and blending into the mainstream is not generally available to those of African or Asian ancestry.

Gender

From infancy onward, we confront a world that has different expectations of us, depending upon whether we are male or female (Stern & Karraker,

1989). Such characteristics as strength, will, and anger are expected more of males, delicacy and nurturing of females. Cultural expectations may build on and exaggerate existing biological predispositions, although the confounding of expectation with biology makes it difficult to know just where the effects of biology end and the effects of socialization begin. Psychologists use the term *sex* to refer to biological differences and **gender** to refer to socially determined differences between males and females.

Feminist criticisms of psychological theories have claimed that there is a male bias to traditional understandings of personality. In terms that we have considered previously, the individualism that predominates in Western culture and also in psychological models of personality and health is more characteristic of men; women are more collective (Eagly, 1987b; Triandis, 1990). Feminist understanding is more connected and empathic, based on defining the self in terms of relationships with other people. Traditional (masculine) understanding is more objective and separate from others. Do we not expect that when they leave home for the first time, college women will maintain closer ties with their families than college men do? Various research strategies may help or hinder us in understanding phenomena such as gender.

Although gender and race/ethnicity appear as separate headings in this chapter, real people cannot be so tidily categorized. Gender affects whites, African Americans, Hispanics, and others in different ways (Greene, 1994a). The experience of being a woman is different, depending upon whether one is African American or white, Christian or Jewish, Quebecois or native American. To be a man, likewise, is a different experience depending upon ethnic categories. Unfortunately, research on women has often ignored women of color or has treated their experience as a secondary issue (Reid & Kelly, 1994). Minority women confront the dilemma that cultural images of beauty are based on white features. Behavioral expectations, too, divide minority from majority women. Whereas white women have sought increased access to work in recent decades, many minority women who have had to work to support themselves and their families have not found work a path to liberation. In addition to race and ethnicity, gender is also affected by such factors as social class and generation (Stack, 1986).

Gender and Culture

Freud thought that his psychoanalytic discussion of gender described a biologically determined, universal pattern, in which males were morally more advanced and females motivated by envy of men. Critics have argued that Freud's ideas were accurate only for societies that are patriarchal, based on a tradition of male power and privilege. Freud's description of male development centers on the hypothesis that young boys experience a rivalry with their fathers for their mother's affection (the Oedipus conflict). This conflict, which occurs at age 3 to 5, is resolved successfully if the boy

RESEARCH STRATEGIES   ●---

Do Methods of Research Limit Our Investigations? The Case for a Diversity of Methods

As we have seen in the Research Strategies sections throughout this book, researchers are aware that the way they conduct their investigations influences their findings. They take precautions to avoid methods that may distort results or lead to unreliable findings. Is it possible, though, that researchers overlook some aspects of personality because of limited methods? That is the charge of some critics. The same methods that are designed to control extraneous influences on our measures unfortunately also narrow the focus of our research. Perhaps, like a search party with only an incomplete idea about where we will find our treasure, we ought to spread our efforts a little wider.

Many psychologists who have written about diverse populations suggest that our methods should be expanded. Some critics suggest that to understand women, we need to adopt *feminist research methods* to compensate for traditional approaches that overlook women's experience (Nielsen, 1990; Reinharz, 1992). Similar considerations apply to ethnic and other cultural groups. When we reach beyond the predominantly white, middle-class, college educated (or college student) samples most readily available to researchers, the survey questions or other data being tested by the

researchers may not be meaningful to those being tested. How is a subject to convey that perception when a researcher has provided only multiple-choice questions and sees only an encoded and scored data point to represent the person who participated in the study? How is a subject to say that the questions are pointless, or beside the point of his or her own experience? How, sometimes, is a subject quite different from the researcher even to get into the sample of subjects?

Consider a study on the causes of academic underachievement, designed by a researcher who intends to study achievement motivation and academic self-efficacy to see how well they predict college grades. What might be some overlooked issues? Joe, who is too financially strapped to afford a book until midsemester, is is never asked a question that permits him to make that point. Sally, who has slept very little because her best friend has just learned she has AIDS and turns to Sally for support, is never asked about that issue. Miguel is taking courses that are not interesting to him because he has accepted the advice of those whose racial stereotypes lead them to believe that he would not have a future in physics, his real passion. A researcher who has never lacked the money to buy books, been the emotional anchor for a

yields to his father's authority and accepts the male role as a model for his own aspirations and ethics. Without patriarchy, according to Nancy Chodorow (1978) , the classic Freudian conflict between male child and the father for the affection of the mother would not occur. She disputes Freud's assertion that sex differences in personality are innate. Instead, she friend's anguish, or been the target of racial discrimination will be unlikely to think of these issues when considering academic motivation. The point is that a researcher's theories and hunches about the causes of behavior guide the selection of questions and research design. These theories and hunches may limit the discovery of unanticipated truths. When the researcher's background and life experiences are similar to those of the subjects, this oversight is less likely, because the researcher draws on those similar experiences in choosing theories and methods. When the subjects have different backgrounds and life experiences, however, the researcher may not anticipate what will be found and may not provide the subjects with opportunities to convey unexpected information. In this case, using structured multiple-choice questionnaires, often preferred because of their frequently high reliability, limits the information obtained. More open-ended questions could potentially provide more information.

One obvious strategy for improving this situation is to encourage people with diverse backgrounds to conduct psychological research. Is that enough, or do the methods themselves also limit what can be found? How far can we stretch our openness to unanticipated information from subjects without abandoning science?

Here are some suggestions from feminist researchers, which apply to a variety of issues beyond feminism:
• Emphasize the subjective experience of subjects.
• Study subjects' narrative descriptions. Allowing them the freedom to put their experiences in their own words provides richer information than assessing subjective experience by having people respond to categories provided by the researcher (such as rating their feelings on a 7-point scale from happy to unhappy).
• Use nonmanipulative methods to collect data. For example, do not put subjects in artificial situations where their behavior is influenced by conditions that they do not encounter in their own lives.
• Do not treat the subject as an "object" to be passively studied. Recognize that the subject is in interaction with the researcher and the research project and that trying to be coolly "objective" does not eliminate this interaction but simply changes its character. Of course, the characteristics of the researcher (race, sex, and so on) and his or her behavior will influence the interaction.

In the study of human personality, a diversity of methods provides the best assurance of sound findings. Each method has its limits. Each has its strengths.

proposes that the fact that children are raised by their mothers as the primary caretaker is what produces sex differences. Because they are the same sex as their primary caretaker, girls maintain a sense of close connection and relationship with other people. Boys, perceiving that they are a different sex than their first love object, struggle to achieve a sense of autonomy, and their interpersonal relationships are based on a model of separation. As culture changes and fathers play a greater role in caring for children during the earliest years of life, these socially produced sex differences should diminish, according to Chodorow's model.

Beyond Chodorow's family explanation, others point out that differences in social power produce sex differences, causing the more powerful males to experience themselves as more individual and independent and the less powerful females to emphasize interdependent, collectivist ideas about the self (Lykes, 1985). Lack of power, rather than being female, produces sensitivity to nonverbal cues in others (Snodgrass, 1985; Tavris, 1991), for how else is one to know how to deal with a more powerful person?

Cross-cultural studies suggest that the Oedipus conflict is modified by culture. In traditional China, where male children were highly valued and considerably indulged by their mothers, boys remained closely bonded to their mothers rather than losing maternal nurturance to the father during the Oedipal period (Dien, 1992). A psychiatrist in India reports that the Oedipus complex is different there, with less fear of male retribution (castration) and more salience of the power of the mother (Kakar, 1989). In Mexican-American culture, children are often mothered by more than one woman. This diminishes a boy's rivalry with his father for his mother's love and so transforms the classic Oedipal conflict described by Freud. In addition, understanding psychodynamics in Mexican-American culture requires consideration of grandmothers, aunts, and other family members outside the nuclear family (Segura & Pierce, 1993). Clearly, the early developments that Freud theorized were universal are, in fact, variable across cultures.

Separate or Connected: Gender Differences

Many theorists have described males as more separate and independent and females as more connected to others (Lang-Takac & Osterweil, 1992). In psychoanalytic descriptions, the greater separation or autonomy of males is regarded as evidence of greater psychological maturity. This position strikes feminist scholars as biased (Lerman, 1986b). Many of them have described women's interpersonal connectedness as a strength that deserves greater respect by psychological theorists and therapists (Belenky et al., 1986; Gilligan, 1982; Jordan et al., 1991).

Carol Gilligan (1982) made this case in the area of moral development. She confronted a prevailing theory that considered the highest moral judgments to be based on abstract principles and moral judgments based on interpersonal considerations to be less mature (Kohlberg, 1984). For example, a principle of "life is more important than property" may be used to justify stealing when that is the only way to obtain a drug that would save someone's life. In Kohlberg's model, a decision based on a logical principle is more mature than a decision based on concern for other people's feelings or welfare. That is, abstract thought is higher than interpersonal emotion. Gilligan observed that women's moral decisions typically emphasize specific people, not abstract principles. Furthermore, she asserted that such decisions are not inferior or less mature than the principled decisions of moral men. Women follow a different developmental path in which higher levels of moral judgment involve awareness of the interconnections among people and the implications of one's own actions for many others. Such thinking would consider the dilemma of whether to steal a drug to save a life by considering the implications of this behavior for the person saved, members of that person's family, the owner of the drug, and other people who may be affected. The major impact of Gilligan's theory was to suggest that men and women follow different developmental paths in the moral realm and that women should not be evaluated according to a model that is more suitable for men.

Gilligan's argument has enthusiastic supporters, who see it as a valid response to psychology's undervaluing of women's more interpersonal sense of self. In the realm of psychotherapy, this feminist view has caused some observers to question the assumption that clients should be helped to become more autonomous individuals, less defined in terms of their relationships with others. Gilligan's call for equal valuation of the supposed feminine pattern, however, has some opposition, even among women. Marcia Westkott (1986, 1989) suggests that the rhetoric of interdependence and connectedness makes it more difficult for women to recognize their own needs and separate identities and thus holds back their development. In addition, some researchers argue that the claims of sex differences in moral judgment have been accepted too quickly, given their meager base of empirical evidence (Lifton, 1985).

Are separation and autonomy healthy, or is that a masculine-biased image? Shall we change women to be more like men, or change psychological models of health to describe women as they are? Rhetoric aside, there are reasons to value "masculine" qualities for both sexes. When subjects take the Bem Sex Role Inventory (BSRI), for example, high scores on the masculinity scale are associated with measures of mental health in both sexes, as described shortly.

Sex Role Orientation

Have you ever noticed that when people say what they expect a person to do, they often convey a desire as well as a prediction? When a parent says to a child, "I expected you to clean up your room," or a teacher says, "I expected you to do better on this exam," there is a prescription as well as a prediction. Cultures, as well as individuals, have expectations about behavior, and these expectations also have a demand quality. Cultural expectations that depend upon a person's position or status are called *roles*. Familiar roles include student, teacher, mother or father, and hairdresser.

Expectations that depend upon whether a person is male or female are called **sex role** expectations or, simply, sex roles. Culture teaches people what men and women ought to be like. Consider some stereotyped traditional messages: "Boys shouldn't cry," "Girls should be modest," "Boys should be strong," "Girls should take care of others." Based on such messages, the boy is taught to be strong and unemotional and the girl to be modest and nurturant.

Expectations for males and females are not the same in any culture. You may or may not agree that women are more nurturant and men more independent, but these are common sex role expectations. Men and women are expected to fit the roles, and they are judged more harshly when they do not. Although there are differences in the degree of sex role differentiation from one culture to another, all over the world men are accorded positions of greater power and responsibility for relationships with people outside the family (Spence & Helmreich, 1978). The social roles that women and men occupy in their culture contribute to the expectation that women will be more communal and connected with other people, as they are with the family members for whom they are caretakers, and that men will be more separate, as they often are from the family when they leave each day for outside employment.

Alice Eagly describes these different roles for men and women (that is, the division of labor in the family and in the workplace) as the cause of different expectations by other people and of different beliefs and skills in the individual. These expectations and sex-typed skills and beliefs, in turn, produce sex differences in social behavior. The traditional homemaker wife was assumed to be available to bake cookies for a school fundraiser and to drive children to music lessons, and she was judged by herself and others by the quality of her cooking and the appearance of her home and children. Husbands were expected to be skilled in financial planning and activities outside the home, such as politics. In turn, these external expectations and internal beliefs and skills contribute to sex differences in social behavior, such as the greater nurturance and emotional sensitivity often observed in women and the greater dominance observed in men (Eagly & Wood, 1991). Eagly's ideas describe her **social role model** of behavior. According to Eagly's (1987b) social role analysis, we should acknowledge the impact of these cultural expectations on behavior. Otherwise, we risk drawing the false conclusion that such differences stem from biological causes and are inevitable.

In support of the role interpretation, as opposed to a biological explanation, Eagly garners support from meta-analyses (statistical reviews of many studies) that examine the overall patterns of sex differences. These studies show greater sex differences in situations that accentuate role differences between the sexes. Men are expected to be brave, for example, and in situations where they face strangers in need, men are more helpful than women. When bravery is not an issue—for example, in helping family members—men are not more helpful. Roles other than gender also influence behavior. For example, when business managers participate in studies of leadership style, men and women are similar; leadership style is determined by the work role, not by gender. In contrast, in laboratory experiments that study leadership style among undergraduate subjects, there are greater sex differences. Females show high interpersonal orientation, attending to people's feelings and interpersonal relationships; males show high task orientation, focusing on the job instead of the people. Undergraduates are not really business managers, and in the artificial and ambiguous laboratory setting, they have few clues about how to behave. In this vacuum, their preexisting gender roles are more prominent, and so sex differences are magnified (Eagly & Johnson, 1990; Eagly & Wood, 1991).

Whether consciously or not, people often judge behavior differently, depending upon whether it involves a male or a female. Crying is generally more expected and tolerated in girls, whereas crying boys risk being called sissies. Women are also expected to be more nurturant toward other people's needs. Boasting and effort toward individual goals that might be criticized as self-centered in a female are tolerated and even applauded in a male. We all know people who have resisted these sex role messages, however, and society is changing to give less stereotyped mandates. How can we measure people's acceptance or rejection of society's sex roles?

Sex Role Orientation à la Bem: Masculine, Feminine, Androgynous
A person's acceptance or rejection of culture's sex role messages is called **sex role orientation.** We may accept the traditional masculine or feminine sex roles, we may reject them, or we may combine them. Most of the research on sex role orientation has been conducted using research instruments developed in the United States. Such instruments may not apply worldwide. Still, that limitation applies to most psychological research, and as long as we recognize that the cultural effects of gender may be different in various national and ethnic cultures, the lessons of this research are enlightening.

The most widely used instrument to assess sex role orientation was developed by Sandra Bem (1974). The BSRI asks subjects to indicate, on a 7-point rating scale, how well each adjective on a list describes them. A third of the adjectives were selected because pretesting showed them to be more socially desirable traits for males and another third because they were deemed more desirable for females. (This was based on California undergraduates' assessments in 1973.) To avoid having subjects guess the intent of the instrument, a final third of the adjectives were equally desirable for both sexes.

Masculine and feminine scales are scored separately by computing the extent to which each set of adjectives is similar to subjects' self-descriptions. A person is considered to be masculine if the masculinity score is relatively high compared to the femininity score and feminine if the reverse is true. If both scores are relatively high, the person is called **androgynous,** indicating that he or she has a broader repertoire of traits available and is presumably able to draw from this repertoire to find the most adaptive way of behaving in each situation. Finally, people who are low in both masculinity and femininity are called "undifferentiated" (Bem, 1977) (Fig. 13.1).

Research with the BSRI has documented many differences related to sex role orientation. Androgynous undergraduates report less loneliness and more satisfaction with friendship than other undergraduates (Jones, Bloys & Wood, 1990). Androgynous undergraduates prefer egalitarian over traditional marriages (Pursell, Banikiotes & Sebastian, 1981), and they have more liberal attitudes toward sexual expression (Johnson, 1989). Undergraduate males who are androgynous report feeling more comfortable in dating situations, compared to masculine or undifferentiated males, probably because of the expressive social skills tapped by the femininity scale (Quackenbush, 1990). Female college students high in femininity are more likely to express and want affection, while those high in masculinity want to take control in interpersonal situations (Johnson & Brems, 1989).

Sex roles influence relationships after marriage, too. Androgynous married people handle marital conflict more constructively (Yelsma & Brown, 1985). Several studies report that marital satisfaction is higher when partners are androgynous (Davidson & Sollie, 1987). Sometimes feminine as well as androgynous sex role orientation is also associated with satisfaction, presumably because of the interpersonal relationship qualities (compassionate, loyal, and so on) tapped by the femininity scale (Kalin & Lloyd, 1985; Kurdek & Schmitt, 1986). Masculine people, both men and women, report better sexual functioning and fewer sexual problems (Obstfeld, Lupfer & Lupfer, 1985).

A number of modifications to the Bem conceptualization have been proposed. Some of these changes extend and refine the idea of masculinity and femininity, while others challenge the core assumption that gender is the key issue. Refining the idea that masculinity and femininity are general concepts that apply to many areas of life, some researchers have suggested that we should consider gender orientation in specific domains of life. A woman may be very traditional in her relationships with other people, for example, but "masculine" in her drive for a career as a nuclear physicist. This approach suggests that researchers should measure masculinity and femininity separately in various content areas, such as at home and at work (Chusmir & Koberg, 1990).

Bem's sex role model includes only two factors: feminine and masculine. An alternative model proposes five dimensions in addition to the two proposed by Bem (which are renamed Dominant and Supportive). The five new dimensions are Aesthetic Interests, Mechanical Interests, Feminine

Conventions, Anxiety, and Masculine Conventions (Bernard & Wood, 1990). Fundamentally, such a model challenges a two-factor model as overly simplified. As we learned when considering varying trait models of personality (see Chapter 3), however, the question of how many factors exist often boils down to a choice between fewer broad factors and more numerous specific factors, either choice being reasonable, depending upon our research aims.

Under Another Label: Instrumental and Expressive Traits

Calling a nurturant person "feminine" and an assertive person "masculine" has some justification, because these are commonly accepted cultural meanings of feminine and masculine. It would be more precise, though, to describe the behaviors more directly and to reserve words like masculine and feminine, which are related to roles, for instances in which we know that a person's behavior is motivated to fit the social image of a male or a female. A nurturant person may simply care for someone else and have no thought about femininity. An assertive person may be simply trying to accomplish a task, masculinity aside.

Janet Spence and Robert Helmreich (1978) devised the Personal Attributes Questionnaire (PAQ) to measure sex role orientation based on the idea that masculinity emphasizes instrumental behavior and femininity emphasizes expressive, communal behavior. Like Bem's measure, it is scored for Masculinity and Femininity and permits people to be classified as Masculine, Feminine, Androgynous, or Undifferentiated. Although similar to the BSRI, it differs conceptually in that the masculine and feminine items were not intended to be more desirable for either sex, but simply more common in one than the other.

Students who are androgynous on the PAQ are lower on Neuroticism and higher on Extraversion, Openness, Agreeableness, and Conscientiousness on the NEO Personality Inventory (Ramanaiah & Detwiler, 1992). Clearly, gender roles are related to major personality traits (Fig. 13.2).

Gender Schema Theory

We have cognitive concepts, called schemata, about many important social categories, including gender. Schemata guide our perceptions as we fit new information into these existing categories. Schemata may describe events (such as a first date) or categories of people (such as a rock star or a librarian). While schemata sometimes may be overgeneralized and stereotyped, we could not make sense of all that we experience without some sort of prior categories. Sandra Bem (1984) proposes, in her **gender schema theory,** that the categories "male" and "female" are salient in people's cognitive processes and organize much of their thinking about themselves and their social world.

That we process social information by using prototypical schemata is simply the way our cognitive functioning works. Our culture and social attitudes determine the fact that gender is an important schema, as well as the specific content of our gender schemata. Gender schemata are learned early and are central to perceptions of other people and ourselves. Sandra Bem suggests that society could, and should, stop emphasizing gender in contexts where it is not relevant. Does it matter whether the person who serves our food is a waiter or a waitress?

Comparing individuals, some people are more attuned to gender schemata, and others are less motivated to direct their behavior according to these schemata (Bem, 1987). Information that is consistent with our gender schemata is processed more efficiently, so we remember it more quickly and more accurately. For example, people who are masculine, according to the BSRI, remember more of the adjectives on the masculine scale when given an unexpected memory test. Conversely, people who are feminine remember more of the feminine adjectives. Similar results are found when memory for masculine or feminine behavior, such as ironing or fixing a radio, is tested (Markus et al., 1982; Ruble & Stangor, 1986).

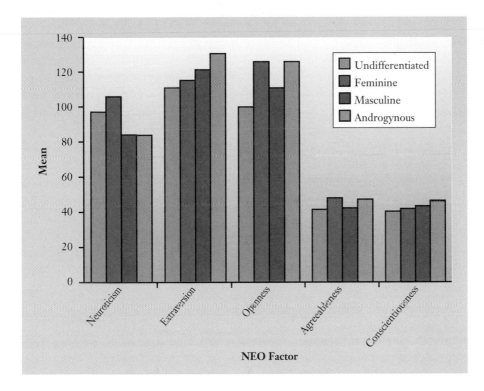

FIGURE 13.2 *Means of sex role groups on the NEO. (Adapted from Ramanaiah & Detwiler, 1992, p. 1217.)*

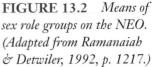

Gender Roles and Psychological Well-Being

Statistics show that females suffer depression more often than males (Lewis, 1985). Is biology the cause, or can it be something about the social role of females that produces this result? Evidence supports the social role interpretation (Rosario et al., 1988). Ravenna Helson and James Picano (1990) ask directly, "Is the traditional role bad for women?" and conclude that it is. Among 21-year old college women who were tested in the late 1950s, traditional role choices (becoming a homemaker without full-time employment outside the home) were associated with well-being, but those same women showed a decline in psychological and physical health by age 43. Greater psychological health was achieved by those who tried to have it all—work and family—although the role-juggling made them tired. The researchers point out that only a longitudinal study could have found such a result. At age 21, there was no hint of the adverse effects of traditional role choices that would emerge for these women over the next two decades. We should also bear in mind that those effects, which occurred during the 1960s and 1970s, may or may not correspond to what women may experience during other historical times.

There is other evidence supporting the conclusion that femininity is not conducive to the highest levels of psychological well-being. Depressed middle-aged women, according to one study, score higher in femininity on the BSRI than a nondepressed group (Tinsley, Sullivan-Guest & McGuire, 1984). Other studies suggest that the presence or absence of what has been labeled masculinity is probably more important than the presence or absence of femininity in producing depression and lower well-being (Bassoff & Glass, 1982). Masculine subjects, both male and female, have been found to have greater personal adjustment and lower levels of depression than feminine subjects (Elpern & Karp, 1984; Harris & Schwab, 1990; Markstrom-Adams, 1989; Nezu, Nezu & Peterson, 1986; Rendely, Holmstrom & Karp, 1984; Welkowitz, Lish & Bond, 1985; Whitley, 1984). One reason for the lower depression and anxiety of masculine individuals is that they more often use effective, problem-focused coping techniques (Brooks, Morgan & Scherer, 1990; Long, 1990; Nezu & Nezu, 1987).

Life events are stronger predictors of depression than sex role (Stoppard & Paisley, 1987). Age also matters. A study comparing working men and women of various ages finds that the positive effect of masculine sex role orientation on life satisfaction is stronger among older adults (Blanchard-Fields & Friedt, 1988). Sex role attitudes can facilitate or constrain a person's ability to find satisfaction through achievement at work.

Achievement

Achievement outside the home may create conflict in traditionally minded females. This conflict may be reflected in females' underestimating their competence for careers, compared to higher perceived competence in males (Poole & Evans, 1989). Psychological masculinity may help females to mobilize their potential for achievement (Taylor & Hall, 1982). Both women and men who are high in masculinity, as assessed by the PAQ, are higher in the motives for Mastery and Competitiveness on a questionnaire measure of orientation to work and family (Adams, Priest & Prince, 1985).

Culture's sex role messages can undermine success for some women. Achievement comes in many forms. The traditionally feminine traits of obedience and compliance may facilitate work that gets good grades in school, but they are not helpful in producing the more assertive achievement that is often required for success beyond school. This could help explain why females often do relatively well in school but do not achieve at comparable levels afterward (Mickelson, 1989). Success that comes from doing what is assigned is more feminine than success that comes from assertive ambition. Among college professors, publication in professional journals is rated as more masculine than feminine (Wiley & Crittenden, 1992). Women who strive for such achievement may experience the sort of conflict between achievement and femininity that is the rationale behind the fear of success motive (discussed in Chapter 7). One study reports that masculine women score especially high in fear of success, probably because they experience the conflict between their achievement striving and feminine role pressures. Androgynous women, whom we would expect to have integrated the potential conflicts between masculinity and femininity, were lowest in fear of success (Major, 1979). A replication study confirmed the effect in a sample of Australian males and females, finding that sex role orientation was a better predictor of fear of success than was gender (Davis, Ray & Burt, 1987).

It is also widely believed that women's achievement is underestimated by other people, a belief bolstered by a widely cited classic study. In this study, Philip Goldberg (1968) found that the same article was judged less favorably if subjects were told it was written by a woman (Joan McKay) than if they were told the author was a man (John McKay). Further studies, however, showed that such biased undervaluation of women's achievement is not very great, especially if judges are given adequate information and if they are competent in the field about which they are making judgments (Swim et al., 1989; Top, 1991). Women do, however, underestimate the role of their own ability in producing achievement. Relative to men, women attribute their successes more to effort and luck and less to ability (Levine, Gillman & Reis, 1982).

Masculine and Feminine: In What Culture?

Ideas about what is desirable for males and for females vary across cultures and can change. In India and Malaysia, cultures that are quite different from that of the United States (where the BSRI instrument was developed), researchers report that students do not agree with American ratings of what is desirable for the two sexes. These two Asian samples classified more traits as neutral rather than masculine or feminine. They did not, however, move any masculine traits to feminine or vice versa, and their responses were consistent with the finding in Western samples that instrumental qualities are seen as more desirable for males and expressive traits as more desirable for females. Expressive traits (altruistic, yielding, eager to soothe hurt feelings) that are considered feminine in the West are, in these Asian samples, considered desirable for both sexes; this finding is consistent with cross-cultural studies showing more interpersonal collective concerns and less independence in Asia than in the West. Also unlike Western samples, the feminine interpersonal traits were held in as high esteem in these cultures as the masculine instrumental traits (Ward & Sethi, 1986).

Whatever the best explanations for gender differences, it is clear that we cannot understand the differences between men and women at an individual level only. We must consider the social context in which the person functions and how social messages about gender-appropriate roles guide and constrain the individual. Gender must be put into context, and each person's self-perception as well as the expectations of that person and the others in a given situation are relevant to this context (Deaux & Major, 1987). When we decide whether to join a particular social club, take a particular course, or engage in any of thousands of other social behaviors, these expectations and self-perceptions spring into action.

Implications of Culture for Psychology

To understand anyone's behavior, we must be mindful of the social expectations with which that person lives: expectations for sex roles, cultural values about individualism and collectivism, the whole fabric of experiences that are patterned by socioeconomic status and by the social climate of the historical time and place. Differences in status and economic well-being are often intertwined with racial and ethnic differences. This confounding can make simple comparisons between groups misleading. When researchers take precautions to control for socioeconomic status when they compare groups, differences are often substantially reduced or eliminated, suggesting that many of what appear to be racial and ethnic effects are in fact due to variations in wealth and status (Kagitçibaşi & Berry, 1989). Awareness of the impact of culture on personality can sensitize theorists to their own cultural assumptions, so that they can more clearly disentangle potential biases from their universal statements.

Culture influences the process of psychotherapy in many ways. For one thing, the expectations that patients bring to their therapists vary from one culture to another. In Asia and the Philippines, clients expect more directiveness and authority from their therapists than in the West (Church, 1987). Assumptions about what is healthy must also be examined in the light of cultural differences. The importance of individuality and achievement varies from one culture to another, and therapists trained in individualistic cultures need to recognize that their images of active individual striving do not constitute universal norms of health. Sometimes it is more sensible to accept the present as it is, knowing that change comes from forces of nature and not only from the individual, as traditional native American and Asian perspectives recognize. When the therapist comes from a different background than the client, ignorance of the client's cultural assumptions may be overcome by providing the therapist with specific cultural training (Scott & Borodovsky, 1990).

Psychological studies of cultural differences have the potential to contribute to better understanding among the world's diverse people, too. For

The "traditional" sex roles of the 1950s and earlier have been criticized as unrealistic models for today. What do you think?

example, one study of power and control found significant differences among cultures. Behavior that people in Singapore and India considered desirable attempts to accomplish goals by exerting power were regarded in Japan, Germany, and the United States as undesirable attempts to dominate and control others (Funkhouser, 1993). Could it be that some of the resentment people feel toward other nationalities is caused by misunderstandings of their intentions? Let us not, though, think of culture only as that which makes us different. Culture is what makes us human.

Over historical time, the dominant motives of a country can change. National surveys show, for example, that the average power motive of U.S. citizens increased from 1957 to 1976 (Veroff et al., 1980). Men's roles have changed as well as women's, and conflicts about success tapped by the fear of success measure are now shared more equally by both sexes (Pedersen & Conlin, 1987). The popular press today describes Generation X post-baby-boomers as less loyal to a particular employer, more environmentally minded, and more concerned with a balance between work and family than past generations. This characterization has some support from research (Burke, 1994). Who knows what coming generations will value and how their world will require revision of our psychological understanding?

SUMMARY

- Personality is influenced substantially by the socially transmitted beliefs and practices that constitute culture.

- Cross-cultural psychology studies the similarities and differences of various groups. Cultural psychology studies the processes by which culture influences personality.

- Comparisons of various nations show differences in families, education, religion, and other social tasks.

- The Japanese concept of *amae* illustrates that dependency is more prevalent and accepted in that culture than in the West.

- Individualist cultures, such as the United States and most developed Western countries, emphasize individual goals. Collectivist cultures, such as those in Asia, emphasize group goals and welfare. These two themes also vary across ethnic groups within a culture.

- Race (a biological variable) and ethnicity (a cultural variable) are related to many personality phenomena, including mental health and identity. Studies of ethnic identity and acculturation emphasize the importance of culture as a factor in self-image and personality.

- Gender (socially determined differences between males and females) influences personality from early life onward. The suggestion that women emphasize connections among people while men emphasize separation and individuality has been much debated.

- Social roles, including sex roles, influence behavior and personality. To varying degrees, people accept their culture's messages about the appropriate behavior for males and females (sex role orientation).

- Gender schema theory emphasizes gender as a salient element in our thinking about ourselves and our social world.

- Gender roles may contribute to psychological difficulties and to conflict about achievement in women.

- The effects of gender depend upon culture.

- The effects of culture are pervasive and make us aware that much of personality can change as society changes.

GLOSSARY

acculturation change in traditions and psychological characteristics as a consequence of direct contact with another culture

amae the Japanese word for dependency as expressed within that culture

androgynous accepting both traits associated with the masculine role and traits associated with the feminine role

bicultural identifying with two ethnic groups

collectivist description of a culture in which group goals and welfare are placed ahead of individual interests

cross-cultural psychology the field of psychology that compares cultures and ethnic groups, examining similarities and differences in psychological functioning among these various groups

cultural psychology the field of psychology that studies the processes by which cultural practices and traditions influence personality and other psychological phenomena

culture the socially transmitted beliefs and practices that influence our behavior and personality

ethnic identity the acceptance as part of one's self-concept the culture of an ethnic group

ethnicity a shared cultural heritage

gender socially determined differences between males and females

gender schema theory Sandra Bem's model emphasizing the categories male and female as salient in people's thinking about themselves and their social world

individualist description of a culture in which a person is expected to place personal goals ahead of the group

race a group of people who are distinct in their genetic makeup as a result of a history of inbreeding in a local geographic area

sex role orientation a person's acceptance or rejection of culture's sex role messages for masculine and feminine behavior

sex role expectations that are derived from the status of being a male or being a female

social role mode Alice Eagly's explanation of behavior that emphasizes the roles, especially gender roles, that people play in society

THOUGHT QUESTIONS

1. Do you think that the role of culture in personality has been considered with sufficient scientific objectivity, or has it been misused as a persuasive device to further people's political agendas?

2. If you have experienced cultures other than your own, what personal impressions were most striking to you? Can these be explained using the concepts from this chapter?

3. What cultural practices in your own culture do you think valuable to export to other cultures? On the other hand, what cultural practices do you think should be changed, and how?

4. Do you think that Japanese *amae* is equally healthy as a style of social interaction, compared with the lower levels of dependency in most Western cultures; or is it evidence of a widespread developmental deficit in Japan? What evidence might be helpful to demonstrate one side or the other of this question?

5. In your own experience, what areas of life seem best described by individualism? What areas are more collectivist?

6. Do you believe that therapists should come from the same culture as their clients? Why or why not?

7. Have you ever experienced culture shock, or surprises when you have interacted with people from a culture different from your own? Describe it.

8. Do you think that multiculturalism is a healthy model for people today?

9. Do you believe that, today, in your culture, males and females are influenced by sex roles? Should they be?

10. Are there aspects of culture other than those discussed in this chapter that you think should be studied (for example, socioeconomic status)?

Conclusion

UNDERSTANDING PERSONALITY FROM A SCIENTIFIC point of view is a daunting task, but like many of life's challenges, the most difficult step is the first one. After hundreds of thousands, perhaps millions, of years on this planet, we humans have begun to think scientifically about ourselves. While there are many unanswered questions, the answers we have found are as exciting as the observations made at a new archeological dig or the first transmissions from a probe into outer space.

Personality research has brought considerable insight into this most personal of the sciences. It appears that we have confirmed the wisdom of some of our prescientific beliefs. The importance of early experience, conveyed in the aphorism, "As the twig is bent, so grows the tree," seems to be substantiated by findings of the early attachment between infant and parent. We have come to believe that relationships with other people are central to our human personality and that these relationships depend in part on our genetic temperament and in part on the way others have interacted with us early in life. The idea that people are not all alike and that they respond differently to the same situation is also confirmed by studies of personality traits and types. It may be that because we observe one another at very close range, we exaggerate our differences (as family members seem to exaggerate the differences among brothers and sisters), but certainly we are not interchangeable. We approach life with different motivations and goals, whether these come from early experience or from our anticipations of the future, and with these individual dynamics, we steer our course through life rather than being pushed and pulled by external forces. This makes life exciting, but it certainly complicates the task of the would-be scientist of personality, who is already daunted by the multitude of influences outside the individual.

A science of personality cannot be fit neatly into a hierarchy of levels of explanation, somewhere between biology and sociology. People are influenced by multiple levels, and they must all be combined into our understandings of personality. Our biological predispositions, reflected in heredity and temperament, have measurable effects throughout our lives; they influence our style of relationships with other people and even our attitudes toward controversial social issues. As we strive toward our goals and experience triumphs and frustrations, the impact of psychological experiences can be measured in physiological analyses of our blood and saliva. Surely the body cannot be ignored if we are to understand personality. At the other extreme, higher level explanations in terms of culture and society must also be included in our studies. Biological predispositions are not expressed in a vacuum but are shaped by the opportunities and frustrations, the images and aspirations transmitted by our culture. Culture varies worldwide and changes rapidly, which further complicates our task.

Between these micro (biological) and macro (cultural) levels we find the more traditionally "psychological" levels: behavior and cognition. It would be overwhelming to include all of biology and culture in our studies, but we must include those factors that influence our behavior, our thoughts, and our subjective experience. We must consider, for example, the hormones that predict aggressive behavior and the genes that seem to be related to sexual orientation. Cultural styles of child-rearing and education, religious life, and political life belong to our study of personality to the extent that they help us to understand individual experience, and not simply that of the group.

The Three Issues: Description, Dynamics, and Development

The complexity of its subject matter and the indistinct boundaries with other disciplines (such as sociology and genetics) pose challenges to this young science, which is wrestling with some basic questions of method and theory to organize its knowledge and plan its agenda for the future. Approaches from other sciences are instructive. In the past, psychologists thought of science as requiring a completely deterministic model, like that of Newtonian physics. Modern physics includes provision for subatomic particles whose individual behavior is indeterminant, although predictions can be made about their behavior in aggregate. In personality, too, there will undoubtedly remain components that cannot be predicted fully; but that should not dissuade us from trying to understand and predict the whole personality. Small changes in subatomic particles can have profound effects, as evidenced by nuclear weapons and power plants. Now, from the study of weather, chaos theory has emerged as a new scientific model. This theory describes a multitude of forces that interact in complex ways, and small factors sometimes influence large results; for example, a butterfly's wings can provide the critical influence to transform complex weather systems. It may not be possible, except in retrospect, to understand where those subtle but powerful forces have been expressed, but at least we now have a scientific model that begins to approach the complexity of our subject matter. Beyond these physical models, when studying humans there is the added complication of conscious thought. People's thoughts, beliefs, and preferences cannot be left out of our models, and there is no theory in the physical sciences that suggests how to include them.

In its brief history as a science, personality has offered many theories, but none has been accepted as a general paradigm for the field. Some, like Freud's psychoanalysis, have guided clinicians in the more-art-than-science endeavors of therapy but have yielded mixed results when subjected to scientific validation. Others, like trait and type approaches, build on everyday conceptions of personality and address some of our questions (how to classify people, for instance) but are not broad enough to cover all our questions about personality. Theories change rapidly as new evidence accumulates, and we are left with many local maps but no atlas. Local maps may be adequate for the research scientist who has specific questions, but they can leave the student of personality, or the integrative theorist, feeling disoriented and overwhelmed.

In the absence of a comprehensive, generally accepted paradigm that can organize what we already know about personality and the directions of future inquiry into a coherent scheme, this book has adopted an interim organization of the field in terms of the issues that personality theory ultimately must address. Three broad issues cross theoretical boundaries: the description, dynamics, and development of personality.

First, we ask the question of *description:* what concepts convey the qualities about people that we seek to understand? How can we say how one person is different from another, without allowing our preconceptions to distort our observations? Is ordinary language adequate, and can people provide trustworthy information if we know what to ask them? How can we understand individuals who may be different from the mainstream and whose lives are so complex that ordinary research questionnaires seem superficial?

Second, we ask the question of *dynamics:* what explains the functioning of personality in particular situations? What forces in us spring into action to produce the distress and symptoms that therapists observe and that are proposed in such clinically derived theories as Freud's psychodynamic approach? On the other hand, how do we adapt, often successfully, to life's stresses and disappointments? How can we understand people's apparently self-initiated striving toward various goals, including achievement, power, and friendship? Are beliefs about the self the key to these central human questions?

Finally, we ask the question of *development:* how does personality emerge and change over time? What genetic and biological determinants shape and constrain the formation of personality? How do these factors interact with experience and cultural forces? What childhood experiences should we take into account to understand, and ultimately to direct, personality formation? How do society's tasks, such as education, work, and love, influence our development and fulfillment? What can we learn about personality by comparing nations, ethnic groups, and genders, and how do the rapid cultural changes that we have all witnessed affect personality?

Description

People have been describing one another for much longer than a science of personality has existed, so it is not surprising that scientific personality descriptions draw heavily from everyday language. The strength of this legacy is that our everyday descriptions involve a set of concepts that is rich and complex. Its limitation is that we may linger too long on the issue of how people perceive themselves, which is not the same as how a science of personality should describe them.

In the main, personality measurement has relied on self-report measures that ask subjects to respond to questionnaires. Despite the highly sophisticated statistical analysis of such measures, they are limited to the extent that some aspects of personality are not obtainable by this method. People sometimes lack insight and distort their self-presentations. The study of self-perception is only one facet of the field of personality, and self-reports may have limited value when researchers are interested in studying other aspects of the field, such as the relationship between personality and physical health or the impact of childhood experience on adult personality. Trait and type schemes that are derived from ordinary language, such as the Big Five factors of personality (Extraversion, Neuroticism, Agreeableness, Conscientiousness, and Openness), provide reliable measures that converge with other people's descriptions of an individual and predict many of that person's behaviors, but researchers also seek to measure behavior directly.

The fundamental question of how we describe personality is not entirely separate from dynamic and developmental questions. People differ not only in how they appear at any given time but also in how they respond to situations and in how they change over the life course. If we describe a person as conservative, for example, this characterization should fit our observations of how the person responds to situations (saving more of his or her lottery winnings than a less conservative person, for example) and of how the person develops over time (making conservative decisions about the different issues that confront a child, an adult, and an elderly person in such areas as physical danger and sexual and financial decisions). Descriptions are, after all, socially constructed (Chapter 1), and by relating these constructs to dynamic situations, to heredity, and to life course or other developmental issues, we can be more certain that they are useful and make valid predictions. Otherwise, how could we claim that they are any more valuable than everyday descriptions of personality?

With respect to the description of personality, we may find that different schemes are necessary for different purposes. The dimensions that people use when describing others in everyday life, such as telling your friends what your parents are like, will not necessarily match the optimal set of dimensions for predicting behavior, for selecting the optimal careers or other social roles for various individuals, or for diagnosing adjustment problems. Furthermore, as we learn more about the causes of behavior, we may find that revised descriptive schemes are desirable to disentangle multiple causes. For example, as scientists learn more about biological and hereditary contributions to personality, we may prefer separate descriptive models that fit each of those dimensions more precisely. If we find that people who are now classified as "introverts" are in fact of two varieties, one with a distinctive inherited physiological pattern and the other without that pattern but with a history of traumatic experience, we will find it more accurate to call these two groups by distinctive names instead of calling them both "introverts."

As concepts become more complex, we will need to use language more precisely. For example, in speaking of "traits," we will need to recognize that the dimensions of the perceiver do not necessarily correspond to the causes within the individual. We may categorize people along a dimension of conscientiousness, for example, and that dimension may be adequate for predicting which people will complete tasks on time without supervision. This finding does not imply, however, that we understand why some people are conscientious and others are not. One person may be conscientious because of a childhood history of punishment for behavior the parent labeled as irresponsible; another may be conscientious because of commitment to a much-desired future goal. Perceiving people is not the same as understanding them. Here is another example. A "masculine" or "feminine" person may be that way because of acceptance of gender roles in society, but the match between the person's characteristics and the gender roles is not proof that one causes the other. Advances in theory will be necessary to guide research and will tell us more precise ways of using language as scientists.

Most personality descriptions focus on the study of differences between individuals (nomothetic research), but as we saw in Chapter 5, intensive studies of individuals themselves (idiographic research) have also been conducted in both therapeutic and academic settings. Idiographic approaches are less constrained by the need to have comparable measures (such as self-reports) from all subjects, and they often study narratives, which permit people to tell the stories of their lives in full detail. It is not enough to support our science with impressive statistical predictions; we also wish to know whether a particular person will complete a task, commit a crime, and so on. Such an understanding of individuals will always remain an elusive goal because of the large number of variables going into the prediction and because of idiosyncrasies of the individual that prevent what we know about one person from helping us to understand another. The goal of understanding individuals, however, helps to define the scope of what personality researchers need to study; whatever impacts individual lives, from neurotransmitter effects on moods to the challenges of a lost job, is grist for our theoretical mill.

Dynamics

We can describe cars and computers by saying how they look, but for real understanding, we must observe them in action. How does a car handle on the road? What programs does a computer run? What does each do well, and what risks a crash? The same kinds of questions apply to personality. How does it function; what are its dynamics? What are the limitations to its adaptive functioning? These are questions of personality dynamics.

With respect to the *dynamics* of personality, we are trying to understand how people function. We do not turn dials or press keys as we would with a machine, but people do respond to a variety of situations in their lives, and dynamic questions ask how these responses work. People are complex; they seek goals and adapt to situational demands at both unconscious and conscious levels. These levels combine in complex ways that change from one situation to the next. If we understand these processes, we can intervene effectively to shape the desired outcome. How would you motivate a slow employee or help a person to recover from a personal tragedy? People's beliefs and thoughts (cognitive processes) are important in many dynamic explanations, so a dynamic approach would listen to the employee's description of the job or the stressed person's dilemma. For many theorists, cognitions about the self are key concepts that explain striving and adjustment, so we would ask people to describe themselves, their abilities, and their expected future selves. In addition, emotion plays a key role in increasing our understanding of personality dynamics, because emotion has implications ranging from the physiological (with its relationship to health and disease) to the social (with its implications for social perceptions and behavior).

Many of the dynamic topics studied by personality psychologists relate to people's successful or unsuccessful attempts to adapt to life's demands; thus, they are of particular interest to therapists. In fact, therapists from Freud onward have contributed many ideas to our understanding of personality dynamics as they have explored the origins and alleviation of dysfunctional patterns. As with all studies of special populations, whether therapy patients or college students or middle-class whites, we cannot presume that the findings generalize to all other groups of people, until evidence is presented to support such generalization. Perhaps at a broad theoretical level we may be similar: all pursuing goals, all continuing more or less effectively to use the adaptive coping methods we have learned in the past. When we get down to specifics, however, there is more diversity: we seek different goals and cope in different ways. We have different self-concepts and different sets of beliefs about what we can accomplish and what we can't. Our behavior and even our physical health are diverse. So our studies of personality dynamics may emphasize either the differences among people or their similarities, depending upon the specificity or generality of our concepts and the situations in which we make observations.

Development

Unlike computers and cars, people change over time. Questions of personality *development* address these changes. Time brings both change and continuity, depending upon where you look. Research has provided evidence of considerable continuity over time, so that early signs of adult personality are already observable in childhood and, in the form of temperament, even in infancy. Studies of heredity provide evidence of genetic effects on personality that are far stronger than personality theories have traditionally anticipated, because most major theorists have focused their attention on family interactions and experiences in childhood and beyond.

The contributions of heredity and physiological factors to development are making headlines (for example, in discoveries of genetic influences on homosexuality), but the impact of heredity often varies depending upon the social context. Researchers are now trying to understand how biological predispositions *interact* with various experiences to shape personality. There are many practical gains to be derived from such research; for example, we can hope to learn how we can influence children's behavior to fulfill their potential talent and intelligence rather than succumbing to impulsive antisocial behavior. Some research points to the potential of schools to improve the outlook of high-risk individuals; what of other cultural enterprises and institutions?

The cultural context is immensely important for our species; we cannot understand a person without understanding the culture that person lives in. The culture both provides the opportunity for the expression of personality and contributes significantly to the formation of personality. Culture influences family structure and the early messages we learn in our families. Development from childhood onward presents us with cultural tasks and supports in school, work, marriage, politics, and religion, among other areas. Although the multiplicity of cultural forms and the rapidity of cultural change complicate our task enormously, we cannot fully understand personality without taking culture into account. And so those who study personality must be in close communication with sociologists and historians as well as with biologists and physiologists.

In its relationship with other fields, such as sociology and history, personality has obvious political implications. It helps us to understand the personalities of political leaders, their motivations, their reactions to situations, and how they change over time. Other political implications emerge from considering how personality is influenced by social tasks and opportunities; some observers believe that social change would enhance the personality development of women, ethnic and racial minorities, and other deprived groups. The idea that personality is influenced by genetics raises controversy because social attitudes toward gay rights, crime, and other behaviors have traditionally been based on the assumption of choice, not genetic determination. Even learned behavior has political implications: who should control the models to which children are exposed? If we strive to have a politically neutral field of study, we will need either to have tunnel vision or simply to deny political implications. Perhaps it is helpful to take a long view and to recognize that personality understandings are complex and in flux. There should not be a quick leap from a single finding to a political conclusion. Yet we cannot claim to be wholly objective, either.

As we learn more about the causes of personality by studying its development, we will undoubtedly need to revise our descriptive schemes and our dynamic statements. At the same time, we need some tentative understandings of description and dynamics before we can study personality development effectively.

Research Strategies in Perspective

In many ways, science has become the new authority in controversial matters. Research and statistics carry a weight of persuasion in a world of uncertainty and controversy. Correctly conducted and rightly interpreted, science largely deserves this prestige, but science can be badly conducted, too, and then it can mislead or even be dangerous. Although we cannot all master the tools of research design and statistics, it is impossible to study an empirical field such as personality without some familiarity with its research strategies and their strengths and limitations.

Total objectivity is rare indeed; however, the conclusions based on research are strengthened when careful methodological precautions are taken. Ensuring that our measurements are reliable and valid and that our subjects are representative of people to whom we will apply our findings is a basic goal of researchers. For this reason, studies of adults in the community and national samples add much insight that cannot be obtained from college student samples alone (Ward, 1993). Statistical methods, including factor analysis and path analysis, have been developed to permit sophisticated descriptions of the relationships among variables. Longitudinal studies help us to determine whether personality remains consistent or changes over time, as well as what influences (such as education) contribute to change. We can test whether one factor actually causes changes in another by using experimental methods and sophisticated longitudinal designs. Other designs help sort out the impact of heredity on personality from the influence of the environment. When many studies have been conducted to test a particular hypothesis, we may find, using meta-analytic procedures, that relationships occur only part of the time and that outside variables can explain why a relationship sometimes occurs and sometimes doesn't. The descriptions that are accurate for some groups of people may not fit other groups, although it is sometimes easy to overemphasize the differences and lose sight of the similarities.

Studying individuals rather than groups is a challenging task, and researchers have developed systematic methods to expand the insights of case studies and psychobiography. It is humbling to realize that as much observation and analysis can be required to study one individual as to conduct research on large groups of people. Our broader studies may always be limited to only some aspects of much more complicated lives, and there are no guarantees that our choices about what to study and what to omit are always the best choices. Our professional journals tell us more about work than about friendship, more about achievement than about dependency, and more about self-esteem than about responsibility. Researchers who are more attuned to other aspects of the diversity of human personality may make different choices, and the growth of our field may come as much from exploring such diverse viewpoints as from building on its current foundations.

Despite the contributions of sound research methods to the study of personality, methods can only put our theoretical ideas to the test. They cannot tell us what to theorize or what use to make of the observations we derive by using the methods. Psychologists who work in applied settings, as therapists, counselors, or consultants, bring insights that supplement the implicit personality theories that each of us has and that often provide unacknowledged direction to research. Furthermore, such applied settings offer an arena for testing whether our understanding of personality, so often based on studies of students in college and university environments, is also valid in the diverse and complex world where ordinary people spend their lives.

What Will the Future Bring?

It is difficult enough to understand the present state of a discipline and surely foolhardy to try to predict its future with any precision. Our rapidly expanding knowledge about personality would make any mere snapshot misleading. The field is more like an unfinished motion picture—a movie with unresolved threads of plot and scenes that will seem out of place when the perspective of hindsight is available. Like viewers of an engaging film, we will guess what lies in store.

One prediction seems safe: developments in other fields will influence our discipline. Advances in genetic studies and in physiology may reveal the mechanisms underlying individual differences. Perhaps, as current findings suggest, more of the personality manifestations that intrigue us will be shown to be strongly influenced by biology, which will cause us to rethink our explanations of personality in terms of experience. (Of course, biology probably interacts with experience to determine most outcomes.) A more complete view of personality would have to include biological influences not only as causes of personality but as an intrinsic part of personality; this would be an expansion of our now largely cognitive views.

We may also look to fields that take a more macrolevel approach, such as sociology and anthropology, to expand our growing awareness of the role of culture in shaping personality. We may anticipate that personality theorists and researchers will increasingly consider the social context of personality, including cultural variation and the impact of the sociological facts of life within each population and on each individual. This approach will require increased study of populations outside the college environment as well as continued effort to develop measures, and to use them, in other populations. We will need to include researchers who are intimately familiar with these other populations to avoid misperceiving them through our own cultural lenses. Perhaps we will come to think of the emphasis on the individual personality in our theories as a cultural creation, a biased view typical only of individualist cultures that will be revised as the West comes to understand the collectivism of Asian (and other) cultures. As diverse cultural perspectives are recognized, it seems reasonable to expect that the personal dimensions of our field may cause other cultural groups to protest angrily at having been excluded and misunderstood, as has occurred when women and ethnic minorities have voiced their differences from traditional approaches. Such inclusion has sensitized us to the need to consider the fear of success as well as its glory and to consider acculturation, social class, and power inequities as significant influences on some people's personalities. These political voices can potentially sharpen our consideration of scientific objectivity and encourage critical evaluation of the extent to which our science is or should be influenced by social values.

What will be the role of theory in the future of personality? Theory and observations go hand in hand, each influencing the other, and so we may expect theories to evolve as research continues. With the emphasis on empirical testing that is the mark of modern personality investigation, perhaps we will automatically be mindful of the close relationship between theory and its related observations. In the early days of personality study, when systematic observations in this field were just beginning to accumulate, it was naturally tempting to assume that the new theories would have broad application. Freud generalized from his limited observations of a select population of clients in the unique setting of psychoanalytic therapy, claiming that the dynamics he had observed applied to all people. Now, with more observations that can validate or invalidate our theoretical predictions, we are less bold but more precise.

We may expect that applied uses of personality concepts will result from increased knowledge, in therapy, business, education, and other areas. Furthermore, these applications in the complex real world will continue to raise questions for research and theory, pushing us beyond the simplified understandings of our subject pools.

Another prediction is that some of the relationships between variables we now espouse will be proved invalid as time brings changes in the people we study and perhaps also in our methods of observation. We have already seen dramatic reversals in some reported findings. Consider these examples. In the 1950s, it was reported that African Americans had lower self-esteem than whites; today, this is no longer found. In the 1970s, it was reported that females had a higher level of fear of success than males and that this caused them to achieve at lower levels in their careers. Soon thereafter, sex differences in the fear of success were no longer found consistently. It is not always clear in which cases changed results indicate that culture has brought change to the people that we study and in which cases the change occurs because early studies are flawed and additional investigation corrects our observational errors. In either case, we must be somewhat tentative about accepting the results of research, realizing that what is reported may not describe all people for all time and that, until findings are replicated with sufficient attention to measurement, sampling, and other research considerations, it is possible that they are only half true. With sufficient replication, using the methods of science to produce the most unbiased findings researchers can obtain, and considering diverse perspectives to see beyond the myopia of our own individual experience, we are more likely to achieve objectivity. Science, despite its systematic discipline, simply tests and refines what we have already thought, or at best prepares us to learn something new by telling us where to look.

Like all sciences that base knowledge on empirical observation, the field of personality strives for objective and verifiable statements that explain what we have observed and anticipate new observations. There are, however, many considerations in studying personality that make the lessons of other sciences only partially relevant. For one thing, we stumble constantly over the question of consciousness. Our descriptions of personality depend more than is often acknowledged upon the conscious self-reports of subjects. As David McClelland's studies of motivation demonstrate (see Chapter 7), conscious reports do not predict behavior in the same way as do alternative measures, such as projective tests. Alternative modes of data collection, such as measures of people's actual behaviors, have been used less often because they are less convenient.

As we have seen, cultural factors influence personality, and they are now gaining serious consideration by theorists and researchers. The researcher's prior convictions about personality may be even more difficult to submit to the empirical test, because such convictions are not simply a matter of scientific belief but the basis for a sense of self-worth and personal values. In the field of motivation, researchers studied the need for achievement and at first resisted the apparently absurd idea of fear of success. Once fear of success was proposed, however, many researchers (especially women) who could identify with its proposed dynamics accepted this idea wholeheartedly and with relatively little scientific skepticism. It became a bandwagon (Mednick, 1989). It is easy to accept incomplete evidence as support for what we already believe while rejecting evidence when it would challenge our prior convictions.

Consciousness, culture, and personal convictions pose special obstacles to a science of personality, but they do not preclude it. I like to think they raise the ante of this game of science, promising that as we learn new truths about personality, we will enhance not only our science but also ourselves and others whom we influence. Whether this is best accomplished by changing individuals, modifying society, taking biological functioning into account, or other strategies that we may discover in the future is, in a comprehensive science of personality, largely an empirical question.

SUMMARY

- In the absence of an accepted paradigm, we have organized our study of personality into three issues: description, dynamics, and development.

- Research strategies provide valuable tools for attaining more objective knowledge, but they must be carefully evaluated.

- Personality is a rapidly changing field. Its future is likely to be influenced by developments in other fields, and these developments can be expected to cast doubt on some of the findings that we now accept.

THOUGHT QUESTIONS

1. Explain why our study of personality was organized around description, dynamics, and development. Can you suggest an alternative organization?

2. Considering the material covered in this book, identify one finding about the description of personality that you found interesting or surprising.

3. Considering the material covered in this book, identify one finding about the dynamics of personality that you found interesting or surprising.

4. Considering the material covered in this book, identify one finding about the development of personality that you found interesting or surprising.

5. Propose a topic or question about the description of personality that you think deserves further study.

6. Propose a topic or question about the dynamics of personality that you think deserves further study.

7. Propose a topic or question about the development of personality that you think deserves further study.

8. Sometimes students protest that they do not want to study the methods of research, but only the results. Evaluate this position and the importance of knowing research methods.

9. You've considered many research results in this book. Are there any that you think would no longer be replicated today? Which ones?

10. What fields outside of psychology (biology? genetics? sociology? history?) do you think ought to be required for personality students? Explain why you think these fields are important to understanding personality.

Factor Analysis

THE SEARCH FOR UNDERLYING BASIC DIMENSIONS of personality requires advanced statistical techniques. Nature, including human nature, does not reveal its secrets to the casual observer. The statistical technique of *factor analysis* is a basic tool for researchers seeking to identify the fundamental traits of personality. Factor analysis builds on the correlation coefficients that we examined in Chapter 2. Researchers often compute the correlations among many variables and present these in a correlation matrix. (For an example of a correlation matrix, see the multitrait-multimethod matrix in the Research Strategies box, Chapter 3.) When several measures converge (as evidenced by positive correlations among them), it is often more convenient to use a single composite score instead of the several measures. Rather than look at a subject's self-rating on a list of adjectives that include *kind*, *trusting*, *cooperative*, *forgiving*, and *not rude*, a researcher would simply consider a the person's score on the composite measure called Agreeableness (one of the Big Five personality factors).

How can we know which measures converge? Most fundamentally, we look for correlations among them. That process can be tedious, however, and the judgments that one person makes about which items to combine might not be the same as another person's. Factor analysis is a systematic procedure that simplifies this process. This statistical method can take a large set of correlations and reduce it to manageable dimensions.

The mathematical calculations of factor analysis are complicated. In practice, they require computers and a number of technical decisions. Conceptually, though, the technique is not so mysterious. It assumes that any measured score is influenced by several hidden causes. One underlying cause can influence two or more measured variables. When this happens, the two measured variables will be correlated. The underlying causes are not directly visible, but they can be inferred by examining the correlations among variables. When found, these underlying causes are called factors.

After a factor analysis has been conducted, we know how many dimensions are represented in the data and how closely each item corresponds to each dimension. This correspondence is expressed as a *factor loading* of that item on the factor. For example, a factor analysis of people's self-ratings on several adjectives showed that these ratings correspond to the Big Five factors. High factor loadings indicate that the adjective belongs to that factor. High negative loadings indicate that rejecting the adjective is indicative of that factor. As shown in Table A.1, the Extraversion factor is characterized by agreeing with some items (*talkative, sociable*) and disagreeing with others (*quiet, shy*). The other four factors also have corresponding adjectives, indicated by the boldface factor loadings.

Factor analysis is often useful in the development of personality tests (Briggs & Cheek, 1986; Comrey, 1988). Through factor analysis, we can look beneath the surface of measured traits to discover the underlying factors that determine them. In the words of researchers who have developed the five-factor model, "Factor analysis . . . systematizes the quest for those basic requirements of scientific constructs, convergent and discriminant validity" (Costa & McCrae, 1992a, p. 654). Many personality tests are scored by adding together all the items to compute one score. Other tests provide several subscores; for example, the NEO-PI provides scores for five factors: Neuroticism, Extraversion, Openness, Conscientiousness, and Agreeableness. Factor analysis can be used to confirm that a test measures one dimension or several, and it is often used when tests are being developed or revised to help select items that correspond to the intended factors. There is no guarantee that the factors found when a test is administered to one group of people will be the same as those found for another group of people, although there is often similarity.

Factor Rotation

To understand some of the complications in comparing models of personality, a rather esoteric point about the method of factor analysis must be made. Factors that are discovered in factor analysis can be presented in equivalent alternative forms. By analogy, we can think of 5 as "1 + 4," "2 + 3," "3.18 + 1.82," and so on. All amount to the same thing. In graph

TABLE A.1   Big Five Factors of American Natural Language

	Big Five factor				
	E	*A*	*N*	*C*	*O*
Quiet	**−79**	07	−06	03	−14
Shy	**−67**	08	13	−07	−08
Talkative	**65**	05	03	−02	−02
Sociable	**70**	16	−12	−05	−06
Kind	−07	**68**	−08	−02	−16
Cooperative	−02	**56**	−06	00	−15
Cold	−25	**−51**	01	−04	−15
Rude	11	**−58**	06	−10	−13
Worrying	−14	−09	**67**	05	−06
Nervous	−22	07	**65**	−03	−09
Stable	−04	26	**−59**	17	−01
Relaxed	01	17	**−75**	02	−03
Thorough	−01	−04	02	**58**	−20
Efficient	00	−02	−09	**53**	−21
Careless	07	−16	−01	**−44**	−05
Disorganized	−08	05	−03	**−61**	−04
Original	12	−06	−08	02	**56**
Artistic	−04	16	09	−10	**50**
Imaginative	14	−06	−00	−09	**48**
Simple	−02	21	18	−11	**−37**

Note: E, Extraversion; A, Agreeableness; N, Neuroticism; C, Conscientiousness; O, Openness. All loadings multiplied by 100. Loadings ≥ |30| are in boldface.

Adapted from Benet & Waller, 1995, p. 708.

form, this equivalence corresponds to rotating the vertical and horizontal axes. This can be done without losing any information. For example, we usually define places on a map in terms of the dimensions of north-south and east-west. It would be possible to define locations in terms of northeast-southwest and northwest-southeast instead. If a town happened to have streets laid out in these directions, it would be more convenient to

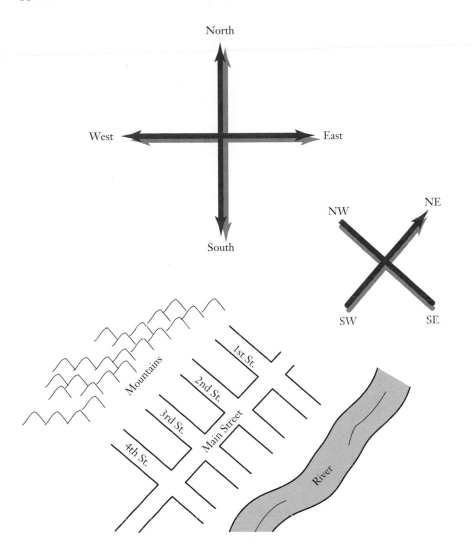

FIGURE A.1
*Alternative rotations convey
the same information, but
sometimes one rotation is
more useful than other.*

give directions to a driver in those terms, although an observer from a satellite would probably find the north-south dimensions more convenient (Fig. A.1). Statisticians tell us that some of the differences among the various factor models of personality correspond to such differences in rotation.

The general problem of locating points in space is not limited to two dimensions. By adding height, we can consider three dimensions. Those who live in very large metropolitan areas are familiar with the need to find an office not only by location on the two-dimensional ground but also by height. On what floor of the skyscraper is the office?

A circumplex model, such as that of Wiggins (see Chapter 3), diagrams all the rotations of a two-factor model. For a three-factor model, we would need to show a sphere instead of a circle. What about a four- or five-factor model? Even solid geometry cannot help us to visualize this problem.

That's too bad, because it would be helpful to have a visual image of factor models such as the Big Five personality traits.

Summary

Factor analysis is a complex yet useful statistical tool in personality research. The following points summarize what should be known by non-statisticians when reading personality research:

1. Factor analysis is a statistical procedure that builds on the correlation coefficient.

2. Factor analysis examines a correlation matrix and identifies a smaller number of dimensions (factors) based on correlations among the variables.

3. Factor loadings tell how closely a particular item or variable corresponds to a general factor.

4. Factor analysis is used to develop personality tests. It guides test developers in deciding whether to score a test as one scale or as a larger number of factors.

5. The same underlying factors can be described differently if the factors are rotated.

REFERENCES

Abelson, R. P. (1981). Psychological status of the script concept. *American Psychologist,* *36,* 715–729.

Abrams, D., Carter, J., & Hogg, M. A. (1989). Perceptions of male homosexuality: An application of social identity theory. *Social Behaviour, 4,* 253–264.

Abramson, L., McClelland, D. C., Brown, D., & Kelner, S. (1991). Alexithymic characteristics and metabolic control in diabetic and healthy adults. *Journal of Nervous and Mental Disease, 179,* 490–494.

Acklin, M. W. (1993). Rorschach classics in contemporary perspective: Series introduction. *Journal of Personality Assessment, 61,* 196–197.

Acklin, M. W., Bibb, J. L., Boyer, P., & Jain, V. (1991). Early memories as expressions of relationship paradigms: A preliminary investigation. *Journal of Personality Assessment, 57,* 177–192.

Acklin, M. W., Sauer, A., Alexander, G., & Dugoni, B. (1989). Predicting depression using earliest childhood memories. *Journal of Personality Assessment, 53,* 51–59.

Adams, J., Priest, R. F., & Prince, H. T. (1985). Achievement motive: Analyzing the validity of the WOFO. *Psychology of Women Quarterly, 9,* 357–369.

Ader, R., & Cohen, N. (1993). Psychoneuroimmunology: Conditioning and stress. *Annual Review of Psychology, 44,* 53–85.

Adler, A. (1927). *Understanding human nature* (W. B. Wolfe, Trans.). New York: Fawcett. (Original work published 1921)

Adler, A. (1950). *The practice and theory of individual psychology* (2nd ed. rev.) (P. Radin, Trans.) . London: Routledge & Kegan Paul.

Adorno, T. W., Frenkel-Brunswick, E., Levinson, D. J., & Sanford, R. N. (1950). *The authoritarian personality.* New York: Harper & Row.

Ahadi, S., & Diener, E. (1989). Multiple determinants and effect size. *Journal of Personality and Social Psychology, 56,* 398–406.

Ainsworth, M. D. S. (1989). Attachments beyond infancy. *American Psychologist, 44,* 709–716.

Ainsworth, M. D. S., Blehar, M. C., Waters, E., & Wall, S. (1978). *Patterns of attachment: A psychological study of the strange situation.* Hillsdale, N.J.: Erlbaum.

Aldwin, C. M., Levenson, M. R., Spiro, A., III, & Bossé, R. (1989). Does emotionality predict stress? Findings from the Normative Aging Study. *Journal of Personality and Social Psychology, 56*, 618–624.

Aldwin, C. M., & Revenson, T. A. (1987). Does coping help? A reexamination of the relation between coping and mental health. *Journal of Personality and Social Psychology, 53*, 337–348.

Alexander, I. E. (1988). Personality, psychological assessment, and psychobiography. *Journal of Personality, 56*, 265–294.

Alexander, I. E. (1990). *Personology: Method and content in personality assessment and psychobiography.* Durham: Duke University Press.

Alexander, M. J., & Higgins, E. T. (1993). Emotional trade-offs of becoming a parent: How social roles influence self-discrepancy effects. *Journal of Personality and Social Psychology, 65*, 1259–1269.

Allport, G. W. (1931). What is a trait of personality? *Journal of Abnormal and Social Psychology, 25*, 368–372.

Allport, G. W. (1937). *Personality: A psychological interpretation.* New York: Henry Holt.

Allport, G. W. (1950). *The individual and his religion.* New York: Macmillan.

Allport, G. W. (1955). *Becoming: Basic considerations for a psychology of personality.* New Haven, Conn.: Yale University Press.

Allport, G. W. (Ed.). (1965). *Letters from Jenny.* New York: Harcourt Brace Jovanovich.

Allport, G. W. (1966). Traits revisited. *American Psychologist, 21*, 1–10.

Allport, G. W. (1968). Is the concept of self necessary? In C. Gordon & K. J. Gergen (Eds.), *The self in social interaction: Vol. 1. Classic and contemporary perspectives* (pp. 25–32). New York: Wiley.

Allport, G. W., & Odbert, H. S. (1936). Trait-names: A psycho-lexical study. *Psychological Monographs, 47* (1, Whole No. 211).

Allport, G. W., & Ross, J. M. (1967). Personal religious orientation and prejudice. *Journal of Personality and Social Psychology, 5*, 432–443.

Alper, T. G. (1974). Achievement motivation in college women: A now-you-see-it-now-you-don't phenomenon. *American Psychologist, 29*, 194–203.

Alter-Reid, K., Gibbs, M. S., Lachenmeyer, J. R., Sigal, J., & Massoth, N. A. (1986). Sexual abuse of children: A review of the empirical findings. *Clinical Psychology Review, 6*, 249–266.

Amabile, T. M., Hill, K. G., Hennessey, B. A., & Tighe, E. M. (1994). The Work Preference Inventory: Assessing intrinsic and extrinsic motivational orientations. *Journal of Personality and Social Psychology, 66*, 950–967.

Amaro, H., Russo, N. F., & Pares-Avila, J. A. (1987). Contemporary research on Hispanic women: A selected bibliography of the social science literature. *Psychology of Women Quarterly, 11*, 523–532.

Ambady, N., & Rosenthal, R. (1992). Thin slices of expressive behavior as predictors of interpersonal consequences: A meta-analysis. *Psychological Bulletin, 111*, 256–274.

Amelang, M., & Borkenau, P. (1986). The trait concept: Current theoretical considerations, empirical facts, and implications for personality inventory construction. In A. Angleitner & J. S. Wiggins (Eds.), *Personality assessment via questionnaires: Current issues in theory and measurement* (pp. 7–34). Berlin: Springer-Verlag.

Amirkhan, J. H. (1990). A factor analytically derived measure of coping: The Coping Strategy Indicator. *Journal of Personality and Social Psychology, 59*, 1066–1074.

Amirkhan, J. H. (1994). Criterion validity of a coping measure. *Journal of Personality Assessment, 62*, 242–261.

Andersen, S. M., & Cole, S. W. (1990). "Do I know you?": The role of significant others in general social perception. *Journal of Personality and Social Psychology, 59*, 384–399.

Andersen, S. M., & Klatzky, R. L. (1987). Traits and social stereotypes: Levels of categorization in person perception. *Journal of Personality and Social Psychology, 53*, 235–246.

Anderson, C. A., & Sedikides, C. (1991). Thinking about people: Contributions of a typological alternative to associationistic and dimensional models of person perception. *Journal of Personality and Social Psychology, 60*, 203–217.

Anderson, J. W. (1981). Psychobiographical methodology: The case of William James. In L. Wheeler (Ed.), *Review of personality and social psychology: Vol. 2* (pp. 245–272). Beverly Hills: Sage.

Anderson, N. B., McNeilly, M., & Myers, H. (1993). A biosocial model of race differences in vascular reactivity. In J. Blascovich & E. S. Katkin (Eds.), *Cardiovascular reactivity to psychological stress and disease* (pp. 83–108). Washington, D.C.: American Psychological Association.

Anderson, W. (1975). The self-actualization of Richard M. Nixon. *Journal of Humanistic Psychology, 15*(1), 27–34.

Aneshensel, C. S., Frerichs, R. R., & Clark, V. A. (1981). Family roles and sex differences in depression. *Journal of Health and Social Behavior, 22*, 379–393.

Angleitner, A., Buss, D. M., & Demtröder, A. I. (1990). A cross-cultural comparison using the Act Frequency Approach (AFA) in West Germany and the United States. *European Journal of Personality, 4*, 187–207.

Angleitner, A., & Demtröder, A. I. (1988). Acts and dispositions: A reconsideration of the Act Frequency Approach. *European Journal of Personality, 2*(2), 121–141.

Angleitner, A., Ostendorf, F., & John, O. P. (1990). Towards a taxonomy of personality descriptors in German: A psycho-lexical study. *European Journal of Personality, 4*, 89–118.

Ansbacher, H. L., & Ansbacher, R. R. (Eds.). (1956). *The individual psychology of Alfred Adler: A systematic presentation in selections from his writings.* New York: Harper Torchbooks.

Antrobus, J. (1991). Dreaming: Cognitive processes during cortical activation and high afferent thresholds. *Psychological Review, 98*, 96–121.

Apostal, R., & Marks, C. (1990). Correlations between the Strong-Campbell and Myers-Briggs scales of introversion-extraversion and career interests. *Psychological Reports, 66*, 811–816.

Archer, S. L., & Waterman, A. S. (1988). Psychological individualism: Gender differences or gender neutrality? *Human Development, 31*, 65–81.

Argentero, P. (1989). Second-order factor structure of Cattell's 16 Personality Factor Questionnaire. *Perceptual and Motor Skills, 68*, 1043–1047.

Ariam, S., & Siller, J. (1982). Effects of subliminal oneness stimuli in Hebrew on academic performance of Israeli high school students: Further evidence on the adaptation-enhancing effects of symbiotic fantasies in another culture using another language. *Journal of Abnormal Psychology, 91*, 343–349.

Aries, E. J., & Olver, R. R. (1985). Sex differences in the development of a separate sense of self during infancy: Directions for future research. *Psychology of Women Quarterly, 9*, 515–531.

Armstead, C. A., Lawler, K. A., Gorden, G., Cross, J., & Gibbons, J. (1989). Relationship of racial stressors to blood pressure responses and anger expression in Black college students. *Health Psychology, 8*, 541–556.

Aronson, E. (1982). Modifying the environment of the desegregated classroom. In A. J. Stewart (Ed.), *Motivation and society* (pp. 319–336). San Francisco: Jossey-Bass.

Aronson, E., et al. (1978). *The jigsaw classroom.* Beverly Hills, Calif.: Sage.

Asch, S. E. (1946). Forming impressions of personality. *Journal of Abnormal and Social Psychology, 41*, 258–290.

Asch, S. E., & Zukier, H. (1984). Thinking about persons. *Journal of Personality and Social Psychology, 46*, 1230–1240.

Ashmore, R. D. (1990). Sex, gender, and the individual. In L. A. Pervin (Ed.), *Handbook of personality: Theory and research* (pp. 486–526). New York: Guilford.

Ashmore, R. D., & Del Boca, F. K. (1979). Sex stereotypes and implicit personality theory: Toward a cognitive-social psychological conceptualization. *Sex Roles, 5*, 219–248.

Ashton, P. (1986). Motivation training and personal control: A comparison of three intervention strategies. *Education, 106*, 454–461.

Assor, A. (1989). The power motive as an influence on the evaluation of high and low status persons. *Journal of Research in Personality, 23*, 55–69.

Atkinson, J. W. (1953). The achievement motive and recall of interrupted and completed tasks. *Journal of Experimental Psychology, 46*, 381–390.

Atkinson, J. W. (Ed.). (1958). *Motives in fantasy, action, and society: A method of assessment and study.* Princeton, N.J.: D. Van Nostrand.

Atkinson, J. W. (1966). Motivational determinants of risk-taking behavior. In J. W. Atkinson & N. T. Feather (Eds.), *A theory of achievement motivation* (pp. 11–29). New York: Wiley.

Atkinson, J. W. (1982). Motivational determinants of thematic apperception. In A. J. Stewart (Ed.), *Motivation and society* (pp. 3–40). San Francisco: Jossey-Bass.

Atkinson, J. W., & Birch, D. (1978). The dynamics of achievement-oriented activity. In J. W. Atkinson & J. O. Raynor (Eds.), *Personality, motivation, and achievement* (pp. 143–197). Washington: Hemisphere.

Atkinson, J. W., & McClelland, D. C. (1948). The projective expression of needs. II. The effect of different intensities of the hunger drive on thematic apperception. *Journal of Experimental Psychology, 38*, 643–658.

Ault, R. L., Jr., Hazelwood, R. R., & Reboussin, R. (1994). Epistemological status of equivocal death analysis. *American Psychologist, 49,* 72–73.

Aviezer, O., Van IJzendoorn, M. H., Sagi, A., & Schuengel, C. (1994). "Children of the dream" revisited: 70 years of collective early child care in Israeli kibbutzim. *Psychological Bulletin, 116,* 99–116.

Azibo, D. A. (1988). Personality, clinical, and social psychological research on Blacks: Appropriate and inappropriate research frameworks. *Western Journal of Black Studies, 12,* 220–233.

Bagley, C. R. (1991). Factor structure of temperament in the third year of life. *Journal of General Psychology, 118*(3), 291–297.

Baguma, P., & Furnham, A. (1993). The Protestant work ethic in Great Britain and Uganda. *Journal of Cross-Cultural Psychology, 24,* 495–507.

Baird, L. L. (1990). A 24-year longitudinal study of the development of religious ideas. *Psychological Reports, 66,* 479–482.

Bakan, D. (1966). *The duality of human existence: Isolation and communion in Western man.* Boston: Beacon.

Baker, L. A., & Daniels, D. (1990). Nonshared environmental influences and personality differences in adult twins. *Journal of Personality and Social Psychology, 58,* 103–110.

Baker, L. J., Dearborn, M., Hastings, J. E., & Hamberger, K. (1984). Type A behavior in women: A review. *Health Psychology, 3,* 477–497.

Balay, J., & Shevrin, H. (1988). The subliminal psychodynamic activation method: A critical review. *American Psychologist, 43,* 161–174.

Baldwin, M. W. (1992). Relational schemas and the processing of social information. *Psychological Bulletin, 112,* 461–484.

Balkin, J. (1986). Contributions of family to men's fear of success in college. *Psychological Reports, 59,* 1071–1074.

Balkin, J. (1987). Contributions of friends to women's fear of success in college. *Psychological Reports, 61,* 39–42.

Ballou, M. B. (1990). Approaching a feminist-principled paradigm in the construction of personality theory. *Women and Therapy, 9,* 23–40.

Bandura, A. (1977). Self-efficacy: Toward a unifying theory of behavioral change. *Psychological Review, 84,* 191–215.

Bandura, A. (1978). The self system in reciprocal determinism. *American Psychologist, 33,* 344–358.

Bandura, A. (1980). Gauging the relationship between self-efficacy judgment and action. *Cognitive Therapy and Research, 4,* 263–268.

Bandura, A. (1990a). Perceived self-efficacy in the exercise of control over AIDS infection. *Evaluation and Program Planning, 13,* 9–17.

Bandura, A. (1990b). Selective activation and disengagement of moral control. *Journal of Social Issues, 46(1),* 27–46.

Bandura, A., Adams, N. E., Hardy, A. B., & Howells, G. N. (1980). Tests of the generality of self-efficacy theory. *Cognitive Therapy and Research, 4,* 39–66.

Bandura, A., Cioffi, D., Taylor, C. B., & Brouillard, M. E. (1988). Perceived self-efficacy in coping with cognitive stressors and opioid activation. *Journal of Personality and Social Psychology, 55,* 479–488.

Bandura, A., Reese, L., & Adams, N. E. (1982). Microanalysis of action and fear arousal as a function of differential levels of perceived self-efficacy. *Journal of Personality and Social Psychology, 43,* 5–21.

Bandura, A., Taylor, C. B., Williams, S. L., Mefford, I. N., & Barchas, J. D. (1985). Catecholamine secretion as a function of perceived coping self-efficacy. *Journal of Consulting and Clinical Psychology, 53,* 406–414.

Banks, H. C., & Juni, S. (1991). Defense mechanisms in minority African-American and Hispanic youths: Standardization and scale reliabilities. *Journal of Personality Assessment, 56,* 327–334.

Barefoot, J. C., Siegler, I. C., Nowlin, J. B., Peterson, B. L., Haney, T. L., & Williams, R. B., Jr. (1987). Suspiciousness, health, and mortality: A follow-up study of 500 older adults. *Psychosomatic Medicine, 49,* 450–457.

Barends, A., Westen, D., Leigh, J., Silbert, D., & Byers, S. (1990). Assessing affect-tone of relationship paradigms from TAT and interview data. *Psychological Assessment, 2,* 329–332.

Barnard, C. P., & Hirsch, C. (1985). Borderline personality and victims of incest. *Psychological Reports, 57,* 715–718.

Barnett, R. C., Brennan, R. T., Raudenbush, S. W., & Marshall, N. L. (1994). Gender and the relationship between marital-role quality and psychological distress. *Psychology of Women Quarterly, 18,* 105–127.

Baron, S. H., & Pletsch, C. (Eds.) (1985). *Introspection in biography.* Hillsdale, N.J.: Erlbaum.

Barrett, P., & Kline, P. (1982). An item and radial parcel factor analysis of the 16 PF questionnaire. *Personality and Individual Differences, 3,* 259–270.

Barrick, M. R., & Mount, M. K. (1991). The Big Five personality dimensions and job performance: A meta-analysis. *Personnel Psychology, 44*(1), 1–26.

Barris, R. (1987). Relationships between eating behaviors and person/environment interactions in college women. *Occupational Therapy: Journal of Research, 7,* 273–288.

Barry, G. M. (1991). Consulting with contrary types. *Organization Development Journal, 9*(1), 61–66.

Bartussek, D., Diedrich, O., Naumann, E., & Collet, W. (1993). Introversion-extraversion and Event-Related Potential (ERP): A test of J. A. Gray's theory. *Personality and Individual Differences, 14,* 565–574.

Baruch, G. K., & Barnett, R. (1986). Role quality, multiple role involvement, and psychological well-being in midlife women. *Journal of Personality and Social Psychology, 51,* 578–585.

Bass, B. M., & Farrow, D. L. (1977). Quantitative analyses of biographies of political figures. *Journal of Psychology, 97,* 281–296.

Bass, R. F. (1987). The generality, analysis, and assessment of single-subject data. *Psychology in the Schools, 24,* 97–104.

Bassoff, E. S., & Glass, G. V. (1982). The relationship between sex roles and mental health: A meta-analysis of twenty-six studies. *Counseling Psychologist, 10,* 105–112.

Bates, J. E. (1994). Introduction. In J. E. Bates & T. D. Wachs (Eds.), *Temperament: Individual differences at the interface of biology and behavior* (pp. 1–14). Washington, D.C.: American Psychological Association.

Batson, C. D. (1990). Good Samaritans—or priests and Levites? Using William James as a guide in the study of religious prosocial motivation. *Personality and Social Psychology Bulletin, 16,* 758–768.

Batson, C. D., & Ventis, W. L. (1982). *The religious experience: A social-psychological perspective.* New York: Oxford University Press.

Baumeister, R. F. (1987). How the self became a problem: A psychological review of historical research. *Journal of Personality and Social Psychology, 52,* 163–176.

Baumeister, R. F. (1988). Should we stop studying sex differences altogether? *American Psychologist, 43,* 1092–1095.

Baumeister, R. F. (1991). On the stability of variability: Retest reliability of metatraits. *Personality and Social Psychology Bulletin, 17,* 633–639.

Baumeister, R. F., & Cairns, K. J. (1992). Repression and self-presentation: When audiences interfere with self-deceptive strategies. *Journal of Personality and Social Psychology, 62,* 851–862.

Baumeister, R. F., Heatherton, T. F., & Tice, D. M. (1993). When ego threats lead to self-regulation failure: Negative consequences of high self-esteem. *Journal of Personality and Social Psychology, 64,* 141–156.

Baumeister, R. F., & Tice, D. M. (1988). Metatraits. *Journal of Personality, 56,* 571–598.

Baumeister, R. F., Tice, D. M., & Hutton, D. G. (1989). Self-presentational motivations and personality differences in self-esteem. *Journal of Personality, 57,* 547–579.

Baumgardner, A. H. (1990). To know oneself is to like oneself: Self-certainty and self-affect. *Journal of Personality and Social Psychology, 58,* 1062–1072.

Baumrind, D. (1971). Current patterns of parental authority. *Developmental Psychology Monographs, 4*(2, Pt. 2).

Beck, N. C., McRae, C., Henrichs, T. F., Sneider, L., et al. (1989). Replicated item level factor structure of the MMPI: Racial and sexual differences. *Journal of Clinical Psychology, 45,* 553–560.

Belenky, M. F., Clinchy, B. M., Goldberger, N. R., & Tarule, J. M. (1986). *Women's ways of knowing: The development of self, voice, and mind.* New York: Basic Books.

Belle, D. (1985). Ironies in the contemporary study of gender. In A. J. Stewart & M. B. Lykes (Eds.), *Gender and personality: Current perspectives on theory and research* (pp. 312–317). Durham, N.C.: Duke University Press.

Belsky, J. (1993). Etiology of child maltreatment: A developmental-ecological analysis. *Psychological Bulletin, 114,* 413–434.

Belsky, J., Fish, M., & Isabella, R. A. (1991). Continuity and discontinuity in infant negative and positive emotionality: Family antecedents and attachment consequences. *Developmental Psychology, 27,* 421–431.

Belsky, J., Steinberg, L., & Draper, P. (1991a). Childhood experience, interpersonal development, and reproductive strategy: An evolutionary theory of socialization. *Child Development, 62,* 647–670.

Belsky, J., Steinberg, L., & Draper, P. (1991b). Further reflections on an evolutionary theory of socialization. *Child Development, 62,* 682–685.

Bem, D. J., & Allen, A. (1974). On predicting some of the people some of the time: The search for cross-situational consistencies in behavior. *Psychological Review, 81,* 506–520.

Bem, D. J., & Funder, D. C. (1978). Predicting more of the people more of the time: Assessing the personality of situations. *Psychological Review, 85*, 485–501.

Bem, S. L. (1974). The measurement of psychological androgyny. *Journal of Consulting and Clinical Psychology, 42*, 155–162.

Bem, S. L. (1977). On the utility of alternative procedures for assessing psychological androgyny. *Journal of Consulting and Clinical Psychology, 45*, 196–205.

Bem, S. L. (1984). Androgyny and gender schema theory: A conceptual and empirical integration. *Nebraska Symposium on Motivation, 32*, 179–226.

Bem, S. L. (1987). Gender schema theory and the romantic tradition. In P. Shaver & C. Hendrick (Eds.), *Sex and gender* (pp. 251–271). Newbury Park, Calif.: Sage.

Benet, V., & Waller, N. G. (1995). The big seven factor model of personality description: Evidence for its cross-cultural generality in a Spanish sample. *Journal of Personality and Social Psychology, 69*, 701–718.

Bennett, P., & Carroll, D. (1990). Stress management approaches to the prevention of coronary heart disease. *British Journal of Clinical Psychology, 29*, 1–12.

Benson, H., Malhotra, M. S., Goldman, R. F., Jacobs, G. D., & Hopkins, P. J. (1990). Three case reports of the metabolic and electroencephalographic changes during advanced Buddhist meditation techniques. *Behavioral Medicine, 16*, 90–95.

Bergeman, C. S., Chipuer, H. M., Plomin, R., Pedersen, N. L., McClearn, G. E., Nesselroade, J. R., Costa, P. T., & McCrae, R. R. (1993). Genetic and environmental effects on Openness to Experience, Agreeableness, and Conscientiousness: An adoption/ twin study. *Journal of Personality, 61*, 159–179.

Berglas, S., & Jones, E. E. (1978). Drug choice as a self-handicapping strategy in response to noncontingent success. *Journal of Personality and Social Psychology, 36*, 405–417.

Bergman, L. R., & Magnusson, D. (1986). Type A behavior: A longitudinal study from childhood to adulthood. *Psychosomatic Medicine, 48*, 134–142.

Bernard, L. C., & Wood, J. (1990). Further observations on the multidimensional aspects of masculinity-femininity: The Multidimensional Sex Role Inventory-Revised. *Journal of Social Behavior and Personality, 5*, 205–224.

Berry, D. S., & Brownlow, S. (1989). Were the physiognomists right? Personality correlates of facial babyishness. *Personality and Social Psychology Bulletin, 15*, 266–279.

Berry, J. M. (1989). Cognitive efficacy across the life span: Introduction to the special series. *Developmental Psychology, 25*, 683–686.

Berry, J. W. (1990). Psychology of acculturation. In J. J. Berman (Ed.), *Nebraska Symposium on Motivation: Vol. 37. Cross-cultural perspectives* (pp. 201–234). Lincoln: University of Nebraska Press.

Berry, J. W., & Bennett, J. A. (1992). Cree conceptions of cognitive competence. *International Journal of Psychology, 27*, 73–88.

Berry, J., Kim, U., Power, S., Young, M., & Bujaki, J. (1989). Acculturation attitudes in plural societies. *Applied Psychology, 38*, 185–206.

Berzonsky, M. D. (1992). Identity style and coping strategies. *Journal of Personality, 60*, 771–788.

Berzonsky, M. D., Rice, K. G., & Neimeyer, G. J. (1990). Identity status and self-construct systems: Process X structure interactions. *Journal of Adolescence, 13*, 251–263.

Best, D. L., & Ruther, N. M. (1994). Cross-cultural themes in developmental psychology: An examination of texts, handbooks, and reviews. *Journal of Cross-Cultural Psychology, 25*, 54–77.

Betancourt, H., & López, S. R. (1993). The study of culture, ethnicity, and race in American psychology. *American Psychologist, 48*, 629–637.

Bhagat, R. S., Allie, S. M., & Ford, D. L., Jr. (1991). Organizational stress, personal life stress and symptoms of life strains: An inquiry into the moderating role of styles of coping. *Journal of Social Behavior and Personality, 6*, 163–184.

Bijnen, E. J., & Poortinga, Y. H. (1988). The questionable value of cross-cultural comparisons with the Eysenck Personality Questionnaire. *Journal of Cross-Cultural Psychology, 19*(2), 193–202.

Bijnen, E. J., Van der Net, T. Z., & Poortinga, Y. H., (1986). On cross-cultural studies with the Eysenck Personality Questionnaire. *Journal of Cross-Cultural Psychology, 17*(1), 3–16.

Blaine, B., & Crocker, J. (1995). Religiousness, race, and psychological well-being: Exploring social psychological mediators. *Personality and Social Psychology Bulletin, 21*, 1031–1041.

Blanchard-Fields, F., & Friedt, L. (1988). Age as a moderator of the relation between three dimensions of satisfaction and sex role. *Sex Roles, 18*, 759–768.

Blankfield, R. P. (1991). Suggestion, relaxation, and hypnosis as adjuncts in the care of surgery patients: A review of the literature. *American Journal of Clinical Hypnosis, 33,* 172–186.

Block, J. (1961). *The Q-sort method in personality assessment and psychiatric research.* Springfield, Ill: Charles C. Thomas.

Block, J. (1971). *Lives through time.* Berkeley, Calif.: Bancroft Books.

Block, J. (1989). Critique of the act frequency approach to personality. *Journal of Personality and Social Psychology, 56,* 234–245.

Block, J. (1993). Studying personality the long way. In D. C. Funder, R. D. Parke, C. Tomlinson-Keasey, & K. Widaman (Eds.), *Studying lives through time: Personality and development* (pp. 9–41). Washington, D.C.: American Psychological Association.

Block, J. H., Gjerde, P. F., & Block, J. H. (1991). Personality antecedents of depressive tendencies in 18-year-olds: A prospective study. *Journal of Personality and Social Psychology, 60,* 726–738.

Blum, G. S. (1989). A computer model for unconscious spread of anxiety-linked inhibition in cognitive networks. *Behavioral Science, 34,* 16–45.

Blustein, D. L., Devenis, L. E., & Kidney, B. A. (1989). Relationship between the identity formation process and career development. *Journal of Counseling Psychology, 36,* 196–202.

Bolger, N. (1990). Coping as a personality process: A prospective study. *Journal of Personality and Social Psychology, 59,* 525–537.

Bond, L. (1987). The Golden Rule settlement: A minority perspective. *Educational Measurement: Issues and Practice, 6*(2), 18–20.

Booth-Kewley, S., & Friedman, H. S. (1987). Psychological predictors of heart disease: A quantitative review. *Psychological Bulletin, 101,* 343–362.

Booth-Kewley, S., Rosenfeld, P., & Edwards, J. E. (1992). Impression management and self-deceptive enhancement among Hispanic and non-Hispanic White Navy recruits. *Journal of Social Psychology, 132,* 323–329.

Bores-Rangel, E., Church, A. T., Szendre, D., & Reeves, C. (1990). Self-efficacy in relation to occupational consideration and academic performance in high school equivalency students. *Journal of Counseling Psychology, 37,* 407–418.

Borkenau, P., & Liebler, A. (1992a). The cross-modal consistency of personality: Inferring strangers' traits from visual or acoustic information. *Journal of Research in Personality, 26,* 183–204.

Borkenau, P., & Liebler, A. (1992b). Trait inferences: Sources of validity at zero acquaintance. *Journal of Personality and Social Psychology, 62,* 645–657.

Borkenau, P., & Müller, B. (1992). Inferring act frequencies and traits from behavior observations. *Journal of Personality, 60,* 553–573.

Borkenau, P., & Ostendorf, F. (1987). Retrospective estimates of act frequencies: How accurately do they reflect reality? *Journal of Personality and Social Psychology, 52,* 626–638.

Borkenau, P., & Ostendorf, F. (1990). Comparing explanatory and confirmatory factor analysis: A study on the 5-factor model of personality. *Personality and Individual Differences, 11,* 515–524.

Bornstein, M. H., Gaughran, J. M., & Seguí, I. (1991). Multimethod assessment of infant temperament: Mother questionnaire and mother observer reports evaluated and compared at five months using the Infant Temperament Measure. *International Journal of Behavioral Development, 14*(2), 131–151.

Botwin, M. D., & Buss, D. M. (1989). Structure of act-report data: Is the five-factor model of personality recaptured? *Journal of Personality and Social Psychology, 56,* 988–1001.

Bouchard, T. J., Lykken, D. T., McGue, M., Segal, N. L., & Tellegen, A. (1990). Sources of human psychological differences: The Minnesota Study of Twins Reared Apart. *Science, 250,* 223–228.

Bouchard, T. J., & McGue, M. (1990). Genetic and rearing environmental influences on adult personality: An analysis of adopted twins reared apart. *Journal of Personality, 58,* 263–292.

Bowers, K. S. (1984). On being unconsciously influenced and informed. In K. S. Bowers & D. Meichenbaum (Eds.), *The unconscious reconsidered* (pp. 227–272). New York: Wiley.

Bowlby, J. (1969). *Attachment and loss, Vol. 1. Attachment.* London: Hogarth.

Bowlby, J. (1988). Developmental psychiatry comes of age. *American Journal of Psychiatry, 145,* 1–10.

Boyer, L. B. (1988). Effects of acculturation on the personality traits of aged Chiricahua and Mescalero Appaches: A Rorschach study. *British Journal of Projective Psychology, 33*(2), 2–17.

Boyle, G. J. (1987). Content similarities and differences in Cattell's Sixteen Personality Factor Questionnaire,

Eight State Questionnaire, and Motivation Analysis Test. *Psychological Reports, 60,* 179–186.

Boyle, G. J. (1988). Contribution of Cattellian psychometrics to the elucidation of human intellectual structure. *Multivariate Experimental Clinical Research, 8,* 267–273.

Boyle, G. J. (1989). Re-examination of the major personality-type factors in the Cattell, Comrey and Eysenck scales: Were the factor solutions by Noller et al. optimal? *Personality and Individual Differences, 10,* 1289–1299.

Boyle, G. J., Stanley, G. V., & Start, K. B. (1985). Canonical/redundancy analyses of the Sixteen Personality Factor Questionnaire, the Motivation Analysis Test, and the Eight State Questionnaire. *Multivariate Experimental Clinical Research, 7,* 113–122.

Bradshaw, C. K. (1990). A Japanese view of dependency: What can *amae* psychology contribute to feminist theory and therapy? *Women and Therapy, 9,* 67–86.

Brand, C. R., & Egan, V. (1989). The "Big Five" dimensions of personality? Evidence from ipsative, adjectival self-attributions. *Personality and Individual Differences, 10,* 1165–1171.

Brems, C. (1990). Defense mechanisms in clients and non-clients as mediated by gender and sex-role. *Journal of Clinical Psychology, 46,* 669–475.

Brems, C., & Johnson, M. E. (1990). Reexamination of the Bem Sex-Role Inventory: The Interpersonal BSRI. *Journal of Personality Assessment, 55,* 484–498.

Brescia, W., & Fortune, J. C. (1989). Standardized testing of American Indian students. *College Student Journal, 23*(2), 98–104.

Breuer, J., & Freud, S. (1955). Studies on hysteria. In J. Strachey (Ed. and Trans.), *The standard edition of the complete psychological works of Sigmund Freud (Vol. 2).* London: Hogarth Press. (Original work published 1925)

Brewer, B. W. (1993). Self-identity and specific vulnerability to depressed mood. *Journal of Personality, 61,* 343–364.

Brief, D. E., & Comrey, A. L. (1993). A profile of personality for a Russian sample: As indicated by the Comrey Personality Scales. *Journal of Personality Assessment, 60,* 267–284.

Briggs, S. R., & Cheek, J. M. (1986). The role of factor analysis in the development and evaluation of personality scales. *Journal of Personality, 54,* 106–148.

Briggs, S. R., Cheek, J. M., & Buss, A. H. (1980). An analysis of the Self-Monitoring Scale. *Journal of Personality and Social Psychology, 38,* 679–686.

Bringle, R. G., & Bagby, G. J. (1992). Self-esteem and perceived quality of romantic and family relationships in young adults. *Journal of Research in Personality, 26,* 340–356.

Brink, T. L. (1975). The case of Hitler: An Adlerian perspective on psychohistory. *Journal of Individual Psychology, 31,* 23–31.

Brody, N. (1987). Introduction: Some thoughts on the unconscious. *Personality and Social Psychology Bulletin, 13,* 293–298.

Broehl, W. G., Jr., & McGee, V. E. (1981). Content analysis in psychohistory: A study of three lieutenants in the Indian Mutiny, 1957–58. *Journal of Psychohistory, 8,* 281–306.

Bromley, D. B. (1990). Academic contributions to psychological counselling. 1. A philosophy of science for the study of individual cases. *Counselling Psychology Quarterly, 3,* 299–308.

Brooks, P. R., Morgan, G. S., & Scherer, R. F. (1990). Sex role orientation and type of stressful situation: Effects on coping behaviors. *Journal of Social Behavior and Personality, 5,* 627–639.

Broucek, F. (1979). Efficacy in infancy: A review of some experimental studies and their possible implications for clinical theory. *International Journal of Psychoanalysis, 60,* 311–316.

Broughton, R. (1984). A prototype strategy for construction of personality scales. *Journal of Personality and Social Psychology, 47,* 1334–1346.

Broughton, R., Trapnell, P. D., & Boyes, M. C. (1991). Classifying personality types with occupational prototypes. *Journal of Research in Personality, 25,* 302–321.

Brown, J. D., & Mankowski, T. A. (1993). Self-esteem, mood, and self-evaluation: Changes in mood and the way you see you. *Journal of Personality and Social Psychology, 64,* 421–430.

Browne, A., & Finkelhor, D. (1986). Impact of child sexual abuse: A review of the research. *Psychological Bulletin, 99,* 66–77.

Bruch, M. A., Hamer, R. J., & Heimberg, R. G. (1995). Shyness and public self-consciousness: Additive or interactive relation with social interaction? *Journal of Personality, 63,* 47–63.

Bruhn, A. R. (1990). Cognitive-perceptual theory and the projective use of autobiographical memory. *Journal of Personality Assessment, 55,* 95–114.

Bruhn, A. R. (1992a). The Early Memories Procedure: A projective test of autobiographical memory, Part 1. *Journal of Personality Assessment, 58,* 1–15.

Bruhn, A. R. (1992b). The Early Memories Procedure: A projective test of autobiographical memory, Part 2. *Journal of Personality Assessment, 58,* 326–346.

Bub, J., & Bub, D. (1988). On the methodology of single-case studies in cognitive neuropsychology. *Cognitive Neuropsychology, 5,* 565–582.

Bubenzer, D. L., Zimpfer, D. G., & Mahrle, C. L. (1990). Standardized individual appraisal in agency and private practice: A survey. *Journal of Mental Health Counseling, 12,* 51–66.

Buchanan, D. R., & Taylor, J. A. (1986). Jungian typology of professional psychodramatists: Myers-Briggs Type Indicator analysis of certified psychodramatists. *Psychological Reports, 58,* 391–400.

Bulhan, H. A. (1985). Black Americans and psychopathology: An overview of research and theory. *Psychotherapy, 22,* 370–378.

Bunce, S. C., Larsen, R. J., & Cruz, M. (1993). Individual differences in the excitation transfer effect. *Personality and Individual Differences, 15,* 507–514.

Bunge, M. (1990). What kind of discipline is psychology: Autonomous or dependent, humanistic or scientific, biological or sociological? *New Ideas in Psychology, 8*(2), 121–137.

Buri, J. R. (1991). Parental Authority Questionnaire. *Journal of Personality Assessment, 57,* 110–119.

Burke, R. J. (1994). Generation X: Measures, sex and age differences. *Psychological Reports, 74,* 555–562.

Burlew, A. K., & Smith, L. R. (1991). Measures of racial identity: An overview and a proposed framework. *Journal of Black Psychology, 17,* 53–71.

Buss, A. H. (1980). *Self-consciousness and social anxiety.* New York: W. H. Freeman.

Buss, A. H. (1989). Personality as traits. *American Psychologist, 44,* 1378–1388.

Buss, A. H., & Finn, S. E. (1987). Classification of personality traits. *Journal of Personality and Social Psychology, 52,* 432–444.

Buss, A. H., & Plomin, R. (1984). *Temperament: Early developing traits.* Hillsdale, N.J.: Erlbaum.

Buss, D. M. (1981). Sex differences in the evaluation and performance of dominant acts. *Journal of Personality and Social Psychology, 40,* 147–154.

Buss, D. M. (1984). Evolutionary biology and personality psychology: Toward a conception of human nature and individual differences. *American Psychologist, 39,* 1135–1147.

Buss, D. M. (1991). Evolutionary personality psychology. *Annual Review of Psychology, 42,* 459–491.

Buss, D. M., & Craik, K. H. (1980). The frequency concept of dispositions: Dominance and dominant acts. *Journal of Personality, 48,* 379–392.

Buss, D. M., & Craik, K. H. (1981). The act frequency analysis of interpersonal dispositions: Aloofness, gregariousness, dominance, and submissiveness. *Journal of Personality, 49,* 175–192.

Buss, D. M., & Craik, K. H. (1983a). The act frequency approach to personality. *Psychological Review, 90,* 105–126.

Buss, D. M., & Craik, K. H. (1983b). Act prediction and the conceptual analysis of personality scales: Indices of act density, bipolarity, and extensity. *Journal of Personality and Social Psychology, 45,* 1081–1095.

Buss, D. M., & Craik, K. H. (1985). Why *not* measure that trait? Alternative criteria for identifying important dispositions. *Journal of Personality and Social Psychology, 48,* 934–946.

Buss, D. M., & Craik, K. H. (1989). On the cross-cultural examination of acts and dispositions. *European Journal of Personality, 3,* 19–30.

Buss, D. M., & Schmitt, D. P. (1993). Sexual strategies theory: An evolutionary perspective on human mating. *Psychological Review, 100,* 204–232.

Buss, H. M. (1990). The different voice of Canadian feminist autobiographers. *Biography, 13,* 154–167.

Butler, A. C., Hokanson, J. E., & Flynn, H. A. (1994). A comparison of self-esteem lability and low trait self-esteem as vulnerability factors for depression. *Journal of Personality and Social Psychology, 66,* 166–177.

Butler, T., Giordano, S., & Neren, S. (1985). Gender and sex-role attributes as predictors of utilization of natural support systems during personal stress events. *Sex Roles, 13,* 515–524.

Bütz, M. R. (1992). The fractal nature of the development of the self. *Psychological Reports, 71,* 1043–1063.

Byrne, D. G. (1987). Personality, life events and cardiovascular disease. *Journal of Psychosomatic Research, 31,* 661–671.

Campbell, D. T., & Fiske, D. W. (1959). Convergent and discriminant validation by the multitrait-multimethod matrix. *Psychological Bulletin, 56,* 81–105.

Campbell, J. B., & Heller, J. F. (1987). Correlations of extraversion, impulsivity and sociability with sensation seeking and MBTI-introversion. *Personality and Individual Differences, 8,* 133–136.

Campbell, J. D. (1990). Self-esteem and clarity of the self-concept. *Journal of Personality and Social Psychology, 59,* 538–549.

Campbell, J. F. (1988). The primary personality factors of younger adolescent Hawaiians. *Genetic, Social, and General Psychology Monographs, 114,* 141–171.

Campbell, J. F. (1991). The primary personality factors of Hawaiian, middle adolescents. *Psychological Reports, 68,* 3–26.

Campbell, J. F. (1992). Quantitative differences between male and female Hawaiian early adolescents in their primary factors of personality. *Psychological Reports, 71,* 19–27.

Cann, D. R., & Donderi, D. C. (1986). Jungian personality typology and the recall of everyday and archetypal dreams. *Journal of Personality and Social Psychology, 50,* 1021–1030.

Cantor, N. (1990). From thought to behavior: "Having" and "doing" in the study of personality and cognition. *American Psychologist, 45,* 735–750.

Cantor, N., & Kihlstrom, J. F. (1987). *Personality and social intelligence.* Englewood Cliffs, N.J.: Prentice-Hall.

Cantor, N., & Mischel, W. (1979a). Prototypes in person perception. In L. Berkowitz (Ed.) *Advances in experimental social psychology* (Vol. 12, pp. 3–52). New York: Academic Press.

Cantor, N., & Mischel, W. (1979b). Prototypicality and personality: Effects on free recall and personality impressions. *Journal of Research in Personality, 13,* 187–205.

Cantor, N., Norem, J., Langston, C., Zirkel, S., Fleeson, W., & Cook-Flannagan, C. (1991). Life tasks and daily life experience. *Journal of Personality, 59,* 425–451.

Cantor, N., & Zirkel, S. (1990). Personality, cognition, and purposive behavior. In L. A. Pervin (Ed.), *Handbook of personality: Theory and research* (pp. 135–164). New York: Guilford.

Caprara, G. V. (1987). The disposition-situation debate and research on aggression. *European Journal of Personality, 1,* 1–16.

Caprara, G. V., Barbaranelli, C., & Comrey, A. L. (1992). Validation of the Comrey Personality Scales on an Italian sample. *Journal of Research in Personality, 26,* 21–31.

Carlisle-Frank, P. (1991). Examining personal control beliefs as a mediating variable in the health-damaging behavior of substance use: An alternative approach. *Journal of Psychology, 125,* 381–397.

Carlson, J. G. (1985). Recent assessments of the Myers-Briggs Type Indicator. *Journal of Personality Assessment, 49,* 356–365.

Carlson, J. G. (1989). Affirmative: In support of researching the Myers-Briggs Type Indicator. *Journal of Counseling and Development, 67,* 484–486.

Carlson, R. (1971). Where is the person in personality research? *Psychological Bulletin, 75,* 203–219.

Carlson, R. (1980). Studies of Jungian typology: II. Representations of the personal world. *Journal of Personality and Social Psychology, 38,* 801–810.

Carlson, R. (1981). Studies in script theory: I. Adult analogs of a childhood nuclear scene. *Journal of Personality and Social Psychology, 40,* 501–510.

Carlson, R. (1982). Personology lives! *Contemporary Psychology, 27,* 7–8.

Carlson, R. (1988). Exemplary lives: The uses of psychobiography for theory development. *Journal of Personality, 56,* 105–138.

Carlson, R., & Brincka, J. (1987). Studies in script theory: III. Ideology and political imagination. *Political Psychology, 8,* 563–574.

Carlson, R., & Levy, N. (1973). Studies of Jungian typology: I. Memory, social perception, and social action. *Journal of Personality, 41,* 559–576.

Carlson, R., & Williams, J. (1984). Studies of Jungian typology: III. Personality and marriage. *Journal of Personality Assessment, 48,* 87–94.

Carnelley, K. B., Pietromonaco, P. R., & Jaffe, K. (1994). Depression, working models of others, and relationship functioning. *Journal of Personality and Social Psychology, 66,* 127–140.

Carroll, L. (1987). A study of narcissism, affiliation, intimacy, and power motives among students in business administration. *Psychological Reports, 61,* 355–358.

Cartwright, D., & Mori, C. (1988). Scales for assessing aspects of the person. *Person-Centered Review, 3,* 176–194.

Carver, C. S., Reynolds, S. L., & Scheier, M. F. (1994). The possible selves of optimists and pessimists. *Journal of Research in Personality, 28,* 133–141.

Carver, C. S., & Scheier, M. F. (1994). Situational coping and coping dispositions in a stressful transaction. *Journal of Personality and Social Psychology, 66,* 184–195.

Carver, C. S., Scheier, M. F., & Weintraub, J. K. (1989). Assessing coping strategies: A theoretically based approach. *Journal of Personality and Social Psychology, 56,* 267–283.

Caspi, A. (1987). Personality in the life course. *Journal of Personality and Social Psychology, 53,* 1203–1213.

Caspi, A. (1993). Why maladaptive behaviors persist: Sources of continuity and change across the life course. In D. C. Funder, R. D. Parke, C. Tomlinson-Keasey, & K. Widaman (Eds.), *Studying lives through time: Personality and development* (pp. 343–376). Washington, D.C.: American Psychological Association.

Caspi, A., & Bem, D. J. (1990). Personality continuity and change across the life course. In L. A. Pervin (Ed.), *Handbook of personality: Theory and research* (pp. 549–575). New York: Guilford.

Caspi, A., Bem, D. J., & Elder, G. H., Jr. (1989). Continuities and consequences of interactional styles across the life course. *Journal of Personality, 57,* 375–406.

Caspi, A., Elder, G., & Bem, D. J. (1987). Moving against the world: Life-course patterns of explosive children. *Developmental Psychology, 23,* 308–313.

Caspi, A., Elder, G., & Bem, D. J. (1988). Moving away from the world: Life-course patterns of shy children. *Developmental Psychology, 24,* 824–831.

Caspi, A., & Herbener, E. S. (1990). Continuity and change: Assortative marriage and the consistency of personality in adulthood. *Journal of Personality and Social Psychology, 58,* 250–258.

Caspi, A., Herbener, E. S., & Ozer, D. J. (1992). Shared experiences and the similarity of personalities: A longitudinal study of married couples. *Journal of Personality and Social Psychology, 62,* 281–291.

Casselden, P. A., & Hampson, S. E. (1990). Forming impressions from incongruent traits. *Journal of Personality and Social Psychology, 59,* 353–362.

Cattell, R. B. (1943). The description of personality: I. Foundations of trait measurement. *Psychological Review, 50,* 559–594.

Cattell, R. B. (1960). The multiple abstract variance analysis equations and solutions: For nature-nurture research on continuous variables. *Psychological Review, 67,* 353–372.

Cattell, R. B. (1965). *The scientific analysis of personality.* Baltimore: Penguin.

Cattell, R. B. (1973). *Personality and mood by questionnaire.* San Francisco: Jossey-Bass.

Cattell, R. B. (1986). The 16PF personality structure and Dr. Eysenck. *Journal of Social Behavior and Personality, 1,* 153–160.

Cattell, R. B. (1990). Advances in Cattellian personality theory. In L. A. Pervin (Ed.), *Handbook of personality: Theory and research* (pp. 101–110). New York: Guilford.

Cattell, R. B., & Brennan, J. (1984). The cultural types of modern nations, by two quantitative classification methods. *Sociology and Social Research, 68,* 208–235.

Cattell, R. B., Eber, H. W., & Tatsuoka, M. M. (1970). *Handbook for the Sixteen Personality Factor Questionnaire (16PF).* Champaign, Ill.: Institute for Personality and Ability Testing.

Cattell, R. B., & Krug, S. E. (1986). The number of factors in the 16PF: A review of the evidence with special emphasis on methodological problems. *Educational and Psychological Measurement, 46,* 509–522.

Cattell, R. B., Rao, D. C., & Schuerger, J. M. (1985). Heritability in the personality control system: Ego strength (C), super ego strength (G) and the self sentiment (Q_3); by the MAVA model, Q-data, and maximum likelihood analyses. *Social Behavior and Personality, 13,* 33–41.

Cattell, R. B., Schuerger, J. M., & Klein, T. W. (1982). Heritabilities of ego strength (Factor C), super ego strength (Factor G), and self-sentiment (Factor Q_3) by multiple abstract variance analysis. *Journal of Clinical Psychology, 38,* 769–779.

Cattell, R. B., Vaughan, D. S., Schuerger, J. M., & Rao, D. C. (1982). Heritabilities, by the multiple abstract variance analysis (MAVA) model and objective test measures, of personality traits U.I.23, capacity to mobilize, U.I.24, anxiety, U.I.26, narcistic ego, and U.I.28, asthenia, by maximum-likelihood methods. *Behavior Genetics, 12,* 361–378.

Cella, D. F., DeWolfe, A. S., & Fitzgibbon, M. (1987). Ego identity status, identification, and decision-making style in late adolescents. *Adolescence, 22,* 849–861.

Cervone, D. (1991). The two disciplines of personality psychology. *Psychological Science, 2,* 371–377.

Chapman, M., & Skinner, E. A. (1989). Children's agency beliefs, cognitive performance, and conceptions of effort and ability: Individual and developmental differences. *Child Development, 60,* 1229–1238.

Chapman, M., Skinner, E. A., & Baltes, P. B. (1990). Interpreting correlations between children's perceived control and cognitive performance: Control, agency, or means-ends beliefs? *Developmental Psychology, 26,* 246–253.

Chehrazi, S. (1986). Female psychology. *Journal of the American Psychoanalytic Association, 34,* 111–162.

Chen, J., & Goldsmith, L. T. (1991). Social and behavioral characteristics of Chinese only children: A review of research. *Journal of Research in Childhood Education, 5,* 127–139.

Chess, S. (1986). Early childhood development and its implications for analytic theory and practice. *American Journal of Psychoanalysis, 46,* 123–148.

Cheung, P. C., Conger, A. J., Hau, K., Lew, W. J. F., & Lau, S. (1992). Development of the Multi-Trait Personality Inventory (MTPI): Comparison among four Chinese populations. *Journal of Personality Assessment, 59,* 528–551.

Choca, J. P., Shanley, L. A., Peterson, C. A., & Van Denburg, E. (1990). Racial bias and the MCMI. *Journal of Personality Assessment, 54,* 479–490.

Chodorow, N. (1978). *The reproduction of mothering.* Berkeley: University of California Press.

Church, A. T. (1987). Personality research in a non-Western culture: The Philippines. *Psychological Bulletin, 102,* 272–292.

Chusmir, L. H. (1985). Short-form scoring for McClelland's version of the TAT. *Perceptual and Motor Skills, 61,* 1047–1052.

Chusmir, L. H., & Azevedo, A. (1992). Motivation needs of sampled Fortune-500 CEOs: Relations to organization outcomes. *Perceptual and Motor Skills, 75,* 595–612.

Chusmir, L. H., & Koberg, C. S. (1990). Dual sex role identity and its relationship to sex role conflict. *Journal of Psychology, 124,* 545–555.

Ciardiello, J. A. (1985). Beethoven: Modern analytic views of the man and his music. *Psychoanalytic Review, 72,* 129–147.

Clarke, J. H. (1988). The influence of external perception of control on freshman priorities and progress. *Journal of College Student Development, 29,* 560–562.

Clausen, J. S. (1991). Adolescent competence and the shaping of the life course. *American Journal of Sociology, 96,* 805–842.

Cloninger, C. R. (1986). A unified biosocial theory of personality and its role in the development of anxiety states. *Psychiatric Developments, 3,* 167–226.

Cloninger, C. R. (1987a). Neurogenetic adaptive mechanism in alcoholism. *Science, 236,* 410–416.

Cloninger, C. R. (1987b). A systematic method for clinical description and classification of personality variants: A proposal. *Archives of General Psychiatry, 44*(6), 573–588.

Cloninger, C. R., Przybeck, T. R., & Svrakic, D. M. (1991). The Tridimensional Personality Questionnaire: U.S. normative data. *Psychological Reports, 69,* 1047–1057.

Cloninger, C. R., Sigvardsson, S., & Bohman, M. (1988). Childhood personality predicts alcohol abuse in young adults. *Alcoholism Clinical and Experimental Research, 12,* 494–505.

Cloninger, S. C. (1993). *Theories of personality: Understanding persons.* Englewood Cliffs, N.J.: Prentice-Hall.

Coccaro, E. F. (1995, January/February). The biology of aggression. *Scientific American,* 38–47.

Coccaro, E. F., Bergeman, C. S., & McClearn, G. E. (1993). Heritability of irritable impulsiveness: A study of twins reared together and apart. *Psychiatry Research, 48,* 229–242.

Cohen, S., & Williamson, G. M. (1991). Stress and infectious disease in humans. *Psychological Bulletin, 109,* 5–24.

Cohn, L. D. (1991). Sex differences in the course of personality development: A meta-analysis. *Psychological Bulletin, 109,* 252–266.

Cole, T. R., & Premo, T. (1987). The pilgrimage of Joel Andrews: Aging in the autobiography of a Yankee farmer. *International Journal of Aging and Human Development, 24*(2), 79–85.

Coleman, S. R., & Salamon, R. (1988). Kuhn's *Structure of Scientific Revolutions* in the psychological journal literature, 1969–1983: A descriptive study. *Journal of Mind and Behavior, 9,* 415–445.

Coles, R. (1989). *The call of stories: Teaching and the moral imagination.* Boston: Houghton Mifflin.

Collins, W. A., & Gunnar, M. R. (1990). Social and personality development. *Annual Review of Psychology, 41,* 387–416.

Colvin, C. R. (1993). "Judgable" people: Personality, behavior, and competing explanations. *Journal of Personality and Social Psychology, 64,* 861–873.

Colvin, C. R., & Block, J. (1994). Do positive illusions foster mental health? An examination of the Taylor and Brown formulation. *Psychological Bulletin, 116,* 3–20.

Colvin, C. R., & Funder, D. C. (1991). Predicting personality and behavior: A boundary on the acquaintanceship effect. *Journal of Personality and Social Psychology*, *60*, 884–894.

Compas, B. E. (1987). Coping with stress during childhood and adolescence. *Psychological Bulletin*, *101*, 393–403.

Compas, B. E., Howell, D. C., Phares, V., Williams, R. A., & Giunta, C. T. (1989). Risk factors for emotional/behavioral problems in young adolescents: A prospective analysis of adolescent and parental stress and symptoms. *Journal of Consulting and Clinical Psychology*, *57*, 732–740.

Comrey, A. L. (1988). Factor-analytic methods of scale development in personality and clinical psychology. *Journal of Consulting and Clinical Psychology*, *56*, 754–761.

Conley, J. J. (1984a). The hierarchy of consistency: A review and model of longitudinal findings on adult individual differences in intelligence, personality and self-opinion. *Personality and Individual Differences*, *5*, 11–25.

Conley, J. J. (1984b). Longitudinal consistency of adult personality: Self-reported psychological characteristics across 45 years. *Journal of Personality and Social Psychology*, *47*, 1325–1333.

Conley, J. J. (1984c). Relation of temporal stability and cross-situational consistency in personality: Comment on the Mischel-Epstein debate. *Psychological Review*, *91*, 491–496.

Conn, S. R., & Ramanaiah, N. V. (1990). Factor structure of the Comrey Personality Scales, the Personality Research Form-E, and the five factor model. *Psychological Reports*, *67*, 627–632.

Contrada, R. J., Leventhal, H., & O'Leary, A. (1990). Personality and health. In L. A. Pervin (Ed.), *Handbook of personality: Theory and research* (pp. 638–669). New York: Guilford.

Cook, H. (1985). Effects of subliminal symbiotic gratification and the magic of believing on achievement. *Psychoanalytic Psychology*, *2*, 365–371.

Cooley, C. H. (1902). *Human nature and the social order.* New York: Scribner.

Coombs, W. N., & Schroeder, H. E. (1988). Generalized locus of control: An analysis of factor analytic data. *Personality and Individual Differences*, *9*, 79–85.

Cooper, H. M. (1979). Statistically combining independent studies: A meta-analysis of sex differences in conformity research. *Journal of Personality and Social Psychology*, *37*, 131–146.

Cooper, S. H., Perry, J. C., & Arnow, D. (1988). An empirical approach to the study of defense mechanisms: I: Reliability and preliminary validity of the Rorschach Defense Scales. *Journal of Personality Assessment*, *52*, 187–203.

Cooper, S. H., Perry, J. C., & O'Connell, M. O. (1991). The Rorschach Defense Scales: II. Longitudinal perspectives. *Journal of Personality Assessment*, *56*, 191–201.

Corsini, R. J. (1986). The present science of personality: Comments on Eysenck's article. *Journal of Social Behavior and Personality*, *1*, 483–488.

Costa, P. T., Jr. (1991). Clinical use of the five-factor model: An introduction. *Journal of Personality Assessment*, *57*, 393–398.

Costa, P. T., Jr., Busch, C. M., Zonderman, A. B., & McCrae, R. R. (1986). Correlations of MMPI factor scales with measures of the five factor model of personality. *Journal of Personality Assessment*, *50*, 640–650.

Costa, P. T., Jr., & McCrae, R. R. (1985). *The NEO Personality Inventory manual.* Odessa, Fla.: Psychological Assessment Resources.

Costa, P. T., Jr., & McCrae, R. R. (1988a). From catalog to classification: Murray's needs and the five-factor model. *Journal of Personality and Social Psychology*, *55*, 258–265.

Costa, P. T., Jr., & McCrae, R. R. (1988b). Personality in adulthood: A six-year longitudinal study of self-reports and spouse ratings on the NEO Personality Inventory. *Journal of Personality and Social Psychology*, *54*, 853–863.

Costa, P. T., Jr., & McCrae, R. R. (1989). Personality continuity and the changes of adult life. In M. Storandt & G. R. VandenBos (Eds.), *The adult years: Continuity and change* (pp. 41–77). Washington, D.C.: American Psychological Association.

Costa, P. T., Jr., & McCrae, R. R. (1992a). Four ways five factors are basic. *Personality and Individual Differences*, *13*, 653–665.

Costa, P. T., Jr., & McCrae, R. R. (1992b). *Revised NEO Personality Inventory (NEO-PI-R) and NEO Five-Factor Inventory (NEO-FFI) professional manual.* Odessa, Fla.: Psychological Assessment Resources.

Costa, P. T., McCrae, R. R., & Dye, D. A. (1991). Facet scales for agreeableness and conscientiousness: A revision of the NEO Personality Inventory. *Personality and Individual Differences*, *12*, 887–898.

Côté, J. E. (1986). Identity crisis modality: A technique for assessing the structure of the identity crisis. *Journal of Adolescence, 9,* 321–335.

Côté, J. E. (1993). Foundations of a psychoanalytic social psychology: Neo-Eriksonian propositions regarding the relationship between psychic structure and cultural institutions. *Developmental Review, 13,* 31–53.

Côté, J. E., & Levine, C. (1988a). A critical examination of the ego identity status paradigm. *Developmental Review, 8,* 147–184.

Côté, J. E., & Levine, C. (1988b). The relationship between ego identity status and Erikson's notions of institutionalized moratoria, value orientation stage, and ego dominance. *Journal of Youth and Adolescence, 17,* 81–99.

Côté, J. E., & Levine, C. (1989). An empirical test of Erikson's theory of ego identity formation. *Youth and Society, 20,* 388–414.

Côté, J. E., & Levine, C. G. (1992). The genesis of the humanistic academic: A second test of Erikson's theory of identity formation. *Youth and Society, 23,* 387–410.

Cousins, S. (1989). Culture and self-perception in Japan and the United States. *Journal of Personality and Social Psychology, 56,* 124–131.

Cox, T., & McCay, C. (1982). Psychosocial factors and psychophysiological mechanisms in the aetiology and development of cancers. *Social Science and Medicine, 16,* 381–396.

Craig-Bray, L., & Adams, G. R. (1986). Different methodologies in the assessment of identity: Congruence between self-report and interview techniques? *Journal of Youth and Adolescence, 15*(3), 191–204.

Cramer, D. (1990a). Disclosure of personal problems, self-esteem, and the facilitativeness of friends and lovers. *British Journal of Guidance and Counselling, 18,* 186–196.

Cramer, D. (1990b). Self-esteem and close relationships: A statistical refinement. *British Journal of Social Psychology, 29,* 189–191.

Cramer, D. (1993). Personality and marital dissolution. *Personality and Individual Differences, 14,* 605–607.

Cramer, P. (1987). The development of defense mechanisms. *Journal of Personality, 55,* 597–614.

Cramer, P. (1988). The Defense Mechanism Inventory: A review of research and discussion of the scales. *Journal of Personality Assessment, 52,* 142–164.

Cramer, P. (1991). Anger and the use of defense mechanisms in college students. *Journal of Personality, 59,* 39–55.

Cramer, P., & Blatt, S. J. (1990). Use of the TAT to measure change in defense mechanisms following intensive psychotherapy. *Journal of Personality Assessment, 54,* 236–251.

Cramer, P., & Gaul, R. (1988). The effect of success and failure on children's use of defense mechanisms. *Journal of Personality, 56,* 729–742.

Crawford, C. B., & Anderson, J. L. (1989). Sociobiology: An environmentalist discipline? *American Psychologist, 44,* 1449–1459.

Crawford, M., & Marecek, J. (1989). Feminist theory, feminist psychology: A bibliography of epistemology, critical analysis, and applications. *Psychology of Women Quarterly, 13,* 477–491.

Creel, R. (1980). Radical epiphenomenalism: B. F. Skinner's account of private events. *Behaviorism, 8,* 31–53.

Crews, D. J., & Landers, D. M. (1987). A meta-analytic review of aerobic fitness and reactivity to psychosocial stressors. *Medicine and Science in Sports and Exercise, 19*(5, Suppl), 114–120.

Crick, F., & Mitchison, G. (1983). The function of dream sleep. *Nature, 304,* 111–114.

Crick, N. R., & Dodge, K. A. (1994). A review and reformulation of social information-processing mechanisms in children's social adjustment. *Psychological Bulletin, 115,* 74–101.

Crocker, J. (1993). Memory for information about others: Effects of self-esteem and performance feedback. *Journal of Research in Personality, 27,* 35–48.

Crocker, J., & Major, B. (1989). Social stigma and self-esteem: The self-protective properties of stigma. *Psychological Review, 96,* 608–630.

Crockett, J. B., & Crawford, R. L. (1989). The relationship between Myers-Briggs Type Indicator (MBTI) Scale scores and advising style preferences of college freshmen. *Journal of College Student Development, 30,* 154–161.

Cronbach, L. J. (1955). Processes affecting scores on "understanding others" and "assumed similarity." *Psychological Bulletin, 52,* 177–193.

Cronbach, L. J. (1957). The two disciplines of scientific psychology. *American Psychologist, 12,* 671–684.

Cronbach, L. J. (1975). Beyond the two disciplines of scientific psychology. *American Psychologist, 30,* 116–127.

Cronbach, L. J., & Gleser, G. C. (1957). *Psychological tests and personnel decisions.* Urbana: University of Illinois.

Cronbach, L. J., & Meehl, P. E. (1955). Construct validity in psychological tests. *Psychological Bulletin, 52,* 281–302.

Cross, S. E., & Markus, H. R. (1990). The willful self. *Personality and Social Psychology Bulletin, 16,* 726–742.

Croyle, R. T. (1992). Appraisal of health threats: Cognition, motivation, and social comparison. *Cognitive Therapy and Research, 16,* 165–182.

Csikszentmihalyi, M. (1993). *The evolving self: A psychology for the third millennium.* New York: HarperCollins.

Curry, C., Trew, K., Turner, I., & Hunter, J. (1994). The effect of life domains on girls' possible selves. *Adolescence, 29,* 133–150.

Cushman, P. (1990). Why the self is empty: Toward a historically situated psychology. *American Psychologist, 45,* 599–611.

Cyphers, L. H., Phillips, K., Fulker, D. W., & Mrazek, D. A. (1990). Twin temperament during the transition from infancy to early childhood. *Journal of the American Academy of Child and Adolescent Psychiatry, 29,* 392–397.

D'Agostino, P. R. (1991). Spontaneous trait inferences: Effects of recognition instructions and subliminal priming on recognition performance. *Personality and Social Psychology Bulletin, 17,* 70–77.

Dabbs, J. M., Jr., & Ruback, R. B. (1988). Saliva testosterone and personality of male college students. *Bulletin of the Psychonomic Society, 26,* 244–247.

Dabbs, J. M., Jr., Frady, R. L., Carr, T. S., & Besch, N. F. (1987). Saliva testosterone and criminal violence in young adult prison inmates. *Psychosomatic Medicine, 49,* 174–182.

Darvill, T. J., Johnson, R. C., & Danko, G. P. (1992). Personality correlates of public and private self consciousness. *Personality and Individual Differences, 13,* 383–384.

Darwin, C. (1872). *The expression of the emotions in man and animals.* London: J. Murray.

Dattell, A. R., & Neimeyer, R. A., (1990). Sex differences in death anxiety: Testing the emotional expressiveness hypothesis. *Death Studies, 14,* 1–11.

Davidson, B., & Sollie, D. L. (1987). Sex-role orientation and marital adjustment. *Social Behavior and Personality, 15,* 59–69.

Davidson, R. J., Ekman, P., Saron, C. D., Senulis, J. A., & Friesen, W. V. (1990). Approach-withdrawal and cerebral asymmetry: Emotional expression and brain physiology, I. *Journal of Personality and Social Psychology, 58,* 330–341.

Davidson, R. J., & Fox, N. A. (1989). Frontal brain asymmetry predicts infants' response to maternal separation. *Journal of Abnormal Psychology, 98,* 127–131.

Davies, M. F. (1985). Self-consciousness and paranormal belief. *Perceptual and Motor Skills, 60,* 484–486.

Davis, C., & Yager, J. (1992). Transcultural aspects of eating disorders: A critical literature review. *Culture, Medicine and Psychiatry, 16,* 377–394.

Davis, D. L., Grove, S. J., & Knowles, P. A. (1990). An experimental application of personality type as an analogue for decision-making style. *Psychological Reports, 66,* 167–175.

Davis, G. L., Hoffman, R. G., & Nelson, K. S. (1990). Differences between Native Americans and Whites on the California Psychological Inventory. *Psychological Assessment, 2,* 238–242.

Davis, M., Ray, J. J., & Burt, J. S. (1987). Sex roles and fear of success: A general population study. *Personality and Individual Differences, 8,* 431–432.

Deaux, K. (1984). From individual differences to social categories. Analysis of a decade's research on gender. *American Psychologist, 39,* 105–116.

Deaux, K., & Major, B. (1987). Putting gender into context: An interactive model of gender-related behavior. *Psychological Review, 94,* 369–389.

deChesnay, M. (1985). Father-daughter incest: An overview. *Behavioral Sciences and the Law, 3,* 391–402.

Deci, E. L., & Ryan, R. M. (1985). *Intrinsic motivation and self determination in human behavior.* New York: Plenum.

DeKay, W. T., & Buss, D. W. (1992). Human nature, individual differences, and the importance of context: Perspectives from evolutionary psychology. *Current Directions in Psychological Science, 1,* 184–189.

Dell, P. F. (1988a). Not reasonable skepticism, but extreme skepticism. *Journal of Nervous and Mental Disease, 176,* 537–538.

Dell, P. F. (1988b). Professional skepticism about multiple personality. *Journal of Nervous and Mental Disease, 176,* 528–531.

deMause, L. (1988). On writing childhood history. *Journal of Psychohistory, 16,* 135–171.

DePaulo, B. M. (1992). Nonverbal behavior and self-presentation. *Psychological Bulletin, 111,* 203–243.

Derryberry, D., & Rothbart, M. K. (1988). Arousal, affect, and attention as components of temperament. *Journal of Personality and Social Psychology, 55,* 958–966.

Derryberry, D., & Tucker, D. M. (1991). The adaptive base of the neural hierarchy: Elementary motivational controls on network function. In R. Dienstbier (Ed.), *Nebraska symposium on motivation 1990: Vol. 38. Perspectives on Motivation* (pp. 69–164). Lincoln: University of Nebraska Press.

Desharnais, R., Bouillon, J., & Godin, G. (1986). Self-efficacy and outcome expectations as determinants of exercise adherence. *Psychological Reports, 59,* 1155–1159.

Deutsch, F. M., Lussier, J. B., & Servis, L. J. (1993). Husbands at home: Predictors of paternal participation in childcare and housework. *Journal of Personality and Social Psychology, 65,* 1154–1166.

DeWaele, J. P., & Harré, R. (1979). Autobiography as a psychological method. In G. P. Ginsburg (Ed.), *Emerging strategies in social psychological research.* New York: Wiley.

Dewe, P., Cox, T., & Ferguson, E. (1993). Individual strategies for coping with stress at work: A review. *Work and Stress, 7,* 5–15.

Dewhurst, K., & Beard, A. W. (1970). Sudden religious conversions in temporal lobe epilepsy. *British Journal of Psychiatry, 117,* 497–507.

Dickinson, A. M. (1989). The detrimental effects of extrinsic reinforcement on "intrinsic motivation." *Behavior Analyst, 12,* 1–15.

Dickson, D. H., & Kelly, I. W. (1985). The "Barnum effect" in personality assessment: A review of the literature. *Psychological Reports, 57,* 367–382.

Dien, D. (1992). Gender and individuation: China and the West. *Psychoanalytic Review, 79,* 105–119.

Digman, J. M. (1989). Five robust trait dimensions: Development, stability, and utility. *Journal of Personality, 57,* 195–214.

Digman, J. M. (1990). Personality structure: Emergence of the five-factor model. *Annual Review of Psychology, 41,* 417–440.

Digman, J. M., & Inouye, J. (1986). Further specification of the five robust factors of personality. *Journal of Personality and Social Psychology, 50,* 116–123.

Digman, J. M., & Takemoto-Chock, N. K. (1981). Factors in the natural language of personality: Reanalysis, comparison, and interpretation of six major studies. *Multivariate Behavioral Research, 16,* 149–170.

Dion, K. L., & Yee, P. H. (1987). Ethnicity and personality in a Canadian context. *Journal of Social Psychology, 127,* 175–182.

Dixon, M., Brunet, A., & Laurence, J. R. (1990). Hypnotizability and automaticity: Towards a PDP model of hypnotic responding. *Journal of Abnormal Psychology, 99,* 336–343.

Dixon, T. M., & Baumeister, R. F. (1991). Escaping the self: The moderating effect of self-complexity. *Personality and Social Psychology Bulletin, 17,* 363–368.

Dohrenwend, B. S., & Dohrenwend, B. P. (1974). *Stressful life events: Their nature and effects.* New York: Wiley.

Doi, T. (1973). *The anatomy of dependence* (J. Bester, Trans.). Tokyo: Kodansha International. (Original work published 1971)

Dolan, B. (1991). Cross-cultural aspects of anorexia nervosa and bulimia: A review. *International Journal of Eating Disorders, 10,* 67–78.

Dolan, C. A., Sherwood, A., & Light, K. C. (1992). Cognitive coping strategies and blood pressure responses to real-life stress in healthy young men. *Health Psychology, 11,* 233–240.

Dollard, J., & Miller, N. E. (1950). *Personality and psychotherapy: An analysis in terms of learning, thinking and culture.* New York: McGraw-Hill.

Domino, G., & Affonso, D. D. (1990). A personality measure of Erikson's life stages: The inventory of psychosocial balance. *Journal of Personality Assessment, 54,* 576–588.

Donley, R. E., & Winter, D. G. (1970). Measuring the motives of public officials at a distance: An exploratory study of American presidents. *Behavioral Science, 15,* 227–236.

Doty, R. M., Peterson, B. E., & Winter, D. G. (1991). Threat and authoritarianism in the United States, 1978–1987. *Journal of Personality and Social Psychology, 61,* 629–640.

Dovidio, J. F., Evans, N., & Tyler, R. B. (1986). Racial stereotypes: The contents of their cognitive representations. *Journal of Experimental Social Psychology, 22,* 22–37.

Drasgow, F. (1987). Study of the measurement bias of two standardized psychological tests. *Journal of Applied Psychology, 72,* 19–29.

Duberstein, P. R., & Talbot, N. L. (1992). Parental idealization and the absence of Rorschach oral imagery. *Journal of Personality Assessment, 59,* 50–58.

Dubow, E. F., Huesmann, L. R., & Eron, L. D. (1987). Childhood correlates of adult ego development. *Child Development, 58,* 859–869.

Duck, S. (1993, August). *The meaning of [everyday] life: Relaters as scientists and vice versa.* Paper presented at the meeting of the American Psychological Association, Toronto.

Dukes, W. F. (1965). $N = 1$. *Psychological Bulletin, 64,* 74–79.

Duncan, R. C., Konefal, J., & Spechler, M. M. (1990). Effect of neurolinguistic programming training on self-actualization as measured by the Personal Orientation Inventory. *Psychological Reports, 66,* 1323–1330.

Dunning, D., & Cohen, G. L. (1992). Egocentric definitions of traits and abilities in social judgment. *Journal of Personality and Social Psychology, 63,* 341–355.

Dunning, D., Perie, M., & Story, A. L. (1991). Self-serving prototypes of social categories. *Journal of Personality and Social Psychology, 61,* 957–968.

Durel, L. A., Carver, C. S., Spitzer, S. B., Llabre, M. M., Weintraub, J. K., Saab, P. G., & Schneiderman, N. (1989). Associations of blood pressure with self-report measures of anger and hostility among Black and White men and women. *Health Psychology, 8,* 557–575.

Dweck, C. S. (1991). Self-theories and goals: Their role in motivation, personality, and development. In R. A. Dienstbier (Ed.), *Nebraska symposium on motivation, 1990.* Lincoln: University of Nebraska Press.

Dweck, C. S., & Leggett, E. L. (1988). A social-cognitive approach to motivation and personality. *Psychological Review, 95,* 256–273.

Dzewaltowski, D. A. (1989). Toward a model of exercise motivation. *Journal of Sport and Exercise Psychology, 11,* 251–269.

Eagly, A. H. (1978). Sex differences in influenceability. *Psychological Bulletin, 85,* 86–116.

Eagly, A. H. (1987a). Reporting sex differences. *American Psychologist, 42,* 756–757.

Eagly, A. H. (1987b). *Sex differences in social behavior: A social role interpretation.* Hillsdale, N.J.: Erlbaum.

Eagly, A. H., Ashmore, R. D., Makhijani, M. G., & Longo, L. C. (1991). What is beautiful is good, but . . . : A meta-analytic review of research on the physical attractiveness stereotype. *Psychological Bulletin, 110,* 109–128.

Eagly, A. H., & Carli, L. L. (1981). Sex of researchers and sex-typed communications as determinants of sex differences in influenceability: A meta-analysis of social influence studies. *Psychological Bulletin, 90,* 1–20.

Eagly, A. H., & Chrvala, C. (1986). Sex differences in conformity: Status and gender role interpretations. *Psychology of Women Quarterly, 10,* 203–220.

Eagly, A. H., & Crowley, M. (1986). Gender and helping behavior: A meta-analytic review of the social psychological literature. *Psychological Bulletin, 100,* 283–308.

Eagly, A. H., & Johnson, B. T. (1990). Gender and leadership style: A meta-analysis. *Psychological Bulletin, 108,* 233–256.

Eagly, A. H., & Steffen, V. J. (1986). Gender and aggressive behavior: A meta-analytic review of the social psychological literature. *Psychological Bulletin, 100,* 309–330.

Eagly, A. H., & Wood, W. (1991). Explaining sex differences in social behavior: A meta-analytic perspective. *Personality and Social Psychology Bulletin, 17,* 306–315.

Eccles, J. S. (1989). Bringing young women to math and science. In M. Crawford & M. Gentry (Eds.), *Gender and thought: Psychological perspectives* (pp. 36–58). New York: Springer-Verlag.

Edel, L. (1953–1971). *Henry James.* Philadelphia: Lippincott.

Edelson, M. (1985). The hermeneutic turn and the single case study in psychoanalysis. *Psychoanalysis and Contemporary Thought, 8,* 567–614.

Eisenberg, N., & Lennon, R. (1983). Sex differences in empathy and related capacities. *Psychological Bulletin, 94,* 29–39.

Eisenberger, R., Kuhlman, D. M., & Cotterell, N. (1992). Effects of social values, effort training, and goal structure on task persistence. *Journal of Research in Personality, 26,* 258–272.

Eisenberger, R., & Selbst, M. (1994). Does reward increase or decrease creativity? *Journal of Personality and Social Psychology, 66,* 1116–1127.

Ekman, P. (1993). Facial expression and emotion. *American Psychologist, 48,* 384–392.

Ekman, P. (1994). Strong evidence for universals in facial expressions: A reply to Russell's mistaken critique. *Psychological Bulletin, 115,* 268–287.

Ekman, P., Davidson, R. J., & Friesen, W. V. (1990). The Duchenne smile: Emotional expression and brain physiology, II. *Journal of Personality and Social Psychology, 58,* 342–353.

Elder, G. H., Jr., & MacInnis, D. J. (1983). Achievement imagery in women's lives from adolescence to adulthood. *Journal of Personality and Social Psychology, 45,* 394–404.

Elizabeth, P. (1983). Comparison of psychoanalytic and a client-centered group treatment model on measures of anxiety and self-actualization. *Journal of Counseling Psychology, 30,* 425–428.

Ellenberger, H. F. (1972). The story of "Anna O": A critical review with new data. *Journal of the History of the Behavioral Sciences, 8,* 267–279.

Elliot, A. J., & Harackiewicz, J. M. (1994). Goal setting, achievement orientation, and intrinsic motivation: A mediational analysis. *Journal of Personality and Social Psychology, 66,* 968–980.

Elms, A. C. (1988a). Freud as Leonardo: Why the first psychobiography went wrong. *Journal of Personality, 56,* 19–40.

Elms, A. C. (1988b, August). *The psychologist as biographer.* Paper presented at the meeting of the American Psychological Association, Atlanta, Ga.

Elpern, S., & Karp, S. A. (1984). Sex-role orientation and depressive symptomatology. *Sex Roles, 10,* 987–992.

Emde, R. N. (1992). *Amae,* intimacy, and the early moral self. *Infant Mental Health Journal, 13,* 34–42.

Emmons, R. A. (1986). Personal strivings: An approach to personality and subjective well-being. *Journal of Personality and Social Psychology, 51,* 1058–1068.

Emmons, R. A. (1991). Personal strivings, daily life events, and psychological and physical well-being. *Journal of Personality, 59,* 453–472.

Emmons, R. A., & King, L. A. (1989). Personal striving differentiation and affective reactivity. *Journal of Personality and Social Psychology, 56,* 478–484.

Endler, N. S., & Edwards, J. M. (1986). Interactionism in personality in the twentieth century. *Personality and Individual Differences, 7,* 379–384.

Engebretson, T. O., Matthews, K. A., & Scheier, M. F. (1989). Relations between anger expression and cardiovascular reactivity: Reconciling inconsistent findings through a matching hypothesis. *Journal of Personality and Social Psychology, 57,* 513–521.

Entwistle, D. R. (1972). To dispel fantasies about fantasy-based measures of achievement motivation. *Psychological Bulletin, 77,* 377–391.

Epstein, A. W. (1982). Observations on the brain and dreaming. *Biological Psychiatry, 17,* 1207–1215.

Epstein, A. W. (1987). The phylogenesis of the "ego," with remarks on the frontal lobes. *American Journal of Psychoanalysis, 47,* 161–166.

Epstein, J. A., & Harackiewicz, J. M. (1992). Winning is not enough: The effects of competition and achievement orientation on intrinsic interest. *Personality and Social Psychology Bulletin, 18,* 128–138.

Epstein, S. (1979). The stability of behavior: I. On predicting most of the people much of the time. *Journal of Personality and Social Psychology, 37,* 1097–1126.

Epstein, S. (1980). The stability of behavior: II. Implications for psychological research. *American Psychologist, 35,* 790–806.

Epstein, S. (1985). The implications of cognitive-experiential self-theory for research in social psychology and personality. *Journal for the Theory of Social Behaviour, 15*(3), 283–310.

Epstein, S. (1990). Cognitive-experiential self-theory. In L. A. Pervin (Ed.), *Handbook of personality: Theory and research* (pp. 165–192). New York: Guilford.

Epstein, S. (1994). Integration of the cognitive and the psychodynamic unconscious. *American Psychologist, 49,* 709–724.

Epstein, S., Lipson, A., Holstein, C., & Huh, E. (1992). Irrational reactions to negative outcomes: Evidence for two conceptual systems. *Journal of Personality and Social Psychology, 62,* 328–339.

Epstein, S., & O'Brien, E. J. (1985). The person-situation debate in historical and current perspective. *Psychological Bulletin, 98,* 513–537.

Erikson, E. H. (1950). *Childhood and society.* New York: Norton.

Erikson, E. H. (1958). On the nature of clinical evidence. *Daedalus, 87,* 65–87.

Erikson, E. H. (1959). Identity and the life cycle. Selected papers. *Psychological Issues, 1* (Monograph 1). New York: International Universities Press.

Erikson, E. H. (1962). *Young man Luther: A study in Psychoanalysis and History.* New York: Norton.

Erikson, E. H. (1968). *Identity: Youth and crisis.* New York: Norton.

Erikson, E. H. (1969). *Gandhi's truth: On the origins of militant nonviolence.* New York: Norton.

Erikson, E. H. (1975). *Life history and the historical moment.* New York: Norton.

Erikson, E. H. (1982). *The life cycle completed: A review.* New York: Norton.

Erwin, E. (1980). Psychoanalytic therapy: The Eysenck argument. *American Psychologist, 35,* 435–443.

Etaugh, C., & Nekolny, K. (1990). Effects of employment status and marital status on perceptions of mothers. *Sex Roles, 23,* 273–280.

Evans, D. W. (1994). Self-complexity and its relation to development, symptomatology and self-perception during adolescence. *Child Psychiatry and Human Development, 24,* 173–182.

Evans, R. G. (1982). Defense mechanisms in females as a function of sex-role orientation. *Journal of Clinical Psychology, 38,* 816–817.

Exner, J. E. (1986). *The Rorschach: A comprehensive system, Vol. 1* (rev. ed.). New York: Wiley.

Eyman, J. R., & Eyman, S. K. (1991). Personality assessment in suicide prediction. *Suicide and Life-Threatening Behavior, 21,* 37–55.

Eysenck, H. J. (1954). The science of personality: Nomothetic! *Psychological Review, 61,* 339–342.

Eysenck, H. J. (1967). *The biological basis of personality.* Springfield, Ill: Charles C. Thomas.

Eysenck, H. J. (1979). The conditioning model of neurosis. *Behavioral and Brain Sciences, 2,* 155–199.

Eysenck, H. J. (1986a). Can personality study ever be scientific? *Journal of Social Behavior and Personality, 1,* 3–19.

Eysenck, H. J. (1986b). Cross-cultural comparisons: The validity of assessment by indices of factor comparison. *Journal of Cross Cultural Psychology, 17,* 506515.

Eysenck, H. J. (1988). Personality, stress and cancer: Prediction and prophylaxis. *British Journal of Medical Psychology, 61,* 57–75.

Eysenck, H. J. (1990a). Biological dimensions of personality. In L. A. Pervin (Ed.), *Handbook of personality: Theory and research* (pp. 244–276). New York: Guilford.

Eysenck, H. J. (1990b). Genetic and environmental contributions to individual differences: The three major dimensions of personality. *Journal of Personality, 58,* 245–261.

Eysenck, H. J. (1991). Dimensions of personality: 16, 5 or 3? Criteria for a taxonomic paradigm. *Personality and Individual Differences, 12,* 773–790.

Eysenck, H. J. (1992a). The effects of psychotherapy: An evaluation. *Journal of Consulting and Clinical Psychology, 60,* 659–663. (Reprinted from 1952 *Journal of Consulting Psychology, 16,* 319–324.)

Eysenck, H. J. (1992b). Four ways five factors are *not* basic. *Personality and Individual Differences, 13,* 667–673.

Eysenck, H. J. (1993). Creativity and personality: Suggestions for a theory. *Psychological Inquiry, 4,* 147–178.

Eysenck, S. B., & Abdel-Khalek, A. M.(1989). A cross-cultural study of personality: Egyptian and English children. *International Journal of Psychology, 24,* 1–11.

Eysenck, H. J., & Eysenck, M. W. (1985). *Personality and individual differences: A natural science approach.* New York: Plenum.

Eysenck, H. J., & Eysenck, S. B. G. (1975). *Manual of the Eysenck Personality Questionnaire.* San Diego: Edits.

Eysenck, S. B. G., Eysenck, H. H., & Barrett, P. (1985). A revised version of the Psychoticism scale. *Personality and Individual Differences, 6,* 21–29.

Eysenck, S. B., & Haapasalo, J. (1989). Cross-cultural comparisons of personality: Finland and England. *Personality and Individual Differences, 10,* 121–125.

Eysenck, S. B., & Kozeny, J. (1990). Cross-cultural comparisons of personality: Czech and English subjects. *Studia Psychologica, 32,* 255–259.

Eysenck, S. B., & Tambs, K. (1990). Cross-cultural comparison of personality: Norway and England. *Scandinavian Journal of Psychology, 31*(3), 191–197.

Eysenck, S. B., von Knorring, A. L., & von Knorring, L. (1988). A cross-cultural study of personality: Swedish and English children. *Scandinavian Journal of Psychology, 29*(3,4), 152–161.

Fadiman, J. (1993). Who's minding the store? A comment on Frick's defense of unitary personality. *Journal of Humanistic Psychology, 33*(2), 129–133.

Fagan, P. J., Wise, T. N., Schmidt, C. W., Jr., Ponticas, Y., Marshall, R. D., & Costa, P. T., Jr. (1991). A comparison of five-factor personality dimensions in males with sexual dysfunction and males with paraphilia. *Journal of Personality Assessment, 57,* 434–448.

Faggen, J. (1987). Golden Rule revisited: Introduction. *Educational Measurement: Issues and Practice, 6*(2), 5–8.

Fagley, N. S., & Miller, P. M. (1990). Investigating and reporting sex differences: Methodological importance, the forgotten consideration. *American Psychologist, 45,* 297–298.

Fairbairn, W. D. (1952). *An object-relations theory of the personality.* New York: Basic Books.

Fairfield, B. (1990). Reorientation: The use of hypnosis for life-style change. *Individual Psychology, 46,* 451–458.

Falbo, T., & Polit, D. F. (1986). Quantitative review of the only child literature: Research evidence and theory development. *Psychological Bulletin, 100,* 176–189.

Falk, A. (1985). Aspects of political psychobiography. *Political Psychology, 6,* 605–619.

Fava, M., Littman, A., & Halperin, P. (1987). Neuroendocrine correlates of the Type A behavior pattern: A review and new hypotheses. *International Journal of Psychiatry in Medicine, 17,* 289–307.

Feingold, A. (1992). Gender differences in mate selection preferences: A test of the parental investment model. *Psychological Bulletin, 112,* 125–139.

Feixas, G., & Villegas, M. (1991). Personal construct analysis of autobiographical texts: A method presentation and case illustration. *International Journal of Personal Construct Psychology, 4,* 51–83.

Feldman, S. S., & Rosenthal, D. A., (1990). The acculturation of autonomy expectations in Chinese high schoolers residing in two Western nations. *International Journal of Psychology, 25,* 259–281.

Fenigstein, A., Scheier, M. F., & Buss, A. H. (1975). Public and private self-consciousness: Assessment and theory. *Journal of Consulting and Clinical Psychology, 43,* 522–527.

Fernandez, E., & Turk, D. C. (1989). The utility of cognitive coping strategies for altering pain perception: A meta-analysis. *Pain, 38*, 123–135.

Field, M. J. (1960). *Search for security.* London: Faber and Faber.

Finkelhor, D. (1979). *Sexually victimized children.* New York: Free Press.

Finkelhor, D., Hotaling, G., Lewis, I. A., & Smith, C. (1990). Sexual abuse in a national survey of adult men and women: Prevalence, characteristics, and risk factors. *Child Abuse and Neglect, 14*, 19–28.

Fisher, S., & Greenberg, S. (1977). *The scientific credibility of Freud's theories and therapy.* New York: Basic Books.

Fiske, S. T. (1993). Social cognition and social perception. *Annual Review of Psychology, 44*, 155–194.

Fitzpatrick, J. J. (1976). Erik H. Erikson and psychohistory. *Bulletin of the Menninger Clinic, 40*, 295–314.

Fleming, J. (1982). Projective and psychometric approaches to measurement: The case of fear of success. In A. J. Stewart (Ed.), *Motivation and society* (pp. 63–96). San Francisco: Jossey-Bass.

Fleming, J., & Horner, M. S. (1992). The motive to avoid success. In C. P. Smith (Ed.), *Motivation and personality: Handbook of thematic content analysis* (pp. 179–189). New York: Cambridge University Press.

Flora, S. R. (1990). Undermining intrinsic interest from the standpoint of a behaviorist. *Psychological Record, 40*, 323–346.

Foa, U. G., & Foa, E. G. (1974). *Societal structures of the mind.* Springfield, Ill: Charles C. Thomas.

Folkman, S., & Lazarus, R. S. (1991). Coping and emotion. In A. Monat & R. S. Lazarus (Eds.), *Stress and coping: An anthology* (3rd ed., pp. 207–227). New York: Columbia University Press.

Försterling, F. (1985). Attributional retraining: A review. *Psychological Bulletin, 98*, 495–512.

Försterling, F. (1986). Attributional conceptions in clinical psychology. *American Psychologist, 41*, 275–285.

Fourqurean, J. M., Meisgeier, C., & Swank, P. (1990). The link between learning style and Jungian psychological types: A finding of two bipolar preference dimensions. *Journal of Experimental Education, 58*, 225–237.

Francis, L. J. (1991). Personality and attitude towards religion among adult churchgoers in England. *Psychological Reports, 69*, 791–794.

Francis, L. J. (1992). Is psychoticism really a dimension of personality fundamental to religiosity? *Personality and Individual Differences, 13*, 645–652.

Francis, L. J., & Pearson, P. R. (1993). The personality characteristics of student churchgoers. *Personality and Individual Differences, 15*, 373–380.

Frank, G. (1992). The response of African Americans to the Rorschach: A review of the research. *Journal of Personality Assessment, 59*, 317–325.

French, E. G., & Lesser, G. S. (1964). Some characteristics of the achievement motive in women. *Journal of Abnormal and Social Psychology, 68*, 119–128.

Freud, S. (1953). The interpretation of dreams. In J. Strachey (Ed. and Trans.), *The standard edition of the complete psychological works of Sigmund Freud* (Vol. 4, pp. 1–338; *Vol. 5*, pp. 339–621). London: Hogarth Press. (Original work published 1900)

Freud, S. (1957). Leonardo da Vinci: A study in psychosexuality. In J. Strachey (Ed. and Trans.), *Standard edition of the complete psychological works of Sigmund Freud* (*Vol. 11*). London: Hogarth Press. (Original work published 1910)

Freud, S. (1958). *On creativity and the unconscious.* New York: Harper & Row. (Original work published 1925)

Freud, S. (1959). *Moses and monotheism.* New York: Vintage Books. (Original work published 1939)

Freud, S. (1963). *Three case histories.* New York: Macmillan.

Freud, S., & Bullitt, W. C. (1966). *Thomas Woodrow Wilson: Twenth-eighth president of the United States.* Boston: Houghton Mifflin.

Frick, R. B. (1982). The ego and the vestibulocerebellar system: Some theoretical perspectives. *Psychoanalytic Quarterly, 51*, 93–122.

Frick, W. B. (1993). Subpersonalities: Who conducts the orchestra? *Journal of Humanistic Psychology, 33*(2), 122–128.

Friedland, N., & Keinan, G. (1991). The effects of stress, ambiguity tolerance, and trait anxiety on the formation of causal relationships. *Journal of Research in Personality, 25*, 88–107.

Friedman, H. S., & Booth-Kewley, S. (1987a). The "disease-prone personality": A meta-analytic view of the construct. *American Psychologist, 42*, 539–555.

Friedman, H. S., & Booth-Kewley, S. (1987b). Personality, Type A behavior, and coronary heart disease: The role of emotional expression. *Journal of Personality and Social Psychology, 53*, 783–792.

Friedman, H. S., & Miller-Herringer, T. (1991). Nonverbal display of emotion in public and in private: Self-monitoring, personality, and expressive cues. *Journal of Personality and Social Psychology, 61*, 766–775.

Friedman, M., & Rosenman, R. H. (1974). *Type A behavior and your heart.* New York: Knopf.

Friedman, W. J., Robinson, A. B., & Friedman, B. L. (1987). Sex differences in moral judgments? A test of Gilligan's theory. *Psychology of Women Quarterly, 11,* 37–46.

Fudin, R. (1986). Subliminal psychodynamic activation: Mommy and I are not yet one. *Perceptual and Motor Skills, 63,* 1159–1179.

Funder, D. C. (1983). Three issues in predicting more of the people: A reply to Mischel and Peake. *Psychological Review, 90,* 283–289.

Funder, D. C. (1987). Errors and mistakes: Evaluating the accuracy of social judgment. *Psychological Bulletin, 101,* 75–90.

Funder, D. C. (1991). Global traits: A neo-Allportian approach to personality. *Psychological Science, 2,* 31–39.

Funder, D. C., & Block, J. (1989). The role of ego-control, ego-resiliency, and IQ in delay of gratification in adolescence. *Journal of Personality and Social Psychology, 57,* 1041–1050.

Funder, D. C., Block, J. H., & Block, J. (1983). Delay of gratification: Some longitudinal personality correlates. *Journal of Personality and Social Psychology, 44,* 1198–1213.

Funder, D. C., & Colvin, C. R. (1988). Friends and strangers: Acquaintanceship, agreement, and the accuracy of personality judgment. *Journal of Personality and Social Psychology, 55,* 149–158.

Funder, D. C., & Dobroth, J. M. (1987). Differences between traits: Properties associated with inter-judge agreement. *Journal of Personality and Social Psychology, 52,* 409–418.

Funder, D. C., Parke, R. D., Tomlinson-Keasey, C., & Widaman, K. (1993). *Studying lives through time: Personality and development.* Washington, D.C.: American Psychological Association.

Funder, D. C., & Sneed, C. D. (1993). Behavioral manifestations of personality: An ecological approach to judgmental accuracy. *Journal of Personality and Social Psychology, 64,* 479–490.

Funkhouser, G. R. (1993). A self-anchoring instrument and analytical procedure for reducing cultural bias in cross-cultural research. *Journal of Social Psychology, 133,* 661–673.

Furnham, A., Bond, M., Heaven, P., Hilton, D., Lobel, T., Masters, J., Payne, M., Rajamanikam, R., Stacey, B., & Van Daalen, H. (1993). A comparison of Protestant Work Ethic beliefs in thirteen nations. *Journal of Social Psychology, 133,* 185–197.

Furnham, A., & Schofield, S. (1987). Accepting personality test feedback: A review of the Barnum effect. *Current Psychological Research and Reviews, 6*(2), 162–178.

Furnham, A., & Stringfield, P. (1993). Personality and work performance: Myers-Briggs Type Indicator correlates of managerial performance in two cultures. *Personality and Individual Differences, 14,* 145–153.

Gaines, S. O., Jr., & Reed, E. S. (1995). Prejudice: From Allport to DuBois. *American Psychologist, 50,* 96–103.

Gallup, G. G., Jr. (1970). Chimpanzees: Self-recognition. *Science, 167,* 86–87.

Gallup, G. G., Jr. (1977). Self-recognition in primates: A comparative approach to the bidirectional properties of consciousness. *American Psychologist, 32,* 329–338.

Gangestad, S. W., Simpson, J. A., DiGeronimo, K., & Biek, M. (1992). Differential accuracy in person perception across traits: Examination of a functional hypothesis. *Journal of Personality and Social Psychology, 62,* 688–698.

Gangestad, S., & Snyder, M. (1985). "To carve nature at its joints": On the existence of discrete classes in personality. *Psychological Review, 92,* 317–349.

Garcia, M. E., Schmitz, J. M., & Doerfler, L. A. (1990). A fine-grained analysis of the role of self-efficacy in self-initiated attempts to quit smoking. *Journal of Consulting and Clinical Psychology, 58,* 317–322.

Gardner, H. (1983). *Frames of mind: The theory of multiple intelligences.* New York: Harper Collins.

Gecas, V. (1989). The social psychology of self-efficacy. *Annual Review of Sociology, 15,* 291–316.

Geen, T. R. (1992). Facial expressions in socially isolated nonhuman primates: Open and closed programs for expressive behavior. *Journal of Research in Personality, 26,* 273–280.

Geisler, C. (1985). Repression: A psychoanalytic perspective revisited. *Psychoanalysis and Contemporary Thought, 8,* 253–298.

Gerbing, D. W., & Tuley, M. R. (1991). The 16PF related to the five-factor model of personality: Multiple-indicator measurement versus the a priori scales. *Multivariate Behavioral Research, 26,* 271–289.

Gergen, K. J. (1985). The social constructivist movement in modern psychology. *American Psychologist, 40,* 266–275.

Gergen, K. J., & Gergen, M. M. (1988). Narrative and the self as relationship. In L. Berkowitz (Ed.), *Advances in experimental social psychology* (Vol. 21, pp. 17–56). Orlando, Fla.: Academic Press.

Geschwind, N. (1979). Editorial: Behavioural changes in temporal lobe epilepsy. *Psychological Medicine, 9,* 217–219.

Gilligan, C. (1982). *In a different voice: Psychological theory and women's development.* Cambridge, Mass.: Harvard University Press.

Giltinan, J. M. (1990). Using life review to facilitate self-actualization in elderly women. *Gerontology and Geriatrics Education, 10,* 75–83.

Gjerde, P. F. (1993). Depressive symptoms in young adults: A developmental perspective on gender differences. In D. C. Funder, R. D. Parke, C. Tomlinson-Keasey, & K. Widaman (Eds.), *Studying lives through time: Personality and development* (pp. 256–288). Washington, D.C.: American Psychological Association.

Glaser, B. G., & Strauss, A. L. (1967). *The discovery of grounded theory: Strategies for qualitative research.* Chicago: Aldine.

Gleick, J. (1987). *Chaos: Making a new science.* New York: Penguin Books.

Gleser, G. C., & Ihilevich, D. (1969). An objective instrument to measure defense mechanisms. *Journal of Consulting and Clinical Psychology, 33,* 51–60.

Goebel, B. L., & Boeck, B. E. (1987). Ego integrity and fear of death: A comparison of institutionalized and independently living older adults. *Death Studies, 11,* 193–204.

Goffman, E. (1959). *The presentation of self in everyday life.* New York: Doubleday.

Goffman, E. (1967). *Interaction ritual: Essays on face-to-face behavior.* Garden City, N.Y.: Anchor.

Goisman, R. M. (1983). Therapeutic approaches to phobia: A comparison. *American Journal of Psychotherapy, 37,* 227–234.

Gold, D., Andres, D., & Schwartzman, A. E. (1987). Self-perception of personality at midlife in elderly people: Continuity and change. *Experimental Aging Research, 13,* 197–202.

Goldberg, L. R. (1981). Language and individual differences: The search for universals in personality lexicons. In L. Wheeler (Ed.), *Review of personality and social psychology* (Vol. 2, pp. 141–165). Beverly Hills, Calif.: Sage.

Goldberg, L. R. (1990). An alternative "description of personality": The Big-Five factor structure. *Journal of Personality and Social Psychology, 59,* 1216–1229.

Goldberg, P. (1968). Are women prejudiced against women? *Transaction, 5,* 28–30.

Goldberg, S. R., & Henningfield, J. E. (1988). Reinforcing effects of nicotine in humans and experimental animals responding under intermittent schedules of IV drug injection. *Pharmacology, Biochemistry and Behavior, 30,* 227–234.

Goldfried, M. R., Greenberg, L. S., & Marmar, C. (1990). Individual psychotherapy: Process and outcome. *Annual Review of Psychology, 41,* 659–688.

Goldsmith, H. H., & Alansky, J. A. (1987). Maternal and infant temperamental predictors of attachment: A meta-analytic review. *Journal of Consulting and Clinical Psychology, 55,* 805–816.

Goldsmith, H. H., Buss, A. H., Plomin, R., Rothbart, M. K., Thomas, A., Chess, S., Hinde, R. A., & McCall, R. B. (1987). What is temperament? Four approaches. *Child Development, 58,* 505–529.

Goodspeed, R. B., & DeLucia, A. G. (1990). Stress reduction at the worksite: An evaluation of two methods. *American Journal of Health Promotion, 4,* 333–337.

Gordon, C. (1968). Self-conceptions: Configurations of content. In C. Gordon & K. J. Gergen (Eds.), *The self in social interaction: Vol. 1. Classic and contemporary perspectives* (pp. 115–136). New York: Wiley.

Gould, D., Hodge, K., Peterson, K., & Giannini, J. (1989). An exploratory examination of strategies used by elite coaches to enhance self-efficacy in athletes. *Journal of Sport and Exercise Psychology, 11,* 128–140.

Graham, S. (1992). "Most of the subjects were White and middle class": Trends in published research on African Americans in selected APA journals, 1970–1989. *American Psychologist, 47,* 629–639.

Gray, J. A. (1987). Perspectives on anxiety and impulsivity: A commentary. *Journal of Research in Personality, 21,* 493–509.

Green, G. D. (1990). Is separation really so great? *Women and Therapy, 9,* 87–104.

Greenberg, J., Solomon, S., Pyszczynski, T., Rosenblatt, A., Burling, J., Lyon, D., Simon, L., & Pinel, E. (1992). Why do people need self-esteem? Converging evidence that self-esteem serves an anxiety buffering function. *Journal of Personality and Social Psychology, 63,* 913–922.

Greene, B. A. (1985). Considerations in the treatment of black patients by white therapists. *Psychotherapy, 22,* 389–393.

Greene, B. A. (1992). Racial socialization as a tool in psychotherapy with African American children. In L. A. Vargas & J. D. Koss-Chioino (Eds.), *Working with culture: Psychotherapeutic interventions with ethnic minority children and adolescents* (pp. 63–81). San Francisco: Jossey-Bass.

Greene, B. (1994a). An African American perspective on racism and antisemitism within feminist organizations. In J. Adleman & G. M. Enguidanos-Clark (Eds.), *Racism in the lives of women: Testimony, theory, and guides to practice*. New York: Haworth Press.

Greene, B. (1994b). Institutional racism in the mental health professions. In J. Adleman & G. M. Enguidanos-Clark (Eds.), *Racism in the lives of women: Testimony, theory and guides to practice*. New York: Haworth Press.

Greenfield, P. M., & Childs, C. P. (1991). Developmental continuity in biocultural context. In R. Cohen & A. W. Siegel (Eds.), *Context and development* (pp. 135–159). Hillsdale, N.J.: Erlbaum.

Greeno, C. G., & Maccoby, E. E. (1986). How different is the "different voice"? *Signs, 11*, 310–316.

Greenwood, J. D. (1994). A sense of identity: Prolegomena to a social theory of personal identity. *Journal for the Theory of Social Behaviour, 24*, 25–46.

Greer, S., & Watson, M. (1985). Towards a psychobiological model of cancer: Psychological considerations. *Social Science and Medicine, 20*, 773–777.

Gross, J. (1989). Emotional expression in cancer onset and progression. *Social Science and Medicine, 28*, 1239–1248.

Grossarth-Maticek, R., & Eysenck, H. J. (1990). Personality, stress and disease: Description and validation of a new inventory. *Psychological Reports, 66*, 355–373.

Grotevant, H. D., & Adams, G. R. (1984). Development of an objective measure to assess ego identity in adolescence: Validation and replication. *Journal of Youth and Adolescence, 13*, 419–438.

Grubb, H. J., & Ollendick, T. H. (1986). Cultural-distance perspective: An exploratory analysis of its effect on learning and intelligence. *International Journal of Intercultural Relations, 10*, 399–414.

Gruber, H. E. (1989). The evolving systems approach to creative work. In D. B. Wallace & H. E. Gruber (Eds.), *Creative people at work: Twelve cognitive case studies* (pp. 3–43). New York: Oxford University Press.

Grünbaum, A. (1984). *The foundations of psychoanalysis: A philosophical critique*. Berkeley: University of California Press.

Grych, J. H., & Fincham, F. D. (1992). Interventions for children of divorce: Toward greater integration of research and action. *Psychological Bulletin, 111*, 434–454.

Gudjonsson, G. H. (1979). The use of electrodermal responses in a case of amnesia. *Medicine, Science, and the Law, 19*, 138–140.

Guerin, D. W., & Gottfried, A. W. (1994). Developmental stability and change in parent reports of temperament: A ten-year longitudinal investigation from infancy through preadolescence. *Merrill-Palmer Quarterly, 40*, 334–355.

Guisinger, S., & Blatt, S. J. (1994). Individuality and relatedness: Evolution of a fundamental dialectic. *American Psychologist, 49*, 104–111.

Gunnar, M. R., Mangelsdorf, S., Larson, M., & Hertsgaard, L. (1990). Attachment, temperament, and adrenocortical activity in infancy: A study of psychoendocrine regulation. *Developmental Psychology, 25*, 355–363.

Gustafson, R., & Källmén, H. (1990). Alcohol, subliminal stimulation, and disinhibitory processes. *Perceptual and Motor Skills, 70*, 495–502.

Gynther, M. D. (1989). MMPI comparisons of Blacks and Whites: A review and commentary. *Journal of Clinical Psychology, 45*(6), 878–883.

Haaga, D. A. F., Dyck, M. J., & Ernst, D. (1991). Empirical status of cognitive theory of depression. *Psychological Bulletin, 110*, 215–236.

Haan, N., Millsap, R., & Hartka, E. (1986). As time goes by: Change and stability in personality over fifty years. *Psychology and Aging, 1*(3), 220–232.

Hall, J. A. (1978). Gender effects in decoding nonverbal cues. *Psychological Bulletin, 85*, 845–875.

Hall, J. A. (1987). On explaining gender differences: The case of nonverbal communication. In P. Shaver & C. Hendrick (Eds.) *Sex and gender*. Newbury Park, Calif.: Sage.

Halpin, G., Simpson, R. G., & Martin, S. L. (1990). An investigation of racial bias in the Peabody Picture Vocabulary Test-Revised. *Educational and Psychological Measurement, 50*, 183–189.

Hamaguchi, E. (1985). A contextual model of the Japanese: Toward a methodological innovation in Japan studies. *Journal of Japanese Studies, 11*, 289–321.

Hampson, S. E. (1988). *The construction of personality: An introduction* (2nd ed.). New York: Routledge.

Hampson, S. E., John, O. P., & Goldberg, L. R. (1986). Category breadth and hierarchical structure in personality: Studies of asymmetries in judgments of trait implication. *Journal of Personality and Social Psychology, 51,* 37–54.

Hanin, Y., Eysenck, S. B., Eysenck, H. J., & Barrett, P. (1991). A cross-cultural study of personality: Russia and England. *Personality and Individual Differences, 12,* 265–271.

Harackiewicz, J. M., & Elliot, A. J. (1993). Achievement goals and intrinsic motivation. *Journal of Personality and Social Psychology, 65,* 904–915.

Hardaway, R. A. (1990). Subliminally activated symbiotic fantasies: Facts and artifacts. *Psychological Bulletin, 107,* 177–195.

Haring, M. J., Stock, W. A., & Okun, M. A. (1984). A research synthesis of gender and social class as correlates of subjective well-being. *Human Relations, 37,* 645–657.

Harrington, D. M., Block, J. H., & Block, J. (1987). Testing aspects of Carl Rogers's theory of creative environments: Child-rearing antecedents of creative potential in young adolescents. *Journal of Personality and Social Psychology, 52,* 851–856.

Harrington, T. F. (1986). The construct validity of the career decision-making system cross-culturally. *International Journal for the Advancement of Counselling, 9,* 331–339.

Harris, J. G., Jr. (1980). Nomovalidation and idiovalidation: A quest for the true personality profile. *American Psychologist, 35,* 729–744.

Harris, T. L., & Schwab, R. (1990). Sex-role orientation and personal adjustment. *Journal of Social Behavior and Personality, 5,* 473–479.

Hattie, J., & Cooksey, R. W. (1984). Procedures for assessing the validities of tests using the "known-groups" method. *Applied Psychological Measurement, 8,* 295–305.

Haugaard, J. J., & Emery, R. E. (1989). Methodological issues in child abuse research. *Child Abuse and Neglect, 13,* 89–100.

Hazan, C., & Shaver, P. (1987). Romantic love conceptualized as an attachment process. *Journal of Personality and Social Psychology, 52,* 511–524.

Headey, B., & Wearing, A. (1989). Personality, life events, and subjective well-being: Toward a dynamic equilibrium model. *Journal of Personality and Social Psychology, 57,* 731–739.

Headey, B., & Wearing, A. (1990). Subjective well-being and coping with adversity. *Social Indicators Research, 22,* 327–349.

Heft, L., Thoresen, C. E., Kirmil-Gray, K., Wiedenfeld, S. A., Eagleston, J. R., Bracke, P., & Arnow, B. (1988). Emotional and temperamental correlates of Type A in children and adolescents. *Journal of Youth and Adolescence, 17,* 461–475.

Helms, J. E. (1984). Toward a theoretical explanation of the effects of race on counseling: A Black and White model. *Counseling Psychologist, 12*(4), 153–165.

Helson, R. (1993). Comparing longitudinal studies of adult development: Toward a paradigm of tension between stability and change. In D. C. Funder, R. D. Parke, C. Tomlinson-Keasey, & K. Widaman (Eds.), *Studying lives through time: Personality and development* (pp. 93–119). Washington, D.C.: American Psychological Association.

Helson, R., & Moane, G. (1987). Personality change in women from college to midlife. *Journal of Personality and Social Psychology, 53,* 176–186.

Helson, R., & Picano, J. (1990). Is the traditional role bad for women? *Journal of Personality and Social Psychology, 59,* 311–320.

Hendrick, C., & Hendrick, S. (1986). A theory and method of love. *Journal of Personality and Social Psychology, 50,* 392–402.

Hendrick, S., & Hendrick, C. (1987). Love and sex attitudes and religious beliefs. *Journal of Social and Clinical Psychology, 5,* 391–398.

Henley, S., & Furnham, A. (1989). The Type A behaviour pattern and self-evaluation. *British Journal of Medical Psychology, 62,* 51–59.

Herbert, T. B., & Cohen, S. (1993). Stress and immunity in humans: A meta-analytic review. *Psychosomatic Medicine, 55,* 364–379.

Herek, G. M. (1987). Religious orientation and prejudice: A comparison of racial and sexual attitudes. *Personality and Social Psychology Bulletin, 13,* 34–44.

Herman, J. (1981). *Father-daughter incest.* Cambridge, Mass.: Harvard University Press.

Hermans, H. J. M. (1987). The dream in the process of valuation: A method of interpretation. *Journal of Personality and Social Psychology, 53,* 163–175.

Hermans, H. J. M. (1988). On the integration of nomothetic and idiographic research methods in the study of personal meaning. *Journal of Personality, 56,* 785–812.

Hermans, H. J. M. (1991). The person as co-investigator in self-research: Valuation theory. *European Journal of Personality, 5*, 217–234.

Hermans, H. J. M., & Bonarius, H. (1991a). The person as co-investigator in personality research. *European Journal of Personality, 5*, 199–216.

Hermans, H. J. M., & Bonarius, H. (1991b). Static laws in a dynamic psychology? *European Journal of Personality, 5*, 245–247.

Hermans, H. J. M., Kempen, H. J. G., & van Loon, R. J. P. (1992). The dialogical self: Beyond individualism and rationalism. *American Psychologist, 47*, 23–33.

Hermans, H. J. M., Rijks, T. I., & Kempen, H. J. G. (1993). Imaginal dialogues in the self: Theory and method. *Journal of Personality, 61*, 207–236.

Herrnstein, R. J., & Murray, C. (1994). *The bell curve: Intelligence and social class in American life.* New York: Free Press.

Hersen, M., & Barlow, D. H. (1976). *Single-case experimental design: Strategies for studying behavioral change.* New York: Pergamon Press.

Hewstone, M., Hantzi, A., & Johnston, L. (1991). Social categorization and person memory: The pervasiveness of race as an organizing principle. *European Journal of Social Psychology, 21*, 517–528.

Hicks, L. E. (1984). Conceptual and empirical analysis of some assumptions of an explicitly typological theory. *Journal of Personality and Social Psychology, 46*, 1118–1131.

Hicks, L. E. (1985). Is there a disposition to avoid the fundamental attribution error? *Journal of Research in Personality, 19*, 436–456.

Higgins, E. T. (1987). Self-discrepancy: A theory relating self and affect. *Psychological Review, 94*, 319–340.

Higgins, E. T. (1989). Continuities and discontinuities in self-regulatory and self evaluative process: A developmental theory relating self and affect. *Journal of Personality, 57*, 407–444.

Higgins, E. T., Bond, R. N., Klein, R., & Strauman, T. (1986). Self-discrepancies and emotional vulnerability: How magnitude, accessibility, and type of discrepancy influence affect. *Journal of Personality and Social Psychology, 51*, 5–15.

Higgins, E. T., Roney, C. J. R., Crowe, E., & Hymes, C. (1994). Ideal versus ought predilections for approach and avoidance: Distinct self-regulatory systems. *Journal of Personality and Social Psychology, 66*, 276–286.

Hilgard, E. R. (1965). *Hypnotic sysceptibility.* New York: Harcourt, Brace and World.

Hilgard, E. R. (1976). Neodissociation theory of multiple control systems. In G. E. Schwartz & D. Shapiro (Eds.), *Consciousness and self-regulation: Advances in research.* Vol. 1 (pp. 137–171). New York: Plenum.

Hiller, J. E. (1989). Breast cancer: A psychogenic disease? *Women and Health, 15*(2), 5–18.

Hjelle, L. A., & Bernard, M. (1994). Private self-consciousness and the retest reliability of self-reports. *Journal of Research in Personality, 28*, 52–67.

Hobson, J. A. (1988). *The dreaming brain.* New York: Basic Books.

Hodapp, V., Heiligtag, U., & Störmer, S. W. (1990). Cardiovascular reactivity, anxiety and anger during perceived controllability. *Biological Psychology, 30*, 161–170.

Hoffman, C., Mischel, W., & Baer, J. S. (1984). Language and person cognition: Effects of communicative set on trait attribution. *Journal of Personality and Social Psychology, 46*, 1029–1043.

Hoffman, C., & Tchir, M. A. (1990). Interpersonal verbs and dispositional adjectives: The psychology of causality embodied in language. *Journal of Personality and Social Psychology, 58*, 765–778.

Hoffman, L. W. (1986). Work, family, and the child. In M. S. Pallak & R. Perloff (Eds.), *Psychology and work: Productivity, change, and employment* (pp. 169–220). Washington, D.C.: American Psychological Association.

Hoffman, L. W. (1991). The influence of the family environment on personality: Accounting for sibling differences. *Psychological Bulletin, 110*, 187–203.

Hofstede, G. (1980). *Culture's consequences: International differences in work-related values.* Beverly Hills: Sage.

Hofstee, W. K. B. (1990). The use of everyday personality language for scientific purposes. *European Journal of Personality, 4*, 77–88.

Hofstetter, C. R., Sallis, J. F., & Hovell, M. F. (1990). Some health dimensions of self-efficacy: Analysis of theoretical specificity. *Social Science and Medicine, 31*, 1051–1056.

Holahan, C. J., & Moos, R. H. (1987). Personal and contextual determinants of coping strategies. *Journal of Personality and Social Psychology, 52*, 946–955.

Holahan, C. K. (1988). Relation of life goals at age 70 to activity participation and health and psychological well-being among Terman's gifted men and women. *Psychology and Aging, 3*, 286–291.

Holden, G. (1991). The relationship of self-efficacy appraisals to subsequent health related outcomes:

A meta-analysis. *Social Work in Health Care*, *16*(1), 53–93.

Holland, J. L. (1985). *Making vocational choices: A theory of vocational personalities and work environments.* Englewood Cliffs, N.J.: Prentice-Hall.

Hollinger, C. L., & Fleming, E. S. (1985). Social orientation and the social self-esteem of gifted and talented female adolescents. *Journal of Youth and Adolescence*, *14*, 389–399.

Hollinger, C. L., & Fleming, E. S. (1988). Gifted and talented young women: Antecedents and correlates of life satisfaction. *Gifted Child Quarterly*, *32*, 254–259.

Holloway, S. D., & Machida, S. (1991). Child-rearing effectiveness of divorced mothers: Relationship to coping strategies and social support. *Journal of Divorce and Remarriage*, *14*, 179–201.

Holmes, T. H., & Masuda, M. (1974). Life changes and illness susceptibility. In B. S. Dohrenwend & B. P. Dohrenwend (Eds.), *Stressful life events: Their nature and effects.* New York: Wiley.

Holmes, T. H., & Rahe, R. H. (1967). The social readjustment rating scale. *Journal of Psychosomatic Research*, *11*, 213–218.

Holroyd, J. (1985–1986). Hypnosis applications in psychological research. *Imagination, Cognition and Personality*, *5*(2), 103–115.

Holzman, P. S. (1985). Psychoanalysis: Is the therapy destroying the science? *Journal of the American Psychoanalytic Association*, *33*, 725–770.

Horner, M. S. (1972). Toward an understanding of achievement related conflicts in women. *Journal of Social Issues*, *28*, 157–175.

Horner, M. S., & Fleming, J. (1992). A revised scoring manual for the motive to avoid success. In C. P. Smith (Ed.), *Motivation and personality: Handbook of thematic content analysis* (pp. 190–204). New York: Cambridge University Press.

Hornstein, G. A. (1992). The return of the repressed: Psychology's problematic relations with psychoanalysis, 1909–1960. *American Psychologist*, *47*, 254–263.

Horowitz, L. M., Sampson, H., Siegelman, E. Y., Wolfson, A., & Weiss, J. (1975). On the identification of warded-off mental contents: An empirical and methodological contribution. *Journal of Abnormal Psychology*, *84*, 545–558.

Horwood, L. J., & Fergusson, D. M. (1986). Neuroticism, depression and life events: A structural equation model. *Social Psychiatry*, *21*, 63–71.

House, R. J., Spangler, W. D., & Woycke, J. (1991). Personality and charisma in the U.S. presidency: A psychological theory of leader effectiveness. *Administrative Science Quarterly*, *36*, 364–396.

Houston, B. K., Smith, M. A., & Cates, D. S. (1989). Hostility patterns and cardiovascular reactivity to stress. *Psychophysiology*, *26*, 337–342.

Houts, A. C., Cook, T. D., & Shadish, W. R. (1986). The person-situation debate: A critical multiplist perspective. *Journal of Personality*, *54*, 52–105.

Howard, G. S. (1991). Cultural tales: Narrative approach to thinking, cross-cultural psychology, and psychotherapy. *American Psychologist*, *46*, 187–197.

Howard, G. S., Youngs, W. H., & Siatczynski, A. M. (1989). A research strategy for studying telic human behavior. *Journal of Mind and Behavior*, *10*, 393–411.

Howarth, E., & Zumbo, B. D. (1989). An empirical investigation of Eysenck's typology. *Journal of Research in Personality*, *23*, 343–353.

Huesmann, L. R., Eron, L. D., Lefkowitz, M. M., & Walder, L. O. (1984). Stability of aggression over time and generation. *Developmental Psychology*, *20*, 1120–1134.

Hughes, M., & Demo, D. H. (1989). Self-perceptions of Black Americans: Self-esteem and personal efficacy. *American Journal of Sociology*, *95*, 132–159.

Hui, C. H., & Triandis, H. C. (1986). Individualism-collectivism: A study of cross-cultural researchers. *Journal of Cross-Cultural Psychology*, *17*, 225–248.

Hull, J. G., Van Treuren, R. R., & Virnelli, S. (1987). Hardiness and health: A critique and alternative approach. *Journal of Personality and Social Psychology*, *53*, 518–530.

Huot, B., Makarec, K., & Persinger, M. A. (1989). Temporal lobes signs and Jungian dimensions of personality. *Perceptual and Motor Skills*, *69*, 841–842.

Hutterer, R. (1990). Authentic science: Some implications of Carl Rogers's reflections on science. *Person Centered Review*, *5*, 57–76.

Hutton, H. E., Miner, M. H., Blades, J. R., & Langfeldt, V. C. (1992). Ethnic differences on the MMPI Overcontrolled-Hostility Scale. *Journal of Personality Assessment*, *58*, 260–268.

Hutton, P. H. (1983). The psychohistory of Erik Erikson from the perspective of collective mentalities. *Psychohistory Review*, *12*, 18–25.

Hyde, J. S. (1981). How large are cognitive gender differences? A meta-analysis using ω^2 and *d*. *American Psychologist*, *36*, 892–901.

Hyde, J. S. (1984). How large are gender differences in aggression? A developmental meta-analysis. *Developmental Psychology, 20,* 722–736.

Hyde, J. S., Fennema, E., & Lamon, S. J. (1990). Gender differences in mathematics performance: A meta-analysis. *Psychological Bulletin, 107,* 139–155.

Hyde, J. S., Fennema, E., Ryan, M., Frost, L. A., & Hopp, C. (1990). Gender comparisons of mathematics attitudes and affect: A meta-analysis. *Psychology of Women Quarterly, 14,* 299–324.

Hyde, J. S., Klein, M. H., Essex, M. J., & Clark, R. (1995). Maternity leave and women's mental health. *Psychology of Women Quarterly, 19,* 257–285.

Hyde, J. S., & Linn, M. C. (1988). Gender differences in verbal ability: A meta-analysis. *Psychological Bulletin, 104,* 53–69.

Hyland, M. E. (1989). There is no motive to avoid success: The compromise explanation for success-avoiding behavior. *Journal of Personality, 57,* 665–693.

Hyland, M. E., Curtis, C., & Mason, D. (1985). Fear of success: Motive and cognition. *Journal of Personality and Social Psychology, 49,* 1669–1677.

Hyland, M. E., & Dann, P. L. (1988). Converging evidence that fear of success is multidimensional. *Current Psychology Research and Reviews, 7,* 199–206.

Hyland, M. E., & Mancini, A. V. (1985). Fear of success and affiliation. *Psychological Reports, 57,* 714.

Ihilevich, D., & Gleser, G. C. (1986). *Defense mechanisms: Their classification, correlates, and measurement with the Defense Mechanism Inventory.* Owossow, Mich.: DMI Associates.

Immelman, A. (1993). The assessment of political personality: A psychodiagnostically relevant conceptualization and methodology. *Political Psychology, 14,* 725–741.

Irvine, S. H., & Berry, J. W. (Eds.). (1988). *Human abilities in cultural context.* New York: Cambridge University Press.

Ivancevich, J. M., & Matteson, M. T. (1988). Type A behaviour and the healthy individual. *British Journal of Medical Psychology, 61,* 37–56.

Izard, C. E. (1993). Four systems for emotion activation: Cognitive and noncognitive processes. *Psychological Review, 100,* 68–90.

Izard, C. E. (1994). Innate and universal facial expressions: Evidence from developmental and cross-cultural research. *Psychological Bulletin, 115,* 288–299.

Jacklin, C. N. (1981). Methodological issues in the study of sex-related differences. *Developmental Review, 1,* 266–273.

Jacklin, C. N. (1989). Female and male: Issues of gender. *American Psychologist, 44,* 127–133.

Jacobsen, T., Edelstein, W., & Hofmann, V. (1994). A longitudinal study of the relation between representations of attachment in childhood and cognitive functioning in childhood and adolescence. *Developmental Psychology, 30,* 112–124.

Jaeger, R. M. (1987). NCME opposition to proposed Golden Rule legislation. *Educational Measurement: Issues and Practice, 6*(2), 21–22.

Jaffe, L. S. (1990). The empirical foundations of psychoanalytic approaches to psychological testing. *Journal of Personality Assessment, 55,* 746–755.

James, J. B., & Paul, E. L. (1993). The value of archival data for new perspectives on personality. In D. C. Funder, R. D. Parke, C. Tomlinson-Keasey, & K. Widaman (Eds.), *Studying lives through time: Personality and development* (pp. 45–63). Washington, D.C.: American Psychological Association.

James, W. (1950). *The principles of psychology* (2 vols.). New York: Dover. (Original work published 1890 by Holt)

Janoff-Bulman, R. (1989). Assumptive worlds and the stress of traumatic events: Applications of the schema construct. *Social Cognition, 7,* 113–136.

Jemmott, J. B., III (1987). Social motives and susceptibility to disease: Stalking individual differences in health risks. *Journal of Personality, 55,* 267–298.

Jemmott, J. B., III, Hellman, C., McClelland, D. C., Locke, S. E., Kraus, L., Williams, R. M., & Valeri, C. R. (1990). Motivational syndromes associated with natural killer cell activity. *Journal of Behavioral Medicine, 13,* 53–73.

Jenkins, C. D., Zyzanski, S. J., & Rosenman, R. H. (1979). *Manual for the Jenkins Activity Survey.* New York: Psychological Corporation.

Jenkins, S. R. (1987). Need for achievement and women's careers over 14 years: Evidence for occupational structure effects. *Journal of Personality and Social Psychology, 53,* 922–932.

Jenkins, S. R. (1994). Need for power and women's careers over 14 years: Structural power, job satisfaction, and motive change. *Journal of Personality and Social Psychology, 66,* 155–165.

Jennings, J. L. (1986). The revival of "Dora": Advances in psychoanalytic theory and technique. *Journal of the American Psychoanalytic Association, 34,* 607–635.

Jex, S. M., & Gudanowski, D. M. (1992). Efficacy beliefs and work stress: An exploratory study. *Journal of Organizational Behavior, 13,* 509–517.

John, O. P. (1990). The "big five" factor taxonomy: Dimensions of personality in the natural language and in questionnaires. In L. A. Pervin (Ed.), *Handbook of personality: Theory and research* (pp. 66–100). New York: Guilford.

John, O. P., Angleitner, A., & Ostendorf, F. (1988). The lexical approach to personality: A historical review of trait taxonomic research. *European Journal of Personality, 2,* 171–203.

John, O. P., Hampson, S. E., & Goldberg, L. R. (1991). The basic level in personality-trait hierarchies: Studies of trait use and accessibility in different contexts. *Journal of Personality and Social Psychology, 60,* 348–361.

John, O. P., & Robins, R. W. (1994). Accuracy and bias in self-perception: Individual differences in self-enhancement and the role of narcissism. *Journal of Personality and Social Psychology, 66,* 206–219.

Johnson, E. H. (1989). The role of the experience and expression of anger and anxiety in elevated blood pressure among black and white adolescents. *Journal of the National Medical Association, 81,* 573–584.

Johnson, E. H., & Broman, C. L. (1987). The relationship of anger expression to health problems among Black Americans in a national survey. *Journal of Behavioral Medicine, 10,* 103–116.

Johnson, J. T., & Shulman, G. A. (1988). More alike than meets the eye: Perceived gender differences in subjective experience and its display. *Sex Roles, 19,* 67–79.

Johnson, M. E. (1989). Sex-role orientation and attitudes toward sexual expression. *Psychological Reports, 64,* 1064.

Johnson, M. E., & Brems, C. (1989). Differences in interpersonal functioning as related to sex-role orientation. *Psychology: A Journal of Human Behavior, 26*(4), 48–52.

Jones, A. C. (1985). Psychological functioning in black Americans: A conceptual guide for use in psychotherapy. *Psychotherapy, 22,* 363–369.

Jones, D. C., Bloys, N., & Wood, M. (1990). Sex roles and friendship patterns. *Sex Roles, 23,* 133–145.

Jones, E. E., & Berglas, S. (1978). Control of attributions about the self through self-handicapping strategies: The appeal of alcohol and the role of underachievement. *Personality and Social Psychology Bulletin, 4,* 200–206.

Jones, E. E., & Nisbett, R. (1971). The actor and the observer: Divergent perceptions of the causes of behavior. In E. E. Jones, D. Kanouse, H. Kelley, R. Nisbett, S. Valins, & B. Weiner (Eds.), *Attribution: Perceiving the causes of behavior* (pp. 79–94). Morristown, N.J.: General Learning Press.

Jones, E. E., & Windholz, M. (1990). The psychoanalytic case study: Toward a method for systematic inquiry. *Journal of the American Psychoanalytic Association, 38,* 985–1015.

Jones, M. (1993). Influence of self-monitoring in dating motivations. *Journal of Research in Personality, 27,* 197–206.

Jones, N. S. C. (1990). Black/white issues in psychotherapy: A framework for clinical practice. *Journal of Social Behavior and Personality, 5,* 305–322.

Jordan, J. V., Kaplan, A. G., Miller, J. B., Stiver, I. P., & Surrey, J. L. (1991). *Women's growth in connection: Writings from the Stone Center.* New York: Guilford Press.

Jorm, A. F. (1987). Sex differences in neuroticism: A quantitative synthesis of published research. *Australian and New Zealand Journal of Psychiatry, 21*(4), 501–506.

Joseph, S., Cairns, E., & McCollam, P. (1993). Political violence, coping, and depressive symptomatology in Northern Irish children. *Personality and Individual Differences, 15,* 472–473.

Josephs, R. A., Markus, H. R., & Tafarodi, R. W. (1992). Gender and self-esteem. *Journal of Personality and Social Psychology, 63,* 391–402.

Judd, C. M., & Park, B. (1993). Definition and assessment of accuracy in social stereotypes. *Psychological Review, 100,* 109–128.

Jung, C. G. (1954). Marriage as a psychological relationship. In C. G. Jung, *The development of personality* (pp. 187–201). Princeton, N.J.: Princeton University Press. (Original work published 1931)

Jung, C. G. (1959). *Aion: Researches into the phenomenology of the self* (2nd ed.) (R. F. C. Hull, Trans.). Princeton, N.J.: Princeton University Press.

Jung, C. G. (1974). *Dreams* (W. McGuire, Ed.; R. F. C. Hull, Trans.). Princeton, N.J.: Princeton University Press.

Juni, S. (1982). The composite measure of the Defense Mechanism Inventory. *Journal of Research in Personality, 16,* 193–200.

Juni, S. (1993). Rorschach content psychometry and fixation theory. *Genetic, Social, and General Psychology Monographs, 119,* 77–98.

Kagan, J., Reznick, J. S., & Snidman, N. (1988). Biological bases of childhood shyness. *Science, 240,* 167–171.

Kagan, J., & Snidman, N. (1991). Infant predictors of inhibited and uninhibited profiles. *Psychological Science, 2,* 40–44

Kagitçibaşi, Ç., & Berry, J. W. (1989). Cross-cultural psychology: Current research and trends. *Annual Review of Psychology, 40*, 493–531.

Kakar, S. (1989). The maternal-feminine in Indian psychoanalysis. *International Review of Psycho-Analysis, 16,* 355–362.

Kalimo, R., & Vuori, J. (1990). Work and sense of coherence: Resources for competence and life satisfaction. *Behavioral Medicine, 16,* 76–89.

Kalin, R., & Lloyd, C. A. (1985). Sex role identity, sex-role ideology and marital adjustment. *International Journal of Women's Studies, 8*(1), 32–39.

Kalthoff, R. A., & Neimeyer, R. A. (1993). Self-complexity and psychological distress: A test of the buffering model. *International Journal of Personal Construct Psychology, 6,* 327–349.

Kamarck, T. W., Manuck, S. B., & Jennings, J. R. (1990). Social support reduces cardiovascular reactivity to psychological challenge: A laboratory model. *Psychosomatic Medicine, 52,* 42–58.

Kanner, A. D., Coyne, J. C., Schaefer, C., & Lazarus, R. S. (1981). Comparisons of two modes of stress measurement: Daily hassles and uplifts versus major life events. *Journal of Behavioral Medicine, 4,* 1–39.

Karoly, P., & Lecci, L. (1993). Hypochondriasis and somatization in college women: A Personal Projects Analysis. *Health Psychology, 12,* 103–109.

Kaun, D. E. (1991). Writers die young: The impact of work and leisure on longevity. *Journal of Economic Psychology, 12,* 381–399.

Keiser, R. E., & Prather, E. N. (1990). What is the TAT? A review of ten years of research. *Journal of Personality Assessment, 55,* 800–803.

Kelly, E. L., & Conley, J. J. (1987). Personality and compatibility: A prospective analysis of marital stability and marital satisfaction. *Journal of Personality and Social Psychology, 52,* 27–40.

Kelly, G. A. (1955). *The psychology of personal constructs* (Vols. 1 and 2). New York: Norton.

Kendall-Tackett, K. A., Williams, L. M., & Finkelhor, D. (1993). Impact of sexual abuse on children: A review and synthesis of recent empirical studies. *Psychological Bulletin, 113,* 164–180.

Kenny, D. A. (1991). A general model of consensus and accuracy in interpersonal perception. *Psychological Review, 98,* 155–163.

Kenny, D. A., & Albright, L. (1987). Accuracy in interpersonal perception: A social relations analysis. *Psychological Bulletin, 102,* 390–402.

Kenny, D. A., & Campbell, D. T. (1989). On the measurement of stability in over-time data. *Journal of Personality, 57,* 445–481.

Kenny, D. A., Horner, C., Kashy, D. A., & Chu, L. (1992). Consensus at zero acquaintance: Replication, behavioral cues, and stability. *Journal of Personality and Social Psychology, 62,* 88–97.

Kenrick, D. T. (1987). Gender, genes, and the social environment. In P. C. Shaver & C. Hendrick (Eds.), *Review of Personality and Social Psychology* (Vol. 8, Sex and gender, pp. 14–43). Beverly Hills, Calif.: Sage.

Kenrick, D. T., & Dantchik, A. (1983). Interactionism, idiographics, and the social psychological invasion of personality. *Journal of Personality, 51,* 286–307.

Kenrick, D. T., & Funder, D. C. (1988). Profiting from controversy: Lessons from the person-situation debate. *American Psychologist, 43,* 23–34.

Kenrick, D. T., & Stringfield, D. O. (1980). Personality traits and the eye of the beholder: Crossing some traditional philosophical boundaries in the search for consistency in all of the people. *Psychological Review, 87,* 88–104.

Kernberg, O. F. (1976). *Object-relations theory and clinical psychoanalysis.* New York: Jason Aronson.

Kernis, M. H., Cornell, D. P., Sun, C., Berry, A., & Harlow, T. (1993). There's more to self-esteem than whether it is high or low: The importance of stability of self-esteem. *Journal of Personality and Social Psychology, 65,* 1190–1204.

Kerr, H. D. (1993). White liver: A cultural disorder resembling AIDS. *Social Science and Medicine, 36,* 609–614.

Keutzer, C. S. (1984). The power of meaning: From quantum mechanics to synchronicity. *Journal of Humanistic Psychology, 24*(1), 80–94.

Khamis, V. (1993). Victims of the intifada: The psychosocial adjustment of the injured. *Behavioral Medicine, 19,* 93–101.

Kiesler, D. J. (1983). The 1982 Interpersonal Circle: A taxonomy for complementarity in human transactions. *Psychological Review, 90,* 185–214.

Kihlstrom, J. (1984). Conscious, subconscious, unconscious: A cognitive perspective. In K. S. Bowers & D. Meichenbaum (Eds.), *The unconscious reconsidered* (pp. 149–211). New York: Wiley.

Kihlstrom, J. F. (1990). The psychological unconscious. In L. A. Pervin (Ed.), *Handbook of personality: Theory and research* (pp. 445–464). New York: Guilford.

Kimble, G. A. (1989). Psychology from the standpoint of a generalist. *American Psychologist, 44,* 491–499.

King, L. A., & Emmons, R. A. (1990). Conflict over emotional expression: Psychological and physical correlates. *Journal of Personality and Social Psychology, 58,* 864–877.

King, L. A., & Emmons, R. A. (1991). Psychological, physical, and interpersonal correlates of emotional expressiveness, conflict, and control. *European Journal of Personality, 5,* 131–150.

Kirchler, E. (1989). Everyday life experiences at home: An interaction diary approach to assess marital relationships. *Journal of Family Psychology, 2,* 311–336.

Kirkpatrick, L. A. (1993). Fundamentalism, Christian orthodoxy, and intrinsic religious orientation as predictors of discriminatory attitudes. *Journal for the Scientific Study of Religion, 32,* 256–268.

Kirmayer, L. J., & Robbins, J. M. (1993). Cognitive and social correlates of the Toronto Alexithymia Scale. *Psychosomatics, 34,* 41–52.

Kirsch, I. (1980). "Microanalytic" analyses of efficacy expectations as predictors of performance. *Cognitive Therapy and Research, 4,* 259–262.

Kissinger, H. (1979). *The White House Years.* Boston: Little, Brown.

Kitayama, S., & Markus, H. R. (1992, May). *Construal of the self as cultural frame: Implications for internationalizing psychology.* Paper presented at the symposium Internationalization and Higher Education, University of Michigan, Ann Arbor, Mich.

Klein, H. A. (1987). The relationship of temperament scores to the way young adults adapt to change. *Journal of Psychology, 121,* 119–135.

Klein, S. B., Loftus, J., & Plog, A. E. (1992). Trait judgments about the self: Evidence from the encoding specificity paradigm. *Personality and Social Psychology Bulletin, 18,* 730–735.

Kline, P. (1987). The experimental study of the psychoanalytic unconscious. *Personality and Social Psychology Bulletin, 13,* 363–378.

Kline, P. (1988). The cross-cultural measurement of personality. In G. K. Verma & C. Bagley (Eds.), *Cross-cultural studies of personality, attitudes and cognition* (pp. 3–40). London: Macmillan.

Kline, P., & Lapham, S. L. (1992). The PPQ: A study of its ability to discriminate occupational groups and the validity of its scales. *Personality and Individual Differences, 13,* 225–228.

Kneier, A. W., & Temoshok, L. (1984). Repressive coping reactions in patients with malignant melanoma as compared to cardiovascular disease patients. *Journal of Psychosomatic Research, 28,* 145–155.

Knowles, E. S., & Sibicky, M. E. (1990). Continuity and diversity in the stream of selves: Metaphorical resolutions of William James's one-in-many-selves paradox. *Personality and Social Psychology Bulletin, 16,* 676–687.

Kobasa, S. C. (1979). Stressful life events, personality, and health: An inquiry into hardiness. *Journal of Personality and Social Psychology, 37,* 1–11.

Kobasa, S. C., Maddi, S. R., & Courington, S. (1981). Personality and constitution as mediators in the stress-illness relationship. *Journal of Health and Social Behavior, 22,* 368–378.

Kobasa, S. C., Maddi, S. R., & Kahn, S. (1982). Hardiness and health: A prospective study. *Journal of Personality and Social Psychology, 42,* 168–177.

Kobasa, S. C., Maddi, S. R., & Puccetti, M. C. (1982). Personality and exercise as buffers in the stress-illness relationship. *Journal of Behavioral Medicine, 5,* 391–404.

Koch, S. (1981). The nature and limits of psychological knowledge: Lessons of a century qua "science." *American Psychologist, 36,* 257–269.

Kochanska, G. (1991). Socialization and temperament in the development of guilt and conscience. *Child Development, 62,* 1379–1392.

Koenig, H. G. (1990). Research on religion and mental health in later life: A review and commentary. *Journal of Geriatric Psychiatry, 23,* 23–53.

Koestner, R., & McClelland, D. C. (1992). The affiliation motive. In C. P. Smith (Ed.), *Motivation and personality: Handbook of thematic content analysis* (pp. 205–210). New York: Cambridge University Press.

Koestner, R., Franz, C., & Weinberger, J. (1990). The family origins of empathic concern: A 26-year longitudinal study. *Journal of Personality and Social Psychology, 58,* 709–717.

Koestner, R., Zuckerman, M., & Koestner, J. (1987). Praise, involvement, and intrinsic motivation. *Journal of Personality and Social Psychology, 53,* 383–390.

Kohlberg, L. (1981). *Essays on moral development. Vol. 1. The philosophy of moral development: Moral stages and the idea of justice.* San Francisco: Harper & Row.

Kohlberg, L. (1984). *The psychology of moral development.* San Francisco: Harper & Row.

Kornfeld, A. D. (1990). Shared versus system exemplars in the teaching of psychology. *Psychological Reports, 67,* 795–799.

Kraft, T. (1992). Counteracting pain in malignant disease by hypnotic techniques: Five case studies. *Contemporary Hypnosis, 9,* 123–129.

Krampen, G., Effertz, B., Jostock, U., & Müller, B. (1990). Gender differences in personality: Biological and/or psychological? *European Journal of Personality, 4,* 303–317.

Kratochwill, T. R. (Ed.). (1978). *Single subject research.* New York: Academic Press.

Krippendorff, K. (1980). *Content analysis.* Beverly Hills: Sage.

Kroeger, O., & Thuesen, J. M. (1988). *Type talk: The 16 personality types that determine how we live, love, and work.* New York: Delta.

Kroger, J. (1986). The relative importance of identity status interview components: Replication and extension. *Journal of Adolescence, 9,* 337–354.

Kroger, J., & Haslett, S. J. (1988). Separation-individuation and ego identity status in late adolescence: A two-year longitudinal study. *Journal of Youth and Adolescence, 17,* 59–79.

Krosnick, J. A., Betz, A. L., Jussim, L. J., & Lynn, A. R. (1992). Subliminal conditioning of attitudes. *Personality and Social Psychology Bulletin, 18,* 152–162.

Krueger, J., & Rothbart, M. (1988). Use of categorical and individuating information in making inferences about personality. *Journal of Personality and Social Psychology, 55,* 187–195.

Kruglanski, A. W. (1989). The psychology of being "right": The problem of accuracy in social perception and cognition. *Psychological Bulletin, 106,* 395–409.

Kuhn, T. S. (1970). *The structure of scientific revolutions* (2nd ed.). Chicago: University of Chicago Press.

Kunda, Z., & Sherman-Williams, B. (1993). Stereotypes and the construal of individuating information. *Personality and Social Psychology Bulletin, 19,* 90–99.

Kurdek, L. A., & Schmitt, J. P. (1986). Interaction of sex role self-concept with relationship quality and relationship beliefs in married, heterosexual cohabiting, gay, and lesbian couples. *Journal of Personality and Social Psychology, 51,* 365–370.

Lachman, M. E., & Leff, R. (1989). Perceived control and intellectual functioning in the elderly: A 5-year longitudinal study. *Developmental Psychology, 25,* 722–728.

Lachman, S. J., & Bass, A. R. (1985). A direct study of halo effect. *Journal of Psychology, 119,* 535–540.

LaFromboise, T., Coleman, H. L. K., & Gerton, J. (1993). Psychological impact of biculturalism: Evidence and theory. *Psychological Bulletin, 114,* 395–412.

Laird, J. D. (1974). Self-attribution of emotion: The effects of expressive behavior on the quality of emotional experience. *Journal of Personality and Social Psychology, 29,* 475–486.

Lamb, M. E. (1987). Predictive implications of individual differences in attachment. *Journal of Consulting and Clinical Psychology, 55,* 817–824.

Lamiell, J. T. (1981). Toward an idiothetic psychology of personality. *American Psychologist, 36,* 276–289.

Lamiell, J. T. (1987). *The psychology of personality: An epistemological inquiry.* New York: Columbia University Press.

Lamiell, J. T. (1991). Valuation theory: The self-confrontation method, and scientific personality psychology. *European Journal of Personality, 5,* 235–244.

Landrine, H. (1992). Clinical implications of cultural differences: The referential versus the indexical self. *Clinical Psychology Review, 12,* 401–415.

Landy, F. J. (1986). Stamp collecting versus science: Validation as hypothesis testing. *American Psychologist, 41,* 1183–1192.

Lang-Takac, E., & Osterweil, Z. (1992). Separateness and connectedness: Differences between the genders. *Sex Roles, 27,* 277–289.

Langer, E. J. (1989). *Mindfulness.* Reading, Mass.: Addison-Wesley.

Lanham, B. B. (1988). Freedom, restraint, and security: Japan and the United States. *Ethos, 16,* 273–284.

Larkin, J. E. (1991). The implicit theories approach to the self-monitoring controversy. *European Journal of Personality, 5,* 15–34.

Larrieu, J., & Mussen, P. (1986). Some personality and motivational correlates of children's prosocial behavior. *Journal of Genetic Psychology, 147,* 529–542.

Larsen, R. J., & Diener, E. (1987). Affect intensity as an individual difference characteristic: A review. *Journal of Research in Personality, 21,* 1–39.

Larsen, R. J., Diener, E., & Emmons, R. A. (1986). Affect intensity and reactions to daily life events. *Journal of Personality and Social Psychology, 51,* 803–814.

Lassner, J. B., Matthews, K. A., & Stoney, C. M. (1994). Are cardiovascular reactors to asocial stress also reactors to social stress? *Journal of Personality and Social Psychology, 66*, 69–77.

Latack, J. C., & Havlovic, S. J. (1992). Coping with job stress: A conceptual evaluation framework for coping measures. *Journal of Organizational Behavior, 13*, 479–508.

Lay, C. H., Knish, S., & Zanatta, R. (1992). Self-handicappers and procrastinators: A comparison of their practice behavior prior to an evaluation. *Journal of Research in Personality, 26*, 242–257.

Lazarus, R. S. (1993). From psychological stress to the emotions: A history of changing outlooks. *Annual Review of Psychology, 44*, 1–21.

Lazarus, R. S., & Folkman, S. (1984). *Stress, appraisal, and coping*. New York: Springer.

Leahey, T. H. (1992). The mythical revolutions of American psychology. *American Psychologist, 47*, 308–318.

Leak, G. K., & Christopher, S. B. (1982). Freudian psychoanalysis and sociobiology: A synthesis. *American Psychologist, 37*, 313–322.

Leak, G. K., & Fish, S. (1989). Religious orientation, impression management, and self-deception: Toward a clarification of the link between religiosity and social desirability. *Journal for the Scientific Study of Religion, 28*, 355–359.

Leary, M. R., Tambor, E. S., Terdal, S. K., & Downs, D. L. (1995). Self-esteem as an interpersonal monitor: The sociometer hypothesis. *Journal of Personality and Social Psychology, 68*, 518–530.

Leavy, S. A. (1985). Hitler's "table talk" as psychoanalytic source material. *Contemporary Psychoanalysis, 21*, 609–616.

Lecci, L., Karoly, P., Briggs, C., & Kuhn, K. (1994). Specificity and generality of motivational components in depression: A personal projects analysis. *Journal of Abnormal Psychology, 103*, 404–408.

Lee, Y. (1993). Psychology needs no prejudice but the diversity of cultures. *American Psychologist, 48*, 1090–1091.

Lenney, E. (1977). Women's self-confidence in achievement settings. *Psychological Bulletin, 84*, 1–13.

Lennon, R., & Eisenberg, N. (1987). Gender and age differences in empathy and sympathy. In N. Eisenberg & J. Strayer (Eds.), *Empathy and its development* (pp. 195–217). New York: Cambridge University Press.

Lennox, R. (1988). The problem with self-monitoring: A two-sided scale and a one-sided theory. *Journal of Personality Assessment, 52*, 58–73.

Lennox, R. D., & Wolfe, R. N. (1984). Revision of the Self-Monitoring Scale. *Journal of Personality and Social Psychology, 46*, 1349–1364.

Lent, R. W., & Hackett, G. (1987). Career self-efficacy: Empirical status and future directions. *Journal of Vocational Behavior, 30*, 347–382.

Lerman, H. (1986). *A mote in Freud's eye: From psychoanalysis to the psychology of women*. New York: Springer.

Lerner, P. M. (1990). The clinical inference process and the role of theory. *Journal of Personality Assessment, 55*, 426–431.

Lerner, R. M., & Tubman, J. G. (1989). Conceptual issues in studying continuity and discontinuity in personality development across life. *Journal of Personality, 57*, 343–373.

Lester, D. (1986). A cross-cultural test of Sheldon's theory of personality. *Journal of Social Psychology, 126*, 695–696.

Lester, D. (1987). Wife abuse and psychogenic motives in nonliterate societies. *Perceptual and Motor Skills, 64*, 154.

Lester, D. (1989). A neurotransmitter basis for Eysenck's theory of personality. *Psychological Reports, 64*, 189–190.

Lester, D., & Rencher, A. (1993). Aversion to physical touching and personality. *Personality and Individual Differences, 14*, 259–260.

Levine, R., Gillman, M., & Reis, H. (1982). Individual differences for sex differences in achievement attributions? *Sex Roles, 8*, 455–466.

Levinson, D. J. (1986). A conception of adult development. *American Psychologist, 41*, 3–13.

Levinson, H. (1994). Why the behemoths fell: Psychological roots of corporate failure. *American Psychologist, 49*, 428–436.

Levit, D. B. (1991). Gender differences in ego defenses in adolescence: Sex roles as one way to understand the differences. *Journal of Personality and Social Psychology, 61*, 992–999.

Levitz-Jones, E. M., & Orlofsky, J. L. (1985). Separation-individuation and intimacy capacity in college women. *Journal of Personality and Social Psychology, 49*, 156–169.

Lewicki, P. (1983). Self-image bias in person perception. *Journal of Personality and Social Psychology, 45*, 384–393.

Lewicki, P. (1984). Self-schema and social information processing. *Journal of Personality and Social Psychology, 47*, 1177–1190.

Lewis, H. B. (1985). Depression vs. paranoia: Why are there sex differences in mental illness? In A. J. Stewart

& M. B. Lykes (Eds.), *Gender and personality: Current perspectives on theory and research* (pp. 62–90). Durham, N.C.: Duke University Press.

Lewis, M. (1989). Cultural differences in children's knowledge of emotional scripts. In P. Harris & C. Saarni (Eds.), *Children's understanding of emotion* (pp. 350–373). New York: Cambridge University Press.

Lewis, T. D. (1983). Gordon Liddy: A life style analysis. *Individual Psychology: Journal of Adlerian Theory, Research and Practice, 39,* 259–273.

Lewis, T. T. (1985). Gordon Allport's eclectic humanism: A neglected approach to psychohistory. *Psychohistory Review, 13*(2,3), 33–41.

Lieberson, S. (1991). Small N's and big conclusions: An examination of the reasoning in comparative studies based on a small number of cases. *Social Forces, 70,* 307–320.

Lifton, P. D. (1985). Individual differences in moral development: The relation of sex, gender, and personality to morality. *Journal of Personality, 53,* 306–334.

Lin, C. C., & Fu, V. R. (1990). A comparison of child-rearing practices among Chinese, immigrant Chinese, and Caucasian-American parents. *Child Development, 61,* 429–433.

Lincoln, B. (1994). A Lakota Sun Dance and the problematics of sociocosmic reunion. *History of Religions, 34,* 1–14.

Linden, W., Chambers, L., Maurice, J., & Lenz, J. W. (1993). Sex differences in social support, self-deception, hostility, and ambulatory cardiovascular activity. *Health Psychology, 12,* 376–380.

Lindsey, K. P., & Paul, G. L. (1989). Involuntary commitments to public mental institutions: Issues involving the overrepresentation of blacks and assessment of relevant functioning. *Psychological Bulletin, 106,* 171–183.

Linn, M. C., & Petersen, A. C. (1985). Emergence and characterization of sex differences in spatial ability: A meta-analysis. *Child Development, 56,* 1479–1498.

Linn, R. L., & Drasgow, R. (1987). Implications of the Golden Rule settlement for test construction. *Educational Measurement: Issues and Practice, 6*(2), 13–17.

Linville, P. W. (1987). Self complexity as a cognitive buffer against stress-related illness and depression. *Journal of Personality and Social Psychology, 52,* 663–676.

Lippa, R., & Connelly, S. (1990). Gender diagnosticity: A new Bayesian approach to gender-related individual differences. *Journal of Personality and Social Psychology, 59,* 1051–1065.

Lipton, E. (1990). Representing sexuality in women artists' biographies: The cases of Suzanne Valadon and Victorine Meurent. *Journal of Sex Research, 27*(2), 81–94.

Little, B. R., Lecci, L., & Watkinson, B. (1992). Personality and personal projects: Linking Big Five and PAC units of analysis. *Journal of Personality, 60,* 501–525.

Lobel, T. E., & Winch, G. L. (1986). Different defense mechanisms among men with different sex role orientations. *Sex Roles, 15,* 215–220.

Locke, E. A., & Taylor, M. S. (1991). Stress, coping, and the meaning of work. In A. Monat & R. S. Lazarus (Eds.), *Stress and coping: An anthology* (3rd ed., pp. 140–157). New York: Columbia University Press.

Loehlin, J. C. (1987). Twin studies, environment differences, age changes. *Behavioral and Brain Sciences, 10,* 30–31.

Loehlin, J. C. (1992). *Genes and environment in personality development.* Newbury Park, Calif.: Sage.

Loevinger, J. (1966). The meaning and measurement of ego development. *American Psychologist, 21,* 195–206.

Loevinger, J. (1985). Revision of the Sentence Completion Test for ego development. *Journal of Personality and Social Psychology, 48,* 420–427.

Loewenberg, P. (1988). Psychoanalytic models of history: Freud and after. In W. M. Runyan (Ed.), *Psychology and historical interpretation.* New York: Oxford University Press.

Loftus, E. F. (1993). The reality of repressed memories. *American Psychologist, 48,* 518–537.

Long, B. C. (1990). Relation between coping strategies, sex-typed traits, and environmental characteristics: A comparison of male and female managers. *Journal of Counseling Psychology, 37,* 185–194.

Lorimer, R. (1976). A reconsideration of the psychological roots of *Gandhi's Truth. Psychoanalytic Review, 63,* 191–207.

Lubin, B., Larsen, R. M., Matarazzo, J. D., & Seever, M. (1985). Psychological test usage patterns in five professional settings. *American Psychologist, 40,* 857–861.

Lumpkin, J. R. (1985). Health versus activity in elderly persons' locus of control. *Perceptual and Motor Skills, 60,* 288.

Lundy, A. (1985). The reliability of the Thematic Apperception Test. *Journal of Personality Assessment, 49,* 141–145.

Lundy, A. (1988). Instructional set and Thematic Apperception Test validity. *Journal of Personality Assessment, 52*, 309–320.

Lupfer, M. B., Clark, L. F., & Hutcherson, H. W. (1990). Impact of context on spontaneous trait and situational attributions. *Journal of Personality and Social Psychology, 58*, 239–249.

Luthar, S. S., & Blatt, S. J. (1993). Dependent and self-critical depressive experiences among inner-city adolescents. *Journal of Personality, 61*, 365–386.

Lyddon, W. J. (1991). Socially constituted knowledge: Philosophical, psychological, and feminist contributions. *Journal of Mind and Behavior, 12*, 263–279.

Lykes, M. B. (1985). Gender and individualistic vs. collectivist bases for notions about the self. *Journal of Personality, 53*, 356–383.

Lykes, M. B., & Stewart, A. J. (1986). Evaluating the feminist challenge to research in personality and social psychology: 1963–1983. *Psychology of Women Quarterly, 10*, 393–411.

Lykken, D. T., & Tellegen, A. (1993). Is human mating adventitious or the result of lawful choice? A twin study of mate selection. *Journal of Personality and Social Psychology, 65*, 56–68.

Lyness, S. A. (1993). Predictors of differences between Type A and B individuals in heart rate and blood pressure reactivity. *Psychological Bulletin, 114*, 266–295.

Lynn, R., Yamauchi, H., & Tachibana, Y. (1991). Attitudes related to work of adolescents in the United Kingdom and Japan. *Psychological Reports, 68*, 403–410.

Lynn, S. J., & Rhue, J. W. (1988). Fantasy proneness: Hypnosis, developmental antecedents, and psychopathology. *American Psychologist, 43*, 35–44.

Lynn, S. J., Rhue, J. W., & Weekes, J. R. (1990). Hypnotic involuntariness: A social cognitive analysis. *Psychological Review, 97*, 169–184.

Lyon, L. S. (1985). Facilitating telephone number recall in a case of psychogenic amnesia. *Journal of Behavior Therapy and Experimental Psychiatry, 16*, 147–149.

Mabry, C. H. (1993). Gender differences in ego level. *Psychological Reports, 72*, 752–754.

Maccoby, E. E. (1991). Different reproductive strategies in males and females. *Child Development, 62*, 676–681.

Maccoby, E. E., & Jacklin, C. N. (1974). *The psychology of sex differences*. Stanford, Calif.: Stanford University Press.

Maccoby, E. E., & Jacklin, C. N. (1980). Sex differences in aggression: A rejoinder and reprise. *Child Development, 51*, 964–980.

MacDougall, J. M., Dembroski, T. M., Dimsdale, J. E., & Hackett, T. P. (1985). Components of Type A, hostility, and anger-in: Further relationships to angiographic findings. *Health Psychology, 4*, 137–152.

Mack, J. E. (1971). Psychoanalysis and historical biography. *Journal of the American Psychoanalytic Association, 19*, 143–179.

Mack, J. E. (1980). Psychoanalysis and biography: Aspects of a developing affinity. *Journal of the American Psychoanalytic Association, 28*, 543–562.

MacKay, D. G. (1973). Aspects of the theory of comprehension, memory and attention. *Quarterly Journal of Experimental Psychology, 25*, 22–40.

MacNair, R. R., & Elliott, T. R. (1992). Self-perceived problem-solving ability, stress appraisal, and coping over time. *Journal of Research in Personality, 26*, 150–164.

Magnusson, D. (1990). Personality development from an interactional perspective. In L. A. Pervin (Ed.), *Handbook of personality: Theory and research* (pp. 193–222). New York: Guilford.

Magnusson, D., & Törestad, B. (1993). A holistic view of personality: A model revisited. *Annual Review of Psychology, 44*, 427–452.

Major, B. (1979). Sex-role orientation and fear of success: Clarifying an unclear relationship. *Sex Roles, 5*, 63–70.

Major, B., Cozzarelli, C., Sciacchitano, A. M., Cooper, M. L., Testa, M., & Mueller, P. M. (1990). Perceived social support, self-efficacy, and adjustment to abortion. *Journal of Personality and Social Psychology, 59*, 452–463.

Makarec, K., & Persinger, M. A. (1993). Bilingual men but not women display verbal memory weaknesses but not figural memory differences compared to monolinguals. *Personality and Individual Differences, 15*, 531–536.

Malgady, R. G., Rogler, L. H., & Constantino, G. (1987). Ethnocultural and linguistic bias in mental health evaluation of Hispanics. *American Psychologist, 42*, 228–234.

Malinosky-Rummell, R., & Hansen, D. J. (1993). Long-term consequences of childhood physical abuse. *Psychological Bulletin, 114*, 68–79.

Malm, L. (1993). The eclipse of meaning in cognitive psychology: Implications for humanistic psychology. *Journal of Humanistic Psychology, 33*(1), 67–87.

Mandler, G., & Nakamura, Y. (1987). Aspects of consciousness. *Personality and Social Psychology Bulletin, 13,* 299–313.

Mangelsdorf, S., Gunnar, M., Kestenbaum, R., Lang, S., & Andreas, D. (1990). Infant proneness-to-distress temperament, maternal personality, and mother-infant attachment: Associations and goodness of fit. *Child Development, 61,* 820–831.

Manicas, P. T., & Secord, P. F. (1983). Implications for psychology of the new philosophy of science. *American Psychologist, 38,* 399–413.

Maoz, Z., & Shayer, A. (1987). The cognitive structure of peace and war argumentation: Israeli Prime Ministers versus the Knesset. *Political Psychology, 8,* 575–604.

Maqsud, M. (1992). Psychoticism, extraversion, and neuroticism among Batswana adolescents. *Journal of Social Psychology, 132,* 275–276.

Marceil, J. C. (1977). Implicit dimensions of idiography and nomothesis: A reformulation. *American Psychologist, 32,* 1046–1055.

Marcia, J. E. (1966). Development and validation of ego-identity status. *Journal of Personality and Social Psychology, 3,* 551–558.

Marecek, J. (1989). Introduction [to special issue: Theory and method in feminist psychology]. *Psychology of Women Quarterly, 13,* 367–377.

Marin, G. V., Marin, G., Otero-Sabogal, R., Sabogal, F., & Perez-Stable, E. (1987). *Cultural differences in attitudes toward smoking: Developing messages using the theory of reasoned action* (Techn. Rep.). (Available from Box 0320, 400 Parnassus Ave., San Francisco, Calif. 94117).

Markstrom-Adams, C. (1989). Androgyny and its relation to adolescent psychosocial well-being: A review of the literature. *Sex Roles, 21,* 325–340.

Markus, H. (1977). Self-schemata and processing information about the self. *Journal of Personality and Social Psychology, 35,* 63–78.

Markus, H., Crane, M., Bernstein, S., & Sidali, M. (1982). Self-schemas and gender. *Journal of Personality and Social Psychology, 42,* 38–50.

Markus, H. R., & Kitayama, S. (1991). Culture and the self: Implications for cognition, emotion, and motivation. *Psychological Review, 98,* 224–253.

Markus, H., & Nurius, P. (1986). Possible selves. *American Psychologist, 41,* 954–969.

Markus, H., & Wurf, E. (1987). The dynamic self-concept: A social psychological perspective. *Annual Review of Psychology, 38,* 299–337.

Marmot, M. G., & Syme, S. L. (1976). Acculturation and coronary heart disease in Japanese Americans. *American Journal of Epidemiology, 104,* 225–247.

Martin, R. B., Guthrie, C. A., & Pitts, C. G. (1993). Emotional crying, depressed mood, and secretory immunoglobulin A. *Behavioral Medicine, 19,* 111–114.

Martindale, C., Covello, E., & West, A. (1986). Primary process cognition and hemispheric asymmetry. *Journal of Genetic Psychology, 147,* 79–87.

Martinetti, R. F. (1985). Cognitive antecedents of dream recall. *Perceptual and Motor Skills, 60,* 395–401.

Masling, J. (1992). The influence of situational and interpersonal variables in projective testing. *Journal of Personality Assessment, 59,* 616–640. (Original work published 1960)

Maslow, A. H. (1966). *The psychology of science: A reconnaissance.* New York: Harper & Row.

Maslow, A. H. (1968). *Toward a psychology of being* (2nd ed.). New York: D. Van Nostrand.

Maslow, A. H. (1987). *Motivation and personality* (3rd ed.). New York: Harper & Row. (Original work published 1954)

Mason, A., & Blankenship, V. (1987). Power and affiliation motivation, stress, and abuse in intimate relationships. *Journal of Personality and Social Psychology, 52,* 203–210.

Masson, J. M. (1984). *The assault on truth: Freud's suppression of the seduction theory.* New York: Farrar, Straus & Giroux.

Masson, J. M. (1990). *Final analysis: The making and unmaking of a psychoanalyst.* New York: Addison-Wesley.

Matheny, A. P., Riese, M. L., & Wilson, R. S. (1985). Rudiments of infant temperament: Newborn to 9 months. *Developmental Psychology, 21,* 486–494.

Matthews, G. (1989). The factor structure of the 16PF: Twelve primary and three secondary factors. *Personality and Individual Differences, 10,* 931–940.

Matthews, G., & Amelang, M. (1993). Extraversion, arousal theory and performance: A study of individual differences in the EEG. *Personality and Individual Differences, 14,* 347–363.

Matthews, K. A. (1982). Psychological perspectives on the Type A behavior pattern. *Psychological Bulletin, 91,* 293–323.

Mauro, R., Sato, K., & Tucker, J. (1992). The role of appraisal in human emotions: A cross-cultural study. *Journal of Personality and Social Psychology, 62,* 301–317.

McAdams, D. P. (1980). A thematic coding system for the intimacy motive. *Journal of Research in Personality*, *14*, 413–432.

McAdams, D. P. (1982). Intimacy motivation. In A. J. Stewart (Ed.), *Motivation and society* (pp. 133–171). San Francisco: Jossey-Bass.

McAdams, D. P. (1985). *Power, intimacy, and the life story: Personological inquiries into identity.* Chicago: Dorsey Press.

McAdams, D. P. (1988). Biography, narrative, and lives: An introduction. *Journal of Personality*, *56*, 1–18.

McAdams, D. P. (1990). Unity and purpose in human lives: The emergence of identity as a life story. In A. I. Rabin, R. A. Zucker, R. A. Emmons, & S. Frank, (Eds.), *Studying persons and lives* (pp. 148–200). New York: Springer-Verlag.

McAdams, D. P., Booth, L., & Selvik, R. (1981). Religious identity among students at a private college: Social motives, ego stage, and development. *Merrill Palmer Quarterly*, *27*, 219–239.

McAdams, D. P., & Bryant, F. B. (1987). Intimacy motivation and subjective mental health in a nationwide sample. *Journal of Personality*, *55*, 395–413.

McAdams, D. P., & Constantian, C. A. (1983). Intimacy and affiliation motives in daily living: An experience sampling analysis. *Journal of Personality and Social Psychology*, *45*, 851–861.

McAdams, D. P., Jackson, R. J., & Kirshnit, C. (1984). Looking, laughing and smiling in dyads as a function of intimacy motivation and reciprocity. *Journal of Personality*, *52*, 261–273.

McAdams, D. P., Lensky, D. B., Daple, S. A., & Allen, J. (1988). Depression and the organization of autobiographical memory. *Journal of Social and Clinical Psychology*, *7*, 332–349.

McAdams, D. P., Lester, R. M., Brand, P. A., McNamara, W. J., & Lensky, D. B. (1988). Sex and the TAT: Are women more intimate than men? Do men fear intimacy? *Journal of Personality Assessment*, *52*, 397–409.

McAdams, D. P., & Powers, J. (1981). Themes of intimacy in behavior and thought. *Journal of Personality and Social Psychology*, *40*, 573–587.

McAdams, D. P., Ruetzel, K., & Foley, J. M. (1986). Complexity and generativity at mid-life: Relations among social motives, ego development, and adults' plans for the future. *Journal of Personality and Social Psychology*, *50*, 800–807.

McAdams, D. P., & Vaillant, G. E. (1982). Intimacy motivation and psychosocial adaptation: A longitudinal study. *Journal of Personality Assessment*, *46*, 586–493.

McCall, R. B. (1990). Infancy research: Individual differences. *Merrill Palmer Quarterly*, *36*(1), 141–157.

McCann, S. J. H. (1990a). Authoritarianism and preference for the presidential candidate perceived to be higher on the power motive. *Perceptual and Motor Skills*, *70*, 577–578.

McCann, S. J. H. (1990b). Threat, power, and presidential greatness: Harding to Johnson. *Psychological Reports*, *66*, 129–130.

McCartney, K., Harris, M. J., & Bernieri, F. (1990). Growing up and growing apart: A developmental meta-analysis of twin studies. *Psychological Bulletin*, *107*, 226–237.

McCaulley, M. H. (1990). The Myers-Briggs Type Indicator: A measure for individuals and groups. *Measurement and Evaluation in Counseling and Development*, *22*, 181–195.

McClelland, D. C. (1961). *The achieving society.* New York: Free Press.

McClelland, D. C. (1965). N Achievement and entrepreneurship: A longitudinal study. *Journal of Personality and Social Psychology*, *1*, 389–392.

McClelland, D. C. (1975). *Power: The inner experience.* New York: Irvington.

McClelland, D. C. (1979). Inhibited power motivation and high blood pressure in men. *Journal of Abnormal Psychology*, *88*, 182–190.

McClelland, D. C. (1980). Motive dispositions: The merits of operant and respondent measures. *Review of Personality and Social Psychology*, *1*, 10–41.

McClelland, D. C. (1985). *Human motivation.* Glencoe, Ill: Scott, Foresman and Company.

McClelland, D. C. (1986). Some reflections on the two psychologies of love. *Journal of Personality*, *54*, 334–353.

McClelland, D. C. (1989). Motivational factors in health and disease. *American Psychologist*, *44*, 675–683.

McClelland, D. C., Alexander, C., & Marks, E. (1982). The need for power, stress, immune function, and illness among male prisoners. *Journal of Abnormal Psychology*, *91*, 61–70.

McClelland, D. C., Atkinson, J. W., Clark, R. A., & Lowell, E. L. (1953). *The achievement motive.* New York: Appleton-Century-Crofts.

McClelland, D. C., & Boyatzis, R. E. (1982). Leadership motive pattern and long-term success in management. *Journal of Applied Psychology, 67,* 737–743.

McClelland, D. C., & Burnham, D. H. (1976, March/April). Power is the great motivator. *Harvard Business Review,* 100–110.

McClelland, D. C., Davis, W. B., Kalin, R., & Wanner, E. (1972). *The drinking man: Alcohol and human motivation.* New York: Free Press.

McClelland, D. C., Floor, E., Davidson, R. J., & Saron, C. (1980). Stressed power motivation, sympathetic activation, immune function, and illness. *Journal of Human Stress, 6*(2), 11–19.

McClelland, D. C., & Franz, C. E. (1992). Motivational and other sources of work accomplishments in mid-life: A longitudinal study. *Journal of Personality, 60,* 679–707.

McClelland, D. C., & Jemmott, J. B., III (1980). Power motivation, stress, and physical illness. *Journal of Human Stress, 6*(4), 6–15.

McClelland, D. C., & Koestner, R. (1992). The achievement motive. In C. P. Smith (Ed.), *Motivation and personality: Handbook of thematic content analysis* (pp. 143–152). New York: Cambridge University Press.

McClelland, D. C., Koestner, R., & Weinberger, J. (1989). How do self-attributed and implicit motives differ? *Psychological Review, 96,* 690–702.

McClelland, D. C., & Krishnit, C. (1988). The effect of motivational arousal through films on salivary immunoglobulin A. *Psychology and Health, 2,* 31–52.

McClelland, D. C., Patel, V., Stier, D., & Brown, D. (1987). The relationship of affiliative arousal to dopamine release. *Motivation and Emotion, 11,* 51–66.

McClelland, D. C., Ross, G., & Patel, V. (1985). The effect of an academic examination on salivary norepinephrine and immunoglobulin levels. *Journal of Human Stress, 11*(2), 52–59.

McClelland, D. C., & Winter, D. G. (1969). *Motivating economic achievement.* New York: Free Press.

McCornack, S. A., & Parks, M. R. (1990). What women know that men don't: Sex differences in determining the truth behind deceptive messages. *Journal of Social and Personal Relationships, 7,* 107–118.

McCrae, R. R. (1982). Consensual validation of personality traits: Evidence from self-reports and ratings. *Journal of Personality and Social Psychology, 43,* 293–303.

McCrae, R. R. (1984). Situational determinants of coping responses: Loss, threat, and challenge. *Journal of Personality and Social Psychology, 46,* 919–928.

McCrae, R. R. (1990). Traits and trait names: How well is Openness represented in natural languages? *European Journal of Personality, 4,* 119–129.

McCrae, R. R. (1991). The five-factor model and its assessment in clinical settings. *Journal of Personality Assessment, 57,* 399–414.

McCrae, R. R. (1993). Moderated analyses of longitudinal personality stability. *Journal of Personality and Social Psychology, 65,* 577–585.

McCrae, R. R., & Costa, P. T., Jr. (1989a). More reasons to adopt the five-factor model. *American Psychologist, 44,* 451–452.

McCrae, R. R., & Costa, P. T., Jr. (1989b). Reinterpreting the Myers-Briggs Type Indicator from the perspective of the five-factor model of personality. *Journal of Personality, 57,* 17–40.

McCrae, R. R., & Costa, P. T., Jr. (1986). Personality, coping, and coping effectiveness in an adult sample. *Journal of Personality, 54,* 385–405.

McCrae, R. R., & Costa, P. T., Jr. (1987). Validation of the five-factor model of personality across instruments and observers. *Journal of Personality and Social Psychology, 52,* 81–90.

McCrae, R. R., & Costa, P. T., Jr. (1988). Recalled parent-child relations and adult personality. *Journal of Personality, 56,* 417–434.

McCrae, R. R., & Costa, P. T., Jr. (1989a). Rotation to maximize the construct validity of factors in the NEO Personality Inventory. *Multivariate Behavioral Research, 24,* 107–124.

McCrae, R. R., & Costa, P. T., Jr. (1989b). The structure of interpersonal traits: Wiggins's circumplex and the five-factor model. *Journal of Personality and Social Psychology, 56,* 586–595.

McCrae, R. R., & Costa, P. T., Jr. (1991a). Adding *Liebe und Arbeit*: The full five factor model and well-being. *Personality and Social Psychology Bulletin, 17,* 227–232.

McCrae, R. R., & Costa, P. T., Jr. (1991b). The NEO Personality Inventory: Using the five-factor model in counseling. *Journal of Counseling and Development, 69,* 367–372.

McCrae, R. R., Costa, P. T., & Busch, C. M. (1986). Evaluating comprehensiveness in personality systems: The California Q-Set and the five-factor model. *Journal of Personality, 54,* 430–446.

McGee, R., Williams, S., & Elwood, M. (1994). Depression and the development of cancer: A meta-analysis. *Social Science and Medicine, 38,* 187–192.

McGregor, L., Eveleigh, M., Syler, J. C., & Davis, S. F. (1991). Self-perception of personality characteristics and the Type A behavior pattern. *Bulletin of the Psychonomic Society, 29,* 320–322.

McGue, M., & Lykken, D. T. (1992). Genetic influence on risk of divorce. *Psychological Science, 3,* 368–373.

McHugh, M. C., Koeske, R. D., & Frieze, I. H. (1986). Issues to consider in conducting nonsexist psychological research: A guide for researchers. *American Psychologist, 41,* 879–890.

McIntosh, D. N., Silver, R. C., & Wortman, C. B. (1993). Religion's role in adjustment to a negative life event: Coping with the loss of a child. *Journal of Personality and Social Psychology, 65,* 812–821.

McKay, J. R. (1992). Affiliative trust–mistrust. In C. P. Smith (Ed.), *Motivation and personality: Handbook of thematic content analysis* (pp. 254–265). New York: Cambridge University Press.

McKillop, K. J., Jr., Berzonsky, M. D., & Schlenker, B. R. (1992). The impact of self-presentations on self-beliefs: Effects of social identity and self-presentational context. *Journal of Personality, 60,* 789–808.

McLarty, M. H. (1990). An examination of modern psychology through two philosophies of knowledge. *Psychological Record, 40,* 273–288.

McLeod, C. R., & Vodanovich, S. J. (1991). The relationship between self-actualization and boredom proneness. *Journal of Social Behavior and Personality, 6*(5), 137–146.

McMahon, R. C., Kelley, A., & Kouzekanani, K. (1993). Personality and coping styles in the prediction of dropout from treatment for cocaine abuse. *Journal of Personality Assessment, 61,* 147–155.

McNally, R. J., Litz, B. T., Prassas, A., Shin, L. M., & Weathers, F. W. (1994). Emotional priming of autobiographical memory in post-traumatic stress disorder. *Cognition and Emotion, 8,* 351–367.

McNulty, S. E., & Swann, W. B., Jr. (1994). Identity negotiation in roommate relationships: The self as architect and consequence of social reality. *Journal of Personality and Social Psychology, 67,* 1012–1023.

Mead, G. H. (1934). *Mind, self, and society* (C. W. Morris, Ed.). Chicago: University of Chicago Press.

Mednick, M. T. (1989). On the politics of psychological constructs: Stop the bandwagon, I want to get off. *American Psychologist, 44,* 1118–1123.

Meehl, P. E. (1990). Why summaries of research on psychological theories are often uninterpretable. *Psychological Reports, 66,* 195–244.

Meehl, P. E. (1992). Factors and taxa, traits and types, differences of degree and differences in kind. *Journal of Personality, 60,* 117–174.

Mehrabian, A., Young, A. L., & Sato, S. (1988). Emotional empathy and associated individual differences. *Current Psychology Research and Reviews, 7*(3), 221–240.

Meissner, W. W. (1990). Foundations of psychoanalysis reconsidered. *Journal of the American Psychoanalytic Association, 38,* 523–557.

Menard, S. (1991). *Longitudinal research.* Newbury Park, Calif.: Sage.

Merenda, P. F. (1987). Toward a four-factor theory of temperament and/or personality. *Journal of Personality Assessment, 51,* 367–374.

Mershon, B., & Gorsuch, R. L. (1988). Number of factors in the personality sphere: Does increase in factors increase predictability of real-life criteria? *Journal of Personality and Social Psychology, 55,* 675–680.

Meyer, B. C. (1987). Notes on the uses of psychoanalysis for biography. *Psychoanalytic Quarterly, 56,* 287–316.

Meyer, J. M., Heath, A. C., Eaves, L. J., Mosteller, M., & Schieken, R. M. (1988). The predictive power of Cattell's personality questionnaires: An eighteen month prospective study. *Personality and Individual Differences, 9,* 203–212.

Mickelson, R. A. (1989). Why does Jane read and write so well? The anomaly of women's achievement. *Sociology of Education, 62,* 47–63.

Milgram, S. (1974). *Obedience to authority: An experimental view.* New York: Harper & Row.

Miller, J. G., & Bersoff, D. M. (1992). Culture and moral judgment: How are conflicts between justice and interpersonal responsibilities resolved? *Journal of Personality and Social Psychology, 62,* 541–554.

Miller, J. G., Bersoff, D. M., & Harwood, R. L. (1990). Perceptions of social responsibilities in India and in the United States: Moral imperatives or personal decisions? *Journal of Personality and Social Psychology, 58,* 33–47.

Miller, L. (1988). Behaviorism and the new science of cognition. *Psychological Record, 38,* 3–18.

Miller, L. (1989). On the neuropsychology of dreams. *Psychoanalytic Review, 76,* 375–401.

Miller, R. S., & Leary, M. R. (1992). Social sources and interactive functions of emotion: The case of embarrassment. In M. S. Clark (Ed.), *Emotion and social behavior* (pp. 202–221). Newbury Park, Calif.: Sage.

Miller, T. R. (1991). The psychotherapeutic utility of the five-factor model of personality: A clinician's experience. *Journal of Personality Assessment, 57,* 415–433.

Mischel, H. N., & Mischel, W. (1983). The development of children's knowledge of self-control strategies. *Child Development, 54,* 603–619.

Mischel, W. (1968). *Personality and assessment.* New York: Wiley.

Mischel, W. (1984). On the predictability of behavior and the structure of personality. In R. A. Zucker, J. Aronoff, & A. I. Rabin (Eds.), *Personality and the prediction of behavior* (pp. 269–305). New York: Academic Press.

Mischel, W. (1990). Personality dispositions revisited and revised: A view after three decades. In L. A. Pervin (Ed.), *Handbook of personality: Theory and research* (pp. 111–134). New York: Guilford.

Mischel, W. (1992). Looking for personality. In S. Koch & D. E. Leary (Eds.), *A century of psychology as science* (pp. 515–526). Washington, D.C.: American Psychological Association.

Mischel, W., & Peake, P. K. (1982). Beyond déjà vu in the search for cross-situational consistency. *Psychological Review, 89,* 730–755.

Mischel, W., & Peake, P. K. (1983). Some facets of consistency: Replies to Epstein, Funder, and Bem. *Psychological Review, 90,* 394–402.

Mischel, W., Shoda, Y., & Peake, P. K. (1988). The nature of adolescent competencies predicted by preschool delay of gratification. *Journal of Personality and Social Psychology, 54,* 687–696.

Mischel, W., Shoda, Y., & Rodriguez, M. L. (1989). Delay of gratification in children. *Science, 244,* 933–938.

Mishler, E. G. (1990). Validation in inquiry-guided research: The role of exemplars in narrative studies. *Harvard Educational Review, 60,* 415–442.

Moes, E. C. (1990). Validation in the eyes of men: A psychoanalytic interpretation of paternal deprivation and the daughter's desire. *Melanie Klein and Object Relations, 81,* 43–65.

Moffitt, K. H., & Singer, J. A. (1994). Continuity in the life story: Self-defining memories, affect, and approach/avoidance personal strivings. *Journal of Personality, 62,* 21–43.

Moore, J. (1985). Some historical and conceptual relations among logical positivism, operationism, and behaviorism. *Behavior Analyst, 8,* 53–63.

Moore, J. (1990). On mentalism, privacy, and behaviorism. *Journal of Mind and Behavior, 11,* 19–36.

Moos, R. H. (1986). Work as a human context. In M. S. Pallak & R. Perloff (Eds.), *Psychology and work: Productivity, change, and employment* (pp. 5–52). Washington, D.C.: American Psychological Association.

Moot, S. A., III, Teevan, R. C., & Greenfeld, N. (1988). Fear of failure and the Zeigarnik effect. *Psychological Reports, 63,* 459–464.

Morawski, J. G. (1985). The measurement of masculinity and femininity: Engendering categorical realities. *Journal of Personality, 53,* 196–223.

Morgan, C. D., & Murray, H. A. (1962). Thematic apperception test. In H. A. Murray, *Explorations in personality* (pp. 530–545). New York: Oxford University Press. (Original work published 1938)

Morris, T., & Greer, H. S. (1980). A "Type C" for cancer? *Cancer Detection and Prevention, 3*(1), 102. (Abstract)

Moser, K., & Gerth, A. (1986). Construction and validation of a power motive questionnaire. *Psychological Reports, 58,* 83–86.

Moskowitz, D. S. (1990). Convergence of self-reports and independent observers: Dominance and friendliness. *Journal of Personality and Social Psychology, 58,* 1096–1106.

Moskowitz, D. S. (1993). Dominance and friendliness: On the interaction of gender and situation. *Journal of Personality, 61,* 387–409.

Moskowitz, D. S., & Schwarz, J. C. (1982). Validity comparison of behavior counts and ratings by knowledgeable informants. *Journal of Personality and Social Psychology, 42,* 518–528.

Moskowitz, G. B., & Roman, R. J. (1992). Spontaneous trait inferences as self-generated primes: Implications for conscious social judgment. *Journal of Personality and Social Psychology, 62,* 728–738.

Moyerman, D. R., & Forman, B. D. (1992). Acculturation and adjustment: A meta-analytic study. *Hispanic Journal of Behavioral Sciences, 14,* 163–200.

Mudrack, P. E. (1993). The Protestant work ethic and Type A behaviour: Overlap or orthogonality? *Personality and Individual Differences, 14,* 261–263.

Mullen, M. K. (1994). Earliest recollections of childhood: A demographic analysis. *Cognition, 52,* 55–79.

Multon, K. D., Brown, S. D., & Lent, R. W. (1991). Relation of self-efficacy beliefs to academic outcomes: A meta-analytic investigation. *Journal of Counseling Psychology, 38,* 30–38.

Munroe, R. L., & Munroe, R. H. (1992). Friendliness: Sex differences in East African dreams. *Journal of Social Psychology, 132,* 401–402.

Munter, P. O. (1975). Psychobiographical assessment. *Journal of Personality Assessment, 39,* 424–428.

Murray, H. A. (1938). *Explorations in personality: A clinical and experimental study of fifty men of college age.* New York: Oxford University Press.

Murray, H. A. (1940). What should psychologists do about psychoanalysis? *Journal of Abnormal and Social Psychology, 35,* 150–175.

Murray, J. B. (1990). Review of research on the Myers-Briggs Type Indicator. *Perceptual and Motor Skills, 70*(3, Pt 2), 1187–1202.

Murrey, G. J., Cross, H. J., & Whipple, J. (1992). Hypnotically created pseudomemories: Further investigation into the "memory distortion or response bias" question. *Journal of Abnormal Psychology, 101,* 75–77.

Musser, L. M., & Browne, B. A. (1991). Self-monitoring in middle childhood: Personality and social correlates. *Developmental Psychology, 27,* 994–999.

Mutén, E. (1991). Self-reports, spouse ratings, and psychophysiological assessment in a behavioral medicine program: An application of the five-factor model. *Journal of Personality Assessment, 57,* 449–464.

Myers, I. B., & McCaulley, M. H. (1985). *Manual: A guide to the development and use of the Myers-Briggs Type Indicator.* Palo Alto, Calif.: Consulting Psychologists Press.

Nadon, R., Laurence, J., & Perry, C. (1991). The two disciplines of scientific hypnosis: A synergistic model. In S. J. Lynn & J. W. Rhue (Eds.), *Theories of hypnosis* (pp. 485–519). New York: Guilford.

Nakagawa, M., Lamb, M. E., & Miyaki, K. (1992). Antecedents and correlates of the strange situation behavior of Japanese infants. *Journal of Cross-Cultural Psychology, 23,* 300–310.

Nash, M. R. (1987). What, if anything, is regressed about hypnotic age regression: A review of the empirical literature. *Psychological Bulletin, 102,* 42–52.

Nash, M. R. (1988). Hypnosis as a window on regression. *Bulletin of the Menninger Clinic, 52,* 383–403.

Natsoulas, T. (1981). Basic problems of consciousness. *Journal of Personality and Social Psychology, 41,* 132–178.

Natsoulas, T. (1983). Perhaps the most difficult problem faced by behaviorism. *Behaviorism, 11,* 1–26.

Negy, C., & Woods, D. J. (1993). Mexican- and Anglo-American differences on the Psychological Screening Inventory. *Journal of Personality Assessment, 60,* 543–553.

Neimeyer, G. J. (1988). Cognitive integration and differentiation in vocational behavior. *Counseling Psychologist, 16,* 440–475.

Neimeyer, G. J. (1989). Applications of repertory grid technique to vocational assessment. *Journal of Counseling and Development, 67,* 585–589.

Neimeyer, G. J. (1992). Personal constructs in career counseling and development. *Journal of Career Development, 18,* 163–173.

Neimeyer, G. J., & Rareshide, M. B. (1991). Personal memories and personal identity: The impact of ego identity development on autobiographical memory recall. *Journal of Personality and Social Psychology, 60,* 562–269.

Neimeyer, R. A. (1992). Constructivist approaches to the measurement of meaning. In G. J. Neimeyer (Ed.). *Handbook of constructivist assessment.* Newbury Park, CA: Sage.

Nelson, J. G. (1992). Class clowns as a function of the Type T psychobiological personality. *Personality and Individual Differences, 13,* 1247–1248.

Nelson, K. (1993). The psychological and social origins of autobiographical memory. *Psychological Science, 4,* 7–14.

Newman, L. S., Higgins, E. T., & Vookles, J. (1992). Self-guide strength and emotional vulnerability: Birth order as a moderator of self-affect relations. *Personality and Social Psychology Bulletin, 18,* 402–411.

Newman, L. S., & Uleman, J. S. (1990). Assimilation and contrast effects in spontaneous trait inference. *Personality and Social Psychology Bulletin, 16,* 224–240.

Nezu, A. M., & Nezu, C. M. (1987). Psychological distress, problem solving, and coping reactions: Sex role differences. *Sex Roles, 16,* 205–214.

Nezu, A. M., Nezu, C. M., & Peterson, M. A. (1986). Negative life stress, social support, and depressive symptoms: Sex roles as a moderator variable. *Journal of Social Behavior and Personality, 1,* 599–609.

Nichtern, S. (1985). Gandhi: His adolescent conflict of mind and body. *Adolescent Psychiatry, 12,* 17–23.

Niedenthal, P. M., Setterlund, M. B., & Wherry, M. B. (1992). Possible self-complexity and affective reactions to goal-relevant evaluation. *Journal of Personality and Social Psychology, 63,* 5–16.

Nielsen, J. M. (1990). *Feminist research methods: Exemplary readings in the social sciences.* Boulder: Westview Press.

Nigg, J. T., & Goldsmith, H. H. (1994). Genetics of personality disorders: Perspectives from personality and psychopathology research. *Psychological Bulletin*, *115*, 346–380.

Nisbett, R. E., & Wilson, T. D. (1977). Telling more than we can know: Verbal reports on mental processes. *Psychological Review*, *84*, 231–259.

Nitis, T. (1989). Ego differentiation: Eastern and Western perspectives. *American Journal of Psychoanalysis*, *49*, 339–346.

Nixon, S. J., & Parsons, O. A. (1990). Application of the Tridimensional Personality Questionnaire to a population of alcoholics and other substance abusers. *Alcoholism: Clinical and Experimental Research*, *14*, 513–517.

Nolen-Hokesema, S. (1987). Sex differences in unipolar depression: Evidence and theory. *Psychological Bulletin*, *101*, 259–282.

Noller, P., Law, H., & Comrey, A. (1987). Cattell, Comrey, and Eysenck personality factors compared: More evidence for the five robust factors? *Journal of Personality and Social Psychology*, *53*, 775–782.

Noller, P., Law, H., & Comrey, A. L. (1988). Factor analysis of the Comrey Personality Scales in an Australian sample. *Multivariate Behavioral Research*, *23*, 397–411.

Norcross, J. C. (1991). Prescriptive matching in psychotherapy: An introduction. *Psychotherapy*, *28*, 439–443.

Norman, W. T. (1963). Toward an adequate taxonomy of personality attributes: Replicated factor structure in peer nomination personality ratings. *Journal of Abnormal and Social Psychology*, *66*, 574–583.

Norman, W. T., & Goldberg, L. R. (1966). Raters, ratees, and randomness in personality structure. *Journal of Personality and Social Psychology*, *4*, 681–691.

Nunes, E. V., Frank, K. A., & Kornfeld, D. S. (1987). Psychologic treatment for the Type A behavior pattern and for coronary heart disease: A meta-analysis of the literature. *Psychosomatic Medicine*, *49*, 159–173.

O'Gorman, J. G., & Hattie, J. A. (1986). Confirmation of the factor structure of the EPQ using an Australian sample. *Personality and Individual Differences*, *7*, 897–898.

O'Hear, A. (1989). *Introduction to the philosophy of science*. Oxford, U.K.: Clarendon Press.

O'Leary, A. (1985). Self-efficacy and health. *Behavior Research and Therapy*, *23*, 437–452.

O'Leary, A. (1990). Stress, emotion, and human immune function. *Psychological Bulletin*, *108*, 363–382.

O'Leary, A. (1992). Self-efficacy and health: Behavioral and stress-physiological mediation. *Cognitive Therapy and Research*, *16*, 229–245.

O'Toole, B. I., & Stankov, L. (1992). Ultimate validity of psychological tests. *Personality and Individual Differences*, *13*, 699–716.

Obstfeld, L. S., Lupfer, M. B., & Lupfer, S. L. (1985). Exploring the relationship between gender identity and sexual functioning. *Journal of Sex and Marital Therapy*, *11*, 248–258.

Ofshe, R. J. (1992). Inadvertent hypnosis during interrogation: False confession due to dissociative state: Misidentified multiple personality and the satanic cult hypothesis. *International Journal of Clinical and Experimental Hypnosis*, *40*, 125–156.

Ogbonnaya, A. O. (1994). Person as community: An African understanding of the person as an intrapsychic community. *Journal of Black Psychology*, *20*, 75–87.

Oggins, J., Veroff, J., & Leber, D. (1993). Perceptions of marital interaction among black and white newlyweds. *Journal of Personality and Social Psychology*, *65*, 494–511.

Omodei, M. M., & Wearing, A. J. (1990). Need satisfaction and involvement in personal projects: Toward an integrative model of subjective well-being. *Journal of Personality and Social Psychology*, *59*, 762–769.

Orne, M. T. (1959). The nature of hypnosis: Artifact and essence. *Journal of Abnormal and Social Psychology*, *58*, 277–299.

Orne, M. T. (1971). Hypnosis, motivation, and the ecological validity of the psychological experiment. In W. J. Arnold & M. M. Page (Eds.), *Nebraska symposium on motivation, 1970*. Lincoln: University of Nebraska Press.

Ornstein, R. (1991). *The evolution of consciousness: Of Darwin, Freud, and cranial fire: The origins of the way we think*. New York: Touchstone.

Osborne, J. W., Maguire, T. O., & Angus, N. (1987). Private self-consciousness as a moderator variable. *Psychological Reports*, *60*, 303–312.

Osipow, S. H. (1986). Career issues through the life span. In M. S. Pallak & R. Perloff (Eds.), *Psychology and work: Productivity, change, and employment* (pp. 137–168). Washington, D.C.: American Psychological Association.

Otto, R. K., Poythress, N., Starr, L., & Darkes, J. (1993). An empirical study of the reports of APA's peer review panel in the Congressional review of the U.S.S. *Iowa* incident. *Journal of Personality Assessment*, *61*, 425–442.

Ovcharchyn, C. A., Johnson, H. H., & Petzel, T. P. (1981). Type A behavior, academic aspirations and academic success. *Journal of Personality*, *49*, 248–250.

Overholser, J. C. (1993). Idiographic, quantitative assessment of self-esteem. *Personality and Individual Differences, 14,* 639–646.

Oyserman, D., & Markus, H. (1990). Possible selves and delinquency. *Journal of Personality and Social Psychology, 59,* 112–125.

Oyserman, D., & Saltz, E. (1993). Competence, delinquency, and attempts to attain possible selves. *Journal of Personality and Social Psychology, 65,* 360–374.

Ozer, D. J. (1987). Personality, intelligence, and spatial visualization: Correlates of mental rotations test performance. *Journal of Personality and Social Psychology, 53,* 129–134.

Ozer, D. J., & Gjerde, P. F. (1989). Patterns of personality consistency and change from childhood through adolescence. *Journal of Personality, 57,* 483–507.

Ozer, E. M., & Bandura, A. (1990). Mechanisms governing empowerment effects: A self-efficacy analysis. *Journal of Personality and Social Psychology, 58,* 472–486.

Padilla, A. M. (1988). Early psychological assessments of Mexican-American children. *Journal of the History of the Behavioral Sciences, 24,* 111–117.

Paludi, M. A. (1984). Psychometric properties and underlying assumptions of four objective measures of fear of success. *Sex Roles, 10,* 765–781.

Palys, T. S., & Little, B. R. (1983). Perceived life satisfaction and the organization of personal project systems. *Journal of Personality and Social Psychology, 44,* 1221–1230.

Park, B., & Judd, C. M. (1989). Agreement on initial impressions: Differences due to perceivers, trait dimensions, and target behaviors. *Journal of Personality and Social Psychology, 56,* 493–505.

Parker, J. G., & Asher, S. R. (1987). Peer relations and later personal adjustment: Are low-accepted children at risk? *Psychological Bulletin, 102,* 357–389.

Passini, F. T., & Norman, W. T. (1966). A universal conception of personality structure? *Journal of Personality and Social Psychology, 4,* 44–49.

Paterson, R. J., & Moran, G. (1988). Attachment theory, personality development, and psychotherapy. *Clinical Psychology Review, 8,* 611–636.

Patterson, D. R., Everett, J. J., Burns, G. L., & Marvin, J. A. (1992). Hypnosis for the treatment of burn pain. *Journal of Consulting and Clinical Psychology, 60,* 713–717.

Patton, D., Barnes, G. E., & Murray, R. P. (1993). Personality characteristics of smokers and ex-smokers. *Personality and Individual Differences, 15,* 653–664.

Paul, R. (1985). Freud and the seduction theory: A critical examination of Masson's *The Assault on Truth. Journal of Psychoanalytic Anthropology, 8,* 161–187.

Paulhus, D. L., & Bruce, M. N. (1992). The effect of acquaintanceship on the validity of personality impressions: A longitudinal study. *Journal of Personality and Social Psychology, 63,* 816–824.

Paunonen, S. V. (1989). Consensus in personality judgments: Moderating effects of target-rater acquaintanceship and behavior observability. *Journal of Personality and Social Psychology, 56,* 823–833.

Paunonen, S. V. (1991). On the accuracy of ratings of personality by strangers. *Journal of Personality and Social Psychology, 61,* 471–477.

Paunonen, S. V., Jackson, D. N., Trzebinsky, J., & Forsterling, F. (1992). Personality structure across cultures: A multimethod evaluation. *Journal of Personality and Social Psychology, 62,* 447–456.

Pavelchak, M. A. (1989). Piecemeal and category-based evaluation: An idiographic analysis. *Journal of Personality and Social Psychology, 56,* 354–363.

Pavkov, T. W., Lewis, D. A., & Lyons, J. S. (1989). Psychiatric diagnoses and racial bias: An empirical investigation. *Professional Psychology: Research and Practice, 20,* 364–368.

Pedersen, D. M., & Conlin, T. (1987). Shifts in fear of success in men and women from 1968 to 1987. *Psychological Reports, 61,* 36–38.

Pennebaker, J. W., & Beall, S. K. (1986). Confronting a traumatic event: Toward an understanding of inhibition and disease. *Journal of Abnormal Psychology, 95,* 274–281.

Pennebaker, J. W., Colder, M., & Sharp, L. K. (1990). Accelerating the coping process. *Journal of Personality and Social Psychology, 58,* 528–537.

Pennebaker, J. W., Kiecolt-Glaser, J. K., & Glaser, R. (1988). Disclosure of traumas and immune function: Health implications for psychotherapy. *Journal of Consulting and Clinical Psychology, 56,* 239–245.

Peplau, L. A., & Conrad, E. (1989). Beyond nonsexist research: The perils of feminist methods in psychology. *Psychology of Women Quarterly, 13,* 379–400.

Persinger, M. A. (1983). Religious and mystical experiences as artifacts of temporal lobe function: A general hypothesis. *Perceptual and Motor Skills, 57,* 1255–1262.

Persinger, M. A. (1984). Striking EEG profiles from single episodes of glossolalia and transcendental mediation. *Perceptual and Motor Skills, 58,* 127–133.

Persinger, M. A., & Valliant, P. M. (1985). Temporal lobe signs and reports of subjective paranormal experiences in a normal population: A replication. *Perceptual and Motor Skills, 60,* 903–909.

Persky, V. W., Kempthorne-Rawson, J., & Shekelle, R. B. (1987). Personality and risk of cancer: 20-year follow-up of the Western Electric study. *Psychosomatic Medicine, 49,* 435–449.

Pervin, L. A. (1985). Personality: Current controversies, issues, and directions. *Annual Review of Psychology, 36,* 83–114.

Pervin, L. A. (1990). A brief history of modern personality theory. In L. A. Pervin (Ed.), *Handbook of personality: Theory and research* (pp. 3–18). New York: Guilford.

Peterson, C., & Seligman, M. E. P. (1987). Explanatory style and illness. *Journal of Personality, 55,* 237–265.

Peterson, C., Seligman, M. E. P., & Vaillant, G. E. (1988). Pessimistic explanatory style is a risk factor for physical illness: A thirty-five-year longitudinal study. *Journal of Personality and Social Psychology, 55,* 23–27.

Peterson, J. B., Weiner, D., Pihl, R. O., Finn, P. R., & Earleywine, M. (1991). The Tridimensional Personality Questionnaire and the inherited risk for alcoholism. *Addictive Behaviors, 16,* 549–554.

Phares, V., & Compas, B. E. (1992). The role of fathers in child and adolescent psychopathology: Make room for daddy. *Psychological Bulletin, 111,* 387–412.

Philogene, G. (1994). "African American" as a new social representation. *Journal for the Theory of Social Behaviour, 24,* 89–109.

Phinney, J. S. (1990). Ethnic identity in adolescents and adults: Review of research. *Psychological Bulletin, 108,* 499–514.

Phinney, J. S. (1991). Ethnic identity and self-esteem: A review and integration. *Hispanic Journal of Behavioral Sciences, 13,* 193–208.

Pichot, P. (1984). Centenary of the birth of Hermann Rorschach. *Journal of Personality Assessment, 48,* 591–596.

Piechowski, M. M., & Tyska, C. (1982). Self-actualization profile of Eleanor Roosevelt, a presumed nontranscender. *Genetic Psychology Monographs, 105,* 95–153.

Piedmont, R. L. (1988). An interactional model of achievement motivation and fear of success. *Sex Roles, 19,* 467–490.

Piedmont, R. L. (1989). The Life Activities Achievement Scale: An act-frequency approach to the measurement of motivation. *Educational and Psychological Measurement, 49,* 863–874.

Piedmont, R. L. (1993). A longitudinal analysis of burnout in the health care setting: The role of personal dispositions. *Journal of Personality Assessment, 61,* 457–473.

Pincs, A. M., & Aronson, E. (1988). *Career burnout: Causes and cures.* New York: Free Press.

Pletsch, C. (1985). Subjectivity and biography. In S. H. Baron & C. Pletsch (Eds.), *Introspection in biography* (pp. 355–360). Hillsdale, N.J.: Erlbaum.

Plomin, R., Coon, H., Carey, G., DeFries, J. C., & Fulker, D. W. (1991). Parent-offspring and sibling adoption analyses of parental ratings of temperament in infancy and childhood. *Journal of Personality, 59,* 705–732.

Plomin, R., Pedersen, N. L., McClearn, G. E., Nesselroade, J. R., & Bergeman, C. S. (1988). EAS temperaments during the last half of the life span: Twins reared apart and twins reared together. *Psychology and Aging, 3*(1), 43–50.

Pois, R. A. (1990). The case for clinical training and challenges to psychohistory. *Psychohistory Review, 18,* 169–187.

Polit, D. F., & Falbo, T. (1987). Only children and personality development: A quantitative review. *Journal of Marriage and the Family, 49,* 309–325.

Poole, M. E., & Evans, G. T. (1989). Adolescents' self-perceptions of competence in life skill areas. *Journal of Youth and Adolescence, 18,* 147–173.

Popper, K. (1959). *The logic of scientific discovery.* New York: Basic Books.

Povinelli, D. J. (1993). Reconstructing the evolution of mind. *American Psychologist, 48,* 493–509.

Poythress, N., Otto, R. K., Darkes, J., & Starr, L. (1993). APA's expert panel in the Congressional review of the USS *Iowa* incident. *American Psychologist, 48,* 8–15.

Pozzuto, R. (1982). Toward an Adlerian psychohistory. *Individual Psychology, 38,* 261–270.

Pratkanis, A. R., & Greenwald, A. G. (1985). How shall the self be conceived? *Journal for the Theory of Social Behavior, 15,* 311–329.

Prescott, C. A., Johnson, R. C., & McArdle, J. J. (1991). Genetic contributions to television viewing. *Psychological Science, 2,* 430–431.

Price, J., Sloman, L., Gardner, R., Gilbert, P., et. al. (1994). The social competition hypothesis of depression. *British Journal of Psychiatry, 164,* 309–315.

Primavera, J. P., III, & Kaiser, R. S. (1992). Non-pharmacological treatment of headache: Is less more? *Headache, 32*, 393–395.

Pugh, G. M., & Boer, D. P. (1989). An examination of culturally appropriate items for the WAIS-R Information subtest with Canadian subjects. *Journal of Psychoeducational Assessment, 7*, 131–140.

Pulkkinen, L. (1992). Life-styles in personality development. *European Journal of Personality, 6*, 139–155.

Pursell, S., Banikiotes, P. G., & Sebastian, R. J. (1981). Androgyny and the perception of marital roles. *Sex Roles, 7*, 201–215.

Quackenbush, R. L. (1990). Sex roles and social-sexual effectiveness. *Social Behavior and Personality, 18*, 35–40.

Ramanaiah, N. V., & Detwiler, F. R. J. (1992). Psychological androgyny and the NEO Personality Inventory. *Psychological Reports, 71*, 1216–1218.

Ramanaiah, N. V., Heerboth, J. R., & Jinkerson, D. L. (1985). Personality and self-actualizing profiles of assertive people. *Journal of Personality Assessment, 49*, 440–443.

Rammsayer, T., Netter, P., & Vogel, W. H. (1993). A neurochemical model underlying differences in reaction times between introverts and extraverts. *Personality and Individual Differences, 14*, 701–712.

Raskin, R., Novacek, J., & Hogan, R. (1991). Narcissism, self-esteem, and defensive self-enhancement. *Journal of Personality, 59*, 19–38.

Rauste-von Wright, M., & Frankenhaeuser, M. (1989). Females' emotionality as reflected in the excretion of the dopamine metabolite HVA during mental stress. *Psychological Reports, 64*, 856–858.

Ray, J. J. (1986). Measuring achievement motivation by self-reports. *Psychological Reports, 58*, 525–526.

Read, S. J., Jones, D. K., & Miller, L. C. (1990). Traits as goal-based categories: The importance of goals in the coherence of dispositional categories. *Journal of Personality and Social Psychology, 58*, 1048–1061.

Reeve, J., Olson, B. C., & Cole, S. G. (1987). Intrinsic motivation in competition: The intervening role of four individual differences following objective competence information. *Journal of Research in Personality, 21*, 148–170.

Reid, P. T., & Kelly, E. (1994). Research on women of color: From ignorance to awareness. *Psychology of Women Quarterly, 18*, 477–486.

Reinharz, S. (1992). *Feminist methods in social research.* New York: Oxford University Press.

Reise, S. P., & Waller, N. G. (1993). Traitedness and the assessment of response pattern scalability. *Journal of Personality and Social Psychology, 65*, 143–151.

Rendely, J. G., Holmstrom, R. M., & Karp, S. A. (1984). The relationship of sex-role identity, life style, and mental health in suburban American homemakers: 1. Sex role, employment and adjustment. *Sex Roles, 11*, 839–848.

Rendon, D. (1987). Understanding social roles from a Horneyan perspective. *American Journal of Psychoanalysis, 47*, 131–142.

Reno, R. R., & Kenny, D. A. (1992). Effects of self-consciousness and social anxiety on self-disclosure among unacquainted individuals: An application of the social relations model. *Journal of Personality, 60*, 79–94.

Resnick, M. N., & Nunno, V. J. (1991). The Nuremberg mind redeemed: A comprehensive analysis of the Rorschachs of Nazi war criminals. *Journal of Personality Assessment, 57*, 19–29.

Rhee, E., Uleman, J. S., Lee, H. K., & Roman, R. J. (1995). Spontaneous self-descriptions and ethnic identities in individualistic and collectivistic cultures. *Journal of Personality and Social Psychology, 69*, 142–152.

Rhodes, N., & Wood, W. (1992). Self-esteem and intelligence affect influenceability: The mediating role of message reception. *Psychological Bulletin, 111*, 156–171.

Rholes, W. S., Jones, M., & Wade, C. (1988). Children's understanding of personal dispositions and its relationship to behavior. *Journal of Experimental Child Psychology, 45*, 1–17.

Richards, P. S. (1994). Religious devoutness, impression management, and personality functioning in college students. *Journal of Research in Personality, 28*, 14–26.

Ricoeur, P. (1977). The question of proof in Freud's psychoanalytic writings. *Journal of the American Psychoanalytic Association, 28*, 397–417.

Rideout, C. A., & Richardson, S. A. (1989). A team-building model: Appreciating differences using the Myers-Briggs Type Indicator with developmental theory. *Journal of Counseling and Development, 67*, 529–533.

Riemann, R., & Angleitner, A. (1993). Inferring interpersonal traits from behavior: Act prototypicality versus conceptual similarity of trait concepts. *Journal of Personality and Social Psychology, 64*, 356–364.

Riemann, R., Grubich, C., Hempel, S., Mergl, S., & Richter, M. (1993). Personality and attitudes towards current political topics. *Personality and Individual Differences, 15*, 313–321.

Riese, M. L. (1987). Temperament stability between the neonatal period and 24 months. *Developmental Psychology, 23*, 216–222.

Rigby, C. S., Deci, E. L., Patrick, B. C., & Ryan, R. M. (1992). Beyond the intrinsic-extrinsic dichotomy: Self-determination in motivation and learning. *Motivation and Emotion, 16*, 165–185.

Riger, S. (1992). Epistemological debates, feminist voices: Science, social values, and the study of women. *American Psychologist, 47*, 730–740.

Rintala, M. (1984). The love of power and the power of love: Churchill's childhood. *Political Psychology, 5*, 375–389.

Ritzler, B., Zillmer, E., & Belevich, J. (1993). Comprehensive system scoring discrepancies on Nazi Rorschachs: A comment. *Journal of Personality Assessment, 61*, 576–583.

Roberts, B. W., & Donahue, E. M. (1994). One personality, multiple selves: Integrating personality and social roles. *Journal of Personality, 62*, 199–218.

Robles, R., Smith, R., Carver, C. S., & Wellens, A. R. (1987). Influence of subliminal visual images on the experience of anxiety. *Personality and Social Psychology Bulletin, 13*, 399–410.

Rogers, C. R. (1959). A theory of therapy, personality, and interpersonal relationships, as developed in the client-centered framework. In S. Koch (Ed.), *Psychology: A study of a science: Vol. 3. Formulations of the person and the social context* (pp. 185–256). New York: McGraw-Hill.

Rogers, C. R. (1961a). Ellen West—and loneliness. *Review of Existential Psychology and Psychiatry, 1*, 94–101.

Rogers, C. R. (1961b). *On becoming a person: A therapist's view of psychotherapy.* Boston: Houghton Mifflin.

Rogers, C. R. (1969). *Freedom to learn: A view of what education might become.* Columbus, Ohio: Chas. E. Merrill.

Rogers, C. R. (1973). Some new challenges. *American Psychologist, 28*, 379–387.

Rogers, C. R. (1974). Can learning encompass both ideas and feelings? *Education, 95*, 103–114.

Roglić, G., Pibernik-Okanović, M., Prašek, M., & Metelko. (1993). Effect of war-induced prolonged stress on cortisol of persons with Type II diabetes mellitus. *Behavioral Medicine, 19*, 53–59.

Rogoff, B., & Chavajay, P, (1995). What's become of research on the cultural basis of cognitive development? *American Psychologist, 50*, 859–877.

Rokeach, M. (1981). *The three Christs of Ypsilanti: A psychological study.* New York: Columbia University Press.

Romer, D., Gruder, C. L., & Lizzadro, T. (1986). A person-situation approach to altruistic behavior. *Journal of Personality and Social Psychology, 51*, 1001–1012.

Ronan, G. F., Colavito, V. A., & Hammontree, S. R. (1993). Personal problem-solving system for scoring TAT responses: Preliminary validity and reliability data. *Journal of Personality Assessment, 61*, 28–40.

Rooney, J. P. (1987). Golden Rule on "Golden Rule." *Educational Measurement: Issues and Practice, 6*(2), 9–12.

Root, M. P. P. (1990). Resolving "other" status: Identity development of biracial individuals. *Women and Therapy, 9*, 185–205.

Rorer, L. G. (1990). Personality assessment: A conceptual survey. In L. A. Pervin (Ed.), *Handbook of personality: Theory and research* (pp. 693–720). New York: Guilford.

Rosario, M., Shinn, M., Mørch, H., & Huckabee, C. B. (1988). Gender differences in coping and social supports: Testing socialization and role constraint theories. *Journal of Community Psychology, 16*, 55–69.

Rosenberg, S. D., Schnurr, P. P., & Oxman, T. F. (1990). Content analysis: A comparison of manual and computerized systems. *Journal of Personality Assessment, 54*, 298–310.

Rosenberg, S., & Jones, R. (1972). A method for investigating and representing a person's implicit theory of personality: Theodore Dreiser's view of people. *Journal of Personality and Social Psychology, 22*, 372–386.

Rosenman, R. H. (1990). Type A behavior pattern: A personal overview. *Journal of Social Behavior and Personality, 5*, 1–24.

Rosenman, R. H., Brand, R. J., Jenkins, C. D. et al. (1975). Coronary heart disease in the Western Collaborative Group Study: Final follow-up experience of 8½ years. *Journal of the American Medical Association, 233*, 872–877.

Rosenman, S. (1989). Guardians, ferrets and defilers of the treasure: The Masson-Freudians controversy. *Journal of Psychohistory, 16*, 297–321.

Rosenthal, R. (1966). *Experimenter effects in behavioral research.* New York: Appleton-Century-Crofts.

Rosenthal, R. (1978). Combining results of independent studies. *Psychological Bulletin, 85*, 185–193.

Rosenthal, R. (1979). The "File Drawer Problem" and tolerance for null results. *Psychological Bulletin, 86,* 638–641.

Rosenthal, R. (1984). *Meta-analytic procedures for social research.* Beverly Hills, Calif.: Sage.

Rosenzweig, S. (1958). The place of the individual and of idiodynamics in psychology: A dialogue. *Journal of Individual Psychology, 14,* 3–21.

Rosnow, R. L., & Rosenthal, R. (1989). Statistical procedures and the justification of knowledge in psychological science. *American Psychologist, 44,* 1276–1284.

Ross, M. (1989). Relation of implicit theories to the construction of personal histories. *Psychological Review, 96,* 341–357.

Rothbaum, F., & Weisz, J. R. (1994). Parental caregiving and child externalizing behavior in nonclinical samples: A meta-analysis. *Psychological Bulletin, 116,* 55–74.

Rotter, J. B. (1966). Generalized expectancies for internal versus external control of reinforcement. *Psychological Monographs, 80* (1, Whole No. 609).

Rotter, J. B. (1975). Some problems and misconceptions related to the construct of internal versus external control of reinforcement. *Journal of Consulting and Clinical Psychology, 43,* 56–67.

Rotter, J. B. (1990). Internal versus external control of reinforcement: A case history of a variable. *American Psychologist, 45,* 489–493.

Rowe, D. C., Vazsonyi, A. T., & Flannery, D. J. (1994). No more than skin deep: Ethnic and racial similarity in developmental process. *Psychological Review, 101,* 396–413.

Rubinstein, B. B. (1980). The problem of confirmation in clinical psychoanalysis. *Journal of the American Psychoanalytic Association, 28,* 397–417.

Ruble, D. N., Fleming, A. S., Hackel, L. S., & Stangor, C. (1988). Changes in the marital relationship during the transition to first time motherhood: Effects of violated expectations concerning division of household labor. *Journal of Personality and Social Psychology, 55,* 78–87.

Ruble, D. N., & Stangor, C. (1986). Stalking the elusive schema: Insights from developmental and social-psychological analyses of gender schemas. *Social Cognition, 4,* 227–261.

Ruf, B. M., & Chusmir, L. H. (1991). Dimensions of success and motivation needs among managers. *Journal of Psychology, 125,* 631–640.

Runco, M. A., Ebersole, P., & Mraz, W. (1991). Creativity and self-actualization. *Journal of Social Behavior and Personality, 6*(5), 161–167.

Runyan, W. M. (1981). Why did Van Gogh cut off his ear? The problem of alternative explanations in psychobiography. *Journal of Personality and Social Psychology, 40,* 1070–1077.

Runyan, W. M. (1982a). In defense of the case study method. *American Journal of Orthopsychiatry, 52,* 440–446.

Runyan, W. M. (1982b). *Life histories and psychobiography: Explorations in theory and method.* New York: Oxford University Press.

Runyan, W. M. (1983). Idiographic goals and methods in the study of lives. *Journal of Personality, 51,* 413–437.

Runyan, W. M. (1987). The growth of literature in psychohistory: A quantitative analysis. *Psychohistory Review, 15,* 121–135.

Runyan, W. M. (1988a). Alternatives to psychoanalytic psychobiography. In W. M. Runyan (Ed.), *Psychology and historical interpretation* (pp. 219–244). New York: Oxford University Press.

Runyan, W. M. (1988b). Progress in psychobiography. *Journal of Personality, 56,* 295–326.

Runyan, W. M. (1990). Individual lives and the structure of personality psychology. In A. I. Rabin, R. A. Zucker, R. A. Emmons, & S. Frank (Eds.), *Studying persons and lives* (pp. 10–40). New York: Springer.

Rushton, J. P. (1985). Differential K theory: The sociobiology of individual and group differences. *Personality and Individual Differences, 6,* 441–452.

Rushton, J. P. (1987). An evolutionary theory of health, longevity, and personality: Sociobiology and r/K reproductive strategies. *Psychological Reports, 60,* 539–549.

Rushton, J. P., Fulker, D. W., Neale, M. C., Nias, D. K. B., & Eysenck, H. J. (1986). Altruism and aggression: The heritability of individual differences. *Journal of Personality and Social Psychology, 50,* 1192–1198.

Russell, J. A. (1994). Is there universal recognition of emotion from facial expression? A review of the cross-cultural studies. *Psychological Bulletin, 115,* 102–141.

Russell, R. J. H., & Wells, P. A. (1994). Personality and quality of marriage. *British Journal of Psychology, 85,* 161–168.

Ruth, W. J., Mosatche, H. S., & Kramer, A. (1989). Freudian sexual symbolism: Theoretical considerations and an empirical test in advertising. *Psychological Reports, 64,* 1131–1139.

Ryan, R. M., Rigby, S., & King, K. (1993). Two types of religious internalization and their relations to religious orientations and mental health. *Journal of Personality and Social Psychology, 65*, 586–596.

Rychlak, J. F. (1981a). Logical learning theory: Propositions, corollaries, and research evidence. *Journal of Personality and Social Psychology, 40*, 731–749.

Rychlak, J. F. (1981b). *A philosophy of science for personality theory* (2nd ed.). Malabar, Fla.: Robert E. Krieger Publishing Company.

Rychlak, J. F. (1984). Logical learning theory: Kuhnian anomaly or medievalism revisited? *Journal of Mind and Behavior, 5*, 389–416.

Rychlak, J. F. (1988). *The psychology of rigorous humanism.* (2nd ed.). New York: New York University Press.

Ryckman, R. M., Robbins, M. A., Thornton, B., Gold, J. A., & Kuehnel, R. H. (1985). Physical self-efficacy and actualization. *Journal of Research in Personality, 19*, 288–298.

Salovey, P. (1992). Mood-induced self-focused attention. *Journal of Personality and Social Psychology, 62*, 699–707.

Saltman, V., & Solomon, R. (1982). Incest and the multiple personality. *Psychological Reports, 50*, 1127–1141.

Sampson, E. E. (1989). The challenge of social change for psychology. *American Psychologist, 44*, 914–921.

Sánchez-Bernardos, M. L., & Sanz, J. (1992). Effects of the discrepancy between self-concepts on emotional adjustment. *Journal of Research in Personality, 26*, 303–318.

Sande, G. N., Goethals, G. R., & Radloff, C. E. (1988). Perceiving one's own traits and others': The multifaceted self. *Journal of Personality and Social Psychology, 54*, 13–20.

Sanderman, R., Eysenck, S. B., & Arrindell, W. A. (1991). Cross-cultural comparisons of personality: The Netherlands and England. *Psychological Reports, 69*, 1091–1096.

Sappington, A. A. (1990). Recent psychological approaches to the free will versus determinism issue. *Psychological Bulletin, 108*, 19–29.

Sarason, S. B. (1989). The lack of an overarching conception in psychology. *Journal of Mind and Behavior, 10*, 263–279.

Saudino, K. J., & Eaton, W. O. (1991). Infant temperament and genetics: An objective twin study of motor activity level. *Child Development, 62*, 1167–1174.

Scarr, S. (1987). Personality and experience: Individual encounters with the world. In J. Aronoff, A. I. Rabin, and R. A. Zucker (Eds.), *The emergence of personality* (pp. 49–78). New York: Springer.

Scarr, S., & McCartney, K. (1983). How people make their own environments: A theory of genotype-environment effects. *Child Development, 54*, 424–435.

Schaefer, E. S., & Burnett, C. K. (1987). Stability and predictability of quality of women's marital relationships and demoralization. *Journal of Personality and Social Psychology, 53*, 1129–1136.

Schepeler, E. (1990). The biographer's transference: A chapter in psychobiographical epistemology. *Biography, 13*, 111–129.

Schibuk, M., Bond, M., & Bouffard, R. (1989). The development of defenses in childhood. *Canadian Journal of Psychiatry, 34*, 581–588.

Schiedel, D. G., & Marcia, J. E. (1985). Ego identity, intimacy, sex role orientation, and gender. *Developmental Psychology, 21*, 149–160.

Schlenker, B. R., & Leary, M. R. (1982). Social anxiety and self-presentation: A conceptualization and model. *Psychological Bulletin, 92*, 641–669.

Schlenker, B. R., & Weigold, M. F. (1990). Self-consciousness and self-presentation: Being autonomous versus appearing autonomous. *Journal of Personality and Social Psychology, 59*, 820–828.

Schmied, L. A., & Lawler, K. A. (1986). Hardiness, Type A behavior, and the stress-illness relation in working women. *Journal of Personality and Social Psychology, 51*, 1218–1223.

Schmieder, R. E., Rüddel, H., Schächinger, H., Bruns, J., & Schulte, W. (1993). Renal hemodynamics and cardiovascular reactivity in the prehypertensive stage. *Behavioral Medicine, 19*, 5–12.

Schneider, D. (1973). Implicit personality theory: A review. *Psychological Bulletin, 79*, 294–309.

Schneider, R. H., Egan, B. M., Johnson, E. H., Drobny, H., & Julius S. (1986). Anger and anxiety in borderline hypertension. *Psychosomatic Medicine, 48*, 242–248.

Schnell, R. L. (1980). Contributions to psychohistory: IV. Individual experience in historiography and psychoanalysis: Significance of Erik Erikson and Robert Coles. *Psychological Reports, 46*, 591–612.

Schnurr, P. P., Rosenberg, S. D., Oxman, T. E., & Tucker, G. J. (1986). A methodological note on content analysis: Estimates of reliability. *Journal of Personality Assessment, 50*, 601–609.

Schroeder, D. H., & Costa, P. T., Jr. (1984). Influence of life event stress on physical illness: Substantive effects or methodological flaws? *Journal of Personality and Social Psychology, 46,* 853–863.

Schroth, M. L. (1985). The effect of differing measuring methods on the relationship of motives. *Journal of Psychology, 119,* 213–218.

Schuerger, J. M., Zarrella, K. L., & Hotz, A. S. (1989). Factors that influence the temporal stability of personality by questionnaire. *Journal of Personality and Social Psychology, 56,* 777–783.

Schulz, R., & Schlarb, J. (1987–1988). Two decades of research on dying: What do we know about the patient? *Omega, 18,* 299–317.

Schunk, D. H. (1989). Self-efficacy and achievement behaviors. *Educational Psychology Review, 1,* 173–208.

Scott, N. E., & Borodovsky, L. G. (1990). Effective use of cultural role taking. *Professional Psychology: Research and Practice, 21,* 167–170.

Sedikides, C. (1992). Changes in the valence of the self as a function of mood. In M. S. Clark (Ed.), *Emotion and social behavior* (pp. 271–311). Newbury Park, Calif.: Sage.

Sedikides, C. (1993). Assessment, enhancement, and verification determinants of the self-evaluation process. *Journal of Personality and Social Psychology, 65,* 317–338.

Seegmiller, R. A., & Epperson, D. L. (1987). Distinguishing thinking-feeling preferences through the content analysis of natural language. *Journal of Personality Assessment, 51*(1), 42–52.

Segura, D. A., & Pierce, J. L. (1993). Chicana/o family structure and gender personality: Chodorow, familism, and psychoanalytic sociology revisited. *Signs, 19,* 62–91.

Selkin, J. (1994). Psychological autopsy: Scientific psychohistory or clinical intuition? *American Psychologist, 49,* 74–75.

Selye, H. (1946). The general adaptation syndrome and the diseases of adaptation. *Journal of Clinical Endocrinology, 6,* 117–120.

Selye, H. (1991). History and present status of the stress concept. In A. Monat & R. S. Lazarus (Eds.), *Stress and coping: An anthology* (3rd ed., pp. 21–35). New York: Columbia University Press.

Semin, G. R., & Fiedler, K. (1988). The cognitive functions of linguistic categories in describing persons: Social cognitions and language. *Journal of Personality and Social Psychology, 54,* 558–568.

Semin, G. R., & Krahé, B. (1987). Lay conceptions of personality: Eliciting tiers of a scientific conception of personality. *European Journal of Social Psychology, 17,* 199–209.

Serlin, R. C. (1987). Hypothesis testing, theory building, and the philosophy of science. *Journal of Counseling Psychology, 34,* 365–371.

Setterlund, M. B., & Niedenthal, P. M. (1993). "Who am I? Why am I here?": Self-esteem, self-clarity, and prototype matching. *Journal of Personality and Social Psychology, 65,* 769–780.

Sexton, T. L., & Tuckman, B. W. (1991). Self-beliefs and behavior: The role of self-efficacy and outcome expectation over time. *Personality and Individual Differences, 12,* 725–736.

Shaffer, J. W., Graves, P. L., Swank, R. T., & Pearson, T. A. (1987). Clustering of personality traits in youth and the subsequent development of cancer among physicians. *Journal of Behavioral Medicine, 10,* 441–447.

Shapiro, S. B. (1985). An empirical analysis of operating values in humanistic education. *Journal of Humanistic Psychology, 25*(1), 94–108.

Shedler, J., & Block, J. (1990). Adolescent drug use and psychological health. *American Psychologist, 45,* 612–630.

Sheldon, W. H. (1942). *The varieties of temperament: A psychology of constitutional differences.* New York: Harper.

Shelton, S. H. (1990). Developing the construct of general self-efficacy. *Psychological Reports, 66,* 987–994.

Shevrin, H., & Dickman, S. (1980). The psychological unconscious: A necessary assumption for all psychological theory? *American Psychologist, 35,* 421–434.

Shields, S. A. (1987). Women, men, and the dilemma of emotion. In P. Shaver & C. Hendrick (Eds.), *Sex and gender* (pp. 229–250). Newbury Park, Calif.: Sage.

Shiller, V. M., Izard, C. E., & Hembree, E. A. (1986). Patterns of emotion expression during separation in the strange-situation procedure. *Developmental Psychology, 22,* 378–383.

Shipley, T. E., Jr., & Veroff, J. (1958). A projective measure of need for affiliation. In J. W. Atkinson (Ed.), *Motives in fantasy, action, and society: A method of assessment and study* (pp. 83–104). Princeton, N.J.: Van Nostrand.

Shneidman, E. S. (1994). The psychological autopsy. *American Psychologist, 49,* 75–76.

Shor, R. E., & Orne, M. T. (1962). *Harvard Group Scale of Hypnotic Susceptibility, Form A.* Palo Alto, Calif.: Consulting Psychologists Press.

Shostrom, E. L. (1964). An inventory for the measurement of self-actualization. *Educational and Psychological Measurement, 24*, 207–218.

Showers, C. (1992). Compartmentalization of positive and negative self-knowledge: Keeping bad apples out of the bunch. *Journal of Personality and Social Psychology, 62*, 1036–1049.

Shulim, J. I. (1977). The birth of Robespierre as a revolutionary: A Horneyan psychohistorical approach. *American Journal of Psychoanalysis, 37*, 343–350.

Shulman, D. G. (1990). The investigation of psychoanalytic theory by means of the experimental method. *International Journal of Psycho-Analysis, 71*, 487–498.

Shulman, D. G., & Ferguson, G. R. (1988). An experimental investigation of Kernberg's and Kohut's theories of narcissism. *Journal of Clinical Psychology, 44*, 445–451.

Shuptrine, F. K., Bearden, W. O., & Teel, J. E. (1990). An analysis of the dimensionality and reliability of the Lennox and Wolfe Revised Self-Monitoring Scale. *Journal of Personality Assessment, 54*, 515–522.

Shweder, R. A. (1975). How relevant is an individual difference theory of personality? *Journal of Personality, 43*, 455–484.

Shweder, R. A. (1990). Cultural psychology: What is it? In J. W. Stigler, R. A. Shweder, & G. Herdt (Eds.), *Cultural psychology: Essays on comparative human development* (pp. 1–43). New York: Cambridge University Press.

Shweder, R. A., & Sullivan, M. A. (1993). Cultural psychology: Who needs it? *Annual Review of Psychology, 44*, 497–523.

Siegler, I. C., Zonderman, A. B., Barefoot, J. C., Williams, R. B., Jr., Costa, P. T., Jr., & McCrae, R. R. (1990). Predicting personality in adulthood from college MMPI scores: Implications for follow-up studies in psychosomatic medicine. *Psychosomatic Medicine, 52*, 644–652.

Silon, B. (1992). Dissociation: A symptom of incest. *Individual Psychology, Journal of Adlerian Theory, Research and Practice, 48*, 155–164.

Silverman, L. H. (1983). The subliminal psychodynamic activation method: Overview and comprehensive listing of studies. In J. Masling (Ed.), *Empirical studies of psychoanalytic theories. Vol. 1.* (pp. 69–100). Hillsdale, N.J.: Analytic Press.

Silverman, L. H., & Weinberger, J. (1985). Mommy and I are one: Implications for psychotherapy. *American Psychologist, 40*, 1296–1306.

Silverman, L. H., Ross, D. L., Adler, J. M., & Lustig, D. A. (1978). Simple research paradigm for demonstrating subliminal psychodynamic activation: Effects of Oedipal stimuli on dart-throwing accuracy in college males. *Journal of Abnormal Psychology, 87*, 341–357.

Silverstein, S. M. (1993). Methodological and empirical considerations in assessing the validity of psychoanalytic theories of hypnosis. *Genetic, Social, & General Psychology Monographs, 119*(1), 5–54.

Simonton, D. K. (1990). Personality and politics. In L. A. Pervin (Ed.), *Handbook of personality: Theory and research* (pp. 670–692). New York: Guilford.

Singer, J. E., & Davidson, L. M. (1991). Specificity and stress research. In A. Monat & R. S. Lazarus (Eds.), *Stress and coping: An anthology* (pp. 36–47). New York: Columbia University Press.

Singer, J. L., & Bonanno, G. A. (1990). Personality and private experience: Individual variations in consciousness and in attention to subjective phenomena. In L. A. Pervin (Ed.), *Handbook of personality: Theory and research* (pp. 419–444). New York: Guilford.

Singh, K. (1990). Toughmindedness in relation to birth order, family size, and sex. *Individual Psychology, 46*, 82–87.

Sipps, G. J., & Alexander, R. A. (1987). The multifactorial nature of extraversion-introversion in the Myers-Briggs Type Indicator and Eysenck Personality Inventory. *Educational and Psychological Measurement, 47*, 543–552.

Sipps, G. J., & DiCaudo, J. (1988). Convergent and discriminant validity of the Myers-Briggs Type Indicator as a measure of sociability and impulsivity. *Educational and Psychological Measurement, 48*, 445–451.

Skaalvik, E. M. (1986). Sex differences in global self-esteem: A research review. *Scandinavian Journal of Educational Research, 30*(4), 167–179.

Skaggs, E. B. (1945). Personalistic psychology as science. *Psychological Review, 52*, 234–238.

Skinner, B. F. (1950). Are theories of learning necessary? *Psychological Review, 57*, 193–216.

Skinner, B. F. (1987). Whatever happened to psychology as the science of behavior? *American Psychologist, 42*, 780–786.

Skitka, L. J., & Tetlock, P. E. (1993). Providing public assistance: Cognitive and motivational processes underlying liberal and conservative policy preferences. *Journal of Personality and Social Psychology, 65*, 1205–1223.

Slife, B. D. (1981). The primacy of affective judgment from a teleological perspective. *American Psychologist, 36,* 221–222.

Slife, B. D., & Rychlak, J. F. (1982). Role of affective assessment in modeling aggressive behavior. *Journal of Personality and Social Psychology, 43,* 861–868.

Smith, B. M. (1990). The measurement of narcissism in Asian, Caucasian, and Hispanic American women. *Psychological Reports, 67,* 779–785.

Smith, C. P. (Ed.). (1992a). *Handbook of thematic content analysis.* New York: Cambridge University Press.

Smith, C. P. (1992b). Introduction: Inferences from verbal material. In C. P. Smith (Ed.), *Handbook of thematic content analysis* (pp. 1–17). New York: Cambridge University Press.

Smith, C. P. (1992c). Reliability issues. In C. P. Smith (Ed.), *Handbook of thematic content analysis* (pp. 126–139). New York: Cambridge University Press.

Smith, E. R., Stewart, T. L., & Buttram, R. T. (1992). Inferring a trait from a behavior has long-term, highly specific effects. *Journal of Personality and Social Psychology, 62,* 753–759.

Smith, H. (1985). The sacred unconscious, with footnotes on self-actualization and evil. *Journal of Humanistic Psychology, 25*(3), 65–80.

Smith, J. A. (1994). Reconstructing selves: An analysis of discrepancies between women's contemporaneous and retrospective accounts of the transition to motherhood. *British Journal of Psychology, 85,* 371–392.

Smith, M. B. (1994). Selfhood at risk: Postmodern perils and the perils of postmodernism. *American Psychologist, 49,* 405–411.

Smith, T. W. (1992). Changing racial labels: From "Colored" to "Negro" to "Black" to "African American." *Public Opinion Quarterly, 56,* 496–514.

Snarey, J., & Lydens, L. (1990). Worker equality and adult development; The kibbutz as a developmental model. *Psychology and Aging, 5,* 86–93.

Snodgrass, S. E. (1985). Women's intuition: The effect of subordinate role on interpersonal sensitivity. *Journal of Personality and Social Psychology, 49,* 146–155.

Snyder, M. (1974). Self-monitoring of expressive behavior. *Journal of Personality and Social Psychology, 30,* 526–537.

Snyder, M., Tanke, E. D., & Berscheid, E. (1977). Social perception and interpersonal behavior: On the self-fulfilling nature of social stereotypes. *Journal of Personalty and Social Psychology, 35,* 656–666.

Sohier, R. (1985–1986). Homosexual mutuality: Variation on a theme by Erik Erikson. *Journal of Homosexuality, 12*(2), 25–38.

Sohn, D. (1982). Sex differences in achievement self-attributions: An effect-size analysis. *Sex Roles, 8,* 345–357.

Sorrentino, R. M., Hewitt, E. C., & Raso-Knott, P. A. (1992). Risk-taking in games of chance and skill: Informational and affective influences on choice behavior. *Journal of Personality and Social Psychology, 62,* 522–533.

Sorrentino, R. M., Short, J. C., & Raynor, J. O. (1984). Uncertainty orientation: Implications for affective and cognitive views of achievement behavior. *Journal of Personality and Social Psychology, 46,* 189–206.

Spangler, W. D. (1992). Validity of questionnaire and TAT measures of need for achievement: Two meta-analyses. *Psychological Bulletin, 112,* 140–154.

Spangler, W. D., & House, R. J. (1991). Presidential effectiveness and the leadership motive profile. *Journal of Personality and Social Psychology, 60,* 439–455.

Spanos, N. P. (1994). Multiple identity enactments and multiple personality disorder: A sociocognitive perspective. *Psychological Bulletin, 116,* 143–165.

Spanos, N. P., Burgess, C. A., Cross, P. A., & MacLeod, G. (1992). Hypnosis, reporting bias, and suggested negative hallucinations. *Journal of Abnormal Psychology, 101,* 192–199.

Spanos, N. P., Burnley, M. C. E., & Cross, P. A. (1993). Response expectancies and interpretations as determinants of hypnotic responding. *Journal of Personality and Social Psychology, 65,* 1237–1242.

Spanos, N. P., Cross, W. P., Menary, E. P., Brett, P. J., & de Groh, M. (1987). Attitudinal and imaginal ability predictors of social cognitive skill-training enhancements in hypnotic susceptibility. *Personality and Social Psychology Bulletin, 13,* 379–398.

Spanos, N. P., & McLean, J. (1986). Hypnotically created pseudomemories: Memory distortions or reporting biases? *British Journal of Experimental and Clinical Hypnosis, 3,* 155–159.

Spanos, N. P., Radtke, H. L., Hodgins, D. C., Stam, H. J., & Bertrand, L. D. (1983). The Carleton University Responsiveness to Suggestion Scale: Normative data and psychometric properties. *Psychological Reports, 53,* 523–535.

Spanos, N. P., Sims, A., de Faye, B., Mondoux, T. J., & Gabora, N. J. (1992–1993). A comparison of hypnotic and nonhypnotic treatments for smoking. *Imagination, Cognition and Personality, 12*, 12–43.

Spearman, C. (1927). *The abilities of man.* New York: Macmillan.

Spence, J. T., & Helmreich, R. L. (1978). *Masculinity and femininity: Their psychological dimensions, correlates, and antecedents.* Austin: University of Texas Press.

Spence, J. T., & Helmreich, R. L. (1980). Masculine instrumentality and feminine expressiveness: Their relationships with sex role attitudes and behaviors. *Psychology of Women Quarterly, 5*, 147–163.

Spence, J. T., & Robbins, A. S. (1992). Workaholism: Definition, measurement, and preliminary results. *Journal of Personality Assessment, 58*, 160–178.

Spencer, M. B., & Markstrom-Adams, C. (1990). Identity processes among racial and ethnic minority children in America. *Child Development, 61*, 290–310.

Spengler, P. M., & Strohmer, D. C. (1994). Stability of a 4 x 6 repertory grid for measuring cognitive complexity. *Journal of Constructivist Psychology, 7*, 137–145.

Spenner, K. I., & Featherman, D. L. (1978). Achievement ambitions. *Annual Review of Sociology, 4*, 373–420.

Sperling, M. B. (1987). Ego identity and desperate love. *Journal of Personality Assessment, 51*, 600–605.

Sperling, M. B., & Berman, W. H. (1991). An attachment classification of desperate love. *Journal of Personality Assessment, 56*, 45–55.

Sperling, M. B., Berman, W. H., & Fagen, G. (1992). Classification of adult attachment: An integrative taxonomy from attachment and psychoanalytic theories. *Journal of Personality Assessment, 59*, 239–247.

Sperry, R. W. (1986). Science, values, and survival. *Journal of Humanistic Psychology, 26*(2), 8–23.

Sperry, R. W. (1987). Structure and significance of the consciousness revolution. *Journal of Mind and Behavior, 8*, 37–65.

Sperry, R. W. (1990). Structure and significance of the consciousness revolution. *Person-Centered Review, 5*, 120–129.

Spinhoven, P., & Van Wijk, J. (1992). Hypnotic age regression in an experimental and clinical context. *American Journal of Clinical Hypnosis, 35*, 40–46.

Sroufe, L. A., Carlson, E., & Shulman, S. (1993). Individuals in relationships: Development from infancy through adolescence. In D. C. Funder, R. D. Parke, C. Tomlinson-Keasey, & K. Widaman (Eds.), *Studying lives through time: Personality and development* (pp. 315–342). Washington, D.C.: American Psychological Association.

Sroufe, L. A., Fox, N. E., & Pancake, V. R. (1983). Attachment and dependency in developmental perspective. *Child Development, 54*, 1615–1627.

Staats, A. W. (1987). Humanistic volition versus behavioristic determinism: Disunified psychology's schism problem and its solution. *American Psychologist, 42*, 1030–1032.

Staats, A. W. (1993). Personality theory, abnormal psychology, and psychological measurement: A psychological behaviorism. *Behavior Modification, 17*, 8–42.

Stack, C. B. (1986). The culture of gender: Women and men of color. *Signs, 11*, 321–324.

Stava, L. J., & Jaffa, M. (1988). Some operationalizations of the neodissociation concept and their relationship to hypnotic susceptibility. *Journal of Personality and Social Psychology, 54*, 989–996.

Steele, R. S. (1977). Power motivation, activation, and inspirational speeches. *Journal of Personality, 45*, 53–64.

Stein, K. F. (1994). Complexity of self-schema and responses to disconfirming feedback. *Cognitive Therapy and Research, 18*, 161–178.

Steklis, H. D., & Walter, A. (1991). Culture, biology, and human nature: A mechanistic approach. *Human Nature, 2*, 137–169.

Stelmack, R. M. (1990). Biological bases of extraversion: Psychophysiological evidence. *Journal of Personality, 58*, 293–311.

Stern, M., & Karraker, K. H. (1989). Sex stereotyping of infants: A review of gender labeling studies. *Sex Roles, 20*, 501–522.

Sternberg, K. J., & Lamb, M. E. (1992). Evaluations of attachment relationships by Jewish Israeli day-care providers. *Journal of Cross-Cultural Psychology, 23*, 285–299.

Stewart, A. J., & Chester, N. L. (1982). Sex differences in human social motives: Achievement, affiliation, and power. In A. J. Stewart (Ed.), *Motivation and society* (pp. 172–218). San Francisco: Jossey-Bass.

Stewart, A. J., Franz, C., & Layton, L. (1988). The changing self: Using personal documents to study lives. *Journal of Personality, 56*, 41–74.

Stewart, A. J., & Lykes, M. B. (1985). Conceptualizing gender in personality theory and research. *Journal of Personality, 53*, 93–101.

Stewart, R. A., & Beatty, M. J. (1985). Jealousy and self-esteem. *Perceptual and Motor Skills, 60*, 153–154.

Stifler, K., Greer, J., Sneck, W., & Dovenmuehle, R. (1993). An empirical investigation of the discriminability of reported mystical experiences among religious contemplatives, psychotic inpatients, and normal adults. *Journal for the Scientific Study of Religion, 32,* 366–372.

Stiles, W. B., Shapiro, D. A., & Elliott, R. (1986). "Are all psychotherapies equivalent?" *American Psychologist, 41,* 165–180.

Stock, J., & Cervone, D. (1990). Proximal goal-setting and self-regulatory processes. *Cognitive Therapy and Research, 14,* 483–498.

Stone, P. J., Dunphy, D. C., Smith, M. S., & Ogilvie, D. M. (1966). *The General Inquirer: A computer approach to content analysis.* Cambridge, Mass.: MIT Press.

Stoppard, J. M., & Paisley, K. J. (1987). Masculinity, femininity, life stress, and depression. *Sex Roles, 16,* 489–496.

Storms, P. L., & Spector, P. E. (1987). Relationships of organizational frustration with reported behavioural reactions: The moderating effect of locus of control. *Journal of Occupational Psychology, 60,* 227–234.

Strauman, T. J. (1990). Self-guides and emotionally significant childhood memories: A study of retrieval efficiency and incidental negative emotional content. *Journal of Personality and Social Psychology, 59,* 869–880.

Streitmatter, J. (1993). Gender differences in identity development: An examination of longitudinal data. *Adolescence, 28,* 55–66.

Strelau, J. (1987). Emotion as a key concept in temperament research. *Journal of Research in Personality, 21,* 510–528.

Strickland, B. R. (1989). Internal-external control expectancies: From contingency to creativity. *American Psychologist, 44,* 1–12.

Strube, M. J. (1990). In search of the self: Balancing the good and the true. *Personality and Social Psychology Bulletin, 16,* 699–704.

Stumpf, H. (1993). The factor structure of the Personality Research Form: A cross-national evaluation. *Journal of Personality, 61,* 27–48.

Styra, R., Sakinofsky, I., Mahoney, L., Colapinto, N. D., & Currie, D. J. (1993). Coping styles in identifiers and nonidentifiers of a breast lump as a problem. *Psychosomatics, 34,* 53–60.

Sue, S. (1983). Ethnic minority issues in psychology: A reexamination. *American Psychologist, 38,* 583–592.

Sue, S. (1988). Psychotherapeutic services for ethnic minorities. *American Psychologist, 43,* 301–308.

Suedfeld, P., Corteen, R. S., & McCormick, C. (1986). The role of integrative complexity in military leadership: Robert E. Lee and his opponents. *Journal of Applied Social Psychology, 16,* 498–507.

Suinn, R. M., Ahana, C., & Khoo, G. (1992). The Suinn-Lew Asian Self-Identity Acculturation Scale: Concurrent and factorial validation. *Educational and Psychological Measurement, 52,* 1041–1046.

Sullivan, H. W. (1953). *The interpersonal theory of psychiatry.* New York: Norton.

Sullivan, T., & Schneider, M. (1987). Development and identity issues in adolescent homosexuality. *Child and Adolescent Social Work, 4,* 13–24.

Suls, J., & Fletcher, B. (1985). The relative efficacy of avoidant and nonavoidant coping strategies: A meta-analysis. *Health Psychology, 4,* 249–288.

Sundberg, N. D., Goldman, M. S., Rotter, N. J., & Smyth, D. A. (1992). Personality and spirituality: Comparative TATs of high-achieving Rajneeshees. *Journal of Personality Assessment, 59,* 326–339.

Švrakić, D. M., Przybeck, T. R., & Cloninger, C. R. (1991). Further contribution to the conceptual validity of the unified biosocial model of personality: U.S. and Yugoslav data. *Comprehensive Psychiatry, 32,* 195–209.

Swann, W. B., Jr., Hixon, J. G., & De La Ronde, C. (1992). Embracing the bitter "truth": Negative self-concepts and marital commitment. *Psychological Science, 3,* 118–121.

Swede, S. W., & Tetlock, P. E. (1986). Henry Kissinger's implicit theory of personality: A quantitative case study. *Journal of Personality, 54,* 617–646.

Swim, J., Borgida, E., Maruyama, G., & Myers, D. G. (1989). Joan McKay versus John McKay: Do gender stereotypes bias evaluations. *Psychological Bulletin, 105,* 409–429.

Takeuchi, D. T., Kuo, H. S., Kim, K., & Leaf, P. J. (1989). Psychiatric symptom dimensions among Asian Americans and Native Hawaiians: An analysis of the Symptom Checklist. *Journal of Community Psychology, 17,* 319–329.

Talwar, R., Schwab, J., & Lerner, R. M. (1989). Early adolescent temperament and academic competence: Tests of "direct effects" and developmental contextual models. *Journal of Early Adolescence, 9,* 291–309.

Tang, T. L. (1993). A factor analytic study of the Protestant Work Ethic. *Journal of Social Psychology, 133,* 109–111.

Tashakkori, A. (1993). Gender, ethnicity, and the structure of self-esteem: An attitude theory approach. *Journal of Social Psychology, 133*, 479–488.

Tavris, C. (1991). The mismeasure of woman: Paradoxes and perspectives in the study of gender. In J. D. Goodchilds (Ed.), *Psychological perspectives on human diversity in America* (pp. 89–136). Washington, D.C.: American Psychological Association.

Taylor, G. J., Bagby, R. M., Ryan, D. P., Parker, J. D. A., Doody, K. F., & Keefe, P. (1988). Criterion validity of the Toronto Alexithymia Scale. *Psychosomatic Medicine, 50*, 500–509.

Taylor, H., & Cooper, C. L. (1989). The stress-prone personality: A review of the research in the context of occupational stress. *Stress Medicine, 5*, 17–27.

Taylor, M. C., & Hall, J. A. (1982). Psychological androgyny: Theories, methods, and conclusions. *Psychological Bulletin, 92*, 347–366.

Taylor, S. E., & Brown, J. D. (1988). Illusion and well-being: A social psychological perspective on mental health. *Psychological Bulletin, 103*, 193–210.

Taylor, S. E., & Brown, J. D. (1994). Positive illusions and well-being revisited: Separating fact from fiction. *Psychological Bulletin, 116*, 21–27.

Taylor, S. E., Kemeny, M. E., Aspinwall, L. G., Schneider, S. G., Rodriguez, R., & Herbert, M. (1992). Optimism, coping, psychological distress, and high-risk sexual behavior among men at risk for acquired immunodeficiency syndrome (AIDS). *Journal of Personality and Social Psychology, 63*, 460–473.

Tegano, D. W. (1990). Relationship of tolerance of ambiguity and playfulness to creativity. *Psychological Reports, 66*, 1047–1056.

Tellegen, A., & Atkinson, G. (1974). Openness to absorbing and self-altering experiences ("absorption"), a trait related to hypnotic susceptibility. *Journal of Abnormal Psychology, 83*, 268–277.

Tellegen, A., Lykken, D. T., Bouchard, T. J., Jr., Wilcox, K. J., Segal, N. L., & Rich, S. (1988). Personality similarity in twins reared apart and together. *Journal of Personality and Social Psychology, 54*, 1031–1039.

Temoshok, L. (1987). Personality, coping style, emotion and cancer: Towards an integrative model. *Cancer Surveys, 6*, 545–567.

Tennen, H., & Affleck, G. (1990). Blaming others for threatening events. *Psychological Bulletin, 108*, 209–232.

Tesser, A. (1993). The importance of heritability in psychological research: The case of attitudes. *Psychological Review, 100*, 129–142.

Tetlock, P. E., Armor, D., & Peterson, R. S. (1994). The slavery debate in antebellum America: Cognitive style, value conflict, and the limits of compromise. *Journal of Personality and Social Psychology, 66*, 115–126.

Thomas, C. B. (1988). Cancer and the youthful mind: A forty-year perspective. *Advances, 5*(2), 42–58.

Thompson, V. L. S. (1995). The multidimensional structure of racial identification. *Journal of Research in Personality, 29*, 208–222.

Thoresen, C. E., & Low, K. G. (1990). Women and the Type A behavior pattern: Review and commentary. *Journal of Social Behavior and Personality, 5*, 117–133.

Thoresen, C. E., & Powell, L. H. (1992). Type A behavior pattern: New perspectives on theory, assessment, and intervention. *Journal of Consulting and Clinical Psychology, 60*, 595–604.

Thornhill, R., & Thornhill, N. W. (1992). The evolutionary psychology of men's coercive sexuality. *Behavioral and Brain Sciences, 15*, 363–421.

Thornton, B. (1992). Repression and its mediating influence on the defensive attribution of responsibility. *Journal of Research in Personality, 26*, 44–57.

Thurstone, L. L. (1938). *Primary mental abilities.* Chicago: University of Chicago Press.

Tice, D. M. (1992). Self-concept change and self-presentation: The looking glass self is also a magnifying glass. *Journal of Personality and Social Psychology, 63*, 435–451.

Tieger, T. (1980). On the biological basis of sex differences in aggression. *Child Development, 51*, 943–963.

Tinsley, E. G., Sullivan-Guest, S., & McGuire, J. (1984). Feminine sex role and depression in middle-aged women. *Sex Roles, 11*, 25–32.

Tloczynski, J. (1993). Is the self essential? Handling reductionism. *Perceptual and Motor Skills, 76*, 723–732.

Tobacyk, J. J. (1992). Changes in locus of control beliefs in Polish university students before and after democratization. *Journal of Social Psychology, 132*, 217–222.

Tobacyk, J. J., & Tobacyk, Z. S. (1992). Comparisons of belief-based personality constructs in Polish and American university students: Paranormal beliefs, locus of control, irrational beliefs, and social interest. *Journal of Cross-Cultural Psychology, 23*, 311–325.

Tomarken, A. J., Davidson, R. J., & Henriques, J. B. (1990). Resting frontal brain asymmetry predicts affective responses to films. *Journal of Personality and Social Psychology, 59,* 791–801.

Tomkins, S. S. (1962). *Affect, imagery, and consciousness.* New York: Springer Verlag.

Tomkins, S. S. (1979a). *Affect, imagery, and consciousness* (Vol. 3). *New* York: Springer-Verlag.

Tomkins, S. S. (1979b). Script theory: Differential magnification of affects. In H. E. Howe, Jr., and R. A. Dienstbier (Eds.), *Nebraska symposium on motivation, 1978* (Vol. 26, pp. 201–236). Lincoln: University of Nebraska Press.

Tomkins, S. S. (1987). Script theory. In J. Aronoff, A. I. Rabin, and R. A. Zucker (Eds.), *The emergence of personality* (pp. 147–216). New York: Springer.

Tompkins, L. D., & Mehring, T. (1989). Competency testing and the international student: A common sense approach to detecting cultural bias in testing instruments. *Journal of Multicultural Counseling and Development, 17*(2), 72–78.

Top, T. J. (1991). Sex bias in the evaluations of performance in the scientific, artistic, and literary professions: A review. *Sex Roles, 24,* 73–106.

Torgersen, A. M. (1987). Longitudinal research on temperament in twins. *Acta Geneticae Medicae et Gemellologiae Twin Research, 36,* 145–154.

Torki, M. A. (1994). Associations between personality and stress reactions during and after invasion of Kuwait. *Psychological Reports, 74,* 667–673.

Torney-Purta, J. (1984). Annotated bibliography of materials for adding an international dimension to undergraduate courses in developmental and social psychology. *American Psychologist, 39,* 1032–1042.

Torrey, J. W. (1987). Phases of feminist re-vision in the psychology of personality. *Teaching of Psychology, 14,* 155–160.

Towson, S. M., & Zanna, M. P. (1982). Toward a situational analysis of gender differences in aggression. *Sex Roles, 8,* 903–914.

Trapnell, P. D., & Wiggins, J. S. (1990). Extension of the Interpersonal Adjective Scales to include the Big Five dimensions of personality. *Journal of Personality and Social Psychology, 59,* 781–790.

Tresemer, D. W. (1974, March). Fear of success: Popular but unproven. *Psychology Today, 7,* 82–84.

Triandis, H. C. (1972). *The analysis of subjective culture.* New York: Wiley.

Triandis, H. C. (1988). Collectivism v. individualism: A reconceptualization of a basic concept in cross-cultural social psychology. In G. K. Verma & C. Bagley (Eds.), *Cross-cultural studies of personality, values, and cognition* (pp. 60–95). London: Macmillan.

Triandis, H. C. (1989). The self and social behavior in differing cultural contexts. *Psychological Review, 96,* 506–520.

Triandis, H. C. (1990). Cross-cultural studies of individualism and collectivism. In J. J. Berman (Ed.), *Nebraska Symposium on Motivation: Vol. 37. Cross-cultural perspectives* (pp. 41–133). Lincoln: University of Nebraska Press.

Triandis, H. C., Bontempo, R., Villareal, M. J., Asai, M., & Lucca, N. (1988). Individualism and collectivism: Cross-cultural perspectives on self-ingroup relationships. *Journal of Personality and Social Psychology, 54,* 323–338.

Triandis, H. C., Leung, K., Villareal, M., & Clack, F. (1985). Allocentric vs. idiocentric tendencies: Convergent and discriminant validation. *Journal of Research in Personality, 19,* 395–415.

Triandis, H. C., McCusker, C., & Hui, C. H. (1990). Multimethod probes of individualism and collectivism. *Journal of Personality and Social Psychology, 59,* 1006–1020.

Trice, A. D., Haire, J. R., & Elliott, K. A. (1989). A career locus of control scale for undergraduate students. *Perceptual and Motor Skills, 69,* 555–561.

Trice, A. D., & Milton, C. T. (1987). Locus of control as a predictor of procrastination among adults in correspondence courses. *Perceptual and Motor Skills, 65,* 1002.

Trickett, P. K., & Putnam, F. W. (1993). Impact of child sexual abuse on females: Toward a developmental, psychobiological integration. *Psychological Science, 4,* 81–87.

Trivers, R. L. (1971). The evolution of reciprocal altruism. *Quarterly Review of Biology, 46,* 35–57.

Trivers, R. (1972). Parental investment and sexual selection. In B. Campbell (Ed.), *Sexual selection and the descent of man* (pp. 136–179). Chicago: Aldine.

Trivers, R. (1985). *Social evolution.* Menlo Park, Calif.: Benjamin/Cummings.

Trope, Y., Cohen, O., & Alfieri, T. (1991). Behavior identification as a mediator of dispositional inference. *Journal of Personality and Social Psychology, 61,* 873–883.

True, R. M. (1949). Experimental control in hypnotic age regression. *Science, 110,* 583.

Trzebinski, J. (1985). Action-oriented representations of implicit personality theories. *Journal of Personality and Social Psychology, 48,* 1266–1278.

Tucker, I. F. (1991). Predicting scores on the Rathus Assertiveness Schedule from Myers-Briggs Type Indicator categories. *Psychological Reports, 69,* 571–576.

Tucker, R. C. (1985). A Stalin biographer's memoir. In S. H. Baron & C. Pletsch (Eds.), *Introspection in biography: The biographer's quest for self-awareness* (pp. 249–271). Hillsdale, N.J.: Analytic Press.

Tuckman, B. W., & Sexton, T. L. (1990). The relation between self-beliefs and self-regulated performance. *Journal of Social Behavior and Personality, 5,* 465–472.

Turban, D. B., & Keon, T. L. (1993). Organizational attractiveness: An interactionist perspective. *Journal of Applied Psychology, 78,* 184–193.

Turner, M. B. (1967). *Philosophy and the science of behavior.* New York: Appleton-Century-Crofts.

Tzeng, O. C., Ware, R., & Chen, J. (1989). Measurement and utility of continuous unipolar ratings for the Myers-Briggs Type Indicator. *Journal of Personality Assessment, 53,* 727–738.

Underwood, B., & Moore, B. S. (1981). Sources of behavioral consistency. *Journal of Personality and Social Psychology, 40,* 780–785.

Vaillant, G. E., & Drake, R. E. (1985). Maturity of ego defenses in relation to DSM III axis II personality disorder. *Archives of General Psychiatry, 42,* 597–601.

Van De Water, D., & McAdams, D. P. (1989). Generativity and Erikson's "belief in the species." *Journal of Research in Personality, 23,* 435–449.

Van der Does, A. J., & Van Dyck, R. (1989). Does hypnosis contribute to the care of burn patients? Review of the evidence. *General Hospital Psychiatry, 11,* 119–124.

van der Ploeg, H. M., Kleijn, W. C., Mook, J., van Donge, M., Pieters, A. M. J., & Leer, J. H. (1989). Rationality and antiemotionality as a risk factor for cancer: Concept differentiation. *Journal of Psychosomatic Research, 33,* 217–225.

Van Wicklin, J. F. (1990). Conceiving and measuring ways of being religious. *Journal of Psychology and Christianity, 9,* 27–40.

Vander Mey, B. J. (1988). The sexual victimization of male children: A review of previous research. *Child Abuse and Neglect, 12,* 61–72.

Vander Mey, B. J., & Neff, R. L. (1982). Adult-child incest: A review of research and treatment. *Adolescence, 17,* 717–735.

Vazquez-Nuttall, E., Romero-Garcia, I., & de Leon, B. (1987). Sex roles and perceptions of femininity and masculinity of Hispanic women: A review of the literature. *Psychology of Women Quarterly, 11,* 409–425.

Verma, G. K., & Mallick, K. (1988). Problems in cross-cultural research. In G. K. Verma & C. Bagley (Eds.), *Cross-cultural studies of personality, attitudes and cognition* (pp. 96–107). London: Macmillan Press.

Veroff, J. (1958). Development and validation of a projective measure of power motivation. In J. W. Atkinson (Ed.), *Motives in fantasy, action, and society: A method of assessment and study* (pp. 105–116). Princeton, N.J.: Van Nostrand.

Veroff, J., Depner, C., Kulka, R., & Douvan, E. (1980). Comparison of American motives: 1957 versus 1976. *Journal of Personality and Social Psychology, 39,* 1249–1262.

Veroff, J., & Feld, S. (1970). *Marriage and work in America: A study of motives and roles.* New York: Van Nostrand Reinhold.

Veroff, J., McClelland, L., & Ruhland, D. (1975). Varieties of achievement motivation. In M. T. S. Mednick, S. S. Tangri, & L. W. Hoffman (Eds.), *Women and achievement: Social and motivational analyses* (pp. 172–205). Washington, D.C.: Hemisphere.

Veroff, J., Reuman, D., & Feld, S. (1984). Motives in American men and women across the adult life span. *Developmental Psychology, 20,* 1142–1158.

Viglione, D. J., Brager, R., & Haller, N. (1991). Psychoanalytic interpretation of the Rorschach: Do we have better hieroglyphics? *Journal of Personality Assessment, 57,* 1–9.

Vinacke, W. E., Shannon, K., Palazzo, V., Balsavage, L., & Cooney, P. (1988). Similarity and complementarity in intimate couples. *Genetic, Social, and General Psychology Monographs, 114*(1), 51–76.

Viney, L. L. (1981). Experimenting with experience: A psychotherapeutic case study. *Psychotherapy, 18,* 271–278.

Vitaliano, P. P., Russo, J., Carr, J. E., Maiuro, R. D., & Becker, J. (1985). The Ways of Coping Checklist: Revision and psychometric properties. *Multivariate Behavioral Research, 20,* 3–26.

Voland, E., & Voland, R. (1989). Evolutionary biology and psychiatry: The case of anorexia nervosa. *Ethology and Sociobiology, 10,* 223–240.

Vollhardt, L. T. (1991). Psychoneuroimmunology: A literature review. *American Journal of Orthopsychiatry, 61,* 35–47.

Vonk, R., & Heiser, W. J. (1991). Implicit personality theory and social judgment: Effects of familiarity with a target person. *Multivariate Behavioral Research*, *26*, 69–81.

Vroege, J. A., & Aaronson, N. K. (1994). Type A behavior and social support among employed women. *Behavioral Medicine*, *19*, 169–173.

Wagstaff, G. F., Vella, M., & Perfect, T. (1992). The effect of hypnotically elicited testimony on jurors' judgments of guilt and innocence. *Journal of Social Psychology*, *132*, 591–595.

Waite, R. G. L. (1977). *The psychopathic God: Adolf Hitler*. New York: Basic Books.

Walker, A., Jr. (Ed.). (1991). *Thesaurus of psychological index terms* (6th ed.). Arlington, Va.: American Psychological Association.

Wallace, E. R., IV (1986). Determinism, possibility, and ethics. *Journal of the American Psychoanalytic Association*, *34*, 933–974.

Wallace, E. R., IV (1989). Pitfalls of a one-sided image of science: Adolf Grünbaum's *Foundations of Psychoanalysis*. *Journal of the American Psychoanalytic Association*, *37*, 493–529.

Wallerstein, R. S. (1986). Psychoanalysis as a science: A response to the new challenges. *Psychoanalytic Quarterly*, *55*, 414–451.

Wallerstein, R. S. (1989). The Psychotherapy Research Project of the Menninger Foundation: An overview. *Journal of Consulting and Clinical Psychology*, *57*, 195–205.

Walsh, B. W., & Peterson, L. E. (1985). Philosophical foundations of psychological theories: The issue of synthesis. *Psychotherapy*, *2*, 145–153.

Ward, C., & Sethi, R. R. (1986). Cross-cultural validation of the Bem Sex Role Inventory. *Journal of Cross-Cultural Psychology*, *17*, 300–314.

Ward, E. A. (1993). Generalizability of psychological research from undergraduates to employed adults. *Journal of Social Psychology*, *133*, 513–519.

Ward, R. A., & Loftus, E. F. (1985). Eyewitness performance in different psychological types. *Journal of General Psychology*, *112*, 191–200.

Waterman, A. S. (1982). Identity development from adolescence to adulthood: An extension of theory and a review of research. *Developmental Psychology*, *8*, 341–358.

Waterman, A. S., Geary, P. S., & Waterman, C. K. (1974). Longitudinal study of changes in ego identity status from the freshman to the senior year at college. *Developmental Psychology*, *10*, 387–392.

Watkins, C. E., Jr., & Hector, M. (1990). A simple test of the concurrent validity of the Social Interest Index. *Journal of Personality Assessment*, *55*, 812–814.

Watson, D., & Clark, L. A. (1984). Negative affectivity: The disposition to experience aversive emotional states. *Psychological Bulletin*, *96*, 465–490.

Watson, D., & Pennebaker, J. W. (1989). Health complaints, stress, and distress: Exploring the central role of negative affectivity. *Psychological Review*, *96*, 234–254.

Watson, D., & Tellegen, A. (1985). Toward a consensual structure of mood. *Psychological Bulletin*, *98*, 219–235.

Watson, D., Clark, L. A., & Tellegen, A. (1988). Development and validation of brief measures of positive and negative affect. The PANAS scales. *Journal of Personality and Social Psychology*, *54*, 1063–1070.

Watson, P. J., Hood, R. W., Morris, R. J., & Hall, J. R. (1984). Empathy, religious orientation, and social desirability. *Journal of Psychology*, *117*, 211–216.

Weber, M. (1958). *The Protestant ethic and the spirit of capitalism*. New York: Scribner.

Weekes, J. R., Lynn, S. J., Green, J. P., & Brentar, J. T. (1992). Pseudomemory in hypnotized and task-motivated subjects. *Journal of Abnormal Psychology*, *101*, 356–360.

Weiland, S. (1989). Aging according to biography. *Gerontologist*, *29*, 191–194.

Weinberg, R. S., Hughes, H. H., Critelli, J. W., England, R., & Jackson, A. (1984). Effects of preexisting and manipulated self-efficacy on weight loss in a self-control program. *Journal of Research in Personality*, *18*, 352–358.

Weinberger, J. (1986). Comment on Robert Fudin's paper "Subliminal psychodynamic activation: Mommy and I are not yet one." *Perceptual and Motor Skills*, *63*, 1232–1234.

Weiner, B. (1985). An attributional theory of achievement motivation and emotion. *Psychological Review*, *92*, 548–573.

Weiner, B. (1990). Attribution in personality psychology. In L. A. Pervin (Ed.), *Handbook of personality: Theory and research* (pp. 465–485). New York: Guilford.

Weiner, B. (1991). On perceiving the other as responsible. In R. A. Dienstbier (Ed.), *Nebraska symposium on motivation, 1990*. Lincoln: University of Nebraska Press.

Weiner, B., Frieze, I. H., Kukla, A., Reed, L., Rest, S., & Rosenbaum, R. M. (1971). *Perceiving the causes of success and failure.* Morristown, N.J.: General Learning Press.

Weiss, J. (1987). The Golden Rule bias reduction principle: A practical reform. *Educational Measurement: Issues and Practice, 6*(2), 23–25.

Weiss, J. (1988). Testing hypotheses about unconscious mental functioning. *International Journal of Psychoanalysis, 69,* 87–95.

Weisz, J. R., Weiss, B., Alicke, M. D., & Klotz, M. L. (1987). Effectiveness of psychotherapy with children and adolescents: A meta-analysis for clinicians. *Journal of Consulting and Clinical Psychology, 55,* 542–549.

Weitz, R. (1989). Uncertainty and the lives of persons with AIDS. *Journal of Health and Social Behavior, 30,* 270–281.

Welkowitz, J., Lish, J. D., & Bond, R. N. (1985). The Depressive Experiences Questionnaire: Revision and validation. *Journal of Personality Assessment, 49,* 89–94.

Wells-Parker, E., Miller, D. I., & Topping, J. S. (1990). Development of control-of-outcome scales and self-efficacy scales for women in four life roles. *Journal of Personality Assessment, 54,* 564–575.

Werner, P. D., & Pervin, L. A. (1986). The content of personality inventory items. *Journal of Personality and Social Psychology, 51,* 622–628.

West, S. G. (1986). Methodological developments in personality research: An introduction. *Journal of Personality, 54,* 1–17.

Westen, D., Lohr, N., Silk, K. R., Gold, L., & Kerber, K. (1990). Object relations and social cognition in borderlines, major depressives, and normals: A Thematic Apperception Test analysis. *Psychological Assessment, 2,* 355–364.

Westkott, M. (1986). Historical and developmental roots of female dependency. *Psychotherapy, 23,* 213–220.

Westkott, M. (1989). Female relationality and the idealized self. *American Journal of Psychoanalysis, 49,* 239–250.

Wheeler, L. (1988). My year in Hong Kong: Some observations about social behavior. *Personality and Social Psychology Bulletin, 14,* 410–420.

White, M. S. (1985). Ego development in adult women. *Journal of Personality, 53,* 561–574.

White, P. (1980). Limitations on verbal reports of internal events: A refutation of Nisbett and Wilson and of Bem. *Psychological Review, 87,* 105–112.

White, P. A. (1988). Knowing more about what we can tell: "Introspective access" and causal report accuracy 10 years later. *British Journal of Psychology, 79*(1), 13–45.

White, R. W. (1959). Motivation reconsidered: The concept of competence. *Psychological Review, 66,* 297–333.

Whitley, B. E., Jr. (1984). Sex-role orientation and psychological well-being: Two meta-analyses. *Sex Roles, 12,* 207–225.

Whitworth, R. H., & Perry, S. M. (1990). Comparison of Anglo- and Mexican-Americans on the 16PF administered in Spanish or English. *Journal of Clinical Psychology, 46,* 857–863.

Wiebe, D. J. (1991). Hardiness and stress moderation: A test of proposed mechanisms. *Journal of Personality and Social Psychology, 60,* 89–99.

Wiederman, M. W., & Allgeier, E. R. (1993). The measurement of sexual-esteem: Investigation of Snell and Papini's (1989) Sexuality Scale. *Journal of Research in Personality, 27,* 88–102.

Wiersma, U. J. (1992). The effects of extrinsic rewards in intrinsic motivation: A meta-analysis. *Journal of Occupational and Organizational Psychology, 65,* 101–114.

Wiggins, J. S. (1979). A psychological taxonomy of trait-descriptive terms: The interpersonal domain. *Journal of Personality and Social Psychology, 37,* 395–412.

Wiggins, J. S. (1984). Cattell's system from the perspective of mainstream personality theory. *Multivariate Behavioral Research, 19,* 176–190.

Wiggins, J. S., & Broughton, R. (1991). A geometric taxonomy of personality scales. *European Journal of Personality, 5,* 343–365.

Wild, C. (1965). Regression in the service of the ego. *Journal of Personality and Social Psychology, 2,* 161–169.

Wild, T. C., Enzle, M. E., & Hawkins, W. L. (1992). Effects of perceived extrinsic versus intrinsic teacher motivation on student reactions to skill acquisition. *Personality and Social Psychology Bulletin, 18,* 245–251.

Wiley, M. B., & Crittenden, K. S. (1992). By your attributions you shall be known: Consequences of attributional accounts for professional and gender identities. *Sex Roles, 27,* 259–276.

Wilson, D., Sibanda, J., Sibanda, P., & Wilson, C. (1989). Second-order factor structure of Cattell's High School Personality Questionnaire among Zimbabwean schoolboys. *Journal of Social Psychology, 129,* 419–420.

Wilson, S. C., & Barber, T. X. (1983). The fantasy-prone personality: Implications for understanding imagery, hypnosis, and parapsychological phenomena. In A. A. Sheikh (Ed.), *Imagery: Current theory, research, and application* (pp. 340–390). New York: Wiley.

Wilson, S. R. (1988). The "real self" controversy: Toward an integration of humanistic and interactionist theory. *Journal of Humanistic Psychology*, (1), 39–65.

Windle, M. (1989a). Predicting temperament-mental health relationships: A covariance structure latent variable analysis. *Journal of Research in Personality, 23*, 118–144.

Windle, M. (1989b). Temperament and personality: An exploratory interinventory study of the DOTS-R, EASI-II, and EPI. *Journal of Personality Assessment, 53*, 487–501.

Winter, D. G. (1973). *The power motive.* New York: Free Press.

Winter, D. G. (1987). Leader appeal, leader performance, and the motive profiles of leaders and followers: A study of American presidents and elections. *Journal of Personality and Social Psychology, 52*, 196–202.

Winter, D. G. (1988). The power motive in women—and men. *Journal of Personality and Social Psychology, 54*, 510–519.

Winter, D. G. (1991). A motivational model of leadership: Predicting long-term management success from TAT measures of power motivation and responsibility. *Leadership Quarterly, 2*(2), 67–80.

Winter, D. G. (1993). Power, affiliation, and war: Three tests of a motivational model. *Journal of Personality and Social Psychology, 65*, 532–545.

Winter, D. G., & Carlson, L. A. (1988). Using motive scores in the psychobiographical study of an individual: The case of Richard Nixon. *Journal of Personality, 56*, 75–103.

Winter, D. G., Hermann, M. G., Weintraub, W., & Walker, S. G. (1991a). The personalities of Bush and Gorbachev at a distance: Follow-up on predictions. *Political Psychology, 12*, 457–464.

Winter, D. G., Hermann, M. G., Weintraub, W., & Walker, S. G. (1991b). The personalities of Bush and Gorbachev measured at a distance: Procedures, portraits, and policy. *Political Psychology, 12*(2), 215–245.

Winter, L., & Uleman, J. S. (1984). When are social judgments made? Evidence for the spontaneousness of trait inferences. *Journal of Personality and Social Psychology, 47*, 237–252.

Wittig, M. A. (1985) Meta-theoretical dilemmas in the psychology of gender. *American Psychologist, 40*, 800–811.

Wollman, N., & Stouder, R. (1991). Believed efficacy and political activity: A test of the specificity hypothesis. *Journal of Social Psychology, 13*, 557–566.

Wood, J. V., Giordano-Beech, M., Taylor, K. L., Michela, J. L., & Gaus, V. (1994). Strategies of social comparison among people with low self-esteem: Self-protection and self-enhancement. *Journal of Personality and Social Psychology, 67*, 713–731.

Wortman, C. B., & Silver, R. C. (1989). The myths of coping with loss. *Journal of Consulting and Clinical Psychology, 57*, 349–357.

Wright, J. C., & Mischel, W. (1987). A conditional approach to dispositional constructs: The local predictability of social behavior. *Journal of Personality and Social Psychology, 53*, 1159–1177.

Wright, J. C., & Mischel, W. (1988). Conditional hedges and the intuitive psychology of traits. *Journal of Personality and Social Psychology, 55*, 454–469.

Wright, W. J. (1985). Personality profiles of four leaders of the German Lutheran Reformation. *Psychohistory Review, 14*, 12–22.

Wright, R. (1994). *The moral animal: Evolutionary psychology and everyday life.* New York: Random House.

Wrightsman, L. S. (1981). Personal documents as data in conceptualizing adult personality development. *Personality and Social Psychology Bulletin, 7*, 367–385.

Wurgaft, L. D. (1976). Erik Erikson: From Luther to Gandhi. *Psychoanalytic Review, 63*, 209–233.

Wylie, L., & Forest, J. (1992). Religious fundamentalism, right-wing authoritarianism and prejudice. *Psychological Reports, 71*, 1291–1298.

Yang, K., & Bond, M. H. (1990). Exploring implicit personality theories with indigenous or imported constructs: The Chinese case. *Journal of Personality and Social Psychology, 58*, 1087–1095.

Yeagle, E. H., Privette, G., & Dunham, F. Y. (1989). Highest happiness: An analysis of artists' peak experience. *Psychological Reports, 65*, 523–530.

Yee, A. H., Fairchild, H. H., Weizmann, F., & Wyatt, G. E. (1993). Addressing psychology's problems with race. *American Psychologist, 48*, 1132–1140.

Yelsma, P., & Brown, C. T. (1985). Gender roles, biological sex, and predisposition to conflict management. *Sex Roles, 12*, 731–747.

Zahn-Waxler, C., & Radke-Yarrow, M. (1990). The origins of empathic concern. *Motivation and Emotion, 14*, 107–130.

Zahn-Waxler, C., Radke-Yarrow, M., Wagner, E., & Chapman, M. (1992). Development of concern for others. *Developmental Psychology, 28,* 126–136.

Zajonc, R. B. (1980). Feeling and thinking: Preferences need no inferences. *American Psychologist, 35,* 151–175.

Zakowski, S. G., McAllister, C. G., Deal, M., & Baum, A. (1992). Stress, reactivity, and immune function in healthy men. *Health Psychology, 11,* 223–232.

Zane, N. W. S., Sue, S., Hu, L., & Kwon, J. H. (1991). Asian-American assertion: A social learning analysis of cultural differences. *Journal of Counseling Psychology, 38,* 63–70.

Zeanah, C. H., Anders, T. F., Seifer, R., & Stern, D. N. (1989). Implications of research on infant development for psychodynamic theory and practice. *Journal of the American Academy of Child and Adolescent Psychiatry, 28,* 657–668.

Zeidner, M. (1989). Social anxiety among Jewish and Arab students in Israel. *Journal of Social Psychology, 129,* 415–418.

Zeldow, P. B., Daughtery, S. R., & McAdams, D. P. (1988). Intimacy, power, and psychological well-being in medical students. *Journal of Nervous and Mental Disease, 176,* 182–187.

Zillman, D., & Bryant, J. (1974). Effect of residual excitation on the emotional response to provocation and delayed aggressive behavior. *Journal of Personality and Social Psychology, 30,* 782–791.

Zimmerman, M. A. (1989). The relationship between political efficacy and citizen participation: Construct validation studies. *Journal of Personality Assessment, 53,* 554–566.

Živković, M. (1982). Dream test. *Perceptual and Motor Skills, 55,* 935–938.

Zuckerman, M. (1990a). The psychophysiology of sensation seeking. *Journal of Personality, 58,* 313–345.

Zuckerman, M. (1990b). Some dubious premises in research and theory on racial differences: Scientific, social, and ethical issues. *American Psychologist, 45,* 1297–1303.

Zuckerman, M., Bernieri, F., Koestner, R., & Rosenthal, R. (1989). To predict some of the people some of the time: In search of moderators. *Journal of Personality and Social Psychology, 57,* 279–293.

Zuckerman, M., Gioioso, C., & Tellini, S. (1988). Control orientation, self-monitoring, and preference for image versus quality approach to advertising. *Journal of Research in Personality, 22,* 89–100.

Zuckerman, M., Koestner, R., DeBoy, T., Garcia, T., Marcsca, B. C., & Sartoris, J. M. (1988). To predict some of the people some of the time: A reexamination of the moderator variable approach in personality theory. *Journal of Personality and Social Psychology, 54,* 1006–1019.

Zuckerman, M., Kuhlman, D. M., & Camac, C. (1988). What lies beyond E and N? Factor analyses of scales believed to measure basic dimensions of personality. *Journal of Personality and Social Psychology, 54,* 96–107.

Zullow, H. M., Oettingen, G., Peterson, C., & Seligman, M. E. P. (1988). Pessimistic explanatory style in the historical record: CAVing LBJ, presidential candidates, and East versus West Berlin. *American Psychologist, 43,* 673–682.

and Ability Testing, Inc., P. O. Box 1188 Champaign, Illinois, U. S. A. 61824–1188. All rights reserved. Reproduced by permission. "16PF™ " is a trademark belonging to IPAT; **98:** H. J. Eysenck & M. W. Eysenck. (1985). *Personality and individual differences: A natural science approach*. New York: Plenum (pp. 14–15). Copyright © 1985 by the Plenum Publishing Corporation. Adapted with permission; **99:** Archive Photos. **100:** J. S. Wiggins. (1979). A psychological taxonomy of trait-descriptive terms: The interpersonal domain. *Journal of Personality and Social Psychology, 37,* 395–412. (p. 399) Copyright © 1979 by the American Psychological Association. Adapted with permission; **119:** Joseph Rodriguez/Black Star; **121:** Bonnie Kamin; **124:** J. S. Hyde. (1981). How large are cognitive gender differences? A meta-analysis using ω^2 and *d. American Psychologist, 36,* 892–901. Copyright © 1981 by the American Psychological Association. Adapted with permission; **128:** Eastcott & Momatiuk/Woodfin Camp & Associates; **135:** The Library of Congress; **146:** The National Archives; Leonardo da Vinci/Art Resource; **161:** UPI/Bettman; **164:** Mark Daughhetee, 1985, "The Sin of Gluttony"; **169:** Reuters/Bettman; **171:** R. A. Neimeyer. (1992). Constructivist approaches to the measurement of meaning. In G. J. Neimeyer (Ed.). *Handbook of constructivist assessment.* Copyright © 1992 by Sage Publication, Inc. Reprinted by permission of Sage Publications, Inc.; **192:** Stephen Shames/Matrix; **201:** Adapted from J. Kihlstrom (1985). Conscious, subconscious, unconscious: A cognitive perspective. In K. S. Bowers & D. Meichenbaum (Eds.), *The unconscious reconsidered* (pp. 149–211). New York: Wiley. **205:** Oskar Diethelm Historical Library, Cornell Medical College, New York Hospital; **210:** April Saul; **218:** Lewis Hine, 1910, "Newsies at Skeeter's Branch, St. Louis, Missouri," Ford Motor Collection, Metropolitan Museum; **221:** Eugene Richards/Magnum Photos; **233:** Adapted from Chapter 4 in D. C. McClelland, J. W. Atkinson, R. A. Clark, & E. L. Lowell (1953.) *The Achievement Motive.* New York: Appleton-Century Crofts. (Reissued in 1976 by Irvington Publishers, Inc., New York, NY.) Copyright by John W. Atkinson; **239:** Digital image © Corbis Media/Hulton Deutsch;

241: Brian Bailey/TSI; **256:** Eugene Richards/ Magnum Photos; **259:** *Journal of Human Stress, 11*(2), 52–59. (1985). Reprinted with permission of the Helen Dwight Reid Educational Foundation. Published by Heldref Publications, 1319 Eighteenth St., N. W., Washington, D. C. 20036–1802. Copyright © 1985; **267:** Douglas C. Pizac/AP; **273:** Bonnie Kamin; **279:** The Dorothea Lange Collection, Oakland Museum; **296:** "A Nightmare on Elm Street," MOMA Film Stills Archive; **302:** Bruce Davidson/ Magnum Photos; **320:** Bill Aron/Tony Stone Images; **323:** April Saul; **329:** B. R. Little, L. Lecci & B. Watkinson (1992). Personality and personal projects: Linking Big Five and PAC units of analysis. *Journal of Personality, 60,* 501–525. Copyright © 1992 by Duke University Press. Adapted with permission; **333:** A. Bandura, L. Reese & N. E. Adams (1982). Microanalysis of action and fear arousal as a function of differential levels of perceived self-efficacy. *Journal of Personality and Social Psychology, 43,* 5–21 (p. 10) Copyright © 1982 by the American Psychological Association. Adapted with permission; **351:** The National Archives; **361:** A. Caspi, G. Elder & D. J. Bem (1987). Moving against the world: Life-course patterns of explosive children. *Developmental Psychology, 23,* 308–313. Copyright © by the American Psychological Association. Reprinted with permission; **375:** Michael Amendolia/News Limited; **380:** Gary S. Chapman; **390:** Liz McAuley/ Tony Stone Images; **407:** Archive Photos; **409:** D. Watson & A. Tellegen (1985). Toward a consensual structure of mood. *Psychological Bulletin, 98,* 219–235. (p. 221). Copyright © 1985 by the American Psychological Association. Reprinted with permission; **411:** Tony Stone Images; **423:** George Eastman House; **427:** Howard Grey/Tony Stone Images; **429:** G. J. Neimeyer (1992). Personal constructs in career counseling and development. *Journal of Career Development, 18*(3), 163–173. Copyright © 1992 by Plenum Publishing Corporation. Adapted with permission; **435:** Eugene Richards; **439:** "Mrs. Doubtfire," Kobal Collection; **462:** Leonard Freed/Magnum Photos; **483:** Archive Photos.

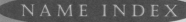